DESMOND BALL AND DAVID HORNER began assembling pieces of Australia's Soviet spy jigsaw in the late 1970s when David Horner obtained a copy of General Blamey's top secret January 1945 letter to the minister for the Army. In 1987 Desmond Ball learnt about the Australian connection with 'Venona', the US and UK signals intelligence operation which decrypted substantial portions of the KGB's cable traffic during and immediately after the war. In 1992 the links between Blamey's file and Venona began to emerge. Four years of research followed: in archives in the UK, USA, Canada and Australia, where the authors gained special access to classified documents; and interviewing many of those involved. In 1996 the US government began releasing decrypts of Australian-sourced material. The jigsaw was almost complete . . .

Desmond Ball is a special professor at the Strategic and Defence Studies Centre, ANU, where David Horner is a senior fellow. Among Desmond Ball's books are *A Suitable Piece of Real Estate: American Installations in Australia* (1980), *Pine Gap* (1988) and, with Jeffrey Richelson, *The Ties that Bind: Intelligence Cooperation Between the UKUSA Countries* (1985). David Horner's many books include *Inside the War Cabinet* (1996), *High Command* (1982) and, with Joanna Penglase, *When the War Came to Australia* (1992).

BREAKING THE CODES

*Australia's KGB network,
1944–1950*

Desmond Ball and
David Horner

ALLEN & UNWIN

Copyright © Desmond Ball and David Horner 1998

All rights reserved. No part of this book may be reproduced or transmitted in any form or by any means, electronic or mechanical, including photocopying, recording or by any information storage and retrieval system, without prior permission in writing from the publisher.

First published in 1998 by
Allen & Unwin
9 Atchison Street
St Leonards NSW 2065
Australia
Phone: (61 2) 9901 4088
Fax: (61 2) 9906 2218
E-mail: frontdesk@allen-unwin.com.au
Web: http://www.allen-unwin.com.au

National Library of Australia
Cataloguing-in-Publication entry:

Ball, Desmond, 1947– .
  Breaking the codes: Australia's KGB spy network 1944–1950.

  Bibliography.
  Includes index.
  ISBN 1 86448 578 7.

  1. Soviet Union. Komitet gosudarstvenno*i bezopasnosti—History.
  2. Espionage, Soviet—Australia—History. 3. National security—
  Australia. 4. Australia—Foreign relations. 5. Australia—Strategic
  aspects. I. Horner, D.M. (David Murray), 1948– . II. Title.

327.1247094

Set in 10/12 pt Arrus by DOCUPRO, Sydney
Printed and bound by South Wind Production (s) Pte Ltd, Singapore

10 9 8 7 6 5 4 3 2 1

Contents

List of figures and illustrations	vii
Acronyms and abbreviations	x
Preface	xiv

1 'there are leakages of information from Australia'
   SIGINT AND COUNTER-ESPIONAGE ... 1

2 'one directing organisation is most urgent'
   THE FORMATION OF AUSTRALIA'S SECURITY SERVICE ... 11

3 'our security system has failed to cope'
   THE SECURITY SERVICE AND THE WAR WITH JAPAN ... 29

4 'our only means of gauging Japanese espionage'
   THE DEVELOPMENT OF SIGINT IN AUSTRALIA ... 48

5 'a grave threat to national security'
   THE FIRST SECURITY LEAKS ... 73

6 'the source was the Soviet Minister'
   GENERAL BLAMEY'S LETTER ... 92

7 'is there any great difference?'
   MOSCOW CENTRE AND SOVIET INTELLIGENCE ... 115

8 'there was no mistaking the men'
   THE ARRIVAL OF THE RUSSIANS ... 125

9 'the CIS has no standing'
   POSTWAR SECURITY AND INTELLIGENCE IN AUSTRALIA   147

10 'reading dozens of messages'
   OPERATION VENONA: BREAKING RUSSIAN CODES   177

11 'KLOD has communicated detailed information'
   VENONA AND SOVIET ESPIONAGE IN AUSTRALIA   203

12 'Wally Clayton was the great Pooh-Bah'
   THE COMMUNIST PARTY AND CLAYTON   217

13 'absorbed with Russianism'
   THE DEVELOPMENT OF THE KLOD GROUP   232

14 'his friends in the NOOK'
   SOVIET ESPIONAGE IN EXTERNAL AFFAIRS   252

15 'our enquiries have met with no success'
   BRITAIN'S SPYCATCHERS COME TO AUSTRALIA   274

16 'identification of the spymaster has been made'
   ASIO AND 'THE CASE'   295

17 'a clincher for Clayton as a spy'
   THE END OF 'THE CASE'   313

18 'every counter-intelligence man's dream
   THE IMPORTANCE OF 'THE CASE'   337

Appendix 1   AMF Weekly Intelligence Review No. 118,
             4 November 1944   354
Appendix 2   Department of Information Background
             Service   364
Appendix 3   Security in the Western Mediterranean and
             the Eastern Atlantic: Report of
             post-hostilities planning staff,
             19 May 1945   366

Notes   377
Bibliography   430
Index   445

List of figures and illustrations

Letter from General Sir Thomas Blamey to the acting minister for the army, 6 January 1945	xx
Commander R.B.M. Long, wartime director of Naval Intelligence	19
Lieutenant-Colonel Eric Longfield Lloyd, director of the Security Service	20
Lieutenant-Colonel Colyn Cohen, Army liaison officer in the Commonwealth Security Service	21
The minister for the Army, Percy Spender and Major R.F.B. Wake, head of the Security Service, Queensland	24
Members of the War Cabinet, December 1941	27
Charles Kevin, assistant secretary in the department of the Army	32
Sir George Knowles, solicitor-general and secretary of the Attorney-General's department	34
Brigadier William Simpson, director-general of the Commonwealth Security Service	36
General Sir Thomas Blamey with Brigadier John Rogers, director of Military Intelligence	37
Lieutenant-Colonel Robert Little, assistant director of Military Intelligence	41
Telegraphists at HMAS *Harman* Naval Communications Station, Canberra	51
Paymaster Captain Eric Nave, the 'father' of Australian Sigint	54

Victoria Barracks, Melbourne, June 1943	56
Major-General Spencer B. Akin, chief signal officer, SWPA, with Major-General Colin Simpson, signal officer-in-chief, AMF	62
Senior officers of the Central Bureau, Brisbane, 1945	63
General Sir Thomas Blamey at the Central Bureau, Brisbane, 1944	64
Kalinga signals intercept station, July 1945	66
Lieutenant-General Frank Berryman, chief of staff, Advanced Land Headquarters	74
Major-General Wang Chih, Brisbane, August 1944	75
Brigadier John Rogers, director of Military Intelligence, August 1944	93
Senator James Fraser, acting minister for the Army, in New Guinea, April 1945	93
Frank Forde, minister for the Army and deputy prime minister, 1941–46	96
The Soviet Embassy, Canberra	126
Feodor Nosov, TASS representative, Sydney, 1943–50	131
J.B. (Ben) Chifley, prime minister, 1945–49	148
Dr H.V. Evatt, minister for External Affairs and attorney-general, 1941–49	150
Dr John Burton, secretary of the department of External Affairs, 1947–49	151
Sir Frederick Shedden, secretary of the department of Defence, 1937–56	154
Brigadier Bertrand Combes, director of Military Intelligence, December 1945	159
Brigadier Frederick Chilton, July 1944	163
Lieutenant-Commander J.E. Poulden, director of the postwar Defence Signals Bureau	168
Captain Charles Spry, April 1940	170
The KGB's encryption system	187
US Army Security Agency headquarters, Arlington Hall, Virginia	190
Gene Grabeel	191
Meredith Gardner and the 'young ladies' at Arlington Hall	192
Brigadier-General Carter W. Clarke, assistant chief of US Army Intelligence	194
FBI Special Agent Robert J. Lamphere	194
Venona decrypt of the cable from Canberra to Moscow, 19 March 1946	204
Venona decrypt of the cable from Moscow to Canberra, 5 June 1948	207
The KLOD network	212

Walter Clayton (KLOD), 1955	221
Katharine Susannah Prichard, 'an influential ACADEMICIAN'	234
Alfred Hughes (BEN)	241
Ian Milner (BUR), 1971	255
Jim Hill (TOURIST), 1954	263
Ric Throssell (FERRO)	269
Sir Percy Sillitoe, director-general of MI5, 1946–53	275
Sir Roger Hollis, director-general of MI5, 1956–65	278
Professor Sir Kenneth Bailey, solicitor-general and secretary of the Attorney-General's department	289
Justice Geoffrey Reed, director-general of ASIO, 1949–50	292
Organisation of ASIO, 1949–50	296
'Agincourt', ASIO headquarters, Sydney, 1949–50	299
Ray Whitrod, head of ASIO's counter-espionage operations in Sydney, 1949–50	300
Sir Frederick Shedden and Major-General Robert Macon, deputy chief US Army Field Forces, April 1949	303
Colonel Charles Spry, director-general of Security, July 1950	314
G.R. Richards, ASIO deputy director-general (operations) and Colonel Charles Spry, director-general of Security, 1954	317
Ric Throssell	321
Wally Clayton	329

Acronyms and abbreviations

ADMI	Assistant Director of Military Intelligence
AFSA	Armed Forces Security Agency
AGS	Allied Geographical Section
AIB	Allied Intelligence Bureau
AIC	Australian Intelligence Corps
AIF	Australian Imperial Force
ALLY	Australian Labour League of Youth
ALP	Australian Labor Party
AMF	Australian Military Forces
AMTORG	Soviet Trading Company
ANZAC	Australian and New Zealand Army Corps
ASA	US Army Security Agency
ASIS	Australian Secret Intelligence Service
ASIO	Australian Security Intelligence Organisation
ASWG	Australian Special Wireless Group
ATIS	Allied Translator and Interpreter Section
AWA	Amalgamated Wireless (Australasia) Ltd
AWAS	Australian Women's Army Service
BOAC	British Overseas Airways Corporation
BRUSA	Britain United States of America Agreement
CGS	Chief of the General Staff
Cheka	All-Russian Extraordinary Commission for Combating Counter-Revolution and Sabotage
CIA	Central Intelligence Agency
CIB	Commonwealth Investigation Branch

CIS	Commonwealth Investigation Service
CJI	Controller of Joint Intelligence
CMF	Citizen Military Forces
COIC	Combined Operational Intelligence Centre
COMINT	Communications intelligence
COMINTERN	Communist International
CPA	Communist Party of Australia
CPGB	Communist Party of Great Britain
CPSU	Communist Party of Soviet Union
CPUSA	Communist Party of the United States of America
CSIR	Council for Scientific and Industrial Research
CSS	Commonwealth Security Service
DCI	Director of Central Intelligence
DDMI	Deputy Director of Military Intelligence
DF	Direction finding
DCI	Director of Central Intelligence
DMI	Director of Military Intelligence
DNI	Director of Naval Intelligence
DSB	Defence Signals Branch
EM	Emigres work in Soviet intelligence
EYL	Eureka Youth League
FBI	Federal Bureau of Investigation
FECB	Far East Combined Bureau
FELO	Far East Liaison Office
FRUMEL	Fleet Radio Unit Melbourne
GCCS	Government Code and Cipher School
GCHQ	Government Communications Headquarters
GHQ	General Headquarters (SWPA)
GRU	Soviet Military Intelligence
GS	General Staff
GSO	General Staff Officer
GUGB	Main Administration of State Security
INO	Foreign Intelligence Department of Cheka
INU	Foreign Intelligence Directorate (Inostrannoye Upravlenie)
IO	Foreign Section of Cheka
IPR	Institute of Pacific Relations
ISGS	Intelligence Section of the General Staff
IYC	International Youth Council
JIB	Joint Intelligence Bureau
JIC	Joint Intelligence Committee
KGB	Committee of State Security (Komitet Gosudarstvennoy Bezopasnosti)
KI	Committee of Information (Komitet Informatsii)
LHQ	Land Headquarters

MGB	Ministry of State Security (Ministerstvo Gosudarstvennoy Bezopasnosti)
MHz	Megahertz
MIS	Military Intelligence Service (US Army)
MI5	British security service (Military Intelligence, section 5)
MI6	British Secret Intelligence Service
MPI	Military Police Intelligence
MVD	Soviet Ministry of Internal Affairs (Ministerstvo Vnutrennikh Del)
NCO	Non-Commissioned Officer
NKGB	People's Commissariat of State Security
NKVD	People's Commissariat for Internal Affairs
MVD	Ministry of Internal Affairs (Ministerstvo Vnutrennikh Del)
NSA	National Security Agency
NSW	New South Wales
OGPU	Unified State Political Directorate (Soviet security service 1923–34)
OMS	International Liaison Department of the Comintern
OTC	Overseas Telecommunications Commission
OTP	One-time pad
PHP	Post-Hostilities Planning (Committee)
PMG	Postmaster General's Department
QC	Queen's Counsel
RAAF	Royal Australian Air Force
RAB	Radio Analysis Bureau
RAF	Royal Air Force
RAN	Royal Australian Navy
RANVR	Royal Australian Navy Volunteer Reserve
RCE	Royal Commission on Espionage
RCMP	Royal Canadian Mounted Police
RDF	Radio direction finding
RIS	Russian Military Intelligence Service
RN	Royal Navy
RSS	Radio Security Service
RU	Soviet Intelligence Bureau
SIB	Special Intelligence Bureau
Sigint	Signals intelligence
SIS	US Army Signal Intelligence Service
SLO	Security Liaison Officer
SLU	Special Liaison Unit
SSO	Special security officers
SWPA	South West Pacific Area
T/A	Traffic analysis

TASS	Telegraphic Agency of the Soviet Union (Telegranfnoie Agentstvo Sovietskavo Soiuza)
UKUSA	United Kingdom, the United States of America, Canada, Australia and New Zealand (Agreement)
USASA	US Army Security Agency
USASIS	US Army Signal Intelligence Service
VYP	Victorian Youth Parliament
WAAAF	Women's Auxiliary Australian Air Force
W/T	Wireless telegraphy

Preface

THIS BOOK DEALS WITH THE most important espionage case in Australia's history. From 1943–49, a group of about ten people, all of whom were members of the Communist Party of Australia or close acquaintances of communists, provided information and documentary material to the Soviet State Security Service, commonly known as the KGB. The material that was given to Moscow included not only information about domestic Australian political matters, foreign policy, and the structure and activities of the Australian wartime Security Service, but also British and US documents concerning postwar strategic planning which had been passed to Canberra from London.

The Australian government was apprised of the information leaks in January 1945. Signals intelligence (Sigint) activities, involving the interception and decryption of foreign signals, had 'definitely proved' the leakages, but their 'method and origin' remained to be ascertained. Within four years, however, US and British cryptanalysts had, in an operation code-named Venona, decrypted substantial portions of the KGB cable traffic between Moscow and Canberra in 1943–48; these decrypts provided an extraordinary picture of Soviet espionage activities in Australia, including the identities of the Australian agents and contacts involved.

The authors have been involved in research and analysis of Australian defence history, Soviet espionage, and Allied signals intelligence (Sigint) and cryptanalytic activities during the Second World War since the early 1970s. In an article in *Australian Outlook* in

1978, David Horner first revealed that in 1945 General Sir Thomas Blamey had advised the Australian government of Soviet espionage in Australia, but despite efforts by several historians, few other details have been brought to light.[1] In 1987, during discussions in Washington about the origins of the UKUSA arrangements promulgated in 1947–48 for postwar Sigint cooperation between the United Kingdom, the United States, Australia and Canada, Desmond Ball was told about the Australian Venona operation, in which US and later British cryptanalysts decrypted substantial portions of the KGB's cable traffic between Moscow and Canberra between 1943 and 1948, and was shown an example of the decrypts.

In 1992 we decided to write a book on Sigint and counter-espionage, using the Soviet espionage operation in Australia in 1943–49 and the investigation into it from 1944 to 1950 as a case study. We were excited by the historic importance of the project, and perhaps also by the elements of detection involved. But it was a daunting exercise, which would require research not only in Australia but also in Britain and the US and, to the extent possible, in Moscow as well.

There were other considerations that also induced caution. We were very concerned that the nature of the evidentiary material would make the story especially difficult to pursue. The interception and decryption of radio and cable traffic is the most sensitive of the 'sources and methods' employed by intelligence agencies. Much of the intelligence collected and produced by the Allied Sigint authorities during the war remained publicly unavailable, including that which had aroused Blamey's concerns in late 1944. It was unlikely that either the US or the UK would officially release information about their postwar Sigint activities, and it seemed inconceivable that copies of decrypts of the enciphered KGB cable traffic for the period would become publicly available.

This is a story of major importance in Australian historiography. In April 1954 two KGB officers from the Soviet embassy in Canberra, Vladimir and Evdokia Petrov, defected to Australia, bringing with them sketchy stories of Soviet espionage in Australia over the previous ten years. The Menzies government made political capital out of the subsequent Royal Commission on Espionage in Australia and won the next federal election. Indeed, it continued to use anti-communism and the construction of 'Red scares' for political purposes throughout the 1950s and 1960s.

For many years some politicians and partisan historians have claimed that the Petrov defection was engineered by Menzies or the security authorities in order to win the 1954 election.[2] The respected historian, Russel Ward, in a widely circulated general book on Australian history, wrote that the Petrov affair was 'probably organised by a self-appointed group of conspirators, responsible to no one but themselves'.³ Others have claimed that Petrov brought little information with him, and that he merely repeated what the Australian security authorities wanted him to say.

Like ripples from a stone thrown into a pond, the theories of conspiracy move outwards from the Petrov defection. The security authorities—embodied in the Australian Security Intelligence Organisation (ASIO)—have been seen to be pursuing a political agenda of their own, manufacturing and exaggerating the communist threat to maintain conservative governments in power. Furthermore, as part of the Western intelligence community, the Australian security and intelligence organisations have been more inclined to follow the bidding of their Allied partners than the wishes of the Australian government.

Another of the ripples of conspiracy that radiate from the Petrov defection is the assertion that there was no Soviet espionage in Australia in the 1940s. Since ASIO had been set up in 1949 to deal with this espionage, it had thus been set up on a lie. ASIO had been established not to counter a real espionage threat, but to maintain political surveillance over ordinary law-abiding Australians, to further the interests of the Allied intelligence community and to keep the conservatives in power.

Over the last twenty years many of these conspiracy theories have been discredited, but the key element in their persistence is the denial that in the 1940s the Soviets were conducting espionage in Australia with the help of Australian citizens. Since the evidence of this espionage relies on the Venona intercepts, and since the security authorities were adamant that the Venona operation remain secret, it was not possible to provide absolute proof of the espionage. The absence of this proof allowed critics such as the historian Frank Cain, to argue, in 1991, that there 'were no decrypts of Soviet diplomatic traffic from Canberra to Moscow implicating' Ian Milner—one of the spies revealed by the Venona material. Cain claimed that the documents released to Australian archives by ASIO over recent years had been 'carefully vetted . . . to sustain this yarn'.⁴ A little later he elaborated on his argument:

> The accusation against the unfortunate Milner hangs on the vague allegation about information in an unimportant British document being detected in the intercept of radio traffic going to Moscow. It was very thin evidence to hang a man on, more so when the decrypt has not been produced . . . There were no such decrypts.⁵

He explained the formation of ASIO as follows:

ASIO was established in 1949 by the Australian Labor Party government in response to the US imposition of an embargo on the transfer of all classified information to Australia. There was a series of inter-relating factors involving the US Defense Department, the US Navy, the State Department and the newly established CIA which led to an exaggerated emphasis being placed on the rumour of Soviet spying in Australia in 1945.[6]

Others too have followed this line. For example, the historian Gregory Pemberton has written that the 'Decrypts . . . simply could not have existed in this case.'[7] These arguments have been widely accepted. The official history of the Australian Labor Party, published in 1991, states that ASIO 'was reluctantly established by Chifley after pressure from the British and American governments and trumped-up allegations of security breaches unscrupulously dramatized by Fadden [the leader of the Country Party].'[8] Our story will show that the allegations of security breaches were not trumped up, that there was a real espionage ring and that ASIO was established specifically to deal with it.

When, in 1992–93, following the collapse of the Soviet Union, Comintern files from the 1930s and early 1940s were opened in Moscow, they showed unequivocally that members of the US Communist Party had conducted espionage for the Soviet Union.[9] Those who had previously denied the existence of such espionage now had to shift ground: some members of the party evidently did steal material from official US government files and give it to the Soviets, but they were not 'spies'; their 'involvement in anything that could be called espionage was ad hoc, amateurish and sporadic'.[10] The information that they would have given Moscow was in any case unimportant, being mainly reports about communist activities or general political policies.[11]

Similar arguments have been put forward about the Australian spies—that the information passed to the Soviets was of little or no value and could not harm Australian security. Indeed, in the interests of open diplomacy there was advantage in allowing the Soviets access to Australian planning documents. Our story will show that the material passed to the Soviets could well have cost the lives of Australian servicemen, and gave the Soviets an immense advantage during the Cold War.

The subject of espionage in Australia, including the role of Australians in such activities, is politically controversial and has generated an enormous literature. It encompasses questions of the loyalty of members of the Communist Party and of the wisdom of government decisions to ban the party. As mentioned above, it includes the defection of the Petrovs and the subsequent royal commission. And it involves discussion of the capabilities and activities of intelligence and security agencies, the integrity of their officers, and the possibilities of their involvement in political machinations. None of this literature is definitive; very little is authoritative; most is contaminated in some fashion by the surrounding political controversy; much is polemical; some is untruthful. All of this literature had to be comprehended, but almost none of it directly or authoritatively addressed the subject of this book.

The exceptions deserve special credit. The most authoritative book on the defection of the Petrovs and the subsequent royal commission is by Robert Manne; it includes a chapter on 'the case'.[12] However, the Petrov affair is essentially a postscript to this story, which could be told even if the Petrov defections and the royal commission had never occurred. Until 1996 there were two published accounts of operations Bride and Venona, which involved the decryption of substantial sections of KGB radio and cable traffic for selected periods from 1940 to 1948—by Robert Lamphere, who was the senior FBI officer involved in the Venona operation from September 1947 to 1955;[13] and by Peter Wright, who was involved in some of the later phases of the operation.[14] However, these accounts did not pursue the Australian side of the Bride/Venona operation. In 1989, Christopher Andrew published an article on 'The Growth of the Australian Intelligence Community and the Anglo-American Connection', which has several pages recounting some details of this story,[15] but it is more tantalising than satisfying, and calls out for further explication and discussion. In 1991, Richard Hall published *The Rhodes Scholar Spy*, a path-breaking effort relating the decryption operation to the uncovering of espionage activity in Australia in 1944–48, but this is a journalistic work, undocumented, marred by some important inaccuracies, and substantially incomplete. David McKnight's *Australia's Spies and Their Secrets*, published in 1994, provides much new and fascinating detail about 'the case', but it was written without access to any of the Venona material.[16]

By the early 1990s, by which time the case was half a century old, there were hundreds of people in the US, Britain and Australia who had been involved in some aspect of it (whether on the cryptanalytic or counter-espionage sides). Most of them had retired from public office, and many were prepared to be interviewed. Indeed, we were somewhat concerned, given the age of those who had been personally involved in the story, that this number would soon decrease rapidly. We made extensive efforts to interview a wide range of people who were involved in the story and are very grateful for their assistance. The names of those who were happy to be quoted are listed in the bibliography.

While these interviews were crucial to our understanding of the story, we were always conscious that it would be incomplete without obtaining copies of the decrypts. Then, in early 1995 we were informed that the US National Security Agency (NSA) was preparing to release most of its holdings of Venona decrypts, including many of the cables between Moscow and Canberra. In October 1995 the NSA released copies of two decrypted cables from Moscow to Canberra (12 September 1943 and 2 December 1943), and in October 1996 it released copies of another 187. This represents a small proportion of the Australian Venona material. Venona was from 1947 a joint US–British cryptanalytic effort, and the British Government Communications Headquarters (GCHQ) has remained adamant that most of the decrypted Moscow–Canberra traffic, including some decrypted by US cryptanalysts, should be withheld. For example, few of the decrypts of 1943–44 traffic have been released, and some extremely significant ones in March–April 1946 also remain unpublished. Nonetheless, the release of the limited number of decrypts has enabled us to complete the story with authoritative evidence.

Those committed to conspiracy theories and frame-ups are unlikely to be dissuaded by any evidence. New documentary revelations are for such people only further manifestations of a conspiracy; insofar as they clarify certain events, it is only to suggest tangential intrigue. Frank Cain was still arguing in October 1996 that the information was planted on Vladimir Petrov. He was not convinced that the Venona decrypts 'provided unanswerable justification for the Petrov affair and the subsequent clamp-down on the Left in Australia'. He wanted to know 'just where the decrypts have been all this time'.[17] He thought that it was still far from certain that Petrov was even a spy.[18]

In completing this study we have incurred many debts of gratitude. In addition to the participants who provided us with first-hand information (listed in the bibliography), we would like to thank others who helped us through research, administrative support and advice: Steve Bates, Robert L. Benson (Office of Security, US National Security Agency), Emma Casswell, Edward J. Drea (chief of research and analysis, US Army Center of Military History), Renee Frank (Public Affairs Office, US National Security Agency), Richard Hall, Colonel John Herlihy (DMI Australian Army in 1993), Ian Livingstone, Maree Millan, Susan Prendergast, Jeffrey T. Richelson, David Sissons, Ian Smith (and the staff at the Australian War Memorial), Karen Smith, Moira Smythe (and the staff at the Australian Archives), Joe Straczek, Karin von Strokirch, Elza Sullivan, Robert Swan and Helen Wilson. We are particularly grateful to Mr David Sadleir, director-general of Security, for giving us special access to relevant material still held by ASIO.

ULTRA
TOP SECRET AND PERSONAL
6 January, 1945

My dear Acting Minister,

As you know, the Allied Intelligence Organisation is now world wide and operates through many various channels, some of which are so secret that as little as possible in regard to them is set out on paper.

One of its functions is to counter, as far as possible, the collection of Intelligence by the enemy. In the course of this service it has been definitely proved that there are leakages of information from Australia which have their origin apparently in Canberra.

As examples of this, the following are brought to notice.

(i) A Special Spy Report from HARBIN on 24th November, 1944 gave details concerning General MacArthur's plans for certain operations in the Philippines.

The source of this report was given as the Soviet Ambassador in Australia.

(ii) Another HARBIN Special Intelligence Report dated 2nd December gave information of a similar nature.

The source given in this case was Soviet Minister in Australia.

(iii) A news background sheet, which was distributed to Newspaper Editors by the Department of Information, contained certain information. This information dealt with the utilisation of Australian Forces. The matter has already been dealt with in correspondence between the acting Minister for Defence and the Minister for Information.

This item of news was also the subject of a HARBIN Intelligence Report in practically identical terms with those of the background news sheet.

(iv) Details of the Army Intelligence Service estimate of Japanese strength in the Philippines, issued in the AMF Weekly Intelligence Summary on 4 November, 1944, were known in full in TOKIO on 11th November.

This information is believed to have been transmitted from Sydney.

Action is being taken to restrict the dissemination of information that may be published in the Army Intelligence Summary by limiting the information contained therein and by limiting further the number of recipients.

It is suggested that you might consider it desirable that such action as can be taken at Canberra, to limit the association of official personnel with foreign representatives, is put in train.

The matter is recognised as one of great delicacy since, apparently, allied official channels play an important part in the transmission of information.

The cases given above are samples of many that have recently come to notice.

Yours faithfully,

General
Commander-in-Chief
Australian Military Forces

Senator J M Fraser,
Acting Minister for the Army.

Letter from General Sir Thomas Blamey to the acting minister for the Army, 6 January 1945. It was this letter that first informed the government of the leakages of information from Australia. (3DRL 6643, item 2/59)

1

'there are leakages of information from Australia'

SIGINT AND COUNTER-ESPIONAGE

ON 6 JANUARY 1945, IN a 'Top Secret and Personal' letter, General Sir Thomas Blamey, the commander-in-chief of the Australian Military Forces (AMF), informed Senator James Fraser, acting minister for the Army, that in the course of Allied intelligence operations, 'it has been definitely proved that there are leakages of information from Australia which have their origin apparently in Canberra'. Four examples of such leakages—'samples of many that have recently come to notice'—were given in the letter, including details of Allied plans for certain operations in the Philippines and details of recent Australian Army Intelligence estimates of Japanese strength there. In several cases the source was given as the 'Soviet Minister in Australia'. Blamey informed Fraser that 'every effort is, of course, being made to ascertain the method and origin of these transmissions'.[1] Although Blamey had been careful not to reveal it, his information had been gained through the interception and decryption of Japanese radio communications by the Allied signals intelligence (Sigint) organisation.

Thus began one of the most fascinating stories in the annals of espionage and counter-espionage—a story which involved the international cooperation of several of the world's most secret intelligence organisations; the most arcane intelligence operations and techniques; the deaths of Australian servicemen in the South-West Pacific Area; the propagation of seeds of suspicion in Moscow, Washington and London which flowered into the Cold War; and the establishment of postwar intelligence agencies within the framework of the UKUSA arrangements which continue to the present day.

This book is about the relationship between two different intelligence activities—Sigint and counter-espionage. Sigint involves the collection and production of intelligence by the interception of communications or monitoring of another country's radio or electronic signals, and is generally the most important source of intelligence available to governments and their defence establishments. Communications intelligence (Comint), the branch of Sigint with which this book is mainly concerned, has been officially defined as follows:

> Comint activities shall be construed to mean those activities which produce Comint by interception and processing of foreign communications passed by radio, wire, or other electronic-magnetic means . . . and by the processing of foreign encrypted communications, however transmitted. Interception comprises search, intercept, and direction-finding. Processing comprises range estimation, transmitter operator identification, signal analysis, traffic analysis, cryptanalysis, decryption, study of plain text, the fusion of these processes, and the reporting of the results.[2]

Although Sigint was of major importance in the Second World War, its full value was not acknowledged until the publication of Frederick Winterbotham's book *The Ultra Secret*, in 1974.[3] Since then a plethora of books has examined the history and techniques of Sigint and also the effect of Sigint or special intelligence (as it was known) on strategic decision-making and military operations.[4] Sigint has been described as 'the missing dimension of most diplomatic history',[5] but only in very recent times—since the mid 1970s—has its role in counter-espionage been acknowledged.

Sigint is almost as old as radio communications. Even before the First World War, as soon as radio started to be used for diplomatic and military communications, several countries (including Britain and Russia) established intercept stations and cryptanalytic offices for reading foreign diplomatic communications.[6] During the war, many countries developed capabilities for intercepting, decrypting and analysing military radio traffic, and Sigint contributed crucially to the outcomes of several campaigns on both the eastern and western fronts. The most dramatic such cases occurred on the eastern front, where Sigint was the principal factor in the German defeat of the Russians at Tannenberg and subsequent battles, which in turn led eventually to the collapse of the Tsarist regime. As David Kahn has argued, 'the establishment of Communist power, perhaps the supreme fact of contemporary history, was assisted to a certain degree by the cryptanalysis of Tsarist secret communications'.[7]

The US and the major European powers retained their Sigint and cryptanalytic agencies after the end of the war, but their organisational structures and the targets of their various activities changed greatly during the 1920s and '30s. Constrained by governmental indifference and at times hostility, the US Sigint agencies concentrated on trying to break the codes and ciphers of the Japanese foreign service, Navy and Army. Britain was more concerned with Germany and the Soviet Union, but did not ignore Japan.

Britain's outstanding cryptanalytic success in the Second World War was the breaking of the ciphers of the German Enigma encryption machine. The information from this source was given the security classification of Ultra Top Secret and eventually became known as Ultra. Possession of it gave Britain, and later the US, an extraordinary insight into Axis planning, movements and intentions. Ultra was thus invaluable to Allied planning and operations. Indeed, at the end of the war, the British prime minister, Winston Churchill, told King George VI, at a meeting with Sir Stewart Menzies, head of MI6 (Britain's secret intelligence service), that 'it was thanks to Ultra that we won the war'.[8]

Churchill was exaggerating: Ultra by itself did not win the war. Once the Soviet Union survived the first German offensives in 1941, and the US entered the war in December of that year, the Allies would eventually have won even without Ultra. But, Ultra did stave off several defeats between 1940 and 1942. It was an 'invaluable accessory' in planning Allied strategic initiatives from 1942 to 1945, including Operation Overlord, the Allied landings in Normandy in June 1944; it contributed decisively to Allied victories in numerous battles and campaigns; and it may well have shortened the war by two or three years.[9] Ultra was crucial to Montgomery's successes against Rommel in north Africa in 1941–42.[10] The Allied success against the German U-boats in the north Atlantic and Mediterranean in the second half of 1941 was 'achieved entirely on the basis of Ultra',[11] which also contributed to the success of the subsequent Allied naval offensive in the north Atlantic.[12]

Sigint was equally important in the Pacific War. It enabled the US Navy to win major strategic victories in the Coral Sea in May 1942 and at Midway the following month.[13] These were the principal turning points in the Pacific War. Eventually the Allies were able to build up an almost complete picture of the Japanese order of battle. In the areas closest to Australia, the Allied forces under General Douglas MacArthur, commander-in-chief of the South-West Pacific Area (SWPA), were thus able to strike where the Japanese were weakest.[14] Without Sigint the Allied losses would have been significantly greater. The US submarine campaign against the Japanese merchant fleet plying between Southeast Asia and the homeland was aided by Sigint and resulted in the loss of more than a thousand Japanese vessels.[15] In turn this had a devastating effect on Japan's economy, and also on its ability to resupply its forces in the Central and South-West Pacific. At the strategic level, the Americans had decrypted the Japanese diplomatic radio traffic, and the resulting information, known as Magic, helped the Allies understand the intentions of Japan and, through the reports of the Japanese ambassador in Berlin, of Germany as well.[16]

Through the end of the war and the onset of the Cold War, Sigint remained crucially important. Alerted by Allied wartime successes, the Soviet Union was more careful of communications security than the Germans and Japanese had been, but the Allies had gained in expertise and experience. As the Cold War developed, the Soviet Union acquired nuclear weapons and long-range delivery systems, and as the policies of nuclear deterrence were pursued, the US, the UK and their allies established a worldwide Sigint network for intercepting Soviet diplomatic, intelligence and military signals. The system was based upon a series of agreements about the sharing of collection and cryptanalytic tasks and the exchange of signals intelligence. These are generally referred to collectively as the UKUSA agreement (instituted in 1947–48), and constitute the most important secret international intelligence cooperation regime ever organised. Throughout the Cold War, Sigint provided the UKUSA allies with unique intelligence about Soviet strategic-weapons developments (e.g. the interception of telemetry generated in ballistic-missile test launches), critical intelligence for US nuclear war plans (e.g. electronic intelligence about Soviet air defence deployments and capabilities), and the most important source of strategic early warning (e.g. interception of mobilisation, dispersal and launch commands).

The effectiveness of Sigint related directly to the extent to which its success could be kept secret. If an adversary learned that its signals were being intercepted and decrypted, then he would immediately change his codes and make his systems more difficult to penetrate. During the war, secrecy was achieved in two ways. First, stringent rules were introduced for the handling of Ultra material. Those handling the material were sworn to secrecy, and measures were taken to minimise the chances that officers who were aware of the secret might be captured. Initially, only commanders at the highest levels were given Ultra material; they were allowed to read it but not retain it. Eventually British and American procedures were standardised. The success of these procedures is demonstrated by the fact that secrecy about Ultra was maintained until the 1970s.

Second, measures had to be taken to ensure that Allied operations were not conducted in a way that might reveal that they were based on foreknowledge of the enemy's intentions. In the 1970s much prominence was given to a claim that Churchill allowed German bombers to flatten Coventry for fear of revealing that he knew about the attack in advance.[17] This claim was shown to be false, but there were other instances where the Allies made sacrifices to preserve Sigint secrecy. For example, Britain knew that the Germans would attack the island of Crete, with airborne troops on 20 May 1941 and Major-General Freyberg, the Allied commander on Crete, was warned. But he was also told not to show by his troop dispositions that he knew an attack was imminent. He applied this rule so rigidly that the Germans were able to seize an airfield, fly in their troops and win the battle.[18] In the second half of 1942, British aircraft and submarines took heavy toll of the German and Italian ships resupplying north Africa from Italy. Forewarned by Ultra when the convoys were leaving Italy, what route they were taking and which convoys were carrying vital fuel, the British nonetheless made sure a spotter aircraft appeared over each convoy before it was attacked, in an attempt to persuade the Germans that it was this plane that had detected the ships. Eventually the Germans concluded that the British had a network of agents in Italian ports.[19] There were occasions in the battle of the Atlantic when convoys were not diverted away from German submarine wolf packs for fear that the Germans might deduce that their codes had been broken. In July 1945, when the Pacific war had only one month to run, the US cruiser *Indianapolis* was sunk by a Japanese submarine in the Philippine Sea and its loss was not discovered for 84 hours. In fact, US codebreakers had intercepted the message from the Japanese submarine to Tokyo reporting the sinking (of a 'battleship'), but the message was given restricted circulation and the rescue efforts were delayed.[20]

Thirty years passed before the existence of the Ultra secret was revealed in Winterbotham's book, and it was another decade before its profound implications could be incorporated into the history of the Second World War. A major contribution to this process was the publication of the multi-volume official history of *British Intelligence in the Second World War*, which appeared between 1979 and 1990.[21] There are numerous other publications on Sigint in both the European and Pacific theatres. Accounts of Sigint operations and successes in the postwar period are less numerous, primarily because the end of the Cold War is still very recent history and many of the techniques and organisations are still in use.

The secrecy of Venona—the Allied cryptanalytic operation that exposed Soviet espionage activities after the war—was even greater than that accorded to Ultra. During the war, of course, it had been necessary to distribute Ultra intelligence to dozens of US, British and other Allied commands and agencies, on a worldwide scale and in an expeditious fashion. The only people who needed to know about Venona, however, were the cryptanalysts and the Sigint personnel who supported them in obtaining, decrypting and translating Soviet traffic, and those intelligence and counter-espionage personnel who were directly involved in exploitation of the Venona material. Some prime ministers and presidents were told about the Venona decrypts, at least in general terms, including British prime minister Attlee in 1947, and Australian prime ministers Chifley in February 1949 and Menzies in 1950; others, such as President Truman, were not told.[22] In 1954–55, following the defection of Vladimir and Evdokia Petrov, the royal commission on espionage was established to inquire into and report upon any espionage or related activities conducted by the Soviet Union in Australia, but the commissioners were never informed of the existence of the Venona material, and were unable to identify several Soviet agents and contacts mentioned in papers brought out by Petrov (e.g. BEN and PODRUGA), even though these had been identified in the Venona operation some six years before. In 1983, when Justice R. M. Hope was asked to review the activities of the Australian intelligence and security agencies, he asked to be briefed about the Venona material, which he had learned about during his first royal commission on intelligence and security in 1974–77; his request was denied by the US and British intelligence authorities. The existence of the Venona material was first publicly reported in May 1980,[23] and in 1986 former FBI special agent Robert Lamphere published his detailed account of the Venona operation.[24] But it was only in July 1995, some four decades after the event, that the US government officially revealed the operation and began to release copies of Venona decrypts.

The other half of this story concerns counter-espionage. Counter-espionage encompasses all those activities, techniques and methods involved in countering the espionage plans and operations of foreign intelligence agencies. These include Sigint activities such as radio monitoring, direction finding (DF) and cryptanalytic activities, as well as technical surveillance techniques such as telephone tapping, bugging homes and offices, and long-range audio surveillance techniques; professional interrogation methods; the use of 'double agents' within an espionage network or 'defectors in place' within adversary intelligence agencies; protective security measures such as vetting, security clearances and controlling the distribution of documents in order to restrict tightly access to the information sought by adversary intelligence agencies; and the personal skills involved in learning as much as possible about those people identified as being involved in espionage—their work, movements, political interests, family and friends, motivations, characters and mind-sets.

Sir Percy Sillitoe, the one-time head of Britain's counter-espionage organisation, MI5, once remarked that 'counter-espionage was the most dreary, uninspiring and over-rated occupation imaginable'. The 'mystery and excitement of cloak and dagger operations was more in the public's imagination than to be found in fact, and stemmed from a natural awe of the unknown'.[25] Counter-espionage is necessarily also a very secret and sensitive activity. Carelessness can cause an adversary to wind up his espionage operation before one has detected its full dimensions or collected sufficient evidence about the people involved. Often, indeed, a counter-espionage agency will decide to make no evident moves regarding an espionage operation, preferring to monitor it passively and learn more about its structure, intentions and tradecraft. The agency knows that the elimination of one operation will only lead to the establishment of another, involving unknown agents, since important matters are at stake; a known network can be used to feed false or misleading information to an adversary; and it may even be possible to 'double' some of the agents to work against their foreign employer, but only if total secrecy is maintained. Sooner or later, however, most counter-espionage activities are expected to result in the break-up of the espionage operation and the arrest and trial of complicit participants.

It was inevitable that Sigint would play a role in counter-espionage. Espionage activities generally involve regular and extensive communications and the maintenance of complex but secret communications networks and facilities. An intelligence headquarters must be able to communicate fairly directly with its agents in order to provide direction (and sometimes encouragement), to arrange meetings and organise contact points, and to ensure proper tradecraft is being practised; the agents obviously have to transmit their information and documents to their controllers. Since the value of much intelligence is perishable, some means of rapid communication, such as radio or cable, is invariably required.

Espionage activities can be compromised in many ways. They can be revealed by defectors, discovered by double agents, or exposed by poor tradecraft, personal indiscretions, or chance observations by security authorities. Most often, however, they are compromised by weaknesses in their communications systems, techniques and practices. Radio transmissions are monitored by various signals-surveillance, intercept and DF means. Traffic analysts identify the channels, circuits and frequencies used by adversary intelligence agencies. Cryptanalysts can sometimes even decrypt the most secret messages of these agencies, revealing whole espionage networks and their memberships.

The exploitation of these weaknesses requires close and effective cooperation between Sigint and counter-espionage authorities. Richard Sorge, who has been called 'perhaps the greatest spy of all time',[26] was compromised when in 1941 the Japanese counter-intelligence radio-monitoring service intercepted and located the source of his radio transmissions, but the identification and capture of Sorge and his colleagues involved extensive surveillance and secret police work.[27] The Lucy ring and the Rote Kapelle (or 'Red Orchestra'), the most successful GRU (Soviet Military Intelligence) networks in Europe during the Second World War, were broken by the German Abwehr (Military Intelligence) and Gestapo (Secret State Police) by a variety of Sigint, surveillance and interrogation means. In the case of the Lucy ring, the Abwehr had intercepted and analysed some 5500 clandestine wireless signals exchanged between Moscow and three illicit transmitters in Switzerland; Swiss cryptanalysts had also successfully decrypted numerous signals, and a Swiss radio surveillance unit had located the transmitters. The Swiss Bundespolizei (Federal Police) were able to break up and arrest most of the members of the ring in November 1943.[28] In the case of the Rote Kapelle—a much larger organisation, with elements in Belgium, the Netherlands and France as well as Germany itself—its existence and the location of some of its important facilities were discovered by radio surveillance and DF activities. Most of its members were captured in late 1942, having been tracked down by the Abwehr and Gestapo through a combination of radio monitoring activities, physical surveillance and brutal interrogation methods; most were killed or imprisoned, but some were used in a 'Funkspiel' or 'radio playback game' in which false information was passed to Moscow.[29]

One of the most amazing episodes in cooperation between Sigint and counter-espionage activities was the 'Double-Cross' (or XX) operation in which MI5 'actively ran and controlled the German espionage system' in Britain from 1939 to 1945 (and which remained a secret until 1972). By intercepting and decrypting Abwehr radio transmissions to agents sent to Britain, and by locating these agents and turning most of them into double agents (while executing or secretly incarcerating those who refused to cooperate), the British authorities were able to feed the German High Command false information about bombing damage, battle outcomes and, most importantly, Allied plans for the Normandy landings (Operation Overlord).[30]

Cooperation between Sigint and counter-espionage agencies is never easy. Both activities depend upon a tight compartmentalisation whereby details of particular operations, sources and methods are restricted to the minimum number of officers with a 'need to know'. Sigint authorities are inevitably concerned that counter-espionage efforts designed to follow up cryptanalytic breaks and perhaps even lead to arrests and trials will compromise the code-breaking activity itself. Within the Sigint community, there is rarely any doubt that preservation of cryptanalytic secrets is far more important than particular counter-espionage successes.

This book is a case study of the role of Sigint in counter-espionage, as revealed in the cracking of Australia's most serious espionage case between 1944 and 1949. Inevitably, it is a complex story, which cannot be fully understood without an explanation of the background of the various organisations and people involved. For instance, one of the reasons why the Soviet intelligence services targeted Australia in the mid 1940s was because of lax Australian security; equally, Australia's failure to react effectively to news of the security leaks can be attributed to the shortcomings in its security organisation. Since there are no other comprehensive accounts, we found it necessary to describe the formation and development of the Australian security service and the changes to the security services after the Second World War.

Similarly, although a number of books have explained some aspects of Australian or Allied Sigint in the South West Pacific Area, there is no single, detailed, authoritative account of the development of the Australian Sigint organisations. To help readers understand how these organisations developed and operated and also how they could be used for counter-espionage, we trace the formation of Sigint organisations in Australia during the Second World War and explain how they cooperated with Allied organisations and how they were restructured after the war.

There are two other important strands in the story. The first is the Soviet intelligence structure. Although the history and workings of the Soviet intelligence services might seem remote from the Australian story, it is necessary to know what those services were, how they operated, why they were interested in Australia, and how their work there meshed with their other operations around the world. The second strand is Venona, the Allied cryptanalytic operation that provided incontrovertible evidence of Soviet espionage activities. This operation was so amazing, and of such fundamental importance to the uncovering of Soviet espionage, that its story needs to be told in considerable detail.

Finally, we bring all these strands together to show how the spies were uncovered and how the security authorities reacted. Despite the array of different organisations—the security services, the Sigint organisations, the Soviet intelligence services, and the various governments and military structures—this is essentially a story of people. In Australia, people such as Eric Longfield Lloyd and Robert Wake, who appear early in the story through their involvement with security in the 1920s, played important roles in the late 1940s. The key figures in the postwar Sigint organisations in Britain, Australia and the US developed their expertise during the Second World War. On the government side, Dr Herbert Vere Evatt was the Australian minister for External Affairs and attorney-general from 1941 to 1949. As attorney-general he was responsible for the various security organisations. But as minister for External Affairs he presided over a department which harboured some of the spies. The various directors of military intelligence and their staffs reappear throughout the story, including men like Bertrand Combes, John Rogers and Charles Spry, who also headed the Australian Security and Intelligence Organisation (ASIO). From Britain there are the members of MI5, whose presence in Australia indicated how seriously they viewed the threat from Soviet espionage, and the members of the British Sigint organisations. The first of these to assist Australia was the Australian-born Eric Nave in 1940, but later British experts helped establish the postwar Defence Signals Branch. There are the Russians, with their dual roles—ostensibly working as diplomats or journalists, but in reality members of Soviet intelligence. One, Viktor Zaitsev, had already made a significant contribution to espionage as the controller of the famous Richard Sorge in Japan in 1941. And to complete the picture there are the Australian spies, informers and facilitators. Some, such as Walter Clayton, Katharine Susannah Prichard, Ian Milner, Jim Hill and Alfred Hughes worked consciously for the Soviet Union; others, perhaps naively, passed information to members of the Australian Communist Party without inquiring too closely what happened to it.

The purpose of this book is to provide a comprehensive and authoritative account of events that have never before been told in detail. Nonetheless, there are still many gaps and inconsistencies. Where these gaps have appeared we have generally allowed them to stand—they too are part of the story. Indeed, incomplete information is a feature of both Sigint and counter-espionage. With one or two exceptions, such as in trying to determine how information from the Soviet minister in Canberra reached Tokyo in 1944, we have made little effort to indulge in speculation. The story that unfolds is one that is important to an understanding of both Australian history and the wider history of the Cold War.

2

'one directing organisation is most urgent'

THE FORMATION OF AUSTRALIA'S SECURITY SERVICE

ESPIONAGE AND COUNTER-ESPIONAGE were not important factors in the early defence plans of the new Commonwealth of Australia. While spying on one's enemy—or more prosaically, gathering military intelligence—is perhaps as old as organised warfare, Australia in the late nineteenth and early twentieth centuries was largely immune from the espionage threat. By contrast, espionage was well entrenched in Europe as part of both warfare and peacetime military preparations. The European governments and their Defence ministries fully understood the dangers of espionage, and the years leading up to the First World War saw an increase in peacetime espionage in Europe. A popular book in England was Erskine Childers's *The Riddle of the Sands*, published in 1903, which described how two British yachtsmen uncovered a German invasion plot which was being abetted by a British traitor. Within a few years Britain had become obsessed with spies and spying, but as one historian has noted, 'the German spy scare which gripped Britain in the years before the war was entirely without foundation'.[1] In response to this hysteria, in 1909 Britain established its counter-espionage agency, later known as MI5 (Military Intelligence, section 5), which was active during the First World War.

Australia's defence structure and geography, however, provided little incentive for foreign espionage. Unlike Britain before the First World War, Australia did not build battleships like the *Dreadnought*, the details of which would have been valuable to a possible enemy. If an enemy wanted to know about the Commonwealth Military

Forces, which were composed of part-time militiamen, he had only to read the published reports of the various inspector-generals. Australia's only real experience of espionage had been in 1902, when Major William Bridges was sent, at the request of the British government, to look at military developments in the French colony of New Caledonia.[2] Once the war began, Australia had no role in strategic decision-making. Nor was it likely that any country was contemplating an invasion, so a potential enemy was unlikely to be determining possible landing places or prospective targets.

Over the next 40 years Military Intelligence and other counter-espionage or security intelligence organisations were to expand considerably, until by 1943 they were to face a real, unexpected and dangerous espionage threat. To understand how the organisations coped with this threat it is necessary to know how they developed both before the Second World War and under the pressures of that war.

THE ORIGIN OF AUSTRALIA'S COUNTER-ESPIONAGE ORGANISATIONS

Although rational consideration might have led to the view that the threat of espionage was relatively low, the outbreak of the First World War brought immediate public disquiet about the threat of espionage and sabotage, particularly by enemy nationals living in Australia. Foreign nationals, known as 'aliens', were therefore rounded up and placed in internment camps. Meanwhile, concerned members of the public were alert for incidents such as spies signalling by lights to enemy ships offshore.

The chief agency responsible for dealing with the threat of espionage was Military Intelligence. This organisation had developed before the war, initially as the separate Australian Intelligence Corps (AIC), and later as the Intelligence Section of the General Staff (ISGS).[3] At first Military Intelligence was concerned with the provision of maps and other topographical information, and it was not until the outbreak of war that it began to think seriously about security issues such as keeping track of aliens, preventing sabotage, and censoring letters and other communications going abroad. By March 1916 the director of Military Intelligence, Major Edmund Piesse, was responsible for the drafting and enforcing of War Precautions Act regulations, postal and press censorship, counter-espionage, surveillance of enemy aliens and strategic intelligence of political and military developments in the East Asian region.[4] Naval Intelligence, under Lieutenant-Commander John Latham, was focused more narrowly on naval concerns such as eliminating the leakage of information about ship movements and preventing sabotage.

In February 1916, at the behest of the British Counter-Espionage Bureau (later that year named MI5), an Australian Counter-Espionage Bureau (soon to change its name to the Special Intelligence Bureau—SIB) was established under the direction of the governor-general's official secretary, Major George Steward. This organisation had a very small staff and relied on assistance from state police forces. Steward saw his roles as the detection of espionage, the provision of advice to the government and to the police on legislation, and what he called 'Control'—that is, the surveillance of foreign travellers.[5]

In December 1917 another body, the Commonwealth Police, was established, to investigate matters concerning Commonwealth property and facilities. The federal government did not trust the state police forces to deal with what it saw as possible subversive organisations such as the Industrial Workers of the World. The Commonwealth Police, like the SIB, was small, but unlike the SIB, it had no role in counter-espionage.

During the war the main activities of the security intelligence organisations were the conduct of censorship, the identification and internment of enemy aliens, and the surveillance of possibly subversive organisations. The Australian official history, published in 1936, concluded:

> The efficiency of the intelligence section of the Defence Department, aided by the vigilance of the censorship, saved the country from the enemy within the gates. If there had been real spying, it is hardly likely that the officers whose business it was to detect it would have failed to find instances. . . We may with confidence accept the verdict of an official intelligence report that 'in the main it may be taken that spies in the ordinary accepted sense of the term were not identified here'.[6]

With the advantage of hindsight, and the recent revelations of the way Soviet spies have operated in Britain and other countries since the beginning of the 1940s, one would now be hesitant to conclude, as Ernest Scott did in 1936, that there were no spies in Australia. But scant evidence has appeared to suggest that any important espionage was taking place there. No doubt the work of the security intelligence organisations was effective in eliminating the threat from enemy nationals or those who had an obvious reason for supporting Germany or its allies. However, there may have been other reasons why there was little if any espionage. Australia was remote from Europe, communications with Europe were difficult and subject to interception, and, most importantly, Australia was not involved in strategic policy-making or even operational planning, and thus had few secrets to be stolen.[7] That is, of course, if one assumed that the enemy was Germany and its allies; but if Japan was a potential enemy then it might have found the details of Australia's defences to be of interest.

After the First World War, the security intelligence organisations moved their focus even more strongly towards countering subversion. The success of the communist revolution in Russia and the formation of the Soviet Union raised the possibility that communists in Australia might be fomenting revolution. Frank Cain has written extensively on what he calls 'political surveillance' by the security organisations both during the First World War and in the inter-war period, noting that this was their main role during the 1920s and '30s.[8]

The principal organisation conducting this political surveillance in the immediate postwar period was the successor to the SIB, the Commonwealth Investigation Branch (CIB), which moved from the governor-general's office to the attorney-general's department and absorbed many of the investigators from the Commonwealth Police when that body was abolished in August 1919. Major Harold Jones, who had been Steward's deputy, became the director of the CIB. During the 1920s the CIB took over much of the work that Military Intelligence had performed during the war. Also, in 1925 the Commonwealth Police was reformed as a uniformed force. Known as 'peace officers', its members were responsible for enforcing Commonwealth laws and for providing security, where necessary, on Commonwealth premises.

While Military Intelligence and the CIB placed most emphasis on counter-subversion, counter-espionage was not completely overlooked. In 1920 a conference of senior Australian commanders from the First World War identified a possible threat of invasion by Japan.[9] Between 1919 and 1926 Military Intelligence and the CIB detected Japanese agents operating around the Newcastle area.[10] The high point came in 1920, when prime minister William Morris Hughes directed Captain Eric Longfield Lloyd, the head of Military Intelligence in NSW, and Major Piesse, now head of the Pacific Branch in the prime minister's department, to investigate reports of Japanese activity at Newcastle.

Despite the evidence of some Japanese espionage, throughout the 1920s the CIB concentrated on surveillance of the Communist Party of Australia (CPA), which was seen as a much more immediate danger. Then, with the onset of the Great Depression in 1929 along with the election of Labor governments in Canberra and several states, a number of right-wing secret armies were formed to combat a possible communist coup. The activities of these secret armies and their surveillance by the CIB exacerbated the tensions between the CIB and Military Intelligence. During the First World War difficulties had arisen between the military and civilian security intelligence organisations over the duplication of work and at times lack of consultation. The state police forces had complained that they did not have enough staff to carry out the often duplicated, but at times conflicting, tasks they received from the various agencies. After the war these problems had continued, and further difficulties had arisen within the CIB, whose state branches often operated independently from head office in Canberra.

The secret armies, such as the Old and New Guards in NSW and the League of National Security in Victoria, inflamed relations within the security organisations because they were largely formed from former or serving military officers who resented the fact that they might have been placed under surveillance by the CIB. In their view the paramount threat was the Communist Party. In response to the CIB's concerns, in 1931, on the instructions of the Labor prime minister, James Scullin, the Military Board directed all members of the Staff Corps and Instructional Corps not to associate with nor assist any of the secret armies.[11] Later Major Jones, the director of the CIB, was to claim that the hostility of Military Intelligence towards his branch stemmed from its inquiries into the League of National Security.[12]

In fact, by comparison with its concern about the communists, the CIB took little action against the secret armies. Furthermore, many of its officers had been officers in Military Intelligence. Jones had joined the part-time AIC in Victoria in 1910 when he was working for the federal Taxation department. The head of the CIB in Victoria, Major Roland Browne, had joined the AIC in Western Australia in 1912. He had been wounded in action in the First World War and after the war had continued serving in the ISGS. The head of the CIB in NSW, Lieutenant-Colonel Eric Longfield Lloyd, had been awarded the Military Cross in the First World War and joined Military Intelligence after he was wounded in 1917. He transferred to the CIB in 1921. He spoke Japanese, and in 1935 became the Australian Trade Commissioner in Tokyo. Lloyd was succeeded as head of the NSW CIB by Lieutenant-Colonel Frederick Galleghan, the commanding officer of a militia infantry battalion, who had served as a soldier in the First World War and been a Customs official in Newcastle.

Military intelligence was not considered an attractive career for regular officers, and although there was a small nucleus of regular officers most intelligence postings were held by militia officers. During the 1920s and '30s there was no separate director of Military

Intelligence at Army Headquarters, and intelligence staff came under the director of Military Operations and Intelligence. From 1934 to 1939 the senior intelligence staff officer at Army Headquarters was Lieutenant-Colonel Bertrand Combes. Born in 1894, he was a Royal Military College (Duntroon) graduate who had served overseas in the First World War but had been invalided home after being severely wounded at Gallipoli. After attending the staff college at Camberley, in 1930 he became the senior intelligence staff officer in NSW. Under Combes, Military Intelligence stepped up its interest in the CPA, and in August 1934 he directed that militia officers or selected civilians in country towns be appointed as military reporting officers to report on possible communist sympathisers.[13]

Military Intelligence was divided into three main sections. 'Ia' dealt with information; 'Ib', security; and 'Ic', censorship. Between the wars very little attention was paid to Ia. The War Book allowed for the Army's control of postal and telegraphic censorship in time of war, but there was no work for the Ic staff before the war. The main focus of the intelligence staff was therefore Ib. The Army intelligence staff were concerned not just with security within the Army, but also with subversion and possible enemy espionage in the general community. Before the war they kept watch over Nazi sympathisers and members of the CPA.

In 1935 Major W. J. R. (Jack) Scott, a militia officer, was appointed the senior Military Intelligence officer in the headquarters of the 2nd Military District (NSW). He had been awarded the DSO in the First World War and had commanded militia infantry battalions during the 1920s. Scott, who had been the military chief of the Old Guard and had briefly been in the New Guard, approached certain citizens to undertake voluntary work with Military Intelligence and recruited eleven men in 1939 to widen his information-gathering network.[14] In April 1939 he took up full-time duty to supervise the NSW section of the Military Police Intelligence (MPI) organisation, which had been established the previous year and consisted of sections of military personnel working closely with sections of the state police forces. In NSW, the MPI section consisted of 30 (later 50) policemen, 28 military personnel and eighteen field security police. Its formation was facilitated by the state police commissioner, William MacKay, who had been in charge of aggressive police investigations into the New Guard in the early 1930s. The arrangement in NSW was not replicated in the other states, where the civilian police were involved to varying degrees. Nor was there consistent and effective cooperation between Military Intelligence and the CIB. Cain has claimed, without providing any compelling evidence, that the CIB was an 'efficient organisation',[15] but it still had a relatively small staff.

While Military Intelligence and the CIB spent much time watching the CPA and the Nazis, in the late 1930s the Japanese stepped up their intelligence gathering around the northern Australian coast and in New Guinea and the Solomon Islands.[16] Military and Naval Intelligence were aware of many of these activities but were unable to prevent them. For example, the crews of pearl luggers operating in northern Australian waters often included senior Japanese naval officers in disguise.

The difficulty in preventing Japanese espionage underlined the problem, in a democracy, of preventing a possible enemy from gathering information when its agents did not act illegally. But it also showed up the weaknesses in the Australian counter-espionage organisation. The historical consultant to the 1977 Royal Commission, Jacqueline Templeton, concluded that 'Australia entered World War II ill-equipped for security and intelligence work'.[17] Certainly, the work of the various security intelligence organisations was in need of some rationalisation.

FORMATION OF THE SECURITY SERVICE

As early as 1936, the department of Defence had pressed for an interdepartmental committee to examine the question of national intelligence, but it was not until February 1939 that a committee, with limited membership, reported that it was 'strongly of the opinion that an efficient Security Intelligence Organisation is an essential adjunct to National Security'. There was no systematic cooperation between Defence and the CIB, it found, and insufficient use was made of the state police forces.[18] No action was taken on this recommendation, but there was continuing disquiet among the security organisations. For example, in June 1939 Major Scott wrote to the attorney-general, William Morris Hughes, criticising both Naval and Military Intelligence as well as the CIB. The organisations were understaffed and lacked trained personnel, he said, and there was inadequate cooperation between the states. He described the useful role of MI5 in Britain. On 8 August 1939 the director of the CIB, Jones, wrote to Hughes and complained about the lack of cooperation among the three branches of security intelligence, and by mid August the Attorney-General's department was considering the wisdom of transferring its responsibility for 'national security intelligence' to the department of Defence.[19]

When war broke out, these concerns were initially supplanted by others of more pressing urgency. On advice from the CIB and Military Intelligence, enemy aliens were rounded up and placed in internment camps controlled by the Army. Furthermore, censorship procedures had to be established. In September 1939 the government set up a department of Information which had responsibility for the press, broadcasting and films, but postal and telegraphic censorship remained with the Army.

These activities caused an increase in the size of the intelligence sections of the three services. According to the War Book, in time of war the Army was responsible for internal security; the state police and other related security bodies were to cooperate with them and at their direction in preserving this security. With this broad responsibility, a number of part-time militia intelligence officers changed to full-time work. Lieutenant-Colonel Combes was promoted to colonel and became director of Military Operations and Intelligence.

The expansion of the intelligence staff was complicated by the formation of the Second Australian Imperial Force (2nd AIF) for service overseas. Major-General Sir Thomas Blamey was appointed general officer commanding the 6th Australian Division, and many keen militia officers transferred to the AIF. Then, in April 1940, the AIF was expanded with the formation of the 1st Australian Corps, with Blamey as commander. In view of the lack of regular Army intelligence officers, the key intelligence appointments went to militia officers. The senior intelligence officer was Major John Rogers, a 45-year-old industrial chemist and oil company executive who had had limited experience in the militia intelligence corps during the early 1920s but had served under Blamey on the headquarters of both the 1st Australian Division and the Australian Corps in France in 1918. He and the other corps intelligence officers served throughout the fighting in the Middle East during 1940 and 1941, and most were later to figure prominently in Military Intelligence.

The director of Naval Intelligence (DNI) was Lieutenant-Commander Rupert Long, a 40-year-old permanent naval officer who had been assistant DNI from 1936 to 1939 and had in fact acted as DNI during this period.[20] Long's responsibilities covered all aspects of intelligence, including the establishment of the coastwatcher organisation. With naval reporting officers at major ports, he established his own security intelligence organisation. There were a few major differences between the Army and naval intelligence organisations. Since it was unlikely that the Australian Army would have to fight within Australia, the Military Intelligence staff in Australia did not pay much attention to operational intelligence. That was handled by the intelligence staff of the 1st Australian Corps, which from mid 1940 was in the Middle East. By contrast, naval operations might take place around Australia, so the DNI was

Commander R.B.M. ('Cocky') Long, the wartime director of Naval Intelligence. In 1940 he argued that it was 'most urgent' that 'one directing organisation' be formed to deal with internal security. (AWM 107007)

concerned to develop procedures and organisations to detect an approaching enemy.

The Royal Australian Air Force (RAAF) intelligence organisation was less well-formed than those of the other two services. The Chief of the Air Staff was concerned primarily about the security of civil establishments manufacturing items that were essential to the RAAF, and about the security of coastal airfields remote from direct Army control.[21]

Perhaps the most pressing security concern in the first months of the war was the activities of the CPA. In August 1939 the Soviet Union had signed a non-aggression pact with Hitler's Germany, and communists in Australia were being told to keep out of the Army and to boycott the export of war materials.[22] In January 1940 prime minister Menzies, who was also minister for Defence Coordination, convened a meeting at Army Headquarters to consider the activities of the CPA. Chaired by Colonel Combes, the conference included representatives of the three services, the CIB, the department of Information and the state police forces; it recommended against banning the CPA, but urged stricter control of its activities.[23]

Concerned at the lack of 'one directing organisation', which he considered 'most urgent', the DNI, Lieutenant-Commander Long, arranged for a meeting with representatives of Military and Air Force Intelligence to reconsider the interdepartmental report from February 1939, on which no action had been taken.[24] After a number of meetings and recommendations from the chiefs of staff, on 5 June the War Cabinet agreed to set up a defence security organisation responsible to the three chiefs of staff.[25] It is probable that this plan

Lieutenant-Colonel Eric Longfield Lloyd. In March 1941 he was appointed the first director of the Security Service. He became one of three directors in the reformed Commonwealth Security Service in 1942, and after the war became director of the Commonwealth Investigation Service. (NLA)

was opposed by attorney-general Hughes and by the solicitor-general, Sir George Knowles, who were concerned that the defence security organisation would not take account of the concerns of the CIB; in any case no further action was taken.[26]

The lack of action was caused by the intense bureaucratic struggle between the competing organisations—Hughes, Knowles and Jones on the one side, and the new minister for the Army, Percy Spender, and the chiefs of staff on the other. Finally, at a conference in December— attended by Knowles; Brigadier Combes, who had recently been made assistant chief of the general staff; Colonel Kenneth Mackenzie, the director of Military Operations and Intelligence; Lieutenant-Colonel Jones, the director of the CIB; and Lieutenant-Colonel Longfield Lloyd, the deputy director of the CIB, who had recently concluded his term as Australian Trade Commissioner in Japan—Combes proposed a compromise under which a new organisation, to be known as the Security Service, would be formed.[27] It would be functionally overseen by the Attorney-General's department and operationally by the Army. Its director was expected to be Longfield Lloyd, who was acceptable both to Hughes and Knowles, and to Combes and the Army as a result of his long association with Military Intelligence.[28]

The War Cabinet approved the establishment of the Security Service on 18 February 1941, Lloyd was approved as director on 5 March,[29] and on 31 March the Security Service officially opened at the Patents Office in Canberra. From the beginning it faced considerable obstacles. It lacked office space, telephones and clerical staff. Lloyd appointed deputy directors in each state, but since these were mainly former militia officers the new organisation became heavily

Lieutenant-Colonel Colyn Cohen, the Army liaison officer in the Commonwealth Security Service from 1941 to 1945. He controlled a network of informers in Newcastle before the war and until he moved to Canberra in 1941. (AWM 3DRL 7732)

dependent on the military. Each service was to nominate representatives in the new organisation, but by the middle of the year the Navy had withdrawn its representative. There was only grudging cooperation from the CIB, which refused to pass over its ciphers to communicate with London, and retained its files. The Army, too, was reluctant to make personnel available, although it did nominate a representative, Major Colyn Cohen, who was soon promoted to lieutenant-colonel and who was to remain with the organisation until after the end of the war.

Born in 1896, Cohen had served as an infantry officer in the First World War and had been almost blinded by mustard gas at Villers-Bretonneux in 1918.[30] He read with great difficulty, always wore dark glasses, and carried a cane. After the war he had gained a law degree at Sydney University and had returned to Newcastle to join the legal firm of Braye Cragg Cohen. In 1923 he joined the militia as an intelligence officer concerned with internal security in Newcastle and remained there until 1941. As the senior Military Intelligence officer in Newcastle he worked with Major Scott, the head of the MPI in Sydney, to build up a network of informers in the period before the war.[31] In 1941 he moved to Canberra with his wife, who had special permission to drive his car on official business.[32]

INQUIRIES INTO THE SECURITY SERVICE

Forty years after Federation, Australia had at last established a security service, but in truth, little had been achieved by the formation of yet another security organisation, and most of the work continued to be undertaken by the Army. On 4 July 1941 the War Cabinet directed that an inquiry be made into the Security Service. At the request of the minister for the Army, Percy Spender, its scope was extended to cover Military Intelligence, about which he was 'very dissatisfied'.[33] The officer selected to carry out the inquiry was Lieutenant-Colonel John Mawhood, whose appointment was endorsed at a War Cabinet meeting on 9 July 1941.

Mawhood was a British officer who had arrived in Australia in December 1940 as head of Mission 104, which had been sent from the UK to establish and train independent military companies in Australia.[34] The Army vigorously opposed Mawhood's selection to conduct the inquiry, believing he had neither the capacity nor the character to carry out his tasks. Eventually, the War Cabinet decided to restrict the investigation to the Security Service and not to include Military Intelligence, and at the suggestion of the chief of the general staff, Lieutenant-General Sturdee, it engaged Alexander Duncan, the chief commissioner of the Victoria Police, to undertake the investigation. Sir George Knowles arranged for him to be assisted by Mawhood.

Duncan's report was not completed until January 1942, but on 18 October 1941 Mawhood submitted a separate report to Knowles.[35] He began with the comment that he was 'most unfavourably impressed and disturbed' by what he had seen and learned about the work of Military Intelligence since he had arrived in Australia. The main weaknesses were in policy and personnel. There was no clearly defined policy and 'no proper conception of what Military Intelligence really means'.

With respect to personnel, he observed that 'good intelligence demands an alert and vigorous brain', yet 'no one could claim that Military Intelligence at Army Headquarters is remarkable in that direction'. The director of Military Intelligence, Colonel James A. Chapman, who had been promoted to fill the newly created position on 1 July 1941, was not 'big enough for the job; quite bluntly, he has not the personality, intellect, education, or training necessary for this important post'. Mawhood claimed that Brigadier Combes, who was 'responsible for the creation of the Intelligence organisation as it is presently constituted', had 'surrounded himself by henchmen of the calibre of Longfield Lloyd, Cohen, Scott, and Powell, all of whom are now Lieutenant-Colonels'. He continued:

> I am convinced from reliable and independent sources that close investigation into the antecedents of certain of the men named in this report would produce remarkable disclosures. It should be

borne in mind that these men, openly or under cover, were at one time active members of the New Guard.

Mawhood went on to criticise the Security Service, which he said had been set up as a compromise between the CIB and the Army. Longfield Lloyd was not the right man, as he 'possessed neither the intelligence, personality, nor knowledge requisite for the task'. While Air Intelligence still maintained a measure of support for the Security Service, Naval Intelligence had withdrawn its representative and had severed relations with it, as had the CIB and the state police forces. Mawhood suggested that a director-general of Security should be appointed; he recommended Commander Long, the DNI.

While Mawhood had given the Army plentiful reason to distrust him, there was much truth in his claim that there were grave shortcomings in the security intelligence organisation. Its lack of effectiveness in counter-espionage was demonstrated by the incident concerning Major Hashida of the Japanese Army. Hashida visited Australia from January to March 1941, ostensibly as a heavy industry expert. Despite the fact that he was under surveillance by Military Intelligence and state police officers, he visited and took notes on important defence and industrial facilities in Queensland, NSW, Victoria, South Australia and Western Australia. The extent of his espionage was revealed when he was arrested by Netherlands East Indies authorities in Batavia (Jakarta) on his return journey to Japan, and his notebooks were made available to Australian authorities.[36]

By mid 1941 it was clear that war with Japan was likely, and the need to coordinate Australian intelligence and security activities with those of the British in the Far East became urgent. CIB director Jones continued as the principal liaison officer with MI5 in London and refused to hand over his ciphers to the Security Service. Long, however, was in direct communication with Royal Navy authorities. The Army had not established a separate Intelligence Directorate at Army Headquarters until Chapman was appointed DMI on 1 July. The Air Force followed suit in August, and on 18 September Wing Commander Gerald Packer became the new director.[37]

In an effort to improve cooperation in the Far East, in August the DMI directed Lieutenant-Colonel Robert Frederick Bird (Bob) Wake to visit Singapore to establish links with the Far East Combined Bureau (FECB) and, in particular, the Far Eastern Security Service. Wake was well placed to carry out this task, as he was deputy director of the CIB in Brisbane as well as head of both the Security Service and Military Intelligence in Queensland. Wake was to be a key and controversial figure in the efforts to uncover Soviet

The minister for the Army, Percy Spender, during an inspection of Northern Command, Brisbane, in 1941. On the right in civilian clothes is Major R.F.B. Wake, the head of the Security Service in Queensland. Wake was also deputy director of the Commonwealth Investigation Bureau and head of Military Intelligence in Queensland. Later he would be director Sydney in the new Australian Security Intelligence Organisation, responsible for investigating 'the case'. (Mrs E. Wake)

espionage in the late 1940s. Born in Melbourne in 1900, he joined the Navy as a clerical assistant in 1918 and later became a clerk in the Naval Intelligence Office.[38] In 1934 he became the principal assistant to Longfield Lloyd, then the deputy director of the CIB in NSW, and in 1936 he was transferred to Brisbane to head the CIB in Queensland and the Northern Territory.[39] There was no Military Police Intelligence unit in Queensland, but early in 1939 he was commissioned in the militia, and soon after the outbreak of war, with the rank of major, he became the senior Military Intelligence officer in the state while still retaining his civilian appointment. Wake had a dominating personality and great energy but, as his widow recalled, he was 'very much a law unto himself', and Army officers criticised him for not wearing his uniform. According to his wife, Elizabeth, some of them resented his rapid promotion from lieutenant to lieutenant-colonel in about three years.[40]

Using his various appointments, Wake had arranged for the Army's Field Security Police to carry out investigations for the CIB and Security Service. As his responsibilities covered not only Queensland but also New Guinea and the Solomon Islands, he had a good knowledge of the coastwatcher organisation. His mission to Singapore was supported by DNI Long, who had known him when they both worked in intelligence in Sydney and who called him 'Hereward' after the Anglo-Saxon rebel known as 'the Wake'.[41] Wake visited Singapore from 28 August to 12 September and, as well as establishing relations with the Far Eastern Security Service, arranged for Chapman and Long to visit the FECB later in the year.[42]

Between 10 and 23 October 1941, Colonel G. E. Grimsdale from the FECB visited Australia and wrote a detailed report on its intelligence structure. His comments provide a valuable contemporary picture:

> It was difficult in the short time available to get a complete and accurate picture of the somewhat complicated security organisation. The normal peace time work was in the hands of the Commonwealth Investigation Board [sic], a civil department corresponding in principle in many respects to M. I. 5. In war time this organisation was, for various reasons, found to be inadequate for Defence Security purposes. In the absence of any other suitable organisation, defence security was therefore largely taken over by Military Intelligence. Hence the presence of M. I. officers at the Passport Control Office at Darwin . . . This has naturally thrown a great strain on the resources of the M. I. Directorate, and in my opinion, has so increased the direct responsibilities of the D. M. I. as to throw an undue burden onto one man, to the possible detriment of the I (a) [i.e information] side of his work.

Grimsdale went on to describe the formation of the Security Service, but noted that a shortage of personnel meant Military Intelligence still had to do most of the work. 'The latter has also recently organised a small body of picked men from all ranks of civil and military life into a Field Security Police, known now as the "Field Security Wing", of which each Military Command and District has a proportion.'[43] To an outsider such as Grimsdale, it was clear that the security intelligence organisation in Australia had considerable shortcomings, so much would hinge on the outcome of the Duncan inquiry.

CHANGE OF GOVERNMENT

During the period of the Duncan inquiry the government changed twice. On 29 August Arthur Fadden replaced Menzies as prime minister, but otherwise the ministerial appointments remained. Then, after a vote of no confidence in the House of Representatives, on 7 October the Labor Party formed a new government. John Curtin, who had been leader of the opposition since 1935, became prime minister and minister for Defence Coordination. The members of the War Cabinet included Curtin, Frank Forde (minister for the Army), Joseph 'Ben' Chifley (Treasurer), Herbert Vere Evatt (attorney-general and minister for External Affairs), John Beasley (minister for Supply and Development and later minister for Supply and Shipping), Norman Makin (minister for the Navy and minister for Munitions), Arthur Drakeford (minister for Air and minister for Civil Aviation) and John Dedman (minister for War Organisation of Industry).

The War Cabinet was concerned with all aspects of the war effort, but matters of a more strategic nature were considered by the Advisory War Council, which included members of both the government and the opposition. The Advisory War Council could not make decisions but, since it included five key members of the War Cabinet, decisions of the council could be ratified as decisions of the War Cabinet, and in practice it did have an executive function. The secretary of both the War Cabinet and the Advisory War Council was Frederick Shedden, who, since he was also secretary of the department of Defence, was in a powerful position to influence the decisions of the War Cabinet. Curtin relied heavily on his advice.

As attorney-general, Evatt was responsible for the CIB and the Security Service, and was to be a key figure in matters concerning security intelligence for the next decade. Born in 1894, he had trained as a barrister at Sydney University and had been a member of the NSW Legislative Assembly from 1925 to 1930, when he resigned to become a High Court judge—at 36, the youngest person ever so appointed. (He had been appointed a King's Counsel in 1929.) In 1940 he resigned from the High Court and was elected to the federal House of Representatives. A brilliant lawyer and noted historian, Evatt was passionate about civil liberties and had an idealistic approach to international affairs, but he could be abrasive and ambitious, and had chaotic work habits. These characteristics were to be reflected in his approach to security intelligence.

Evatt's appointment as attorney-general may, in fact, have been of concern to some members of the Security Service. In December 1920 Longfield Lloyd of the CIB had advised Piesse, the head of the Pacific Branch in the Prime Minister's department, that during the First World War Evatt had come 'under most unfavourable notice' by the security authorities when his correspondence and that of a friend, Vere Gordon Childe, a noted socialist and pacifist, were reviewed by the censor. According to Lloyd, he had been reliably informed that in 1920, when Evatt was asked by prime minister Hughes to investigate the 'Japanese question' in California, Evatt had 'bragged about the commission allegedly given him'. The informant, Campbell, had described Evatt 'as an unscrupulous man

Members of the Australian War Cabinet watch the governor-general, Lord Gowrie, sign the proclamation which declared that a state of war existed between Australia and Japan, December 1941. From left: the minister for the Army, F.M. Forde, the prime minister, John Curtin, Lord Gowrie, the treasurer, J.B. Chifley and the minister for External Affairs, Dr H.V. Evatt. (AWM 10688)

much given to utilizing all things to his ends only'.[44] It is likely that the informant was Professor Arthur Campbell, who by 1941 was dean of the faculty of Law at Adelaide University, the South Australian state censor and the state deputy director of the Security Service. During the First World War he had been a district censor and state publicity censor in NSW.

Even before he became minister in October 1941, Evatt made it clear that he was concerned about civil liberties. On 15 June 1940, at the urging of Military Intelligence, the CPA had been declared an illegal organisation, and two communists, Horace Ratcliff and Max Thomas, had been jailed for not observing National Security Regulations.[45] On their release in May 1941 they were promptly interned, and when they appealed to the advisory committee they were supported by Evatt, who said that he had 'every reason to question the value of reports by so-called Military Intelligence'.[46] Germany's attack on the Soviet Union in June 1941 changed the CPA's attitude towards the war, and in October 1941 Ratcliff and Thomas were released. Shortly before the attack on Pearl Harbor, Evatt refused to allow the Japanese consulate in Melbourne to be 'bugged'.

The minister for the Army, Frank Forde, lacked Evatt's academic credentials and ideological commitment to civil liberties. As a conscientious administrator, but one who put his loyalty to his party before personal advancement, he was likely to follow advice from his department on security issues. Since the Army still retained a heavy responsibility for security, especially postal and telegraphic censorship, he would be involved in security issues for the remainder of the war.

Thus, on the eve of war with Japan, Australia had a new and untried government. The Security Service was in a state of limbo as it waited for the outcome of the Duncan inquiry and was subject to keen competition from the CIB and the three armed services. So far the security intelligence organisations had been unsuccessful in detecting cases of enemy espionage. They were all to face a much greater challenge once Japan entered the war and moved closer to Australia.

3

'our security system has failed to cope'

THE SECURITY SERVICE AND THE WAR WITH JAPAN

THE OUTBREAK OF WAR WITH Japan in December 1941 provided the Australian security intelligence organisations with a range of new challenges. Initially there was no panic, but as the Japanese advanced through Malaya, the Philippines and the Netherlands East Indies, seized Singapore and landed at Rabaul, Timor and Ambon, it became obvious that there was a real threat of invasion. By February and March 1942 the mood of the government changed to one of alarm. There was talk of scorched-earth policies in some states and considerable public disquiet.

During 1940 and 1941 there had been occasional German raiders in Australian waters, but by mid 1942 Japanese submarines were active near Australia, and the security of information such as convoy timings became crucial. Another change was the establishment of a major Allied headquarters, General Headquarters South West Pacific Area, in Australia, with control over important Allied operations. The security of information about future intentions, deployments of units and force structures would be critical.

In December 1941, however, these concerns lay in the future. The first priority was the internment of Japanese aliens. Before the war dossiers had been created on the thousands of Germans, Italians and other Europeans in Australia, and many were interned. In the early part of the war Military Intelligence and the CIB had identified which aliens were be interned, but later this function was taken over by the Security Service. The Army administered the internment camps and until mid 1942 controlled aliens and internment policy.

In early 1942 the Italian farmers in northern Queensland were also interned, as this was a likely area of Japanese invasion. The maximum number of internees at any particular time, 6780, was reached in September 1942 (including 1029 Germans, 3651 Italians and 1036 Japanese).[1]

The threat of invasion prompted a stepping-up of security within the civilian population. Citizens were arrested, or warned, for writing unpatriotic letters (which had been detected by mail censorship) and for breaking any of the many National Security Regulations. The security services kept close watch on organisations such as those professing friendship with foreign countries, unusual religious sects and extreme political parties.

The most celebrated case of possible subversion concerned the anti-British and highly nationalistic Australia First Movement. In March 1942 four of its members were arrested in Perth and sixteen in Sydney. Two members in Perth were found guilty in a criminal court of conspiring to assist the enemy, while the remainder were detained under National Security Regulations.[2] Responsibility for the arrests in NSW was taken by the Military Police Intelligence section.[3] At the end of the war a judicial inquiry determined that the recommendation for the detention of the eight people in Sydney had not been justified. The Australian official war historian, Paul Hasluck, concluded: 'The detention of some of the 21 persons concerned was undoubtedly the grossest infringement of individual liberty made during the war and the tardiness in rectifying it was a matter of shame to the democratic institution and to the authorities concerned'.[4] Some members of Military Intelligence were unrepentant. One wrote soon after the war: 'In view of the conditions then operating and the possibility of almost immediate invasion of Australia by Japanese forces, the action taken was regarded as justified.'[5]

THE DIRECTOR-GENERAL OF SECURITY

These were some of the attitudes in circulation when, on 7 January 1942, Duncan forwarded his report to attorney-general Evatt. There were considerable weaknesses in the report and Duncan, a former Scotland Yard policeman, did not appear to understand the Australian federal system.[6] Duncan was critical of the security intelligence organisation, especially the CIB, and argued that there was insufficient coordination between the various agencies, personnel were untrained and inexperienced, and the organisation was incompetent and inefficient. He recommended expanding the area of responsibility of the Security Service and the appointment of a director-general of Security with wide-ranging powers and responsibilities, answering directly to the attorney-general. He suggested as a candidate the NSW police commissioner, William MacKay. From reading the Duncan and Mawhood reports, Templeton concluded that 'when Japan entered the war in December 1941, Australia's Security Service was in a chaotic state'.[7]

While the government was considering Duncan's report, in response to an inquiry in the Advisory War Council by the former Army minister, Percy Spender, it sought further advice from the armed services as to the possibility that enemy agents might have sent short-wave broadcasts to ships at sea. The services' reports outlined the various measures then in operation, including the monitoring of radio traffic, restrictions on telephone calls, the scrutiny of cables and censorship of mail. The Navy urged that immediate steps be taken 'to create a Commonwealth Security Service under the direction of a trained and experienced officer'.[8]

Duncan's report caused more problems than it solved, as the agencies under investigation all rushed to defend their records and promote their cases to their own ministers. Jones thought the report was 'very misleading'.[9] Knowles wrote a sixteen-page critique in which he argued that Duncan had tended to take the Army's view on many issues. He thought Lloyd was 'not big enough' for the position of director-general, adding that he was 'so much under the domination of the Army that were he placed in charge, the militarization of the combined establishment would be inevitable'. Knowles did not favour MacKay and recommended an officer of his department instead.[10]

By this stage the director of Military Intelligence, Colonel Chapman, had been sent to another appointment in Darwin and been replaced by Colonel Caleb Roberts, a militia intelligence officer who had been awarded the Military Cross in the First World War. As an engineer with the Victorian Country Roads Board, Roberts had been required to travel frequently around the state, so he had been well placed to organise the state's military reporting officers during the 1930s.[11] He told the chief of the general staff, Lieutenant-General Sturdee, that MacKay was not suitable as director-general of the Security Service.[12] In turn, Sturdee advised the minister for the Army that Brigadier Combes was the best candidate.[13] DNI Long was later to recommend Sir Owen Dixon, a justice of the High Court of Australia and chairman of the Shipping Control Board, as director-general.[14]

In this environment of bureaucratic in-fighting, another figure appeared who was to have considerable influence for several years. This was an assistant secretary in the department of the Army, J. Charles Kevin. A member of the English and NSW Bars, Kevin

Charles Kevin (foreground), the assistant secretary in the department of the Army, who in 1942 drafted the plans for the new Commonwealth Security Service. Later he was transferred to the Security Service and conducted a critical review of its effectiveness. (AWM 42293)

was on loan from the Australian high commissioner's office in London, and with a lawyer's mind he set about providing some alternative ideas. A note in a department of Army file, perhaps written by Kevin, set out the problem:

> I start from the fact that—(a) not one enemy agent has been caught; (b) not one case of espionage has been uncovered in Australia. From this it follows either—(i) that Australia is free from espionage, or (ii) that enemy agents are active here but that our Security system has failed to cope with them. If (i) is true, then Australia is the only belligerent to have escaped the enemy's attention.[15]

The note went on to state that (i) was in fact unlikely to be true, and that one single, centralised security intelligence organisation was needed.

Kevin drafted a letter to Evatt from Army minister Forde, who signed it on 5 March 1942. The letter argued for a single organisation and that it was immaterial whether it came under the attorney-general or the minister for the Army. The Duncan report, it remarked, contained little that would bring about the desired result, namely 'a ruthlessly efficient and quick moving body which will counter the dangers which are walling up around Australia and inside Australia'. Forde's letter continued:

> I recognise, of course, that these proposals involve the removal of Military Intelligence from a great many security matters, the elimination of the existing security service, and the confining of the CIB to control of peace officers and domestic departmental

investigations of a non-security character .. [However, the time frame for the] creation of an adequate security organisation is unfortunately not a matter of weeks, but of days.[16]

Armed with Kevin's notes, Forde presented the argument to the War Cabinet on 9 March, saying there was not the slightest doubt that enemy agents were operating in Australia, but the present 'organisation is unable to uncover them and, in fact, does not know where to look for them'.[17] Forde secured approval to form a new, expanded security service to be named the Commonwealth Security Service (CSS) and to have executive as well as advisory powers. Since it was 'important to impress the civil rather than the military stamp upon the proposed organisation, owing to necessity for public confidence in the reasonable protection of civil rights and liberty', Evatt thought the director-general should report to the attorney-general rather than to the minister for the Army. Since Duncan had recommended MacKay as director-general, his services would be sought from the NSW government for a period of six months. However, as Evatt was shortly to leave on an overseas visit, he agreed that in his absence Forde would have responsibility for the new organisation.[18] It was therefore left to Kevin to tie up the administrative details.

Over the next few months the arrangements were determined in a series of conferences. MacKay wanted his headquarters to be in Sydney and his representatives to be the state police commissioners.[19] This was opposed by Forde, who ruled that the headquarters was to be in Canberra and was 'not to perform merely a nominal role but is to be the nerve centre of your organisation'. It was to absorb the records of the other security organisations and to maintain 'constant and real control' over the state branches, which would each be headed by an assistant director. The CSS was to be responsible for communications with MI5 in London.[20]

CSS headquarters was established in the Patents Office in Canberra with the telegraph address of 'Compositely'. It had three directors: Longfield Lloyd, Major Beauchamp Tyrell, who had been in Military Intelligence in Sydney since the beginning of the war, and Wake, who was given responsibility for the Fighting Services. The state deputy directors were Commander J. C. McFarlane (Qld), S. C. Taylor (NSW), Lieutenant-Colonel S. F. Whittington (Vic), J. H. Kirkman, (SA), Lieutenant-Colonel H. D. Mosely (WA), and Judge P. L. Griffiths (Tas). In Canberra there were eight principals with functional responsibilities. In addition, there were to be three service liaison officers, but in the first instance only Lieutenant-Colonel Cohen was appointed. The United States forces were represented by Lieutenant-Colonel William Clark, the assistant military

Sir George Knowles, the solicitor-general and secretary of the Attorney-General's department during the Second World War. He had little rapport with his minister, Dr Evatt, and obstructed the development of the Commonwealth Security Service. (NLA)

attaché at the US Embassy in Canberra; later he was succeeded by Lieutenant-Colonel Earl C. Stewart.

While no doubt a capable policeman, MacKay was a poor choice as director-general. He tended to see the CSS as part of a police empire and wanted to retain his post as police commissioner. He was also probably a victim of the feud between the department of the Army and the Attorney-General's department. While the CSS was administratively part of the latter, its director-general answered directly to the minister, thus cutting the departmental secretary, Sir George Knowles, out of the line of command. Knowles had joined the Attorney-General's department in 1907 and had been secretary and solicitor-general since 1932. He had little rapport with Evatt, but was still a powerful bureaucrat. Knowles reduced the Security Service budget allocation from over £255 000 to £100 000, was difficult over the transfer of clerical staff and the provision of office accommodation, and ensured that the CIB did not hand over its files to the CSS.[21] By May MacKay felt compelled to write to Forde that 'it was impossible . . . to work in conjunction with Sir George Knowles'.[22]

Denied civil staff, MacKay had to call upon members of the MPI, who were transferred from the NSW police, and 163 members of the Army, on loan for three months. The Army was opposed to the practice of having its personnel subject to an outside body, and on 2 September advised that officers seconded to the CSS would have to take up civil appointments and would lose their pension benefits. The other ranks in the CSS would have to leave the Army altogether.[23]

In early September MacKay announced that when his six-month term expired on 21 September he would not seek reappointment. However, at a meeting on 15 September 1942 with the secretary of the department of the Army, Frank Sinclair, and several senior Army officers, he made a last attempt to resolve the problem of using Army personnel.[24] Nine days later, Evatt wrote to Forde seeking to retain the Army men in the CSS, and the majority of these men subsequently became members of a new establishment known as the Security Service, Australian Intelligence Corps.[25] Thus the Security Service had gained additional staff which were charged to the Army budget.

By this time Brigadier William Simpson, who had served with the AIF in the Middle East, had been appointed director-general of Security. According to one account, Simpson 'was a school and university associate of Dr Evatt',[26] which perhaps explains why Evatt was at last willing to accept a military officer as head of the CSS. Simpson had been born in 1894, the same year as Evatt, and they had both attended Fort Street High School in Sydney and Sydney University, from which they received their law degrees. Simpson had served in the First AIF as an engineer officer and had continued as a legal officer in the militia between the wars. From the outbreak of the Second World War to early 1941 he had been the senior legal officer in Eastern Command (NSW); he had then become deputy judge advocate-general of the AIF in the Middle East. He held a similar position from the time he returned to Australia in July 1942 until his appointment to the Security Service. With Simpson as director-general, the Army found it easier to accept his control over its personnel, but it would not give up its efforts to reduce this drain on its manpower.

THE NEW ALLIED COMMAND AND INTELLIGENCE STRUCTURE

Simpson's appointment reflected the fact that in mid 1942 a completely new set of command military relationships had been established in Australia. In 1939 and 1940 the AIF, with some of the Army's most capable officers, had been dispatched to the Middle East, but with the outbreak of war in the Far East these officers and men had started to return to Australia, and in March 1942 the Army command structure was reshaped. The Military Board was disbanded, General Blamey became commander-in-chief of the Australian Military Forces, and the former members of the Military Board became his principal staff officers.

Brigadier William Simpson, in Palestine in May 1942, when he was deputy judge advocate-general of the AIF. In September 1942 he was appointed director-general of the Commonwealth Security Service and later clashed with Blamey over the use of Army personnel in the Security Service. In January 1945 Military Intelligence briefed him on Ultra and the leakage of information. (AWM 24172)

The arrangements were complicated further with the arrival in March of General MacArthur as commander-in-chief of the South West Pacific Area (SWPA). He assumed command of all Allied forces in Australia, New Guinea and the surrounding waters. While MacArthur's naval and air commanders were American officers, the commander of the Allied Land Forces was Blamey, who retained his post as commander-in-chief.[27] Initially MacArthur's General Headquarters SWPA was located in Melbourne, where it was close to Blamey's Land Headquarters (LHQ), as well as the headquarters of the other services. MacArthur was not comfortable with the fact that an Australian officer commanded American land forces in the SWPA, but since the Australian Army provided the overwhelming majority of the land forces, it was unavoidable that Blamey should exercise command. In any case, the Australian Army bore the brunt of the hard fighting in Papua in 1942, including on the Kokoda Trail, at Milne Bay, and at Buna, Gona and Sanananda.

From the time when MacArthur arrived in Australia, the government looked to him as its principal adviser on strategic issues. In theory the two senior organisations controlling the Australian war effort were the War Cabinet and the Advisory War Council, but after MacArthur arrived another body—the Prime Minister's War Conference—was formed. It consisted of Curtin, MacArthur, and anyone else Curtin decided to invite. Its secretary was Frederick Shedden, who, as he was also secretary of the War Cabinet, the Advisory War Council and the department of Defence, was in an immensely powerful position.

As Australia's senior military officer, Blamey was extremely

General Sir Thomas Blamey, commander-in-chief of the Australian Military Forces, in discussion with his director of Military Intelligence, Brigadier John Rogers, in August 1944. They had served together in the First World War. Rogers accompanied Blamey to the crucial meeting in Canberra on 17 January 1945 at which the security leaks were discussed. (AWM 100210)

frustrated by the fact that the government's principal adviser on strategic matters was an American general. In April 1942 he won the right to approach the prime minister directly on certain issues, but he found that Curtin tended to accept MacArthur's advice rather than his. Nevertheless, for two years Blamey was on good terms with Curtin, and relations did not begin to deteriorate until he accompanied Curtin on a visit to the US and Britain in April and May 1944.

The return of the AIF formations and the arrival of the Americans also brought a restructuring of the intelligence system. In July the Allied Intelligence Bureau (AIB) was set to up to control Allied special operations, coastwatching and the dissemination of propaganda in the SWPA. Colonel Roberts was appointed Controller of the AIB, and Brigadier John Rogers, who had returned from the Middle East, became the Australian DMI.[28] AIB included sections responsible for special operations in the Philippines, the Netherlands East Indies, New Guinea and other areas of the SWPA. It also included Secret Intelligence Australia, which was partly controlled by the British Secret Intelligence Service in London. Its task was to conduct espionage, as distinct from the special operations carried out by the other sections of AIB. Initially the Far East Liaison Office

(FELO), which had the task of disseminating propaganda in the SWPA, was part of AIB, but in September 1942 it came under the supervision of Land Headquarters. A full discussion of the AIB is beyond the scope of this book, but it should be kept in mind that security was only part of a wide range of intelligence activities carried out by the Australian and American forces in the SWPA.[29]

Intelligence in the SWPA was coordinated by GHQ SWPA, where the principal players were MacArthur's chief of staff, Major-General Richard Sutherland, his G2, or assistant chief of staff intelligence, Brigadier-General Charles Willoughby, and MacArthur's chief signals officer, Brigadier-General Spencer Akin. GHQ SWPA directly supervised AIB, the Allied Translator and Interpreter Section (ATIS), the Allied Geographical Section (AGS), Central Bureau (which was responsible for signals intelligence) and a small radar organisation called Section 22. Within the headquarters was the Combined Operational Intelligence Centre (COIC), staffed by officers of the three Australian services, which partly duplicated the work of Willoughby's G2 (Intelligence Section).

Each of the Allied forces had its own intelligence organisation, directed primarily at providing operational intelligence to naval fleets, air groups and army formations. The Royal Australian Navy had its Directorate of Naval Intelligence, headed by Commander Long, in Melbourne. It liaised closely with those elements of the intelligence structure which affected naval operations or required naval support. The US Navy in Australia also had its intelligence organisation, whose key component was its Fleet Radio Unit in Melbourne (FRUMEL).

From modest beginnings, the Air Force intelligence structure was built up into a highly organised and effective network. According to some accounts, a solid foundation was laid by the capable Wing Commander Packer in late 1941 and early 1942. By late 1942, Air Commodore Joseph Hewitt was the head of Allied Air Forces intelligence in Brisbane.

The Australian Army's intelligence organisation was headed by its Directorate of Military Intelligence, with intelligence staffs at each level of command, including the Lines of Communications Area headquarters in each state.

Each service also had its own security or counter-intelligence staffs, responsible for internal security. As we have seen, the Army had wider security responsibilities, which included postal and telegraphic censorship. Security functions in Army field units were undertaken by field security sections and field censorship sections. Within the US forces, security and counter-intelligence came under Colonel Elliott R. Thorpe, assistant chief of staff G2 at the headquarters of US Forces Far East, based in Melbourne, and later in

Sydney and Brisbane.[30] The commanding officer of the US Counter-Intelligence Corps in Australia was Major Albert L. Vreeland, who from April 1943 had his headquarters in Brisbane.[31]

While thousands of personnel were working in a score of different intelligence agencies, the really crucial intelligence was provided by the interception and decryption of enemy radio traffic. Since this activity is of central importance to our story, it is described in detail in the next chapter.

The restructuring of the Allied intelligence organisations in mid 1942 corresponded to the move of GHQ SWPA and Advanced LHQ to Brisbane in late July and August 1942. Blamey flew frequently between his two headquarters in Brisbane and Melbourne. The LHQ staff in Melbourne was headed by the chief of the general staff, Lieutenant-General John Northcott, who represented Blamey on the Chiefs of Staff Committee and in the War Cabinet and the Advisory War Council. Advanced LHQ in Brisbane was headed by Blamey's chief of staff, Lieutenant-General Frank Berryman, who was concerned with planning and supporting Australian operations.

Like the remainder of the LHQ staff, the intelligence staff was split between Melbourne and Brisbane. Brigadier Rogers was located in Brisbane with his new deputy, Colonel Kenneth Wills; his staff were concerned with intelligence policy, control of interpreters, operational intelligence, records and intelligence personnel, field security and field censorship.[32] Rogers flew between the two headquarters, but spent most of his time either in Brisbane or visiting the intelligence staffs at forward army and corps headquarters in New Guinea or on the Atherton Tableland.

Rogers and Wills were the dominant figures in Australian intelligence during the war. Rogers had gained Blamey's confidence in the First World War and maintained it during their long association in the Second. A smooth operator, able to get the best out of his subordinates and to work well with allies, he made a highly effective DMI, but most observers agreed that Wills had the superior intellect. Wills had anticipated the Japanese advance over the Kokoda Trail in 1942 but had not been able to persuade MacArthur or Blamey.[33] Although he was not as personable as Rogers, he was a capable deputy who handled the most difficult matters, such as security breaches and staffing; Rogers himself described Wills as 'the Power behind the Throne'.[34] Later, as controller of the AIB, he transformed it into an invaluable contributor to Allied operations in 1945.

In Melbourne the intelligence staff was headed by the assistant director of military intelligence (ADMI), Lieutenant-Colonel Robert Little, a militia officer who had been awarded the DSO as an artillery officer in the First World War. He looked after matters such as internees, liaison with the civilian CSS, postal and telegraphic censorship and the decoding of Japanese diplomatic radio traffic. In August 1943, Colonel Wills proposed a scheme for rotating the senior appointments in the Intelligence Corps, but he strongly suggested retaining Little as ADMI 'for his excellent knowledge of organisation and routine—and his Y work (Diplomatic)'.[35] The latter comment referred to the diplomatic signals intercept section, which will be described in the next chapter.

This intelligence structure remained largely unchanged during 1943 and 1944. Throughout 1943, the Australian Army played the predominant role, repulsing the Japanese thrust towards Wau, capturing Salamaua, landing at Nadzab and Lae, moving into the Ramu Valley, thrusting into the Finisterre Ranges, storming ashore at Finschhafen and seizing Sattelberg. In all this the US Army had a minor part, even if the bulk of the naval and air support was provided by the Americans. But in early 1944 the situation changed. The Australian Army was exhausted and its divisions began to return to Australia for a rest while the US forces began a spectacular advance along the north coast of New Guinea. By the end of July 1944 MacArthur's forces had reached the western end of New Guinea and were poised to attack the Philippines in October. The war in the Pacific now had only one more year to run.

THE SECURITY SERVICE AT WAR

What role had the Security Service played during the period from late 1942 to late 1944, in which the Japanese had been halted and then pushed back in a series of major offensives? Although Simpson enjoyed better relations with the Army than MacKay, he was not without problems. For example, MacKay insisted on recalling many members of the MPI back to the NSW police and was loath to give the CSS access to files originally gathered by the MPI.[36] There were also problems of coordination with the services' security organisations, which retained responsibility for security in operational areas, as well as with the American Counter-Intelligence Corps. Since northern Queensland, the Northern Territory and northern Western Australia were potentially operational areas, the military commanders in those areas believed that they should be responsible for security in their areas. The key area was Queensland, where the major headquarters were located and where most units were training for future operations.

In early 1943 Lieutenant-Colonel Wake, who by then was director of counter-subversion at the CSS headquarters in Canberra, was sent back to Queensland to take control of security there. Wake had been

Lieutenant-Colonel Robert Little, assistant director of Military Intelligence, 1943–45, was responsible for security, internees and censorship and controlled the diplomatic Sigint section in Victoria Barracks, Melbourne. (AWM 120553)

interfering in the operations in several states, causing two senior officers, Tyrell and Whittington, to resign, so Simpson was pleased to move him away from Canberra.[37] Wake expanded the Security Service in Queensland and instituted security checks on civilians and members of the armed forces. He also claimed that Allied personnel had been penetrated by enemy agents. Before long the Army commanders in Queensland were complaining that Wake was interfering in their affairs. Indeed, the more the Army looked into Wake's record the more concerned it became, until by July 1943 Army staff had put together a litany of complaints. The first was that in 1940, when Wake had applied for transfer to the AIF, he had claimed in writing that he had served with British and French security organisations in the First World War.[38] Furthermore, he had been seen wearing ribbons representing war service, even though he had been too young to join up then and there was no record that he had. The chief commissioner of the Queensland police had complained that Wake had employed unreliable staff—including one man who had embezzled money and others who should have been interned as aliens—and that he 'played politicians to the limit'. Towards the end of 1942 Wake had returned to Brisbane, incorrectly advised the staff at the headquarters of the Queensland Lines of Communications Area that his task was 'to tie up all Security arrangements' in north Queensland, and set himself up in an office in Townsville before returning to Canberra. Once he officially became head of security in Queensland in early 1943, there were further complaints about his work. For example, staff of the US

Counter-Intelligence Corps claimed that while in Queensland they had been shadowed by members of the Security Service.

The Navy, too, was concerned about Wake. Although Commander Long, the DNI, had previously had a high opinion of Wake, he now thought that Wake's staff were tapping his telephone conversations. He arranged a burglary of the CSS offices in Brisbane and spirited out files on himself and Simpson.[39] Interviewed by an Army investigator on 5 July 1943, Long said the Navy had lost all confidence in Wake 'and it is considered that Wake has morally degenerated, particularly during the last 12 months'.[40] According to Templeton's study of the Security Service prepared for the 1977 Royal Commission on Intelligence and Security:

> In July 1943, the Army submitted a case against [Wake] alleging that his counter-espionage work had got quite out of hand and that officers of the security service, the Army and the US Army suspected that they were being shadowed and spied on by Wake's agents, whose 'concentration was on visiting Australian, US and English Service Officers and also security service officers. Suspicions of continuous dogging of movement were more than feared in the case of such officers as the Commander In Chief [Blamey] and other Senior Officers.'[41]

On 1 September 1943, Rogers arranged a meeting of Australian and American security officers in Brisbane at which it was proposed to establish an Allied Security Bureau.[42] Simpson refused to cooperate, the US withdrew and the bureau was never established. Apparently the US had 'intimated that if Col Wake was permitted to attend Inter-Allied Services Conferences they would not be able to be present'.[43]

Blamey wrote to Attorney-General Evatt to complain about Wake, while in the meantime Wake was reduced to his substantive Army rank of lieutenant and in October 1943 placed on the reserve of officers. At the end of the year Evatt appointed Justice Reed, of South Australia, to conduct a court of inquiry into the charges against Wake. The full results of this inquiry are not known, but according to some sources the accusation about the service ribbons failed because the date on which it was claimed Wake had worn the ribbons was wrong.[44] While the inquiry was still sitting, Brigadier Eugene Gorman, a prominent Melbourne Queen's Counsel who was serving as the chief inspector of the Army, advised Blamey that he was concerned that 'the Army had no right of representation and . . . I feared the charges admitted by Wake were likely to be brushed aside as not meriting evidence. I feared also a finding that his very bad conduct in this respect would be set down as merely enthusiasm to join the AIF.'[45]

Gorman's fears were justified. Astonishingly, Wake remained as the head of the Security Service in Queensland, although the Army gained responsibility for the area north of Townsville, where most of the troops were located.[46] The history of the Security Service claims that Wake retained his 'influence over Simpson . . . purely by virtue of his superior experience', but also quotes the views of a former military liaison officer in the Service that 'some sort of blackmail has also been suggested'.[47] Simpson retained his high opinion of Wake, and when he relinquished the position of director-general in October 1945 he wrote a glowing recommendation to the chairman of the Public Service Board:

> Wake . . . is himself an expert investigator with an exceptional capacity of training investigators and filling them with his own enthusiasm. . . . Any reference to Mr Wake's duties as Deputy Director of Queensland would be incomplete without a reference to the difficulties with which he had to contend through what I believe to be the jealousies of certain Army officers with whom he was previously associated as a Military officer. I am satisfied that these difficulties were not of Mr Wake's creation and to a very great extent were caused by the jealousy of smaller men . . . I have at all times received from Mr Wake the utmost efficiency and cooperation and can only speak of his services during the period I was Director-General in the very highest terms.[48]

This endorsement runs contrary to every other report we encountered during the preparation of this book. Yet Wake continued in charge of security in Queensland until 1949, when the Australian Security Intelligence Organisation was formed and he became, in effect, the chief investigator of Soviet espionage in Australia.[49]

In late 1942 Charles Kevin was transferred from the department of the Army to help establish an Organisations Section in the CSS. This was a sophisticated analytical element, staffed by highly educated researchers, whose role was to investigate various organisations within Australia.[50] Asked by Simpson to review the work of the CSS, Kevin found it to be completely inept. He concluded in September or October 1943: 'the unpalatable fact is that the Service has been unable to locate one known enemy agent or one major instance of sabotage'.[51] Another senior officer found that the staff were incompetent and 'being ignorant of international affairs were incapable of assessing the significance to Australia of events abroad'.[52] In November 1943 Simpson centralised the work of counter-espionage and established a group of special investigators.

It is difficult to obtain a clear picture of the work of the CSS during 1943 and 1944, but in March 1944 Captain Alan Hillgarth, RN, the chief of the intelligence staff of the Eastern Fleet at Ceylon, visited Australia and reported on his observations. He wrote that

Simpson was 'a fat but energetic barrister with real experience of active service in both wars'. He was responsible directly to the attorney-general, who did not interfere in his work, and while he had the power of 'arrest and detention without trial', he did not 'abuse his power'. Hillgarth thought that Simpson was doing a 'sound job, in the face of many difficulties, including attempted political influence', but found that his 'personal assistant Lieutenant Kevin RANVR' was 'perhaps the brains of this concern'.[53]

Following the arguments about Wake's role, relations between the CSS and the Army continued to deteriorate. Although Simpson was an Army officer, he filled a civilian appointment, and Army critics were later to complain that he acted as an Army officer when it suited him and at other times emphasised that he was the director-general of a civilian organisation. The Army's day-to-day relations with the CSS were maintained by the intelligence staff at LHQ in Melbourne and at the Lines of Communications Area headquarters in the respective states. Although the three services had liaison officers in Canberra, the most important to our story was Lieutenant-Colonel Cohen, a frequent visitor to LHQ in Melbourne, where his principal contact was the ADMI, Lieutenant-Colonel Little, and to Advanced LHQ in Brisbane, whose senior security officer, Major Max Phillips, liaised with the CSS in that state and advised Rogers on security issues. Mrs Cohen recalled that her husband 'did not have much faith in Brigadier Simpson or in [the] Security Service'; he disliked Simpson and the feeling was reciprocated.[54]

By August 1944, when Blamey was under pressure from the prime minister to release men to industry, he attempted to have the 312 Army members of the Security Service returned to the Army. The issue was still under dispute when in September 1944 Simpson retired from the Army. He remained as director-general in a purely civil appointment, thus strengthening Blamey's hand in his move to have the Army men returned to his control. As a result, when the case of the security leakages arose at the end of 1944, Blamey and the Army were still in conflict with the director-general of security.

The Security Service was in conflict with the Army over another matter. As well as the more traditional tasks of security—watching subversive organisations, vetting staff, ensuring security procedures were followed and liaising with the censorship authority—the service was also responsible for ensuring that unauthorised information was not passed out of Australia by radio. Early in the war small listening posts were established within the general post offices in Brisbane, Sydney, Melbourne, Adelaide and Perth to monitor clandestine radio traffic on frequency bands not monitored by the three armed services. These posts reported to the Navy. In addition, the Army had a special intercept station at Park Orchards, near Ringwood on the eastern outskirts of Melbourne, which kept a careful watch over Japanese frequencies.[55] Although there were a few cases of irresponsible youths caught transmitting in the early days of the war, no secret communications were detected.[56] This, at any rate, was the Navy's claim, but Lieutenant Colonel F. J. M. Stratton, of the British Radio Security Service (RSS), who visited Australia in 1943, was not convinced that 'the evidence on which they based their statement was sufficient'. He reported that the Security Service was the 'one body in Australia seriously anxious about the possibility of leakage of information from Australia by means of radio'.[57]

The Navy was unwilling to give up its control of the post office stations and opposed the setting up of a Discrimination Unit other than its own, but after a meeting on 25 May 1943 between Brigadier Simpson and members of the signal officer in chief's staff the Army agreed to assist.[58] It had already formed several Type C Sections of the Australian Special Wireless Group to intercept Australian service radio traffic and check on careless operating or leakages of information. The signal officer in chief, Major-General Colin Simpson, agreed that these sections could also be used to intercept radio transmissions of unknown origin. Later two Type D Sections, Nos 66 and 67, with the express purpose of intercepting suspicious radio transmissions, were established at Darwin and at Yadjin, near Atherton in Queensland, respectively. Both stations were equipped with direction-finding capabilities. The intercept station at HMAS *Harman*, near Canberra, was also used to monitor illicit radio traffic.[59]

Lieutenant-Colonel Alastair (Mic) Sandford, the senior Australian officer in the Allied Central Bureau, took the key role in establishing the Australian Radio Security Service. During a four-month visit to Britain in mid 1943 he made contact with the British RSS and on return advised that Britain and India would 'play' with the Australian RSS only so long as it was controlled by the Australian Army.[60] The problem was that while the Army was responsible for radio security in the operational areas, the CSS was responsible for civilian radio security. Eventually, in December 1943, the Defence Committee authorised the formation of the 1st Australian Discrimination Unit,[61] and on 11 February 1944 the Committee set out the CSS's responsibilities for radio security:

> The Director-General of Security is responsible for all Radio Security measures in Australia and the area under Commonwealth control . . . The direction of interception undertaken by wireless sections raised for Radio Security work will be the responsibility of the Director General of Security . . . The Discrimination Unit

will be located at Canberra and under the direct control of the Director-General of Security . . .⁶²

Commanded by Captain Robert McNamara, the Discrimination Unit was formed at Indooroopilly, Queensland in February 1944 and the following month moved to Canberra where it was housed in an old hospital in the suburb of Acton.⁶³ Copies of all intercepted traffic, including logs from the five post office listening sites, were sent to the unit whose staff of eight women from the Australian Women's Army Service and four men were to 'discriminate' between illicit and non-illicit transmissions. The unit was supplied with the call-signs and frequencies of all Allied units and these were kept on a card index system with 10 000 entries.⁶⁴

The unit worked for the Security Service and issued tasks to the Type D Sections. All unusual traffic of a military nature intercepted on service channels was forwarded to Major William Hill, the staff officer (special wireless) on Major-General Simpson's staff (Hill had been one of the early members of the 4th Australian Special Wireless Section serving in Greece, Crete and Syria in 1941). Other suspicious traffic was forwarded to Captain (later Major) Clive Ogilvie, the radio security officer on the staff of the director-general of security, across the Molonglo River in the Patents Office. In the second half of 1944 Hill, Ogilvie and Sandford visited England for special training by the British RSS.

Another early member of the 4th Special Wireless Section was Warrant Officer Keith Hart, who by 1944 was second in command of the Discrimination Unit. As far as he can recall, the listening stations never intercepted radio transmissions from any foreign embassies. But at one stage, because of the skip distance involved, they were requested by London to intercept transmissions from two German agents in China whose call-signs were HOK and PAK.⁶⁵ The activities of these agents were the subject of a 27-page report prepared by the US Army Military Intelligence Service in February 1945.⁶⁶ No Japanese radio agents were discovered broadcasting from Australia.⁶⁷

A bitter dispute broke out between the CSS and the Central Bureau that was never resolved satisfactorily. In April 1944 Brigadier Simpson wrote to DMI Rogers, explaining that either 'Sandford and his organisation are deliberately "not playing" with my organisation', or 'Sandford and his organisation are incompetent to play their part in Radio Security so far as it concerns catching illicit wireless.' Unless the dispute was straightened out in ten days, Simpson proposed 'to inform my Minister that there is no method in existence by which illicit wireless can be found in Australia, and state my reasons.'⁶⁸ Rogers told Simpson that there was a third alternative—that the

British RSS was not prepared to cooperate with the CSS.[69] Early the following year Simpson accused Sandford (inaccurately) of receiving a personal allowance from the British Foreign Office.[70]

The activities of the Discrimination Unit raised questions about the role that signal interception might play not only in preventing the transmission of illegal radio messages but, if the messages could be deciphered, in uncovering enemy espionage as well. The Security Service had no part in this activity. But before we discuss the role of signals intelligence in counter-espionage we should outline the formation of the signals intelligence organisation in Australia.

4

'our only means of gauging Japanese espionage'

THE DEVELOPMENT OF SIGINT IN AUSTRALIA

SIGNALS INTELLIGENCE, OR SIGINT, WAS a crucial factor in shaping the Pacific War from its outbreak in December 1941 until the cessation of hostilities in August 1945. But less well known is the role it played in counter-espionage. Although security services and counter-espionage organisations generally apply a range of security and control measures in wartime, these efforts have rarely been successful against a determined and careful enemy agent. Foreign nationals or aliens might be interned, but little can be done about an agent who has been a resident for many years, perhaps under an assumed name, or about a native-born citizen who, for whatever reason, has decided to help the enemy.

The weak link in such espionage is the transmission of information to the enemy country. In Chapter 3 we discussed the chief measures taken against this in Australia during the Second World War: mail and telegraphic censorship, and the monitoring of radio transmissions. While these measures may have limited the circulation of information, however, they did not actually identify any enemy agents. The best way of doing this was by reading the enemy's correspondence, and without an Allied agent in the enemy's camp, the most effective means was to intercept and decipher the enemy's radio and cable traffic. The prime purpose of such interception was the gathering of intelligence that might be valuable in strategic decision-making or in the conduct of operations, but clearly it could have a secondary role—the exposure of enemy espionage.

The value of Sigint in counter-espionage was emphasised by

Vice-Admiral Sir Geoffrey Layton, the commander-in-chief of the Royal Navy's China Station, in a cable to the Admiralty on 14 June 1941, when he lamented the lack

> of information regarding Japanese espionage and of effective counter-measures. Almost our only means at present of gauging extent and success of Japanese espionage is derived from special intelligence sources, which may for technical reasons dry up at any moment, and are in any case limited to intelligence transmitted through consular channels.

Layton added that Sigint had revealed a 'continuous stream of military and shipping intelligence through consuls'.[1] The prerequisite for gathering this sort of intelligence was an effective Sigint organisation, and such an organisation took much time and effort to establish.

THE GENESIS OF SIGINT IN AUSTRALIA

Before the Second World War the Australian government had no embassies overseas and relied on Britain for intelligence and foreign policy advice. In time of war it was expected that the Australian services would dovetail into the British services, and the latter saw no need to foster an Australian intelligence-gathering capability which would have duplicated their own and only wasted resources. With a severe shortage of funds, it is not surprising, then, that the Australian services made little progress in developing a Sigint organisation of their own, and although at the time of the Munich crisis in 1938 an attempt was made to form an inter-service Sigint organisation, the attempt was abandoned.[2] Thus at the outbreak of war Australia had no Sigint or cryptanalytic capability.

The main work of developing one was initiated by the Navy. Through their connections with the Royal Navy, both the director of naval intelligence, Commander Long, and the director of signals communications, Commander Jack Newman, had become aware of the extent and value of British Sigint. For example, in March 1939 Newman represented Australia at a conference in Singapore on the 'Organisation of Wireless Intelligence in the Far East'.[3]

Following this meeting, plans were put in train to establish a radio direction-finding (D/F) station at HMAS *Coonawarra*, near Darwin, as part of Britain's Far East D/F organisation. The reports of D/F bearings were to be forwarded to the chief of the intelligence staff, Far East, in Singapore.[4] Equipment was installed towards the end of 1939 and the station began operations on 26 February 1940.[5]

It is possible that the RAN had already established a limited D/F capability at Victoria Barracks, Melbourne, but this was never likely to be capable of providing the extent of interception required.[6]

With the establishment of the D/F station at *Coonawarra*, Newman turned his attention to the Navy's wireless telegraphy (W/T) receiving station at HMAS *Harman*, near Canberra, which until then had been 'confined to Naval communications'. On 14 May he wrote to the chief of naval staff suggesting that 'other work of considerable value could be performed if equipment and personnel' were made available.[7] 'The type of work contemplated is mostly of a "W/T Intelligence" nature, but does not include cryptography.' He noted that the radio traffic of Italian merchant ships had already been intercepted, but proper 'Y' procedure (as Sigint collection was known at the time) could only be carried out if suitable equipment was made available. Newman's approach was strongly supported by DNI Long, as it would allow 'for the regular interception of traffic from Shore Stations in Japan and her Mandated Islands and from Japanese ships'. Long also realised that the interception of radio messages might have a counter-espionage role; as he put it: 'A watch on this activity might well provide sufficient evidence to reveal enemy agents in Australia, or more probably, the Netherlands East Indies.'[8] Approval was given, and by October 1940 *Harman* had four full-time and six part-time 'Y' operators, and *Coonawarra* had four part-time ones. This was a modest beginning, but plans were afoot to increase the staff by early 1941.[9]

The Royal Australian Navy had previously sent any coded messages it collected to the Far East Combined Bureau (FECB) in Singapore for decryption, but Long and Newman realised that there could be value in Australia possessing its own cryptanalytic staff.[10] At their instigation, on 12 December 1939 the chief of naval staff, Admiral Sir Ragnar Colvin, wrote to the other two service chiefs suggesting that such an organisation be set up in Australia 'on the lines of the Government Code and Cypher School in London, with a view to breaking down enemy codes and cyphers'.[11] The chief of the air staff, Air Vice-Marshal S. J. Goble, thought that Australia would not be justified in setting up such an organisation, but the chief of the general staff, Lieutenant-General E. K. Squires, was more encouraging.[12] He considered that Australia should at least have a nucleus organisation 'against the contingencies of operations in and about Australia and her territories. The work is clearly of a highly skilled nature and much practice is necessary, and the sooner a commencement can be made the better.'

Apparently Squires had already initiated some action, for, according to a later Australian Army signal officer-in-chief, Major-General Colin Simpson, 'The history of interception in Australia by Army

Telegraphists of the Royal Australian Navy and the Women's Royal Australian Naval Service at HMAS Harman *Naval Communications Station near Canberra. In May 1940 the director of Signals Communications, Commander Jack Newman, recommended that* Harman *begin intercept work. By October 1940* Harman *had four full-time and six part-time 'Y' operators. (AWM 9234)*

Signals dates from September 1939 when a detachment of Signals 3 Div C.M.F. was detailed at the request of GS Intelligence to intercept enemy wireless transmissions.'[13] It is not clear what this organisation did, but it was likely that its staff were working on a part-time basis. On 31 January 1940 they were mobilised for full-time duty and were then administered by Southern Command signals in Melbourne.[14] Located initially at Albert Park, the wireless interception unit soon moved to Park Orchards.[15] It monitored enemy overseas press broadcasts and forwarded the material to Army headquarters.

When the 1st Australian Corps was formed in April 1940, the then Colonel Simpson was appointed chief signal officer. A pharmacist by profession, he had served with pioneer units and the 3rd Division Signals Company in the First World War, during which he had earned the Military Cross, and had been commanding officer of the 3rd Division signals from 1935 to 1939. At the request of the War Office, Australia was asked to form a Special Wireless Section Type B for service with the 1st Australian Corps signals, and Simpson selected Captain Jack Ryan, the chief engineer of radio station 3AW in Melbourne, who was also an officer in the 3rd

Division signals, as its commander. The 4th Australian Special Wireless Section, as the new unit was eventually known, began training at Seymour in Victoria in June, and embarked for the Middle East in December 1940 with a strength of two officers and 87 other ranks.[16]

Under direction from Squires, the Australian Army had also taken action to establish the nucleus of a cryptanalytic organisation when, in January 1940, the Military Intelligence staff at Eastern Command in Sydney had asked Professor Thomas Room, professor of Pure Mathematics at Sydney University, and Mr Richard Lyons, a senior lecturer in Mathematics, to begin studying foreign codes.[17] (Perhaps the Australian Army had been alerted to the need for cryptanalysis when, at the suggestion of the War Office, Major Roy Kendall, a regular Australian Signal Corps officer, had attended a one-month course in cryptography at the end of his training in England in March 1939.[18] Back in Australia he had worked under Colonel Combes, the director of Military Operations and Intelligence, at Army Headquarters, first as the GSO2 Signals and then as the GS Intelligence—the position previously held by Combes.) Soon the Sydney University group was joined by Professor Dale Trendall, the 31-year-old professor of Greek, and by Captain Athanasius Treweek, a 28-year-old lecturer in Greek and a militia artillery officer. They began practising on Japanese consular telegrams made available by Amalgamated Wireless (Australasia) Ltd (AWA), the main radio telegraph company in Sydney. By October 1941 the intelligence staff at Eastern Command were reporting that the 'cypher-breaking group' was producing 'exceedingly good results'.[19] At one weekend session in 1941 the section succeeded in breaking the Japanese LA code, a low-grade code used for consular traffic, but this had been slow going.[20]

The matter of establishing a cryptanalytic organisation actually to provide information to the Australian services did not seem to be pursued with any urgency. On 15 February 1940 the Defence Committee considered Admiral Colvin's letter of December 1939, and as a result, on 11 April the prime minister cabled the British government. He noted that while there seemed 'no valid reasons for setting up a full-scale cryptographic organisation in Australia', it appeared desirable to examine the feasibility 'of establishing a nucleus organisation'.[21] He sought the British government's advice, but by the time its reply arrived on 15 October 1940 the RAN had already begun to set up a small unit; the reply merely noted that if the Australians wanted to continue in that direction they could send 'suitable men (or women)' to attend a training course in Britain.[22]

The Special Intelligence Bureau

The RAN's cryptanalytic organisation was built around the extraordinary expertise of Paymaster-Commander Eric Nave, RN. Born in 1899, Nave had joined the RAN in 1917 and in 1921 had been sent to Japan to study Japanese.[23] He displayed a remarkable aptitude, and from 1925 to 1927 served on loan to the Royal Navy in the China Fleet, investigating Japanese wireless telegraphy. According to an Admiralty 'in-house' history, 'Japanese Naval Sigint work began' with the appointment of Nave to the flagship of the China station.[24] In 1927 Nave started work at the Government Code and Cypher School (GCCS) in London. Later the GCCS would move to Bletchley House in Buckinghamshire, where it would play the key role in breaking the German Enigma cipher during the Second World War. According to Nave's own account, he 'founded' the GCCS Japanese Naval Section. In 1931 he transferred to the Royal Navy and returned to the China station, working on Japanese codes. Two years later he was back at GCCS, where he stayed until 1937, when he again returned to the Far East, joining the FECB at Hong Kong. Nave accompanied the main body of the FECB when it was transferred to Singapore in 1939. By this time the FECB had made considerable progress in reading the main Japanese naval ciphers, as well as having some success with army ciphers being used in China.

Extended service in the tropics had affected Nave's health, and in February 1940 he was sent on leave to Australia, bringing with him a wealth of knowledge and experience of Japanese cryptography. Colvin had been the British naval attaché in Tokyo when Nave had been studying Japanese there, so he was sympathetic to Nave's work. Encouraged by Long and Newman, Nave continued studying various Japanese codes using material forwarded from Singapore, as well as Japanese naval traffic from the mandated islands and Japanese commercial shipping traffic collected by HMAS *Harman* and *Coonawarra*.

Overseas radio broadcasts were also monitored by a receiving station set up by the Postmaster-General's department (PMG) at Mont Park, near the present La Trobe University in the north-eastern suburbs of Melbourne, with the broadcasts relayed by landline to an office, known as 'the Listening Post', in Collins Street, Melbourne. The Listening Post had been established about July 1940 following a series of conferences with Navy and Army authorities, and it monitored broadcasts from Berlin, Rome, Moscow, Tokyo and American stations. Its reports were delivered by messenger to the Intelligence divisions of the Navy and Army.[25]

Paymaster Captain Eric Nave is generally known as the 'father' of Australian Sigint. He was an Australian naval officer who transferred to the Royal Navy where he specialised in Japanese codes and ciphers. He returned to Australia in 1940 and set up the RAN Sigint organisation. (Mrs M. Nave)

Towards the end of October 1940, Admiral Colvin and several senior naval officers attended a conference in Singapore to consider the defence of the Far East. Commander Long suggested that the RAN obtain advice from the intelligence staff in Singapore as to how best use could be made of Australia's intelligence resources. In a memorandum, Long noted that the RAN now had two direction-finding stations—*Harman* and *Coonawarra*—while Nave was working on cryptanalysis. In an attached note, Nave explained that his work would be assisted by the provision of another interpreter and a second clerk.[26] Soon after, Nave was joined by Paymaster-Lieutenant Keith Miller.

In January 1941 the head of the FECB, Captain F. J. Wylie, RN, visited Australia and discussed plans to cooperate with the Dutch at Batavia (Jakarta) and to improve the interchange of intelligence between Australia and the FECB. Wylie said he had no real objection to Australia's starting its own 'cryptographic intelligence organisation', but that 'it should be controlled from Singapore'.[27] He added that while he had already received valuable support from Nave's small organisation, he thought Nave should be given more assistance; this would allow him to 'deal more expeditiously with important matters', and 'provide to some extent against possible interruption of surface mail communication with Singapore'.[28] At about the same time, Nave began discussions with the Army's small cipher section at Sydney University to see whether it would be able to cooperate with his section.

Meanwhile, in March 1941 Commander Newman attended a communications conference in Singapore, where he examined the work of the FECB. He noted that it had two sections, 'W' section, which dealt with direction-finding and traffic analysis, and 'Y' section, which concentrated on cryptanalysis. He recommended that Australia install and operate additional D/F and interception stations. The FECB advised Newman that 'the Consular and Diplomatic codes were now so complicated that a large staff of experts is required to obtain results, and that anything of interest read from this or other codes or cyphers would be forwarded to Naval Board'. The FECB recognised Nave's expertise, however, and was willing to send him cryptanalytic information in return for his assistance.[29]

Supported by Long, Nave pressed ahead with his efforts to establish a cryptanalytic section, and in April his staff was increased by one interpreter and one clerk.[30] Soon afterwards, A. B. (Jim) Jamieson, who had spent eight years in Japan, returned to Australia on the last ship to sail from Japan to Australia before war broke out. He recalled a 'mysterious request' to see 'an officer [Nave] who was dressed in plain clothes. He told me he had just been authorised to set up a cryptographic unit in the RAN. He certainly knew Japanese very well, very well indeed.'[31] As a Paymaster-Lieutenant, Jamieson joined the group. Known as the Special Intelligence Bureau (SIB), it was established in Victoria Barracks, Melbourne, and sought to obtain information by radio interception, direction-finding, traffic analysis and cryptanalysis. It cooperated with the FECB in Singapore and with Dutch authorities in the Netherlands East Indies.

Nave continued his efforts to expand his organisation and in June, at the request of the chief of naval staff, the chief of the general staff sought approval from his minister to call up the members of the Sydney University group and transfer them to Nave's bureau.[32] As a result, in mid 1941 Nave was joined by Treweek, now a major, and Room and Lyons, who remained civilians. Another member was Lieutenant Ian Longfield Lloyd, son of the Security Service director. In July, Room and Jamieson were sent to the FECB in Singapore for four months' training.[33]

With this limited staff, Nave's SIB could do little more than supplement the work of the FECB in Singapore and the GCCS at Bletchley Park, but it was able to break the cipher of the Japanese mission in Australia and send the key to Bletchley. The Australians had some important successes. In September they intercepted a message instructing the Japanese consul-general to find another neutral country to look after Japanese interests, but Nave later claimed that the secretary to the chief of naval staff failed to pass on the information to the government.[34]

By this time the RAAF had also entered the field of special intelligence. In July 1941 seven experienced RAAF radio operators and two Army operators began a special course at Victoria Barracks,

Victoria Barracks on St Kilda Road, Melbourne, (photographed in June 1943) contained the headquarters of the three Australian Services and the department of Defence. The Services' cryptanalytic sections were established within the barracks area. From the beginning of 1943 the Australian diplomatic section was located on the top floor of the centre three-storey section of A block shown in the photograph. (AWM 52350)

Melbourne, concentrating on the Japanese *kana* code—the Japanese version of the Morse code.[35] After completing their training, in September 1941 the RAAF group was established at Darwin and began sending its intercepts to Nave's SIB in Melbourne. About the same time the RAAF set up a small cryptanalytic section in Melbourne under Flight Lieutenant H. Roy Booth to work on the material collected at Darwin.[36] Formerly a Sydney solicitor, Booth had recently returned to Australia from Singapore, where he had been attached to the RAF.

On 19 November 1941 the SIB received a Japanese circular advising all overseas posts that in the event of a national emergency they would be warned in a shortwave broadcast by a coded message indicating that diplomatic relations with America, the Soviet Union or Britain were to be severed. Treweek doubted whether the SIB was actually reading the Japanese diplomatic cipher at that time and thought it might have been translated in Singapore.[37] The message—the famous 'winds execute' message—would be in the form of a weather broadcast with the words 'east wind, rain', 'north wind, cloudy' or 'west wind, clear'. On 28 November the acting chief of naval staff, Commodore J. W. Durnsford, passed this information and the earlier message about the need for another neutral mission to the secretary of the department of Defence, Frederick Shedden. It was seen by Prime Minister Curtin later that day.[38] The director of Military Intelligence immediately made arrangements to reinforce the staff at Park Orchards to keep watch for the coded message. Treweek said later that he could 'remember the excitement as everyone waited for the "winds execute" message. Jamieson and others were given receivers to take home so that they could extend the watch.'[39]

On 2 December 1941 the Japanese Foreign Ministry sent a telegram to its consulate in Melbourne directing it to burn all its codes and ciphers and report when this had been completed. The SIB decoded the message on 4 December. The chief of naval staff, Admiral Sir Guy Royle, was absent from Melbourne, on a visit to Singapore, so Nave took the message to the second naval member, Commodore Durnsford. He recalled the conversation:

> 'Important piece of information, Nave!'
> 'Very important, sir!'
> 'How long do you think we've got?'
> 'Well, it's a matter of days. Probably at the weekend. The Japanese think all the Americans have fat heads on Sunday morning and that's probably when they'll strike.'[40]

Durnsford promptly sent a copy of the message to Shedden, adding that a message had also been intercepted from the Japanese consulate indicating that its codes had been destroyed.[41]

In recent years there have been claims in a number of books that in the early hours of 4 December 1941 Lieutenant Longfield Lloyd, on duty at the Park Orchards station, received the intercepted Japanese message, 'East wind, rain', indicating that war with the United States was imminent.[42] Whether or not the 'winds execute' message was received in Washington has been a matter of historical debate for many years, but the most authoritative sources tend to discount the stories that it was received.[43] Captain Nave's own autobiography makes no mention of the receipt of the 'winds execute' message in Australia. Furthermore, Lieutenant Jamieson recalls that he and Lloyd were at one of the interception stations and says they never received the 'winds execute' message.[44]

There is, however, an interesting and unusual twist in the available evidence. On his copy of the intercepted message of 19 November, Frederick Shedden drew a line beside the message 'West wind, rain' (meaning that the Japanese were going to attack Thailand, Malaya or the Netherlands East Indies) and wrote: 'Advised by Army duty officer 8.15 a.m. this had been received and noted by General Staff, FGS, 8/12'.[45] Of course by this time the Japanese had already attacked Pearl Harbor and landed in northern

Malaya. Nonetheless, whatever the fate of the 'winds execute' message, the SIB had provided ample warning to the Australian government—a substantial achievement for the new organisation.

4TH AUSTRALIAN SPECIAL WIRELESS SECTION, MIDDLE EAST

By the outbreak of war in the Pacific the Australians had developed some limited expertise in what was known as special intelligence. Meanwhile, in the Middle East the 4th Australian Special Wireless Section was gaining practical experience in actual operations. In April 1941 it was deployed to Greece, where it was attached to a British unit, No. 101 Special Wireless Section. During the German attack it intercepted and broke the German air codes and reported on German tactical movements.[46]

After the evacuation from Greece, the Australian section was attached to the headquarters of the Allied force on Crete, where it was joined by Lieutenant A. W. (Mic) Sandford, the unit's first intelligence officer.[47] Corporal Geoffrey Ballard, a member of the section, vividly recalled the new arrival:

> Lieutenant Sandford made an immediate impression on the whole Section. In that unreal atmosphere, most of us wondered what had stuck us. Well-to-do member of the Adelaide 'establishment', extrovert, cosmopolite, raconteur, he was at ease with everyone. His heady conversation, wild exaggerations and endless fund of stories brought a bright new element into our lives . . . [He] quickly gained the respect of the whole Section by his cryptographic skill and single-minded dedication to the task, and during the battle and march out of Crete, he showed that he was courageous and utterly fearless.[48]

During the battle the section provided a stream of tactical intelligence to the Allied commander, General Freyberg, who also had access to the highly secret Ultra intelligence from Bletchley Park, which gave him the higher-level operational picture.

After the Crete campaign, the section was deployed to Palestine, where it was attached to the headquarters of the 1st Australian Corps for the Syrian campaign. It supplied valuable intelligence on the Vichy French order of battle and tactics.[49] After the successful conclusion of the campaign and the signing of the armistice, the Australian divisions moved into Syria and the Wireless Section was located in a large house at Souq-el-Gharb near Aley in the hills above Beirut.

According to the British official history of intelligence in the

Second World War, on 22 June 1941, the day the Germans attacked the Soviet Union, all British work on Russian codes and ciphers was stopped.[50] However, it is known that on 19 July the Australian Special Wireless Section began intercepting Russian radio traffic, which was sent by dispatch rider each day to the British No. 2 Wireless Company at Sarafand, near Tel Aviv in Palestine. Australian operators were trained to intercept the Russian traffic by the British unit.[51] In August a detachment was sent to Aleppo in northern Syria to watch Turkish radio traffic and the section began watching British radio stations in Syria to detect breaches of security. On 24 October the section was ordered to cease work on the Russian traffic and begin monitoring German traffic in the Soviet Union to obtain a complete picture of German medium-frequency transmissions, to collect 'Playfair' material for the British unit at Heliopolis, and to collect Enigma material for Bletchley Park.[52] The RAF's principal Sigint centre in the Middle East was at Heliopolis, in Cairo.[53] During part of this period Sandford was detached to work with a British Sigint unit in the Western Desert, and spent some time at Heliopolis. While in Syria the section was supervised by the British No. 2 Wireless Company, which had been located at Sarafand since 1923 and was the main British Army Sigint centre in the Middle East.[54]

After the outbreak of war in the Far East, the section turned its attention to training on the Japanese *kana* code in anticipation of an eventual return to Australia, and for a brief period in December it also intercepted Rumanian radio traffic. On 4 February 1942 the unit embarked at Suez for the journey back to Australia.

Establishing an Allied Sigint Organisation

The Japanese victories in December 1941 and early 1942 threw the Allied intelligence organisations in the Pacific into turmoil. The cryptanalytic section of the FECB had to leave Singapore for Colombo and Kilindini in East Africa; the latter group later moved to New Delhi. The British wanted the FECB to come to Australia, but Newman said facilities were not available.[55] Nave was later to lament that he had not been consulted about this decision.[56]

The following month the US Navy's 'Cast' code-breaking unit at Corregidor in the Philippines moved by submarine, first to Java and then to Australia. This group of some 75 men, under the command of Lieutenant John M. Lietwiler, had possessed the Purple machine, which could read the Japanese diplomatic code, as well as the slightly simpler Red machine, but these machines were destroyed before the unit left the Philippines. It comprised experienced codebreakers who soon began applying their skills in Melbourne, initially under Lieutenant-Commander Redfield Mason, and then under Lieutenant-Commander Rudolph Fabian, who had served in the Philippines.[57] Fabian's unit was established on the middle floor of the heavily guarded Monterey flats in Queens Road, South Yarra, near Albert Park, and liaison was organised with Nave's SIB. The US Navy unit was eventually known as Fleet Radio Unit Melbourne (FRUMEL).[58] FRUMEL became part of the US Navy's intelligence system, under which intelligence and information useful for the breaking of enemy codes was transferred freely between Washington, Hawaii and Melbourne.

Soon after the outbreak of war in the Far East the SIB had been joined by Professor Trendall from Sydney, who Nave remembered was 'the best' of the men from Sydney University in his flair for cryptographic work.[59] Later Trendall was to develop the Trencode for use by Allied operatives working behind enemy lines. When he died in 1995 an obituary observed that he was 'widely regarded as Australia's foremost classical scholar'.[60]

Gradually the SIB was expanded with the arrival of British officers evacuated from the Far East such as E. T. Biggs, who had been in the British embassy in Tokyo; Henry Archer, the former British consul-general at Harbin, in Manchuria; Hubert Graves; Lieutenant-Commander Alan Merry; and the FECB's brilliant and eccentric Arthur Cooper, with his pet gibbon. The section worked on both Japanese service and diplomatic codes. Then, as FRUMEL began operations, the uniformed members of the SIB, such as Nave, Miller, Jamieson, Merry and Treweek, joined the Americans on the middle floor of the Monterey Building, while the remaining members moved to the top floor to concentrate on diplomatic traffic, although they also worked on service traffic if it was available. The Directorate of Signal Communications, under Commander Newman, was on the ground floor.[61] Newman and Fabian had joint control of the US/RAN FRUMEL staff. The Americans would not allow civilians to work with their organisation.[62]

The Australian SIB worked closely with FRUMEL but was not integrated with it. Ronald Bond, then a corporal in the SIB, recalls that on several occasions the SIB passed information to the Americans about ships leaving Saigon and Hanoi which the US Navy submarines used to telling effect. The SIB could not handle 'machine enciphered' intercepts but instead passed them either to the Americans downstairs or to London.[63]

When General MacArthur arrived in Australia in March 1942, the special intelligence organisation underwent a further change, for accompanying him were Lieutenant-Colonel Joseph R. Sherr and a few members of the 2nd Signal Service Company, which had provided the US Army's Sigint service in the Philippines.[64] Most members of the 2nd Signal Service Company were killed or captured. It did not take MacArthur long to realise that one of his most pressing requirements was the development of effective Sigint, and on 1 April, ten days after arriving in Melbourne, he radioed Washington:

> Investigation discloses that a central allied signal intelligence section is required for the interception and cryptanalyzing of Japanese intelligence. The time delay and transmission uncertainties incident to sending interpreted material to Washington and elsewhere dictate that this work be handled locally. Allied forces here are organizing such a bureau.

He went on to request that trained staff be sent to Australia to supplement the 'few individuals that I have brought from the Philippines'.[65]

MacArthur's initiatives complemented those of the Australian Army. On 3 March the DMI, Colonel Roberts, recommended the establishment of an organisation to intercept Japanese military signals traffic.[66] Meanwhile, Captain Ryan and his 4th Special Wireless Section had returned to Australia on the same ship as the 1st Australian Corps's chief signal officer, Brigadier Simpson, and a senior intelligence officer, Lieutenant-Colonel Wills, and during the voyage they had developed plans for an enlarged Sigint organisation.[67] On arrival, the 4th Special Wireless Section—now designated the 5th—was located at Park Orchards along with the small Diplomatic and Press Intercept Section, under Lieutenant J. Jennings.[68]

On 30 March 1942 discussions began with US officers and Australian Army and Air Force officers about forming a 'Research and Control Centre'.[69] The driving force was Captain Sandford, who called to see MacArthur's chief signal officer, Brigadier-General Spencer B. Akin, on 1 April. At Sandford's instigation, Roberts wrote to the deputy chief of the general staff to recommend establishing a central bureau:

> An intercept section depends upon a crytographic and research centre for the success of its results due to the impossibility of long range investigation in forward areas. Where No. 5 W/T Section was operating in the Middle East it was constantly fed not only with broken cyphers but with identifications, frequencies, call signs, forecasts etc which are absolutely vital and which were all supplied by the Central Bureau GHQ, MF.[70]

On 6 April a further meeting was held chaired by Brigadier Simpson, now the Australian Army's signal officer-in-chief, and including the key US and Australian signals and intelligence officers from all three services.[71] Finally, on 15 April, a combined Allied organisation, the

Major-General Spencer B. Akin, chief signal officer, SWPA, (left) with Major-General Colin Simpson, signal officer-in-chief, AMF, in Melbourne in March 1943. Simpson was instrumental in establishing the Australian Army's Sigint organisation. Akin was responsible for the Central Bureau, the Allied Sigint organisation. (AWM 64497)

Central Bureau, was established in a large house called Cranleigh at 225 Domain Road, South Yarra. It operated under the direction of Akin, with Lieutenant-Colonel Sherr as the executive officer. The necessary cryptanalysts requested by MacArthur left the US the following day on the last scheduled clipper flight to Hawaii.[72]

The Australian Army component of Central Bureau came from the Australian Special Wireless Group (ASWG) and included some British personnel who had escaped from Singapore. Leaving the Press and Diplomatic Section at Park Orchards, the ASWG was formed at Bonegilla, in northern Victoria, from the 5th Special Wireless Section, which moved there in May and was responsible for the recruiting and training of intercept operators. The RAAF component consisted of personnel assigned from Victoria Barracks, Melbourne. There were three assistant directors, Major Abraham Sinkov of the US Army, who arrived a little later; Major A. W. Sandford of the Australian Army; and Squadron Leader Roy Booth of the RAAF. The Central Bureau's authorised expenditure was £50 000 from the US Army, and £25 000 from each of the Australian Army and the RAAF. The Australian government provided the US funds and debited the US under the Reverse Lend Lease program.[73]

The US Navy's cryptanalytic section, FRUMEL, did not join

Senior officers of the Central Bureau at Archerfield Aerodrome, Brisbane, in July 1945. From left: Wing Commander H. Roy Booth, RAAF, deputy director Central Bureau; Lieutenant Colonel Alastair Wallace (Mic) Sandford, AIF, deputy director Central Bureau; Squadron Leader W. (Bill) J. Clarke, RAAF, chief signals officer Central Bureau; Lieutenant-Colonel Jack Ryan, wearing First World War ribbons, commanding officer of the Australian Special Wireless Group. (AWM P1443/71/45)

MacArthur's Central Bureau, and although it passed some information to MacArthur's headquarters, Fabian forwarded most of his intercepted material to US Navy headquarters in Washington and Hawaii. This was a severe irritant to MacArthur's chief of intelligence, Brigadier-General Willoughby, who was also annoyed to find that the Central Bureau was not under his control. It came directly under MacArthur's chief of staff, the abrasive Major-General Richard Sutherland.

Before long, a widespread Sigint organisation had evolved. In August 1942 Major (later Lieutenant-Colonel) Jack Ryan was appointed commanding officer of the ASWG at Bonegilla, where, assisted by twelve British operators who had escaped from Singapore, he hurried to train new Special Wireless Sections Type B for deployment to operations. In June 1942 the 51st Section went to Darwin and the 52nd Section, staffed mainly with women of the Australian Women's Army Service (AWAS), went to Mornington, south of Melbourne. The following month the first elements of the 55th Section started to arrive in New Guinea.[74] Later in the war the 54th Section went to Darwin, the 55th Section to New Guinea, and the 56th Section to Perth. In May 1943 the headquarters of the ASWG moved to Kalinga, near Brisbane.

General Sir Thomas Blamey during a visit to the Central Bureau in Brisbane on 25 February 1944. Left to Right (back row) Major R.E. Porter, AIF, ADC to Blamey; Colonel H.S. Doud, US Army, deputy director of Central Bureau; Wing Commander H. Roy Booth, RAAF, deputy director; Lieutenant-Colonel A.W. Sandford, AIF, deputy director. (front row) Brigadier J.D. Rogers, AIF, director of Military Intelligence; Blamey; Major-General Spencer B. Akin, US Army Signals Corps, director of Central Bureau. (AWM P1443/71/17)

The RAAF also had a number of wireless units, and the 1st Wireless Unit began operations at Townsville in April 1942, from where it moved to New Guinea and eventually to the Philippines. By the end of the war there were five other RAAF wireless units operating in Darwin, Hollandia and the Philippines.[75] Intercept information was also fed to the Central Bureau by the US 126th Signal Radio Company, which began work in Melbourne in April 1942 and later moved to Brisbane and eventually to the Philippines. Three other US companies served in the SWPA in 1944 and 1945.[76]

In September 1942 Central Bureau moved to Brisbane, where it set up at 21 Henry Street, Ascot, and in huts on the Ascot racecourse. About this time it was joined by Nave, who had had a dramatic row with Fabian, and Professor Room. The Central Bureau had four tasks: it provided MacArthur with radio intelligence derived from Japanese military signals; it was responsible for Allied communications security in MacArthur's command; it worked with the US Signal Intelligence Service in Washington to solve Japanese army codes; and it 'supplied and exchanged intelligence with the US Navy and the British in adjacent theatres as appropriate'.[77] In late 1942 the bureau deployed to the field small intelligence sections, known as Australian Special Intelligence Personnel Sections, with traffic analysis and cryptographic personnel, linguists and drivers. These sections were attached to the Special Wireless Sections as the intelligence component.[78]

Although the Central Bureau gained in effectiveness during the latter part of 1942, MacArthur's most important intelligence on Japanese naval operations still came from FRUMEL, which also provided him with the Magic Summaries containing the intercepts of Japanese diplomatic traffic, decrypted in Washington. MacArthur, however, was determined to have his own access to diplomatic traffic, and on 31 December 1942 he told General George C. Marshall, chief of staff of the US Army in Washington, that since his intercept organisation was becoming better organised the time had come to intercept and decode 'Japanese traffic of the greater East Asia Administration and other correspondence of the highest plane of diplomatic and military agencies'. He intended to set up a completely separate agency under his own signals officer, Sooey, and it was to report directly to him.[79]

Apparently the Navy stopped passing Magic information to MacArthur because of an instruction from US Naval Headquarters, which had become worried about the 'Army's mishandling of radio intercept intelligence'.[80] As a result, the Central Bureau was reorganised as the GHQ agency to control operationally all intercept and D/F units in the South West Pacific Area. The only exception was the naval intercept organisation, which was regarded as distinct from the land and air agencies. On 30 January 1943 the new organisation of the Central Bureau was instituted and Major (soon to be Lieutenant-Colonel) Sandford was confirmed as executive officer.[81]

Reflecting Blamey's determination to have his own source of diplomatic intelligence, in November 1942 the Australian diplomatic section in the Monterey Building was transferred to A Block at Victoria Barracks, where it reported to Lieutenant-Colonel Robert Little, the ADMI at Army headquarters in Melbourne.[82] The civilian women, Misses Robertson, Shearer and Eldridge, were transferred from the department of the Navy to the department of the Army. Later Lieutenant Ronald Bond succeeded Trendall (who had recruited him) as head of the cryptanalytic section, which was joined by other young men who had been students of Trendall or Treweek.[83] These included Eric Barnes, later professor of Mathematics at Adelaide University, and John Davies, professor of French at Adelaide.[84] It was hard to find suitable linguists and several, including the section head, Archer, collapsed through over-work.[85]

The aerials and wireless operating compound of the Australian Special Wireless Group camp at Kalinga, near Brisbane, in July 1945. Formed at Bonegilla in 1942 the ASWG had sections at Darwin, Mornington (Victoria), Perth, and in New Guinea. (AWM 69982)

The 52nd Australian Special Wireless Section at Mornington intercepted Japanese diplomatic traffic from places such as French Indo-China, Tokyo, Harbin (Manchuria), Afghanistan, Peru, Chile and German-occupied capitals such as Budapest, and this material was sent daily to Victoria Barracks by landline. Several Japanese agents were identified in Chile and Peru.[86] This information was passed to Blamey, the DMI in Brisbane, and to other Australian, US and New Zealand intelligence agencies. Nave recalled later that when he had been in the SIB the Australian Defence officials had been wary of passing the intelligence from these sources to Evatt and the department of External Affairs, as they mistrusted their security. Indeed the 'Y Precis' was not shown to the External Affairs secretary, Hodgson, until June 1943, and he was not permitted to show it to his minister.[87]

While the Australian diplomatic section remained a small unit throughout the war, the Central Bureau became the largest signals intelligence organisation in the theatre, numbering over 1000 men and women by the end of 1943. More than 100 intercept stations and other Sigint facilities were established in Australia during the war. Organising this Sigint network had been an outstanding achievement, and was to pay rich dividends on the battlefield.

SIGINT AND OPERATIONS

The importance of Sigint to Allied operations during the crucial months in mid 1942 cannot be overstated. At this stage the Central Bureau had made little progress with the Japanese Army codes, and the most significant breaks came from the US Navy, which intermittently broke the main Japanese fleet code, JN25, as well as other codes. The US Navy intelligence centres at Washington, Hawaii and Melbourne cooperated to produce Ultra intelligence—not to be confused with the intelligence deciphered at Bletchley Park—and this was passed rapidly to MacArthur's GHQ as well as to South Pacific Command, which was responsible for operations in the area of the Solomon Islands, New Hebrides, Fiji and New Zealand.

Forewarned by Naval Ultra, a US naval force from South Pacific Command, supported by Australian and American ships of MacArthur's command, intercepted a Japanese invasion force bound from Rabaul to Port Moresby. In several battles in the Coral Sea on 7 and 8 May 1942, planes from American aircraft carriers sank one Japanese carrier and damaged another, at the price of one carrier of their own lost and one damaged. Although this was not a decisive tactical victory, it forced the Japanese to call off their seaborne invasion of Port Moresby and reduced the number of Japanese carriers available for the thrust towards Midway Island in the central Pacific planned for the following month.

However good the intelligence might have been, the crucial factor was whether the intelligence staff believed it. In the lead-up to the battle of the Coral Sea, MacArthur's chief of intelligence, Charles Willoughby, had produced contradictory assessments as to whether the Japanese were really planning an invasion.[89] A similar thing happened when on 19 May FRUMEL intercepted a radio message from Tokyo to Japanese headquarters in Rabaul. As 'enemy air strength in the Australia area at present will make it impossible to keep Moresby supplied by the sea route between Rabaul and Moresby after the latter is occupied', the Rabaul command was ordered to investigate a land route from the north coast of New Guinea to Port Moresby.[90] This message, which one senior codebreaker called 'one of the three most important to be decoded in the war', formed the basis of a General Headquarters Intelligence Summary on 23 May 1942.[91] But on Willoughby's advice, neither MacArthur nor Blamey took the intelligence entirely seriously, even though some reinforcements were sent to Port Moresby.

Perhaps an even more important interception was the one warning the US Navy that the Japanese fleet intended to attack Midway in early June. As a result the Americans were waiting and sank four Japanese carriers for the loss of the *Yorktown*, which had been hurriedly repaired after being damaged in the Coral Sea a month earlier. Years later Treweek, then at FRUMEL in the Monterey building, remembered going home to his wife in their flat in Melbourne and telling her, 'Japan has just lost the war! I can't tell you more! Japan has just lost the war!'[92] This great victory changed the naval balance in the Pacific, for instead of seizing New Caledonia, Fiji and Samoa, the Japanese decided to press ahead with their plans to capture Port Moresby. The victory also gave the Americans the confidence to begin planning a major counter-offensive in the South and South-West Pacific. Earlier, on 18 April, a Magic Summary, comprising decrypted Japanese diplomatic traffic, had informed MacArthur and the Australian government that a Japanese report of the discussions between the Japanese foreign minister and the German ambassador in Tokyo indicated there was no plan to invade Australia.[93]

Despite intercepted information that the Japanese intended to land at Buna on the north coast of Papua and advance on Port Moresby via Kokoda, Willoughby provided erratic assessments and eventually, according to Drea, 'reversed himself and declared that the Japanese purpose was to consolidate areas they already had, not to invade new ones'.[94] Thus, when the Japanese landed on the night of 21 July, the Allies were caught off guard, leading to the epic fighting retreat along the Kokoda Trail.

Better intelligence was provided about the Japanese plans to land at Milne Bay. MacArthur reinforced the area first, and when the Japanese landed towards the end of August his Australian forces were able to achieve a major victory over a Japanese amphibious landing. During these battles MacArthur's Sigint organisation had been able to gain an important advantage over the Japanese by intercepting Japanese Air Force messages, so that usually the Allies were ready for air attacks.[95]

By the end of 1942, as MacArthur's Australian and US forces gained the initiative in Papua, and the South Pacific forces took control at Guadalcanal in the Solomon Islands, Ultra was providing the most important intelligence in the South and South-West Pacific. In early 1943 it had two major triumphs. The first was the warning that the Japanese at Rabaul planned to reinforce their troops in the Lae–Salamaua area of New Guinea.[96] Allied aircraft were waiting, and in the battle of the Bismarck Sea in early March, eight Japanese transports and four destroyers were sunk. The Japanese lost some 3000 men. The second coup was the interception of the itinerary of Admiral Yamamoto, commander-in-chief of the Japanese fleet. Acting on this information, on 18 April 1943 US fighters intercepted and shot down his bomber in the Solomon Islands.

Having secured bases on the north coast of Papua and at Guadalcanal, the Allies were able to strike at the Japanese bases with their growing air forces and to make better use of their naval forces. This enabled them to mount major offensives in both the New Guinea and Solomons areas during 1943. By April 1944 the

Australians had taken Salamaua, Lae and Finschhafen, and had advanced to Madang.

In early 1944 Central Bureau began to break the Japanese Army codes consistently, and as the year progressed MacArthur's intelligence staff had increasingly reliable intelligence about the Japanese Army order of battle. Sometimes MacArthur made good use of this information, for example in planning the leap forward to Hollandia, in western New Guinea, in April 1944, secure in the knowledge that the Japanese were massing their forces farther east in the Madang–Wewak area.[97] Although at times MacArthur was inclined to ignore Ultra when it did not suit his plans, there was no doubt that the Central Bureau's output was crucial to the success of his campaigns, especially the destruction of the Japanese Air Force in the New Guinea area in March 1944. Ultra saved thousands of lives, it had the potential to shorten the war, and it would have been a disaster if the Japanese learned that their codes were being broken.

PREPARING FOR THE FINAL CAMPAIGNS

In September 1944, as the war entered its final phases, MacArthur's forces stood poised to invade the Philippines. While his forces had advanced along the north coast of New Guinea the Australians had been left well behind, and towards the end of 1944 they were given the task of relieving US forces in the New Guinea area. The Australian First Army (3rd, 5th, 6th and 11th Divisions) operated in New Guinea, New Britain and Bougainville, while Blamey held the 1st Australian Corps (7th and 9th Divisions) in readiness to assist MacArthur in the Philippines.

As US forces prepared for the invasion in October, MacArthur moved his advanced headquarters forward to Hollandia. It was clear that once Manila was secured the Americans intended to transfer the Central Bureau, with all of its IBM machines, there and that the Australians would be left without this important resource. These fears were expressed by the Australian DMI, Brigadier Rogers, and Lieutenant-Colonel Sandford of the Central Bureau at a series of important intelligence conferences in London in September 1944.[98]

That same month an advanced detachment of Central Bureau moved forward to Hollandia, but the majority of the personnel remained behind in Brisbane.[99] The Australians tried to maintain about half the total strength of the Central Bureau in an effort to ensure that if the Australian component was separated out it could still form a viable organisation.[100] Blamey's Advanced Land Headquarters in Brisbane began to move forward to Hollandia as well, but arrangements were complicated further when MacArthur's forces landed at Leyte in October and he progressively moved his advanced headquarters there.

These developments brought a number of changes in the intelligence organisation. For example, in June 1944 the Allied Intelligence Bureau was split in two. The Philippines section remained directly under GHQ, while the remainder became mainly an Australian responsibility. Blamey had been concerned about Colonel Roberts's capacity to control the AIB, and in October 1944 the Australian DDMI, Colonel Wills, was promoted to brigadier to command the AIB. At about the same time the intelligence staff at Advanced LHQ accompanied the main headquarters staff to Hollandia. Wills was not immediately replaced. Instead, day-to-day intelligence matters at Advanced LHQ were handled by several highly competent lieutenant-colonels, such as Reginald Holmes and Charles (Basil) Finlay.

There were still tasks, such as liaison with other intelligence organisations, that needed to be managed in Brisbane, and on 15 December 1944 Brisbane Section LHQ, comprising mainly intelligence personnel, opened at Coronation Drive in the city centre. On 14 January 1945 Lieutenant-Colonel Phillip Sadler arrived from DMI in Melbourne to command the section temporarily, and on 18 January, Lieutenant-Colonel Evan Mander-Jones, the chief instructor of the LHQ School of Military Intelligence at Southport, south of Brisbane, was promoted to colonel and given the additional appointment of DDMI Brisbane Section LHQ.[101] Most of the Ultra intelligence continued to be generated in Brisbane, which was also the central point for communications with Washington and London.

By late 1944 the procedure for handling Ultra information had been refined considerably. In early 1943 the US War Department had tried to bring signals intelligence organisations around the world under more centralised control, to ensure that Ultra would be handled in a uniform way and minimise the chance of a leak compromising the whole operation. To this end it sent special security officers (SSOs) to each of the major overseas commands. Their role was not to intercept and decrypt enemy signals, but to pass Ultra intelligence to its recipients in the most secure manner possible. The first SSOs arrived in the South West Pacific Area in December 1943, but MacArthur insisted that they come under his control for administration and discipline, and they were not given access to Central Bureau. It was not until the latter months of 1944 that they were able to institute some of the necessary security measures.

Under the new arrangements, the senior SSO, Lieutenant-Colonel James Ashby Jr, was located at Hollandia to receive the Ultra material from Brisbane and deliver it to MacArthur's headquarters. Another SSO, Major John R. Thompson, was stationed in Brisbane with a small staff to send the messages by cipher to Ashby, as well as to SSOs at the headquarters of the Far East Air Force, the 6th US Army and later the 8th US Army. These latter headquarters were also in the Hollandia area, and the first two accompanied MacArthur to Leyte in October. It was planned that the sorting of the Ultra information in Brisbane would be carried out by G2 staff from GHQ, but because of staff shortages, Thompson's SSO personnel assisted with this task.[102]

Within the Australian forces, the security and handling of Ultra information was the responsibility of Special Liaison Unit No 9 (SLU9), which arrived from Britain in December 1944 and was based in Brisbane. The unit commander was Squadron-Leader Bob Yendall, but the key appointment of Special Intelligence Security Officer was held by Squadron-Leader Sidney Burley, RAF.[103] SLU detachments were deployed with Blamey's Advanced LHQ at Hollandia and later Morotai, with the headquarters of the First Army at Lae, with the 1st Tactical Air Force at Morotai, and at the Headquarters North-West Area RAAF in Darwin.[104] Major Thompson and Burley worked together harmoniously in Brisbane. The Australian intelligence staff, the staff of Central Bureau and the SSOs were to play important roles in efforts to trace the leakage of information in late 1944 and early 1945.

As we saw in Chapter 3, by the end of 1944 a widespread security network had been set up in the SWPA, but it was not necessarily well equipped to handle intelligence leaks. At the top level, prime minister Curtin was sick and his deputy, Forde, lacked authority. MacArthur, the government's chief adviser on military matters, had left Australia, and the government did not have full confidence in Blamey, who had fallen out badly with several ministers. Senior Army officers distrusted Evatt, his personal staff and certain members of the department of External Affairs. Yet, as attorney-general, Evatt was responsible for the Security Service.

Where the leakages concerned Ultra information, newly introduced regulations meant that few people could be told of their full seriousness or of how they had been discovered. In apportioning blame, there would be jealousies between the Americans and the Australians. As early as 1942 the Americans had unjustly accused the Australian intelligence staff of leaking Ultra information.[105] Moreover, there was already a dispute between the Army and the Security Service. In northern Queensland, and perhaps in other areas too, Military Intelligence staff were conducting security work already being undertaken by the Security Service.

As Australia entered the last year of the war, the possibility of espionage, subversion or sabotage probably appeared lower than at any time in the previous five years; aliens had been rounded up, Italy had joined the Allies, the war had moved away from Australian shores and victory was in sight. On the other hand, as we saw in Chapter 3 there is no evidence that the Security Service would have been capable of countering such threats. It must have come as a considerable shock to the Security Service and the Cabinet when they learned in early 1945 that top-level information was being leaked to the Japanese. Significantly, the first warning of the leaks came not from the Security Service, but from the Americans, and the source of this information was signals intelligence. Even more worrying was that if the Japanese assessed the leaked information promptly it would reveal the existence of Ultra.

5

'a grave threat to national security'

THE FIRST SECURITY LEAKS

THE CONSTANT FEAR OF ALLIED intelligence staffs during the war was that the enemy would find out about the success of their Sigint operations. This would be disastrous for Allied campaigns, and perhaps even to the course of the war. It is easy, then, to imagine how Lieutenant-General Frank Berryman, the chief of staff Advanced LHQ at Hollandia, reacted when on 2 October 1944 MacArthur's intelligence chief Willoughby told him that the Chinese military liaison officer at Advanced LHQ might have been given access to Ultra information and that this might have been leaked to the Japanese.

Berryman was only too aware of the dangers, for that same day he had signed a certificate placing himself on the distribution list for the GHQ Special Intelligence Bulletins, which were used to disseminate intelligence based on Ultra.[1] This was part of a general improvement in the handling of Ultra information, brought about by the arrival of the SSOs in the SWPA. The news that liaison officer Major-General Wang Chih might have been the source of a leak was disturbing.[2] But it may not have come as a complete surprise to Berryman, because for some time the Australian Army had been careful about the information it made available to Wang.

THE CHINESE LIAISON OFFICERS IN AUSTRALIA

The Second World War was fought by an unequal alliance of Allied coalition partners. The inner group comprised the US, Britain and

Lieutenant-General Frank Berryman, chief of staff, Advanced Land Headquarters. In October 1944 he was dismayed to learn that Ultra information might have been passed to the Chinese liaison officer, and in turn this information might have been leaked to the Japanese. (Sir Frank Berryman)

its dominions, which shared intelligence, including the highly secret Ultra. The other alliance partners were trusted to a lesser degree. In Australia, for example, the Dutch, Free French and Nationalist Chinese representatives were generally kept at arm's length and were certainly not given access to Ultra. Wang had been able to gain some access to it by late 1944 only after a long process of cultivating his American and Australian Allies.

Two and a half years earlier, on 3 April 1942, Prime Minister Curtin had approved the appointment of two Chinese military liaison officers with the Australian Military Forces, and a little later Captain Wang Chih-Kuang of the Chinese Navy, and Lieutenant-Colonel Wang Chih of the Chinese Army, had arrived as liaison officers. Both Wangs had served with MacArthur in the Philippines. In October Captain Wang was appointed naval attaché to the Chinese legation in Australia, but Lieutenant-Colonel Wang remained as Chinese military liaison officer to the AMF. Both men were located at the Chinese consulate at 10 Queen Street in Melbourne.[3]

Wang Chih had been born at Changsha, in Hunan Province, in 1906 and had been educated in China and later the US. After graduating with a degree in history, he was admitted to the US Military Academy at West Point and, in 1932, graduated twelfth in a class of 266. He returned to China and by 1934 was commanding an engineer battalion. In 1938, at a time when the Chinese communists were cooperating with the Nationalist government, he was ordered to lead a reinforcement demolition company operating with the Red Army behind enemy lines, destroying Japanese depots and

Major-General Wang Chih and two unidentified US officers, Brisbane, August 1944. Wang passed information to Chungking using ciphers that could be broken by the Japanese. (P.J. Sadler)

communications. Wang had come from the same area in China as the leader of the communists, Mao Zedung, who tried his best to persuade Wang to join the party. Wang refused 'because of my firm belief in freedom and democracy, which was probably the result of my American training'.[4]

By 1939 Wang was the commander of an infantry regiment which fought a number of battles against the Japanese. Then in May 1941 he was sent by Nationalist leader Generalissimo Chiang Kai-shek as a military liaison officer with the US forces in the Philippines. So as not to upset the American hierarchy, Colonel Wang was temporarily demoted to lieutenant-colonel for this new assignment. After the outbreak of war between Japan and the US he remained in the Philippines before being evacuated from Corregidor to Australia in mid April, one month after MacArthur had fled.

It was not long before senior Australian officers were expressing some concern about Wang. In December 1942, when Blamey heard that he had attended a staff conference at LHQ in Melbourne, the general was quick to remind his staff that foreign liaison officers, including British officers, were not to attend Australian conferences.[5] Allied authorities had good reason to be wary of passing information to a representative of the Chinese Nationalist government. As early as August 1941 a decrypted Japanese diplomatic message from Hsinking (where General Umezu Yoshijiroo, the commander-in-chief of the Japanese Kwantung Army in Manchuria, had his headquarters) to Bangkok had shown that the Japanese had access to intelligence from the Soviet ambassador at the Nationalist capital at Chunking.[6]

In December 1942 the Allied Translator and Interpreter Section translated a Japanese intelligence report captured near Milne Bay in New Guinea which gave details of Allied shipping movements into Milne Bay, including the numbers, dates and hours when Australian corvettes were due to leave the convoy. The source was given as the 'Chinese military attache, Melbourne'.[7] Further investigation indicated that this probably referred to the naval attaché, and the Australian Naval Board assured MacArthur's headquarters that it had given the Chinese 'no information whatsoever concerning Allied Naval dispositions or movements'.[8] The US Intelligence staff took up the matter with Colonel Wang, who discussed it with Captain Wang, and on 2 January 1943 replied that the latter had

> said that since the codes in his use are suspected to be broken, he has immediately ceased to use and has advised Chungking Headquarters to immediately cease to use the codes in question. He has also reported the fact to the Chungking Headquarters, and has asked for a full investigation.[9]

Colonel Wang was by now with LHQ in Brisbane, where he came to the attention of the deputy director of security for Queensland, Robert Wake. Initially Wang had discussed with the Security Service the possibility of its providing an agent to work with the Chinese community in Brisbane. On 9 March 1943 Wake reported to Brigadier Simpson, the director-general of security in Canberra, that Wang was 'very social' in his activities and that his choice of friends was 'not of the best from a Security viewpoint'.[10] The next day Wake reported further that Wang

> is suffering from a form of anglophobia which has been accentuated since his arrival in Australia by the off-hand manner in which he alleges certain Australian officers have treated him . . . Wang is somewhat of a 'strutter' and Australians as a whole do not pay respect to rank and probably Wang feels that he has been singled out to what is really part of a national characteristic. But irrespective of the causes, the result is that Wang not only feels that full respect is not paid to his rank but also that he is on occasions slighted socially.

Wake added that Wang was 'intensely anti-Communist' and regarded the Australian government 'as almost semi-Communist or at least too sympathetic towards Leftist thought'.[11]

On 2 April 1943 Wake warned Simpson that the Royal Australian Navy regarded Wang with a considerable degree of suspicion and had protested at his use of a private cipher for communication with Chungking.[12] That same day, Major-General Berryman, then DCGS at Advanced LHQ, sought clarification of Wang's role. By this stage Wang had an office in the LHQ building at St Lucia in Brisbane; he lived in private accommodation even though his assistant, Lieutenant Nan Yu Lu, lived in the LHQ officers' mess.[13] Berryman was informed by the Australian intelligence staff that Wang 'should be permitted only such facilities for gathering information according to the degree of goodwill and co-operation he displays in conforming to requirements concerning method of transmitting information to China'. As a liaison officer it was expected that Wang would use communication channels prescribed by the Australian Army, but it was realised that he could not be prevented from using Captain Wang Chih-Kuang or the Chinese legation to transmit information without Australian knowledge.[14]

In response to Wake's suspicions, in September 1944 Simpson advised the deputy directors of security in each state that in July 1943 the Allied Translator and Interpreter Section had translated a 1942 Japanese intelligence report captured by Allied forces which said, 'The Resident Attache for Chungking made the following report on the 17th'—namely that there were 11 000 Americans on Guadalcanal and over 7000 on Tulagi, the Australian Army presence at Port Moresby had been increased by 2500, and the Australian naval squadron was safeguarding the resupply of Milne Bay. This information had been detailed in an Allied intelligence document on the 11th of the month—presumably August 1942.[15] A little later Simpson corrected his letter to say that Captain Wang had sent the information to Chungking by a cipher that had been broken by the Japanese.[16] Presumably this incident was the one described earlier in this chapter. It is clear from this account that initially Simpson and the Security Service had been told neither about the security breach in December 1942, nor that the source had been Captain Wang. This was the only time a leak was attributed directly to Captain Wang, but Naval Intelligence thought he was 'unreliable and unscrupulous and that it was dangerous to pass him information of a security nature'. It was believed that at times he 'drank to excess, and under the influence of drink was very loose in his talk'.[17]

While the Security Service was watching Captain Wang, it was also watching the Australia–China Cooperation Association, which had been formed in 1939 to encourage closer relations with and provide assistance to China. The membership consisted for the most part of Australian citizens 'with liberal views', but included some persons of partly Chinese origin. The Security Service noted that a number of members of the Communist Party belonged to the association, but it was not regarded as a 'communist subsidiary'. It also noted that the association's 'publicity officer', George Burchett, was a communist, and that his son, Wilfred Burchett, a war correspondent with Australian Associated Press, had sent photographs from China for use in his father's lecture tours.[18]

While the Allies provided a tremendous amount of military aid to China, senior Allied officials were alert to ways in which they might be able to obtain some assistance in return. For example, from late 1942 to late 1943 Colonel Wang was closely involved in discussions with MacArthur's headquarters over a proposal by the Allied Intelligence Bureau (AIB) to insert Chinese agents into the Netherlands East Indies from Australia. Towards the end of 1943 he visited Chungking to finalise plans, but for various reasons, including Dutch opposition, the scheme was dropped.[19]

WANG'S EFFORTS TO OBTAIN INFORMATION

Although Wang had spent much time on the ill-fated project to insert Chinese agents into the East Indies, his main role was exchanging military information between Chungking and GHQ. This task had begun as soon as he had arrived in Australia in 1942 and had continued throughout 1943. For example, in July 1943 he had passed on to GHQ the locations and identities of Japanese forces in China, Indo-China and Burma. In return he had sought the identities of Japanese units in the South West Pacific Area. GHQ was willing to pass on information gained from translated documents and prisoners of war, but not from Ultra sources.[20] In February 1944 Wang returned to Australia from China and in March, on behalf of Chiang Kai-shek, he visited US Admiral Chester Nimitz in Hawaii to try to persuade him to invade Formosa. On his return to Australia he redoubled his efforts to gain Allied information.

Lieutenant-Colonel Phillip Sadler was the general staff officer grade one intelligence at LHQ from August 1942 until 9 March 1944, when he took over from Colonel Wills as the senior intelligence officer at New Guinea Force headquarters. He recalls that shortly before he went to New Guinea—possibly in February 1944—Central Bureau decoded signals between Wang and Chungking which contained information on the Japanese order of battle that had been gained from Ultra intercepts. This raised two concerns: first, Wang was not supposed to have access to Ultra information; and second, if the Japanese had intercepted Wang's signals they might learn that their own signals traffic was being intercepted. There were immediate top-level meetings between MacArthur, Blamey and Rogers, and as a result Wang was denied access to both the LHQ and GHQ intelligence sections.[21]

Wang had not been given specific access to Ultra information, but had made good use of his access to the LHQ intelligence section. The deputy head of the LHQ intelligence 'Japanese order of battle' section was Major George Batchelor.[22] On the wall of his office was a large map of the SWPA on which was marked Japanese locations determined from Ultra intelligence. This map was covered with a blind, which was supposed to be raised only when Batchelor had his door closed and locked. On one occasion when Wang entered the room, the door was open but the blind was up.[23]

The impact of this event can be gauged from a note in the files of Colonel Wills, who had preceded Sadler as senior intelligence officer on New Guinea Force headquarters:

> I heard a rather grim story regarding the possibility of trouble for your blokes a few weeks back. GHQ told the war correspondents that the Japs had been presented with some comprehensive information in a rather unfortunate manner.[24]

In an effort to regain access to the intelligence staff, Colonel Wang held a big party in a Brisbane hotel to which he invited Willoughby, Rogers and their staffs. About this time he was promoted to major-general—a further excuse for a celebration. Wang spoke English perfectly and had sufficient money to entertain lavishly. His Buick car made him popular with women and he also had a weekender at the Gold Coast.[25]

On 18 July 1944 General Wang made a formal request to LHQ for a summary of the organisation tables of Australian infantry and mechanised forces.[26] The DMI, Brigadier Rogers, advised LHQ staff that the policy of the Combined Chiefs of Staff was that 'Intelligence information supplied by the United States and Great Britain to the Chinese should be strictly limited to Intelligence needed by the Chinese in the prosecution of the war against Japan.'[27]

While LHQ was considering Wang's request, he made a further appeal to GHQ for details of enemy land and air forces in the Philippines and Formosa.[28] Willoughby replied that Formosa was not within the South West Pacific theatre, and the only information on the Philippines that could be released was that obtained from captured enemy documents. All other information, 'because of its source of origin', was classified Top Secret. The general policy was to release data of tactical and strategic significance to current operations, but matters concerning enemy orders of battle would be 'handled by proper staff agencies between London, India, Chungking and Washington'.[29]

Some idea of the Australian attitude towards Wang at this time can be gained from a memorandum Simpson sent to his deputy directors-general in Sydney, Melbourne and Brisbane on 1 September 1944:

> It is the considered opinion of certain well-informed Allied officers that General Wang should not be trusted with any information; in fact some quarters go further and express the view that no secret information should be given to Chinese representatives in this country, if only because the secret information which they pass on to Chungking has reached the Japanese from that point. This material would normally go from Australia to Chungking in the Chinese diplomatic bag or cipher.
> A further statement which has been made in high places is that 'Chinese are either giving or permitting secret information to reach the Japanese. Japanese received particulars of the numbers of B29s (in China) and the time of their take off to bomb Japan. They could only have received this information from a Chinese source. Chinese representatives in Australia should not be given any information'[30] . . . it would be as well if the closest possible attention were given to this gentleman and you are therefore instructed by intermittent surveillance and other means to obtain a full picture of his associates and activities in your [area]. Until further instructed you are requested to regard General Wang as a person of more than usual Security interest.[31]

On 30 November, LHQ informed Wang that the First Army, under Lieutenant-General Vernon Sturdee, consisted of the 3rd, 5th and 6th Divisions; the Second Army was administrative only and was commanded by Major-General Herbert Lloyd; and the 1st Australian Corps, under Lieutenant-General Sir Leslie Morshead, consisted of the 7th and 9th Divisions. Wang was not told what brigades were in each division nor their locations.[32]

As well as seeking information, in July 1944 Wang sought permission from the Australian Army to send messages to Chungking by cipher. However, the chief cipher officer, Lieutenant-Colonel Laurence Christie, examined Wang's code books and concluded that they did not meet Australian security requirements. Considering Chungking's remote location, for at least part of the way any communications would have to be by radio.[33] On 7 September, after receiving advice from Willoughby, Blamey informed Wang that his messages to Chungking would have to be sent in Australian Army ciphers. He could either give his messages in plain English to the Australian Army for ciphering, or he could put the messages in his own private cipher for translation into Australian Army ciphers and subsequent dispatch. Wang was happy with this arrangement.[34]

Years later a senior Australian Army cryptographer was to express astonishment at this arrangement: 'If Wang was a person of evil intent towards us, an incipient Red or an adherent to the Puppet Regime in

Manchuria, I wager that "he was happy with this arrangement", for such a procedure would have been a cryptographer's bonanza!' Then again, he added, chief cipher officer Christie 'was, I regret to say, of limited perspicacity and inventiveness'.[35]

Despite these precautions (or perhaps because of them), by October 1944 it was clear that information from Wang was still reaching the Japanese, and urgent action was now necessary. On 6 October Willoughby wrote to Rogers, the Australian DMI (with a copy to Berryman), drawing his attention to a radio message from the War Department in Washington which stated that the Chinese intelligence staff had said the Japanese 30th, 81st, 100th, 102nd, 103rd and 105th Divisions were located in the Philippines. The source was given as Major-General Wang Chih in Brisbane. At that time the information had an Ultra classification.

Willoughby reported that Wang had approached the head of his G2 Philippines sub-section in Brisbane, Colonel Stephen Mellnik, to verify the existence of these divisions, and that Mellnik had warned Wang against relaying his information. (Mellnik had been a classmate of Wang's at West Point and had served with him in the Philippines. Mellnik had been captured by the Japanese, had escaped, had joined the Filipino guerillas, and had been taken off the Philippines by submarine in July 1943.[36]) When Wang said he had obtained the information from the order of battle section at Advanced LHQ, the matter was brought to the attention of Lieutenant-Colonel Lewis, the head of that section.

Faced with this evidence, Willoughby warned Wang in writing not to delve into the enemy order of battle, which was based on secret sources. As Willoughby told Rogers:

> It is evidence from this radio, that he [Wang] sent this information on in spite of our admonition. This is not the first indiscretion from this quarter. I am afraid that he may pick operational dates, objectives, etc., and report them in this fashion.

Willoughby suggested that Rogers take action to prevent access to Order of Battle Annexes, the *AMF Weekly Intelligence Review* and the GHQ Monthly Enemy Dispositions paper. He concluded:

> There is evidence of Jap troop movements affecting an operational area, in which we are interested. This may be coincidence. Assuming that such information was relayed by the same channel (as is the case of the Divisions), the likelihood of it falling into enemy's hands is a grave possibility. We have evidence from captured Jap documents of leakages via the Chinese Military Attache, Melbourne.[37]

Clearly Willoughby was angry about the leaks, and on 19 October he wrote to the deputy chief of staff of the US Forces in Australia:

> On several occasions Maj Gen Chih Wang . . . has committed indiscretions or worse, and he once disregarded a written admonition from me not to report certain secret matter.
> In view of the above he should not be allowed to occupy an office in the same building with any SWPA offices.
> If this be the case at present, it is desired that he be required to move to another location.[38]

Not surprisingly, when Wang asked to be allowed to join GHQ at Hollandia he was told that 'everything was so over crowded in Hollandia that there was no room for him'.[39] These precautions seemed sufficient to ensure Wang would not be the source of any further leaks.

THE *AMF WEEKLY INTELLIGENCE REVIEW*

Yet the leaks continued. Over a month later, on 22 November, the special security officer at GHQ, Lieutenant-Colonel Ashby, informed Berryman that Ultra sources had shown that further information had been leaked to the enemy. As Berryman noted in his diary:

> This is unfortunate as evidence points to us as a possible source of leakages and coming on the incident of a previous leakage thro' Chungking where Landops [Advanced LHQ] was quoted as the source of leakage.[40]

This evidence of a new series of leaks was particularly worrying. The Allied Sigint organisation had only just decrypted a message from Tokyo which seemed to indicate that the contents of the *AMF Weekly Intelligence Review* No. 118 for the period 27 October to 3 November 1944 were known in full in Tokyo on 11 November.[41] The Ultra report showed that on 11 November Tokyo had sent out an intelligence summary that stated:

> The enemy's appreciation of Japanese strength in the Philippines at the beginning of November (D4 report sent on November the 7th).
> (1) Air strength (as of November the 3rd):
>   Northern Sector: 281 planes
>   Central Sector: 107 planes
>   Southern Sector: 61 planes
>   Total 449 planes

(2) Ground strength (as of November the 1st):
   Luzon Island: 161,200 men
   Central Sector: 51,900 men
   Southern Sector   60,900 men
                  Total 274,000 men[42]

The *AMF Review* consisted of five parts. Part 1 was a brief summary of significant events. Part 2 formed the main part of the *Review* and included a summary of operations by areas, strengths and dispositions of enemy forces, enemy organisation, enemy equipment, tactics, extracts from captured documents and other general information. Part 3 dealt with other fronts, Part 4 covered topographical information, and Part 5 dealt with security. In *Review* No. 118, Part 1 covered one page; Part 2, 26 pages; Parts 3 and 4 were omitted, and Part 5 was one page long. The key information, the estimate of enemy strengths in the SWPA, particularly the Philippines, on 1 November 1944, was on page 12 in Part 2.[43]

At this stage the Allied intelligence staff had not identified 'D 4', who had apparently sent the report, but it was known that Wang had been given access to at least part of the *Review*. After issue No. 120, publication of the *Review* was suspended.[44] The reason was given in the Advisory War Council two months later, on 8 February 1945, when John McEwen asked when the *Review*, 'which had been temporarily suspended in November last' would be resumed. Minister Evatt replied that:

> publication of the Summary was in abeyance, pending the outcome of enquiries which were being made on matters raised by the Commander-in-Chief, Australian Military Forces, concerning leakages of military information attributed to diplomatic sources in Australia.[45]

The evidence of this new and even more dangerous leak demanded General Blamey's personal intervention, and at 11 a.m. on 24 November, in Brisbane, he spoke by secraphone with the DMI in Melbourne 're copies from AWA of Chinese sigs'. An hour later Blamey discussed the matter with General Akin, the director of Central Bureau,[46] then wrote immediately to the head of Amalgamated Wireless (Australasia) in Sydney, which was responsible for transmitting overseas radio cables from Australia:

> It is requested that in the interest of the defense of the Commonwealth and of the cause of the United Nations that you make available at once to Major General S.B. Akin, Chief Signal Officer, General Headquarters, Southwest Pacific Area, photographic copies of all incoming and outgoing messages of the Chinese Government, its Military, Naval and other representatives

in Australia, and of the Bank of China and any other Chinese agencies during the period November 1–8 1944 (both dates inclusive). Your compliance with this request has the full approval of General Headquarters, Southwest Pacific Area, and is a most urgent military necessity.[47]

The fact that defence was spelt with an 's', in the American fashion, suggests the letter was drafted by Akin and typed in his office.[48]

On the same day, Ashby in Hollandia gave Berryman a report of the leaks, and General Sutherland, MacArthur's chief of staff, told Berryman he was convinced that the *AMF Review* was the source. Berryman would not admit that LHQ might be at fault, as he thought it was possible that there were other leaks since 'GHQ itself is not security minded'.[49] The following day Ashby showed Berryman a signal from Akin to Colonel S. S. Auchincloss, Akin's deputy in Hollandia, stating that Wang had regularly received *AMF Reviews* containing Ultra information. Berryman immediately signalled the DMI in Brisbane asking whether Wang had received Part 2 of the *Review*.[50]

By 26 November Akin had arrived in Hollandia; he disclosed that Ultra information had been in Part 1 of the *Review* and that he had discussed the matter with Blamey in Brisbane.[51] The next day Lieutenant-Colonel Sandford, the Australian assistant director of Central Bureau, arrived in Hollandia and discussed the security of Ultra information with Berryman.[52] After receiving further information from Brisbane, Berryman reassured Akin that in the three months Wang had been a recipient of the *Review* Ultra information had been restricted to a special appendix which LHQ had not shown to Wang. Akin therefore agreed that most of the information Wang had sent to China would not have been Ultra material.[53] Nevertheless, early in December Berryman ordered his senior intelligence officer in Hollandia, Lieutenant-Colonel Reginald Holmes, to prepare a shorter distribution list for the *Review*.[54]

Investigation showed that while Wang had been given a copy of Part 2 of the *Review* (which included the estimates of the enemy strength in the SWPA), Berryman was right in his claim that the information Wang saw was not based on Ultra material. The *Review* stated that the Japanese strength in the crucial Leyte–Samar–Masbate area was 13 000. The GHQ *Special Intelligence Bulletin* of 10 October (which was based on Ultra) put the Japanese strength there at almost 27 000. In fact, it was a little over 20 000, so the data was probably not based on Ultra sources. (Nevertheless, in broad terms, Allied intelligence was remarkably accurate. The GHQ *Special Intelligence Bulletin* stated that the Japanese 16th, 26th, 30th, 100th, 102nd, 103rd and 105th Divisions [plus three independent brigades and the 115th Division which could not be located] were in the Philippines. The *Review* listed exactly the same divisions but did not mention the unlocated 115th. In fact, the Japanese had all the first seven divisions plus two more, the 2nd and 8th, but not the 115th, in the Philippines.[55])

After the Americans landed at Leyte on 20 October, Willoughby believed the Japanese were withdrawing from the island. However, on 1 November information was received that in fact they were reinforcing the island. There followed an extremely tense period while the US intelligence staff tried to identify the new arrivals. The Japanese 1st Division was not identified until 6 November, and this posed a considerable threat to General Krueger's Sixth US Army.[56] Allied estimates of the Japanese strength would therefore have been of immense value to the Japanese commander in Manila.

A WIDER SECURITY PROBLEM

While Berryman was making every effort to tighten procedures for the handling of Ultra information and ensure that it was not made available to General Wang, Blamey was dealing with an even more worrying security breach—one which indicated that the problem went beyond that posed by the Chinese and did not necessarily involve the *AMF Weekly Intelligence Review*. On 6 November the department of Information had issued a circular headed 'Background Service New Series', which was apparently disseminated to the editors of the capital city newspapers.[57] After becoming aware of the circular's existence, on 14 November 1944 Blamey wrote to both the minister for Defence and the minister for the Army complaining that while it included information he had given to the department of Information, it also contained additional information—such as the approximate dates of future operations in New Britain, the Solomons and New Guinea, and alterations to the plans for operations in the Philippines—that had not been supplied by the Army. In fact requests by the department for information on future operations had been refused.[58] When the acting minister for Defence, Forde, sought observations from Arthur Calwell, the minister for Information, the latter replied on 24 November that the background service had ceased on 6 November. But, he added, on the last day of its operations, editors in one city only had been given information 'in writing instead of being passed verbally as has always been the rule when referring to military operations'.[59]

Before long Blamey's concern about a possible breach of security was borne out. On 24 November the Allied Sigint organisation intercepted a Japanese message from Harbin to Tokyo which gave details of MacArthur's plans for certain operations in the Philippines. The source of this information was given as the 'Soviet ambassador' in Australia in a message dated 22 November. On 2 December there was a similar report from Harbin and again the source was given as the 'Soviet minister in Australia' and dated 29 November.[60] However, at this stage there was apparently no basis for blaming the leaks directly on the department of Information circular.

Blamey and his intelligence staff were now presented with the possibility that information was being leaked by both the Chinese and the Russians, or that the Chinese and Russians were collaborating. While he pondered how to deal with the Soviet threat, efforts to deal with the Chinese continued. On 30 November senior officials of the Security Service met with the district censor and agreed that, in the interests of national security, 'it might be essential . . . to monitor the telephone of a foreign authority in Melbourne'. It is likely that the 'authority' was the Chinese consulate. The Chinese embassy was in Canberra, but it had consulates in both Melbourne and Sydney. The Soviet Union had an embassy (or legation) in Canberra, but no consulates. The district censor discussed the matter with the Victorian superintendent of telephones and that afternoon confirmed his request in writing.[61]

On 2 December the superintendent of telephones told the district censor that he had passed the request to the Postmaster-General's department. On the advice of a senior official of the department of External Affairs, the request was denied. Two days later the censor was given details of the trunk calls that had originated from the foreign consulate, but was told that the PMG had decided 'that no monitoring of the telephone in question would be permitted unless it was authorised by the Acting Prime Minister'.[62]

Blamey arrived back in Brisbane from the Philippines and New Guinea on the evening of 13 December and next day Sandford told him of further leaks. Sandford explained that Squadron-Leader Burley, the special intelligence security officer, had recently arrived from Britain and was trying to clear up

> a number of extremely difficult breaches of security . . . Not the least of these is the source of information which completes the Japanese 'Harbin Special Intelligence Reports'. As we suspected, the source is the Soviet Ambassador in Australia. Two things are not clear. First, how the Japanese obtain the information from the Soviet and secondly, how the Soviet Ambassador himself obtains the information. An example given in MBJ 30601 is a comparatively innocuous one, but there have been much more dangerous and precise examples in the past.[63]

MBJ messages were intercepts of Japanese radio traffic. The key sentence in MBJ 30601 read: 'Harbin Special Intelligence Report. The Australian government has decided against the despatch of troops to the Philippines until arrangements have been completed for the shipping and aircraft necessary to ensure supplies'.[64]

Continuing his journey, Blamey arrived in Melbourne on Friday 15 December, and the following Monday had an interview with the DMI and Colonel Lindsay Ride, commandant of the British Army Aid Group China, who was on leave in Melbourne.[65] It is reasonable to suspect that both Rogers and Blamey wanted to learn first-hand about the reliability and security-mindedness of Nationalist Chinese officers.

Rogers had further discussions with Blamey the next day and advised him that the *AMF Weekly Intelligence Review* should be republished without red and blue editions. (Only the red edition had Ultra information.) There should be only one edition, and all information from Ultra sources should be eliminated. By late 1944 the *Review* had a distribution list of 202, including the Chinese liaison officer and the Chinese naval attaché.[66] Rogers recommended reducing the list to less than 100. He was not sure about the 15 copies normally distributed to the War Cabinet secretariat, but Blamey thought these copies should still be given out.[67] By the time the *Review* reappeared in February 1945, the list had been cut to 115. Most copies went to major Australian and American headquarters and other military establishments. A small number went to the other services and to British, Canadian, and New Zealand military recipients. The only copies that did not go to a military recipient were the 15 copies for the War Cabinet. There was no copy for the Dutch or Chinese liaison officers in Australia.[68]

Meanwhile the cryptanalysts at the GCCS in Britain had deciphered a Japanese message dated 29 August 1944. Part 1 was missing, but the remainder read:

> Their extent of use must be reduced to a minimum. Moreover, particular care should be taken to see that the source of information is not recorded in Intelligence files, especially in areas which are likely to be involved in battle in the near future. The following is a list of such Intelligence.
>
> Para 1: Information from the military reporting officer in London is D1 Intelligence.
> Para 2: From the military officer in New Delhi—D2 Intelligence.
> Para 3: From the military reporting officer in Ceylon—D3 Intelligence.
> Para 4: From staff officer Noguchi in Sydney—D4 Intelligence.
> Para 5: From the military reporting officer in Melbourne—D5 Intelligence

Para 6: From the military reporting officer in Washington—D6 Intelligence.
Para 7: From the military reporting officer in Ankara—D7 Intelligence.
Para 8: From the general staff (Gunreibu) in Chungking—D8 Intelligence.[69]

By this time Group Captain Frederick Winterbotham, the British government's chief Ultra security officer, had arrived in Brisbane as part of a worldwide inspection of SLUs. As Winterbotham described in his ground-breaking book *The Ultra Secret*, he 'was able, with the cooperation of Colonel Sandford, the young Australian officer in charge whom I had known in London when we were teaching him the job, to sort out some of the distribution problems' so that centres in Melbourne, Delhi and Kandy could get more of what they needed.[70] Winterbotham told Sandford that the implications of the intercept quoting the *AMF Review* were 'obviously so serious and far-reaching' that he would postpone his departure for Britain so as to discuss the matter with the DMI. He said 'the matter is one of serious insecurity on a global scale' and a special section had been set up 'to deal with precisely this type of leakage'.[71]

By mid December 1944, efforts to contain the leaks and to identify the culprits had been restricted to the military and the Security Service, and the attempt to monitor telephones was made within this restricted group of officials. Censorship was supervised by the DMI on behalf of the chief of the general staff. It was carried out in two broad categories. Field censorship was administered by general-staff officers, and in particular by members of the 1st Australian Field Censorship Company. Communications censorship was administered by the controller of postal and telegraph censorship, Phillip Ettelson, a former militia officer in the Army's legal department. Ettelson administered his responsibility through a deputy controller at LHQ and district censors in each Lines of Communication Area (that is, in each state). Liaison officers were provided by each service and by most government departments.[72]

The PMG's refusal to monitor telephones meant that Blamey would have to seek outside assistance, and on 23 December he wrote a carefully considered letter to Forde, acting minister for Defence. (Prime minister Curtin was still in hospital.) Since the minister for the Army had overall responsibility for censorship, Blamey sent a copy of the letter to the acting minister, Senator James Fraser. He said the postal and telegraphic censorship authority was 'being embarrassed' by the PMG's refusal of assistance, then described the actions taken to date and explained that the PMG's attitude constituted 'a grave threat to National Security . . . There is much evidence of a most highly secret character to cause grave misgivings as to leakages of valuable information to the enemy through foreign authorities'. Blamey said that the fact that the PMG had discussed the matter with the department of External Affairs was a 'grave breach of security' and continued:

> I am aware that there is some delicacy in the position, but evidence has accumulated recently which puts it beyond any doubt that important information does reach the enemy from Australia in a very short space of time, and I would suggest that the well-being of our forces in the field should be the paramount consideration in dealing with this question.

He requested that the Post Office be required to accept the request of the censorship authority without further reference.[73]

Blamey was frustrated when on 30 December, Forde wrote pointing out that he should have written to the minister for the Army, who was responsible for censorship. (Blamey had, in fact, sent a copy to the acting minister.) But Forde also forwarded Blamey's letter to the minister for External Affairs and the postmaster-general for their comments. He reminded Blamey that in late 1941 the Army had monitored the telephone of the Japanese legation without the authority of External Affairs.[74] Blamey took no further action for the moment, but would not give up.

So far, he had confined himself to stating, without evidence, that this was a matter of grave national security. He had no wish to explain the source of his information, nor to widen the circle of people who might be aware of the leak. The previous day, 29 December, Blamey had visited Shedden, the influential Defence department and War Cabinet secretary, to discuss 'instances which had come to his notice regarding the leakage of important information of an operational nature to the Japanese'.[75] The information 'was apparently originating from an authoritative source in Australia'. From Shedden's account of the meeting, it is clear that the main topic of the conversation was yet another leak, for an intercepted Japanese message from Harbin had revealed a report couched 'in practically identical terms with those of the background news sheet' about which Blamey had complained the previous month.[76]

It seems that Shedden was at first inclined to dismiss Blamey's claims, and in his note of the meeting he referred to earlier complaints by Blamey about the activities of the Information department, with which Blamey had had a long-running feud. Shedden reminded Blamey that Information had transmitted its material from its main office to the states by teleprinter using 'an elementary code which did not provide for any degree of secrecy'.[77] Perhaps Shedden sensed that Blamey was using the matter of the leaks to score points against old adversaries, as well as to gain some leverage in his argument with the Security Service over Army manning.

Meanwhile, evidence of the leaks mounted. After receiving an intercept on 25 December giving the Australian Army's organisation for operations in New Guinea, Sandford wrote to Little: 'On this auspicious day Imperial General Headquarters feels compelled to make an appropriate present to the Honourable General Staff of the Australian Military Forces'. Rogers asked Winterbotham to send an MI6 security officer from London 'to deal with the problem'. Sandford warned Little that it was 'most imperative of course, that no action whatever be taken until his arrival'.[78] A further intercept on 30 December gave a Japanese report of 16 December on the strength of the British Pacific Fleet then arriving in Australian ports. The report's assessment of two battleships and five cruisers was correct although the assessment of eight aircraft carriers was twice the actual number.[79]

On 2 January, armed with more evidence, Blamey returned to see Shedden, who now suggested that 'in view of the seriousness of this matter' Blamey should agree to one of his officers and one of Shedden's 'collaborating in the preparation of a note for the information of the Prime Minister'. Blamey proposed 'to show his information to the Acting Minister for the Army but he could not supply a copy, as it would disclose the most secret source from which it came'. Shedden said that 'from the information he had revealed to me, other Ministers and Departments might be involved, and it would be essential for the Prime Minister to have the fullest possible information if he were to handle the matter satisfactorily'.[80] He recommended that Blamey write a more detailed letter to the acting minister for the Army, 'in view of the fact that he is the Minister primarily concerned with action to correct the leakages, if they are occurring on a Ministerial level or in another Department'.[81] This was a key sentence, because it indicates that the problem concerned information from a more serious source than that being used by the Chinese liaison officer. It also explains Blamey's strong reaction to the Postmaster-General's department consulting with the department of External Affairs.

Unable to solve the matter within the Army or the department of Defence, Blamey was forced to bring it to the notice of the relevant politicians; but would they listen? Prime minister Curtin was still sick in hospital. The acting prime minister and Defence minister, Forde, had shown little inclination to act positively, and attorney-general Evatt, who was responsible for the Security Service, mistrusted Blamey. Fraser, the acting Army minister was an unknown quantity. A former official of the Western Australian Tramways Employees' Union, he had little experience of military or security matters. Later, after Fraser criticised Army administration in the first half of 1945, Blamey was to write that 'ministerial ineptitude reached an all time low' during Fraser's time as acting minister.[82] Whatever might be the reactions of these politicians, Blamey was convinced that action was needed, and he was determined to get it.

6

'the source was the Soviet Minister'

GENERAL BLAMEY'S LETTER

BLAMEY'S LETTER TO FRASER OF 6 January 1945 is the key piece of evidence concerning both the nature and gravity of the security leaks in late 1944. The letter has been the subject of speculation for some years, but there has been no thorough attempt to describe its effect or analyse its contents.[1] Extensive efforts to find the file from which Blamey drew the material on which he based the letter were unsuccessful for many years, and the file was not released by the Australian government until July 1997.[2] There can be no doubt that Blamey took particular care over the letter's preparation; he discussed the matter with Brigadier Rogers and Lieutenant-Colonel Sandford on 4 January, and explained the situation to Fraser the following day.[3] By that time Blamey had even more evidence.[4]

Knowledge of the letter was kept to a very small circle; Lieutenant George Crowther, for example, who worked for Little on security matters, was officially told nothing of the security breaches. Crowther was a 28-year-old solicitor who numbered among his many influential friends Douglas Menzies, QC, the secretary of the Defence Committee; Zelman Cowen of Naval Intelligence; and members of Blamey's personal staff such as Major Tony Shepherd and Captain Robert Porter. Crippled with polio at a young age, Crowther had been enlisted by Little into Military Intelligence because of his legal background. He was told informally that Blamey had written a letter about a leak of information involving the Japanese order of battle and that knowledge of this had been gained by Allied intercepts. Asked his views on possible sources, Crowther

Left: Brigadier John Rogers, the director of Military Intelligence, Brisbane, August 1944. He had long discussions with Blamey about the leakages of information, and helped draft the crucial letter that Blamey sent to the acting minister for the Army on 6 January 1945. (P.J. Sadler) Right: Senator James Fraser, the acting minister for the Army, during an inspection tour in New Guinea in April 1945. Blamey wrote to him about the security leaks in January 1945, but noted later that 'ministerial ineptitude reached an all-time low' during Fraser's tenure as acting minister. (AWM 18395)

replied that there were four possibilities: the Americans, who were jealous of Australian intelligence capabilities; the Soviets; Evatt and his staff; and possibly the Chinese. When it came out in conversation that the Chinese were indeed under suspicion, Crowther was surprised to learn that they had been given access to sensitive material.[5]

While Blamey was preparing his argument, he would have been further angered to receive a copy of the reply to Forde from the postmaster-general, Senator William Ashley, who said that there had been only two cases when his department had not complied promptly and effectively with the wishes of the censorship authorities. In the first case, a request to monitor the telephone of the consulate of a friendly country, Ashley said External Affairs had advised 'that it was contrary to established practice for the censorship to make such investigations'. In the second, a request for 'the observation of a telephone service installed in the private residence of a high ranking officer of the Australian Military Forces . . . I felt . . . that the case was one where the Postal Department was not justified in providing facilities for monitoring purposes'.[6] Ashley did not explain to Forde that the high-ranking officer was Blamey, who, in late 1944, had requested the monitoring because he believed unauthorised persons were using his phone while he was away.

Blamey was already irritated by this action and no doubt saw Ashley's recent decision as a further example of an uncooperative attitude.[7]

Blamey's 6 January letter, reproduced at the beginning of this book, must be seen in the light of this preceding correspondence. The letter reveals some significant points. First, Blamey got closer than ever before to saying the leaks had been confirmed through highly secret means. Second, the leaks apparently had their origin in Canberra, and particularly with the Soviet minister—there was no mention of Wang or the Chinese. Third, information had been transmitted from Sydney. Fourth, Allied official channels had played an important part in their transmission. Fifth, it was desirable to limit the association of official personnel with foreign representatives.[8] The nature of the material being leaked and its implications will be discussed later in this chapter, but the letter clearly implied that it touched on a momentous matter. Blamey did not refer to the danger posed by the exposure of Allied Sigint operations, but he did highlight the possible involvement of the Soviet minister in the leak, which apparently had reached Tokyo.[9]

THE CANBERRA CABINET MEETINGS

As a result of Blamey's letter, the question of leaks was discussed in Canberra on 9 January at a meeting of the War Cabinet, chaired by Forde.[10] Present were Chifley, Evatt, Beasley, Dedman, Hubert Lazzarini, the minister for Home Security, and Fraser. First, however, the cabinet considered the question of whether the Army members should be withdrawn from the Security Service. The three chiefs of staff and Simpson, the director-general of security, were present for this agenda item. Simpson claimed that the Security Service was 'built around' the military staff, and it was decided to defer a decision so the acting Army minister could submit his observations.[11] The fact that this matter was considered at the same meeting as that which considered the leakage of information has some significance, because just at the time when Blamey was in disagreement with Simpson over Army manning, he was seeking special cooperation from him on the matter of the leakages. During the meeting someone said that censorship staff in India had intercepted messages from Wang to Chungking which revealed that he had passed on information from the *AMF Weekly Intelligence Review*.[12] This was of course a cover for Ultra intelligence.

After Simpson and the chiefs of staff left, the discussion turned to the leaks. Fraser read a statement based on Blamey's letter. While the hand-written notes of the meeting are not comprehensive, they reveal that there had been 'telephone monitoring in Canberra', and given Blamey's accusations about it, the Soviet legation was possibly the subject of this monitoring. The notes also suggest that the ministers were told the British SLU9 had arrived in Australia, and that they were suspicious that it was operating without regard for Australian interests. Blamey was to be asked to state the reasons for his charges about the Soviet legation.[13] The notes reveal how little the politicians knew about Allied intelligence operations. Most—perhaps all—had no knowledge of Ultra. The formal minutes simply state that it was agreed that Forde, Evatt and Fraser would discuss the matter with Simpson and Rogers and would submit a report to the War Cabinet.[14]

After the War Cabinet meeting, on 13 January Shedden met with Blamey and Northcott, the chief of the general staff, and Shedden then set about arranging a meeting of the relevant ministers to discuss the leaks.[15] Blamey met Shedden again on the 15th, and had further discussions with Fraser on the 17th. Then, at 4 o'clock that afternoon, accompanied by Frank Sinclair, the Army secretary, DMI Rogers and his personal assistant, Blamey flew to Canberra.[16] In preparation for the Canberra meeting Rogers had prepared a two-and-a-half-page memo for Blamey listing eleven instances in which information had 'found its way into the hands of the Japanese during November and December. The source of certain items is the Soviet Embassy at Canberra. Other items appear to have come from a Japanese agent in Sydney.'[17]

It is difficult to know exactly what happened that evening. According to Rogers's notes, at 8 p.m. Blamey attended a conference with Forde, Evatt, Rogers, Simpson and Sinclair.[18] Blamey's diary recorded that the main matter of discussion was the 'relationship between Army Intelligence and Security Services, and agreement was reached on the inter-dependent working of the two services. Details of leakages of certain information [was] also discussed in this connection.' At 10 p.m. Blamey had a further meeting with Forde, Evatt and Arthur Calwell, the Information minister, to discuss publicity for the operations of Australian troops. He returned to Melbourne the following morning.[19]

Significantly, Shedden was not present at these meetings, and Sinclair's minutes noted that Blamey read extracts from his Top Secret file and added to the information already supplied by Fraser at the War Cabinet meeting on 9 January.[20] According to Sinclair, the following conclusions were arrived at:

1   There should be more complete co-ordination and collaboration in future between the Army Intelligence

Frank Forde, the minister for the Army and deputy prime minister from 1941 to 1946. As acting prime minister he presided over the War Cabinet that considered the security leaks in January 1945 (AWM 10012)

Authorities and the Director-General of Security in regard to information which comes to the knowledge of the former affecting civil security for which the Director-General of Security has a definite responsibility to the Government. The Director-General of Security is to immediately confer with the Director of Military Intelligence (Brigadier J. Rogers) with a view to ensuring that this objective is achieved.

2   That where, in the opinion of the appropriate Army Authorities or the Director-General of Security, it is essential, either for Defence or Civil Security purposes, respectively, that a private telephone service should be monitored, the necessary measures to this end will be effected with the Postal Authorities through the Chief Communications Censor (Mr Ettelson), whose responsibilities in submitting such a request to the Postal Authorities are to be clearly defined, if such is not already the case.

The minute also noted that if the postal authorities received such a request they were to act on it without question. The postmaster-general was to be given a copy of the minute which was to be signed by Forde and Evatt.[21]

The following morning Rogers met with Simpson for 'two somewhat trying hours' to discuss the issues of Army personnel in the Security Service and the information leaks. Describing this meeting in a memorandum to Blamey, Rogers wrote that Simpson was 'extremely dangerous and puts Ananias completely in the shade'.[22] Referring to Simpson's attempts to resign the previous evening, Rogers suggested that if this happened a possible replacement could be Brigadier Bertrand Combes, the commandant of the Royal Military College, who had long experience in intelligence and security appointments. 'He could be trusted without any doubt with "ULTRA" material and would be acceptable to the people that matter in London.'[23]

The depth of disagreement between Simpson and Blamey is illustrated by Simpson's claims that if Blamey persisted in his attempts to regain the Army personnel, the Security Service 'was finished'. He said he believed that Evatt favoured a civil organisation but staffed with Army personnel paid by the Army. However, 'a civil organization is doomed to failure. Security Service must retain its military colours.'[24]

Rogers's notes on the discussion about the leaks reveal that the previous night Blamey and Rogers had had a separate meeting with Simpson either before or after the meeting with the politicians. Rogers wrote that he gave Simpson a copy of the memorandum Blamey had presented at the War Cabinet conference the previous night, but despite Simpson's direct questions apparently did not describe how Ultra material was derived. Instead he said it was obtained by 'our field sections'. Nevertheless, Rogers told Simpson he would arrange through Colonel Mander-Jones (the DDMI) and Sandford for Simpson to receive 'by safe-hand mail' further information that might come to hand.[25] He also told Simpson the name of the suspected enemy agent in Sydney, but asked him not to try to trace the individual until Rogers had heard from London and then advised him. He asked him not to intercept the communications from the Soviet embassy or the TASS news agency until he had spoken with Generals Akin and Willoughby.

Rogers suggested that Simpson should begin ascertaining which people in Canberra and Sydney were friendly with the Russians and which of them could have access to operational information from GHQ. At Simpson's suggestion, Rogers agreed that he should examine commercial cables from Sydney dispatched abroad at about the time that the estimates of Japanese strength in the Philippines (which appeared in the *AMF Weekly Intelligence Review*) were sent from Australia. 'It is possible that as figures were involved they could be picked up from a "jargonised" message'.[26] The most significant fact from Rogers's memorandum is the evidence that the focus of investigation had moved away from Wang and the Chinese consulate and onto the Soviet diplomatic staff.[27]

THE OUTCOME OF THE CANBERRA MEETINGS

After the meetings in Canberra, Blamey and Rogers initiated a range of measures to assist their investigation. Initially they had been loath to tell Simpson the source of Ultra information, and Rogers sent him a series of memos describing the leaks without giving sources; but apparently they concluded he would have to be told if he were to pursue the investigation properly.[28] On 25 January, after discussions with Squadron Leader Burley, the 'Security Liaison Officer for ULTRA material' in the SWPA, Blamey wrote to Simpson to inform him that as a recipient of Ultra he would have to comply with inter-Allied security regulations and Burley would visit Canberra to inform him of the correct procedures.[29]

On 29 January Burley met Simpson and briefed him on Ultra in general terms. When he explained that the leakage was Chinese, Simpson suspected the reliability of the sources, and even when Burley assured him that the information given by Ultra 'was of the highest reliability' Simpson was still 'inclined to query it'. Burley told Simpson that the information had to be burned after reading, whereupon 'this rather caused him to "get up on his hind legs"', and ask how he could use the material 'adding that he could not be tied down'. When Burley insisted that the material had to be burned Simpson exclaimed, 'Then the stuff is really no good to me . . . What's the point in getting it'. He said that he would have to see the prime minister and Blamey to discuss it more fully. He 'pointed out he was a barrister and tried to convey he "knew all the answers"'. Even though Simpson eventually signed the 'Undertaking', Burley felt compelled to write to Winterbotham and Blamey:

> Personally I do not think Simpson is one who should handle or have access to the Material. He is obviously one who would not hesitate to act first and ask after, especially as he is convinced in his own mind that the source is not reliable. Even so I feel that he will hold back in view of his signing the Undertaking and his legal knowledge of the position should he act otherwise.

While in Canberra Burley also briefed John Hood, the acting secretary of the department of External Affairs in the absence of Hodgson who was acting high commissioner in Ottawa.[30]

Meanwhile, the intelligence staff were still trying to sort out whether there was any connection between the Chinese and the Russians. On 25 January Sandford wrote to Rogers and Little that London had deciphered several messages that gave 'definite proof that the Chungking representatives are the guilty parties. . . It should be understood that there is no direct suggestion that the Chinese in Australia are deliberately passing information to the Japanese. On the contrary, it appears that the Japanese obtain their information through cryptographic study of Chinese cypher communications'.[31] A few days later Little told Simpson that the reference to the 'Japanese agent in Sydney' appeared to be incorrect and the source was the staff officer of the Chinese consulate. He added, however, that it was 'also certain that the Japanese obtain information that originated in the Russian Legation in Australia but . . . there is now nothing to indicate how it reached the Japanese'.[32] The information about the Chinese would have been welcome news to Simpson for, as he explained to Little, he was 'being pressed by his Minister as to how his enquiries were proceeding'.[33]

On 2 February 1945 the CGS, General Northcott, sent a top secret memorandum to the senior formation headquarters in the Australian Army, reminding them that as the ciphers used by the Chinese authorities were 'defective', great care had to be exercised 'to ensure that no information is given to the Chinese Naval and Military Attaches that would be detrimental to the Allied cause in the event of such information falling into the hands of the enemy'. Requests by Chinese attachés to visit operational areas were to be referred, together with reasons for the visit and full proposed itinerary, to LHQ for prior approval.[34]

When Advanced LHQ had moved forward to Hollandia, General Wang had not accompanied it, and by February 1945 he had established himself in Sydney with his assistant Captain Nan Yu Lu.[35] Wang's decision to move to Sydney is strange since there was no major headquarters there: at that stage LHQ was in Melbourne, Advanced LHQ was at Hollandia and GHQ was at Leyte in the Philippines. Wang later said that he had moved because the Chinese consulate-general was in Sydney, and his wife worked there. In any case, he said he was not there for very long.[36]

From the beginning it had not been clear to which headquarters Wang was the liaison officer. Initially he had been attached to the Australian Military Forces, not the Allied Land Forces, but since Australian Army Headquarters became Land Headquarters that distinction was not relevant. Nevertheless, Wang described himself as the chief Chinese military liaison officer in the SWPA, and apparently MacArthur's headquarters accepted him in that capacity. In May 1945, a month after MacArthur established his headquarters in Manila, he visited the Philippines.[37]

Apparently, during the Japanese occupation of the Philippines the Chungking government had maintained an agent there to operate with Filipino guerilas. With the arrival of the Americans in 1945 the Chinese agent presented his credentials to the Americans but, suspicious, they detained him. After representations from the Chungking government and the intervention of General Wang, he was released and flown from Manila to Chungking. According to one report, Wang then asked to be relieved of his position at MacArthur's headquarters, or for another senior officer to be sent from China to represent him in the Philippines while he returned to Sydney. In any case, after a short period in Sydney, Wang rejoined the Manila headquarters.[38]

General Willoughby continued to view Wang with suspicion and drew his activities to the attention of the US counter-intelligence staff in the SWPA.[39] He tried to exclude Wang from the Philippines, claiming that he had 'ample evidence that he picks up information, in irregular, informal, even illegal fashion, that he transmits it immediately and that it is invariably picked up by the Enemy. In spite of repeated warning, he persists in this practice and consequently represents a serious menace to our security.'[40] Nonetheless, Wang joined MacArthur in the Philippines and was present at the Japanese surrender in Tokyo. He remained with MacArthur until May 1946 when he became director of military intelligence at the Chinese ministry of Defence. He was commandant of cadets at the Chinese Military Academy, deputy garrison commander at Tsingtao and, from 1949 to 1964, military counsellor to the President of Taiwan. He finished his career as professor and dean of Chinese Studies at Soochow University in Taipei.

In July 1945, following Wang's departure, the Australian Army decided to make the *AMF Weekly Intelligence Review* available to naval attaché Wang Chih-Kuang. In thanking Blamey, Captain Wang wrote:

> You may rest assured, sir, that any information I may derive from this Review will be sent to Chungking via the safe channel of the 'Australian Army Airmail Service', and should I wish to send by signal, which I think is rarely the case, I will certainly enlist Col. Little's advice beforehand.[41]

While the Army had been taking appropriate security measures with the Chinese in the first half of 1945, efforts to monitor Chinese telephones had been less successful. After the meeting in Canberra with members of the War Cabinet on 17 January it appeared that Blamey had achieved some of his aims—the monitoring of telephones and greater cooperation with the Security Service—but there were still considerable problems. On 18 January the *Argus* newspaper reported that Blamey had met with Forde, Evatt and Simpson in Canberra. Drawing attention to this report, Shedden, who had not been at the meeting, disingenuously asked Forde whether it was still necessary to arrange the meeting between Fraser and Evatt to investigate leaks, as directed by the War Cabinet on 9 January.[42]

Shedden's suspicion that all was not running smoothly was confirmed on 20 January when Blamey told him that the 17 January meeting in Canberra had 'centred on a statement by the Director-General of Security of lack of co-operation by the Army with the Security Service. . . Blamey said that the question of a leakage of information at the high level, as suggested by [Senator Fraser at the War Cabinet on 9 January] was not referred to.'[43]

Without Shedden's coordinating hand it appeared unlikely that the government would handle the matter smoothly, and on 24 January he suggested to Forde, who had resumed his post as minister for the Army, that he report to the War Cabinet on what had happened at the meeting in Canberra.[44] By this time Curtin had returned as prime minister, and he chaired meetings of the War Cabinet on 24 January and 9 February and the Advisory War Council on 25 January and 8 February. There is no evidence that Forde and Evatt reported on their investigations or that the leaks were discussed at any of these meetings.

The matter of monitoring telephones in Melbourne was still given low priority. On 30 January Curtin forwarded the postmaster-general's letter of 5 January to Evatt and Forde, the latter in his capacity as minister for the army. But this was just bureaucratic paper shuffling, because Forde had originally received the letter on 5 January when he was acting prime minister.[45]

By April, permission to begin telephone monitoring had still not been granted. After the meeting on 17 January the minute prepared by Sinclair had been signed by Forde and then taken to Evatt for his signature. Evatt read the minute and said he would sign it. He was approached several more times and again agreed to sign, but when he went overseas in March the minute remained unsigned. The postmaster-general had not been informed that he was to react to the Censorship Authority's request. On 7 April Blamey wrote to Shedden to enlist his help, but Shedden replied that he had not been present at the conference and suggested that Blamey approach Forde.[46] Blamey did so, but it is significant that he again drew attention to what he considered to be the most important issue, the PMG's action in referring the matter upwards in the department and to other departments.

> In order to preserve the secrecy of telephone observations, you may recall that I pointed out that it is vital that any reference be kept at an absolute minimum as otherwise, sooner or later, information is bound to leak out and the authorising authority will be embarrassed.[47]

It is not known if permission was finally granted, but if, as is probable, it was, it had taken over four months to accomplish a matter which Blamey had earlier considered to be 'essential in the interests of National Security'.

The issue of the withdrawal of Army personnel from the Security Service was reconsidered at a meeting of the War Cabinet on 9 February.

Forde presented Blamey's view that the Army personnel should be withdrawn or transferred to the Security Service as civilians. Evatt, as attorney-general, presented the opposite view, stating that the director-general could not provide security coverage if he lost the Army personnel. The War Cabinet decided that some personnel could be withdrawn but that most would remain with the Security Service. In turn, the Army was to be allowed a credit in its authorised strength to the extent of the number of personnel on secondment to the Security Service.[48]

This bureaucratic manoeuvring was in some ways incidental to the more fundamental question of what action was being taken to deal with the leaks of information. On 2 February Winterbotham cabled from London that Sir Stewart Menzies, the head of MI6, was prepared to send a senior member of his staff, Lieutenant-Colonel Charles (Dick) Ellis, as his personal representative to assist Rogers for four to six months on all questions bearing on the security of Ultra material.[49] (Ellis, an Australian by birth, but a long-time member of MI6, has been accused in several books as being both a German and Soviet spy.[50] Post war he served in the Australian Secret Intelligence Service.)

Within a few days Rogers cabled back to London that Ellis was no longer required in Australia. It was now clear that the Japanese were deciphering the telegrams from the Chinese staff in Australia. Fortunately, little vital information had reached the Japanese through this source, and as restrictions were applied to the Chinese attachés this information would be restricted even further. Sandford advised that the US joint chiefs of staff 'would prefer the Japanese to concentrate on Chinese ciphers, with which they have achieved success, rather than to divert their efforts on to our own systems'.[51]

The other source of information to the Japanese was the Soviet legation in Canberra. As Sandford noted on 3 February, 'it seems very likely that the despatches of all Soviet diplomatic representatives are sent on from Moscow to Harbin and that the leakage occurs there'.[52] It was thought that the Japanese were not deciphering Soviet ciphers 'as was first supposed'.[53] Already the Australian intelligence staff were sending copies of the Soviet diplomatic cables to Britain, but these developments gave a new urgency to efforts to decipher the Soviet cables. On 5 February Sandford wrote to Little: 'Despite the confirmation of our suspicions concerning the Chinese, it is considered that the Russian Diplomatic traffic will still be required by the United Kingdom'. He asked that arrangements be made with the controller of postal and telegraphic censorship for all traffic to be sent to the Central Bureau 'by bag as before'.[54]

On 8 February Little travelled to Canberra for discussions with Simpson, who was still complaining that the requirement to burn the Ultra material was making it impossible for him to do his job. He was finding it 'quite impossible to remember the contents of those so dealt with, with sufficient accuracy and completeness to take adequate action'. He was hampered further by being shown only paraphrases of the messages. He and his staff needed to compare the full texts of the intercepted messages with the documents from which the information was derived. Again he said that unless given more assistance he would 'be placed in an awkward position with his Minister who . . . has already asked how his enquiries were proceeding'. Little recommended either that Simpson be directed in writing not to make inquiries 'regarding the source from which the Chinese Attaches and Soviet Legation derive their information', or that Simpson be permitted to hold copies of each deciphered message.[55]

On 15 February Sandford cabled Winterbotham to inform him that 'to avoid disastrous' results, Simpson was being instructed to take no action. Winterbotham replied immediately:

> Gravely concerned. Grateful if Rogers will find early opportunity to bring to notice of Simpson that no action may be taken on this type of information whether supplied to you from London and Washington or produced by C. B. without full consultation with the Sigint Boards concerned. The matter of Ultra security is global.[56]

Blamey wrote to Simpson on 17 February asking him to 'take no action in regard to locating the source responsible for the leakage of information through Chinese and Soviet channels until such time as you are further advised'.[57]

Of course this direction did not stop Simpson from continuing his efforts to locate any other sources of espionage. On 8 March Blamey formally advised Simpson that Captain McNamara, the Officer Commanding No. 1 Australian Discrimination Unit, would be responsible for providing relevant intercept information to him.[58] By June 1945 three intercept stations (Darwin, Yadjin and HMAS *Harman*) were operating on behalf of the director-general of security,[59] attempting to monitor any clandestine transmissions from the Soviet embassy in Canberra or the TASS representative in Sydney. As indicated in Chapter 3, no such transmissions were detected.

It is not known what course of inquiry was pursued by the Security Service during the first six months of 1945, but some indication can be gained from a report to the Advisory War Council on 20 June. Percy Spender, an opposition member of the council, had sought information on communist activities in Australia, and Simpson produced a thirteen-page report on the Australian Communist Party. The report included the statement: 'At least one foreign diplomat is known to be acting as an espionage agent for Russia, avowedly because he is a Communist, although a high official of his country in Australia.'[60] It is not clear how the Security Service arrived at its view. Was it through surveillance of foreign diplomatic staff, or was it through an assessment of the leaked material? Before examining possible spies in Australia, it is therefore necessary to assess the evidence presented in Blamey's letter.

THE SOURCE OF THE LEAKS

Blamey's first two examples of material leaked to the Japanese were sourced to the Soviet minister and referred to MacArthur's plans for certain operations in the Philippines. This was particularly sensitive information, and throughout 1944 even Blamey had struggled to determine whether Australian troops would be involved there. Details were known to a very small number of officials in Australia. The Australian government did not learn of MacArthur's plans until he discussed them with Curtin on 30 September 1944.[61] Curtin was not able to pass this information on personally to the War Cabinet, as he then became sick and entered hospital.

The next War Cabinet meeting was held in Canberra on 18 October. It was chaired by Forde and attended by Chifley, the treasurer and minister for Post War Reconstruction; Evatt; Dedman, the minister for War Organisation of Industry; and Lazzarini, the acting minister for Air. The minutes state that the 'War Cabinet noted a summary of the Prime Minister's interview with General MacArthur, Commander-in-Chief Southwest Pacific Area, at Canberra on 30th September 1944, which was read by the Deputy Prime Minister.'[62] The notes of Curtin's meeting with MacArthur had been prepared by Shedden, but it is not known if these notes were distributed to the members of the War Cabinet.

The principal means by which the government was kept up to date with military operations was the provision of weekly printed reports by the chiefs of staff of the three services and copies of the *AMF Weekly Intelligence Review* to the Advisory War Council. On 16 November, for example, the council had before it the chiefs' reports for the weeks ending 21 and 28 October and 4 and 11 November, which, of course, had been circulated earlier, when they had been prepared. At the meeting, the chief of naval staff described the operations of Australian ships in the Philippines campaign and listed Allied and Japanese losses. The chief of the general staff outlined the disposition of Australian troops in New Guinea, New Britain and Bougainville and said that the 5th Division had landed at

Jacquinot Bay (New Britain) on 5 November. He also explained the US operations in the Philippines. The chief of the air staff described RAAF operations in forward areas.[63]

It will be recalled that in their 2 January meeting Shedden and Blamey had discussed the possibility that the leaks might be 'occurring on a Ministerial level or in another Department'.[64] Blamey's letter of 6 January also gives the source of the information about MacArthur's plans as the Soviet minister in Canberra. Only a limited number of ministers and departments were given access to top secret operational information. Leaving aside the ministers for Defence and the three services, the only ministers in the War Cabinet who received this information were Chifley, Evatt, Beasley and Dedman, of whom only Evatt and Beasley were members of the Advisory War Council. It is not suggested that any of these ministers were themselves a security risk, but there is the chance that documents held in their private offices or in their departments might have been seen by someone who could have passed material from them to a Soviet agent.

The third example in Blamey's letter was the information in the news background sheet which was attributed to the same sort of Harbin intelligence report that had been based on information from the Soviet minister in Australia and could have been passed to him by someone in one of the news agencies. Since the USSR was at that time considered to be an ally, it is possible that the TASS representative was shown a copy of the news sheet.

THE HARBIN SPY REPORTS

According to Blamey's letter, the claim that the leaked information came from the Soviet minister in Australia was based on the so-called 'Harbin Spy Reports'. The Japanese forces in Manchuria (or the Japanese puppet state of Manchukuo) were formed into the Kwantung Army, which had its headquarters at Hsinking, as did the Communication Intelligence Group, the Air Force Code Group and the East Asia Communication Investigation League. The headquarters of the Kwantung Army Intelligence Group, however, was located 150km further north at Harbin.[65] The city was a centre for Russian émigrés and a hotbed of spies and intelligence networks. As early as 1941 US Sigint agencies had intercepted Japanese diplomatic messages containing information said to have originated in Moscow, the Soviet embassies in China, Tokyo and the US and the Soviet consulate-general in Harbin. For example, a report sent from Tokyo to the Japanese embassy in Moscow on 13 May 1944 said that the

Japanese consul-general in Harbin had been passing on information from the Soviet consul-general there. US Military Intelligence staff in Washington made the following comment on the intercepted message:

> In the past the Japanese Consul General has sent Tokyo a number of reports about—or purporting to come from—the local Soviet Consulate General. Several of the reports were of a fantastic nature, and suggested either that the Russians were deliberately misleading the Japanese or that the Japanese were buying information from an agent with a well-developed imagination.[66]

On 1 November 1944 the US Army Military Intelligence Service (MIS) in Washington produced a top secret 66-page study of the Japanese Signal Intelligence Service, which stated that Harbin had been quoted as the source of special intelligence reports several times. Most of these were 'in regard to American Army and Fleet operations, and seem to be taken from telegrams of the Soviet Ambassador to Australia . . . They seem to be mostly spy reports and Tokyo considers them valuable enough to pass on to all main army centers.'[67]

Harbin continued to be a valuable source of intelligence for the Japanese. As late as June 1945 the British diplomatic Sigint organisation intercepted a Japanese message from Harbin that said Allied Pacific plans, as 'reported in Soviet Consulate-General circles', had been forwarded to Tokyo.[68]

In September 1945, at the end of the war, the MIS made a further study of the Japanese intelligence system and reported that these messages, known as 'Harbin "A" Intelligence', had obvious inaccuracies; the US intelligence authorities thought that they were fabricated for perhaps monetary gain.[69] The last Harbin A Intelligence report was in August 1944, but soon after, the Americans received evidence of a new series, known as the 'Harbin Special Spy reports', that had been issued by the Japanese Army general staff. The US Magic diplomatic summary for 21 January 1945 noted that the 'Japanese Consul-General in Harbin has for a long time been sending to Tokyo information from an agent who claims to get it from the Soviet Consulate-General'.[70] According to the 1945 MIS report: 'These reports purport to be based on messages from Russian diplomatic representatives in Australia, China, and the United States, and are concerned with general questions of military strategy.' The MIS report said the messages did not appear to be genuine as they contained erroneous Allied orders of battle.[71]

Whether the Americans decided the reports were genuine or not, Blamey found them sufficiently worrying to prompt his letter of 6 January and Rogers was concerned enough to discuss intercepting

Soviet embassy telegrams. Furthermore, as Blamey wrote, the Department of Information news background circular was 'the subject of a Harbin Intelligence Report in practically identical terms with those of the background news sheet'.[72] A mercenary agent in Harbin with a 'well-developed imagination' could hardly have manufactured such a report.

If the Soviet embassy in Australia was in fact the source of information then it could have reached Tokyo in only a limited number of ways. First, the Japanese could have intercepted Soviet cable traffic from Australia. Japanese attempts to break the Soviet codes were the subject of several pages of the MIS report produced on 1 November 1944. Some sections of it have still not been released, but it states that by October 1942 Tokyo had begun a 'study of Russian diplomatic codes and gave a very complete analysis of digit code group structure'. The Japanese were also working on Soviet Army systems. The final sentence of the report reads: 'Other than traffic analysis and general statements as to revelation of intelligence from Soviet messages (some of which were reported as "A" and others as "B" intelligence, . . . [two lines censored] . . . nothing has been revealed in Japanese Army traffic of successes of a purely cryptanalytic nature on the Russian systems.'[73]

The MIS report of September 1945 questions whether the Japanese had had much success with decrypting Soviet codes. It concludes that the Harbin spy reports were probably gained from espionage rather than from intercepting Soviet coded messages. The only possible case of interception was a report from Tokyo, dated 25 January 1945, which stated that according to 'A' intelligence from the Soviet military attaché in Chungking dated 9 January 1945, the Americans were preparing for a landing on the Chinese coast.[74]

Second, the Japanese could have obtained the information from the Soviet embassy in Chungking. The Japanese had a productive spy in the city known as PA, with good access to the Chinese ministry of Foreign Affairs. There is no evidence that he had access to the Soviet embassy in Chungking, and there is no reason why the Soviet embassy in Canberra would send information to Chungking. In any case, PA's reports were sent directly to Tokyo, not through Harbin.[75]

Third, Japanese agents could have obtained the information in Moscow. But if that were the case then the information would not have been sourced to Harbin.

Fourth, a Japanese spy in the Soviet consulate in Harbin could have obtained the information. But there was no reason why Moscow should have passed the information to Harbin.

Fifth, the Soviets could have deliberately passed the information to Japanese agents in Harbin. US intelligence staff had considered the possibility that the earlier Harbin A Intelligence Reports were part of a Soviet deception and misinformation campaign, but had thought the material lacked a consistent pattern.[76] If the later Harbin spy reports were part of such a campaign, designed to maintain a favourable Soviet position on the Siberian–Manchurian border, then the Soviets might well have included genuine material—what intelligence organisations call 'chickenfeed'—that could have little bearing on the border situation. It is known that the Soviets instigated a substantial deception campaign in Siberia in 1945 to persuade the Japanese that they had a smaller force in the Far East, that they could not attack until 1946, and that they would attack in different areas from those they eventually targeted in August 1945.[77] It was in the Soviets' interest to prolong the fighting in the South-West Pacific to enable them to enter the war after the defeat of Germany. Such an action by the Soviet authorities would not have been unusual. On the eve of the battle of Stalingrad in early 1943, Soviet intelligence leaked correct information to the Germans about a forthcoming offensive on the Rzhev Front to divert the Germans away from Stalingrad. According to a senior Soviet intelligence officer in Moscow at the time, '[Marshal] Zhukov, not knowing this disinformation game was being played at his expense, paid a heavy price in the loss of thousands of men under his command.'[78] Recently released information reveals that Zhukov's army lost 500 000 men in this battle, but the defeat was covered up by Stalin.[79] If the leaked material did in fact come from the Soviet embassy in Canberra, the most likely way it would have reached Tokyo was by being passed directly by Soviet authorities to the Japanese.

Leaks through the Chinese

The fourth example in Blamey's letter was the information from the *AMF Weekly Intelligence Review*. This was sent from Sydney and it was known that General Wang had access to copies of the *Review*. But, how was it possible for information gathered by Wang to reach Tokyo?

In January 1944 Captain Jasper Holmes USN at the Joint Intelligence Center in Hawaii wrote to Washington to complain that intelligence based on radio intercepts was being forwarded to Chungking—'we note that very often information that goes there appears again in Japanese intelligence dispatches'.[80] It is not known to what extent MacArthur's staff realised during 1944 that the Japanese had broken much of the Chinese cipher traffic. The MIS report of 1 November 1944 stated:

> There has been remarkably little evidence of the Japanese cryptanalysis of Chinese codes. There are many quotations from Chinese wires, but the source is not given. One exception to this occurs in a Tokyo report to Saipan of 10 May 1944 which gives as the source 'A' information sent out by the Chungking Military Attache in Washington. There is a possibility that this is the same as 'A' intelligence previously referred to as emanating from decryptographic codes, but again it may be the other various meanings assigned to the letter 'A'.[81]

It is likely that US authorities knew more than this report indicates, for the MIS report prepared in September 1945 observed that Japanese cryptanalysts had had considerable success with Chinese codes. Indeed, while 'the full scope of Japanese activities in reading Chinese codes is not known, in those areas where information is available, the Japanese have always been able to read at least some Chinese traffic'. The report stated that by August 1944 the Japanese were reading the ciphers of the Chinese military attachés in Melbourne, Sydney, Washington and London.

> Most of the reports originated by the Chinese military attaches and intercepted by the Japanese have not contained classified information; however, in at least three instances the Japanese have intercepted figures giving Allied estimates of Japanese air strengths. These figures appeared originally in 'secret' intelligence publications which were available to the Chinese. In a number of cases the original Chinese message is available, and it checks closely with the version intercepted and read by the Japanese.[82]

It is now known that the diplomatic code used by the Chinese mission in Tokyo in the 1930s was effectively penetrated by the Japanese Army.[83] After the war the Japanese claimed that they were able to read between 80 and 90 per cent of the relatively uncomplicated Kuomintang codes.[84] Whether the American and Australian intelligence staffs appreciated the ease with which the Japanese could read Chinese cipher traffic is immaterial; they suspected that Chinese ciphers could be broken and therefore directed General Wang to use either Australian or US systems when communicating with Chungking. Wang has since confirmed that he generally used these systems. But he also thought the Americans had exaggerated the Japanese capabilities. He claimed Willoughby had told him that since the Japanese and Chinese languages used the same characters then the Japanese could possibly break his ciphers. But Wang knew there were differences in the languages and that therefore the Japanese would have had trouble with his ciphers. As a result, he had no compunction about using his own ciphers in messages that were sent by commercial cable to Chungking. He also claimed that he did not use the Chinese legation to send his messages to China.[85]

British intelligence authorities were also made aware of the possibility of leaks through the Chinese, and on 21 December 1944 the British diplomatic cryptanalytic organisation at Berkeley Street in London made its first 'break' of a message (dated 9 December) from the Chinese naval attaché in London. The cryptanalysts then went back to decrypt Chinese messages from as early as August 1944.[86] According to an Admiralty 'in-house' history:

> The point of Naval interest was that, as was to be expected, the Chinese Naval Attachés in London and Melbourne especially were passing to Chungking by W/T a considerable amount of true information concerning the establishment, disposition and operations of the British and Allied Fleets. Although the cypher used was graded by B. P. [Bletchley Park] as A.1, it was known both from a Japanese document captured in 1943 and by subsequent breaks of Japanese W/T messages, that the Japanese were reading these ciphers. Here was a serious leakage, and a difficult and delicate matter to straighten out.[87]

Obviously information collected by the Chinese naval attaché in Melbourne, Captain Wang, was also finding its way to Tokyo. The extent of the Japanese penetration of the Chinese ciphers was worse than first thought. For example, on 16 April 1945 the Joint Intelligence Sub-Committee in London reported to the British chiefs of staff that the Japanese were reading messages from the Chinese service attachés in London, New Delhi, Ceylon, Sydney, Melbourne, Washington and Ankara, as well as messages from the Chinese general staff in Chungking to the attachés at these places.[88] Despite this serious situation the Americans resisted British efforts to take action for fear that it might alert the Japanese that they were reading their codes.[89]

THE IMPORTANCE OF THE LEAKS

It is now clear that the leakage of information through the Chinese military attaché was more serious than the MIS report of September 1945 suggests. As we have seen, the contents of the *AMF Weekly Intelligence Review* for 4 November 1944 were known in full in Tokyo on 11 November, despite the Australian Army's attempts to get the Chinese to use its codes and transmission facilities. The main threat to the Allies was the possibility that the leaks might reveal the success of the Allied Sigint operations to the Japanese.

It has not been possible to locate all the intercepted Japanese messages, but the various intercepts that have been released throw some light on the process as well as the nature of the information passed to the Japanese. For example, the volumes of Japanese military attaché traffic that have been released show that the Japanese *Weekly Intelligence Review* No. 95, dated 4 November 1944, was intercepted by the Allied Sigint organisation and apparently decrypted the following day. On 22 November the Japanese vice chief of the general staff sent out a circular giving an assessment of Allied forces in the Pacific. In part, it read: 'The Australian army stationed in the Solomons and in New Guinea comprises 4 to 6 divisions and 150 planes. They are principally garrison forces or are used to relieve the American army.' This message was marked as 'intercepted' on 22 November, 'received' the same day, and 'reviewed' on 1 December.[90] Another message from the Japanese vice chief of the general staff, dated 26 November, stated that the 3rd, 5th, 6th, 7th, 9th and 11th Australian Divisions were located outside Australia, although it added that there were also reports that the 6th and 9th Divisions were still in Australia. This message was 'intercepted' on 29 November, 'received' the same day, and 'translated' on 30 November.[91]

On 19 December 1944 the assistant chief of staff of the Japanese Army in Tokyo sent a message to the Southern Army (in Manila), the 2nd Area Army (Celebes), the 7th Area Army, the 8th Area Army (Rabaul), the 14th Area Army (Manila), and the 19th Army that the Australian Army appeared to have been reduced to five divisions for operations in the New Guinea area. The Japanese thought that the 3rd Australian Division was responsible for Bougainville, the 5th Division for New Britain, and the 6th Division for eastern New Guinea (thought to be in the Lae-Buna area). The 7th Division was thought to be near Madang, the 9th Division at either Hollandia or Biak, and the 11th Division had returned to Australia. The source was given as a D4 Intelligence Report, which Australian intelligence staff identified as 'the staff officer Chinese consulate Sydney'. By February 1945 General Wang and his assistant were based in Sydney. The information was generally accurate, although the 7th and 9th Divisions were training on the Atherton Tableland before moving forward to Morotai, and elements of the 11th Division were near Lae and on Bougainville.[92]

On 16 January 1945 Tokyo warned the Japanese commander in Rabaul of a revised grouping of Australian divisions. Three days later it advised the Southern Army that the Australian Army appeared to be replacing all the American units in the New Guinea area. The source was given as 'D' Intelligence reports and other information.[93]

On 28 March the Chinese liaison officer in Sydney reported to Chungking that the 3rd Australian Division was on the island of Bougainville and that the Australians were conducting operations in three columns—along the coast to the north, eastwards across the island, and along the coast to the south.[94]

On 6 April Tokyo advised Rabaul that according to D4 Intelligence dated 29 March, the Australians estimated there were 35 000 Japanese on the Gazelle Peninsula around Rabaul.[95] In fact, on 1 November 1944 Allied intelligence, based on Ultra sources, had estimated the Japanese strength at 35 000. On 26 June 1945 Brigadier Rogers informed Blamey that the figure had been revised to 49 000. 'This change is due to the receipt recently of more complete information from ULTRA sources.'[96]

Towards the end of April the Chinese liaison officer in Sydney reported to Chungking that reconnaissance flights over the Netherlands East Indies on 24 April by the RAAF had revealed a gradual transfer of the Japanese garrison in the eastern Indies to Malaya.[97] When the Australians went ashore at Brunei in June, the Chinese liaison officer reported what forces the Australians believed they had encountered.[98]

Therefore, despite efforts to restrict access to the liaison officer, and to insist on the use of Australian codes and communications channels, as late as 29 March—and probably well into June—the Japanese were definitely receiving information from the Chinese consulate. It is difficult to gauge to what extent this information placed Australian lives at risk. Certainly, it gave the Japanese commanders in the area an understanding of the forces being arrayed against them, and helped them plan future operations.

There is other evidence that Japanese foreknowledge of Allied operations had a definite effect on their conduct. On 23 April the US Navy cryptanalysis unit in Melbourne (FRUMEL) intercepted and decrypted a Japanese message sent to units at Tarakan and Balikpapan in Borneo. These locations held key oil installations which MacArthur hoped to seize intact. The message warned the Japanese commander that the Allies would soon attack Tarakan and Balikpapan, and told him: 'As quickly as possible all installations [words missing] so that enemy cannot make use of them.' The same day, another US Navy cryptanalysis unit intercepted a message to the chief of the Tarakan branch arsenal, ordering him to 'take all steps necessary in making ready for complete destruction of their oil drilling and oil refining establishments' but to try to maintain the present oil producing capacity 'to the very last'.[99] These two messages were sent to Washington and, after a delay, on 27 April the first one was forwarded to the Central Bureau staff in Brisbane. It was passed immediately to the headquarters of the 1st Australian Corps at Morotai, which was to mount the attack on Tarakan.[100] The Australian historian, Peter Stanley, has suggested, however, that since the initial Japanese demolition order pre-dated the intercepted message by a week, the leak probably originated at GHQ in Manila.[101] On 1 May, Australian troops landed at Tarakan; they lost 215 killed and the airfield and oil installations there were found to be unusable. The Australians landed at Balikpapan on 1 July; they lost 229 killed and again the oil refinery was unusable.

The leaked material thus appears to have fallen into at least two distinct categories. The first was the operational information obtained by General Wang and intercepted by the Japanese during transmission to Chungking. This material had the potential directly to affect Australian operations in the islands. It might have given the Japanese commander in the Philippines a better appreciation of what the Americans knew about the locations of Japanese units and, had the Japanese been more alert, it might have told them their ciphers were being broken by the Allies. Such an outcome might have led to the loss of thousands of lives in the last nine months of the war.

The second category was the information sourced to the Soviet embassy in Canberra. Blamey suggested that the Japanese obtained the department of Information news background sheet through this source, and that the information in it not only gave them a better understanding of the dispositions and intentions of Australian forces in the New Guinea area but provided details of MacArthur's planned operations in the Philippines. In his memo to Blamey of 17 January Rogers listed some instances of other information leaked through the Soviet embassy, including:

- on 19 November—'the Australian government had decided against the despatch of troops to Philippines';
- on 24 November—'Australian forces have taken over from the Americans in the Solomons and New Guinea';
- on 24 November—the US Pacific Fleet was delaying a landing at the eastern tip of the Bicol Peninsula on Luzon;
- on 2 December—the US was 'planning to invade the Camotes Sea north-west of Leyte' (Rogers noted that this was just prior to the US landing on the western coast of Leyte Island);
- on 16 December—the strength of the British Pacific Fleet arriving in Australian ports;
- on 24 December—American losses on Mindoro Island between 15 and 19 December;
- on 26 December—American efforts to reinforce their Mindoro air base; and
- on 29 December—the completion of a torpedo boat base on Mindoro.[102]

The Americans faced a hard fight in the Philippines, and it is difficult to say to what extent that fight was prolonged by the leaked information. An assessment prepared by the MIS in Washington in December 1944 noted that reports of Japanese spy activity usually originated from Tokyo. 'During the current Philippines operations Tokyo has broadcast general information reports to all concerned. Many of these reports treat of projected Allied plans, knowledge of the disclosure of which is critical.'[103]

Even more worrying than the nature of the information finding its way to the Japanese was the fact that the Soviet embassy appeared to be able to gather secret information in Australia. Clearly the Soviets were conducting an espionage operation in Australia and they appeared to be assisted by Australian citizens. Furthermore, this information was being used—whether deliberately or inadvertently—contrary to Australian national interests, possibly to the extent of putting the lives of Australian and American servicemen at risk.

Action could be taken to restrict the leaks through the Chinese liaison officer. In any case, when Wang moved to the Philippines he would no longer have access to information directly affecting Australian operations and he would be an American problem. It appears that after some initial doubts the Allies concluded that the Chinese leaks were caused by insecure ciphers and by Soviet and Japanese agents in Chungking. Wang was not a spy.

Nevertheless, the Chinese connection closely influenced efforts in late 1944 and early 1945 to prevent the leaks and locate their source. Initially Allied intelligence was not able to separate the Chinese and Soviets as the source of the leaks, and Blamey sought permission to monitor the Chinese consulate's telephones. Ultimately, this forced him to bring the leaks, including those through the Soviet embassy, to the government's attention. It may well be that Blamey's evidence of Soviet perfidy was partly circumstantial. Perhaps it was based on hard evidence such as surveillance or radio intercepts, but it might also have been based on long-standing suspicions in the security community.

Efforts to prevent the leaks were hampered by the Allied Sigint organisation's fear that the Japanese would be alerted to the interception of their signal traffic. While the interception of Soviet traffic was less advanced, it was important not to let them know that their espionage had been detected and their traffic was being scrutinised. The outcome was that by 1945 the Security Service moved away from focusing on preventing information from reaching the Germans or Japanese, or from preventing subversion by enemy aliens, and concentrated on the threat from the Soviets. The various security organisations had, of course, been concerned about the communist threat since the 1920s, but now, with the arrival of a Soviet diplomatic presence in Australia, there was a new and real threat to be countered.

7

'is there any great difference?'

MOSCOW CENTRE AND SOVIET INTELLIGENCE

SOVIET ESPIONAGE OPERATIONS IN AUSTRALIA were conducted by two different organisations—the Soviet State Security Service and Soviet Military Intelligence—and it is necessary to understand a little about each of these organisations to appreciate the way they operated in Australia. Although Australia was a long way from the Soviet Union and apparently of little direct strategic interest to it, it presented an attractive espionage target for at least two reasons. First, as an ally of Britain and the US, it shared valuable strategic information from them. Second, Australian security against espionage was weak; the Australian Security Service was unsophisticated and its staff were inexperienced. Furthermore, following the German invasion of the Soviet Union in June 1941, the Soviet Union had become an ally. By 1942, with Australia under threat of Japanese invasion, few members of the Security Service were concerned with watching for Soviet espionage. Although most would have heard of the notorious purges and terror campaigns conducted within the Soviet Union in the late 1930s by the internal security organisation, few would have had any real appreciation of the history, structure, capabilities and intentions of the Soviet espionage organisations.

THE SOVIET STATE SECURITY SERVICE—THE KGB

The Soviet State Security Service had several reorganisations and changes of name between its foundation in December 1917 as the

Cheka (All-Russian Extraordinary Commission for Combating Counter-Revolution and Sabotage) and the establishment of the KGB (Komitet Gosudarstvennoy Bezopasnosti, or Committee of State Security) in March 1954. From July 1941 to April 1943, the relevant agency was the GUGB (Main Administration of State Security) within the NKVD (People's Commissariat for Internal Affairs); from April 1943 to March 1946, it was the NKGB (People's Commissariat of State Security); from March 1946 to October 1947, it was the MGB (Ministerstvo Gosudarstvennoy Bezopasnosti, or Ministry of State Security); from October 1947 to November 1951, it was the KI (Komitet Informatsii, or Committee of Information); and from November 1951 to March 1954 it was the MVD (Ministerstvo Vnutrennikh Del, or Ministry of Internal Affairs).[1]

These changes were in part a reflection of the evolving security and intelligence requirements of the new Soviet government as it defeated the White Armies, established its control throughout the USSR, and developed its policies for support of 'world revolution' in the 1920s. But they also reflected the factional struggles within the Kremlin, and by the late 1930s, under Genrikh Yagoda (1934–36), Nikolay Yezhov (1936–38) and Lavrentiy Beria (1938–43), the State Security Service had become Stalin's main instrument for executing the Great Terror at home, and for hunting down oppositionists (such as Leon Trotsky and other 'Trotskyists') and enforcing Stalinist policies in communist parties abroad. Organisationally, it also reflected the management problems involved in directing and controlling the massive establishments for internal security and foreign intelligence operations.

Domestic operations far outweighed foreign intelligence operations in terms of the attentions of the leadership, the numbers of personnel involved, and the shaping of the organisational structures. The Cheka grew from 23 men in December 1917 to about 262 400 by mid 1921.[2] It expanded rapidly in the late 1920s and early 1930s, when it was responsible for enforcing collectivisation ('dekulakisation')—a process which resulted in at least 14.5 million and probably about 20 million deaths throughout the USSR.[3] In 1936–38, it managed the Great Terror, in which at least another 11 million and more likely around 20 million people were executed or died in the vast network of labour camps ('gulag').[4]

The machinery required for these operations was enormous. When Beria took over as chief of the NKVD in November 1938, he was responsible for the vast gulag, the regular prisons, border troops, internal troops, and railroad troops, as well as internal political security, counter-intelligence, and espionage.[5] By the time Stalin died in 1953, some 11 million people (or more than 5 per cent of the Soviet population) were spying on fellow citizens.[6] In contrast, in 1952 there were some 3000 officers in the Foreign Intelligence Directorate headquarters, plus some 15 000 officers and agents abroad (including thousands of non-Soviet citizens betraying their own countries).[7]

The reorganisations were disruptive, but not nearly so much as the Terror itself. Under Yezhov, the NKVD itself was ruthlessly purged; about 20 000 NKVD personnel perished in 1937–38.[8] In 1938–39, Beria conducted a 'purger's purge', during which Yezhov and about 150 of his colleagues were executed.[9] By 1939, almost all the senior officers who had served in the Cheka/NKVD before 1938 had been killed.

An outstanding feature of the NKVD was its centralised control, and it was this which give its head, Beria, his power and influence. To the NKVD, and later KGB, agents in the field, headquarters was known as Moscow Centre, and orders issued by Moscow Centre were to be feared and obeyed. Although the NKVD had an all-pervading influence on Soviet domestic life, it was its foreign intelligence element which most interested the security staffs of Allied countries like Australia, Britain and the US.

KGB FOREIGN INTELLIGENCE

On 20 December 1920, the Cheka established a Foreign Section (IO), later called the Foreign Department (INO), for foreign intelligence operations.[10] Its activities were initially limited to the surveillance of Russian émigrés abroad (EM work), but it soon established a Disinformation ('Dezinformatsiya') Bureau for spreading false information about the Soviet Union to the foreign press and Western counter-intelligence agencies;[11] and a liaison department for working with the secret intelligence department (OMS) of the Comintern, which was having considerable success with the recruitment of foreign communists and 'fellow travellers'. Many of the NKVD's best foreign agents in the 1930s and 1940s were initially recruited by the Comintern.[12]

Soviet foreign intelligence activities expanded greatly in the late 1930s, initially to conduct 'wet affairs', i.e. the tracking down and execution of Trotskyists and other oppositionists abroad.[13] In early 1939, Beria and his colleagues turned their attention to foreign intelligence collection and, most particularly, the gathering of intelligence on German intentions and the possibilities for a Soviet–German security agreement.[14] From late 1941, the highest priority for intelligence collection operations abroad became information about the US atomic bomb program. As Pavel Sudoplatov (who was appointed a deputy director of the Foreign Department of the NKVD in March 1939 and who served as director of the Administration of Special Tasks and its successor organisations from July 1941 until his arrest in August 1953) has described, the 'illegal network' which he had established in the US and Mexico for locating and assassinating Trotsky served as the basis of the NKVD's atomic espionage operation in the US.[15]

The head of the Soviet foreign intelligence service from 1939 to 1946 was Lieutenant-General Pavel Mikhailovich Fitin (cover-name VIKTOR), who had succeeded Vladimir Georgievich Dekanozov as head of the INO in 1939 and had remained as head of the Foreign Intelligence Directorate, or Inostrannoye Upravlenie (INU), through the successive reorganisations of the NKGB. Fitin was one of the ablest of some 200 young communists with university degrees chosen by the Central Committee at the end of 1938 to replace liquidated NKVD officers.[16] He has been described as 'prudent in the extreme', though, when presenting intelligence to Stalin, 'marginally less servile' than some of his colleagues.[17] Fitin had good reasons for prudence. Two of his three immediate predecessors as heads of Soviet foreign intelligence (A. A. Slutsky and M. Shpigelglas) had been killed in 1938.[18]

Fitin's first task in 1939–41 was to reconstruct the foreign intelligence service and re-establish contacts with its agents abroad. This was a difficult and tricky exercise. Almost all of the OGPU officers who had recruited, controlled, or received information from agents abroad in the 1930s had died in the slaughter of 1937–39, most of them having been convicted as 'German spies'.[19] In the case of Kim Philby, the infamous Soviet agent in the British Foreign Office, for example, there was even a period when no-one at Moscow Centre could even identify or locate him (he was cover-named SONNY, then SOHNCHEN and, from August 1944, STANLEY).[20] The foreign recruits were inevitably regarded with grave suspicion. Indeed, in Philby's case, there were many at Moscow Centre who thought he might be a double agent, really working for MI6, and it was not until August 1944 that he was completely 'rehabilitated'.[21] The INU developed a thirst for personal details about its foreign recruits—their spouses, children, other relatives, personal likes and dislikes, and their mental states—in order to determine their motivations and reliability.

By 1942–43, this reconstruction phase was largely completed, and Fitin turned his attentions to the development of espionage networks in Britain, the US, Canada, Mexico and Australia. Fitin is one of the few senior officers from the Foreign Intelligence Service of the 1930s and 1940s whose portrait hangs, with an accompanying eulogy, on the wall of the Memory Room at the headquarters of the Russian Foreign Intelligence Service.[22]

Fitin was succeeded as head of the INU in 1946 by Lieutenant-General Pyotr Vasilyevich Fedotov (cover-named IVANOV), who, like Fitin, was regarded as 'an intellectual' within the Centre.[23] According to Ilya Dzhirkvelov, who worked at the Centre under Fedotov from 1947 to 1949:

> The qualities that distinguished this man were his intellectual distinction, his intelligence, his charming manners, and his concern for people . . . I was impressed by his powers of logical thinking and his unerring ability to make the correct decision. What really distinguished him from other highly placed KGB officials was that he did not disregard another person's opinion. If someone didn't agree with him he would not give orders but try to persuade him.[24]

In October 1947 Stalin established a new Committee of Information (KI), under the USSR Council of Ministers, which brought together the INU and the foreign intelligence functions of Soviet Military Intelligence (the GRU) into a single organisation responsible for all intelligence collection operations and clandestine activities abroad. The reorganisation was essentially a product of the struggle among Stalin's minions; from Stalin's viewpoint, it weakened the power of Beria and his protégé, Viktor Semyonovich Abakumov, who headed the MGB from 1946 to 1951. Stalin was also influenced by reports from the MGB Resident in Washington in 1947 concerning the establishment of the Central Intelligence Agency (CIA) as the central US agency responsible for foreign intelligence and clandestine operations.[25] The KI was headed successively by top Foreign Ministry officials—Vyacheslav Molotov, J. Malik, Andrey Vyshinskiy, and V. Zorin. The principal KI offices were located in two former Comintern buildings in the Tekstilshchiki District on the outskirts of Moscow, not far from the village of Rostokino. The KI leadership and the First (Anglo-American) Directorate were housed in Building No. 1; and the Second (Europe), Third (Near and Far East), Fourth ('Illegal' Agents) and Fifth (Information Evaluation) Directorates and the EM (Emigrés) Department in Building No. 2.[26]

Fedotov, as a deputy chief of the KI and the senior intelligence official, continued to be in charge of foreign intelligence operations until 1949, when he was replaced by Sergei Romanovich Savchenko.[27] Fedotov became head of the Second Chief Directorate (Counter-intelligence) of the KGB in 1953, but was 'driven out of the KGB' at the end of 1956.[28]

The KI was an organisational failure. In mid 1948, Marshal Bulganin, the minister for the Armed Forces, withdrew the military intelligence elements from the KI and re-established the GRU as an independent service under the direction of his ministry. In December 1948, the MGB took back the SK ('Soviet Colony') and EM (Emigrés) activities, including 'all full time SK and EM workers abroad'.[29] The KI retained control of most foreign intelligence operations until it was disbanded and reabsorbed by the MGB in November 1951.[30]

Savchenko, who remained in charge of foreign intelligence when the INU was reconstituted in the MGB, was less contemplative and more decisive than Fedotov, but he was also much more brutal. He had been head of the NKVD in the Ukraine during the war, and then from 1946 to 1949 head of the MVD in the Ukraine, where he was not only responsible for some of the worst atrocities in the Soviet Union during the 1940s, but was personally involved in some of the executions.[31] He was purged by Beria in March 1953.[32]

The First (Anglo-American) Directorate of the KI was responsible for intelligence operations in the UK, the US, Canada, Australia and the other Commonwealth dominions. It was headed from late 1947 to late 1950 by General Konstantin Mikhailovich Kukin, who had served as Resident in London from 1943 to 1947, where he had overall responsibility for managing the Cambridge group or 'Magnificent Five' (Guy Burgess, Donald Maclean, Kim Philby, Anthony Blunt and John Cairncross).[33] His portrait, too, hangs in the Memory Room of the Russian Foreign Intelligence Service, together with a citation which praises him as 'one of the most outstanding intelligence officers of the 1940s and 1950s'.[34]

From late 1950 to 1951, the head of the First Directorate was Colonel Ivan A. Raina (cover-named YUREV). Raina had been the first head of the Eighth Directorate, which was concerned with the acquisition of information about foreign scientific and technological developments, specifically including atomic energy and atomic weapons[35]—and which by the late 1940s had also become the primary concern of the First Directorate.

Raina maintained a close personal interest in the First Directorate's intelligence activities in Australia. He personally briefed Mrs Evdokia Petrov (cover-named TAMARA) in December 1950, before her departure for Australia;[36] and he personally made available the First Directorate's files on the Australian security service to Vladimir Petrov (cover-named MIHAIL, who was an officer in the MGB).[37] According to Vladimir Petrov, this file (which was 'about an inch thick') contained mainly 'published information' about the formation of ASIO under Mr Justice Reed and the appointment of his successor, Colonel Spry, but it also contained 'a reference to Sir Percy Sillitoe's visit to Australia, including a cable from the USA'.[38]

In 1951, Raina was promoted to deputy chief of the KI,[39] and was succeeded as head of the First Directorate by Colonel Anatoli

Borisovich Gorsky (cover-named KAP, HENRY and VADIM). Gorsky had been posted to London in 1936 as 'a minor technical employee of the Soviet Embassy', but advanced quickly in the London Residency as all the rest of his colleagues were purged in 1937–38. He was appointed Resident in 1939, and served as operational controller of the 'Magnificent Five' until Kukin took them over in mid 1944.[40] He then served (as Anatoli Gromov) as the acting Resident in Washington until 1947.[41] There, from late 1944 until late 1945, he was the controller of Elizabeth Bentley (cover-named GOOD GIRL).[42] Gorsky was dismissed as head of the First Directorate (and discharged from the MVD) in 1953, when it was discovered that his father had been a Tsarist police officer.[43]

Within the First Directorate of the INU and KI, the Second Department was responsible for operations in the UK and the Commonwealth, with separate sections dealing with the UK, Canada, Australia, New Zealand and South Africa. It was headed by Feoktistov from the mid 1940s through 1950.[44] The head of the Australian Section in 1950–51 was German Ivanovich Ashurov, who had previously served abroad, possibly in the US, 'where he had won himself quite a good intelligence reputation'.[45]

From the perspective of the intelligence officers in the Residencies abroad, the various reorganisations at Moscow Centre had little direct impact on their operational activities. As Vladimir Petrov wrote after his defection, 'whether my umbrella was the KI or the MGB made little difference to the job'.[46] Their interest in changes in the power structure and the personalities involved at Moscow Centre was nonetheless intense, because they affected the working relationships between the diplomatic personnel and officers of the various intelligence and security organs within the embassies, and the careers and frequently even the lives of these officers.

From the point of view of foreign agents working for the Russians, the reorganisations were essentially irrelevant. Most of those recruited in the 1930s and 1940s did not know, or, it seems, even care about the bureaucratic structure of the Soviet security and intelligence establishment, or the personalities in the agencies for which they were working. Many of the agents in the US, the 'Magnificent Five' in the UK, and at least some of the agents in Australia were recruited by the Comintern and subsequently passed to the NKVD.[47] A large proportion of the networks established in the US, Canada, the UK and Australia consisted of so-called 'in-the-dark informants', or 'persons responding comparatively readily to unconscious exploitation',[48] such as Party members or fellow travellers who provided agents with information and material which they then passed to the respective Residencies and thence to Moscow Centre—and who remained unaware of this process.

As mentioned, the KI had been formed in 1947 as an umbrella organisation to bring together the Foreign Intelligence Directorate of the MGB (the INU) and the foreign intelligence functions of Soviet Military Intelligence (GRU), but the latter withdrew from the KI in mid 1948. The GRU was a formidable intelligence organisation in its own right and operated its own agents abroad.

SOVIET MILITARY INTELLIGENCE (GRU)

The GRU was established as the Intelligence Bureau (RU) of the Red Army in December 1920. It was headed from March 1924 to mid 1935 by General Yan Karlovich Berzin, who had worked in the Cheka until he joined the RU in December 1920, and who 'moulded it into a professional intelligence organization'.[49] Berzin was arrested and executed in July 1938. There were several chiefs from 1935 to 1941, at least two of whom (General Semen Petrovich Uritskiy, 1935–37, and Yezhov) were also killed during the Great Purge. By the end of the purge, virtually all of the ranking and experienced GRU officers had been executed.[50] Over the decade and a half from 1935 to 1950, there were some twelve chiefs of the GRU—four of whom were executed during the Great Terror.[51] In 1942, when the decision was made to establish a GRU residency in Australia, the chief of the GRU was Ivan Ivanovich Ilichev, who was shot in 1943.[52]

Ilichev was succeeded by Colonel-General Fedor Fedotovich Kuznetsov, who remained chief until April 1946. Kuznetsov was 'a country boy' who came to Moscow to become a factory worker, but who soon joined the Party and embarked on a 'meteoric career'. During the Terror, 'he showed exceptional cruelty'. On his appointment, Stalin asked him whether he could be as good an intelligence officer as he had been at purging the Army, to which he replied: 'Is there any great difference?'[53] He was one of the most brutal but also one of the most successful chiefs of the GRU. He had 'a special role' in the organisation of Stalin's first meeting with Roosevelt and Churchill in Teheran in November 1943 to discuss the shape of the postwar world; he helped to prepare and implement the decisions of the Yalta and Potsdam conferences in 1945; he personally directed operations to steal US atomic secrets; and he presided over the difficult transition from war to peace.[54]

From April 1946 to February 1949, the chief of the GRU was General Sergei Mutveevich Shtemyenko. In 1943, he had been head of the Operations Directorate of the General Staff, in which capacity he was one of the principal Soviet military planners. He was the closest military adviser to Stalin, and accompanied him to Teheran. He is considered to have been 'the most energetic, erudite and merciless of all GRU chiefs'.[55]

Organisationally, the GRU was divided into geographic and functional directorates (e.g. the Radio Intelligence or Sigint Directorate). There were three principal geographic directorates, covering Europe, Asia, and the US/UK/Commonwealth, which were further divided into area branches composed of country desks. Hence, in 1943–47 the GRU Residency in Canberra was managed by and reported to the Australian desk in the Commonwealth Branch of the US/UK Directorate under the First Deputy Chief of the GRU.

The GRU's foreign operations directorates maintained several remarkably well-placed and productive espionage networks around the world during the 1940s—though often, especially at the beginning of the decade, their intelligence was ignored by the Kremlin. The Sorge network in Japan and the Lucy ring and the Rote Kapelle (or 'Red Orchestra') in Switzerland and Germany provided ample advance warning of the German plans and preparations to attack the Soviet Union in June 1941, but the reports went unheeded. Soon after the outbreak of hostilities, the GRU began to produce an impressive volume of high-level intelligence on German war plans and military operations.[56]

The GRU was particularly active in collecting scientific and technological intelligence, including that on atomic research and development, in the UK, Canada and the US. For example, it handled Klaus Fuchs (cover-named REST) while he was in the UK in 1941–43; and it recruited Allan Nunn May (ALEK) in Britain and ran him in Canada (where he provided the GRU, in August 1945, with information on US atomic bomb development and samples of uranium 233 and 235).[57] From late 1943, when Kuznetsov played 'a special role' in organising the Teheran conference, the GRU became very involved with the collection of intelligence on British and US postwar planning.

The GRU tended to place more emphasis than the NKGB on the development of 'illegal' espionage networks—i.e. networks such as the Sorge ring in Japan (until 1940, when a contact with the 'legal' Residency in Tokyo was established) and the Lucy ring and Rote Kapelle in Europe, which operated independently (with their own ciphers and direct radio communications with Moscow) of any 'legal' networks handled by the GRU Residents in Soviet embassies or other diplomatic establishments. In the postwar years, the GRU was particularly concerned to develop 'illegal' networks that would continue to function in the event that hostilities with the West forced the closure of the Residencies. As a GRU tradecraft manual produced in the early 1950s noted:

The operating conditions of a *rezidentsia* will, of course, change in time of war. As is known, the *rezidentsia* under [diplomatic] cover will cease to exist the moment the official Soviet installations shut down. Therefore, one of the most important tasks of the *rezidentsia* under cover is to train during peace-time agents and agent nets to conduct independent communications with the Centre so that they can operate in time of war.[58]

Considering the now well-known activities of spies in Britain, the US, Canada, Japan and Switzerland, it should come as no surprise that both the KGB and the GRU had agents in Australia during and after the Second World War. Perhaps the main difference is that Soviet espionage operations in Australia began a little later than those in other countries, no doubt because there were no diplomatic relations with Australia until 1942, and it took the Soviets some time to appreciate that Australia might provide a convenient window into other Allied activities.

8

'there was no mistaking the men'

THE ARRIVAL OF THE RUSSIANS

DIPLOMATIC RELATIONS BETWEEN AUSTRALIA AND the USSR were established at legation level on 10 October 1942, and the Soviet minister (later ambassador), Andrei Vlasov, presented his credentials in Canberra on 10 March 1943. From the outset, Australia was obviously regarded as a potential source of important intelligence, and arrangements were made to establish both NKGB and GRU Residencies in Canberra. In early 1943, the Soviet government purchased the present embassy compound and buildings at 78 Canberra Avenue in Griffith (just 2km southeast of Parliament House and the principal government office buildings).[1] Surrounded by conifers and thick hedges, the site 'had obviously been chosen with a view to its protection against prying eyes and intruding ears'.[2] A squad of workmen and technicians was sent out from Moscow to carry out various interior alterations, which included the construction of secure rooms for the GRU Residence and a 'secret section' for the NKGB.[3]

As plans were being prepared for the establishment of the NKGB and GRU Residencies in Australia, Moscow Centre must already have decided to establish an NKGB office in Sydney. Sydney was the major centre of Communist Party activity in Australia, but there were also large Party memberships in Melbourne, Brisbane and Perth. Moscow needed confirmation that Sydney was the best place for political and strategic intelligence, and that the distance from Canberra to Sydney and the difficulties of travel and communication between them warranted a separate office in Sydney. The solution

The Soviet Embassy at 78 Canberra Avenue, Griffith, ACT. The site 'had obviously been chosen with a view to its protection against prying eyes and intruding ears'.

was to establish a TASS newsagency office in Sydney and use the correspondent to lay the groundwork for future intelligence operations.

VLADIMIR MIKHEEV

On 11 September 1942 the first TASS correspondent, Vladimir Ivanovich Mikheev, arrived in Fremantle, accompanied by his wife, and went straight on to Sydney.[4] However, he dallied long enough in Perth to meet Katharine Susannah Prichard, a prominent writer and member of the Australian Communist Party. She was later revealed in the Venona decrypts (in which she is referred to as 'an influential ACADEMICIAN') to be a source of information being passed to Moscow, and she no doubt gave him an account of the sorts of assistance he could expect from the Communist Party. Writing from Perth on 3 October 1942, Prichard said she was moving to Sydney and expected to see the Mikheevs in 'a few weeks time'. Letters to her could be sent care of Mikheev, as she would be in touch with him and she might be 'helpful to him in preparing material for the Australian newspapers'.[5]

Little is known about Mikheev's background, but he was undoubtedly charged with scouting out the Australian scene for the Soviet foreign intelligence services and making preparations for NKGB and GRU activities in Australia in 1943. He was probably a member of the GRU rather than the NKGB[6] and, as the Venona material shows, he never cooperated with the NKGB Residency in Canberra.[7] On the other hand, without its own scout in Australia, Moscow Centre would have insisted on being given any information he sent to GRU headquarters in 1942–43 concerning the possibilities, problems and prospects for Soviet espionage operations in

Australia. He was evidently accredited as a war correspondent to 'both the US and Australian Armies and he wore a military uniform'.[8] Initially he lived in a flat at 105 Bayswater Road, Darlinghurst, and later in 1943 moved to Flat 19, 16–18 Kings Cross Road, Darlinghurst, which would serve as the residence and office of the TASS representative and senior KGB officer in Sydney for many years to come.

As a war correspondent Mikheev travelled frequently and widely around Australia. Clive Turnbull, an Australian journalist, remembered meeting him in Melbourne 'during the time that Army GHQ was located' there.[9] On 1 April 1943 he wrote to a member of the Australian department of Information that he would be 'unable to visit Melbourne for quite some time now as I am tied up with my Friends from the Legation whom I am now assisting in the way of helping them learn different aspects of Australia'.[10] Mikheev visited Canberra, Brisbane and other places in northern Australia. In August 1943 he made his last trip in Australia to 'the north'.[11]

While in Sydney, Mikheev was a frequent visitor to the Journalists' Club, where he met many of his contacts and acquaintances. These included the writer Colin Simpson;[12] Rex Chiplin, who has said that he met Mikheev twice;[13] Ian MacInnes, who met him at the club on 'two or three occasions';[14] and Forbes Miller, who met him 'probably three or four times'.[15] Mikheev often went to see Rupert Lockwood (cover-named VORON or WARREN), a prominent Australian communist journalist, 'for advice on personal and journalistic matters'.[16] He met up again with Prichard, who was probably responsible for introducing him to Walter Seddon Clayton, a senior functionary in the Australian Communist Party who (cover-named KLOD) was later revealed in the Venona material as the principal Soviet spymaster.

Mikheev was also a frequent visitor to the central Sydney office of External Affairs minister and Attorney-General Evatt, whose private secretary, Allan Dalziel, was expected to 'keep in contact with him and make him feel at home and render such facilities as I could'[17] and 'to help him settle in with headquarters in Sydney'.[18] Dalziel (cover-named DENIS) introduced Mikheev to several people, including Frederick MacLean.[19] In August 1943, before leaving Australia, Mikheev introduced Dalziel to his successor as TASS correspondent, Feodor Nosov.[20]

SEMYEN MAKAROV

The first NKGB resident in Australia was Semyen Ivanovich Makarov (cover-named EFIM), who arrived on 21 May 1943[21] and quickly established his office in Canberra. When the first Soviet diplomats and NKGB and GRU officers arrived in Canberra, they must have thought they had come to a different world. The battle of Stalingrad had ended with the surrender of the exhausted German troops, but the future of the Soviet Union was still in the balance and life in Moscow was desperate. Canberra was a small country town of only 14 000 people, a disproportionate number of whom were involved in government service. There was still only a handful of other countries with diplomatic missions in Canberra—the UK, the US, the Republic of China, the Netherlands, France, Canada and New Zealand. The people from the Russian embassy were quite identifiable when they ventured outside the embassy grounds. As Ric Throssell has written:

> There was no mistaking the men. They were always in twos and threes; solid, shock-headed fellows in square double-breasted suits that looked as if they had come out of prewar ads for a closing-down sale at a men's emporium, collars too small for honest working-class necks, and ties askew, as if in protest against the concession to bourgeois convention. The gleam of stainless steel teeth had an irresistible fascination. Soviet man. Nothing symbolised the difference between us more than those teeth. They seemed to be the ultimate modernity. Uncompromising. Wholly functional. Efficiency epitomised. And when a Russian smiled it was as if he ceased to be human. Those gleaming rows of mechanical teeth belonged to an automaton. They were the most undiplomatic teeth. You could never quite be at ease with a man with a stainless steel smile.[22]

Born on 3 February 1910, Makarov was about 5'4" to 5'6" tall, 'stocky, square shoulders, large body, short legs', sallow complexion, black hair ('worn long on top and standing well above the forehead'), with a 'medium to full but not large' face and a 'straight, short' nose. He 'walked in an erect manner but with a slow step' and was 'smartly dressed'.[23] His overt posting was initially as an embassy 'clerk', but on 28 April 1947 he was promoted to third secretary and then on 7 November 1948, to second secretary.[24] He was accompanied by his wife, Kiri Vanentinovna and a daughter was born in 1944. Kiri Makarov and their daughter returned to Russia on 25 June 1948, a year before Makarov's own departure.[25]

Makarov's first task was to establish the KGB Residency within the Soviet embassy. He eventually took over the whole of the top floor of the embassy building—with offices for himself and his KGB 'cadre-workers' at the northern end, and the 'secret section' (including the cipher section, safes, dark room, incinerators and reading rooms) at the southern end.[26] According to the 1955 Report of the Royal Commission on Espionage:

the Embassy cipher section was set apart for the M.V.D. Resident and his cipher clerk. Access to the Embassy cipher section, the entrance to which was guarded, was permitted only to very few senior Embassy officials. Access to the M.V.D. room was even more restricted. It was provided with the necessary equipment for photographing documents and developing and printing from negatives. In it was a safe used solely for M.V.D. purposes, to which there were two keys which, when not in use, were kept in the Embassy cipher clerk's safe in a container sealed with a seal held by the M.V.D. cipher clerk. In the M.V.D. safe were deposited the M.V.D. cipher books and documents and the M.V.D. cash. This was kept entirely apart from Embassy funds and used only for M.V.D. purposes and accountable for only to the Moscow Centre.[27]

As the Venona operation would later show, Makarov began to make contact with various Australian Communist Party officials soon after his arrival in 1943. Someone from the Soviet foreign intelligence services in Moscow must have identified Clayton for recruitment as the 'spymaster' in 1942, and someone must have arranged with both him and Makarov to establish their initial contact soon after May 1943. Mikheev, who almost certainly would have met Clayton at the Journalists' Club, is the most likely candidate for this role.

The Commonwealth Security Service had no knowledge of these espionage activities. However, the censorship authorities continued to pass information to the Security Service about the Australian communists. One letter from Marcus Clarke, a senior communist in South Australia, in April 1943, referred to the arrival in Australia of the Soviet legation and said 'he was endeavouring to contact it in order to "facilitate future moves"'.[28] After Blamey's visit to Canberra in January 1945, the Security Service focused more closely on the Soviet mission. Barbara Cohen, who assisted her husband with his Security Service duties because of his blindness, recalled that she was aware that Blamey's visit was concerned with information leaks. She also recalled that Makarov was thought to be an intelligence agent.[29]

Mikheev's successor as TASS representative, Feodor Nosov, became Makarov's 'principal cadre worker' and operated from Sydney. In addition to Nosov, by 1948 Makarov had at least four other KGB officers working for him in the Canberra embassy. The first and most important of these was Gubanov (SANTO), who arrived in Canberra in August 1945 under official cover as embassy clerk. His secret duties included SK and EM work as well as ciphering and other 'technical work' for Makarov and his successor, Valentin Sadovnikov. Gubanov returned to the Soviet Union on 5 March 1951, when his responsibilities were assumed by Evdokia Petrov (TAMARA).[30] The others, in order of their arrival in Australia, included

Vysselsky (VASSILI), who arrived on 6 January 1947 and departed on 24 November 1950, and whose cover was press attaché and later third secretary at the embassy;[31] Krutikov, who was in Australia from 13 August 1948 to 16 October 1950, under the cover of commercial attaché;[32] and Lyudmila Lyalina, who was in Canberra from December 1948 to March 1951 as a typist on the staff of the commercial attaché but who had been co-opted to work with Makarov and then Sadovnikov.[33]

Any assessment of Makarov's espionage activities during his six years in Australia must rest almost entirely on the product of the KLOD group. Makarov himself does not appear to have been very energetic. He did not travel as much as some of his colleagues and, unlike Nosov or his GRU 'neighbour' in the embassy, Viktor Zaitsev, he engaged in little social activity outside of embassy functions. He seemed to have few contacts. According to Evdokia Petrov:

> Makarov failed to establish an independent residency network of agents, but merely collected the intelligence produced by the 'K' group. Whether it was because of this failure, or whether it was because of compromise of the 'K' group . . . Makarov was reprimanded by the C.P.S.U. organisation of his K.I. Directorate on his return to Moscow, and this reprimand was confirmed by the C.P.S.U. organisation for the Committee of Information as a whole.[34]

Makarov left Australia on 24 June 1949. Then in 1950–51 he worked in the First (Anglo-American) Directorate at KI headquarters in Moscow.[35] Whatever the strength of his reprimand in 1949, it was reported to ASIO in July 1952 that Makarov 'had enjoyed a meteoric rise'.[36]

Feodor Andreevich Nosov

The second KGB (then NKGB) 'worker' to be posted to Australia was Feodor Andreevich Nosov (cover-named TEKHNIK, or 'technician'). Nosov was born in Briansk on 24 February 1912 and was by profession a TASS journalist rather than a KGB officer. He had only been 'recruited' by the KGB to serve as a 'contact man' for the KGB in Sydney.[37] Nosov and his wife, Galina, were issued with Soviet passports in Moscow on 8 April 1943, and arrived in Melbourne on the SS *Straat Malakka* on 16 August 1943. In a personal statement lodged on his arrival, Nosov noted that he had had some Army training and that he expected to stay in Australia for one to two years.[38] He was of medium build, 5'5", with brown eyes and thinning brown hair. Galina Nosov was born in Livny on 27 April 1910; she had light brown hair, blue eyes, and was also of medium build.[39]

Feodor Nosov, the TASS representative in Australia from 1943 to 1950. He worked for the KGB and was a frequent visitor to Dr Evatt's office in Sydney. (Australian Archives, CRS A6201/1, item 321)

The Nosovs' flat at 16–18 Kings Cross Road, Darlinghurst, was also the TASS office and had previously been used by Mikheev. Nosov performed his TASS cover role diligently, even becoming treasurer of the Foreign Press Correspondents' Association in Sydney. However, his primary mission was to act as Makarov's 'principal cadre-worker' and as the agent in charge of KGB operations in Sydney. Information and material that he collected as part of his TASS duties was cabled to Moscow. In the case of material obtained from KLOD, Nosov would drive to Canberra and personally deliver it to Makarov or, in 1949–50, to his successor, Sadovnikov. He visited Canberra fairly regularly, attending most official functions and many receptions and cocktail parties, often inviting friends and associates in Sydney to come with him. He seems to have averaged at least a dozen trips to Canberra a year.

Nosov was a bright, pleasant, fairly popular character. During his seven years in Australia, he developed a wide range of contacts—including members of Parliament, government officials, ministerial staff, journalists, writers, trade union officials, Australian communists, and 'friends of Russia'. Nosov's closest Australian friend was Allan Dalziel (DENIS), Evatt's private secretary and Sydney 'representative', to whom he was introduced by Mikheev, who 'brought him [Nosov] to my office . . . and asked me to extend to him any courtesies that would facilitate his work'.[40] According to Dalziel, 'Mr Nosov and I continued a normal and civilised friendship which lasted up until the time of his departure from Australia.'[41] He would often refer to Nosov as 'brother'.[42] He recalled that:

[Nosov] was a gentlemanly and well-behaved person. . . . Mr. and Mrs. Nosov were a typical suburban husband and wife, apparently devoted to each other. They liked to talk and eat and also to go to the pictures or theatre where on occasions, with other Australian friends, I accompanied them. I often referred to Mr. Nosov as looking more like a Methodist Deacon rather than an accredited representative of Tass agency of the Soviet Union. He would laugh at my description.[43]

Dalziel said that his 'primary purpose' in seeing Nosov was to distribute ministerial press statements, but that 'very often' he would visit the Nosovs to talk about Russia and the relative merits of the Soviet and Australian political systems. Dalziel was 'an active Churchman' and 'on two occasions I took [Nosov] and his wife to Church for Christmas Eve church services'.[44]

Nosov was a frequent visitor to Evatt's office in Martin Place, where he got to know several of the staff. For example, Frances Bernie (later identified by Venona decrypts as a Soviet agent, cover-named SESTRA), who worked in Evatt's office from November 1944 to April 1946, said she met Nosov 'several times' and that 'he was a pleasant man to talk to'.[45] However, she later recalled that when she had been alone in her room at Evatt's office Nosov had approached her from behind and placed his arms around her; she 'discreetly showed him her engagement ring in order to stop any further advances being made to her'.[46]

Dalziel also introduced Nosov to his friend Frederick MacLean in 1945 or 1946. MacLean (cover-named LOT) was a journalist who had joined the Communist Party briefly during the war, joined the department of External Affairs in May 1947, and was press officer in its Canberra Political Intelligence and Information Centre from August 1947 until he retired through sickness in February 1952.[47] MacLean met Nosov officially and on several social occasions; he said in November 1954 that although there was something about Galina Nosov that he did not like, he found Nosov 'a good fellow who enjoyed a drink'.[48]

Nosov was a fairly regular visitor to Katharine Susannah Prichard's apartment in Kings Cross, where he met with Australian writers, communists and other 'friends of the Soviet Union', such as Jean Ferguson, Nina Christesen and Dalziel, as well as members of the family such as Ric Throssell, Prichard's son. Both the Nosovs were 'very interested in Australian literature', and particularly the works of Prichard herself.[49] Throssell recalled in July 1954 that he had met Nosov 'at my mother's flat—the last time was just before I left for Moscow [in October 1945]—and he gave me some advice as to the climate and what to wear'.[50] Prichard showed Ric's letters from Moscow to the Nosovs; they commented that he was already, in

January 1946, writing 'like a Russian'.[51] In January 1946, Prichard had a sheepskin coat made for her son which she got his wife, Bea Gallacher, to take with her when she went to join him in Moscow later that month; she wrote to Ric that it had not been easy to find either the sheepskin or a tailor, but that 'in the end' she had enlisted the assistance of Nosov, who she described as 'my usual source of help'.[52]

Nosov had close relations with many journalists, writers and academics. The journalist he knew best was Forbes Miller, chief sub-editor of the *Daily Telegraph* from 1943 to 1952, who had been a member of the Journalists Branch of the Communist Party from 1935 to 1942. In 1943, Nosov arranged for Miller to supply him, for a small fee, with news which might be of interest for him to cable to TASS.[53] This arrangement lasted some six to nine months. Miller visited the Nosovs' flat on about twelve occasions, took them sailing in Sydney Harbour, and accompanied them on other social outings in Sydney; he has noted that Nosov's attitude always appeared to be one of 'diplomatic correctness'.[54] Other journalists and writers he knew—and about whom he reported to Moscow— included Ian MacInnes, who had been a member of the Communist Party until 1950 or 1951, and who had known Nosov in 1945–47;[55] Colin Simpson, who later described Nosov as a 'bright alert personality';[56] Rex Chiplin (CHARLIE), a journalist working for the *Tribune*;[57] and Clement Christesen (CRAB), a lecturer at the University of Melbourne and editor of *Meanjin*, and his wife, Nina Michaelovna Christesen (EVA), who was head of the Russian school at that university. The Christesens were his main social acquaintances in Melbourne.[58] Many of these were the same people who had met Nosov's predecessor, Mikheev.

One of Nosov's closest contacts, according to Vladimir Petrov, was Jean Ferguson (RAPHAEL),[59] who had been a member of the Communist Party since 1940. She was an unpaid secretary of the Australia–Soviet Friendship Society in Sydney, and 'acted as a sort of agent in Sydney for the Soviet Consulate (which was in Canberra) and busied herself as a go-between amongst Communist and Soviet officials'.[60]

Clive Turnbull, who said he had journalistic and 'patriotic' associations with Nosov, described him as 'a little man, somewhat oriental in appearance'.[61] Mark Younger and his wife, who shared a common interest with the Nosovs in Russian music recordings, spent time together in each other's homes; they thought Galina Nosov was 'a very intellectual . . . and intelligent woman'.[62]

Another person Nosov knew 'quite well' was Geoffrey Anderson (YEGER), who had served in the RAAF during the war and won a Distinguished Flying Cross. He served as an official of the Federated

Clerks' Union of Australia and, though never a member of the Communist Party, was very active in 'front' organisations.[63]

An interesting contact was Constantine Tenukest (TIKHON), a naturalised Australian who had been born in Russia in 1906, moved to Prague in 1926 and Australia in 1938, and who worked at the Czech consulate in Sydney from 1943 to 1948. His duties in the consulate included decoding 'important confidential messages' sent from the provisional Czech government in London and then the postwar government in Prague—which gave him access to the Czech ciphers—and dealing with confidential information about the policies and decisions of the Czech government. Tenukest met Nosov in 1944, when he occasionally visited the consulate. In 1945, his visits became much more frequent, and Tenukest and his wife became good friends with the Nosovs. According to Tenukest, Nosov was 'a very communicate [*sic*] person [who] appeared to be very interested in me and most sociable'. Nosov would visit Tenukest at his home during weekends, and the Tenukests had dinner or tea at the Nosovs' on half a dozen occasions. According to Tenukest, 'both Mr and Mrs Nosov were very fond of singing, particularly Ukrainian songs, but they would sing the whole of "Waltzing Matilda" in which they took great pride'.[64]

By about 1947–48, the Nosovs had become homesick and looked forward to being recalled to the Soviet Union.[65] The preparations for their departure must have begun in Moscow in late 1949 or early 1950, for in February 1950 the Soviet Foreign ministry asked the department of External Affairs to provide a visa for Ivan Pakhomov and on 22 March informed it that Pakhomov would replace Nosov as the TASS correspondent in Sydney.[66] When the couple actually left Australia, however, in August 1950, Nosov seems to have been scuttling, although the precise circumstances leading to his departure remain somewhat unclear. Evdokia Petrov said she thought that, probably in 1949, Nosov had reported to Moscow Centre that he had been 'noticed . . . with his contact', and Moscow became concerned about his security and about the Sydney component of the KLOD group.[67]

In 1950, according to Vladimir Petrov (who says he was told this by Pakhomov when Petrov took over the KGB Residency from him in 1951), Nosov was warned by Geoffrey Anderson (YEGER) that 'a large security observation of Nosov was in progress by the Security'.[68] Nosov reported this to the NKGB Resident, Sadovnikov, who informed Moscow Centre. Because Nosov had no diplomatic immunity, he was ordered by Moscow 'to leave immediately for the USSR by aeroplane and not wait for the ship on which he was proposing to travel'.[69] Anderson has acknowledged that he knew Nosov 'quite well' but has denied that he gave any such warning to Nosov, and the Royal Commission on Espionage in 1955 found that it would be improper to conclude on the basis of 'remote hearsay' that Anderson had informed Nosov that he was under security surveillance.[70]

The Nosovs were somewhat unhappy about the turn of events that precipitated their departure. Just before they left, they met Constantine Tenukest and his wife while walking in George Street in central Sydney. According to Tenukest:

> While Mr Nosov appeared very reserved, Mrs Nosov was very agitated and full of condemnation of the Australian society and used words such as 'Fascist', 'Cruel', 'Ungrateful'. Both my wife and I were very surprised for never before had we heard from the Nosovs anything else but 'Hospitable Australian people', 'Friendly Australian people', etc. Mrs Nosov became almost hysterical and Mr Nosov tried to quieten her. That was the last we saw of them.[71]

The Nosovs left Australia on a flight to Rome, en route to the USSR, on 11 August 1950.[72]

Nosov's role as an NKGB/KI cadre-worker was first revealed in the Venona operation in early 1949. By the end of 1949, the Venona material provided considerable detail about his contacts and meetings. For example, the decrypt of a cable from Makarov to Moscow Centre sent on 30 March 1944 disclosed that Nosov had had clandestine meetings with Walter Clayton (KLOD). Other decrypts revealed that Nosov had collected material from Clayton and other members of the KLOD group at the apartment of Katharine Susannah Prichard in Kings Cross.

Of course, these details were not known at the time, but the decrypts reveal that by mid 1945 Nosov believed he was under surveillance by the Commonwealth Security Service. The Security Service files show that it was indeed investigating members of the Soviet legation and the TASS correspondents, Mikheev and Nosov. It will be recalled that among the information apparently passed by the Soviet staff in Harbin to the Japanese was an Australian department of Information background briefing which had been circulated to correspondents such as Nosov. Once the leakage of this information was revealed by Allied intercepts of Japanese signals, Nosov came under immediate suspicion. But as the Venona decrypts show, he was warned. The man most likely to have tipped him off was Constable Alfred Hughes of the Security Service, who was investigating the Soviet representatives in Sydney in mid 1945. Venona later revealed that Hughes (cover-named BEN) was a Soviet agent.

The only information about the MVD's view of Nosov's performance as a cadre-worker has come from Vladimir Petrov, who was reportedly told by Pakhomov that Nosov did very little MVD work during his seven years in Australia and that, despite his wide contacts, he had not exploited the possibilities offered to him.[73] However, it seems that Pakhomov had been kept ignorant about Nosov's primary activity as a contact person for the KLOD group in Sydney. Evdokia Petrov believed that after Nosov reported that he had been 'noticed once with his contact' in 1949, Moscow Centre decided that contact with Nosov's group should be suspended. Mrs Petrov stated in April 1954 that when Pakhomov came to Australia in June 1950 'Nosov did not give him any of his contacts.' Moscow Centre 'instructed Nosov not to tell Pakhomov who his contacts were because Moscow was afraid to endanger [his] group'.[74] Further, from Nosov's departure until Mrs Petrov left the Soviet embassy in April 1954, 'no information or direction came from Moscow about Nosov's group'.[75] But given that Nosov had been recruited by the NKVD for a particular task—to receive information collected by the Sydney members of the KLOD group—and that he had performed it successfully for seven years, then Moscow Centre could not have been displeased with his performance. After Nosov returned to Moscow in August 1950, he evidently went back to more conventional TASS work.[76]

AFTER MAKAROV

Makarov's successor as KI Resident was Valentin Matveevich Mikhailov, alias Sadovnikov (cover-named SAID), who arrived in Australia aboard the *Strathaird* on 7 April 1949.[77] He was described in July 1949 as 'a shortish man, rather thick set, about 35, brownish hair pushed straight back from the forehead, has a broad face, a number of gold teeth, is cheerful, smiles easily, speaks English reasonably well, appears to be well informed, [and] has spent some years in the Soviet Service in Washington'.[78] His wife, Elizaveta (cover-named ZHENA SAID or SAID'S WIFE), who served as a typist in the residency, was described as 'a pleasant, quiet, plumpish woman'.[79]

Sadovnikov was, as one report put it, 'a young man whose success was too much for him'.[80] ASIO was just being established at the time of his appointment, and thus he 'entered upon his task in circumstances very different from those under which Makarov had worked'.[81] But in Moscow Centre at the beginning of 1949, the KLOD group was still considered productive, there was no evidence that the Security Service was aware of the Soviet espionage activities, and the Residency in Canberra must have been regarded as an important KI posting. Sadovnikov's problem was that he was partial to drinking sessions and sexual affairs and used his authority within the embassy and relative freedom of movement outside it to pursue these indulgences.

During the course of Sadovnikov's two-year Residentship, all the MGB/KI cadres who had worked with Makarov returned to Moscow—Nosov in August 1950, Krutikov in October 1950, Vysselsky in November 1950, and Gubanov and Mrs Lyalina in March 1951. In return, at least five new KI personnel were posted to Australia during this period, the best known of whom were Vladimir and Evdokia Petrov, who arrived on 5 February 1951. Vladimir Petrov described Sadovnikov as a 'good' intelligence officer.[82] Nonetheless, in April 1951 he was suddenly recalled to Moscow, ostensibly to report on his work. He left in a hurry, by air on 18 April, under the impression that he would be returning to Australia after a short interval. (His wife stayed in Australia until 27 July.)[83] However, the real reason for his recall was that the ambassador had made a critical report to Moscow about his personal conduct. Sadovnikov had been having an affair with one of his part-time assistants, a young 'embassy typist' who had become pregnant.[84] Furthermore, on a visit to Melbourne, Sadovnikov 'had got drunk and had spent the night in the flat of an Australian', and when confronted by the ambassador about this incident he 'had behaved in an arrogant manner'.[85] There were also rumours that Sadovnikov had been having an affair with the married Rose-Marie Ollier (OLGA), a second secretary at the French embassy whom Moscow Centre supposed that he was recruiting, and with whom he met secretly on some five or six occasions in the countryside outside Canberra.[86] On his return to Moscow, Sadovnikov was charged with misconduct, reprimanded, demoted, and given a desk job in the Australian section of the First (Anglo-American) Directorate.[87]

Following Sadovnikov's hurried return to Moscow in April 1951, Ivan Pakhomov (VALENTIN), Feodor Nosov's successor as both TASS and NKGB/KI representative in Sydney, was appointed 'temporary' KI Resident. However, this was an unsatisfactory arrangement, since the Residency office, operational and support facilities, and lines of communication with Moscow Centre were in the embassy in Canberra. Hence, all the Residency office work devolved to Mrs Petrov, who was entrusted with 'all the KI secret documents and equipment', including the KI ciphers.[88] Pakhomov was also disadvantaged, from the KI/MVD point of view, because he had no diplomatic immunity.[89] In February 1952, he was replaced as 'temporary' Resident by Vladimir Petrov, who served in that capacity until his defection in April 1954.[90]

Pakhomov accomplished little during his ten months as 'temporary' KI/MVD Resident. Sadovnikov had left Australia in a hurry and under the impression that he would be returning soon, so it is unlikely that he briefed Pakhomov properly about his operational activities.[91] Under his TASS cover, he cultivated several journalists such as Rupert Lockwood (VORON) and Fergan O'Sullivan (ZEMLIAK), who was then a journalist working for the *Sydney Morning Herald* and an accredited member of the parliamentary press gallery in Canberra, and was later (April 1953–May 1954) Evatt's press secretary.[92]

However, Pakhomov had no contact with any members of the KLOD group. He does not seem to have paid any attention to the contents of the envelope marked *N* that Sadovnikov left in his safe (which listed the members of the KLOD group and which Vladimir Petrov brought with him when he defected in 1954). According to Mrs Petrov, who enciphered all his communications to Moscow Centre and received all the cables to him from Moscow Centre, the only communication concerning the KLOD group was a cable from Pakhomov complaining that Nosov had not briefed him on any of his contacts when he left (in August 1950) and stating that it was difficult for him to do his work. Moscow Centre did not reply.[93] When Pakhomov handed over the 'temporary' Residentship to Vladimir Petrov in April 1952, he briefed him about eight 'contacts' which Petrov was 'supposed to take over'—but these were mainly people (such as OLGA, YEGER and MONAKH) who had still not been 'actually recruited', as well as FERRO, who 'was an agent who had at one time been very valuable but was now dormant'.[94] There was to be little more progress before the Petrovs defected in 1954.

THE GRU IN AUSTRALIA: VICTOR ZAITSEV

The first GRU Resident was Colonel Victor Sergevitch Zaitsev, who arrived in Canberra on 16 March 1943 and whose overt post at the embassy was that of second secretary.[95] Zaitsev was born in Moscow in 1906. He would have been a junior Army officer during the Great Terror and, in light of his subsequent career, must by 1940 have been a GRU officer of some standing.

Zaitsev, cover-named SERGE, served in Tokyo in 1940–41 under the cover of second secretary and consul at the embassy. His principal task there was to serve as the GRU Residency's contact with the Sorge espionage network in Japan.[96] Richard Sorge (cover-named at various times SONTER, RAMSEY, FIX and INSON) was a German communist who posed convincingly as a Nazi supporter.

He had arrived in Japan in September 1933, and by the time of his arrest in October 1941 had developed what Major-General Charles Willoughby has described as 'the most complete and successful espionage operation in Japanese history' and 'probably . . . the most successful . . . organization of Red Army Intelligence anywhere in the world'.[97]

Sorge was born in Baku in the Russian Caucasus in October 1895, the son of a German father and Russian mother. A German citizen, he had joined the German Communist Party by 1919, joined the Soviet espionage network some time in 1920 and was formally recruited as a Comintern intelligence agent in 1924–25.[98] He transferred from the Comintern to the GRU in 1929, and was sent by General Berzin to Shanghai in 1930 to build up the GRU networks in China.[99] In 1933, with the personal approval of Stalin, he was sent to Tokyo to establish an 'illegal' network to provide intelligence about Japanese strategic intentions and military plans and preparations.[100]

The Sorge network penetrated both the German embassy in Tokyo and high levels of the Japanese government. It provided Moscow with intelligence on a wide range of important subjects, including: Japan's policies towards the Soviet Union, particularly the overriding question of whether or not Japan would attack the Soviet Union; the organisation, armament and order of battle of the Japanese Army and Air Force, especially in Manchuria; developments in Japanese–German relations; Japanese activities in China; Japan's relations with the US and Britain, and particularly the possibility of Japan's going to war with either of them; the influence of the Japanese Army on political affairs; and intelligence on Japanese military and industrial activities in Manchuria.[101]

On 10 May 1941, Sorge warned Moscow that Germany planned to attack the USSR on or about 20 June. (The attack occurred on the 22nd.) Thereafter, his most vital mission was to monitor Japanese war planning and preparations. He was able to assure Moscow in late July and early August 1941 that Japan did not intend to attack the USSR but was planning to drive southward, thus enabling the Siberian forces to be entrained for the German Front and contribute to the successful defence of Moscow.[102] It was for this intelligence that Sorge is sometimes said to have 'single-handedly saved Moscow';[103] in any case he has been ranked as 'perhaps the greatest spy of all time'.[104]

The professional tradecraft practised by Zaitsev in Tokyo in 1940–41 was very sophisticated—and quite instructive for assessing his later activities in Canberra. Zaitsev had the primary responsibility for keeping Sorge and his colleagues supplied with money, film, code and cipher material, and other operating paraphernalia, for passing directions and guidance from GRU Headquarters in Moscow to Sorge, and for collecting most of the espionage material (on rolls of 35mm film) for sending to Moscow. However, he only met Sorge himself once—by happenstance, on 6 August 1941, when both of them visited Max Klausen (FRITZ), who served as both radio operator for Sorge and the 'cut-out' contact person between Sorge and Zaitsev. Later, Sorge professed to finding Zaitsev 'in every respect a typical professional courier [sic!], travelling from country to country'.[105]

Max Klausen, a German communist, joined the Sorge ring in about 1931 and set up its radio communication with a GRU radio station in Vladivostok. He returned to Moscow in August 1933 to attend a 'secret radio school', then rejoined Sorge in Tokyo in November 1935. He established and maintained Sorge's radio communications with stations in the Vladivostok area, transmitting 65 421 words in some 141 transmissions in 1939–41.[106] Zaitsev first met Klausen on 20 October 1940, after Sorge had asked for a link to be established with the Tokyo Residency, since he could not support his network and handle the enormous volume of espionage material through his 'illegal' organisation.[107] Thereafter they met about once a month. Their last meeting was on 10 October 1941, when Klausen gave Zaitsev a map marked with anti-aircraft and searchlight positions.[108] They had planned to meet again on 20 November, but Klausen could not make the rendezvous; he was arrested on 18 October.[109]

The Sorge ring was tracked down and its members captured by the Japanese Kempei Tai (or Military Police) and counter-intelligence authorities through no fault of Zaitsev's. In 1938 the Japanese counter-intelligence radio-monitoring service had detected the transmissions of a clandestine radio, and by mid 1941 radio-monitoring vans had identified Klausen's apartment as the source of the transmissions.[110] Sorge, an inveterate womaniser, could perhaps have escaped, but he dallied over the prospect of a liaison with a beautiful Japanese nightclub dancer.[111] He was hanged on 7 November 1944 and twenty years later was posthumously awarded the supreme decoration of Hero of the Soviet Union.[112] Zaitsev quietly left Japan after the arrests.[113]

Under interrogation by the Japanese police, Klausen identified SERGE as Viktor Zaitsev on 25 December 1941. He described him 'as being about five feet six inches tall, broad shouldered, round faced, and about 30 years old'.[114] Klausen's wife, Anna, who served as a courier for the Sorge ring and who was arrested on 19 November, also identified Zaitsev as the ring's contact officer in the Soviet embassy.[115]

In November 1949, during a subsequent US investigation into 'the Sorge Espionage Ring Case', a Japanese Foreign ministry official,

Ryuhei Honda, who had met Zaitsev 'frequently in 1941', described him as 'heavy set, about 5 foot 6 inches, broad shouldered, in the middle thirties, dark haired, brown eyed, with the features of a Balt or a Ukrainian'.[116] Honda stated that he 'got the impression that [Zaitsev] was not a career diplomat but appeared to be a member of the GRU'.[117]

Zaitsev was in Moscow for less than a year before preparations began for his posting to Australia. Given Zaitsev's experience and standing, the GRU must have had high expectations about the prospects for intelligence activity in Australia. He and his wife, Valeria, were issued limited section diplomatic visas by the US embassy in Kuibyshev on 21 November 1942.[118] The Zaitsevs sailed from Vladivostok to Sydney, via San Francisco, aboard the SS *Felix Dzerjinsky*. When the ship arrived in San Francisco on 22 January 1943 the US authorities noted their arrival but knew nothing more about Zaitsev.[119] The couple arrived in Australia on 16 March.[120] They stayed for nearly five years, but little is known about Zaitsev's espionage activities during this period.

According to Colin Moodie, who served in the international cooperation section of the department of External Affairs in Canberra from February 1943 to January 1944, in March and April 1943 Zaitsev was one of the main officials involved in establishing the Soviet legation and its working relationship with the department.[121] Moodie recalled that Zaitsev was 'a jolly man, portly and shortish with dark hair and a rather bullet head'. He 'spoke fair English', and 'seemed to get on well with those he met'.[122]

On 26 May 1943, Zaitsev and his wife visited Sydney to attend the celebration at Sydney Town Hall of the first anniversary of the signing of the Anglo–Soviet Treaty. 'Enthused applause' broke out when they were introduced to the audience. Zaitsev read a message expressing delight at the 'marvellous victories' achieved by the Allied forces in the twelve months since the treaty was signed, and presented plaques to the Medical Aid to Russia Committee. One of these was given to Hilda Lane, who had organised a Russian choir that sang several songs for the meeting.[123] Lane was then married to Walter Clayton (KLOD), who over the next several months was to organise the espionage network that reported to the NKGB Residency in Canberra.

Zaitsev, who lived with his wife in the Canberra suburb of Forrest, was an affable, sociable, self-assured character. At least during 1943–45, when Russia was Australia's wartime ally and political relations between Canberra and Moscow were quite relaxed, he was an energetic party-goer who obviously enjoyed food, alcohol and song. He was interested in improving his English-language ability, and liked to travel and to discuss Australian politics and foreign policy. Soon after arriving in Australia, Zaitsev arranged to have weekly language lessons with Hope Fitzhardinge (née Hewitt), the wife of Laurence Fitzhardinge, research officer in charge of the Australian reference section at the National Library in 1943–44.[124] Fitzhardinge later recollected that

> At one of the earlier parties at the Soviet Embassy where we had been drinking beer, late in the evening when most of the guests had left, Zaitsev and the remaining guests were drinking alternate tumblers of vodka and cognac. I recall a chap from External Affairs retired very sick. Zaitsev was endeavouring to get me to drink more than he was.[125]

According to Colin Moodie, in the period from April to June 1943 the Russians gave three large receptions at which large volumes of vodka and brandy were drunk, and which were considered 'a great success'. The first one was attended by 'senior people', including Evatt, the External Affairs minister; Colonel Roy Hodgson, the departmental secretary; and John D. L. Hood, head of the political section. Evatt enjoyed the party so much that after leaving he decided to go back with Hodgson to have some more vodka and caviar. Hodgson returned to the department later in the afternoon '"elevated" and easy to deal with, unusually'. Hood later recounted that on that occasion the drinking could not be escaped.[126]

A little later, Paul Hasluck, then head of the department's post-hostilities section decided to host a 'men's party' at his house for the diplomatic representatives at the half-dozen missions then in Canberra. Despite the liquor quotas then in effect, Hasluck and Moodie managed to obtain a nine-gallon barrel of beer, and the party was a fairly wild affair. When it was in full swing, Hasluck's horse was brought into the kitchen to 'add to the gaiety'.[127] Moodie remembers Zaitsev 'with his arms around Hood and Anstey Wynes singing songs in Russian'.[128] Hasluck said later that 'he couldn't think of two more unlikely people to embrace'.[129] Wynes, then head of the international cooperation section and 'general factotum' to Hodgson, a few days after the party said Zaitsev seemed rather freer to do what he wanted than other members of the legation[130]—but at this stage there was not the slightest inkling that he (or any of his colleagues) might be a professional intelligence officer. Zaitsev was much more active than any of his embassy colleagues on the dinner-party circuit in Canberra. He frequently had dinner guests at his own house, as well as visiting others. For example, in 'about 1944 or 1945' he and John Hood had dinner at the home of Stanley Raymond Phippard, a Canberra solicitor.[131]

Zaitsev liked to travel. This was not easy in Australia in 1943–47, but in April 1945 he and Makharov were granted rail priority permits, which were issued by the department of External Affairs to diplomats of high-priority status or who needed to travel frequently.[132] In January 1947, when he was in Sydney to meet an arriving Soviet delegation, he stated in a conversation with a Security Service officer that he had visited Queensland just after his arrival but otherwise had travelled only to Melbourne and Sydney.[133]

As second secretary of the Soviet legation, Zaitsev frequently visited the department of External Affairs in West Block, and sometimes also Evatt's ministerial offices, both in Parliament House and in Sydney. According to Colin Moodie, 'he came into the Department . . . every two or three weeks'.[134] Security within the department was non-existent. External Affairs was eager to deal with the Russians on friendly terms, and Zaitsev was a convivial character. Since he was regarded as having legitimate reason to visit, he needed no escort within the department's offices. Moodie recalled that Zaitsev would just walk in and knock on the doors of the people he wished to talk to—such as Paul Hasluck, John Hood, Anstey Wynes and Ric Throssell.[135] In an interview with an ASIO officer on 22 July 1954, Throssell acknowledged that he had 'met officially Zaitsev' during his 'first year or two in the Department', before he left for Moscow in October 1945.[136]

Apart from the riotous embassy party of 1943, there is no record of any meeting between Zaitsev and Evatt. However, Zaitsev is known to have admired Evatt and evidently maintained some form of contact with him. In January 1947, in a conversation with a Security Service officer in Sydney, he described Evatt as 'a very energetic man' and said 'he had read all Dr Evatt's books'—though not as yet *Injustice Within the Law*, a book about the Tolpuddle Martyrs which Evatt had given him and which he was just reading.[137] In an interview with ASIO officers on 21 June 1950, Beryl Philpott (née Hallett), who had worked in Evatt's office in Sydney from November 1944 to March 1948, stated that 'Zaitseff visited Dalziel'.[138] Allan Dalziel, Evatt's senior representative in Sydney, stated in March 1955 that he had met Zaitsev 'on his arrival in Sydney during the war years and on the infrequent occasions when he came from Canberra on official business [when] he would call at the Ministerial offices'.[139] In January 1947, Dalziel introduced Zaitsev to W. H. Barnwell, an officer in the Security Service whom Dalziel had known for '20 years'.[140] In Barnwell's report of this meeting on 3 January 1947, he noted that Zaitsev 'speaks good English and has an easy, pleasant manner'.[141] An ASIO report of 29 December 1949 notes that Dalziel 'showed secret papers to [Zaitsev] whilst the latter was in his office'.[142]

Zaitsev's departure seems to have been managed from Moscow. On 11 August 1947 the Soviet embassy in Washington DC wrote to the State department requesting that US visas be issued to the Zaitsevs and 'indicating their desire to proceed to the Soviet Union via the United States as soon as the visas were granted'. The US embassy in Canberra was authorised to issue the visas 'as requested' on 14 August.[143] The Zaitsevs left Australia for the UK aboard the SS *Rhexenor* on 4 September;[144] they arrived in the UK on 26 October and departed for Leningrad on 8 November.[145]

In 1947 Zaitsev is reported to have moved to the GRU Residency in Washington, the GRU's most important overseas post, with the cover of press attaché at the embassy.[146] This cannot be confirmed. Although it would have been a logical posting for an officer with his capabilities, experience and achievements, virtually nothing is known about Zaitsev's career and movements after he left the UK for Leningrad in November 1947. Vladimir Petrov recalled in 1954 that he had met Zaitsev in the KI at Rostokino between his return from Australia in November 1947 and mid 1948.[147] In 1949, during a US Army G2 investigation into the Sorge case, both the Military Intelligence section at GHQ Far East Command in Tokyo and the FBI in Washington reported that they knew nothing about Zaitsev other than what the Japanese police and counter-intelligence agencies had found out in December 1941,[148] and the fact that he had passed through San Francisco in January 1943.[149] In May 1951, the FBI reported on Zaitsev's posting to Australia (including his arrival and departure particulars).[150] On 31 July, the bureau's Washington field office reported that a 'stop' had been placed with the department of State 'in order to determine when the subject enters the United States as a Soviet diplomat',[151] but his whereabouts were still unknown in December 1951,[152] and no further information has come to light.

The Australian security intelligence authorities remained unaware that Zaitsev was a GRU officer until at least five years after he left Australia. Charles Spry, then the director-general of ASIO, has said he only learned that Zaitsev was 'important' when he read General Willoughby's book on the Sorge spy case in 1952.[153] In 1954, after his defection, Vladimir Petrov identified Zaitsev to ASIO as 'a GRU cadre-worker'.[154] Colyn Cohen of the Security Service was later to say to Colin Moodie that 'if they had known his full background they would not have let him into the country' in 1943.[155]

Zaitsev's specific espionage activities during his five years in Australia remain matters of speculation. He was presumably too important an officer for the GRU to leave unproductive for such a long time. Two possibilities have been canvassed. One is that he was engaged in setting up some 'illegal' network that was to remain quiescent until the next war but which, for whatever reason, was never activated. It was Vladimir Petrov's firm belief, in 1954, that his GRU 'neighbours' had established an 'illegal apparatus' in Australia.[156] The second possibility is that Zaitsev was running a very high-level agent somewhere in the Australian government.

COMMUNICATIONS BETWEEN THE KGB RESIDENT AND MOSCOW CENTRE

Communications between the Residency in Canberra and Moscow Centre went via two routes—cable and diplomatic bag. During the period when Zaitsev was GRU Resident (1943–47) he had a radio which he used mainly to receive 'military information' from Moscow.[157] But the most secure means of communication with Moscow, to be used as much as possible for the transmission of secret material, was diplomatic bags carried by Soviet diplomatic couriers. Secret messages from Canberra were first encoded and typed, then photographed on 35mm negatives. Cover-names were used to identify the source of the material, and the most important words in the messages were encoded; attachments or 'insertions' containing the codes and (if necessary) the identities and personal details of the cover-names were also photographed on 35mm negatives, sealed in a separate envelope, and sent by the same bag. The original typed messages were to be destroyed by the Resident as soon as Moscow Centre acknowledged receipt of the negatives. Messages from Moscow were kept by the Resident for about a year, after which they were to be destroyed and a certificate of destruction rendered to Moscow.[158]

The limiting factor in the use of the diplomatic bag was the frequency of visits to Canberra by the couriers. The annual plan provided for six courier visits a year, the last of which was generally scheduled for about fifteen or twenty days before the end of the year.[159] In practice, however, the intervals between visits were somewhat irregular, depending on the work commitments of other diplomatic posts en route. Some intervals were longer than three months. In these circumstances, urgent and important material had to be sent by enciphered cable.

From 1943 to 1948 an average of about 290 cables a year were sent from Moscow Centre to the Canberra Residency, and about 530 a year from the Residency to Moscow, or about 70 a month both ways. The cables to Moscow were sent through the Canberra GPO via Overseas Telecommunications at the Sydney GPO.[160] Although they looked like normal cipher-cables between embassy and Foreign Office, they were encrypted in a KGB cipher. The encryption system was later described by the Royal Commission on Espionage:

> The enciphered cables consisted of a series of groups of five digits. The Embassy cipher clerk in Canberra or the Foreign Office clerk in Moscow, as the case might be, was able to decipher only the last group of digits appearing in the cable and from those would learn that the cable was intended for the Resident or the Moscow Centre, and would hand over the cable accordingly. The remainder of the enciphered cable could be deciphered only by a person with access to the M.V.D. cipher book and knowledge of the ciphering technique.
> The 'One Time Pad' cipher system was employed, which means that a particular page of the cipher book was used for one communication only and after use was destroyed so that the breaking of the cipher used in one communication would not enable any other communication to be read.[161]

All cables from Moscow to the embassy in Canberra were addressed to 'SOVPOSOL Canberra', and all cables to Moscow from the embassy were addressed to 'Moscow MININDEL'.[162] The chief cipher clerk in the embassy, or a Foreign ministry cipher clerk in Moscow, would decipher the last group of five numbers by stripping the enciphered group of additives from a key list to indicate the addressee. If the last group deciphered to 11111, it was a straight Foreign ministry/embassy cable; if it was 22222, it was for the GRU; and if it was 66666, it was for the KGB, in which case it was passed to the KGB cipher clerk for decryption.[163] The codebooks were changed at irregular intervals, sometimes after intelligence reports that they or associated material had been compromised. During the period covered by this story, the codebooks were changed in May 1945,[164] in 1948,[165] in 1950, and on 1 September 1953.[166]

Given the use of couriers and diplomatic bags, cover-names, codebooks and 'one-time pads' for cable traffic, together with the procedures for safe handling of cipher materials and for the destruction of the enciphered texts and decipherment drafts, it might have been reasonable to expect that communications between Moscow Centre and the Residency in Canberra were quite secure. However, this cable traffic had been the subject of an intense decryption effort by the US and Britain, and by 1947 some of it was being read.

9

'the CIS has no standing'

POSTWAR SECURITY AND INTELLIGENCE IN AUSTRALIA

THE SECOND HALF OF THE 1940s was a period of extraordinary political, economic and social change, both internationally and in Australia. Internationally, the great wartime coalition between Britain, the United States and the Soviet Union began to fracture as soon as victory in Europe became assured. By 1948, the Cold War had begun. The Soviet Union conducted its first nuclear test explosion in September 1949 (some one or two years earlier than would have been possible without the assistance of the 'atomic spies' in the US and the UK),[1] and a nuclear arms race was looming.

In Australia, the respected and dedicated wartime prime minister, John Curtin, had died in office in July 1945. He was soon succeeded by Joseph Benedict (Ben) Chifley, a former locomotive driver from Bathurst in NSW, who had been treasurer and minister for Post-War Reconstruction in the last Curtin government. He served as prime minister until Labor's defeat by Robert Menzies' conservative Liberal–Country Party coalition in December 1949.[2] The Labor government was determined to implement its policies of political, economic and social reform that had been put on hold during the war, but it was now also faced with the matters of demobilisation and reconstruction.

It was a period of great intellectual ferment, with vigorous competition among a variety of brave new ideas fought out in the media, on university campuses and in the streets, as well as through elections. On the other hand, the governmental machinery for processing ideas into coherent policies and for managing the

J.B. (Ben) Chifley, prime minister, 1945–49. In February 1948 he was informed that the Soviet Union was conducting espionage in Australia, and by September had agreed to set up a security organisation 'similar to MI5'. (NLA)

reconstruction was quite inadequate. New bureaucratic structures and processes had to be organised, and staff recruited for the rapidly expanding public service in Canberra. This activity left little room for concern about postwar security requirements or for any sustained follow-up of the security problems uncovered during the war.

By instinct and background, Chifley was fundamentally interested in domestic economic and social welfare issues, including demobilisation, full employment, soldier land-settlement, public works programs, housing, bank nationalisation, and the provision of social services. However, as treasurer and minister for Post-War Reconstruction from 1942 to 1945, a member of the War Cabinet and (occasionally) the Advisory War Council, and perhaps Curtin's closest personal adviser on crucial war decisions, he had become increasingly involved in external political, economic and strategic matters; and as prime minister during the difficult transition from war to peace and then Cold War, he took them on as his 'inescapable responsibility'.[3] He insisted that Australia's most important external interest was the relationship with Britain, and that, as prime minister, he was the principal Australian link with the British Crown and government. Although he disliked overseas travel and loathed official pomp and ceremony, he visited London in 1946, July 1948, and April–May 1949.[4]

While he was a firm and decisive leader, Chifley specially valued the assistance of John Dedman and Senator Nicholas McKenna in some particular areas of external affairs. Born in Scotland, Dedman was a retired Indian Army officer and farmer, who had been the wartime minister for War Organisation of Industry. In 1945 he succeeded Chifley as minister for Post-War Reconstruction, and in September 1946 additionally became minister for Defence. Chifley had absolute faith in Dedman's integrity and used him as his principal Cabinet aide on economic, defence and security matters.[5] McKenna, by background a lawyer and accountant, was minister for Health and Social Services; he had served as Chifley's 'unofficial assistant' in 1944–46 and remained his closest personal confidant in the Cabinet.[6] Although Chifley was capable of making his own judgments on security and external affairs, he was not able to ignore his energetic External Affairs minister, Evatt.

Evatt and the Department of External Affairs

During the last years of the war, Australian security policy had revolved around two centres of policy-making. The first centred on the department of Defence, which was concerned not just with the prosecution of the war but with the maintenance of good relations with Britain and the US. The key figures in the formation and conduct of this policy were the prime minister, Curtin, and the secretary of the Defence department, Sir Frederick Shedden. The second area of policy-making revolved around Evatt and his department. Evatt was concerned with the development of a more independent Australian approach to foreign affairs and the promotion of the United Nations. The two policy-making centres remained in operation after the war. Although the prime minister was no longer also the minister for Defence, he still had the key role in the development of security policy, especially as it concerned relations with Britain and the US. To a large extent, Chifley, advised by Shedden, continued Curtin's wartime policies. However, with the war over, Defence lost some of its importance; at the same time External Affairs underwent a dramatic expansion in overseas posts, numbers of staff and the topics that it considered.

The key figure was Evatt, who by October 1945 was moving into his fifth year as both External Affairs minister and attorney-general. Chifley was content for Evatt to take the lead on most foreign policy matters, including those concerning postwar international cooperation. Evatt gained international prominence at the United Nations Conference on International Organisation at San Francisco in April 1945, where he was seen as 'the hero of the small nations'.[7] He led the Australian delegation to the Paris Peace Conference in 1946; he chaired the British Commonwealth Conference on the Japanese Peace Conference, which led to the appointment of an Australian to the Allied Control Council; he was chairman of the

Dr H.V. (Bert) Evatt, minister for External Affairs and attorney-general, 1941–49. He was responsible for the Security Service but was notoriously lax about security. One of his secretaries passed information to the Soviet spymaster, Wally Clayton. (AWM 10014)

UN's Atomic Energy Commission and its Palestine Commission and he was elected president of the UN General Assembly in New York in September 1948.[8] He was away from Australia for eleven months between July 1948 and June 1949 (during which time Chifley himself acted as minister for External Affairs).[9] Although Evatt's international activities took him mainly to the UK and the US, he was one of the few Australian political leaders who were closely interested in political and economic developments in postwar Asia and their longer-term implications for Australia.[10]

Evatt's right-hand man with respect to foreign policy matters was Dr John Wear Burton, Jnr., who served as his private secretary and departmental liaison officer from 1941 to 1945 and then, after two years working in the department itself, was secretary from March 1947 until December 1949. Burton was born in Melbourne in March 1915, the son of the Reverend John Wear Burton, president-general of the Methodist Church of Australasia, who during the war had opposed any involvement of Methodist missions in northern Australia and Papua New Guinea in military operations (including coastwatching activities) on Christian pacifist grounds.[11] He obtained a PhD at the London School of Economics (LSE) in 1940 and joined the department of External Affairs on a temporary basis on 30 June 1941, just six months before joining Evatt's office. He was only 32 years old when he was appointed departmental secretary in March 1947.[12]

Evatt and Burton had much in common. They were both energetic, personally ambitious, committed to economic and social reform within Australia and to UN principles in foreign affairs, and

Dr John Burton, the secretary of the department of External Affairs, 1947–49. He opposed the establishment of an Australian security intelligence organisation. He thought that 'Secrecy itself was usually to avoid embarassing someone quoted rather than for any security reason'. (Australian Archives, CRS A6119/79, item 942)

both sometimes pursued their goals with evangelical zeal. They believed in the construction of a new world order in which power politics would be replaced by humanitarian principles, and in which the rights of small countries, particularly those later referred to under the rubric of the Third World, would count equally with those of the superpowers.

Burton has recounted that in 1946–47 'the Department of External Affairs was given virtually no instructions by the Minister except to follow the Purposes and Principles of the United Nations'.[13] Over the next three years, however, he believes that these principles lost out to political expediency. By 1948, Australia was no longer prepared to make foreign policy decisions without the concurrence of London and Washington. And by 1949, 'the guiding instruction was "follow the United States"'.[14] Burton believed that 'Communism, or at least many features of it, is better suited to the immediate and urgent needs of under-developed countries than is Capitalism', that 'the spread of Communism in China, Korea and throughout other Asian areas must be regarded as inevitable', that 'there is no reason to believe that there will ever be an attempt to spread Communism by force', and that 'the reasons for conflict between America and communist centres lie in the refusal of the United States to contemplate adjustments within its own economy'.[15]

Neither Evatt nor Burton had much regard for security. Allan Dalziel, Evatt's principal private secretary in Sydney, later said dryly that Evatt 'was never orderly in the handling of papers and documents'.[16] Ric Throssell, who visited Evatt's office in Sydney in mid

August 1945, has described it as a hive of activity, with visitors coming and going without escort and 'armfuls of official papers [dumped] on the girls' desks'.[17] Secret documents, including intelligence bulletins from the department of External Affairs, papers relating to meetings of the War Cabinet and the Advisory War Council, and papers concerning the activities of the Security Service, were generally not given any special protection. For example, copies of the fortnightly Political Intelligence Summary, prepared by the department of External Affairs from 1944 to 1947 and marked Secret and to 'be destroyed by burning . . . after perusal', were kept among Evatt's personal papers.[18] Lieutenant-Commander D. P. (Paul) McGuire, who headed the Special Branch of FELO in Melbourne during the war, once 'found Evatt's office open and vacant while secret naval documents lay on the desk'.[19] Paul Hasluck, who was in charge of the Australian mission to the United Nations in New York in 1946–47, has recounted how 'after any visit to New York', Evatt's hotel rooms had to be 'ransacked' before the housemaids entered and 'we always retrieved a fair-sized bundle of top secret material'.[20]

Evatt was quite contemptuous of some of the activities of the Security Service. In December 1941, for example, he confirmed to Katharine Susannah Prichard that she was under security surveillance and added that he had told 'the security lads' he did not want information about her.[21] He also freely discussed sensitive security matters with his staff. Some of these individuals were unreliable, and the subjects of the discussions were sometimes made known to the Soviet embassy in Canberra and thence Moscow Centre. In May 1953, for example, Rupert Lockwood (cover-named VORON) typed a 37-page report in the Soviet embassy which was duly forwarded to Moscow Centre and which contained the information that 'In the Security dossier of Allan Dalziel, one of Dr. Evatt's Secretaries, is a photograph of Dalziel coming out of the block of flats in which the Tass office is situated in Sydney'; Lockwood's source for this tidbit was Fergan O'Sullivan (ZEMLIAK), who had just started work as Evatt's press secretary.[22] Dalziel had been photographed by ASIO when leaving Nosov's apartment in December 1949,[23] but it would still have been useful for the KGB in 1953 to have had confirmation of ASIO's interest in Nosov and his contacts two and a half years earlier.

Burton had his own peculiar views about intelligence and security matters. After he became secretary in March 1947, he refused to join the Joint Intelligence Committee (JIC) because he objected to the oath of secrecy required. He reported his attitude to prime minister Chifley and appointed one of his senior officers, Colin Moodie, to represent the department on the JIC.[24] Burton's attitude is hard to fathom because in the month when he took over as secretary he was advised that Australian embassy staff in Moscow had found concealed microphones obviously placed in the embassy by a Soviet intelligence agency.[25] Although the Australian chargé d'affaires protested to the Soviet authorities, Evatt did not want it made public. As Sir Alan Watt, the previous departmental secretary, who was taking over as minister in Moscow, recalled, 'I was personally instructed by the Minister not to mention the matter to anyone.'[26]

In 1948–49 Burton opposed the establishment of an Australian security intelligence organisation because he believed that 'overall' such bodies 'do more harm than good'; they were internally 'very divisive', and could not be trusted to be politically neutral.[27] He did not understand the system of security classification for official documents, and thought that classifications 'reflected not their secrecy so much as their degree of importance', which was usually a short-term political consideration.[28] He believed that, in the case of the department of External Affairs, 'most things are regarded secret whereas in fact there is almost nothing' that was really secret anyway. As he put it: 'Secrecy itself was usually to avoid embarrassing someone quoted rather than for any security reason.'[29]

In the late 1940s, Burton was an active proponent of 'open diplomacy', in which 'our struggle was to get people [i.e. foreign diplomats] to know what was in the files rather than keep it away from them'.[30] It was particularly important for the Soviets to understand the government's dedication to the construction of a new postwar international order. Burton himself had instructed the counsellor at the Soviet embassy to come to his office 'once a week so that I could tell him what our policy was and the policy of some other countries'.[31] He thought that it was the duty of Jim Hill and other officers in his department 'to give certain information to overseas representatives', including the Soviets.[32]

Postwar Strategic Planning

Australian postwar strategic planning involved the development of planning structures in both the departments of External Affairs and Defence, and of some liaison or coordination mechanism between them. It was never a close working relationship. Defence was located in Melbourne, and External Affairs in Canberra. Shedden, who had been involved with intra-Commonwealth defence planning since the early 1930s and who had been secretary of the department of Defence since 1937, was not comfortable with Evatt or Burton.

*Sir Frederick Shedden, secretary of the department of Defence, 1937–56. He was the key figure in establishing the various intelligence organisations in the postwar period. He was the principal adviser on strategic and defence issues to successive prime ministers, Menzies, Curtin, Chifley and Menzies again. (*The Age*, reproduced by permission)*

Some members of External Affairs regarded Defence as uncritically pro-British and pro-American and incapable of distinguishing Australia's interests from those of the UK or the US,[33] while many in Defence were aghast at Burton's views about communism in Asia, Australia's traditional allies, and intelligence and security matters.

In April 1942, while Defence was engrossed in the war effort, a Post-War Reconstruction Section was established in the department of External Affairs. Headed by Paul Hasluck, and initially consisting of only one other officer and a graduate assistant, the section was 'to guide and direct' the department's postwar reconstruction planning activities and to establish procedures for interdepartmental consultation on postwar matters involving External Affairs.[34] It was enlarged and renamed the Post-Hostilities Division in July 1944. By September 1945 it was, with seven officers, the largest division in the department. To meet the urgent need for planning on armistice arrangements, reparations, war crimes and postwar international organisations, Ian Milner and Jim Hill were temporarily appointed to the division from outside the department, while some of the first recruits from the diplomatic cadet scheme inaugurated in 1943—among them Ric Throssell—also went into the division. It was renamed the United Nations Division in early 1946, after several aspects of immediate post-hostilities planning had been addressed, but remained 'one of the most important Divisions of the Department'.[35] The division received copies of all policy-related material produced within the department, copies of papers on postwar planning matters produced by other departments (such as Post-War Reconstruction and Defence) and, most importantly, an enormous volume of papers from London as well as much information from Washington.[36]

At the end of 1944, the Defence Committee proposed to the minister for Defence that a Defence Post-Hostilities Planning (PHP) Committee be established to prepare 'appreciations and plans (other than of a strategical nature) concerning armistice terms and occupation of enemy territories, and to conduct post-war Forces planning'.[37] Representatives of Defence, the armed services and External Affairs met in Canberra on 18 and 19 January to discuss the proposed committee and its relationship to the Post-Hostilities Division, as well as collaboration with New Zealand on postwar defence planning matters.[38] Later in February, the minister for Defence agreed that a representative of External Affairs should serve on the committee. The following month it was agreed that 'there should be a free exchange of all PHP papers between the Defence PHP Committee and the PHP Division of the Department of External Affairs'. Special conditions applied to 'the control and distribution' of documents received from the UK, and in particular the Post-Hostilities Planning Staff of the British Chiefs of Staff Committee, for which Sir Frederick Shedden had accepted personal responsibility.[39]

The formation of the Defence PHP Committee was just one of a range of initiatives, largely driven by Shedden, to restructure the Defence organisation to meet the new challenges of the postwar world. Many of these related to security and intelligence, and indeed Australia's counter-espionage efforts in the period following the end of the Second World War were to be directly affected by the changes to governmental structure and to the security and intelligence organisation. The key organisation was the Security Service, and its fate in this period demonstrates why counter-espionage languished.

The postwar Security Service

It will be recalled that by January 1945 the Security Service was resisting keen pressure to give up its Army personnel. Indeed, at this time, only four months before the end of the war in Europe, and eight months before the Japanese agreed to cease hostilities, the director-general of security, Brigadier Simpson, had made a strong case for maintaining the strength of the Security Service. Situations bringing new security problems in the coming year included the basing of a British fleet in Australia, the likelihood of operations from Australia against Timor and the Netherlands East Indies, the release into the community of large numbers of internees, the introduction of foreign nationals from territories recaptured from the Japanese, and the need to extend Security Service activities to the Australian territories as civil administration was introduced. These arguments for maintaining the strength of the Security Service had been supported by Evatt.[40]

In June 1945 Simpson prepared a thirteen-page report on the Australian Communist Party in which he warned of the dangers it posed to democracy in Australia. This report was considered by the Advisory War Council on 20 June and the acting attorney-general stated that as director-general, Simpson had been instructed to keep careful watch on the activities of the party.[41] By now it was clear that once the war ended the Army personnel would be withdrawn from the Security Service and the need for an organisation of this kind would have to be reconsidered. As a result, in June 1945 J. T. Pinner, a public service inspector, was appointed to chair a committee to investigate and report on the structure, functions, and staffing of both the Security Service and the CIB. Pinner was assisted by A. A. Fitzgerald for both reviews, and by Simpson and Longfield Lloyd for the reviews of the Security Service and CIB respectively.

In considering the Security Service, Simpson made available a report prepared in September 1944 by Lieutenant-Colonel E. A. Airy, a British officer and member of MI5 based at Colombo.[42] Airy had recommended a small postwar security organisation on MI5 lines operating jointly under External Affairs and Defence. Simpson had not agreed with the report and had not shown it to the attorney-general. The Pinner committee also considered a report prepared by Simpson for the attorney-general in April 1945.

The month after the war ended, Pinner reported to the government, recommending that the Security Service and the CIB be merged. The experience of war had

> shown the necessity for some organisation to advise the Government on activities within the country which are or are likely to be of a subversive nature, whether those activities are local in nature or originating from foreign sources. Documents captured from enemy-held territory have confirmed the suspicions that there were in peacetime a not inconsiderable body of enemy espionage agents, German, Japanese and Italian, in this country.[43]

One recommendation was that the radio security section should be returned to the Army:

> The major part of the work of the radio security section now consists of special commitments for Army rather than the search for illicit wirelesses and the Committee is therefore of opinion that any work of this nature which is still necessary might be carried out by the Department of the Army.[44]

On 18 September Simpson explained in a letter to his deputy that a 'small organisation' would be formed 'to deal with subversive associations and counter espionage'. There would be a consolidated record system in Canberra, a 'temporary record system to discriminate what should be retained in the Canberra Central Records', a staff for aliens control, and 'a small investigating staff of, say, four Police'.[45]

It seems that the security services were to be cut back for at least two reasons. First, a massive effort was being made to return as many servicemen as possible to civilian life, and it would have appeared inequitable to demobilise the fighting troops but not those in less active areas. Second, there was a belief in some quarters, and particularly by Evatt, that the security services posed some threat to civil liberties. Once the war was over there would be little need for such services. Yet if the Pinner review's recommendations were followed fully, an identifiable and effective security organisation might have survived. Some of the recommendations, such as the need to retain some of the key staff of the Security Service, were not accepted by the government.

On 24 October Simpson resigned to take up an appointment as a justice of the Supreme Court of the Australian Capital Territory, and the following day CIB director Longfield Lloyd also became director-general of security. It thus fell to Longfield Lloyd to preside over the merger of the two organisations. At that time the Security Service had a strength of 107 civilians and 143 military personnel, but it was planned to reduce the organisation to 86 civilians and 39 military personnel by 7 November.[46]

Some idea of the frustration Longfield Lloyd faced can be gauged from a letter written by the military liaison officer, Lieutenant-Colonel Cohen, on 1 November 1945, in which he described Lloyd as being 'hampered by lack of directions from the Secretary of the Attorney-General's Department'.[47] The following month the Security Service was formally disbanded and its functions were taken over by a small section within the CIB. Later, in early 1947, the organisation was renamed the Commonwealth Investigation Service (CIS).

Some of the senior staff of the Security Service transferred to the CIB. For example, Lieutenant-Colonel Samuel Jackson, who had headed the Security Service in NSW, became assistant director (security) and therefore responsible for the security section within the CIB.[48] Another senior officer to remain with the organisation was Roland S. Browne, the head of the Security Service in Victoria, who moved to Canberra as Lloyd's deputy. Simpson and the Pinner review had recommended the appointment of Robert Wake to head the Security Section, but this was not approved and he continued as head of security in Brisbane. There, as a classified history of the Security Services commented: 'Wake continued to run his own agents (not all of whom were fictional).'[49] Generally, there was a serious loss of expertise and continuity. One senior officer to join the CIB was Brigadier 'Black Jack' (later Sir Frederick) Galleghan, who had served with the Customs department in Newcastle and with the CIB in Sydney before the war and, after distinguished service in Malaya, had been a prisoner of war in Changi. He became a deputy director responsible for NSW in 1946 and 1947.[50]

On the face of it, with long service in Military Intelligence, the CIB and the Security Service, Longfield Lloyd had impressive qualifications to head a security organisation, but he faced great difficulties. He lacked influence with Evatt, and his organisation was given few funds. Brigadier Sir Charles Spry, who as the DMI worked with 'Linger Longer' Lloyd, found him too much of a gentleman for tough security work: 'I didn't think he really knew what went on—he was bullied around.' This view was supported by Brigadier Sir Frederick Chilton, the senior Defence official responsible for intelligence and security, who found Lloyd to be 'ineffectual—noone could take him seriously'. On one occasion Spry witnessed Lloyd being roundly abused by Evatt. Later Spry went to his office to commiserate; 'The trouble is, Charles,' said Lloyd, who was resting his head in his hands, 'the CIS has no standing.'[51]

The end of the war brought the closure or reduction of other security organisations. Postal and Telegraph Censorship ceased to operate, and on 28 September 1945 the secretary of the department of the Army requested that 'all Commonwealth Government Departments be asked to destroy as "secret waste" all reports on, and extracts from, communications scrutinised by the Postal and Telegraph Censorship held by them'.[52] The 1st Australian Discrimination Unit, based in Canberra with the role of examining, on behalf of the Security Service, any suspicious radio messages emanating from within Australia, was disbanded in October 1945.[53] Thus by 1946 much of the wartime security intelligence structure had been dismantled or was in disarray.

THE NEW SECURITY AND INTELLIGENCE STRUCTURE

Just as security intelligence was reorganised after the war, the other intelligence organisations also underwent some major changes, including the formation of several agencies to cover matters which during the war had been dealt with by Allied organisations. For example, Australian and US Army and Air Force signals intelligence

Brigadier Bertrand Combes, director of Military Intelligence, at Victoria Barracks in December 1945. He had long experience in security and intelligence appointments, and prepared the plans for the postwar intelligence organisations. (AWM 120547)

had been controlled by the Central Bureau, whose enormous demands meant that Australia had little scope nor need to develop its own separate signals interception organisation. It is true that the Australian Army had a small diplomatic Sigint organisation in Melbourne that was separate from the Central Bureau, and US and RAN signals intelligence—operating through the US Navy Fleet Radio Unit (FRUMEL) in Melbourne—was also separate from the Central Bureau, but Australia's main effort was entwined with that of the Americans. Another Allied organisation was the Allied Intelligence Bureau, in which the Americans played a substantial role until the last year of the war. The Combined Operational Intelligence Centre, established earlier in the war to coordinate the information gained from the intelligence agencies of the three Australian services, had less American involvement, but in due course some of its functions were taken over by MacArthur's intelligence staff.

Well before the end of the war, Shedden, the Defence department secretary, had taken action to establish postwar intelligence organisations to meet Australian defence requirements. As early as August 1944 he had advised the prime minister to ask the Defence Committee to recommend improvements to joint planning and joint intelligence. In October 1944, after Brigadier Rogers returned from London, an interim Joint Intelligence Committee (JIC) was set up consisting of the directors of intelligence of the three services and charged with considering a postwar joint intelligence organisation. This task was given additional impetus when the British sent a paper to the department of Defence suggesting a Far East Joint Intelligence Bureau in Australia as part of a plan to coordinate intelligence on a Commonwealth-wide basis. The task of developing the organisation in detail was given to Brigadier Bertrand Combes, who was relieved as commandant of the Royal Military College, Duntroon, in July 1945 and seconded to Defence for 'special duties'. Combes had been a key figure in Military Intelligence's involvement in security, particularly the surveillance of Nazi sympathisers and Australian communists before the war; indeed, Major-General Basil Finlay, a later DMI, described him as 'the chief communist chaser'.[54]

Soon after the outbreak of war, Combes was promoted to colonel as Director of Military Operations and Intelligence, and was involved in many of the discussions about the formation of the Security Service. In November 1940, with the rank of brigadier, he became assistant chief of the general staff, and from October 1941 to January 1942 was brigadier general staff at the headquarters of Home Forces. Although he did not serve overseas during the war, Combes had the most extensive background in intelligence and security of any regular officer of his rank.

Combes began by inspecting the various intelligence agencies formed during the war, and on 1 November 1945 he submitted his report, recommending the formation of a joint intelligence organisation and the establishment of links with British intelligence organisations.[55] Combes considered that national intelligence could be divided into six categories: political intelligence, geographic and topographical intelligence, signal intelligence, translation and interrogation, security intelligence, and special intelligence. The latter category referred to clandestine operations behind enemy lines such as had been carried out by the AIB during the war. These forms of intelligence would be best handled on a joint basis, he said. With respect to signals intelligence:

> The modest beginning out of which grew the Central Bureau was made here in 1938. Events during the war proved how wise it had been to lay this foundation in Australia, although the action evoked considerable opposition at the time. The lessons of the war and the probable future influence of atomic and other long range weapons make it more than ever dangerous to concentrate signal intelligence activity in any one part of the Empire. Moreover, technical reasons require a certain degree of dispersal. In fact, Signal Intelligence is an outstanding example of intelligence which should and must be operated on an Empire-wide basis. Australia must take its place in the necessary organisation.[56]

Combes proposed the formation of a Joint Intelligence Committee answering to the Chiefs of Staff Committee and the Defence Committee. It would be supported by a permanent staff consisting of an executive officer and six sections; these would deal with administration, special intelligence, trade and international affairs, geographic information, security and political intelligence. The special intelligence section would cover both signals intelligence and 'special' intelligence.

In proposing a security section, Combes resurrected the notion of a Defence Security Organisation first suggested by the Defence Committee in 1938 and also by the interdepartmental committee he had chaired in 1940. This organisation would cooperate with the security section in the CIB. Surveying the history of proposals for such an organisation to have proper legal power, Combes said:

> Effective peacetime law is thus virtually non-existent. It is not only a serious defect from the defence security point of view, but amounts to a breach of faith with the United Kingdom authorities. Pre-war those authorities refused on occasions to supply secret matter to Australia because of lack of adequate means of protection. They would be quite justified in refusing to do so again.[57]

An interim JIC was already in existence; it consisted of the directors of Intelligence of the three services and a representative from the department of External Affairs. One of the early External Affairs representatives was J. C. R. Proud, who, as a Royal Australian Navy Volunteer Reserve commander, had headed the Far East Liaison Office, the propaganda section within the AIB, during the war. A later representative was J. C. Kevin, who, as an assistant secretary in the department of the Army, had been instrumental in setting up the Commonwealth Security Service in March 1942. The permanent sections proposed by Combes would ultimately require government approval.

During the early months of 1946, Shedden and the chiefs of staff refined their requirements and proposed forming a joint security and intelligence organisation controlled by the JIC, which would report to the Chiefs of Staff Committee or Defence Committee as appropriate,[58] prepare reports and appreciations, and liaise, as necessary, with the Joint Planning Committee and the Defence Scientific Advisory Body.

The joint intelligence organisation itself would consist of three elements. The first, the Joint Intelligence Bureau (JIB), would collate and distribute factual intelligence on economic and political matters, topography and static defences in countries within Australia's region.

The second element was concerned with special intelligence, which was defined as 'the use of any means of intercepting expressed thought' and could include clandestine operations in overseas countries as well as signals intelligence. Both Combes and the DMI in 1946, Colonel Spry, advocated the formation of a secret service for clandestine operations, but Shedden realised that the government would oppose this, and the proposal was put aside.⁵⁹ The chiefs of staff argued that signals intelligence was 'capable of supplying in peace, as in war, information of outstanding importance of a political, economic and military nature', and they recommended the formation of a Signals Intelligence Centre.⁶⁰

The third element was a defence security organisation. The chiefs explained that the need 'for proper security arrangements' had been shown by the defection of a Soviet agent, Igor Gouzenko, in Canada, and other incidents in Britain. They pointed out the need to protect the proposed signals intelligence organisation and the likelihood that Australia might be asked 'to undertake activities connected with most secret equipment and weapons of war. Without an adequate security organisation, it would be unwise to undertake any of these secret commitments and it would be unreasonable to expect the United Kingdom to be satisfied with Australia's undertakings.' These proposals were endorsed by the Defence Committee in April 1946.

When the proposals went before the government, Evatt, as attorney-general, strongly opposed the formation of a defence security organisation on the grounds that a security service in peacetime should be under civilian control and linked with the CIB.⁶¹ Indeed, he told Parliament in March 1946 that when the wartime security service had been 'wound up' there was 'no intention to have a permanent peacetime Security Service such as was necessary in wartime'.⁶²

Support for the formation of joint intelligence organisations came from the British, and when Prime Minister Chifley visited London for a prime ministers' conference in May 1946 the British authorities discussed with him the need to coordinate Commonwealth intelligence. In particular Chifley had discussions with Sir Edward Travis, the director-general of the British Government Communications Headquarters (GCHQ)—the successor of the British wartime signals intelligence organisation (GCCS).⁶³

Soon after he returned, Chifley reported his discussions to the Cabinet, and on 19 July the acting minister for Defence, Forde, recommended to Cabinet that a JIC, a JIB and a Signals Intelligence Centre be established. This proposal was approved but the proposal to set up a defence security organisation was not.⁶⁴ Most of the Cabinet decisions about signals intelligence were made by a subcommittee consisting of Chifley and the minister for Defence—initially Forde and then John Dedman. Evatt was excluded, although, as Shedden put it, he was consulted 'on certain aspects of principle'.⁶⁵ According to one account, the Cabinet decision was 'held up . . . until Dr Evatt was overseas and would have no access to the papers'.⁶⁶ Cabinet also approved the appointment of a Controller of Joint Intelligence (CJI), at assistant secretary level, to control the

Brigadier Frederick Chilton in July 1944 when commanding the 18th Infantry Brigade. In 1946 he was appointed controller of Joint Intelligence. In 1948 he determined that documents leaked to the Soviet Union had been in possession of an official of External Affairs, Ian Milner, and in February 1949 he was (together with Chifley and Shedden) told about the Venona program. He was later secretary of the Repatriation Department. (AWM 67879)

JIB and the Signals Intelligence Centre on behalf of the JIC.[67] The first task, therefore, was to appoint the CJI and the directors of the JIB and the Signals Intelligence Centre. Since the latter title gave away too much about the purpose of the organisation, early in 1947 it was changed to Defence Signals Branch (DSB).

On 28 October 1946 Brigadier Frederick Chilton assumed duties as CJI. Born in 1905, he was a solicitor and militia officer with a distinguished record during the war. He had commanded the 2/2nd Battalion in Libya and Greece in 1941, had been the principal staff officer of Milne Force during the fighting at Milne Bay in 1942, had commanded the 18th Brigade in the Ramu Valley and at Shaggy Ridge in 1943–44, and had landed with his brigade at Balikpapan in 1945. He had then commanded the force that re-established Allied control over Macassar following the Japanese surrender. He lacked direct intelligence experience, but had been an outstanding commander and staff officer, and with his legal training was a clear and logical thinker. He was CJI for less than two years, before becoming second assistant secretary, and later deputy secretary, in the department of Defence. From 1946 until 1958, when he became secretary of the Repatriation department, he was the senior official responsible for oversight of Defence intelligence—including Sigint—as well as for liaison with British and US defence intelligence agencies, including the NSA and GCHQ.

The position of director of the JIB went to Lieutenant-Colonel Allan Fleming, a journalist with the Melbourne *Sun*, who took up his appointment on 5 May 1947. Born in 1912, he had joined the army as a private, was commissioned in late 1939, and served in North Africa and Greece. He was wounded twice and captured twice, each time managing to escape. He had various intelligence appointments and ended the war as the air liaison officer at Advanced Land Headquarters. When Chilton became second assistant secretary in 1948, Fleming succeeded him as CJI, later becoming an assistant secretary, then controller joint service organisations, and national librarian.

The formation of the JIB matched that of a similar organisation in Britain, the JIB (London) headed by Major-General Sir Kenneth Strong, who had been General Eisenhower's head of intelligence in the campaign in north-western Europe. Strong was an advocate of Commonwealth intelligence cooperation and in January 1947 visited Australia for discussions with the Australian JIC and New Zealand representatives. The JIBs established in Melbourne, Wellington and Ottawa were known as JIB (M), JIB (W) and JIB (O) respectively.[68] The JIB (M) was to have a staff of about 120 personnel, but by January 1948 its strength was only 27.[69]

THE POSTWAR SIGINT ORGANISATION

The formation of the DSB was of fundamental importance for Australian defence and security in the postwar period, and the need to develop and maintain an Australian Sigint capability had been recognised for some time. For example, when in September 1944 Brigadier Rogers and Lieutenant-Colonel Sandford had visited England to discuss a number of matters with the British DMI and the head of the Secret Service, one item on the agenda was 'Post war plans and Australia's intelligence responsibilities in the islands of the Pacific and in the islands North of Australia'.[70] By the time the advance headquarters of the Central Bureau moved to Manila in May 1945, the bureau had a total strength of over 4000 staff, three-quarters of them Australians. Initially Blamey was opposed to Australian intercept staff following the Americans northwards, as he felt that the Australian Army would lose its intercept capability; however, after an appeal from the Americans he changed his mind.

Nevertheless, Rogers had earlier commented that 'it was high time that the Americans provided their own sections, both signals and intelligence personnel, to care for their own requirements'.[71]

In March 1945 the head of Britain's GCHQ, Sir Edward Travis, his assistant, Harry (later Sir Francis) Hinsley, the director of Naval Intelligence, Rear-Admiral E. G. N. Rushbrooke, and Commander Clive Loehnis of the Admiralty Operational Intelligence Centre (later director-general of GCHQ from 1960 to 1964), left London on a world tour as the first step towards establishing a postwar Sigint alliance. In April they visited the Diplomatic Section in Melbourne and the Central Bureau's Brisbane staff. They moved on to the USA where they helped lay the foundation of the UKUSA agreement with the Americans.[72]

At the end of the war the Central Bureau was disbanded, but the Australian staff continued their work in a 'rump' organisation. This is made clear in a letter written by Sandford in Brisbane to Berryman on 16 November 1945: 'The affairs of this unit are being wound up very satisfactorily, and our Magnum Opus, a technical history of all our work, is almost complete. I am going to Melbourne in the near future to assist in the formation of the post-war organisation.'[73]

Sergeant Steve Mason was at Kalinga, in Queensland, with the Australian Special Wireless Group when news came in December 1945 that the station there was to close. At the same time the AWAS women at the 52nd Special Wireless Section at Mornington were being discharged, so he had the task of bringing 30 operators from Kalinga to Mornington. He recalls that these 'operators unenthusiastically took over the work that the AWAS had been doing. Everything was low key, Japanese traffic was reduced and no emphasis was placed on chasing it or any other traffic.'[74] However, soon they were tasked to intercept Russian traffic: 'enthusiasm for the work was at a low ebb, but we took mostly Russian high speed traffic. On occasions, with the use of incentives, full logs were produced—I can remember one night's work which yielded more than 1000 messages.'[75] Mornington may have begun intercepting Russian traffic before the end of 1944, but with the end of the war this became its main task.

Most of the Russian traffic intercepted during the war was in plain language. One member of the section recalled that the messages 'were, I think Russian Post Office messages between individuals or else office messages, mainly from economic units in the Far East referring decisions to Moscow for approval or statistics—monumentally banal'.[76] But there is some evidence that on at least one occasion before the end of the war the Australian Special Wireless Group intercepted Soviet diplomatic traffic.[77]

The Russian traffic intercepted at Mornington was taken on Edison wax cylinders and transcribed later. It was then carried by dispatch rider to Victoria Barracks, Melbourne, where it was passed to the Diplomatic Section now headed by Lieutenant-Colonel Sandford. According to another former Central Bureau member, Lieutenant Mostyn Williams, Sandford was located in A Block at Victoria Barracks in the same room as that previously occupied by Professor Trendall. When Sandford left in mid 1946 to join the Anglo-Iranian Oil Company, he was not replaced, because the Central Bureau 'rump was in a state of flux awaiting the formation of the peacetime organisation'. Both Williams and his wife, who also worked in the section, believe that the Russian material was not processed in the section during the war but might have been sent to Britain for processing.[78]

The new embryonic organisation was based on the remaining staffs of both the Central Bureau and FRUMEL, but at this stage it was operating without governmental approval. From the time when Commander Eric Nave had returned to Australia from Singapore in early 1940 through to the discussions between Australian and British intelligence officers in the second half of 1944, the arrival of the British SLU at the end of that year, and Travis's visit in April 1945, Britain had been closely involved with plans to develop an Australian Sigint organisation. This cooperation continued after the war, and at the London Sigint conference in February and March 1946 Australia agreed to provide 65 operating teams, totalling 417 personnel, as its contribution to the global intercept task. These would be shared equally between the services. During 1946 Shedden was in frequent communication with Travis about the formation of an Australian Sigint organisation.[79]

In December 1946 Travis and two senior assistants, Loehnis and Hamish Blair-Cunynghame, who had been a distinguished cryptanalyst at Bletchley Park during the war, visited Australia to discuss the formation of the Sigint organisation and its cooperation with its British counterpart.[80] Representatives from New Zealand were also involved in the discussions. The Melbourne centre and its subordinate intercept stations were allocated a geographical area covering the eastern Indian Ocean and parts of East Asia, Southeast Asia and the Southwest Pacific. Australia would have four intercept and D/F stations: HMAS *Harman*, near Canberra, which would be run by the RAN; Cabarlah, near Toowoomba, Queensland, which would by run by the Army; Pearce, near Perth, which would be run by the RAAF; and a combined services station at Coonawarra, near Darwin.[81] Procedures were established for the exchange and dissemination of the Sigint product and for the standardisation of security regulations, including 'indoctrination oaths'.[82]

The key decision was the appointment of the director of DSB. Four Australians were considered: Captain Nave, Lieutenant-Colonel Sandford and Wing Commander Hugh Berry—who had had important positions in the Central Bureau—and Commander J. B. Newman, RAN, who had been closely involved in Naval Sigint throughout the war. Travis was adamant that a British officer be chosen. On the face of it this was an affront to Australian sovereignty and to the officers concerned, who had had long, distinguished and effective service. On the other hand, it had to be admitted that not all the Australians under consideration might have made an effective head of the DSB. The deciding factor, however, was that Britain would share the product of its intercepts only if it had complete confidence in the DSB's director. Years later Allan Fleming expressed some surprise that Australia should have accepted Travis's demands.[83] Sir Charles Spry, who at the time was a member of the JIC, replied that on the contrary, he was very happy to have a British officer. He knew that Australia would then have the best possible access to British intelligence and that, in due course, an Australian would succeed the British officer.[84]

On 1 April 1947 Lieutenant-Commander J. E. (Teddy) Poulden assumed duty as director of DSB. Regarded as 'one of the ablest signal officers of his generation', Poulden was born in 1915, joined the Royal Navy as a cadet, and later accompanied Churchill as his signals officer in his meeting with President Roosevelt in August 1941.[85] He served at the Royal Navy's Sigint station at Anderson (near Colombo) in Ceylon in 1944–45. He had visited Australia in late 1945 to discuss Australian participation in the postwar Commonwealth Sigint organisation.[86] Poulden's role in the 'hunt' for the enemy agents in Australia was marginal compared with that of British officers attached to the Australian security services (which will be discussed in a later chapter), but he was aware of the Venona operation and liaised with Chilton and the DMI, Spry, on relevant matters. Some of Poulden's Australian staff 'slightly resented the fact that GCHQ had given him his own personal ciphers to communicate with' Travis.[87] It was planned that DSB would have between 300 and 400 personnel, but as late as 1950 it still had only about 200.[88]

Poulden was succeeded as director in April 1950 by Ralph N. Thompson, who remained in the post until 1978—making him the longest-serving head of any Australian intelligence agency. Thompson had served with No. 4 Australian Special Wireless Section, the Army's principal Sigint unit, in Greece, Crete, Lebanon, Syria and Egypt in 1941 and 1942, monitoring German tactical communications. He returned to Australia in March 1942 and went to Darwin, where he was involved in setting up Army and RAAF Sigint facilities. He then went south to Mornington 'to turn a racecourse into an intercept station'.[89] From there, in June he returned to Darwin to

Lieutenant-Commander J.E. (Teddy) Poulden, the first director of the postwar Defence Signals Bureau. Regarded as 'one of the ablest signals officers of his generation', Poulden's presence ensured that Australia had access to British Sigint. (Maj-Gen T.F. Cape)

command No. 51 Section, Australian Special Wireless Group, the main Army Sigint operation in Australia during the war.[90] He worked at Central Bureau in Brisbane during the final stages of the war and then transferred to Melbourne with the rump of Central Bureau; he remained commanding officer of the Australian Special Wireless Group until April 1946.[91]

Fleming, the controller of joint intelligence at the time, has left a clear impression of his decision to appoint Thompson:

> Poulden was in the DSB chair when I took over from Fred Chilton. Poulden as I could see had done and was still doing an excellent job in building up and running DSB, imparting to it the relevant aspects of his own varied experience. He also showed a desirable sensitivity to his role in running an Australian organisation, which had a special problem in starting and growing up as a secret body under the very public rules and staffing procedures of the Public Service Board. However, I thought the time had arrived for the organisation to be led by an Australian. Given our wartime history of Sigint participation, we must have somewhere a 'native' well able to run the show. Given the experienced officers who had carried on into peacetime DSB, and those who had returned to peacetime jobs, I conducted a wide enquiry with Poulden's assistance. The name of Ralph Thompson came up as a likely choice. We talked, and I was able to invite him to leave his peacetime job as a senior officer in the Royal Mint (where he had been pre-war), and become in the change-over period, head of DSB Communications Security.[92]

Thompson was assisted in this role by John Rendle, who had come out from GCHQ, when Poulden left, to serve as both the senior British officer and the special assistant to the director of DSB. Rendle had been an important figure in Britain's Sigint successes during the war. In 1940 he had headed a special Sigint unit established in London to provide Prime Minister Churchill and the chief of MI6 with current Sigint on German Luftwaffe operations.[93] Towards the end of the war he had headed the joint Sigint unit which supported Mountbatten's South-East Asia Command headquarters at Peradeniya, near Kandy, in Ceylon,[94] and in August 1945 visited Australia to liaise with Land Headquarters on Sigint matters.[95] He was later, in 1969, acknowledged by the director of GCHQ to be a central stalwart of the UKUSA Sigint cooperation arrangements.[96]

Responsibility for the oversight of the DSB and JIB rested with the JIC. When sensitive Sigint matters were discussed, a separate JIC (S) was formed which excluded the representative from External Affairs. By way of example, a meeting of the JIC (S) held on 9 February 1949 was attended by Captain G. C. Oldham, RAN, director of Naval Intelligence; Colonel Spry, the DMI; Wing Commander D. Colquhoun, director of RAAF Intelligence; Commander J. Bath, director of Naval Communications; Lieutenant-Colonel W. G. Clementson, representing the director of Signals (Army); Wing Commander J. W. Reddrop, director of Telecommunications and Radar (RAAF); A. P. Fleming, CJI; and Commander Poulden, director of the DSB.[97]

THE ROLE OF MILITARY INTELLIGENCE

As members of the JIC, the directors of intelligence of the three services were closely involved in security and intelligence in the postwar period, and the most important of these, with respect to security and counter-espionage, was the DMI. One lesson from the war was that intelligence was too important a function to be left to amateurs. Before the war Military Intelligence had been manned primarily by militia officers, and this trend had continued during the war. By late 1943 Brigadier Rogers had recognised the need to draw regular officers into intelligence work, and in December 1943 he arranged for Lieutenant-Colonel Charles (Basil) Finlay to join his staff.[98] The following year Finlay moved to Melbourne, where he simultaneously held three appointments: staff officer (special operations) at Army Headquarters, commanding officer of Z Special Unit, and chief of staff of the Services Reconnaissance Department, which was responsible for conducting clandestine operations into Japanese-held Borneo and the Netherlands East Indies. By early

Captain Charles Spry, April 1940. He served as a staff officer in Greece and as a colonel was chief operational staff officer of the 7th Division on the Kokoda Trail in 1942. In 1946 he was appointed director of Military Intelligence and became director-general of ASIO in 1950. (AWM 1294)

1944 Finlay was back at Advanced LHQ as general staff officer grade one (intelligence).

By the last year of the war, Military Intelligence was making preparations for the postwar period. Colonel Mander-Jones, the DDMI and chief instructor of the School of Military Intelligence, and Lieutenant-Colonel Sadler, on the ADMI's staff in Melbourne, were busy preparing an intelligence manual to assist postwar officers.[99] At the end of the war Finlay was transferred from Morotai to Melbourne, where he had the task of gathering material for the embryonic JIB that was being set up under Commander A. S. (Donk) Storey, later director of Naval Intelligence and Security.

At the end of the war Rogers was given the task of heading an Australian military mission to South East Asia Command, and when he returned in October he was discharged from the Army. Already many of the militia and wartime-enlisted intelligence officers were being discharged and regular officers were being transferred in. Rogers was succeeded as DMI by Brigadier Combes, but unfortunately he was in poor health and in April 1946 retired from the Army. For a while Combes was employed by the department of Defence as a consultant on security and intelligence matters, in particular advising Shedden on the structure of the joint intelligence organisation.[100]

Finlay, who was at the directorate when Combes took over, believed that he was being groomed to be the next DMI, but the appointment went to Spry. Finlay and Spry had both been born in 1910 and had graduated together from Duntroon in 1931. Both had served in India between the wars and in the Middle East in

1940 and 1941, but in April 1942 Spry had been promoted to the temporary rank of colonel and had been the chief operational staff officer of the 7th Division during the fighting on the Kokoda Trail. He was therefore slightly senior to Finlay, and had won the confidence of the vice chief of the general staff, Lieutenant-General Sydney Rowell, with whom he had served during the war. For his service on the Kokoda Trail, Spry was awarded the DSO. In recommending the award, his commander, Major-General Allen, said that 'Under the stress of extreme physical and mental strain he was untiring in his efforts, never sparing himself towards the successful prosecution of the campaign.'[101] Spry accompanied Rogers on his mission to South East Asia Command. Following Spry's appointment, Finlay was sent to Canada for training and an exchange appointment. On his return he succeeded Spry as DMI and later reached the rank of major-general.

When Spry took over as DMI, the directorate was in a state of transition from war to peace, and eight regular Army lieutenants with operational service had been identified as future intelligence officers. One of these, Lieutenant Alan Stretton, was serving with the 2/9th Battalion in Borneo when he was ordered to report to a Joint Service Intelligence Course at Puckapunyal. At the end of the course he was promoted to captain and joined the DMI staff in Melbourne. When he arrived he was allotted to work in the security section under Major Max Phillips, who had been the security officer at St Lucia under Rogers in the last years of the war. Another key officer in DMI was Major Colin Brown. Both Brown and Phillips were later to be senior officers in ASIO.

By this time the CIB had been given responsibility for security, but it had neither the resources nor the expertise for the job. With the approval of the prime minister, Spry accepted some responsibility for security.[102] The military officers who had served in the Security Service did not trust the CIB to take over their sources—particularly their sources and undercover agents in the Communist Party—and these, with their records, were passed surreptitiously to the DMI. Spry recalled that he was given an allocation of £11 000 for special purposes such as paying agents, while the CIB had practically no money for such tasks.[103]

Some of these agents were controlled by Lieutenant-Colonel Colyn Cohen, who had returned to his law practice in Newcastle. One agent was run by Lieutenant-Colonel John Prentice, a militia officer who had been general staff officer intelligence in Sydney since 1942. Spry later discovered that Prentice's agent was a phoney and had no real access to the Communist Party.[104]

Stretton has described his introduction to this business:

As soon as I took up my appointment, I was thrown into a world of agents and information. At times I felt that if all agents were withdrawn from certain potentially subversive organizations, there would be no members left . . . I was directed to go to Sydney, make contact with an agent and hand over £400 in cash. Standing on a street corner in Sydney dressed in old clothes, I felt the eyes of the world were on me as I made contact and handed over the parcel.[105]

Several years later Shedden referred to the role of Military Intelligence when he told the US Secretary of State that 'considerable work in the protection of documents, investigation of persons and compilation of dossiers had already been done by Military Intelligence and by the Commonwealth Investigation Service'.[106]

Despite these efforts, counter-espionage efforts were limited. According to Spry, when he became DMI the Soviet embassy in Canberra was not being watched.[107] Nor was Spry briefed about the leakages of information to the Japanese in early 1945. Perhaps Combes had learned of the incident when he was working on special duties in the department of Defence in mid 1945, or after he became DMI, but perhaps he had not. Lieutenant-Colonel Little, who served into 1946 before retiring, was aware of the incident, but apparently no-one thought it important enough to brief Spry. A number of conclusions might be drawn from the fact that Spry was not briefed. Early in 1945 the investigation of possible leaks through the Soviet embassy had been taken over by the Security Service, and it appears likely that the Directorate of Military Intelligence had not pursued that part of the investigation. Therefore, by 1946 the directorate had not been involved in the investigation for over a year. It is likely that neither the DMI, the Security Service, nor its successor, the CIS, had achieved any success in this period. The CIS was left with only a small section to concentrate on counter-intelligence. With substantial changes in staff in both the DMI and the CIS, there had been a loss of institutional memory. Furthermore, the end of the war had brought a momentary loss of urgency in counter-espionage and security activities.

An example of this latter tendency was the difficulty Spry faced in trying to have members of the Communist Party removed from the Army. Soon after he took over as DMI he found that a major who had been posted to work on the development of new equipment in the technical section of the Australian Army Staff in London was an active member of the Communist Party. He was quickly withdrawn to Australia.[108] Spry also discovered communists in the top secret registry of the department of Defence in Melbourne. A little later the directors of intelligence of the three services, Chilton, the CJI, and Professor Sir Kenneth Bailey, the solicitor-general, met with Evatt to discuss the removal of communists from the armed forces. Evatt told Spry that if he was concerned he should just go ahead and remove them from the Army. Spry replied: 'I don't think that my Chief of the General Staff would fall for that, Dr Evatt.'[109] With the approval of the prime minister and the chief of the general staff, Spry initiated a careful study of communist activity in Australia and overseas and kept the government informed of significant developments. He became widely known throughout the Army for his lectures to both regular and (after 1948) Citizen Military Force officers on the threat from communism.

Before the war, Military Intelligence had been seen as an area to be avoided by ambitious officers, but by the late 1940s Spry had used his appointment to great effect. His annual confidential report for the year ending June 1949 was written by the vice chief of the general staff, Lieutenant-General Rowell, and read:

> [Spry] is one of the outstanding officers in the Australian Army. He combines a high standard of professional attainment with equally high personal characteristics and with what is almost a burning zeal to lift the status of the Army as a whole and its general efficiency and well being in particular. In his crusade he is outspoken to the point of bluntness [and displays an] inability to suffer fools gladly.[110]

When he was appointed DMI, Spry was 'indoctrinated' into the workings of signals intelligence. This was particularly important because the JIC, of which the DMI was a member, was responsible for the operation of DSB. Spry's first inkling that signals intelligence might be involved in counter-espionage came in 1947 when Poulden, the director of DSB, brought him a list of names to be checked. Some of these names needed to be checked by the CIS, but Spry knew that neither DSB nor other intelligence agencies trusted the CIS. Indeed, Spry found the special branches of the state police forces more likely to provide information to him than to the CIS.[111]

Chilton, the CJI, found much the same. He recalled that the members of the JIC 'were concerned about the state of security in Australia'. They were worried about the effectiveness of the CIS, which was 'quite inept'. There was much talk in the JIC about the lack of security in various government departments, and how it might be improved.[112]

It is difficult to determine how inept the CIB/CIS actually was, as men like Spry and Chilton were clearly biased against it, but it is probably true that Longfield Lloyd and his deputy, Browne, both with over 25 years' service, were not equipped to handle the changing situation in the postwar period. On the other hand they were starved of funds by the government, with Evatt working on the principle that such an approach would ensure that the CIS would never grow too powerful. Following the publication in June 1946 of the report of the Canadian Royal Commission on Espionage, members of the opposition questioned the government in Parliament about the efficiency of Australia's security services and about the communist threat, but the government was loath to take further action. Eventually, in early 1947 the CIB was reorganised to form one body known as the Commonwealth Investigation Service (CIS), with two sections—Investigation and Security. Nonetheless, Military Intelligence continued to play a key role in security matters.

THE US DENIES INTELLIGENCE TO AUSTRALIA

On 14 January 1947, 'out of the blue', the government received official news from the Australian embassy in Washington that the US was considering formal arrangements under which information could be released.[113] Then, on 25 March 1947, Shedden advised the secretary of the Attorney-General's department that the head of the British Long Range Weapons Organisation had raised the question of security because information about the Guided Weapons Project had to be protected. Three days later Rowell, the vice chief of the general staff, wrote to Shedden recommending that the attorney-general's report

> be sought at an early date so that the whole question of proper security could be settled. Rowell made serious allegations about the CIB claiming that it was not merely incompetent and inefficient but even more serious, that it was unsound. He claimed to have evidence of a well organised subversive organisation endangering national security. He informed the Secretary of Defence rather than the CIB because he believed the CIB could not be trusted. Not only had he ascertained alarming ignorance on CIB's part about the activities and plans of the CPA but also that information was being leaked from the CIB—something admitted by CIB officials themselves. Alarmed that in the light of the creation of the Joint Intelligence Committee and the Long Range Weapons Project national security should be left to such a body, he wanted to see an efficient security organisation with adequate security legislation.[114]

Two months later Sir Henry Tizard, the chairman of the British Defence Research Policy Committee, told Brigadier H. S. Nurse, the Australian Ordnance Board representative in London, that the US 'was worried about the possibility of leakage of secret information from Australia above all countries to which their reports and Defence research and development might go (either direct or through the

UK)'.[115] Immediately the Australian services began to detect a reduction in the inflow of information. Lieutenant-Colonel Basil Finlay was filling an exchange position in the Canadian Army headquarters, dealing with operational planning. In this appointment he had access to US plans, but he was soon posted to a training post where such access was not necessary.[116] Spry had three liaison officers in Washington and was asked to withdraw them.[117]

US concerns about Australian security continued to mount, and on 22 June the Australian ambassador in Washington, Norman Makin, was informed that, following a review of policy on the release of classified information, formal arrangements were being introduced.[118] On 27 June Makin reported to Chifley:

> The United States Service Authorities were only permitted 'on their own', to supply up to and including secret intelligence and technical information requested by an Accredited Australian Service Representative in Washington. In addition, the United States services were authorised to release only top secret information which, on the advice of S.C.A.P. [Supreme Commander for the Allied Powers in Japan, i.e., General Douglas MacArthur], was considered relevant to the occupation forces in Japan. However, if requests were received for other top secret information, the United States services were not authorised to furnish this.[119]

Slowly the US government tightened its release of classified information until, unbeknown to the Australian government, on 27 January 1948 Rear Admiral R. H. Hillenkoetter, the US director of Central Intelligence, sent the following memorandum to the president:

> Indications have appeared that there is a leak, in high government circles in Australia, to Russia. This may, in magnitude, approach that of the Canadian spy expose of last year [sic] insofar as high Australian government officials are concerned. The British Government is now engaged in extensive under-cover investigations to determine just where, in the Australian Government, the leak is.[120]

Australia continued to receive useful information until 11 June 1948, when the US State–Army–Navy–Air Force Coordinating Committee (SANACC) issued a directive prohibiting the armed services from passing on any classified information on their own authority. The Australian chiefs of staff were told of this decision by the Australian service representative in Washington on 2 July.[121] On 21 July the US chiefs of staff agreed to exclude the dominions from the Combined Communications Board. This had the effect of excluding Australia from American Sigint. On 27 July Travis, the head of

GCHQ, said that for the time being he could not provide the Melbourne Sigint Centre with Sigint or other material from the US. The following month the decision was confirmed to withhold all classified information until further notice. Australia had achieved a security grading equivalent to that of India or Pakistan, if not that of the Soviet Union.

This was an extremely serious matter. There was the possibility that Britain might withdraw from the Australian–British Guided Weapons Project and, since US and UK information was inextricably mixed, Australia's whole defence program could be jeopardised. During 1947, plans had been developed to improve defence cooperation between Britain and Australia, and they included the interchange of high-level and secret information. Major-General Sir Leslie Hollis, the chief staff officer to the British ministry of Defence, summed up the approach in a letter to Shedden on 10 March 1947. In it he said that the 'first essential' was to 'treat the Dominion Liaison Oficers in London with complete frankness. By this I mean that we should show them all our Planning and Intelligence papers and give them a complete insight into the way our minds are working on the staff level'.[122] If these arrangements were not to be jeopardised, Australia had to act quickly and positively to rectify the situation.

Frank Cain has argued that the US embargo was applied for reasons that had nothing to do with espionage in Australia, which he believes did not exist. Rather, the US Navy 'was deeply concerned about the development of land-based missile testing ranges' such as was taking place in Australia. He concluded that the embargo was imposed

> for reasons of politics. That is, politics within and without the American Defense Department, politics of rivalry between the various arms of the military services and politics of power played by the new intelligence committees and joint policy committees that were coming to dominate American defence decisions.[123]

The US, he argued, was also deeply suspicious of the Labor government in Australia, which was seen as being soft on communism. He was right about that, but, as the following chapters will show, the Americans and the British indeed had strong evidence of espionage in Australia.

10

'reading dozens of messages'

OPERATION VENONA: BREAKING RUSSIAN CODES

THE EVIDENCE OF SOVIET ESPIONAGE in Australia in the 1940s rested on the most astounding Allied cryptanalytic achievement of the postwar period—the decryption of large portions of Soviet intelligence radio and cable communications for selected periods from 1940 to 1948. This cryptanalytic effort, which began in February 1943 and continued through to October 1980, and which involved British, US and Australian Sigint and counter-espionage agencies, was variously cover-named Operation Bride, Operation Drug and Operation Venona; the resultant decrypts and translations are generally known as Venona material.

The most important breakthroughs included KGB communications between Washington and Moscow, and New York and Moscow, from mid 1944 to May 1945;[1] KGB messages between Moscow and New York in 1942–43;[2] KGB messages between New York and Washington in 1944–45; KGB messages between Moscow and San Francisco, and Moscow and Mexico City, during 1942–46; GRU messages from New York to Washington in 1943; KGB communications between London and Moscow for the week 15 to 21 September 1945;[3] and GRU communications between London and Moscow in 1940–41 (but not decrypted until the 1960s and 1970s).[4] One of the most successful efforts concerned Australian Venona, or the decryption of KGB traffic between Canberra and Moscow for the five-year period from mid 1943. By 1948, so much progress had been made in the Venona operation that, in the case of Canberra–Moscow cables, the US and British cryptanalysts were

177

reading the messages in near real time (soon after the date of transmission).[5] The Venona operation was so crucial to the efforts to crack the Soviet spy ring in Australia that its background, development and conduct need to be described in detail.

THE BRITISH BACKGROUND

Britain began Sigint activities against Russian communications at the very beginning of the Sigint age. After the outbreak of the Russo–Japanese War in 1904, stations were established in India, at Simla and at Abbottabad, some 50km northwest of Rawalpindi, to intercept Russian military and consular radio traffic.[6] By 1907 the Special Section of the Indian Army Intelligence Branch was reading some of the Russian military ciphers, and by 1912 the Army claimed that it had 'succeeded in discovering the Russian, Persian and Chinese Cyphers, and [was] now able to decypher any telegram despatched from, or arriving in, India, or passing along Indian telegraph lines.'[7]

With the outbreak of the First World War in August 1914, the efforts of the British cryptanalysts were concentrated on German signals, but after the Bolshevik takeover of Russia in October 1917 British intelligence authorities became anxious to learn about the policies and plans of the new government, one of whose main goals was to end Russia's involvement in the war. Both Room 40 (the Royal Navy Sigint organisation) and the War Office intercepted Russian diplomatic traffic during the negotiations between Russia and Germany at Brest-Litovsk from December 1917 to March 1918, when they signed an armistice ending the war on the north-eastern front.

One consequence of the revolution was the flight to England of several Russian cryptographers, who joined Room 40 in June 1918 and who were able to reconstruct many of the Tsarist codes and ciphers still being used by the new Bolshevik regime in Moscow. These cryptographers included E. C. (Felix) Fetterlein, who had been the leading cryptanalyst working on British ciphers. He moved from Room 40 to the Government Code and Cypher School (GCCS) when it was established in 1919, and headed the Russian section of GCCS until his retirement in 1938.[8]

In addition to the Home Office radio station at 113 Grove Park in Camberwell, South London, in 1918–20 GCCS established stations elsewhere in Britain, in India (e.g., Jubbulpore) and in the Middle East (e.g., Constantinople in Turkey) to intercept Soviet diplomatic traffic. In 1923, the War Office established a major Sigint station at Sarafand in Palestine, maintained by No. 2 Wireless Company, which became one of the most important stations for interception and cryptanalysis of Soviet service codes and ciphers; it remained operational until after the end of the Second World War.[9] From November 1919, 'the British Cabinet was kept supplied with an impressive volume of Soviet decrypts', which gave the prime minister and the Foreign secretary 'an invaluable insight into Soviet foreign policy'.[10]

In May 1920, as the first move in the establishment of diplomatic relations between Britain and the Soviet Union, a small Soviet trade delegation was established in London. The cryptanalysts at GCCS quickly discovered that the trade delegation was involved in espionage and subversive activities (e.g., funding the pro-Moscow *Daily Herald*). There was intense debate among Cabinet ministers who were outraged by the evidence of Soviet interference in British domestic politics and senior officers from the British security and intelligence community who were concerned about the potential cryptanalytic loss. Eventually, on 18 August 1920 the prime minister, Lloyd George, made public the fact that Britain was reading the Soviet delegation's telegraphic traffic and released copies of eight decrypted messages to the press.[11] On 19 August, *The Times* began its story with the sentence: 'The following wireless messages have been intercepted by the British government.'[12] As a result of this publicity, in early 1921 the Soviets introduced 'new cipher systems' that took Fetterlein and his colleagues several months to break.[13]

In May 1923, the British Foreign secretary, Lord Curzon, denouncing Soviet subversion and anti-British propaganda, issued a protest note to Moscow (known as 'the Curzon ultimatum') which not only quoted a series of Russian intercepts but 'repeatedly—and undiplomatically—taunted the Russians with the successful interception of their communications'.[14] Towards the end of 1923, the Russians again introduced new code and cipher systems which defeated Fetterlein and his colleagues for the best part of a year.[15]

In May 1927, the cryptanalysts at GCCS produced evidence of Soviet espionage in Britain and on 24 May, the prime minister, now Stanley Baldwin, read out in the Commons four Russian telegrams which had 'come into the possession of His Majesty's Government'.[16] In the following days both the Foreign secretary and the Home secretary quoted extensively from intercepted Russian telegrams to support the breaking off of diplomatic relations.[17] To protect the security of its diplomatic and OGPU communications, the Kremlin ordered the adoption of the laborious but theoretically unbreakable 'one-time pad' (OTP) cipher system. Thus, from 1927 to the 1940s, British and American cryptanalysts were unable to decrypt high-grade Soviet communications.[18] A. G. (Alastair)

Denniston, who headed GCCS from its establishment on 1 November 1919 until his retirement in 1944, wrote bitterly that Baldwin's government had 'found it necessary to compromise our work beyond question'.[19]

In 1930, in the US, the Army's Signal Intelligence Service collaborated with the Code and Signal Section of the Navy department in a major effort to solve certain Russian code cablegrams that had been sent from the Amtorg Trading Corporation in New York and its headquarters in Moscow. 'Not a single code telegram' was solved, and in 1931 the cryptanalysts gave up, believing that the OTP traffic was unlikely ever to be read.[20]

The Russian adoption of OTP ciphers and the subsequent loss of access to Russian high-grade diplomatic and intelligence signals traffic for nearly two decades because of the gross misuse of cryptanalytic intelligence by politicians became a legend in the British Sigint community. Henceforth, the British Sigint officers were determined that the dissemination of cryptanalytic materials should be subject to strict regulations, and that cryptanalytic activities should never be compromised for other purposes, including support for counter-espionage and counter-subversion activities. Later, Soviet agents who were exposed by Sigint escaped prosecution thanks to Allied reluctance to reveal the extent of their Sigint successes.

During the 1930s, GCCS continued to have some success with Comintern telegraphy and, increasingly, with low-level Soviet military traffic.[21] With regard to Comintern traffic, Denniston recounted in 1944 that:

> Some time around 1930 our stations picked up a mass of unusual and unknown transmissions, all in cypher except for the 'operators' chat', which was all of the international amateur type.
> The analysis of this traffic was studied closely, and from it emerged a worldwide network of clandestine stations controlled by a station near Moscow. It turned out to be the Comintern network . . . The cryptography attack . . . met with complete success.[22]

These Comintern messages were presumably intercepted at the SIS communications station at Hanslope Park in Buckinghamshire, about 50km from Oxford.

Soviet military signals traffic was intercepted at several major British Sigint stations, including those at Sarafand in Palestine and Abbottabad in the North-West Frontier. By 1940, the latter's 'nearly 200 Royal Signals personnel and an Intelligence Section' were intercepting and reading Red Army traffic in southern USSR.[23]

It has been widely reported, based mainly on a footnote in the official history of British intelligence in the Second World War, that, at the direction of Prime Minister Churchill, 'all work on Russian codes and cyphers was stopped from 22 June 1941, the day on which Germany attacked Russia'.[24] However, this injunction seems to have applied only to the cryptanalysts at GCHQ at Bletchley Park, and even in the case of GCHQ it was not absolute. For example, in October 1942 GCHQ resumed reading the Russian meteorological cipher, which it had broken in 1939, in order to meet the need for daily appreciations of the weather on the Eastern Front.[25] In any event, GCHQ resumed work on Russian diplomatic and intelligence codes and ciphers in June 1944.[26] Moreover, a wide variety of other intercept and cryptanalytic activities concerning Soviet signals traffic—involving NKVD, Red Army, Comintern and broadcast traffic—were kept up between June 1941 and June 1944.

With regard to Soviet military traffic, the British No. 2 Wireless Company at Sarafand continued to work on Red Army signals for at least several months after June 1941. As described in Chapter 4, from July to October 1941 the 4th Australian Special Wireless Section near Beirut intercepted Russian traffic for the Sarafand station.[27]

The SIS also continued to intercept and decrypt Comintern signals traffic. According to the wartime personal assistant to the chief of SIS, even after the ostensible dissolution of the Comintern by Stalin in 1943, SIS intercepted and decrypted 'the instructions that were being sent from the Kremlin to partisan groups and resistance movements under Communist control as to the tactics to be adopted as the day of liberation drew nearer. These messages presented a disturbing picture of Soviet plans for the post-war world.'[28]

In mid 1943, the British authorities decided to improve their capabilities for monitoring Russian radio broadcast stations, including some which transmitted encrypted traffic. As at 24 June 1943, some 61 Russian stations had been identified as being of interest, of which only sixteen were 'usually well received' by monitoring stations in the UK; reception of another seventeen was 'poor', while the other 28 were 'hardly ever heard'.[29] In early June 1943, the British military staff in Teheran was asked to monitor those Russian stations that 'could be heard in Persia' and were not already being 'well received' in the UK.[30] When the station at Sverdlovsk was heard transmitting enciphered traffic, Teheran was requested by London to determine whether the stations at Baku and Yerevan were also transmitting cipher traffic.[31]

The interception of Russian intelligence signals traffic was maintained throughout this period by the Radio Security Service (RSS), which had been established by MI5 in the late 1930s to 'intercept, locate and close down illicit wireless stations operated . . . in Great Britain'.[32] It was administratively a 'special unit' of the branch of military intelligence in the War Office responsible for radio services, but functioned as a unit of MI5's B (or counter-espionage) Division.[33] Its first head was Major (later Colonel) J. P. G. Worlledge, 'the veteran interceptor who, up until 1927, had commanded the No. 2 Wireless Company in Palestine', and its initial headquarters was in Wormwood Scrubs Prison in London.[34]

The RSS soon found that there was little illicit wireless traffic in Britain to intercept, and by December 1939 it had switched most of its resources to monitoring the communications of the German Abwehr 'and associated enemy intelligence and security agencies anywhere in the world'.[35] Early in 1940, the headquarters moved to Arkley View, near Barnet in Middlesex.[36] The RSS's principal intercept stations were located at Arkley and at Hanslope Park.[37] Some cryptanalytic work was done by the RSS's Radio Analysis Bureau at Arkley View, but all intercepted material was also passed directly to GCHQ at Bletchley Park.[38]

In May 1941, the RSS was transferred to the SIS.[39] At its peak, the RSS had 2094 personnel, and employed an additional 1200 voluntary interceptors. Almost half of its resources were engaged in the interception of Abwehr and associated signal traffic, with the remainder divided between 'general search staff' and a discrimination section responsible for distinguishing between illicit and licensed signals.[40]

The RSS recorded 'many thousands of Soviet messages' during this period, including both transmissions from NKVD 'illegal' agents in the UK and transmissions between the Residency in London and Moscow Centre. These intercepts were passed to MI5's B Division and to Section V of MI6, and, from June 1944, to Section IX of MI6.[41]

During the first half of 1944, as D-Day approached, the SIS began to turn its attention to Soviet activities. The Red Army had recaptured Kiev in November 1943, and having held the Germans through the winter of 1943–44, it was now proceeding to eject them from western USSR. Churchill had already become concerned about further Russian intentions; his apprehensions increased as the Red Army entered Poland, Romania and Bulgaria, and neared the East Prussian frontier through the course of 1944.[42] At the end of the year, he advised his Foreign secretary, Anthony Eden, to 'never forget that the Bolsheviks are crocodiles'.[43] 'C', Sir Stewart Menzies, decided to revive the SIS's anti-Soviet operations in early 1944, and in March 1944 established Section IX for this purpose.[44] Its first tasks were to update the SIS files on communism that had 'been on ice' since Felix Cowgill had completed sorting them in August 1939,[45] to analyse the decrypted Comintern traffic being produced by GCHQ,[46] and to process the undeciphered NKVD signals intercepted and recorded by the RSS.⁴⁷ Kim Philby, who had served in Section V under Cowgill since September 1941, was appointed head of Section IX in October 1944⁴⁸—in which capacity he was a personal recipient of the RSS's intercepts of the Soviet intelligence traffic.⁴⁹

US–BRITISH SIGINT COOPERATION

Cooperation between the US and the UK in the area of Sigint was officially instituted in November 1940, when a highly secret agreement was signed providing for 'a full exchange of cryptographic systems, cryptanalytical techniques, direction finding, radio interception, and other technical communication matters pertaining to the diplomatic, military, naval, and air services of Germany, Japan and Italy'.⁵⁰ In January 1941, a small US mission visited Bletchley Park 'for the purpose of establishing technical co-operation with the British cryptanalytic service'.⁵¹ The mission delivered to the GCHQ two Purple machines for decrypting Japanese diplomatic ciphers, two Red machines for decrypting Japanese naval ciphers, and a mixed variety of other Japanese code and cipher material; in return it was given an assortment of advanced intercept, DF and cryptanalytic systems.⁵² By mid 1941, some six months before Pearl Harbor, cooperation between the UK and the US on Sigint operations was unqualified.⁵³ It even included cooperation concerning interception and cryptanalysis of Soviet signal traffic. In December 1942, for example, the US Army chief of staff, General George Marshall, reminded Field Marshal Sir John Dill (chief of the British mission in Washington) that Arlington Hall wanted 'cryptographic material derived from Slavic nations',⁵⁴ and British assistance in securing Russian radio traffic was again requested by the US Army in early 1943.⁵⁵ On 17 May 1943, the arrangements and procedures for Comint cooperation were codified in the BRUSA Agreement—which formed the fundamental basis of UK–US Sigint cooperation into the postwar period.⁵⁶ One of the US Army's main interests in the BRUSA Agreement was its provision for 'US occupational forces in Europe and the Far East to establish and maintain' Sigint facilities for postwar coverage of Soviet radio traffic.⁵⁷

From July 1944, i.e., only a few weeks after GCHQ had resumed cryptanalytic work on Soviet traffic, British and US intelligence and military officials at the highest levels began considering mechanisms and arrangements for postwar Sigint cooperation—of which the Soviet Union was the principal target.⁵⁸ As noted in Chapter 9, Sir Edward Travis, the head of GCHQ, and a group of senior Sigint officers, also visited Australia in April 1945 to discuss postwar Sigint cooperation arrangements. On 12 September 1945, the UK and US Sigint agencies signed the Sigint Continuation Agreement, which extended the wartime Sigint cooperation.[59] On 21 November 1945, the British Chiefs of Staff Committee decided to invite the US to engage in '100% co-operation' in the production of Sigint, and also agreed that 'less than 100% co-operation was not worth having'.[60] The British proposal was accepted by Washington in large part because of the advances GCHQ had already made in cryptanalysis of Soviet 'administrative, military, naval, air and intelligence traffic'.[61] In 1946, the veteran US cryptanalyst William F. Friedman visited Britain to help work out the practical methods of postwar consultation and collaboration. Special liaison offices were established in London and Washington, a personnel exchange scheme was instituted, and arrangements were devised for avoiding duplication of effort and for exchanging cryptanalytic solutions and Sigint material.[62]

In 1944–45, Britain and the US began to establish a worldwide capability for interception of Soviet diplomatic and intelligence signals. In Britain itself, in addition to the RSS/SIS stations at Arkley and Hanslope Park, several large GCHQ and Y Service stations moved to intercepting Soviet signals as their particular area of interest as German signals wound down towards the end of the war in Europe. Forest Moor Mixed Wireless Station, near Harrogate in Yorkshire, which had an 'enormous' antenna field ('about ten miles square'), and which had been used to intercept signals from German forces in Russia, switched to intercepting and recording Russian signals.[63] Even field Y units became involved. For example, No. 11 Special Wireless Section went to San Giorgiu in Italy after the war ended, learnt Russian, and intercepted, recorded and 'eventually broke' the five-figure ciphers being used by Russian units in Russia and Poland.[64] Following the end of the Pacific War in August 1945, Britain established a major Sigint station in Hong Kong, its primary mission being to monitor NKVD radio traffic.[65] By mid 1946, GCHQ had established an interception and cryptanalytic station at Yio Chu Kang in Singapore, and according to Alan Stripp, who worked at the station from August to October 1946, its principal mission was to monitor Russian communications.[66]

By 1945, Canada's major Sigint stations (at, for example, Rockville in Ottawa; West Point Barracks, Victoria; Amherst, Nova Scotia; and Riske Creek in British Columbia) were also all intercepting Soviet signals[67]—including both Soviet diplomatic and intelligence signals and, in the case of the northern intercept stations, military traffic.[68]

In Australia, as we have seen, the Army intercept station at

Mornington began intercepting Russian radio traffic in December 1945. Other Sigint stations in Australia may also have been intercepting Soviet diplomatic and intelligence signals traffic in 1944–45. For example, it has frequently been reported that a station near Darwin had begun to intercept Soviet signals 'in the latter part of 1944'.[69] Ralph Thompson, who became director of the Defence Signals Bureau in April 1950, has confirmed that the RAN station at Coonawarra intercepted Russian traffic from 1946 to 1949 (and later), but he cannot recall whether it had begun this activity before 1946.[70]

In addition to the work of the radio intercept stations, arrangements were also made with the major commercial cable companies to obtain copies of Russian cables. In Britain, for example, a substantial proportion of Russian cable traffic was carried on systems run by Cable & Wireless, and copies of all relevant cables 'routinely went to GCHQ's new post-war home at Eastcote'.[71] In the US, in December 1941, the FBI reached agreement with the major cable companies (such as RCA) to make copies of the cable traffic to certain countries—including the Soviet Union. By the latter part of 1946, 'the FBI was covertly obtaining, directly from the cable companies, cable traffic to and from some thirteen countries'.[72] Secret agreements were worked out after the war by the Army Signal Security Agency and the cable companies whereby the FBI collected the copies of the cable traffic and forwarded 'about half of it to NSA while keeping the rest for itself'.[73] In Australia, Amalgamated Wireless (Australasia) Limited (AWA), the main telegraph company in Sydney, had made Japanese encrypted telegrams available to Army cryptanalysts in Sydney in 1940.[74] As described in Chapter 6, by December 1944 Australian Military Intelligence was passing Russian cables to London, and in January 1945 arrangements were also made for Brigadier Simpson, the director-general of security, to obtain Russian cables dispatched abroad from the GPO in Sydney.[75]

The mechanisms for postwar Sigint cooperation were formalised in two arrangements finalised in 1947–48. The first of these was the establishment of the Commonwealth Sigint Organisation (CSO)—involving the Sigint organisations of the UK, Canada, Australia and New Zealand—which had been agreed at the London Conference on Post-War Commonwealth Sigint Organisation in February–March 1946. Australian participation in the CSO—which involved operational responsibility for all Commonwealth Sigint activity over the area which 'will be Ceylon, Malaya, Hong Kong, New Zealand, Australia and all areas within this perimeter'—was approved by the Chifley government in a Cabinet decision on 12 November 1947.[76]

The second mechanism was the UKUSA Agreement, which actually consists of a series of agreements, exchanges of letters and memoranda of understanding signed by the British, US, Canadian and Australian Sigint organisations signed in 1947–48, and which has been described as 'quite likely the most secret agreement ever entered into by the English-speaking world'.[77] Under the UKUSA and CSO pacts, the five countries involved (the US, Britain, Canada, Australia and New Zealand) carved the Earth into spheres of primary Sigint collection responsibility, with each national Sigint agency assigned specific targets according to its potential for maximum intercept coverage. Cryptanalytic activities were also rationalised; GCHQ took primary responsibility for working on some foreign codes and ciphers, and the US service cryptographic authorities took responsibility for others, but many Soviet codes and ciphers were to be the subject of attention by both the British and US agencies, with liaison and exchange mechanisms established for sharing cryptanalytic solutions as well as decrypted material. The UKUSA Agreement also provided that the participating agencies 'standardize their terminology, codewords, intercept-handling procedures, and indoctrination oaths, for efficiency as well as security'.[78]

THE KGB'S ENCRYPTION SYSTEM

The encryption system used by the KGB in this period was 'theoretically unbreakable', or 'holocryptic'.[79] It involved variants of what was essentially a two-step process, using codebooks and one-time cipher pads. The codebooks contained the letters of the alphabet and thousands of words (in alphabetical order), each accompanied by a four-digit number group. The back part of the codebooks contained the obverse—i.e., the four-digit number groups—accompanied by Russian words. The first step in the cipher process involved converting the words in a given message into the four-digit number groups as listed in the relevant codebook. Where a word was not listed (such as a cryptonym or cover-name, which were often changed), the number groups for each of its letters were used, in which case the letter sequence was prefixed with the number group for the word Spell and ended with the number group for Endspell to alert the addressee.[80] The second step (or super-encipherment) involved addition to these number groups of random five-digit groups (or 'additives') taken from sheets of a one-time pad.[81] The two-step encipherment process is illustrated in Figure 1.

The system was 'holocryptic' in that messages enciphered in such a fashion cannot be read by processes of cryptanalysis—provided the system is used correctly and that the ingredient materials (the plain text, the codebooks or the additives) are not in the

The KGB's encryption system

As an illustration of the two-step encipherment process, involving addition of the code groups and the Gamma (random additives), consider the message: 'KLOD has communicated the detailed information received by him from BEN concerning the Australian Security Service.' (This message is taken from a cable sent from Canberra to Moscow on 1 September 1945, and was one of the first of the Australian Venona messages to be read by Meredith Gardner in mid 1947.)

Four-digit groups for the seven letters in the cover names and the other thirteen words in the message (which includes 'the' twice) would be found in the codebook, as follows:

Code Groups:

B	4762	Australian	4283
E	1646	By	9016
D	2853	Communicated	7236
K	2796	Concerning	5288
L	3154	Detailed	8132
N	3901	From	2379
O	9761	Has	7296
		Him	3247
		Information	9419
		Received	7236
		Security	0962
		Service	4319
		The	6303

The message would then be encoded as follows:

2796 3154 9761 2853 7296 7236 6303 8132 9419 7236 9016 3247 2379 4762 1646 3901 5288 6303 4283 0962 4319

The next step would be addition of the five-digit Gamma groups. For this message of 21 four-digit groups (or 84 digits), the first seventeen five-digit additives on the indicated OTP page would be used and the message enciphered as follows:

Code	27963	15497	61285	37296	72366
Additive	59046	43187	07416	37243	32594
Cipher	76909	58574	68691	64439	04850
Code	30381	32941	97236	90163	24723
Additive	71592	85113	54126	90713	20618
Cipher	01873	17054	41352	80876	44331
Code	79476	21646	39015	28863	03428
Additive	48027	29639	08354	43598	61001
Cipher	17493	40275	37369	61351	64429

Code	30962	4319
Additive	64372	85113
Cipher	94234	28203

The last series of seventeen five-digit groups could then be taken to a commercial cable company for transmittal to Moscow, or (less frequently) transmitted directly by radio.

possession of the cryptanalysts. However, the system was not used correctly: the one-time pads were used more than once! For a few months in early 1942, when the KGB's Central Office for Cryptographic Service in Moscow was under great strain—from both the attacking Germans (who had reached the outer suburbs of Moscow in December 1941) and the practical difficulties of supplying cryptographic materials for the enormous volume of diplomatic, military, trade and intelligence communications for the numerous Soviet posts around the world—it printed duplicate copies of the random additives (gamma) on more than 35 000 pages, which were then assembled and bound in OTPs, and distributed to the various posts in 1942–43.[82] Moreover, at different times between 1944 and 1948, the Allied cryptanalytic and counter-espionage agencies gained possession of extensive pieces of some of the critical materials, including copies of Soviet codebooks and of plain text.

The codebooks were changed at irregular intervals, sometimes occasioned by intelligence that they or associated material had been compromised. The codebook used by the KGB in 1939–41 was never broken.[83] That used in 1941–44 was not attacked successfully until 1953–54.[84] The codebook used from early 1944 to May 1945 proved easier to break, and provided the most significant Venona material in 1946–52.[85] The codebooks were changed again in 1948,[86] in 1950, and on 1 September 1953.[87]

THE US VENONA OPERATION

The US operation 'to examine, and possibly exploit, encrypted Soviet diplomatic communications', later codenamed Venona, began at the headquarters of the US Army's Signal Intelligence Service (USASIS) at Arlington Hall in Virginia on 1 February 1943.[88] (The Signal Intelligence Service was the official name of the US Army's signals interception and cryptanalytic service from 1929 to 1942. From July 1943 to September 1945 it was called the Signal Security Agency. It then became the Army Security Agency (USASA). It merged with the US Navy and Air Force Sigint agencies in May 1949 to form the Armed Forces Security Agency (AFSA), predecessor of the National Security Agency (NSA) established in 1952.[89] The US attack on Soviet signal traffic was started by Miss Gene Grabeel, 'a young Signal Intelligence Service employee who had been a school teacher only weeks earlier', and initially involved the analysis of 'an unsorted collection of thousands of Soviet diplomatic telegrams that had been sent from Moscow to certain of its diplomatic missions and from those missions to Moscow', and which had been 'collected intermittently' by the USASIS since 1939.[90] It soon became apparent that Soviet missions used five cryptographic systems, each of which was allocated exclusively to one of the following subscribers (listed in descending order according to the volume of message traffic that had been collected):

(i) trade representatives, e.g., Lend-Lease, AMTORG, and the Soviet Government Purchasing Commission;
(ii) diplomats, i.e., 'members of the diplomatic corps in the conduct of legitimate Soviet embassy and consular business';
(iii) KGB, i.e., the Soviet intelligence agency, headquarters in Moscow and Residencies abroad;
(iv) GRU, i.e., the Chief Intelligence Directorate of the Soviet General Staff and attachés abroad; and
(v) GRU/Naval and Soviet Naval Intelligence Staff.[91]

According to NSA histories of the Venona project, from the very beginning in February 1943, the analysis of the traffic proved slow and difficult. Then in October 1943, Lieutenant Richard Hallock, a Signal Corps reserve officer who had been a peacetime archaeologist at the University of Chicago, discovered that the 'trade' messages involved extensive use of duplicate key pages. This discovery provided a tool for further analytic progress on the other four cryptographic systems.[92]

Additional 'expert cryptanalysts' joined the Venona project during 1944. These included Cecil Phillips, who, in November 1944, found that in telegrams sent after 1 May that year the KGB code clerks had begun using a new message starting-point indicator system, which gave the OTP page numbers *en clair*. This breakthrough revealed hundreds of instances in which individual pages of OTP additives had been duplicated, and opened the way for the US cryptanalysts to determine the additive values 'for significant parts of hundreds of enciphered telegrams, leaving the coded texts vulnerable to crypto-linguistic code-builders trying to recover the meanings of the four-digit words and phrases'.[93] It was a slow process, however, and 'it was to take almost two more years before parts of any of

Arlington Hall in Virginia, the headquarters of the US Army Security Agency in the 1940s. The Venona project began at Arlington Hall on 1 February 1943. (National Security Agency)

these KGB messages could be read or even recognised as KGB rather than standard diplomatic communications'.[94]

After the end of the war in August 1945, the 'Russian section' at Arlington Hall expanded. Dozens of mathematicians, cryptanalysts, linguists and other technical personnel joined the project. These included Meredith Knox Gardner, who soon began to reconstruct the KGB codebooks. In 1948 the new FBI Venona supervisor, Robert J. Lamphere, described Gardner as:

> unusual and brilliant, not only as a cryptanalyst but also as a linguist. He spoke six or seven languages and was one of the few Western scholars who read Sanskrit. Until the outbreak of World War II he had taught languages at a university in the Southwest. On joining the ASA, Gardner taught himself Japanese in three months, to the amazement of his colleagues. Throughout the war he had worked on breaking the Japanese codes, and after the war was over [Frank] Rowlett [head of the Intelligence Division of the ASA] had put him on the KGB codes. Rowlett told me I'd find Meredith Gardner to be a shy, introverted loner, and that I'd have a hard time getting to know him.[95]

Gardner's introduction to the Venona project was in fact accidental. Towards the end of 1945, he had noticed 'a group of about five young ladies' working on a particular Soviet code, which he was

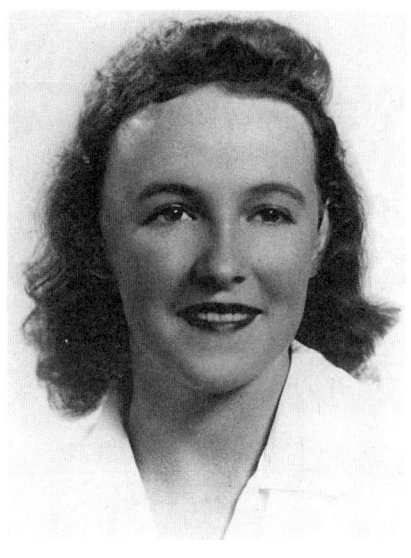

Gene Grabeel. She began work on Soviet diplomatic messages at Arlington Hall on 1 February 1943, and continued in the Venona project until the late 1970s. (National Security Agency)

told might be the NKGB code. He says: 'I strolled over and looked, and lo and behold they had an index printed by the IBM punch card operators' of the frequency of appearance of various uncovered four-digit groups, and 'I just invited myself in.'[96] At this time, the only groups that had been decoded were those for the twelve months, which had recurred regularly near the beginning of each cable and which correlated with the months in which the cables had been sent. Gardner quickly identified the four-digit groups for 'A' (it was, 'not surprisingly', 0001) and 'and' (2682), and 'soon saw ways' of gradually reconstructing the NKGB's codebooks.[97]

In about July 1946, Gardner began to read a few words in NKGB messages that had been sent between the NKGB Residency in New York and Moscow Centre in 1944.[98] On 31 July 1946, for example, he extracted a phrase from a message that had been sent from New York to Moscow on 10 August 1944, and which later analysis proved to be a discussion of clandestine NKGB activity in Latin America.[99]

In about November 1946, Gardner broke the 'spell table' for encoding English letters in the 1944–45 codebook. He could now read significant portions of messages that included English names and phrases. On 13 December 1946, he was able to read an NKGB message that discussed the US presidential election campaign of 1944.[100] On 20 December 1946, he broke into another NKGB message that had been sent to Moscow Centre on 2 December 1944 'which contained a list of names of the leading scientists working on the Manhattan Project—the atomic bomb'.[101] He 'henceforth made rapid progress, reading dozens of messages sent between Moscow and New York in 1944 and 1945'.[102] In late April or early May 1947, Gardner was able

Meredith Gardner and the 'young ladies' in the Venona room at Arlington Hall in about 1948. Gardner was the cryptanalyst/linguist at Arlington Hall who began decrypting NKGB cable traffic in 1946–47 and who revealed the existence of the Soviet espionage network in Australia in 1947. (National Security Agency)

to read two NKGB messages sent in December 1944 that showed that 'someone inside the War Department General Staff was providing highly classified information to the Soviets'.[103]

By mid 1947, Gardner had identified, in addition to the Spell groups, about 15 per cent of the total number of groups in the NKGB codebook. He had found the code groups for some of the addressees and signatories (e.g., VIKTOR at Moscow Centre), and he had found evidence of extensive Soviet espionage activity, not just in the US but also in several other countries, including Australia.[104] He prepared a draft report on his findings on 20 June 1947, and on 22 July he reported that 'the Soviet message traffic contained dozens, probably hundreds of cover-names, including ANTENNA and LIBERAL (later identified as Julius Rosenberg)'.[105]

On 30 August 1947 Gardner sent a ten-page report on the cryptanalytic activity to a handful of senior Army Intelligence (G-2) and ASA officials. The report contained an analysis of some five dozen cover-names, about some of which were substantial pieces of decrypted text with information about the person or the activity involved. It concluded that 'in its present state the traffic tends to arouse curiousity more than it does to satisfy it', but that recovery of the KGB code groups was now progressing rapidly and that regular reports would now be required.[106]

The cryptanalysts at ASA had by April 1947 also broken into the 1945 KGB traffic between Moscow and Canberra. Indeed, it was the 'constant' use of VIKTOR in some 24 Moscow–Canberra cables that enabled him to be identified as the Moscow addressee in other communications. The 'constant Canberra signature' was a code group 'tentatively tagged EFIM'. Gardner had been able to read portions of more than a dozen cables sent between Moscow and Canberra between April and October 1945. These included a cable from Canberra to Moscow (No. 129) on 25 April which contained numerous Spell groups for several Australian States (Victoria and New South Wales) and organisations (e.g., the Association of Scientific Workers of Australia, the Royal Australian Institute of Architects, and the Commonwealth Council for Scientific and Industrial Research); a two-part cable from Canberra to Moscow (Nos. 324–325) on 1 September 1945, which referred to BEN, who 'seems to have furnished information on the Australian Security Service'; and several cables between Moscow and Canberra, in which KLOD occurred some thirteen times, eight times in the sequence 'KLOD has communicated', and from which Gardner concluded that 'KLOD is Canberra's regular purveyor of information'.[107]

Within a few weeks (i.e., around the end of September or early October), Gardner read portions of another Canberra–Moscow cable, which became another milestone in the Venona history. This was evidently cable No. 123, sent on 19 March 1946, in which VIKTOR was informed that KLOD had obtained copies of two documents, 'Security of India and the Indian Ocean' and 'Security in the Western Mediterranean and the Eastern Atlantic', prepared 'by the English Post-Hostilities Planning Staff . . . for the War Cabinet'.[108] It was clear to Gardner that the texts of these documents, or at least large extracts from them, had been transmitted to Moscow in a series of cables sent from Canberra between 22 March and 3 April 1946, and one of the GCHQ liaison officers was asked to obtain copies of the documents from the War Office. The request generated much consternation in London as the War Office sought to find out what the US cryptanalysts wanted the documents for, but they were soon forthcoming. The two documents amounted to some 12 000 words, and comprised the complete text of twenty cables sent between 22 March and 3 April—and enabled Gardner and his colleagues to quickly recover a large proportion of the NKGB's code groups.[109]

By August 1947, US Army Intelligence, G-2, was quite alarmed about the reports from Arlington Hall. On or about 1 September, General Carter W. Clarke, the assistant chief of staff G-2, informed the FBI liaison officer to G-2 that 'the Army had begun to break into Soviet intelligence service traffic, and that the traffic indicated a massive Soviet espionage effort in the US'.[110]

A copy of Gardner's report of 30 August 1947 was also sent to the Joint Counterintelligence Information Center (JCIC), which had been set up 'to exploit current signals intelligence leads' for counter-

Left: Brigadier-General Carter W. Clarke, assistant chief of US Army Intelligence, who was responsible for liaison between ASA, the FBI, the CIA and the Service intelligence agencies on Venona matters. (National Security Agency) Right: Special Agent Robert J. Lamphere, joined the Venona project in 1948 as the FBI's liaison officer and case controller for Venona espionage material. (National Security Agency)

intelligence purposes. The JCIC included representatives from the Army, Navy, and the new CIA. It was evidently not kept abreast of subsequent developments in the Venona operation, but nevertheless, by September 1947 several US agencies (i.e., the Army, Navy, CIA and FBI) were now aware of the operation and of the Soviet espionage activity which it revealed (including the Australian aspects).[111]

On the FBI side, nothing happened until after December 1947, when Special Agent Robert J. Lamphere took over responsibility for the Venona project within the FBI. In September 1947, he had transferred from the Soviet espionage unit of the FBI's New York office to the espionage section of the Domestic Intelligence Division at FBI Headquarters in Washington, D.C., where he was responsible for counter-intelligence operations against Soviet and satellite intelligence operations in the US.[112] By December 1947, the FBI had received copies of decrypted pieces from the KGB New York–Moscow traffic in 1944–45, but the pieces were mostly fragmentary and most of the words were cover-names; while this was 'very intriguing', 'not much had developed because there wasn't much to go on'.[113] Lamphere soon established a close working relationship with Gardner.

The next major breakthrough in this phase of the US Venona operation began in the 'spring of 1948', when Gardner obtained from the FBI 'a mass' of plain text which had been transmitted from New York to Moscow during 1944 and which had been photographed by the FBI during illegal break-ins into the Soviet trade mission in New York in 1944.[114] Gardner was soon able to decipher numerous whole messages and portions of others. These sometimes included whole texts of purloined material, such as telegrams from Prime Minister Churchill to Presidents Roosevelt and Truman in late 1944 and early 1945,[115] and sometimes detailed summaries of documents, such as a technical report on developments in the US nuclear weapons program at Los Alamos[116]—which in turn enabled the reconstruction of new code groups and additives by Gardner and his team.

On 19 October 1948, Gardner and Lamphere had a private meeting at Arlington Hall to discuss the Soviet messages and the counter-espionage implications, and the next day Lamphere officially joined the Venona project full-time as the FBI's liaison officer and case controller for the Venona espionage material.[117] Between late 1948 and early 1951, the Venona decrypts enabled the identification of many of the cover-names in the Moscow–New York and Moscow–Washington traffic. The first identification occurred in December 1948, when SIMA was found to be Judith Coplon, a young Justice department analyst recruited by the KGB in 1944. (Coplan would also become, in March 1949, the first person to be arrested on the basis of a Venona lead.)[118] Several people who had supplied US nuclear secrets to the Soviets in 1944–45 were also identified—such as Klaus Fuchs, identified as REST in August–September 1949,[119] and Harry Gold (cover-named GUS/GOOSE until September 1944, and then ARNO/ARNAUD), David Greenglass (cover-named SHMEL/ BUMBLEBEE until November 1944, and then KALIBR/CALIBRE), Ruth Greenglass (cover-named OSA/WASP), and Julius Rosenberg (cover-named ANTENNA until September 1944 and then LIBERAL), identified in 1950.[120] The identification of the cryptonyms would often allow the decipherment of associated material (e.g., that ERNORMAZ or ENORMOUS referred to 'the US Atomic Energy project' suggested the text would contain US nuclear secrets). HOMER was finally identified as Donald Maclean at the beginning of May 1951.[121]

From 1946 to 1952, the US Venona operation was only able to read KGB traffic which had been encrypted with a codebook used by the KGB from early 1944 to May 1945—and which Arlington Hall had never seen. However, it was able to read a significant proportion of the 1944–45 KGB traffic between Moscow and New York and between New York and Washington. For example, 49 per cent of the message traffic between Moscow and the KGB's New York residency in 1944 was broken.[122] The cryptanalytic achievements of

Gardner and his colleagues were brilliant, but they were aided by a variety of other factors. As the NSA's *Introductory History of Venona* has noted, it was 'the knowledge gained earlier about the extra encipherment layer' that allowed Gardner to break into the KGB's 1944–45 codebook in 1946.[123] In addition, the KGB Residencies in the US made much more use of the duplicated OTP pages in 1944 than in either earlier or later years.[124]

The second phase of the US Venona operation occurred in 1953–54, and involved an attack on KGB messages between New York and Moscow in 1942 and 1943 that employed 'the earlier [i.e., 1941–44] and more difficult codebook'.[125] In 1953, a 'major cryptanalytic breakthrough was made through pure analysis by Dr Samuel P. Chew at NSA, the successor of Arlington Hall'.[126] With this breakthrough, a partially burned codebook used by the KGB Residency in Petsamo in Finland in June 1941 and obtained by Arlington Hall in 1945 was identified as the codebook employed in the Moscow–New York traffic in 1942–43 and was put to use in attacking that traffic.[127]

The cryptanalytic achievements of the US Venona operation in 1943–54 (with respect to Moscow–US traffic from 1942 to 1945) have been summarised in the NSA's *Introductory History of Venona*:

> Arlington Hall's ability to read the Venona messages was spotty, being a function of the underlying code, key changes, and the lack of volume. Of the message traffic from the KGB New York office to Moscow, 49 percent of the 1944 messages and 15 percent of the 1943 messages were readable, but this was true of only 1.8 percent of the 1942 messages. From the 1945 KGB Washington office to Moscow messages, only 1.5 percent were readable. About 50 percent of the 1943 GRU-Naval Washington to Moscow messages were read, but none from any other year.[128]

Within the US intelligence community, knowledge of the Venona operation remained very restricted. Even the CIA was not given copies of the Venona translations until 1953, although a CIA officer, William K. Harvey, had been informed in late 1947. Harvey was a strange-looking, bulging-eyed, 'pear-shaped' man who always carried two pearl-handled pistols and was to become a legendary figure in the CIA.[129] He had moved from the FBI's New York office to join the Soviet section of the new CIA field office in Washington in about September, and was a member of the JCIC, which had received Gardner's report of 30 August.[130] In 1945–47 in New York, he had supervised the FBI handling of Elizabeth Bentley, who (cover-named GOOD GIRL) had worked for the KGB as a courier and auxiliary agent handler since 1941, but who had confessed to the FBI in August 1945—and reported that the KGB was already aware in 1944 of the US effort to break its codes.[131] Harvey was a close friend of Robert Lamphere, whose transfer from New York to Washington he had arranged in September 1947.[132] According to a CIA report:

> [Harvey] gave CIA its first knowledge of NSA's breaking of the Soviet ciphers. Before that, the FBI had restricted knowledge of the break to its British counterpart, MI 5, which, with NSA's agreement, was informed by GCHQ.[133]

THE BRITISH VENONA OPERATION

In June 1944, GCHQ resumed cryptanalytic activities against Soviet high-grade diplomatic and intelligence traffic. By August of that year, there were fifteen cryptanalysts at GCHQ working on Soviet ciphers, and the effort was soon to involve 'many more people'.[134] By 1945, when GCHQ moved from Bletchley Park to Eastcote in the suburbs of north-west London, the interception and cryptanalysis of Soviet signal traffic had become its primary mission. By this time, several dozen cryptanalysts were working on Soviet diplomatic and intelligence ciphers. Indeed, a major consideration in the relocation of the postwar GCHQ to Eastcote was the proximity of the laboratories of the Post Office research department at Dollis Hill,[135] which constructed a variety of primitive computers for attacking Soviet high-grade codes and ciphers, including the OTP systems.

In about August 1945, when the US and British Sigint/cryptologic authorities agreed to collaborate against Soviet communications, GCHQ was 'made aware' of the small Venona program at Arlington Hall.[136] In 1945–46, two GCHQ officers in Washington, Colonel John H. Tiltman and Philip Howse, were kept informed of the slow progress of the project. Tiltman had been the founding head of the Army section at GCCS in 1930. In the 1930s, he had worked on Soviet communications, and had broken the Comintern's encryption system. By 1942, he was head of GCHQ's General Cryptographic Section, and after the BRUSA Agreement in May 1943 he was appointed 'a permanent liaison officer' to the US War department. He remained in Washington until 1954, and was one of the most important figures in the establishment of postwar UK US Sigint cooperation.[137] Philip Howse had been seconded from GCCS to work with the US Navy in Washington on Japanese cryptographic systems in February 1944, and had remained in Washington until early 1946.[138] In June 1946, during a visit to GCHQ, Cecil Phillips gave his British counterparts a detailed briefing on 'the techniques and progress' of the US Venona program.[139]

In early 1947, following the success of Gardner and his colleagues in reading some of the Soviet messages in late 1946, 'a British cryptographer was integrated into the US team'.[140] In May and June 1947 this cryptographer and the special UK liaison officer in Washington were briefed in detail about the progress with Venona, 'especially the Canberra traffic', and 'the GCHQ representative at Arlington Hall began notifying his superiors in the UK about Venona progress in June 1947'.[141] By April 1947, the Venona decrypts had revealed evidence of extensive and serious Soviet espionage in Australia, and by about September the leakage of British documents from Canberra had been revealed. This evidence of Soviet espionage activity in a Commonwealth country led, by about December 1947, to the establishment of a British Venona cryptanalytic team at GCHQ. From 1948, the US and British teams 'worked very closely together, each undertaking different tasks and exchanging integrees at working level'.[142] The operation was headed by Geoffrey Sudbury, a Russian linguist who had been one of the first GCHQ officers to work with the 'Russian section' at Arlington Hall, and who remained in charge for the next two decades.[143]

The relative importance of interception of KGB traffic in the overall British Sigint effort in early 1948 is evinced in a four-page report entitled *Sigint Intelligence Requirements—1948*, which was prepared by the Joint Intelligence Committee (JIC) in April 1948.[144] Sigint on the 'organisation and activities of Soviet espionage and counter-espionage services' was ranked as a 'priority II' requirement second only to Sigint on Soviet strategic offensive and defensive capabilities.[145] Given the substantial allocation of Britain's worldwide Sigint resources required, this prioritisation shows both that the British intelligence authorities were very concerned about Soviet espionage activities and that the British Venona program must already have been producing significant intelligence. Indeed, it was undoubtedly the cryptanalytic successes achieved in 1946–47 that produced the authoritative intelligence about Soviet espionage activities which in turn generated this level of urgency.

In mid 1948, British intelligence liaison authorities in Washington were informed of the achievements of Gardner and his fellow cryptanalysts.[146] The first British intelligence officer to be formally briefed (or 'indoctrinated') on the US Venona operation and its espionage findings was Peter Dwyer, an SIS officer who was posted to Washington in 1947 to serve as liaison officer with the FBI for both MI5 and MI6. (There was a reciprocal arrangement under which the FBI attaché in London, John Cimperman, liaised with both MI5 and MI6.) In early 1948, MI5 appointed its own liaison officer, Dick Thistlethwaite, while Dwyer continued to represent MI6. In mid 1948, Dwyer was informed of the Venona operation, and 'forthwith' Dwyer and Thistlethwaite met with Lamphere to discuss cooperation with respect to Venona activities.[147] In late 1948, Thistlethwaite returned to London and was replaced as the MI5 liaison officer by Geoffrey Patterson;[148] and in November 1949, Dwyer was replaced by Kim Philby as the SIS representative.[149]

The cooperation instituted between the British and US cryptanalytic and counter-intelligence agencies in 1948 proved extremely fruitful. The skills and techniques developed at Arlington Hall were passed to the British Venona team, which in turn took over some of the Venona activities, including further cryptanalytic work on the Canberra–Moscow traffic. A virtually complete set of code groups for the 1944–45 codebook and thousands of duplicated OTP pages were soon collated. Through the first half of 1948, some of the KGB messages on the Canberra–Moscow communications link were being decrypted in near real time.[150] However, in June 1948, the Residency in Canberra used up the last of the duplicated OTP pages. Over the next two years, the cryptanalysts at both GCHQ and Arlington Hall succeeded in decrypting substantial portions of hundreds of KGB cables, as well as fragments of thousands of others, which had been encoded with the 1944–45 and 1945–48 codebooks.

Cooperation was also essential to the counter-intelligence effort, since Soviet espionage activity was effectively worldwide. Some of those identified in the US Venona operation as having spied for the KGB in the US were now living in the UK (e.g. Klaus Fuchs and Donald Maclean), and thus were investigated by MI5.

On the other hand, cooperation also had its pitfalls. Despite the extraordinary degree of compartmentalisation imposed on the Venona operation, the high degree of cooperation meant that Soviet penetration of a critical point in one intelligence or security establishment could compromise intelligence or counter-espionage activities throughout the UKUSA community. As a US intelligence officer has stated with respect to Kim Philby's indoctrination into the UKUSA arrangements and the joint Venona operation, it was 'like opening up a party line to Moscow Center'.[151]

COMPROMISES

The KGB was informed about the British and American efforts to break its codes during 1944. On 29 August 1944, Philby (now cover-named STANLEY) met with 'MAX', his KGB handler from the London Residency. According to a memo on the meeting prepared by MAX for Moscow Centre, Philby reported that there were 'fifteen people working at the "Resort" on our ciphers'.[152] There is no doubt that Philby continued to inform the KGB about GCHQ's work on its codes until he was posted to Istanbul as chief of the MI6 station in Turkey in February 1947, although there was little specific intelligence for him to report during this period. GCHQ had itself made no significant progress; and Meredith Gardner's breaks into the Canberra–Moscow traffic occurred several months after his departure for Istanbul.

In the US, Elizabeth Bentley (GOOD GIRL) informed the FBI in late 1945 that 'the KGB had acquired some limited information about the U.S. effort during 1944'.[153] It seems that the source of this leak was Lauchlin Currie, an administrative assistant to President Roosevelt and a member of the KGB's SILVERMASTER group, who reported in November 1944 that 'the Americans were on the verge of breaking the Soviet code'.[154] In any event, the Soviet codebooks were changed in May 1945.[155]

The books were changed again in 1948. This time, it seems that the KGB had been alerted to the progress of the Venona operation by William Weisband, a Soviet mole at the heart of the Venona operation. Weisband was born in Egypt of Russian parents in 1908, had emigrated to the US and become a US citizen, and had joined the US Army Signal Intelligence Service in 1942. A fluent Russian speaker, he joined the 'Russian section' at Arlington Hall as a 'linguist adviser' in 1945. Meredith Gardner has recalled that Weisband had watched him, in December 1946, as he extracted the list of scientists working on the Manhattan Project from the KGB cable sent from New York to Moscow on 2 December 1944. Weisband, cover-named ZVENO, had been working for the KGB since 1941–42 (and probably earlier). By 1947, he had almost certainly told the KGB that its messages were being read, but his understanding of the cryptanalytic success was 'probably sketchy'.[156] (Weisband was never prosecuted for his betrayal, 'since a public trial would have required revelation of the code breaks'; instead, he was sentenced to a year in jail for failing to answer a summons to appear before a grand jury.)[157]

In August 1949, Kim Philby was asked to return from Istanbul to London prior to being posted to Washington as chief of liaison between MI6 and the US intelligence agencies—the FBI, CIA and NSA. On his first day back in London, Philby checked in at MI6 headquarters at Broadway, and met with Menzies, Easton, and the head of counter-intelligence, Maurice Oldfield, to discuss his forthcoming posting.

Oldfield told Philby that Britain and the US were working together on deciphering Soviet telegrams, and that numerous telegrams sent in 1944 and early 1945 from New York to Moscow and from Moscow to New York had been deciphered. According to a Russian account of Oldfield's briefing based on Philby's recollections:

> Only ten per cent of the telegrams were completely deciphered and of the rest there were fragments and separate words. This was enough to be absolutely certain that in 1944–1945 the Soviet special services were receiving valuable secret information from a source in the British Embassy in Washington and from another source in Los Alamos, where they were working on the atom bomb. The Soviet agent at the British Embassy had the codename 'Homer', and they did not know his real name. Counter-intelligence was working on finding this 'Homer' and discovering the source in Los Alamos . . .
>
> Oldfield . . . told Kim that they had managed to decipher some of the telegrams from late 1944 and early 1945 only very recently—in 1949. Oldfield also told Kim how it was possible to decipher them at all.[158]

According to this same account:

> Kim told his Soviet contact about his talk with Maurice Oldfield . . . Max immediately reported to Moscow on Kim's conversation with Oldfield. But neither Moscow, nor the KGB residence in London, nor Kim Philby could do anything in this situation for the time being. They could only wait and behave with extreme care and caution.[159]

Philby also told Guy Burgess about the decryption operation. Burgess (now cover-named HICKS) was at that time in the Foreign Office; his KGB handler in the Residency was Yuri Ivanovich Modin (cover-named PETER), with whom he met on a weekly basis; he often served as a conduit between Philby and the Residency. According to Modin, the night before Philby departed for Washington 'he sent Burgess to me with [further] news' about the Venona operation.[160]

Philby arrived in Washington on 1 November 1949. The NSA's *Introductory History of Venona* notes that Philby 'occasionally visited Arlington Hall for discussion about Venona; furthermore, he regularly received copies of summaries of Venona translations as part of his official duties'.[161] Philby also established a working relationship with the FBI on the counter-intelligence and counter-espionage aspects of the US Venona operation. He was introduced by Peter Dwyer to Robert Lamphere and fully briefed on the US operation soon after his arrival in Washington. Thereafter, however, according to Lamphere, 'Philby seemed content to leave relations with me to Jeff [sic] Patterson . . . He'd see me not every week, as Dwyer had done, but approximately once a month, and then, if possible, only in conjunction with Jeff Patterson.'[162] This way, Philby was able to monitor the progress of Gardner and Lamphere (as, for example, the identification of HOMER as Donald Maclean unfolded) without seeming too interested.

A wholesale change in Soviet encryption systems was instituted by the KGB's Central Cryptographic Service in 1950, including new codebooks, OTP books and encipherment practices. But no KGB cables transmitted after June 1948 (when the last of the duplicated OTP pages distributed in 1942–43 were used) were decrypted. And from 1951, there were few new breaks into the Soviet traffic prior to 1948, apart from NSA's penetration of the 1941–44 codebook which allowed some of the KGB's 1942–43 New York–Moscow (and some 1943 Canberra–Moscow) cables to be read in 1953–54, and a few subsequent periods when further material became available.

From 1948–49, the principal thrust of the Venona operations in both Britain and the US involved exploiting the decrypts to delineate KGB networks and identify their members in the US, the UK and Australia. It was matched by KGB moves to dismantle its networks and warn its agents as the counter-espionage operations progressed. In New York, in February 1950, Julius Rosenberg (LIBERAL) had discussed with David Greenglass (KALIBR) the need to prepare for a possibly hasty departure from the US; he told him that 'the Russians always tried to stay six months ahead of the FBI' but that 'the FBI might move too swiftly for that much notice'.[163] Two of Rosenberg's colleagues, Joel Barr and Alfred Sarant (one of whom had the cover-name KHYUS or HUGHES and the other METR) 'vanished . . . behind the Iron Curtain', and Harry Gold (GUS), David and Ruth Greenglass (KALIBR and OSA), and Julius and Ethel Rosenberg were preparing to flee when they were arrested, in May–July 1950.[164] Ian Milner (BUR), who had left the Australian department of External Affairs and joined the Security Council Secretariat of the United Nations in New York in January 1947, went to Czechoslovakia in July 1950.

In Washington, at the beginning of May 1951, Gardner and Lamphere learned more about HOMER, the spy in the British embassy in Washington in 1944–45. A cable sent from New York to Moscow on 28 June 1944 revealed that one of the reasons for his frequent visits to New York was that his pregnant wife was there.[165] Philby knew that Donald Maclean's American wife had been living with her mother near New York City, and contrived a plan whereby Guy Burgess, who was then living with Philby in Washington, returned to London to warn Maclean. Burgess and Maclean defected from Britain on Friday 25 May 1951. MI5 had planned to confront Maclean when he arrived at work at Whitehall the next Monday.

The KGB cipher officer responsible for the production and distribution of the duplicated OTP pages was reportedly later shot.[166]

11

'KLOD has communicated detailed information'

VENONA AND SOVIET ESPIONAGE IN AUSTRALIA

BY MID 1949, THE VENONA operation had over the previous two years succeeded in reading substantial portions of the cable traffic between Moscow Centre and the NKGB/KI Residency in Canberra from mid 1943 to mid 1948. It provided an extraordinary picture of Soviet espionage in Australia during that period—rich in detail and of the utmost authority, notwithstanding the fragmentary nature of many of the decrypts and some intriguing gaps that remained to be filled.

By April 1947, Meredith Gardner and his colleagues at Arlington Hall had decrypted portions of several dozen cables sent between Moscow and Canberra from April 1945 to April 1946. As Gardner reported on 30 August 1947, the code group for VIKTOR had been recovered as the addressee on 24 cables to Moscow; one cable from Canberra (No. 191, 10 April 1946) was addressed to PETROV; and 'the constant Canberra signature is a group that has been tentatively tagged EFIM'.[1] He had decrypted several phrases in a cable (No. 129) sent from Canberra to Moscow on 25 April 1945, which reported on scientific associations in Australia and which contained extensive use of groups from the Spell list (e.g., VICTORIA and NEW SOUTH WALES); he had broken into a two-part cable (Nos. 324–325) sent to Moscow on 1 September 1945 in which BEN 'seems to have furnished information on the Australian Security Service'. He had also found thirteen references to KLOD in cables sent from April to October 1945, of which eight contained the sequence 'KLOD has communicated . . .' From this Gardner had concluded that 'KLOD is

VENONA
TOP SECRET

USSR   Ref. No. 3/NBF/T2253
                                                              Issued: /11.1.78
                                                              Copy No.: 501

WAR CABINET DOCUMENTS OBTAINED BY 'KLOD' THROUGH FRIENDS IN 'THE
NOOK': DOCUMENTS PHOTOGRAPHED AND RETURNED (1946)

From: CANBERRA   19 March 1946
To: MOSCOW
No.: 123

   To VIKTOR[i].

   As [6 groups unrecovered] to 'KLOD'[ii] to get the document (the original) on 'Security
of INDIA and the INDIAN Ocean' through his friends in 'the NOOK [ZAKOULOKI]'[iii].
Recently 'KLOD' [6 groups unrecovered] copy of the documents (originals): 'Security of INDIA
and the INDIAN Ocean', Copy No. 78, 14 pages, and 'Security in the Eastern MEDITERRA-
NEAN and the Eastern ATLANTIC', Copy No. 109, 10 pages. Both documents were prepared
by the English Post-Hostilities Planning Staff [7 groups unrecovered] for the War Cabinet. The
documents are dated 19 May 1945 and signed by three people: C.C. A. ALLEN, F. C. CURTIS
and P. WARBURTON. At the same time there is a note on the documents to the effect that
their texts are final and that their circulation has been strictly limited. [2 groups unrecovered]
there is an additional handwritten note to the effect that this copy of the documents is issued
for the personal use of Colonel ROMKE[iv]. Appropriate operational maps are appended to the
documents. The operation of handing over the documents was organised by 'KLOD' in
CANBERRA, where he recently arrived by car (one of the cars he uses to carry out his illegal
work: the latter do(es) not belong to the FRATERNAL[BRATSKAYa][v]. The documents were
handed over to us for 35 minutes. During this time we photographed them and returned them
to 'KLOD'. [9 groups unrecovered] 'KLOD' in [vi] CANBERRA

                              [11 groups unrecovered]
'KLOD'
                              [13 groups unrecovered]
                              [1 group unrecovered]

it would be necessary to transmit immediately to MOSCOW but this will require copious
telegraphic correspondence. We urgently request your instructions.

No. 20[vii]   EFIM[viii]
   Footnotes: [i]   VICTOR: Lt General Pavel Mikhajlovich FITIN
              [ii] KLOD: ie 'CLAUDE'; Walter Seddon CLAYTON.
              [iii] NOOK: Department of External Affairs.
              [iv] Colonel ROMKE Not traced.
              [v]   FRATERNAL: Communist Party.
              [vi] Or 'to'.
              [vii] a.   In reply to this message, VIKTOR asked EFIM to telegraph the
                         text of the documents as soon as possible (MOSCOW's No. 62
                         of 21 March 1946, unpublished).
                    b.   The text of both documents – references P.H.P. (45)15(0) (Final)
                         and P.H.P. (45)6(0) (Final) – was sent in two multi-part messages
                         (CANBERRA's Nos. 126, 127, 129, 131-4, 136, 138, 139 –
                         internal serial No. 21 – of 22–28 March 1946, and Nos.
                         159–163, 165, 166, 169, 171, 175, 178, etc – internal serial No.
                         23 – of 29 March–3 April 1946, both unpublished).
                    c.   A repeat of part of CANBERRA's No. 21 was requested in
                         MOSCOW's No. 71 of 29 March 1946 (3/NBF/T383-1) and sent
                         in CANBERRA's No. 164 of 31 March 1946 (unpublished).
              [viii] EFIM: Semen Ivanovich MAKAROV

*The cable from Canberra to Moscow, 19 March 1946, decrypted at Arlington Hall in September–
October 1947, revealing that the KGB had obtained Top Secret British postwar strategic planning
documents from Canberra. Colonel Romke was actually Colonel H. G. Rourke, the Australian Defence
liaison officer in London.*

Canberra's regular purveyor of information'.² (These decrypts also contained the Spell groups for more than a dozen other names and cryptonyms, including TEKhNIK, PALM, BURNY, SESTRA, YOUNGER, MILNER, KhILL, DZhON and THROSSELL.) In late September or early October 1947, Gardner had broken into the cable sent from Canberra to Moscow on 19 March 1946, which informed VIKTOR that British War Cabinet documents had been obtained through 'friends in the Nook' (i.e., the department of External Affairs) in Canberra. By the beginning of 1948, the cryptanalysts at Arlington Hall were reading some of the Canberra–Moscow traffic in near real time. And by early 1949, by which time both Arlington Hall and GCHQ were working on the Australian Venona material, most of the Canberra–Moscow traffic for 1944–48 that proved recoverable had been decrypted.

The Australian Venona material was relatively modest in quantitative terms. Only a few hundred cables were decrypted to the extent that extensive or meaningful translations were available. (Of these messages, 189 were published by the NSA in October 1995 and October 1996.)³ These amount to about 10 per cent of all the Soviet cables that were deciphered in substantial part throughout the joint US–UK Venona operation. And, given that nearly 5000 cables were sent between Moscow Centre and the Canberra Residency in 1943–48, the decrypts represent only about 5 per cent of this traffic. In addition, however, small groups were broken in more than a thousand other Canberra–Moscow cables, usually involving cable numbers, addressees and signatories, cryptonyms and other words and phrases using groups from the Spell lists. For example, the signature groups were recovered on all the more than 200 messages sent from Moscow to Canberra in the first four months of 1946. (Apart from a circular message sent to Canberra and at least a dozen other Residencies on 7 April 1946 and signed by PETROV, all of these messages were signed by VIKTOR.) Some of the cryptonyms were frequently associated with one or two other words, as in 'To VIKTOR', 'KLOD has communicated . . .', and 'the ACADEMICIAN's son'. Some of these fragments were quite useful. A recovered signature provided a lead for the recovery of an addressee in another cable (e.g. the identification of PETROV as the signature on a cable sent from Moscow on 7 April 1946, which noted Gouzenko's defection in Canada and instructed Residents to tighten security),⁴ while the recurrence of a cryptonym over some period of time suggested sustained rather than sporadic activity, and the recurrence of two cryptonyms close together in various cables suggested some relationship between them (e.g. the 'influential ACADEMICIAN' and FERRO). Mostly, though, the hundreds of fragments were more tantalising than meaningful.

Despite its modest proportions, the Australian Venona operation was very lucrative from both cryptanalytic and counter-espionage points of view. Cryptanalytically, as described in the previous chapter, the transmission of the texts of British War Cabinet documents in cables from Canberra to Moscow in March–April 1946 greatly assisted the recovery by Gardner and his colleagues in late 1947 of a large proportion of the four-digit groups in the KI codebook. From the counter-espionage point of view, the revelations were uniquely important. They described, albeit in segmentary fashion, the chain of command within and between Moscow Centre and the Canberra Residency; the operational tradecraft practised by the KI officers and their agents; the principal Soviet intelligence interests and objectives in Australia; and the membership and workings of the KLOD group, the KI's main source of intelligence in Australia.

OPERATIONAL MATTERS

Nearly all of the cables sent from Moscow to Canberra from August 1943 to June 1946 were signed by VIKTOR (Lieutenant-General Fitin), and nearly all those from October 1946 to June 1948 by either IVANOV (Lieutenant-General Fedotov) or YuREV (Colonel Raina). Cables sent in July–September 1946 were signed by either EVGENEV (Petr Kubatkin) or GENNADIJ (Major-General Gajk Ovakimyan). Sometimes cables dealing with important security matters (e.g., Guzenko's defection) were signed by PETROV (Beria); cables dealing with code and cipher matters were generally signed by ShchEK (Colonel Aleksei Shchekoldin, head of the cipher section, which handled NKGB/KI communications with posts abroad).[5] All the cables to and from Canberra were addressed to or signed by EFIM, but it was evident that TEKhNIK (Fedor Nosov) was the NKGB/KI cadre-worker in regular contact with KLOD. There are occasional references to the NEIGHBOURS (the GRU) in the cables, but it is clear that EFIM knew little about their activities; conversely, though, Moscow Centre had told EFIM on 21 March 1946 that 'in maintaining contact with Zaitsev' he should 'not be too frank with him'.[6]

Moscow Centre insisted that a firm distinction be maintained between 'operational matters' and intelligence material in all communications between Canberra and Moscow. Operational matters, which were the direct responsibility of the head of the NKGB's foreign department, included organisational arrangements, the provision of financial resources, recruitment of particular agents and contacts, directions for intelligence collection, and operational security. As Fitin (VIKTOR) informed the Canberra Residency on 10 April

VENONA
TOP SECRET

USSR   Ref. No.: 3/NBF/T358 (of 15/7/1953)
                                                                        Issued: 1/8/1967
                                                                        Copy No: 201

2ND REISSUE

'C' TO REPORT ON VARIOUS AGENTS (1948)

From: MOSCOW
To: CANBERRA
No: 104   5th June 1948
To EFIM [i].

With reference to No. 40 and No. 41[a]:
1. At the next meeting with 'C[K]'[ii] please ascertain:
(a) What positions 'SISTER[SESTRA]'[iii] and 'BEN[BEN]'[iv] occupy at present and whether they can be used for our work?
(b) [2 groups unrecovered] 'GIRLFRIEND[PODRUGA]' [v] with the work and the possibility of using her in the future.
(c) Where are 'FERRO'[vi] and 'ARTISTE[ARTIST]'[vii] living?
(d) Is it advisable to bring 'FERRO' into our work in view of the fact that his mother is well known in the Commonwealth [SOYuZ][viii] as an influential ACADEMICIAN[AKADEMIK][ix]?
(e) How is it proposed to organise liaison between 'F.'[x] and 'MASTER-CRAFTSMAN[MASTER]'[xi] in view of the fact that they live in different towns?
(f) Will 'C[K]' release 'ARTISTE' from secretarial work if he is suitable for us?

2. Hurry up with getting detailed character reports [KhARAKTERISTIKI] on all candidates recommended by 'C[K]'. Ascertain what experience of working with people under illegal conditions

[59 groups unrecoverable]

No. 1823   IVANOV[xii]
4th June

Note: (a) Not available.

Comments:
[i] EFIM: Semen Ivanovich MAKAROV, at the Soviet Legation/Embassy in CANBERRA from April 1943 to June 1949.
[ii] C[K]:   Presumably CLAUDE[KLOD], i.e. Walter Seddon CLAYTON.
[iii] SISTER: Frances BURNIE.
[iv] BEN: Alfred HUGHES.
[v] GIRLFRIEND: Unidentified covername. Also occurs in MOSCOW's No. 92 of 16th May 1948 (3/NBF/T446).
[vi] FERRO: Richard Prichard THROSSEL, member of the Australian Department of External Affairs.
[vii] ARTISTE: Herbert William TATTERSELL.
[viii] Commonwealth: The Russian for 'Commonwealth of Australia' is 'AVSTRALIJSKIJ SOYuZ' (literally 'Australian Union'). In the context of this message 'SOYuZ' evidently refers to the Commonwealth of Australia and not to the Soviet Union – the word is repeated presumably to avoid any ambiguity. This interpretation is strengthened by the reference to THROSSEL's mother in CANBERRA's No. 363 of 30th September 1945 (3/NBF/T220).
[ix] ACADEMICIAN: Probably a member of the Communist Party.
[x] 'F':   Presumably 'FERRO'.
[xi] MASTER-   Wilbur CHRISTIANSON.
     CRAFTSMAN:
[xii] IVANOV: Lt. Gen. Petr Vasil'evich FEDOTOV.

3/NBF/T358

TOP SECRET

The cable from Moscow to Canberra, 5 June 1948, and decrypted at Arlington Hall soon thereafter requesting reports on various members of the KLOD *group.*

1945, it was 'forbidden to touch on operational questions in intelligence telegrams' and for cipher clerks 'to combine intelligence and operational telegrams in a single message'.[7]

Most of the messages recovered from the Moscow–Canberra traffic in 1943–44 concerned organisational matters, such as organisation of the Residency in Canberra, and the relationships between the Residency on the one hand and 'the FRATERNAL' (the Communist Party of Australia) and 'the local FELLOWCOUNTRYMEN' (members of the Party) on the other. On 21 August 1943, Moscow Centre instructed the Residency to 'pay particular attention to the setting up' of an illegal Residency, 'independently of the local FELLOWCOUNTRYMEN', and to select for the illegal Residency only 'the most reliable and qualified agents who are not under suspicion by the local authorities and whose collaboration with us is known to a very limited number of our agents'.[8] Substantial changes in these relationships were required with the dissolution of the Comintern in September 1943, which removed a major instrument of NKGB foreign operations, but which also clarified the working relations between the Residency and special FELLOWCOUNTRYMEN. As Fitin cabled to Canberra on 12 September, 'a change in circumstances—and in particular the dissolution of the BIG HOUSE [the Comintern]—necessitates a change in the method used by the workers of our residencies to keep in touch with the local FELLOWCOUNTRYMEN organisations on intelligence matters', and that henceforth 'meetings of our workers may take place only with special undercover contacts of the FELLOWCOUNTRYMAN organisations, who are not suspected by the . . . local authorities, exclusively about specific aspects of our intelligence work (acquiring . . . contacts, leads, rechecking of those who are being cultivated, etc.).'[9]

Dozens of the decrypted cables concerned fairly mundane organisational and financial matters. Payments to cover operational expenses were made (in Australian pounds) on a quarterly basis, and generated considerable traffic about the remittances and receipts. For example, cables sent from Moscow on 19 August and 6 September 1945 informed the Residency that £500 had been 'remitted by telegraph . . . as per estimate for the third quarter', and that 'an advance of 300 Australian pounds' had also been remitted 'to cover telegraph expenses in the third quarter [of 1945]'.[10]

Many of the cables from Moscow to Canberra were concerned with operational tradecraft and security. Detailed instructions were given for organising meetings and receiving oral and documentary information, and for communications between Canberra and Moscow. For example, a cable from Moscow to Canberra on 21 August 1943 instructed the Resident that 'the arrangements for making contact' with a cadre-worker (cover-named UCN 44) were as follows:

> *You [i.e., EFIM]*: I knew BOBROV, who studied at the Moscow Textile Institute.
>
> '*UCN 44*': I have a brother, but . . . he did not study at the Textile Institute.[11]

Moscow Centre was often concerned about inadequate security within the Residency. Cables to Canberra complained that there was too much discussion of operational matters within the Residency, that 'operational workers are being initiated into residency matters which bear no relation to the work being carried out by them', and that operational matters were being repeatedly discussed together with intelligence material in Canberra's cables.[12] EFIM was criticised on 30 May 1946 for 'shortcomings' with respect to security rules,[13] and on 8 March 1948 because a report he had written on KLOD which 'quite unnecessarily gave his personal particulars' had been included in a telegram 'with totally inadequate regard for security'.[14]

Moscow Centre attempted to maintain strict control over 'questions of recruitments' and 'work on the development of individuals', but it was frequently frustrated by the enthusiasm of its Australian agents. Cultivation and recruitment of potential agents was supposed to involve a thorough and careful process, with several distinct phases. Detailed biographical material was to be collected and assessed to inform judgments about the trustworthiness and usefulness of particular subjects. When Moscow Centre was satisfied that a subject was providing useful and reliable information, he or she was issued with a cover-name or cryptonym. Walter Seddon Clayton, who had been providing information to the NKGB/KI since 1943, was cover-named KLOD in April 1945; Frances Bernie provided information to Clayton for several months before he told TEKhNIK her identity, and it took another few months for Moscow Centre to name her SESTRA; Ric Throssell was generally referred to as 'the ACADEMICIAN's [Prichard's] son' before being cover-named FERRO in 1947.

The formal recruitment of an individual as a conscious NKGB/KI agent was generally referred to by Moscow Centre as 'bringing [him/her] into our work'.[15] By this time, Moscow could have no doubts about the commitment of the individual. Indeed, formal recruitment was generally associated with other actions (such as cash payments) designed to ensure this commitment. In KLOD's case, for example, EFIM reported to VIKTOR on 5 May 1945:

At the regular meeting with KLOD on 4th May, the latter was given 15 pounds for the first time on the plausible pretext of compensating him for his personal efforts and the expenditure which he incurs when he meets people on assignments of ours. At first KLOD was somewhat taken aback and he declared that he didn't know how to proceed in such a situation, for he had always considered it his duty to help our country. [But he] quickly recovered himself [and] became noticeably more cheerful.

The money was handed over at the end of the conversation. [KLOD] was also told that the money was intended for him personally and [that] no one should know of it.[16]

By mid 1946, and probably before the end of 1945, Moscow Centre had evidently also instituted a category of ATHLETES or probationary agents, who were used to provide information or for other assignments on behalf of the residency, but who were yet to be fully recruited. One of the first of the Australian ATHLETES was cover-named FORMER, and his employment authorised by Moscow Centre in November 1945.[17] In April 1947, Moscow Centre also approved the use of two female ATHLETES, cover-named SPIRITED and GLORY.[18]

The Venona material contains the cryptonyms or cover-names of about two dozen Australians (including non-citizen residents). The allocation of cover-names was the responsibility of Moscow Centre; although they were generally given to people who regularly provided some form of service, it was not necessary for a subject to be either witting or engaged in the provision of information. For example, Jean Ferguson, who met fairly often with TEKhNIK, as well as KLOD and the 'influential ACADEMICIAN', and who was cover-named RAPHAEL, 'was not an agent; RAPHAEL was simply a Communist with a code-name'.[19] Several cover-named informants were unwitting, such as VNUK (GRANDSON) in 1944–45, and FERRO in 1944–45. These were referred to in the jargon of Soviet espionage tradecraft as 'in the dark' informants (or 'persons responding comparatively readily to unconscious exploitation').[20]

THE KLOD GROUP

The Australian Venona material provided detailed descriptions of the arrangements used by the Residency for controlling and contacting agents and receiving information from them. The Resident, Makarov, himself served as controller in only a few particular cases. For example, he was in regular contact in 1944–45 with VNUK (GRANDSON).[21] TEKhNIK in Sydney sometimes also established direct contact with particular agents and sources, such as Katharine Susannah Prichard (the 'influential ACADEMICIAN').

However, these were exceptional and essentially peripheral arrangements. The Australian Venona material clearly depicted KLOD as the central spymaster. Unlike the NKGB/KI operations in the US and Britain, which involved a variety of networks and several local controllers, essentially all the Soviet espionage in Australia was organised by KLOD. He not only proposed and recruited all the important agents, but was also responsible for giving them 'assignments', determining the general contact arrangements within the group, and collecting all the information from them. He was regularly consulted and asked to report by Moscow Centre on the organisational and operational aspects of both current espionage activities and prospective developments.

By February 1945, Clayton had been having 'regular [weekly] meetings' with TEKhNIK for some time. He had provided him with numerous written reports about people and events of interest to Moscow Centre, and he was already being asked to obtain copies of particular official documents. One of his informants was Prichard, who provided him with information she had gleaned from her son. But he was also approaching various secret members of the Communist Party who were able to obtain important official material, often without the foreknowledge of Moscow. For example, he had begun to give Frances Bernie 'detailed instructions on how to conduct herself while working in Evatt's outfit' before he informed TEKhNIK of her involvement. He also later recruited Ian Milner and Jim Hill (KhILL), with the consent of EFIM, but without consultation with Moscow Centre. He often did not inform his controllers about the sources of some of his information.

KLOD's enthusiasm exacerbated Moscow Centre's concerns about his operational security. On 6 October 1945, for example, after KLOD had received and forwarded material from Milner and Hill, Moscow Centre instructed EFIM to tell him to be careful and 'not to burden himself with obtaining information of little importance to us, but to concentrate his attention on essential materials of an operational and intelligence nature'.[22] Later that month, after Gouzenko's defection in Canada, Moscow Centre directed that the frequency of meetings between KLOD and TEKhNIK be cut to once a month, that KLOD should 'maintain only organisational liaison with BEN and the workers of the Australian NOOK', and that no documentary material should be collected until further notice.[23] KLOD and TEKhNIK continued to meet every three or four weeks over the next year. However, in October 1946 Moscow Centre advised EFIM that 'according to information which has reached us' there had been an intensification of counter-intelligence activity in Australia (including

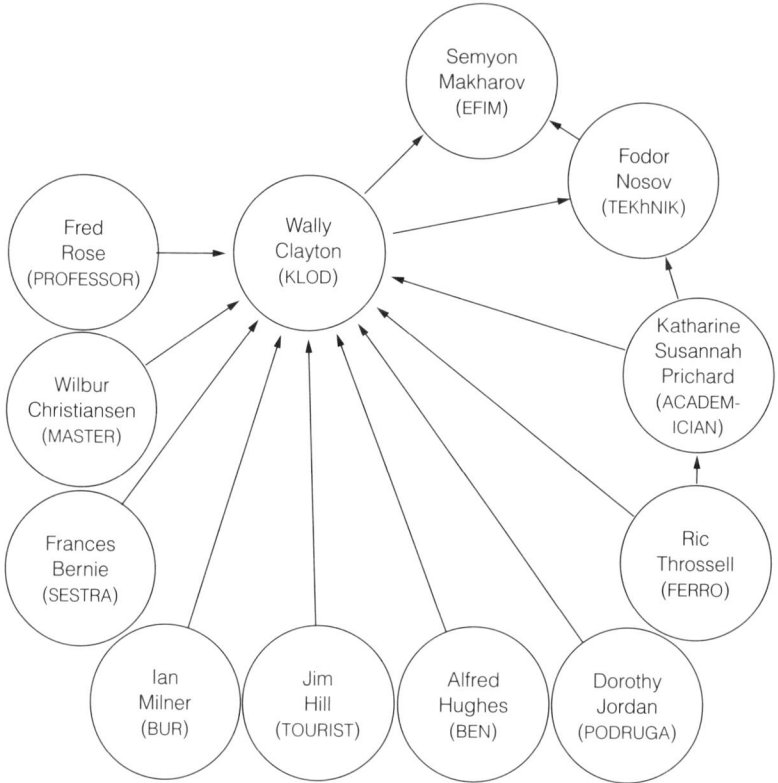

Figure 11.1 *The KLOD network. Some of Clayton's sources were willing agents of the Soviet Union; others were 'in-the-dark' or unwitting informants.*

increased surveillance of the Soviet legation in Canberra). It directed that contact with KLOD be temporarily suspended—and that EFIM 'must explain to KLOD that neither you nor he is threatened by anything specific at the moment and that this temporary suspension of liaison is being undertaken by you as a precautionary measure'.[24]

THE KLOD GROUP IN OPERATION

Moscow Centre directed the intelligence-collection operations in Australia in terms of articulating priorities and asking for specific documents and other particular material. With respect to general priorities, for example, Moscow Centre directed on 20 October 1945 that efforts be concentrated 'only on the department of External Affairs, the political parties and the intelligence and counter-intelligence organisations'.[25] Moscow Centre was always ready to tell EFIM when information and material was of no interest. (For example, he was told on 19 September 1945 that information he had received from PALM, the French consul-general in Sydney, who had been recruited by the NKGB in the US in 1943, 'does not present any interest for us' and that PALM was to be told that 'his information does not satisfy us'.)[26]

KLOD's written reports, together with copies of documents and other material, were supposed to be sent to Moscow by courier. However, EFIM would send by cable lengthy summaries of or extracts from documents which he thought would be of immediate interest to Moscow for operational or intelligence purposes. The most important source of material about operational matters was BEN, who by July 1945 had shown several Security Service files to KLOD, including a file on Mikheev.[27] On 1 September 1945, EFIM sent VIKTOR a long two-part message reporting in detail on documents BEN had provided about the Security Service and which EFIM reckoned were 'of operational value';[28] EFIM was asked by VIKTOR on 15 September to 'express appreciation to KLOD in our name for successful work in this field'.[29]

In September 1945, KLOD arranged with Hill for the latter to provide him with copies of telegrams from the British Foreign Office to the department of External Affairs in Canberra. Over the next twelve months, Hill (TOURIST) gave KLOD copies of hundreds of these telegrams, some dating back to December 1944 but most of them current; detailed résumés of their contents were regularly cabled to Moscow. The purloined cables concerned global diplomatic, strategic and political matters, such as the internal political situations in Bulgaria and Poland, political developments in Iceland and Argentina, and problems in Indonesia. The contact and reporting arrangements worked so efficiently that résumés of cables sent from London to Canberra on 16 October 1945 were cabled to Moscow on 8 November, and the contents of telegrams exchanged between Chifley and Attlee on 23 October were cabled to Moscow on 16 November.[30] On 4 May 1946, EFIM reported that KLOD had obtained British Foreign Office material which 'stated that British troops will remain in Java until the end of this year'.[31] Sometimes EFIM's résumés even included the internal cable numbers of the telegrams from Whitehall (e.g., 'Telegram 1419 of 10 August, 1945').[32]

Moscow Centre frequently directed KLOD, through EFIM, to obtain specific official documents. The most notable such occasion was in early 1946, after Moscow Centre realised that Milner had access to British War Cabinet documents. Basic rules of operational security were violated in order to get two of these to Moscow in the shortest order—*Security in the Western Mediterranean and the Eastern Atlantic*, and *Security of India and the Indian Ocean*, both produced by the post-hostilities planning staff of the War Cabinet in May 1945. On 8 March 1946, EFIM informed VIKTOR that KLOD had 'found out some details of the document which you know about', and that:

> There was one copy of it in the War Department here, held by the Permanent Secretary, Frederick Shedden. The document found its way into the NOOK where it is to be studied and it will be possible to get hold of it once again in the middle of the month.[33]

On 19 March, EFIM told VIKTOR he had obtained copies of both the India/Indian Ocean and Western Mediterranean/Eastern Atlantic documents. According to EFIM:

> The operation of handing over the documents was organised by KLOD in Canberra, where he recently arrived by car (one of the cars he uses to carry out his illegal work . . .). The documents were handed over to us for 35 minutes. During this time we photographed them and returned them to KLOD.[34]

EFIM noted that Moscow had an urgent interest in the documents, but pointed out that to transmit them immediately 'will require copious telegraphic correspondence'. On 21 March, VIKTOR asked EFIM to telegraph the texts of the documents as soon as possible. Their 12 000 words were telegraphed to Moscow in twenty cables sent between 22 March and 3 April.

REORGANISATION OF THE KLOD GROUP, 1947–48

Towards the end of 1947, Moscow Centre decided to revitalise the KLOD group. The development of the group in 1943–46 had involved little planning. KLOD had approached, on his own initiative, members of the Party whom he knew personally and whom he thought could provide useful information—such as Prichard, who had extensive political connections; Frances Bernie 'in Evatt's outfit'; and Alfred Hughes (BEN) in the Security Service. During 1945, as Moscow's interests became better articulated, his efforts had moved to the NOOK, or the department of External Affairs in Canberra, where he had several contacts—including Jim Hill, Ian Milner and Dorothy Jordan (referred to initially as DZhON and later as PODRUGA). He had recruited every one of these without prior consultation with Moscow. He had established a variety of contact, collection and reporting arrangements, some of which involved professional espionage tradecraft but some of which were almost casual. By September 1945, the group was expanding to the point where KLOD was having difficulty 'in maintaining systematic liaison and work with each of his people'.³⁵ In addition to Sydney and Canberra, KLOD also had informants in Melbourne whom he regularly contacted on behalf of Moscow Centre, and this greatly complicated his control and collection activities.³⁶ By 1946–47, some of his earlier informants had become inactive—including SESTRA, BEN, the 'influential ACADEMICIAN', and BUR.

Moscow Centre decided that the group should be rationalised, with perhaps fewer members but a more balanced representation across the areas of operational and intelligence interest, and with tighter arrangements for control and reportage. Several sub-groups were to be established, with their own liaison arrangements, and 'group leaders' were assigned to coordinate activities and simplify KLOD's control and collection functions. KLOD was asked to recommend the group leaders, and to provide 'detailed character descriptions' of them and 'their opportunities'. Two meetings were arranged between EFIM and KLOD (the first in late March and the second on 20 May 1948) to discuss the restructuring and the agents involved. EFIM was instructed to ascertain from KLOD who 'among his old sources whose material he passed us formerly' should be retained, 'apart from PROFESSOR and TOURIST', whom Moscow Centre evidently presumed would continue; the positions presently occupied by SESTRA and BEN, and 'whether they can be used for our work'; 'the opportunities' of PODRUGA and 'the possibility of using her in the future'; the whereabouts of FERRO and the advisability of bringing him 'into our work in view of the fact that his mother is well-known'; and how he 'proposed to organise liaison between FERRO and MASTER in view of the fact that they live in different towns?'³⁷ It was to be a leaner but more dedicated organisation. Whether or not it proceeded, however, the Venona material could not reveal, because the last of the duplicated OTP pages was used by the Canberra Residency in June 1948.

Since early 1948, the cryptanalysts at Arlington Hall had been reading some of the Canberra–Moscow cables soon after transmission. The insights were amazing. Current Soviet espionage activities, and planning for future, more streamlined operations, were being discussed in fascinating detail. By early 1949, however, most of the Canberra–Moscow traffic that was decipherable had been exploited. There were occasional subsequent breaks, as occurred in 1953–54 with respect to messages that used the 1942–44 codebook, when half a dozen cables sent from Moscow to Canberra in August–December 1943 were substantially decrypted. The remaining gaps were immense, however: as much as 95 per cent of the total cable traffic between Moscow and Canberra in 1943–48 was never recovered. Many of the cover-names were never identified, including several ATHLETES (e.g., FORMER, SPIRITED and GLORY), VNUK (GRANDSON), and PROFESSOR (who was referred to by Moscow Centre in May 1948 as one of KLOD's 'old sources', and who was probably Frederick G. G. Rose).[38] But there was another deficiency, of a quite different sort but just as important: the cryptanalysts at Arlington Hall simply had no knowledge of the Australian FRATERNAL, the FELLOWCOUNTRYMEN, the NOOK, or the characters involved in the story they were reading.

12

'Wally Clayton was the great Pooh-Bah'
THE COMMUNIST PARTY AND CLAYTON

THE PRINCIPAL MISSION OF THE Soviet intelligence services in Australia was to collect political, diplomatic, military, scientific and technical intelligence through the employment of cadre workers, collaborators and agents. In accordance with instructions from Moscow Centre, the efforts to recruit collaborators and agents were directed at officers of the department of External Affairs and the armed forces, journalists, scientists, and other public figures. Recruitment was not an easy task. Few of the KGB and GRU officers were fluent in English or confident in dealing with contacts outside of normal embassy activities—though Zaitsev (1943–47) and Nosov (1943–49) were important exceptions. Moreover, Canberra was still very much a 'bush capital', which reinforced the isolation of the Residencies from the Australian community.

Without the Communist Party of Australia (CPA), it is likely that the efforts of Zaitsev, Makarov and their officers and cadre workers would have amounted to nought. As the Australian Venona decrypts showed, the establishment and organisation of NKGB espionage operations in Australia was dependent upon the party and some of its high-ranking functionaries, and all the people who directly or indirectly provided information for Moscow were either members of the party or close relatives of party members.

The Soviet intelligence services were by the 1940s normally disinclined to recruit members of the Communist Party or persons actively associated with party activities, on the wise assumption that such people were likely to have attracted the attentions of the local security services. In Australia, however, the circumstances were different. In the first place, as we have seen, the newly established KGB and GRU Residencies in Canberra found it difficult to develop social contacts within the Australian community. Moreover, they had reason not to be too concerned about the Australian security services during the mid 1940s—which, as an officially commissioned review later reported, were characterised by 'a complete vacuity of objectives, and astonishing ineptitude in execution'.[1] In any event, the party was already well connected in the areas of interest to both the KGB and GRU Residencies, and some party functionaries were more than willing to serve as the conduit between these contacts and the Residencies.

The Communist Party of Australia

The Communist Party of Australia was founded on 30 October 1920, and in August 1922 it was recognised by Moscow as a section of the Communist International (Comintern).[2] During the 1920s, it was a small, isolated group of some 300 members, but its membership began to increase during the Great Depression, and reached about 4000 by 1940.[3]

Through the 1930s and 1940s and into the 1950s, the leaders of the CPA were L. L. Sharkey, J. B. Miles and Richard Dixon. These three composed the national secretariat. In 1930 a Comintern delegate was sent to Australia to reorganise the party and, with 'Moscow's backing', Lance Sharkey became president. From 1932–33, he began to make regular visits to Moscow, maintaining close contact with the Comintern, and from 1935 to 1943 he served on the Comintern's executive committee.[4] J. B. Miles, a former English socialist and a foundation member of the CPA in Queensland, was appointed general secretary of the party in 1931.[5] Richard Dixon joined the party in 1928, was sent to Moscow in 1930, and after his return became assistant party secretary.[6]

In 1930, the executive committee of the Comintern in Moscow advised its member parties that 'legal forms of activity must be combined with systematic illegal work', and that 'all legal parties' should 'immediately undertake measures [to establish] an illegal apparatus'.[7] The illegal work was designed to escape the surveillance of hostile security agencies and protect special party assets from exposure, with members carrying out surveillance and infiltration of other political groups and undertaking other clandestine tasks.[8] It took most parties some time to establish these illegal cores. For example, the CPUSA illegal apparatus was set up in about 1934.[9]

From the mid 1930s, the CPA adhered rigidly to directives from Moscow. In the late 1930s, as war loomed in both Europe and Northeast Asia, it championed the causes of anti-Fascism and world peace. By 1939, as war in Europe appeared inevitable, it advocated the formation of a 'People's Front' involving the USSR and the non-Fascist powers of Europe in an alliance against Nazi Germany. The announcement of the Nazi–Soviet pact in August 1939 came as 'a terrible surprise', and confusion reigned in the CPA for a brief period—compounded by the outbreak of the Second World War in September 1939, and Australia's decision to join Great Britain in the war against Germany.[10] However, the party soon adopted the Comintern policy that the war in Europe was an 'imperialist war', and that 'as the USSR was at peace with Germany, communist duty was to do everything to hinder the war effort, even if it means aiding the military defeat of our own and Britain's soldiers'.[11] Because of its defeatist policies and disruptive activities, the CPA was declared illegal under the Australian National Security (Subversive Associations) Regulations on 15 June 1940.[12]

After 22 June 1941, when Germany attacked the Soviet Union along the entire frontier from the Black Sea to the Baltic, party policy underwent another convolution. The central committee declared that the war had now 'decisively changed in character'.[13] As Lance Sharkey recorded:

> The C. C. [Central Committee] instantly grasped the significance of the attack upon the Soviet Union and its entry into the war. This changed the character of the war into a war of independence on the part of the democratic peoples against fascist imperialist aggression . . .
> The C. C. at once decided for the fullest support of the war, which had now been transformed into a just, a people's war. The C. C. called for the closest relations with and the fullest support for the struggle of the Soviet peoples.[14]

The CPA now became a vigorous supporter of the war effort. The ban on the party was lifted in December 1942. The heroic feats of the Red Army on the Eastern Front greatly increased the party's popularity, and its membership grew rapidly, peaking at 22 000–23 000 in December 1944.[15]

As far as the central committee was concerned, 'full support' for the war was significantly qualified. Dixon, as assistant secretary of the party, reportedly told 'a secret meeting of picked Party leaders' in Melbourne in 1942:

> Although we support the war, that does not mean to say that we forget we are revolutionaries first and last. In public policy we support the war and the imperialist Churchill. But we have other

ends in view. What are these ends? They are to see that Soviet Russia wins the war against Hitler no matter what happens to her allies or how desperate is the military situation on the other fronts. As Communists, we want a Russian victory, not necessarily an Allied victory.[16]

The great majority of the party members at this time were loyal Australians, committed to the defeat of Fascism and the building of a more humane and just social and economic order. Some 4000 served in the Australian Military Forces, and many won decorations and honours.[17] In 1944–45 there was a party cell with more than a dozen members at the RAAF's Headquarters Signals Unit at Frognall in Melbourne.[18] During the final stages of the war, one of the most active Communist Party branches was on Morotai, where Advanced Land Headquarters, HQ 1st Australian Corps and their respective intelligence staffs were located.[19] However, many of the party's leaders remained more committed to assisting the objectives of Soviet foreign policy than to the improvement of social and economic conditions in Australia. Many of the key office-holders in the central committee held their posts at the direction of the Comintern; for them, at least, the interests of the Soviet Union were in principle identical with those of Australian communism and, in practice, paramount.[20] Two members of the central committee in the 1940s who played important roles in this story were Walter Seddon Clayton and Katharine Susannah Prichard.

WALTER SEDDON CLAYTON

Despite the fact that he is now in his 90s and was for many years the subject of intensive surveillance operations by Australian security intelligence authorities, Clayton remains a mysterious figure. From 1940 to 1950, he was engaged in highly illegal activities, initially as a member of the Communist Party when it was a banned organisation and then as its 'spy master'. For much of that period, as well as through the next half decade, he was 'underground', his whereabouts known only to a handful of colleagues. It is not possible to separate his illegal party work from his espionage activities.

Clayton has consistently refused to tell the truth about his activities during the 1940s and early 1950s. He has lied about all of the key matters. He has said that he never engaged in any illegal or 'improper' activity (but that 'Communist activity is never improper'),[21] that 'I have never engaged in espionage',[22] that he had never collected documents or secret information (the party did not need 'little bits of paper'),[23] and that he had never met or known

Walter Clayton at the time of the Royal Commission on Espionage in 1955. In 1944 he was appointed a member of the Central Control Commission of the Communist Party of Australia. With the cover name KLOD he was the KGB's principal spymaster in Australia from 1943 to 1949. (Australian Archives, CRS A6119/79, item 941)

any 'Russians' or 'Soviet citizens'.[24] It is evident from the Venona material, however, that Clayton met with Nosov on numerous occasions (probably more than 100 times), and with Makarov himself at least twice (in late March and on 20 May 1948), and that he also knew Mikheev. But many aspects of Clayton's activities remain known only to himself, and he has evidently decided to take this knowledge to his grave.

His father was Thomas Ernest Clayton, who had been born in Sheffield, England, and after emigrating to New Zealand worked as an ironmonger and then a merchant. His mother was Alice Maud Clayton, née Bean, who was born in New Zealand. Clayton was born in Ashburton, New Zealand on 24 March 1906, and educated at Christ College in Christchurch. He left school at the age of 16, and from 1924 to 1930 he was employed in sports dealers' stores in Christchurch. His last employer there found him 'unsatisfactory' and 'alleged shortages of cash due to him'.[25]

In 1930 Clayton set out to be a 'sports dealer on his own account', but instead, by the end of the year, had embarked for Australia and an entirely different sort of career. The catalyst was Hilda Mary Lane. Born in Paraguay in June 1899, she was the niece of the socialist pioneer William Lane, and became a professional singer.[26] In 1930 she visited New Zealand with an opera company, and Clayton became besotted with her. He followed her to Sydney and then to Melbourne, where they were married on 24 June 1931.[27] Precisely when and how Clayton came to Australia is unknown, since, as a notation on Clayton's ASIO file on 26 July 1954 stated, 'no passport has ever been issued in New Zealand or here for Clayton'.[28]

In 1933, Clayton joined the Communist Party. Like thousands of others, he was shocked at the squalor and inequities of the Great Depression and saw the overthrow of capitalism and the imposition of communism as the answer—but none of his fellow travellers were able to match Clayton in his energetic commitment to the Party or the lengths to which he was prepared to go to serve Moscow. In about 1934 or early 1935 Clayton became a full-time party functionary and organiser in Melbourne.[29] He first came to the notice of the security authorities as a party member in 1936, while he was a member of the Victorian state committee and a district organiser of the northern suburbs in Melbourne (Carlton, North Melbourne, Brunswick, Essendon, Coburg and Moonee Ponds) and also of the Melbourne University and Jewish branches.[30] From 1936 to March 1939, he was very much involved in the party's public activities in Victoria—organising and speaking at public meetings and demonstrations, writing articles and distributing pamphlets. He was arrested at a demonstration on 6 July 1938 and charged with 'offensive behaviour', for which he was fined ten shillings.[31]

In April or May 1939 he moved to Sydney, although the circumstances are unclear. Hilda Lane has said Clayton 'always said that he wanted to live in Sydney', and that Sydney had become 'his permanent home' by 1936.[32] On the other hand, it seems that his move was also prompted by his defeat in a major factional struggle within the party in Victoria.[33] ASIO was later to note that 'when Dixon returned from Moscow in 1937 there was some Party talk that Clayton would be dismissed'.[34]

Once in Sydney, however, Clayton soon rose to the top of the NSW party. He was appointed to the state committee, with particular responsibilities for reorganising finances and organising the sales of the *Workers' Weekly* (later the *Tribune*). He attended the 1939 NSW state conference, and was extensively engaged in public party activities through 1939–40. He was reported to be 'engaged in *all* Party activities' in 1940, including meetings of trade unionists and a meeting 'to organise forces for the protection of Party speakers' at public meetings.[35]

His public activities ceased in late 1941. By then, however, he was fully engaged in 'underground' or clandestine work for the party, which had been declared illegal in June 1940. The Security Service was unable to discover any of Clayton's movements or meetings after 10 October 1941, although it reported on 23 April 1943 that he was 'no doubt still an active executive',[36] and on 31 August 1945 that, since 1941, 'very little concerning him is recorded either here or at Police Headquarters, Sydney', but that he 'is still extremely active in Party work'.[37]

Early in 1940, or perhaps even late in 1939, Clayton was put in charge of preparations for the continued operation of the party in the event that it should be declared illegal. He began arranging for 'secret hide-outs' for party members and assets (such as printing presses) and establishing clandestine means of communication between them. A glimpse of his preparations was obtained on 15 June 1940, when the NSW Police Special Branch raided Clayton's home at 6 Vernon Street in Petersham and found him hiding in the lavatory; 'property found in his possession included instructions for making flat bed press, roller and wax sheets' for the underground production of party papers.[38] During his period underground in 1940–42, he developed clandestine operating techniques such as the use of aliases, 'cut-out' addresses and 'dead drops' for exchanging messages and material with his secret contacts. In 1942, he began using the name 'Sutherland' and the postal address of an unwitting couple (Mr and Mrs C. R. Tennant) at 50 Bundarra Avenue, Bellevue Hill, in Sydney's eastern suburbs, which was known to only 'six or eight associates'[39]—and which was also given to the NKGB/KI residency in Canberra (and subsequently copied and given to ASIO when Vladimir Petrov defected in 1954).[40]

In 1943, Clayton became a member of the CPA central committee, and in 1944 he was appointed a member of the Central Control Commission. He continued in both capacities until August 1951.[41] The commission had been set up around 1931, with the guidance of the Comintern, to be responsible to the central committee for the internal discipline and security of the party. It had five members, who had to have been in the party for at least five years, and who included a chairman and a secretary.[42] During the 1940s, the commission's principal functions were: (i) to ensure the security of the party by making sure that it was not penetrated by government or other external agents and by 'dealing with' any suspect comrades; (ii) to ensure the unity of the party, i.e., to investigate and make decisions on various disciplinary matters among party members; (iii) to ensure the correctness of party decisions and their fulfillment; (iv) to organise and operate the undercover organisation of the party and prepare for its continuance under illegal conditions; and (v) to organise and operate the information-gathering activities of the party. The information collected by the party was of two kinds: information required to inform discussion within the central committee, for use in planning party campaigns, or for publication in the party press; and information that was passed on to the Comintern and, later, the Soviet intelligence organs.[43]

In late 1942, in what remains a puzzling move, Clayton made an aborted attempt to enlist in the 1st Australian Mobile Signals Company. He applied in October 1942, and on 20 November his name was included in a list supplied by the department of the Army to the Security Service for vetting.⁴⁴ Although he was given a clearance,⁴⁵ and although a signal company would have been an interesting place for a person with Clayton's predilections, for some reason he changed his mind—at the same time as the Soviet foreign intelligence organs were preparing to establish their Residencies in Australia—and did not proceed with enlistment.

Precisely when the NKGB established contact with Clayton and when he began to collect information from his associates and contacts for the NKGB cannot be determined, but it was most likely around mid 1943. The first Soviet intelligence officer with whom he met was Vladimir Mikheev, who had arrived in Sydney in September 1942; it is clear that they met in early 1943, and probably also in late 1942. The circumstances of their introduction remain unclear, but they evidently involved both Prichard and Rupert Lockwood (VORON). Prichard had met Mikheev when he stopped over in Fremantle on his way to Sydney in September 1942, and both Clayton and Mikheev visited her apartment after she moved to Sydney at the end of October 1942. Lockwood, who knew Clayton well through his involvement with publication of the *Tribune*, has said that Mikheev 'often came to me for advice often on personal and journalistic matters'.⁴⁶ Lockwood, Clayton and Mikheev were frequent drinkers at the Journalists' Club in Sydney, and Lockwood was keenly aware of Clayton's party interests. In any event, Clayton met the TASS representative, Fedor Nosov, soon after the latter's arrival in Sydney in August 1943.

Initially, Clayton was only one of several 'local FELLOWCOUNTRY-MEN' who provided information to Makarov in Canberra and Nosov in Sydney. His selection as the principal Australian agent followed a cable from Moscow Centre to Canberra on 12 September 1943 in which Lieutenant-General Fitin (VIKTOR) advised Makarov (EFIM) that the dissolution of the Comintern required an overt reduction in legation–party contacts and that henceforth the Residency should maintain covert contact 'only with special reliable undercover contacts of the FELLOWCOUNTRYMAN organisations, who are not suspected by the . . . local authorities'.⁴⁷ As the party organiser responsible for undercover or illegal activities, as well as contact with secret members of the party, Clayton filled the bill nicely.

By the end of 1944, he had established a close clandestine working relationship with Nosov. Regular weekly meetings were organised, at which Clayton was given assignments, reported to Nosov about earlier assignments and gave Nosov notes and copies of material on other matters Clayton deemed important. His assignments at this time included obtaining copies of restricted official documents, ministerial orders, and diplomatic reports (including reports to Canberra from the Australian legation in Moscow), as well as the preparation of 'personal reports' on secret members of the party whom he considered to be prospective informants. In addition to verbal reports, Clayton gave Nosov lengthy notes about political matters which he had either written himself or obtained from party members and associates, and most of whose contents were quite unimportant. Through 1943 and 1944 much of the information Clayton passed to Nosov consisted of poorly informed political gossip written up by Prichard (including information she obtained from Throssell when he joined External Affairs as a cadet in June 1943).

By the beginning of 1945, Moscow Centre was so impressed with Clayton's reliability and ability to obtain official documents and information that it authorised his formal recruitment as an NKGB agent. On 2 February Moscow asked the Residency in Canberra to 'advise whether C. [i.e. Clayton] could not be brought into our work'.[48] Clayton was given the cover-name KLOD in April 1945, and at 'the regular meeting' with Nosov on 4 May he was persuaded to accept money 'on the plausible pretext of compensating him for his personal efforts'.[49] By the end of 1945, Clayton was regularly providing the NKGB with official documents and other information from more than half a dozen informants, including Prichard (and, indirectly, Throssell), Alfred Hughes, Frances Bernie, Ian Milner and Jim Hill.

From 1942 to 1944, Clayton worked in 'a small cubicle like office' in the CPA headquarters at Daking House, in Rawson Place, near Central railway station.[50] In late 1944, when the party headquarters moved to Marx House, at 695 George Street, he occupied an office upstairs, 'in the centre and towards the front of the building'.[51] Much of his party activity during this period involved organising classes for cadres at both Marx House and various party 'safe houses' and weekend camps, as well as ensuring that 'branch tutors' adhered strictly to the party line.[52] Through the mid 1940s he also expanded the purview of the control commission so as to obtain disciplinary authority over significant aspects of the personal affairs of party members—including their changes of jobs (especially if they were public servants), medical problems, marital and sexual issues, and personal disputes between them.[53]

Clayton's wife, Hilda Lane, met the GRU resident, Zaitsev, on 26 May 1943, when she sang several songs at a meeting he attended in Sydney to celebrate the Anglo–Soviet Treaty,[54] but whether this was perchance or by design, indicating some GRU interest in either Clayton or Lane, cannot be determined. Clayton had probably not taken Lane into his confidence anyway. He was, by 1943–44 at least, sexually involved with other women in the party,[55] and deserted Lane just after Christmas 1944. She attested at a hearing in the Supreme Court in Sydney on 30 October 1945 that his desertion 'was a shock to me . . . because I thought that we were happily married', that the only explanation he gave was that 'he didn't like her musical and professional friends', and that 'the home that he left is still available for his occupation and I sincerely desire him to return'.[56] Although she was given an order directing Clayton to return to her, he never obeyed the order, and on 24 April 1947 she was granted a divorce.[57]

After Clayton left Hilda Lane, he lived for several months at 67 Laurel Street, Willoughby, then moved in mid 1945 to 15a Awaba Street, Mosman, which would be his main residence for the next four years.[58] From the beginning of 1945 he lived in a de facto relationship with Shirley May Howard, or Hallett, until her death (aged only 25) on 7 February 1946. She was a well-known Communist Party worker, and for the twelve months before her death she worked as the personal secretary to H. B. Chandler, a member of the political committee.[59] (Makarov informed Moscow of the death of Clayton's 'wife' on 8 March, and advised that 'nothing in KLOD's behaviour has changed' and that 'he is still full of fight'.)[60]

Clayton was 40 years old in 1946. The best contemporary physical description of him was provided by a CIS officer who noticed him in Melbourne on 17 March 1948 and described him as being 5'10" in height, 'reasonably well built', 'completely bald on top . . . [with] very fair hair around [the] sides and back of head', thinnish face, fair complexion, 'wears glasses', and 'dressed in a black suit with a faint stripe, fawn shirt and collar'.[61] His personality was more evanescent. He could be amiable and engaging, but he was more often cold and detached. He was dedicated and energetic, relentless, treacherous, and fearsome to other members of the party.[62] Gloria Garton, who joined the party in Sydney in November 1941, when it was illegal, and who worked as an 'organiser' at party headquarters until 1946, has recounted that 'Wally Clayton was the great Pooh-Bah'.[63] Frances Garrett (née Bernie), who was one of the most active members of the KLOD group in 1945–46, said Clayton was 'as cold as a fish',[64] and described him as a 'shadowy figure; difficult to get to know—wouldn't look at me when I was reporting'.[65] Cecil Sharpley, who often lent his flat in Melbourne to Clayton 'for meetings with secret contacts', has said that 'the mysterious quality in his work . . . was mirrored in his face, which nearly always wore a furtive expression, although Clayton was not unlikeable'.[66] Sharpley described Clayton as 'a fanatic, a plodder—nothing brilliant, but loyal and hard working' and 'completely ruthless and impersonal'.[67]

In 1947 the CPA leadership decided that a secret or 'illegal apparatus' should be re-established, as the onset of the Cold War raised the possibility of the party's being banned again. Clayton was given responsibility for construction of the apparatus. In 1948–49 he put together a network of reliable but little-known party members who were prepared to allow their homes or properties to be used for meetings or hideouts; he established printeries, workshops, and an elaborate system of distribution for illegal newspapers and other party material; and he constructed a complex but fairly secure organisation with aliases, cover addresses and dead drops.[68]

In 1949, Clayton ceased involvement in public activities of the party.[69] He attended a meeting of 'tutors' at Marx House on 13 January 1949,[70] but thereafter his activities were almost all underground. He stopped living at 15a Awaba Street on a regular basis towards the end of 1949, and 'was very seldom in Sydney' in 1950 and 1951.[71]

Clayton's various responsibilities, as secretary of the central control commission, as the official in charge of the party's illegal apparatus and as spymaster of the Soviet espionage network in Australia, complemented each other very nicely. Those of his colleagues in the party who were aware of his clandestine activities simply assumed that this was his illegal work for the party. The agents and contacts from whom he was collecting, almost all of whom were party members, were subject to his disciplinary functions and in some cases might well have believed they were doing no more than providing covert assistance to the party.

There is no doubt that Clayton used his status as a party functionary in attempts to recruit additional members of the KLOD group. For example, in late June 1948 he attempted to recruit George Williamson Legge, who was then working in the political intelligence and information section of the department of External Affairs, on the basis of assisting the party's policy-making process. Legge was introduced to Clayton by a cousin, Jack Legge, who was a member of the party and an associate of Clayton, and who visited him with Clayton one evening at his bed-sitter flat at Acton House in Canberra. According to George Legge:

> He [Clayton] said something like this: 'At times our policy is not always as well informed as it might be, and sometimes we say things or follow lines that are not in fact correct. Now it may be that you could'—I think the term was—'keep us on the rails'.[72]

Legge rebuffed the attempt and had nothing further to do with either his cousin or Clayton.[73]

It also seems that in April 1950, during another visit to Canberra, Clayton attempted to 'suborn' June Barnett, who had joined the department of External Affairs as a cadet in 1948 and become a probationary third secretary in the United Nations division of the department in January 1950. Although she had been a member of the Communist Party from 1944 to 1948, she also refused to provide him with information.[74]

From 1943 to 1949, Clayton was extremely peripatetic. Travel was not easy in Australia in the 1940s, and was quite restricted during 1943–45. However, Clayton was able to travel 'all over Australia', including to Western Australia in 1946 and 1947. He regularly visited Brisbane, Canberra, Melbourne and Adelaide, sometimes for just a couple of days and sometimes for one or two weeks. He would frequently travel by car, sometimes driving to Melbourne down the south coast of NSW, for example, but he often went by plane.[75] In January 1944, for instance, he flew to Cairns on control commission work, even though North Queensland was at this time a closed area which required a permit to enter.[76]

Clayton's schedule during these visits was generally hectic. He would typically call on his party counterparts in the state executives and control commissions. For example, from 1945 to 1949, when, according to Cecil Sharpley, he visited Melbourne about 'every two months', he invariably saw E. F. (Ted) Hill, the main party leader in Victoria, and Richard (Ric) Oke, a member of the state committee and of its organisational committee.[77] He would distribute material from the central committee in Sydney, and he would collect material and party dues to take back to Sydney. In his control commission capacity, he met party members with serious personal problems, and sorted out intra-branch political issues (as, for example, when he went to Cairns in January 1944,[78] and during some of his visits to Canberra in 1946–48);[79] and he investigated matters related to securing the party from external penetration and provocation (as, for example, when he went to Adelaide in January and June 1950).[80] He also visited places that he was using as postal addresses, and cleared or deposited material in various 'dead drops'. Sometimes it took him two or three visits to Melbourne or Canberra to obtain material specially requested by Moscow Centre.[81]

By 1945, Clayton had established a robust system for collecting information and material from the various members of the KLOD group and passing it to the NKGB. His most frequent meetings were with the Sydney members of the group: Prichard, whom he met at both Marx House and her apartment in Darlinghurst; Alfred Thompson Hughes (BEN), whom he met clandestinely; and Frances Bernie (SESTRA), who brought her information and material to him at Marx House.

Through the mid and late 1940s, Clayton usually visited Canberra about a dozen times a year, sometimes by car and sometimes by train, both to collect material from the Canberra members of the KLOD group and to deliver material to Makarov. Sometimes he would drive to Canberra and back to Sydney on the same day, and sometimes he would stay in Canberra overnight. In the mid 1940s he usually stayed at 7 Goreen Street in Reid with Dr Kenneth Hedley Key, an entomologist at the Council for Scientific and Industrial Research (CSIR) and a member of the CPA. Key shared his house with other CPA members, including the undercover *Tribune* correspondent in Canberra.[82] (Jim Hill also lived there in 1946.) It was a good place for Clayton to pick up information about the activities of members of the party in Canberra, to meet with some of his agents and contacts, and to collect other material that was left there for him. By September 1947 Key himself was being 'studied' by the Canberra Residency with a view to prospective recruitment (although there is no evidence that he was ever recruited).[83]

From late 1945 to early 1947, Clayton's most important direct contact in Canberra was Doris Isobel Beeby, who lived at least for the latter part of that period at 18 Myuna Flats in Braddon, near Canberra's Civic Centre. She was born on 31 July 1899, the daughter of Chief Justice Beeby of the Federal Arbitration Court. She had joined the British Communist Party in London in September 1939, and had become a full-time party and trade union organiser when she returned to Australia. In 1945, she was sent to Canberra to help build the Canberra branch of the party, which had about nine members in 1946, as well as to work as *Tribune* correspondent at Parliament House.[84] When Clayton came to Canberra during this period to 'have a look' at the Canberra branch and to discuss *Tribune* matters,[85] it was to Beeby that he called first of all.

At least since early 1944, 18 Myuna Flats had been occupied by various members or supporters of the party, all of whom were sub-tenants to Elfrida Margaret Newbegin, a member of the North Sydney branch who had worked at the CSIR in Canberra in 1943–44 (and later in the department of External Affairs from October 1945 to February 1946).[86] Party members from Sydney often stayed at her flat during brief visits to Canberra. When Beeby lived there, it was also used for regular (secret) meetings of the Canberra branch of the party.[87] Indeed, by 1946, it had become an active meeting place for journalists and young public servants interested in political affairs. Beeby collected material for *Tribune*, but also put aside material specifically for Clayton. According to Clarence William Dakin, who stayed with Beeby for a few days when he came to Canberra in December 1946 looking for a job in the public service (at Newbegin's suggestion), Beeby had scheduled times for private visits by select contacts (usually secret members of the party) in Canberra. She also 'used to travel to Sydney about once a fortnight',[88] but this evidently did not obviate Clayton's need to visit her in Canberra.

In 1948–50, he visited Frederick G. G. Rose, who then lived in Froggatt Street in Turner, 'two or three, or possibly four, times a year'.[89] According to Rose, who was treasurer of the Canberra branch at the time, Clayton would bring him copies of *Tribune* and other party literature to distribute, and would collect any party subscriptions or other 'donations'.[90] Rose had joined the public service in 1937, and joined the Communist Party in Melbourne in 1943. He was posted to Canberra in 1946, and over the next decade worked successively in the department of Territories, the department of Post-War Reconstruction and the department of External Territories. During his sixteen or so years in the public service, he 'had considerable access to classified information'.[91] In March 1956, Spry, the director-general of ASIO, noted that 'there is no positive proof that Rose has actively engaged in espionage', but that 'it appears to me extremely likely that he did so'.[92] He was involved in 'talent spotting' for Clayton (for example, he evidently introduced Clayton to June Barnett at his home during Easter 1950).[93] Rose has denied that he ever passed 'any information of any kind' to Clayton, but his denial is too categoric.[94] It was his function to serve as a Canberra contact point for Clayton, and it would be strange if Clayton's contacts in Canberra did not leave material with Rose for Clayton to collect.

Clayton met sporadically with Makarov in Canberra from 1943 to 1949. In October 1945, Moscow Centre instructed Makarov to tell Clayton not only to be more selective in his collection activities but also to be more careful; to reduce his meetings with Nosov to 'one a month', and to 'maintain only organisational liaison with BEN and the workers of the Australian NOOK'.[95] He also visited Canberra somewhat less frequently over the next several months, although there was no diminution in either the volume or currency of the material he collected from 'his friends in the NOOK'.[96] Indeed, in March 1946 he visited Canberra specifically to collect copies of British War Cabinet documents from Ian Milner which, as Makarov reported to Moscow on 19 March, were 'handed over to us for 35 minutes', photographed and returned to him to give back to Milner.[97] However, from the end of 1945 to March 1946, Clayton generally left his material with Prichard for Nosov to collect, though sometimes he also used 'dead drops' with Nosov. His visits to Canberra then became somewhat more frequent, and for a few months he used Beeby's flat as a safe house for Makarov to collect his material from. In October 1946, when Moscow Centre became aware of 'increased surveillance' of Soviet legations in Commonwealth countries, including Australia specifically, the Canberra Residency was directed to tell Clayton that operations were being temporarily suspended and that he 'should observe great care in the matter of contact with people of whom he has already made use for our common ends'.[98] Over the next year, contact between Clayton and Nosov or Makarov was quite sporadic. On 9 January 1947, for example, Lieutenant-General Fedotov (IVANOV) in Moscow told the Canberra Residency of his concern about a note which Clayton had evidently left at Beeby's flat for Makarov but which had been collected by another Soviet official.[99] From 1945 to 1949, however, Clayton generally communicated with Makarov through dead drops, mainly located in parks in the Braddon/Reid area.

Clayton met with Makarov twice in March and May 1948 to discuss the proposed reorganisation of the KLOD group. At the first meeting, which evidently occurred in late March, Makarov was supposed to ascertain from Clayton 'what the position is of all his people who were working for us and what opportunities they have at the present time', and to obtain his recommendations for 'group leaders', but the meeting was arranged without giving Clayton 'sufficient time to get ready'.[100] The next meeting, on 20 May, involved a detailed discussion of the roles that particular former informants might play in the new organisation.[101]

By the middle of 1949, Clayton would have been apprised that ASIO was aware of the existence of the KLOD group. When Makarov left Australia in June 1949 he knew he was under surveillance. Later in 1949 Nosov reportedly informed Moscow that he had been 'noticed . . . with his contact'.[102] In July 1950 he was told by Rupert Lockwood that one of his agents, Jim Hill, had been confronted by MI5 in London and that the security authorities were planning to arrest him.[103] And by mid 1949, he had established the illegal apparatus in which to effectively disappear.

13

'absorbed with Russianism'

THE DEVELOPMENT OF THE KLOD GROUP

THE INITIAL DEVELOPMENT OF SOVIET espionage activities in Australia in 1944–45, involving the study and recruitment of useful agents and the organisation of efficient and secure means of communication with them, was a slow, careful, tentative, and essentially opportunistic process. Moscow Centre provided detailed instructions about tradecraft to the Residency in Canberra and attempted to maintain managerial authority over both 'operational matters' and the specific nature of the intelligence collected. In practice, however, these matters were determined by the dedication and range of contacts available to the local party functionaries and, in particular, by the opportunities available to Clayton and his willingness and ability to exploit them.

There was no blueprint for the development of the KLOD group. It was not until 1945 that Moscow Centre began to impose some shape on the group, to influence which particular lines of intelligence collection should be pursued, to discard some informants and to seek recruits in specific areas of interest. But in 1944–45, Clayton had the initiative. Sometimes Moscow Centre did not even know the source of the information he was providing.

Most of the material the KLOD group provided in 1944 was not secret. Indeed, one of Clayton's informants had no direct access to secret material. By the beginning of 1945, however, Clayton was spending more of his time trying to obtain documents specifically identified and requested by Moscow Centre, though some of these, such as reports from the Australian legation in Moscow to Canberra about the trade union movement in the Soviet Union, were fairly innocuous.

Clayton's first informants were members of the party or their close relations who were personally known to him and with whom he was already in regular (and usually secret) contact. These included Prichard, Hughes, Bernie and Wilbur Christiansen. Some of Clayton's informants were quite aware that the information they were providing was destined for Moscow, but others were in the dark. In April 1945, Hughes and Bernie, who were in potentially very useful positions, were given cover-names: BEN and SESTRA respectively. Unlike other members of the group, Prichard was not recruited by Clayton but was actively involved in many ways,[1] and worked closely with Clayton in the early development of the group.

KATHARINE SUSANNAH PRICHARD

Prichard was by the 1940s generally acknowledged as 'the most important fiction writer of Australia'.[2] She was also, for half a century, the leading woman communist in Australia, having been a foundation member of the CPA in 1920 and remaining in the party, through all its policy contortions, until her death in October 1969.[3] Born in Levuka in Fiji on 4 December 1883, she left Fiji when she was three and spent her childhood in Melbourne and Launceston. Her father committed suicide in 1907, and the following year, aged 24, she went to London and worked as a freelance journalist. She came back to Australia in 1910, worked for two years with the *Herald* in Melbourne, then returned to London. She was affected by the hunger and plight of London's unemployed, and by 1915, after visiting the Australian Voluntary Hospital near Boulogne in France, 'was consumed with desire to find some way of preventing the diabolical slaughter caused by war'.[4] Also in 1915, she published her first novel, *The Pioneers*, which won a prize for the best Australian novel that year. She returned to Australia in February 1916, determined to devote herself to writing 'about Australia and the realities of life for the Australian people'.[5]

During the latter months of 1915 she met Captain Hugo Throssell, who had won the Victoria Cross for conspicuous bravery at Hill 60 at Gallipoli on 15 August 1915, and who was in London recuperating from his wounds. They were married on 28 January 1919 and moved to Greenmount, near Perth, Western Australia. Their only child, Ric, was born in 1922.

By 1919, both Throssell and Prichard had become active socialists. At victory celebrations in 1919, he declared that the war had

Katharine Susannah Prichard was a leading Australian novelist and a foundation member of the Communist Party of Australia, of which she remained a member until her death in 1969. She is referred to in the Venona material in 1944–45 as 'an influential ACADEMICIAN', *and probably introduced Wally Clayton (*KLOD*) to the first Soviet intelligence officer in Australia, the TASS correspondent, Vladimir Mikheev. (NLA)*

made him a socialist.[6] Prichard was more familiar with Marxist literature and was soon more ideologically committed to communism, but by 1920 they both described themselves as 'Bolsheviks'.[7] She was appointed a foundation member of the CPA in early 1920, and was directed 'to form study circles in Western Australia'.[8] However, the party in Western Australia was 'small and weak'; initially about ten or eleven people came to the study group, 'and these were mostly fossils'. By 1922 the numbers had dwindled 'until there were only four of us one evening . . . [including] myself and my husband'.[9] Nonetheless, the lack of success with the study circles served only to intensify her party efforts. 'No task was too menial for her. No demand too great.'[10] The Marxist ideal required the dedication of both 'brain and body for the workers'.[11]

Prichard's commitment to communism was soon reflected in her novels. Like *The Pioneers*, *Windlestraws* (published in 1916) and *Black Opal* (1921), which established her reputation as a writer, were about people living and working together in harmony with the land, with sexuality a central theme.[12] Although these early novels 'reverberated with a sense of injustice and unspecified commitment to change', they lacked any 'theoretical underpinning'.[13] By the late 1920s, however, the influence of communism on Prichard's writing—in *Working Bullocks* (published in 1926), *The Wild Oats of Han* (1928) and *Coonardoo* (1928)—had become quite conscious. These novels continued to explore the themes of sexuality, the human relationship to the natural world, and injustice, but to more political point. *Coonardoo*, about the doomed love between a white man and a black woman, demanded that Aborigines be recognised as an important and integral part of Australian life.[14] By 1930, Prichard was 'sure', in her own words, that 'there isn't anything worth working for except communism'.[15]

In 1933 she visited the Soviet Union, stopping over on the way in London, where she 'contacted Communist Party Headquarters in England'.[16] In Moscow, from August to November, she shared a small one-bedroom flat with Guido Carlo Luigi Baracchi and Betty Roland, fellow Australian communists who occasionally performed clandestine tasks for the Soviet intelligence services. They had left Australia for Moscow in February 1933, Baracchi's purpose being 'to deliver some highly confidential documents to the party [i.e. Comintern] leaders in the Kremlin'.[17] During a stop-over in London in April, they met Harry Pollitt, the 'top man' in the British Communist Party, who gave Baracchi 'some additional documents to deliver to the Kremlin', and which Roland 'concealed among my lingerie'.[18] In March 1934, Roland carried secret papers from Pollitt and another party official, Palme Dutt, by train across Nazi Germany and delivered them to the OGPU in Leningrad.[19] It was already clear to Roland in 1933 that the OGPU was 'the state's chief instrument of terror' and was 'universally feared', but she thought it was a necessary instrument for building the 'new society', and these Australian communists at least were pleased to work for it.[20]

In November 1933, when Prichard was in London en route back to Australia, Throssell committed suicide. He had been broken by the Depression, his business ventures were failures, and he faced 'the inescapable burden of debt'.[21] Prichard thought she might have contributed to his death; perhaps he had found the unfinished manuscript of her next novel, *Intimate Strangers*, in which the central character was an unwanted husband who took his own life.[22] Whatever, it weighed on her mind 'as an almost insupportable burden of guilt for the rest of her long life'.[23]

She did what was common among communists in the 1930s— 'when the weight of personal suffering seems unbearable, immerse yourself in day to day [party] activity'.[24] Henceforth, her commitment to communism was unqualified. She was soon working furiously for the party, sometimes eighteen hours a day, organising meetings and building up 'spearhead' groups.[25] In her now infrequent novels, through to her goldfields trilogy (*The Roaring Nineties, Golden Miles* and *Winged Seeds*) in the late 1940s, she adopted the literary technique of 'socialist realism'. The passion and the vibrancy of her earlier novels was never repeated. Miles Franklin wrote in 1937 that Prichard was 'a brave soul off the track for the time . . . Now she is . . . absorbed with Russianism to the exclusion or detriment or distortion of Australianism'.[26] In a controversial obituary in 1969,

Dorothy Hewett wrote that after 1933, Prichard 'began her fierce self-immolation in a political dream . . . Her dogma hardened round her like a crystalis [sic] she was never to leave'.[27] Guido Baracchi said of her in 1941 that she was 'taking the final, fatal steps . . . coming to say . . . "Those blokes [in the party hierarchy] know much better than I do"!'[28]

For Prichard, the achievement of communism in Australia meant unquestioned dedication to the Soviet Union. According to her son, Ric Throssell, the Soviet Union remained 'the centre of her ideals for half a century'.[29] She believed in 'the infallibility of the Communist Party of the Soviet Union',[30] and had 'every confidence in the Soviet Government'.[31] Nothing was more important to her than the defence of 'the first Socialist State'.[32] After the German invasion of the Soviet Union in June 1941, she was prepared to support anything that could effectively assist a Soviet victory.[33]

By April 1939, Prichard was a member of the Western Australian state executive of the CPA,[34] and remained one 'all through the period of its illegality'.[35] In July 1942 the Security Service reported that she had 'been receiving lengthy cables from the Soviet Information Bureau and other sources in Moscow'.[36] In September, she met the Soviet intelligence scout Mikheev, on his way to Sydney, and on 3 October she wrote to Moscow stating that she would be moving to Sydney herself in a few weeks time and that letters to her could be sent to Mikheev, as she would be contacting him when she got there.[37] She wrote to Ric, who was then in the Army at Milne Bay, on 7 October 1942, telling him that she was moving to Sydney on 28 October to be nearer to him.[38]

Prichard had long been aware that she was a subject of interest to the security authorities. In Perth in the late 1930s and early 1940s, she had experienced some of the crudest forms of Special Branch and Security Service attentions. In 1932, the police had visited her and taken 'all papers having reference to Communism'.[39] In June 1940, when the CPA was declared illegal, her house was 'ransacked and much of her library removed'.[40] She guessed that her letters were intercepted by the censors and that anything of interest was passed to the Security Service, which was indeed the case.[41] In December 1941, the security interest in her was confirmed by the attorney-general himself. Prichard had called in to Canberra while on a lecture tour of the eastern states for the Australian–Soviet Friendship Society, and had dinner with Evatt and his wife. When she 'started to explain where I had been and what I had been saying on the lecture tour', Evatt stopped her and said: 'You needn't tell me. I've been kept informed by the Security lads of all your movements; had an almost hourly report on where you were going and what you've been saying.'⁴² It was a warning that she must have appreciated when she moved to Sydney.

She lived in Sydney until March 1946, for all but the first few months at Flat 5, 'The Gwydir', 166 Forbes Street, Darlinghurst. It was a lively place, with frequent congregations of radical journalists and academics, novelists and poets, public servants (especially members of the department of External Affairs), CPA functionaries (including Walter Clayton), and 'friends of Russia', who engaged in vigorous and wide-ranging discussions of cultural, social and political ideas and issues. Mikheev and Nosov were also frequent visitors.⁴³

In June 1943, at the 13th National Congress, Prichard was elected (together with Walter Clayton) to the central committee of the CPA. As Ric Throssell has written, 'she played little role in the determination of policy'; rather, 'her role in the Central Committee was primarily concerned with cultural affairs and relations with the USSR'.⁴⁴ Throssell was in Sydney as an External Affairs cadet from June to December 1943 and visited his mother most weekends. He has recounted how among the 'stream' of visitors were 'some of the party leaders and the top men in the communist-led unions', 'grave men' who talked 'as if the political future of the nation depended upon their wisdom', and of whom Prichard told him: 'They are some of the finest men I know.'⁴⁵ He has written that 'the Communist Party was no longer illegal in 1943, but the habit of caution survived among party members', and select officials would sometimes meet privately to discuss 'Party business' in her apartment.⁴⁶ When he saw his mother in Sydney in 1943, Throssell recalled, 'I was not prepared for the change that the war made in her attitudes.'⁴⁷ He worried that his 'kind and gentle mother' had become ruthless, and was prepared to justify torture or whatever means were necessary for the Soviet cause.⁴⁸

Prichard played an important role in the establishment of the KLOD group in 1943–45. She was probably responsible for introducing Mikheev to Clayton in late 1942, and in 1943–45 she was a source of material sent from the KGB Residency in Canberra to Moscow Centre. Most of the material was political gossip, which she would write up in longhand on foolscap paper and give to Clayton to pass to Makarov in Canberra. Much of it consisted of summarised accounts of what Throssell (who had yet formally to join the department) had related to her about the structure, personnel, interests and policies of External Affairs.

Ric Throssell moved to Canberra at the end of 1943, but visited his mother in Sydney fairly often in 1944–45, and some of her discussions with Clayton concerned Throssell's career possibilities. In September 1945, for example, Throssell was told he was to be posted to Moscow; this information, reported by Clayton after a conversation with Prichard, was cabled to Moscow Centre on 30 September.[49] But 'even before he received the appointment', Clayton and Prichard had canvassed Throssell's posting options. Clayton had 'clearly hinted to her that from the point of view of the Party it would be better if he went to a post in Europe, for example in Holland', but 'Prichard . . . very much wanted her son to go to the Soviet Union and had her way'.[50] She sometimes recounted information she had learned from Evatt's secretary Allan Dalziel, whom she regarded as 'a dear—and good friend'.[51] But by 1945, other members of the KLOD group were providing documents and other information of real substance, and Prichard's principal function was to serve as a conduit between Clayton and the various agents and contacts who left material at her apartment.

For a few months, from November 1945 to March 1946, she played another important role in the operations of the group. After October 1945, when Clayton was warned by Moscow Centre to be more cautious, he travelled to Canberra less often and increasingly used Prichard to pass material directly to Nosov. Prichard and Nosov met at least once every couple of weeks during this period.[52]

Prichard was re-elected to the central committee of the party at the 14th National Congress in August 1945, but in March 1946 she resigned and moved back to Perth. In April 1947, she moved to Canberra to live with Throssell,[53] whose posting to Moscow had been cut short by the death of his young wife, Bea. They lived at Elfrida Newbegin's former flat in Braddon until October 1947, when Throssell re-married and Prichard moved back to Perth. Both Throssell and his new wife, Dorothy Jordan (PODRUGA), had visited Doris Beeby at the apartment before Throssell took over the lease.[54]

During her six months in Canberra in 1947, Prichard does not seem to have played any significant role in the activities of the KLOD group, even though it is likely that Clayton met with her on his trips to Canberra during this period. It is evident from the Venona material that Clayton had obtained information from both Throssell and Dorothy Jordan, but whether he had received this from them directly or through Prichard cannot be determined.

Prichard stayed in Western Australia for the rest of her life. The KLOD group appears to have had no connections in the West and, at any event, she worked through the rest of the 1940s on completion of the goldfields trilogy. But she remained firmly committed to communism and to Moscow. In 1966, when the Russian writers Yuri Daniel and Andrei Sinyavsky were prosecuted for distributing anti-Soviet propaganda, she had her first breach with CPA policy. When the central committee issued a statement finding 'the arrest and sentence of these men to be unnecessary and wrong', Prichard supported Moscow and insisted that 'to defend the first Socialist

State was more important than to placate writers and intellectuals with bourgeois leftist conceptions of freedom'.[55] In September 1968, when Soviet forces invaded Czechoslovakia, she again took issue with the central committee, which protested against the invasion, by declaring that 'I have every confidence in the Soviet Government to take every step that's necessary for the defence of Socialism' and that to criticise the invasion was 'counter-revolutionary'.[56] However, she did not leave the party, and paid her last subscription to it just three days before she died, aged 86, on 2 October 1969. She was given a communist funeral, with a Soviet flag draping the coffin; 'the bulk of the . . . mourners was made up of communists'.[57]

There remain many questions about Prichard, including some fundamental ones concerning her views about morality and principle. Throssell has written that his mother lived up to 'the ideal standards of political and personal behaviour which she expected of a true communist',[58] but he is too charitable about some of her lapses. Some of her former party comrades raised questions about her personal integrity when they learned in 1989 that Prichard, who in 1943 was 'a proud member of the Communist Party Central Committee . . . publicly supporting the party policy of everything for the defeat of fascism', and who later wrote (in 1968) that she had thought it 'necessary' that Throssell join the Army, had in fact used her influence with Evatt and Colonel Hodgson to have her son removed 'from the war zone to the security of External Affairs'.[59]

Another incident that also occurred in 1943 throws light on both Prichard's principles and her relationship with Clayton. This involved Jean Devanny, who came to Australia from New Zealand with her husband and their two children in 1929. She was a noted writer of the 1930s and 1940s, an energetic party organiser, a gifted platform orator and 'agitational speaker', and a liberal in sexual matters. Through the late 1930s, she had 'a long affair' with J. B. Miles, the national secretary of the party.[60] In 1941, while working with a group of communist shearers at an isolated bush camp inland from Cairns, Devanny was gang raped. She protested to the Cairns (North Queensland) district committee, but 'influential male comrades used their power to settle sexual scores' with her, and she was expelled (for 'infamous conduct') from the party.[61] In 1943, Devanny warned that unless her expulsion was rescinded, she would publish correspondence she had received from central committee members, and particularly Miles. Clayton, as secretary of the control commission, flew to Cairns (which was still in 'the military war zone') to determine how the matter might be resolved. Clayton has contradicted Devanny's account of their discussions in Cairns (there is no doubt that his role was duplicitous), but she was re-admitted to the party.[62]

Prichard was a member of the central committee with Clayton at this time, and has been widely criticised for not supporting Devanny—and indeed, for contributing to her woes. Devanny had thought that Prichard was a good friend; she saw her both in Brisbane and Sydney at this time, but 'on neither occasion would Katharine Prichard listen to her, or tell her what was happening'.[63] Clayton has said that Prichard was 'in no way . . . whatsoever' involved in the matter, and that whatever her personal views, she would have recognised that it was being handled correctly by the relevant party body (i.e. himself, as secretary of the control commission).[64] Considerations of friendship and justice, of solidarity with a fellow writer and woman, were necessarily subordinate to the authority of the control commission and the party. Indeed, according to Devanny, 'KSP said that what the Party wanted was some sensible older woman to assist the good P [Party] workers that way'.[65]

Alfred Hughes

Clayton's first recruit was Alfred Thompson Hughes, who was given the cover name BEN by Moscow Centre in April 1945, and who was the NKGB's principal source of 'operational intelligence' in Australia. Born in Sydney on 22 March 1900, Hughes attended North Sydney Boys' High, then Sydney Technical College from 1917.[66] Although he was eager to enlist during the First World War, his application was initially rejected because he was under age. Eventually, in June 1918, he was accepted, but was discharged on 31 December without serving overseas.[67] He then worked as a casual labourer at building sites and studied medicine for four years until family financial problems caused him to withdraw from study and join the NSW Police Force.[68]

Hughes was accepted as a probationary constable on 14 May 1924 and confirmed as an ordinary constable on 14 July 1925. He was by this time $5'10\frac{1}{2}''$ tall and weighed 168lb.[69] He was a talented and hard-working officer, but progressed slowly through the ranks. He received the designation of detective in 1933; was promoted to constable 1st class in 1936; and passed the examinations for promotion to sergeant 3rd class in 1940, although he was not promoted to that rank until 1945.[70]

On 4 June 1925 Hughes married Evelyn Margaret Janet Cowell,[71] but they became estranged in 1931, and she applied for a divorce the following year. After they parted, Hughes lived in a boarding house in North Sydney, but continued to support his wife until 1948, when the divorce was granted by the NSW Supreme

Alfred Hughes, a detective sergeant in the NSW Police, joined the Military Police Intelligence section in 1940 and transferred to the Security Service in 1942, where he became responsible for monitoring the activities of the Communist Party in NSW. With the cover name BEN, *he provided Clayton and the KGB with security reports on the KGB's agents in Australia, until he returned to the NSW Police in 1945. He tried unsuccessfully to join ASIO in 1951. (Australian Archives CRS A6119/83, item 1510)*

Court. Cowell later described Hughes as a 'Nationalist' and a 'very deep person who never confided in her'; but who neglected her during their marriage, often not coming home for meals, and whose sole interest was his police work.[72]

On 12 June 1940 Hughes joined the Military Police Intelligence (MPI) section.[73] In 1942, when the Security Service was formed, the section was disbanded and its staff given the option of moving to the Security Service or returning to normal police duties. Hughes chose the Security Service, where he became the chief investigator in the counter-espionage section, responsible for monitoring 'subversive associations and the operations of the Communist Party'.[74] According to a senior colleague in the Security Service at the time:

> Hughes had an excellent knowledge of members of the Communist Party and of its various ramifications . . . Hughes was regarded as the expert. He would see all the reports with regard to the Communist Party and similar subversive organisations, his opinion was constantly asked, and his services used in all investigations dealing with Party members and their activities.[75]

According to another former colleague:

> [Hughes] used to call at Special Branch Headquarters and sit for hours, about two or three times a week, researching Communist Party records to which he had unlimited access. He could easily have extracted documents from files as he was trusted.[76]

His superiors believed that 'Hughes had at least one important agent in the Communist Party.'[77]

In October 1945, Hughes left the Security Service and went back to the NSW Police Force, where he worked in the vice squad for the next fifteen years. On 5 February 1949, he married Margaret Ann Clancy.[78] According to police colleagues in the late 1940s and early 1950s, he had by then developed a 'ruddy complexion' and a large, red nose (which earned him the nickname 'Pickles').[79]

In 1951 Hughes decided to apply to join ASIO. In an undated letter (probably written at the end of May) to the new organisation, he said that he had heard that it was seeking people with experience in criminal investigation, and that he 'had 14 years experience in plain clothes work including 5 years with wartime MPI and Security Service'.[80] ASIO's initial response was to advise Hughes that 'there are no suitable vacancies existing to which you could be appointed'.[81] However, there was evidently some rethinking about this over the next week or so—perhaps arising out of a concern that to reject Hughes outright, when it was known that ASIO was actively recruiting people with his background and experience, might alert him to the Venona-based case being constructed against him. Alternatively, perhaps it was thought that he might reveal, during the application and vetting processes, something about his past activities or contacts. Whatever the reason, on 18 June he was invited, 'if you are still interested', to submit a formal application,[82] which he did on 29 June.[83] However, Hughes did not proceed further with his application, later offering in explanation that 'I was unsettled in my job at the time—things were not so good, but in 1952 they changed for the better', and hence 'I didn't go on with it.'[84]

In the early 1930s, during the Great Depression, the CPA had been able to establish a branch within the Police Force in Sydney. In 1945, it was reported that Hughes was 'a Communist member of long-standing', having joined the party in 'about 1932'.[85] During the war years, and including the period when the Communist Party was illegal, Hughes was reportedly one of two officers in the MPI section and the Security Service (the other was an Army intelligence officer) who were secret members of the Communist Party and whom J. S. Miles described in 1953 as having been 'very useful to the Party'.[86]

Clayton had established secret contact arrangements with Hughes even before the establishment of the NKGB Residency in Canberra in 1943. He evidently informed the NKGB of Hughes's position in 1944, and by the beginning of 1945 Moscow Centre had decided, with some trepidation, to explore the possibility of recruiting him. Clayton was questioned about the possibility by Nosov at a meeting on 15 March, and responded positively.[87] On 5 May, the Canberra Residency reported to Moscow that Hughes, now cover-named BEN, was already 'working secretly' on an assignment from Clayton.[88]

On 3 July 1945, the Canberra Residency cabled to Moscow Centre that 'KLOD has reported that BEN has been bringing a number of items of operational material from the Sydney security organs for him to see', including 'special files on the Soviet Legation and on TASS representatives'.[89] Clayton reported that the former were of little use 'since the main files on the Legation are in Canberra', but that the files on Mikheev and Nosov were more interesting. Mikheev's file, for example, included copies of telegrams he had both sent to and received from Moscow, as well as references to a request by 'American Intelligence' for information about Mikheev and 'his possible connections with the Communists in SYDNEY'.[90] Hughes also provided Clayton with 'a lot of information about the organisational structure of Australia's intelligence organs', and showed him a file on 'Investigation of German Organisations in Sydney' which included 'a detailed account of the activities of the various organisations'.[91]

Indeed, Hughes was able to provide so much documentary material that his NKGB controllers were faced with the question of how to photograph it all. Since Clayton was 'not familiar with the technique of photographing documents', Makarov suggested that Hughes should work directly with Nosov and that the latter should be given a special NKGB camera 'for photographing documents in his flat'.[92] However, Moscow Centre objected to any 'direct liaison' between Hughes and Nosov.[93] In late August 1945, Hughes gave Clayton a lot more information 'concerning the Australian Security Service', including copies of several documents. A lengthy summary of this material, which Makarov considered to be 'of operational value', was cabled to Moscow on 1 September.[94] From Australian Security Service files we know that Simpson, the director-general of Security, had asked his deputy-director in Sydney for a report on Clayton on 8 August. Hughes submitted his report on Clayton to his superior in the Sydney office on 31 August.[95]

Hughes was in a fantastic position. On the one hand, from 1942 to 1945 he was the chief investigator of the Communist Party in New South Wales—not to say of Soviet espionage, which it was also his job to detect. His working responsibilities included attending public meetings of party 'front' organisations, watching the meetings and movements of senior party and 'front' officials, meeting with and interviewing party members, and reporting on these activities. From January 1943 to August 1945, he produced some 30 reports on organisations such as the Eureka Youth League (30 May 1944), or on individuals, such as Vladimir Mikheev (4 May 1945) and Walter Clayton (31 August 1945).[96] He managed to include in these reports at least as much information as would have been expected of him as an experienced detective yet provide nothing that would incriminate these organisations, their members or their activities. He knew exactly how much his colleagues in the Security Service and the NSW Special Branch knew about these matters. He was also able to meet clandestinely with his 'agents' or contacts in the party—whom he consistently refused to identify to his Security Service colleagues or later ASIO investigators. He would have been able to keep Clayton and his NKGB controllers well apprised of security operations against them.

FRANCES BERNIE

Bernie (née Scott) was Clayton's second recruit, and was given the cover-name SESTRA by Moscow Centre in April 1945. Frances Ada Scott was born in Sydney on 22 July 1922 to English migrant parents. She 'did not have an easy childhood', and the family 'had next to nothing in the depression years'.[97] Brought up as a Roman Catholic, she was educated at both public schools and convents and was active in the Young Catholic Association during her youth and in the early part of the war. In 1941, however, she 'felt that Roman Catholicism was not providing the answers to a lot of questions which were confusing my mind, and I felt the need to seek the solution elsewhere'.[98]

In 1941, aged nineteen, she joined the East Sydney Branch of the Communist Party (then an illegal organisation),[99] and was soon actively involved in several 'front' organisations—including, 'almost immediately', the Australian Labour League of Youth (ALLY), the Party's youth organisation. She was 'one of the original organisers' of the Eureka Youth League (EYL) in New South Wales, which was established (from the reorganised ALLY) under the auspices of the central committee in January 1943.[100] By April 1943, she was assistant secretary and hence a member of the state council of the EYL NSW.[101] On 2 September 1943, she was elected assistant secretary of the provisional executive of the recently formed International Youth Committee—a body representing about a dozen trade union, ethnic, religious and other youth groups.[102] By April 1944, she was the assistant national secretary of the EYL.[103]

From 1942 to 1944 Bernie worked as a stenographer at the EYL at 40 Market Street in central Sydney, where she did secretarial and administrative duties and was actively involved in youth rallies and demonstrations organised by the party through the league.[104] Her commitment to communism 'caused a serious domestic upset', as a result of which she left home and moved to a room in Neutral Bay. By 1943, she was a member of the Kings Cross or Darlinghurst Branch of the party.[105] Bernie later stated that:

> At this particular period of my life [i.e., 1942–44] I gave myself entirely to the Communist Party. I had no other interest or occupation and my work for the Communist Party was in every sense a full time work . . . I became intensely pro-Russian in outlook and expression.[106]

Around April 1944, however, Bernie stopped active work for the party. She has said she 'dropped out' because of ill health caused by her tireless party activities, but there is a curious aside to her explanation. It was at that time 'normal Communist Party practice' for functionaries such as Bernie to report their illnesses and plans for leave to more senior officials at party headquarters, then located at Daking House in Rawson Place, near Central railway station. Bernie was told by another party functionary at the EYL, Ida Sherden, that she should see Walter Clayton, whom she found occupying 'a small cubicle like office' in Daking House.[107] Clayton told her that if she ever needed help she should approach the party, and said that 'the Party will help you and when you are better will find you a job if necessary'.[108]

Some months later, on 20 November, Bernie began work as a temporary typist in Evatt's office in Sydney, but the circumstances surrounding her appointment are not completely clear. On 1 and 2 November, the *Sydney Morning Herald* had carried a 'positions vacant' notice for a 'young lady, 21–28 years, competent stenographer, good English, required for Commonwealth Ministerial office, Sydney'.[109] Bernie applied for the job, and was interviewed very soon after by Allan Dalziel, who told her that the advertised position had been filled (by Beryl Hallett) but that he could offer her another, more junior position, which she accepted.[110] On 8 November, Dalziel advised External Affairs that he proposed to employ two new typists (including Bernie); the appointments were approved on 17 November.[111]

Bernie has said that she had applied for the job in Evatt's office on her own initiative. 'I had always been lacking in political perspicacity, and that had been pointed out to me often by the Party; and I thought by taking part in this work I might learn a bit more about politics.'[112] She also felt that 'the Communist Party would be interested in what was happening in any other political party'.[113] More recently, the author David McKnight was told by 'a CPA source' that Clayton 'in fact had arranged the job for her in Evatt's office'.[114] In any event, soon after she began working there, and 'again following normal communist party practices', Bernie reported on her new job to Clayton and agreed that 'if I came across anything which would be of interest to the Communist Party I would bring it to him'.[115]

On 10 February 1945, Bernie married Max Gluck. He was a rabbi's son, born in Vienna on 28 November 1913; driven from Austria by Nazi persecution, he arrived in Australia on 23 May 1939, and was naturalised on 19 November 1945.[116] They had met in 1943, when Gluck visited the EYL office. Gluck has said that although he attended Communist Party meetings in 1943–45, he never really joined the party.[117] This was untrue. As the Canberra Residency informed Moscow Centre on 5 July 1945, on the basis of information provided by Clayton, Gluck 'is a member of the FRATERNAL', who kept his membership secret because of his employment in the Army 'Labour Corps'.[118] Clayton reported that Bernie's marriage 'had had an exceptionally strong favourable influence upon her', making her 'steadier and more serious'.[119]

Bernie continued to work in Evatt's office until 12 April 1946.[120] There were, during her seventeen-month tenure, five or six staff members in the office, including Dalziel and Bernie. Until late 1945, she worked in a small room alone, but during her final several months she shared a room with Beryl Hallett.[121]

According to the Venona material, Clayton told Nosov about Bernie at a meeting on about 20 April 1945, describing her as 'an undercover member' of the party 'who began work four or five months ago at Evatt's as a secretary-typist'. He told Nosov he was 'giving her detailed instruction on how to conduct herself while working in Evatt's outfit', but did not tell him whether she had been providing him with 'any materials'.[122] At a meeting in early July, Clayton gave Nosov additional biographical information about Bernie and described her access to material in Evatt's office. Bernie had brought Clayton copies of correspondence between Dalziel and Evatt, but Makarov reckoned that these were 'of no great interest'. Clayton told Nosov that he needed to do 'a lot of work . . . on her in order to turn her into a worker we can be sure of', and that he had 'begun to carry out work along these lines'; he said that 'for a start he refrained from accepting any documents', but had instructed her to memorise interesting material.[123] Through the next six months, however, she provided Clayton with both verbal reports and documentary material. In October 1945, for example, she 'passed [to Clayton] a mass of internal political material'.[124]

Bernie left the Communist Party shortly after she stopped working in Evatt's office. She wrote to her branch secretary requesting leave of absence for a couple of years, and when it was granted, 'I quietly lapsed from Communist Party activity and have never participated in it since.'[125] She and her husband, who had now changed their surname to Garrett, bought a house in Wahroonga, on the northern outskirts of Sydney, intending to 'settle down and raise a family'.[126]

WILBUR CHRISTIANSEN

Wilbur Norman Christiansen, cover-named MASTER (as in 'master craftsman'), was from the 1940s to the 1970s one of Australia's leading radio physicists. By 1959, when he was made a Fellow of the Australian Academy of Science, he had achieved an international reputation in radio astronomy. His invention of the multiple interferometer antenna system was one of the major advances in radio astronomy in the 1950s.[127] He was probably also one of Clayton's longest-serving informants, starting as early as 1944–45, and he was one of the few informants outside the department of External Affairs in whom Moscow Centre retained an active concern when the KLOD group was reorganised in mid 1948.[128]

Christiansen was born in Melbourne on 9 August 1913. He was educated at Melbourne University, obtaining his BSc in 1933 and his MSc in 1935. At this time he was an active member of the Melbourne University Labor Club, and served as the assistant editor of *Proletariat*, its 'official organ'.[129] He believed, in 1935, that the world was 'moving to a new era of war madness', that the rise of war and fascism in Europe and America was a consequence of 'the development of the general crisis of capitalism', and that the 'organised student movement' had an important role to play in the replacement of capitalism by socialism.[130] He believed in particular in 'the necessity for freedom in science' and the desirability of 'the communist approach' to science, and that all scientific knowledge should be freely available to all people.[131]

In 1936, Christiansen joined Amalgamated Wireless (Australasia) Limited in Melbourne, where he worked for the next eleven years as the supervising engineer in the beam development laboratory at the AWA Radio-Electric Works at Ashfield. AWA had been given responsibility for the construction and operation of the beam (directional high frequency radio-telegraph) international telecommunications system in the 1920s; by the early 1940s more than 40 per cent of Australia's overseas telegraphic traffic was being moved by this system (with the rest going by the underwater cable network).[132] The beam development laboratory worked closely with engineers and technicians at Australia's first international beam transmitting and receiving stations, built by AWA at Ballan and Rockbank, north-west of Melbourne, in 1927.

During the war, AWA 'promptly turned over its extensive resources' to the Australian war effort. More than 20 000 radio-telegraph and radio-telephone transmitters were manufactured, including radio sets for armoured vehicles and tanks, transmitters for RAAF aircraft, ground station transmitters for forward areas and base stations, and sets for the Navy. Radio receivers (including direction-finding equipment) of various types were also produced for the armed services. The research laboratories were responsible for research and advanced development work, and made important contributions in such areas as the design and manufacture of mobile radio systems, the development of radar systems, and 'the design of special equipment for Beam Wireless communications service'.[133] Christiansen himself designed new antenna systems (such as rhombic aerials) for beam propagation.[134]

Whether or not Christiansen was ever a member of the Communist Party is open to question. He has said he 'was never actually a member', but that he 'had general left-wing views', had 'been associated with left-wing things for a long time', had 'associated with Communists . . . in various organizations', and believed that 'the materialist concept of history is the one which fits best with scientific thinking'.[135] However, there are several reports that he was a secret member of the party in Melbourne in 1940–45, including two reports to the security authorities in 1940.[136] In 1958, an informant told ASIO that 'Christiansen was definitely a C.P. of A. member in 1945', but that he was 'a nice old boy' who probably would not have joined the party 'but for his wife'.[137]

On 5 January 1938, Christiansen had married Elsie Mary Hill. She came from a fairly large but very close family. Her father, James Frederick Hill, was a teacher with the Victorian Education department. Her two brothers, Edward Fowler (or Ted), born on 23 April 1915, and James Frederick junior, born in 1918, were respectively major figures in the CPA and the Soviet espionage operations in Australia.

Ted had joined the CPA in about 1937 after being 'spotted' by Clayton at Melbourne University and then recruited by Cecil Sharpley.[138] He was to become over the next couple of decades one of the most prominent communist figures in Australia. Although he and Clayton were not personal friends, they were 'very close' and Clayton would invariably meet with him whenever he came to Melbourne during the 1940s.[139] In 1940–42, when the party was illegal, Ted Hill served 'as a courier and contact man' for the underground members in Melbourne.[140] He also worked with the control commission to enforce discipline and crush deviationism within the party in Victoria.[141] During the war he also recruited promising young people for full-time party work—such as Bernie Taft, who went on to become secretary of the Victorian branch and joint national secretary of the CPA, and who has described Ted Hill as 'intelligent, yet dogmatic and intolerant' and an avowed Stalinist.[142] By the end of the war, he was the dominant figure in the party in Victoria, a position made official in 1949 when he became the Victorian state secretary.[143] He was a member of the central committee from 1948 to 1962 (he was expelled in 1963, as the CPA followed Khrushchev in denouncing the most egregious mistakes and the worst excesses of Stalinism), when he formed the CPA (Marxist/Leninist), which followed the Chinese communist line.[144]

Elsie's other brother, Jim, was by the end of 1945 the most active member of the KLOD group, meeting frequently with Clayton and providing him with a continuous stream of information. Jim Hill and Wilbur Christiansen met during the latter's 'courting days' and became good friends.[145] After 1948, when the Christiansens moved to Sydney, Jim and his family usually stayed with them whenever they visited Sydney.[146]

Christiansen also maintained an active involvement in the trade unions in the scientific and electrical engineering professions, in which many of his associates were party members. In 1943 he was treasurer of the Australian Association of Scientific Workers, whose federal council was located in Melbourne, and which was a party front organisation.[147] According to information Clayton provided to the NKGB in April 1945, 'many of the members of the Federal Council are in the FRATERNAL or are under its influence'.[148] He was reportedly still a member of the association in 1946.[149]

At the beginning of 1948, Christiansen resigned from AWA and moved to Sydney, where he became a senior research officer in the radio astronomy section of the radiophysics division of the CSIRO, which was located at Sydney University. He remained there for the next twelve years, working mainly on the development of large antenna arrays, such as the crossed multiple interferometer, which was the most precise radio astronomy system then developed (and which he used to monitor solar activity as part of Australia's contribution to the International Geophysical Year of 1957–58).[150] He was appointed professor of Electrical Engineering in April 1960.[151]

In April 1948, the CIS began an investigation into Christiansen as a result of information received from the director of signals and the director of Military Intelligence. Spry (the DMI) had been informed by the director of signals about an incident 'during the week ending' 10 April 1948, when two Army signals officers had reportedly been enticed into a luncheon with Christiansen and another colleague. As Spry wrote to Longfield Lloyd on 19 April:

> Soon after the party had assembled, the Army officers were asked questions regarding Army communications, such as channels of communications at home and overseas, and the frequencies used by the Army. [The] questions were so pointed that the officers' suspicions were aroused that they were being deliberately pumped.[152]

Spry told Longfield Lloyd (the director of the CIS) that Christiansen was 'allegedly a known communist and ex-employee of AWA whose services were . . . terminated', and that it had been 'suggested that during the war Christiansen may have been barred from entering service establishments', although, he added, 'I have no idea of the reliability of [this] background information.'[153]

Longfield Lloyd asked the CIS in Sydney to compile a report on Christiansen on 28 April. The response came on 4 June. Based on both CIS files and 'discreet inquiries', it was very flimsy. The files contained the two reports from 1940 that Christiansen was a member of the party, and the inquiries confirmed that he had previously worked at AWA but contradicted the suggestion that he had been discharged; in fact, AWA had been reluctant to lose his services.[154] The investigation into the luncheon concluded that the pointed questions 'have been attributed merely as being of a research nature as among scientists and technicians', and that 'no security significance' should be attributed to the incident.[155] It was a very cursory investigation. As an ASIO report on Christiansen noted in July 1950, there were no file records on Elsie Mary Hill, and 'the relationship of Christiansen to the Hill family was not known by this Office' until it was 'revealed by Christiansen himself' during vetting processes in 1949.[156]

Christiansen's terms of appointment with CSIRO included a provision for permanence after twelve months.[157] However, permanent appointments to the public service now required security checks, in accordance with a new vetting system introduced at British insistence in 1949.[158] As his twelve months came up, Christiansen's case caused both CSIRO and the security authorities some difficulty. The CIS in Sydney was asked to provide a security report on him, and noted on 26 April 1949 that Christiansen 'is recorded at this Office as a suspected member of the Communist Party'.[159] Six months later the CIS 'reported adversely on Christiansen'.[160] The CSIRO was now in a quandary, and in December 1949, it asked ASIO 'to look further into the matter in order that finality should be reached'.[161] The ASIO inquiry found that 'if the question was one of access to secret information it would seem clear that

Christiansen constitutes a security risk', and that 'although access to secret information is not involved at present, there is a possibility that in war time he would normally be given such access'.[162] In August 1950, the CSIRO secretary was 'advised of the facts of the case and ASIO's opinion that, on the evidence, Christiansen should not have access to classified information'.[163] By now, Christiansen had written several letters to the secretary demanding to know why his appointment (and eligibility for superannuation privileges) had not been gazetted.[164] The CSIRO was now 'faced with the problem of finding an answer without referring to Security reasons'.[165] It was towards the end of this inquiry, in July 1950, that Ray Whitrod (an ASIO officer in Sydney) brought to the attention of his colleagues the fact that Christiansen was married to Ted Hill's sister; 'this fact alone', noted the ASIO director Sydney on 9 August, 'presents a security risk as far as Christiansen is concerned'.[166]

By the time, in 1950, that Christiansen's twelve-year-old marriage to Elsie Hill was 'revealed', it had already been deduced by Venona. In a telegram from Moscow to Canberra on 5 May 1948, Makarov had been directed to ask Clayton 'at the next meeting [i.e., on 20 May] . . . to find out about the husband of TOURIST's sister'.[167] This cable was decrypted at Arlington soon after it was sent, and TOURIST had been identified as Jim Hill by the beginning of 1949.

However, there is virtually nothing in the Venona material about when Clayton began obtaining information from Christiansen, or when Christiansen was cover-named MASTER, or whether any of the information obtained from him was ever of value to Moscow. It is possible that he was the source of the information about the Australian Association of Scientific Workers which the Canberra Residency cabled to Moscow on 25 April 1945, detailing the organisational structure and leading personnel in the association, which were evidently of interest to Moscow Centre but which were hardly secret.[168]

There is no doubt, however, that by mid 1948, Christiansen was included by Moscow Centre in the reorganisation of the KLOD group. Indeed, the only question Moscow Centre raised about Christiansen concerned the proposed liaison arrangements between Christiansen and other members of the group in External Affairs.[169]

Christiansen, along with Hughes, Bernie and Prichard, were all of considerable interest to Moscow Centre, and all figured in the Venona traffic. But none were in positions to provide vitally important strategic intelligence (as distinct from the valuable operational information provided by Hughes). It was to the department of External Affairs that Moscow Centre looked for this information, and it was there that KLOD found new recruits.

14

'his friends in the NOOK'

SOVIET ESPIONAGE IN EXTERNAL AFFAIRS

FROM 1945 TO 1948, ACCORDING to the Australian Venona material, the hub of Soviet espionage activity in Australia was the department of External Affairs in Canberra. This was partly opportunistic. On the one hand, Alfred Hughes, who had been able to satisfy much of Moscow Centre's requirement for operational intelligence concerning Australia's counter-espionage activities, left the Security Service in October 1945; and Frances Bernie left Evatt's office in April 1946. On the other hand, there were now several secret members of the party or their associates in External Affairs from whom Clayton was able to obtain important and frequently top secret information—including Ian Milner and Jim Hill.

The focus on External Affairs also reflected the instructions from Moscow in October 1945 to the Canberra Resident to 'concentrate your attention . . . on the Department of External Affairs' as the top priority,[1] and the fact that through 1945 Moscow Centre was gradually succeeding in imposing its authority over Clayton's recruitment and collection activities. By 1948, when it reorganised Clayton's network of informants, the sub-group in External Affairs was its principal interest. By this time, all of Clayton's informants in External Affairs had been given cover-names, indicating that Moscow Centre was satisfied with their reliability and utility, though not necessarily that those concerned were 'witting'. Collectively, the sub-group was referred to by Moscow Centre as 'the workers of the Australian NOOK'.[2]

Ian Milner and Jim Hill worked closely together in providing material to Clayton. Indeed, the occasions on which they first gave him secret documents involved meetings at which only the three of them were present.³ During their first two meetings with Clayton, which the Canberra Residency recounted to Moscow Centre on 29 September 1945, 'MILNER and KhILL told him many interesting things'.⁴ In addition, Hill gave Clayton 'copies of several official telegrams received from the British Foreign Office', and 'a copy of a most secret report of the Australian Department of External Affairs', addressed to Evatt, which covered 'the political and economic situation in South-East Europe' and which 'contains a quantity of . . . secret information received from the British Foreign Office'.⁵ Thereafter, their efforts were somewhat divided. Milner concentrated on providing British postwar strategic planning documents, while Hill provided a regular flow of current British cables about international political developments, as well as copies of official Australian foreign policy documents.

The secret British material was Moscow Centre's primary objective. However, it was also very interested in some Australian information, especially that concerning government policy on the establishment of the United Nations, Indonesia's independence struggle, and the postings of particular External Affairs personnel to the Soviet Union. It was also expressly interested in obtaining copies of telegrams of which both enciphered and plain texts were available, including archival as well as current telegrams, to assist Soviet cryptanalytic efforts against Australian diplomatic ciphers.

With regard to the United Nations, Moscow Centre was eager to capitalise on the possibilities that the establishment of the secretariat in New York provided for its international espionage operations. On 4 May 1946, for example, it asked the Canberra Residency for detailed information about any External Affairs officers who had been or might be appointed to the secretariat (which it cover-named MECCA), including 'detailed personal histories', as well as information about their 'recruiting possibilities'.⁶ In the event that an extant agent moved to New York, Moscow Centre was to be apprised of the 'contact conditions'.⁷ (One of the 'workers of the Australian NOOK', Ian Milner, left the department for New York later in 1946.) In August 1947, Moscow Centre was anxious to obtain detailed information about the composition of the Australian delegation to the opening session of the General Assembly in New York, and in particular whether it might include any of its agents, in which case the Canberra Residency was to 'come to an agreement with these people about the possibility of contact with them in New York'.⁸ (Indeed, Jim Hill had been nominated to accompany Evatt;

he was to stay in New York from 1 September to 26 November 1947.)

Moscow Centre was frequently concerned about the personal welfare and morale of its informants in External Affairs, as well as their operational security. In March 1946, for example, Makarov told Moscow that Clayton had reported 'that his friends in the NOOK are . . . in good spirits and are behaving with great caution'.[9] There was just one incidental cause of disquiet: they had 'recently learnt' of the posting to External Affairs of Captain Mitchell (presumably this should have been Mathews), whom they suspected was 'a representative of counter-intelligence'.[10]

IAN MILNER

In 1945–46, according to the Venona material, the most 'productive' members of the KLOD group were Ian Milner and Jim Hill. Milner, code-named BUR, was then an acting first secretary in the post-hostilities planning (later the United Nations) division of External Affairs in Canberra. Most of the material KLOD obtained from Milner consisted of official British and Australian postwar planning documents, making Milner the foremost member of the group in terms of the strategic importance of the documentary material he supplied.

Ian Frank George Milner was born in Oamaru, 100km south of Christchurch, New Zealand on 6 June 1911. His father, Frank Milner, the rector of a government boarding school in Oamaru, was cold, puritanical, dogmatic and abrasive. He was also an ardent monarchist and imperialist, and was made a CMG (Companion of the Order of St Michael and St George) in 1925; during the Depression he was an active member of the extreme right-wing New Zealand Legion.[11] Much in the son's character can be traced to his father, including a strong will and a determination to be a success, albeit in the opposite political direction.

Ian did his secondary schooling at Waitaki, which was not always a pleasant experience. As a friend (the poet Charles Brasch) later wrote, the rector 'sometimes seemed to treat Ian rather harshly, as to prevent any suspicion of favouritism';[12] on one occasion, he broke a cane on him.[13] But he was a very gifted student, and was able to take the brutality in his stride. He was, in 1929, dux of the school, captain of the cricket team, a member of the rugby team, and the champion school debater.[14]

At Canterbury University College in Christchurch, Milner immediately rebelled against his parents' values. As someone who knew him at the time later said, 'He regarded his father with a mixture

Ian Milner during a visit to New Zealand and Australia in 1971. Milner denied passing information to Clayton. However, the Venona decrypts describe in detail how Milner, cover-named BUR, *obtained various documents for the KGB including British War Cabinet post-hostilities planning documents. Recently released Czech archival records show that he later also worked for Czech intelligence.*

of loathing and horror. Ian would rage against imperialism and the British Empire.'[15] He was deeply affected by the Great Depression, which produced terrible suffering in New Zealand as a result of the collapse of commodity prices. He was introduced to Marxism at the university, and was soon a convert. He was active in the Friends of the Soviet Union, a party front organisation. He continued with his debating interest, wrote poetry, excelled scholastically, and at the end of 1933 won a prestigious Rhodes scholarship to Oxford University.[16]

In 1934, on his way to Oxford, Milner spent about three weeks in the Soviet Union. He was by this time (according to his friend Brasch, who accompanied him) 'a convinced dialectical materialist'.[17] On leaving Russia he wrote that he had seen 'most impressive evidence of a successfully working socialist order'.[18] It is likely that he made contact with the OGPU, and was perhaps even recruited, when he was in Moscow.[19]

Milner was at Oxford from mid 1934 to July 1937, and it is likely that during this period he became a secret member of the Oxford University Branch of the Communist Party. By 1936, in the wake of the Depression and with the rise of fascism on the continent, there were 'hundreds' of members in the Oxford University branch, most of them covert.[20] In August 1935 and July 1936 he visited Vienna, where he witnessed the fascist offensive but remained convinced that the Communist Party represented the wave of the future.[21] In 1937, according to Brasch, Milner had the 'highest hopes for the development of Soviet Russia on Marxist lines; he believed Russia to be the one power whose foreign policy was capable of leading to a just world order'.[22]

Milner graduated from Oxford with a first class honours degree in Politics, Philosophy and Economics (PPE) in June 1937. From October 1937 to August 1939, he worked in the US as a Commonwealth Fund Fellow, first at the University of California at Berkeley, and then, from August 1938, at Columbia University in New York, where he also did work for the Institute of Pacific Relations (IPR).[23]

When Milner returned to New Zealand in August 1939, he was, despite his academic achievements, only able to find a 'backwater' job, producing a history of educational developments in New Zealand for the department of Education. However, with the signing of the Soviet–German non-aggression pact that same month, Milner readily accepted the Comintern line and was happy to devote his attention and energy to the anti-war and anti-conscription movement in New Zealand. On 8 January 1940 he became secretary of the Wellington committee of the Peace and Anti-conscription Council, whose aim was 'to inaugurate a campaign to withdraw New Zealand from the war, to oppose the introduction of any form of conscription, and to protect the welfare and civil liberties of the people of New Zealand'.[24] It was difficult for Milner to be both a conscientious public servant and a vocal anti-war activist. He was reprimanded by the deputy director of Education, informed that his activities with the peace council were officially regarded as 'subversive', and told that if he persisted he would be dismissed.[25] Indeed, it is likely that if he had stayed in New Zealand he would have been arrested.[26]

However, as Milner has recounted, a '*deus ex machina* unbelievably descended on my troubled stage' when, in January 1940, he received a letter from Professor W. MacMahon Ball, head of the department of Political Science at the University of Melbourne (whom Milner had met at the IPR in New York in 1939), inviting him to apply for a lectureship in the department.[27] He was formally appointed on 5 March, and left New Zealand immediately to take up the post.[28] He stopped over in Sydney and spent the day with Rupert Lockwood before proceeding by train to Melbourne.[29]

The Political Science department at Melbourne University was then very small. In 1940, its staff consisted of MacMahon Ball (who, though he remained as nominal head of the department, soon left to head the broadcasting division of the wartime department of Information), Milner and one other full-time colleague; but as the demand grew for training in wartime administration and 'post-war reconstruction', Charles Manning Clark joined them.[30]

Manning Clark, who remained fond of Milner (and visited him in Prague in 1958 and 1984) has said that, once Milner found 'the answer he was looking for in the works of Marx, Engels and Lenin' at Oxford in the mid 1930s, 'he devoted his talents to what he believed to be the noblest cause of all—the liberation of all human beings from their gaolers and their oppressors'. He was, when at Melbourne University, 'convinced he had discovered the truth about history and the future of human society . . . For him the salvation of [the 1917 Bolshevik] revolution against its enemies both within and without the Soviet Union became the greatest good'.[31]

On 12 September 1940, Milner married Margaret Leigh (generally called Margot), a fellow New Zealander, whom he had met as a student at Canterbury and who was senior French mistress at the Woodland Church of England [Girls] Grammar School in Adelaide, South Australia. She had joined the Communist Party in Adelaide in 1938, concerned about 'the growth of Japanese fascism and its invasion of China'.[32] She was reported to the security authorities by a fellow mistress at the school, who described her as 'fanatical' and as 'decidedly dangerous and a fifth columnist'.[33] She stayed in Adelaide for a couple of months after the wedding and then moved to Melbourne in November.[34]

Milner had come to the attention of the Australian security authorities even before he actually arrived in Australia. On 12 March 1940, the officer in charge of the investigation branch of the Attorney-General's department in Melbourne wrote to head office in Canberra, presumably on the basis of information received from the New Zealand authorities, to 'advise that arrangements have been made to have the activities of Milner closely watched'.[35] He next came to notice in June 1940, when the district censor intercepted a letter he had written (and enclosed in an envelope addressed by someone else) to a New York address. The letter contained 'details of peace, anti-conscription and anti-war bodies in New Zealand and names of persons connected with the same'.[36] It was passed to Military Intelligence, Southern Command, who sent it to the Special Branch, who passed it to detectives in Carlton (where Melbourne University is located). On 27 September, the Carlton CIB reported that Milner was regarded as 'an advanced thinker', and that, while no connection had been found between Milner and 'the Communist Party or any Pacificist movement', he did have 'a definite inclination towards a radical political outlook' and was 'associated with a number of agitations in the University'.[37] As far as the security authorities were aware, however, Milner was fairly quiet during his first fifteen months in Australia, though he became an active member of the Council for Civil Liberties and spoke at anti-war meetings; for example, he addressed a convention held by the Christian Pacifist Movement on 14–16 June 1941.[38]

This was in fact his last anti-war speech. Immediately after the German invasion of the Soviet Union on 22 June 1941, he became a dedicated supporter of the war, and, more especially, of the Soviet effort. He spoke at meetings of the Australia–Soviet Friendship

League five times in July and August, and was elected to the committee of the league on 24 August.[39] He was also elected to the committee of the Council for Civil Liberties;[40] he became an active member of the Victorian Youth Parliament, 'a Communist inspired organisation';[41] and he and Margot were the principal organisers of the Civilian Air Raid Defence Committee. This was modelled on the 'deep shelter committees' established in London in 1940, which were intended to discredit the government by calling attention to deficiencies in 'the people's defence'.[42] In early 1942, with the Japanese forces sweeping through Southeast Asia and the Nazis just a few miles from Moscow, Milner thought 'the world was falling about one's ears' and that 'lecturing to students on the techniques of public administration and the American constitution suddenly seemed unreal: fiddling amidst the flames'.[43] He joined the Volunteer Defence Corps, newly formed as a 'home guard'; became a warden at the air raid precaution post in Carlton; and was 'a leading voice for the training of men, women and children in guerilla warfare, which he lectured on and demonstrated'.[44]

In May 1943, he was invited by the Hobart branch of the Australia–Soviet Friendship League, with the foreknowledge of the party, to visit Tasmania. As the director of security, Tasmania, reported on 17 June 1943:

> Milner has come and gone without setting the river on fire . . . He is a superficial young man, intellectually still adolescent, whose head swims with the fumes of Communist wine . . . The performance was another illustration of the deterioration of academic standards in Australia.[45]

In 1944, he was vice president of the Australia–Soviet Friendship League.[46]

What the security authorities did not know at this time, however (though it was 'strongly suspected' by May 1944),[47] was that Milner was a secret but very active member of the Communist Party, having joined the Melbourne University branch soon after his arrival in Melbourne in March 1940. The branch was fairly small in 1940 (there were about fourteen members when Margot Milner arrived at the end of the year),[48] but several members had been friends of Milner's in Wellington in 1939–40.[49] In 1940–41, Milner and his friends formed a 'loose association' within the party in Melbourne, somewhat more relaxed and interested in 'ideas developed through discussion' than either the Victorian or national party leaderships, and in 1941 they were reprimanded for being 'Right Deviationists'.[50]

In 1941–42, when the party was illegal, Milner became the leading (but covert) organiser and recruiter for the University branch, which often met at his flat at 163 Flemington Road in North Melbourne.[51] According to an account given to ASIO on 8 July 1954, Milner would select and 'cultivate' students and, 'after inviting them singly to his home on a social basis, would subsequently invite them to Communist Party study groups or Communist Party Branch meetings'.[52] He would arrange to meet recruits at street corners and escort them to the various secret party meeting places in North Melbourne. (In contrast to his covert activities, Margot 'made no secret of her Communist Party membership and openly courted recruits from the students'.)[53] By 1942, there were about 30 members (mainly students) in the branch.[54]

By 1944, when membership of the University branch reached 100, Milner had become a fairly senior member of the party in Melbourne. On 2–3 December 1944, for example, he attended a secret meeting of the central committee at Upwey in the Dandenong ranges, about 35km east of Melbourne, where the party maintained weekend camping facilities. Milner had just been accepted into the department of External Affairs in Canberra, and as a secret member of the party was obligated to report his new job to the control commission. Indeed, it is likely that he had discussed his application to join External Affairs with his party colleagues before the Upwey meeting; in any case, as his presence at that meeting suggests, his move to Canberra was of interest to at least some members of the central committee.

Milner had applied for the temporary position of special investigation officer in the post-hostilities planning division on 2 October 1944. He had evidently been asked to apply by Paul Hasluck, the director of the division, who had met him at a conference in Canberra earlier in the year.[55] On 1 November, the department decided to offer Milner the job, and he accepted provisionally on 17 November, though he asked for more information about the post from Hasluck,[56] who informed him that:

> The Post-Hostilities Division was created last September to deal mainly with matters relating to the armistice and post-armistice control, international economic and social collaboration, the future world organisation and preparations for the peace conferences . . . Your duties will involve the study of matters related to the armistices and peace settlements and the preparation of suitable submissions [on, for example, draft proposals for a United Nations organisation].[57]

Hasluck also sent Milner 'a statement of the responsibilities and functions of the division', but asked him 'to regard this as confidential and to take care it is not seen by anyone outside the Commonwealth Government service'.[58] Milner wrote to the department formally to accept the position on 28 November, just four days before the meeting at Upwey, stating that he expected 'to take up duties in Canberra in mid January [1945]'.[59]

Late on the night of 2 December, a senior New Zealand official (most likely J. A. Malcolm, the New Zealand supply liaison officer in Melbourne), arrived at Upwey looking for Milner. He told him that his father had died and that 'a Government air priority' had been arranged for him 'to proceed immediately to New Zealand'.[60] The official had first gone to Milner's home in North Melbourne and had been given (with great reluctance) the address of the party camp.

Milner flew to New Zealand on 5 December.[61] He wrote to Hasluck on 4 December and said that he was aiming to be back in Sydney by early January and, after a fortnight's leave, would start work in Canberra 'towards [the] end of January'.[62] On 25 December, he wrote again, saying he planned to reach Sydney in mid January and to have 'a brief holiday and rest-up' before proceeding to Canberra.[63] In fact, he spent some three weeks in Sydney.[64] It is not known whom he (and Margot) met with during this period, but they very likely included Lockwood and Clayton. As the Venona material would show, Milner had certainly made contact with Clayton by March 1945.

Milner began his new job on 12 February 1945, and swore the oath of allegiance the next day. In March, Hasluck went to San Francisco with Evatt for the conference that was to inaugurate the United Nations; he remained overseas for most of the next year, during which period Milner served as acting director of the division (which was renamed the United Nations division in early 1946). In this position he had full access not only to all the files concerning Australian foreign policy making, but also to British postwar planning documents that were provided to External Affairs either directly from Whitehall or via the department of Defence.

Soon after Hasluck was replaced by John Burton as head of the United Nations division in June 1946, Milner began looking for another job. Eighteen months of his two-year initial appointment had passed. He had acted as head of the division for most of that time, and could not have been happy with Burton's appointment over him. Milner disliked Burton. He has said that Burton's 'eyes remained cold and opaque: you couldn't see the man behind them', and that he 'rarely or ever' knew where he was in working with Burton.[65] With Hasluck, his patron, now counsellor-in-charge of the Australian mission at the UN in New York, Milner found himself cut out of 'the normal channels of responsibility'.[66] He applied for a job as a political affairs officer in the UN Security Council Secretariat in New York, and was offered it on 28 September. He was granted leave without pay from the department on 11 November, and was informed a few weeks later that 'the prospects of permanent appointment were not good'.[67] He left Australia in November 1946, and visited New Zealand for a month 'on family matters' before proceeding to New York on 3 January 1947.[68] He had resigned from External Affairs the previous day.[69]

Milner's espionage activity evidently began in September 1945, although it is likely that he had been one of Clayton's unacknowledged informants for some months before this. Together with Jim Hill, he met with Clayton twice in September and 'told him many interesting things' about the classified material accessible to them in External Affairs, especially the secret British material. By February 1946, Milner had told Clayton about the British postwar planning papers from the department of Defence, in particular the War Cabinet document on *Security in the Western Mediterranean and the Eastern Atlantic* which had recently been in his possession. When Moscow Centre asked for a copy of the document, Milner was ready to oblige, borrowing a copy from Defence on 6 March and arranging with Clayton for him to collect it (as well as another on *Security of India and the Indian Ocean*) and pass them to the Canberra residency for photographing on or about 17 March.[70]

Milner worked for the UN in New York for more than three years. The political affairs office of the Security Council Secretariat was at the heart of the UN organisation, and its staff of 30–40 officers was 'perennially overworked'.[71] Just weeks after he began at the UN, he was sent to the Balkans with the Greek Boundary Commission, which was involved in settling border disputes between Greece and Albania, Yugoslavia and Bulgaria. In May 1947 the UN established a Palestine Committee, for which Milner did some work. His most important job was deputy principal secretary of the UN Temporary Commission on Korea (UNTCOK), which was established in September 1947 to supervise 'free elections' in North and South Korea, and which involved his spending considerable time in Seoul.[72]

Milner re-established contact with the MGB in New York on 6 March 1947, and during his 40 months with the UN he 'kept sending us' reports from Palestine, Korea 'and other countries', as well as New York, about 'the activities of minor sections of [the] UN and about some leading officials'.[73] From the end of 1948, when Milner was identified in the US Venona operation, he was placed under close surveillance by the FBI. The FBI maintains a 401-page file on Milner's movements and activities in New York over the next eighteen months, but it remains classified.[74]

In September–October 1949, Milner returned to Australia for four weeks on 'home leave' from the UN, and visited Sydney,

Canberra, Melbourne and Adelaide. ASIO maintained a close watch on him from the day he arrived in Sydney, recording all his movements and contacts. He spent a week in Canberra, where he had 'discussions with the Secretary of External Affairs and other senior public servants'.[75] While there, according to ASIO reports, 'he is believed to have contacted James Frederick Hill on one, and possibly two occasions'.[76] For instance, the Milners attended a dinner party at which Hill was also present on 15 September.[77] When in Melbourne, Milner contacted a known member of the party and associate of both Ted and Jim Hill; and when in Adelaide 'he was closely associated with . . . a prominent Communist'.[78] He left Australia for the US on 12 October 1949.[79]

JIM HILL

James Frederick Hill, commonly known as Jim and code-named TOURIST, was an active member of the KLOD group from 1945 to 1950, during which time he worked in the department of External Affairs in Canberra. He figures in the KI cable traffic, either as TOURIST or by name as KhILL, more than any other member of the group (except for Clayton) over this period. He clearly provided the NKGB/KI with more official material than anyone else, including Milner. Most of this was fairly mundane, such as copies of hundreds of cables from Whitehall to Canberra, but amassed over half a decade they would have given Moscow Centre an important insight into British postwar interests and the development of British and Australian postwar security policies.

Hill was born on 1 April 1918 at Hamilton, Victoria, where his father was principal of Hamilton High School. He had four older brothers and sisters, including Elsie Mary, and Ted.[80] Jim spent his childhood in Geelong and Ballarat, where his father served successively as headmaster of the respective high schools, and did his secondary education at Essendon High School, where his father was also headmaster.

Upon leaving school, in 1933, Hill got a job as a clerk with the Bank of New South Wales in Melbourne, which he held until he resigned on 17 March 1940. He also studied part-time at Melbourne University, from which he graduated with a Law degree on 14 December 1940.

Hill evinced an active interest in politics soon after he started at university. He joined the Moonie Ponds branch of the ALP in 1936, and 'remained a member until late 1940, possibly 1941'.[81] He joined the Communist Party 'in approximately 1937 or 1938',

Jim Hill, leaving the Royal Commission on Espionage in 1954. He was an active member of the KLOD *group from 1945 to 1950 when he worked for the department of External Affairs. He was interrogated by Jim Skardon of MI5 in London in 1950 but denied all allegations of passing information to the Soviet Union. He immediately informed several British and Australian communists, one of whom flew back to Australia to warn Clayton. (Australian Archives CRS A6119/2 item 91)*

and was soon secretary of the Moonee Ponds branch.[82] In 1940–41, he was very active in several front organisations. In October 1941, for example, he was secretary of the Victoria Youth Parliament (VYP), which was a CPA subsidiary organisation[83] and had been described by the attorney-general in August 1940 as being 'merely the Communist Party under another name'.[84] According to Hill, he lost contact with the party when he joined the Army in 1941, and his membership lapsed during 1942.[85] However, if Cecil Sharpley is to be believed, Hill was still in the Party 'in 1942 or 1943 or later'.[86]

Hill enlisted in the Army late in 1941 and served 'in Transport for some months in the Northern Territory', where he transferred to the Army Education Service on 6 June 1942.[87] On 10 January that year, he married Marjorie Irene Royle.[88]

On 10 February 1945, Hill applied for a position as research officer in the post-hostilities planning division of External Affairs.[89] According to one source, he 'joined External Affairs on the introduction of Milner'.[90] On 30 April the acting secretary of External

Affairs, John Hood, wrote to Hill telling him his application had been successful,[91] and to the secretary of the department of the Army, F. R. Sinclair, asking that Hill be released for service in External Affairs, since the establishment of the United Nations made it 'more imperative than ever that additional staff be appointed to the Post Hostilities Planning Division of this Department as soon as possible'.[92] He commenced duty as a temporary research officer with External Affairs on 25 June 1945.[93]

When Hill arrived in Canberra, accommodation was difficult to find. He initially stayed at the Hotel Kingston, while Marjorie and their daughter remained in Melbourne. He moved to several other places over the next year, and in mid 1946 moved to 7 Gooreen Street, Reid, which he leased from Dr Kenneth Hedley Key, and at which Clayton sometimes stayed overnight when he was in Canberra.[94] The Hills moved to 41 Froggatt Street in Turner at the end of 1946.

Hill's principal work associates were Ian Milner, Ric Throssell, Keith Shann and Dr John Burton, who by the end of 1946 had become his chief mentor in the department. In October 1946, Burton recommended that Hill be appointed a permanent public servant in light of Milner's imminent departure, and he was given permanence on 14 February 1947.[95] From May 1946 to February 1949, he was engaged on UN public relations work, including service as departmental liaison officer with the United Nations Association in Australia. He also worked on 'such matters as the drafting of instructions for the Australian Delegation to the United Nations and interpreting documents on disarmament, Military Staff Committee, and atomic energy'.[96] In late 1947 and 1948, he 'was often employed by his Minister in the preparation of material for speeches in Parliament'.[97] In 1948, 'he also toured the Australian States, in company with the Minister's private secretary, Dalziel, with whom Hill was particularly friendly, for the purposes of establishing State Committees of the United Nations Association'.[98] On several occasions, in the absence of the councillor in charge of the UN division, Hill 'temporarily assumed control of the Division'.[99] As we have seen, he served with the Australian Mission to the UN in New York from 1 September to 26 November 1947.[100] According to Evatt, 'while at the U.N.O. Hill appeared to be quite friendly with the Russians', indeed, he became 'very sulky' when Evatt attacked the Soviet foreign minister, Andrey Vishinsky.[101] He also met Milner in New York during this period.[102]

Hill and Clayton evidently established contact soon after Hill moved to Canberra in June 1945, and at the two joint meetings with Milner and Clayton in September, Hill gave Clayton 'copies of several official telegrams received from the British Foreign Office' as well as copies of other secret reports.[103] Hill also gave Clayton 'a series of resumes of various Foreign Office telegrams on rather general political subjects', which was sent to Moscow on 1 October.[104] At another meeting during the first week of October, he handed over copies of Foreign Office telegrams sent to Canberra in May and August, as well as 'a resume of telegrams dating from December 1944 to March 1945 dealing with the situation in Roumania and the attitudes of the British and U.S. Governments', which were sent to Moscow on 10–12 October.[105] Over the next year, Hill gave Clayton something every week or two, mostly recent Foreign Office cables, such as the British telegrams about Argentina and Iceland dated 16 October 1945, which were sent to Moscow on 8 November.[106] By May 1948, as evinced in the Venona material, but probably much earlier, Hill had been given the cover-name TOURIST.[107] He was now regarded by Moscow Centre as a committed agent about whose reliability it had no question, and he was to be the principal agent in External Affairs in the reorganised espionage operations.[108]

Hill's External Affairs career path until 1950 was quite regular. He had become an acting second secretary on 1 September 1947 when he began working with the Australian Mission in New York, and was promoted to second secretary on 15 April 1948; he became acting first secretary on 14 September 1949, and his provisional appointment to that post was gazetted on 10 November 1949.[109] As an ASIO report on 22 November 1949 noted, 'he has outstripped some officers but his promotion has not been spectacular by that Department's standards'.[110] He was not the youngest officer in External Affairs to be promoted to first secretary, but on the other hand no-one else was known to have reached that level from research officer (third secretary) in a shorter time.[111] At the beginning of 1950, the department reported that:

> In his $4\frac{1}{2}$ years service with this Department Mr Hill has proved himself to be a most conscientious and capable officer. He did valuable work with the Australian Mission and United Nations and has continually performed work of a very high standard in the United Nations Division of the Department. His capacity to accept responsibility and his general administrative ability have been clearly exhibited.[112]

Hill was promoted to first secretary on 16 March 1950, but his promotion was not to stand. On 13 December 1949, the CIS told Colin Moodie, the Defence liaison officer in External Affairs, that Hill should be refused a security clearance on the grounds that he was 'a reputed Communist' and brother of Edward Hill, the secretary of the party in Victoria.[113] His promotion was cancelled by the Public Service Board on 1 September 1950.[114]

DOROTHY THROSSELL (NÉE JORDAN)

In the Venona material of 1945–48, there are several mentions of PODRUGA, or FEMALE FRIEND, as a source of information (directly or indirectly) for KLOD, and in 1949 ASIO concluded that PODRUGA was almost certainly Eileen Dorothy Jordan. In 1945, Clayton had reported about her to the NKGB in terms which clearly implied he expected to be able to obtain secret material from her; she was mentioned by name (DZhON) in a cable from Canberra to Moscow on 29 September 1945.[115] However ASIO could never prove that she had ever consciously provided Clayton or the KGB any such material.

Dorothy Jordan was born on 11 April 1919. She obtained an Arts degree at Melbourne University in 1944, and early in 1945 began work in the 'secret records' section of the war organisation of industry division of the department of Post-war Reconstruction in Melbourne. After 'about two months', she moved to Canberra, where she worked in the office of the minister for Post-war Reconstruction for 'about a month' before transferring to External Affairs on 10 August 1945. She worked as a 'records clerk' in the International Cooperation Section, later renamed the legal and consular section, until 9 June 1947, when she transferred to the department of Territories. She resigned from the public service in August 1947 before her marriage to Ric Throssell in October of that year. She lived in Acton House during her first two years in Canberra and moved to Throssell's flat at 18 Myuna Flats when they were married.[116]

Jordan had joined the Melbourne University branch of the Communist Party in 1942.[117] She has said that she lost interest in the Party when she left the university at the end of 1944, and that she 'just let my membership lapse' when she moved to Canberra in 1945.[118]

The information about Jordan in the Venona material is sparse and unrevealing. Clayton had evidently first told the NKGB about her when she was working in the department of Post-war Reconstruction in Melbourne in mid 1945. On 29 September 1945, the Canberra Residency cabled to Moscow Centre that Clayton had 'found out that a young woman Communist called DZhON is working in the Archives Department of the Department of External Affairs', and that:

KLOD reported that, according to his information, the entire diplomatic correspondence of the Australian Department of External Affairs passes through [15 groups unrecovered] who will be able to get hold of copies of enciphered telegrams.[119]

In May and June 1948, when Moscow Centre was planning the reorganisation of the KLOD group, Makarov was instructed to find out from Clayton 'what opportunities' were available to PODRUGA and 'the possibility of using her in the future'.[120] When Jordan was given this cover-name cannot be determined, but it was presumably before she left the public service in August 1947 and possibly as early as late 1945.

On 22 July 1954, Jordan was visited by two ASIO officers, who questioned her about suggestions that 'she had taken papers from External Affairs when she worked in the department and handed them to Communist Party headquarters'.[121] The principal basis of ASIO's suggestions, apart from the unusable Venona material, was Clarence Dakin, who had come to Canberra at the suggestion of party friends in December 1946, had stayed with Doris Beeby for a few days before getting a job in the department of Interior, and who then lived at Acton House until mid July 1947, when he returned to Sydney. Soon after he moved to Acton House he met Jordan, to whom he had been 'mentioned' by Beeby; they became good friends, often visiting each other's rooms and discussing both personal and political matters (at least until about April 1947, when Throssell began to court her).[122] Dakin was interviewed by ASIO on 4 November 1953; he said then (and re-attested at another interview by ASIO on 6 December 1954 and again at the Royal Commission on Espionage on 3–4 February 1955) that Jordan had told him that Beeby had set aside some time one night a week for Jordan to visit her when 'no other persons were to be present', and that Beeby had told her she 'should not bring herself under notice by attending party meetings or party functions'; that Jordan 'always took a briefcase with her when she visited Doris Beeby's flat'; and that 'I was convinced that Dorothy Jordan was passing official information to Doris Beeby'.[123]

Jordan appeared before the royal commission on 4 February 1955. She said she had met Beeby about half a dozen times over a period of some months in 1946–47, that she had only visited Beeby's flat 'two or three times' and that these were 'social gatherings'; she denied that she had ever had any discussions with Dakin about Beeby or her visits to Beeby's flat; and she could not recall anything that might have suggested to Dakin that she was taking information from the department to give to Beeby.[124] The royal commissioners, being unaware of the Venona material, could only report that PODRUGA was 'probably . . . a female', but that 'we were unable to ascertain to whom it referred'.[125]

RIC THROSSELL

The most tragic but also the most intriguing member of the KLOD group was Ric Throssell. He was never a member of the Communist Party, and it is often not possible to separate his actions from those of his mother. Indeed, although there is evidence that Throssell was a source of information for the NKGB/KI from 1945 to 1950, it was Prichard who served for the first part of this period as the conduit for his information. At least until around 1947, Throssell was being unwittingly used by his mother.

He was born on 10 May 1922, at Greenmount, Western Australia, the only child of Prichard and Hugo Throssell. He was eleven when his father committed suicide. After leaving school in 1939, he was awarded a trainee teaching scholarship by the Western Australian Education department. He graduated from the Teachers Training College of Western Australia, with distinction in all subjects, in 1940; and he completed the first year of an Arts degree at the University of Western Australia in 1941.[126]

Throssell began compulsory military training with the Western Australian 11th Divisional Signals at Melville Camp, near Fremantle, on 19 September 1941. He found life in camp to be 'a pointless, dreary routine'[127] and, according to Prichard, by February 1942 he was already 'cursing the system that allowed the war to take place'.[128] He began full-time Army duty on 20 February, and embarked for New Guinea on 27 July 1942.[129] He saw active service as a signalman at Milne Bay in August–September, was promoted to lance corporal on 30 December, and then spent six months at Port Moresby. He returned to Australia on 10 June 1943, and was formally discharged from the Army a month later, having been selected as a diplomatic staff cadet in the department of External Affairs.[130]

The circumstances of Throssell's selection for diplomatic service are illuminating, particularly with respect to the relationship between Throssell and his mother and the critical role she played in his life in the mid 1940s, when he was in his 20s. In early 1943, while in Port Moresby, Throssell applied for a diplomatic cadetship in a scheme which Evatt was introducing into the department; he told his mother about his application, and she was 'enthusiastic'.[131] Throssell wrote an examination paper for the department in a hospital bed while recovering from malaria in Port Moresby, was given a perfunctory interview by his commanding officer, and was somewhat surprised to

Ric Throssell with a portrait of his mother Katharine Susannah Prichard. He joined the department of External Affairs in 1943 and continued in Foreign Affairs and associated agencies until he retired in 1983. The Venona decrypts show that information he told his mother in 1945 was given to Clayton and passed to Moscow. He was later cover named FERRO. *(Canberra Times)*

learn he had been selected.[132] He was to discover some two decades later that his mother had had no compunctions 'about using whatever influence she could marshal in my cause, when she saw the opportunity to remove me from the war zone to the security of External Affairs'.[133] She had evidently contacted Evatt and, under his advice, written to Colonel Hodgson, the departmental secretary, invoking 'every . . . argument she could muster'.[134] However, 'to save my self-esteem, her intervention was kept discreetly secret'.[135] On 17 June, the *Workers' Star* published a congratulatory note about Throssell's selection for the diplomatic service, saying: 'We are sure that he will do fine work for Australia in that sphere as his Communist mother has done, and is doing, in hers.'[136]

Throssell has said that his mother had long been determined 'to leave me to make my decisions',[137] but he was unwilling to acknowledge the extent to which she determined the course of his life. He has said that 'I was never pressed to join the Communist Party, never persuaded to adopt her point of view.'[138] And on 15 March 1948, she wrote to him: 'It does grieve me, of course, that you are not a communist, and don't see eye to eye with me on political matters. Time, maybe, will broaden your outlook.'[139] Throssell's career in External Affairs began on 24 June 1943, when he started a special six-month course at the University of Sydney, which included lectures by people from the department in Canberra about 'diplomatic practice and procedure'.[140] It was during this period that Throssell, who lived in a college at the university, visited his mother at 'The Gwydir' in Darlinghurst, most weekends.[141]

In December 1943, the cadets moved to Canberra to complete their training in the department. Throssell lived in Brassey House, about a kilometre south-east of the department in West Block, where he was assigned to the post-hostilities planning section under the supervision of Paul Hasluck.[142] He was appointed temporary third secretary on 1 March 1944.[143] At first he was mainly involved with preparing 'research papers on every conceivable aspect of world affairs', but in January 1944 he also took part in planning for the Australia–New Zealand security agreement (the ANZAC pact) signed in Canberra that month; later in the year, he worked on the Australian position papers concerning proposals to establish a United Nations organisation, and on the draft UN charter agreed to by representatives of the US, Britain and the Soviet Union in August–September; over the first few months of 1945 he worked on the Australian submissions for the conference in San Francisco in April that finalised the UN charter; and in mid 1945 he was involved in the External Affairs aspects of the investigations into Japanese war crimes.[144] He often visited his mother in Sydney, including when he had to go there on departmental business—as, for example, in August 1945, when Evatt was summoned to a War Cabinet meeting in Sydney and Throssell had 'to take the files to his office in Martin Place'.[145] He continued telling his mother about departmental matters, and their 'family talk' included his posting possibilities.[146]

In 1944–45, one of Clayton's sources of information was Throssell's mother, and, as the Venona material shows, some of the information which she gave Clayton came from Throssell. From Throssell's point of view, he was simply telling his mother what he was learning about the department, its principal subjects of interest, and what he might be doing in his future career. To Moscow Centre, however, the 'influential ACADEMICIAN' and her son were providing important information about the structure of the department of External Affairs, the positions and personalities of various officials, and the Australian foreign policy-making process. All this would have given Moscow a basis for planning its cultivation and recruitment activities, and confirmed that it was possible to obtain official information through clandestine means.

In September 1945, Throssell was informed that he was to be posted to Moscow. He immediately told his mother, she told Clayton, with whom she had had an earlier conversation about the matter, and he told his NKGB controller. On 30 September, the Canberra Residency cabled to Moscow an account of Throssell's posting and the conversations between his mother and Clayton; according to Makarov: 'THROSSEL is described by KLOD as a person of limited intelligence. His relations with his mother are normal. His mother dotes on him.'147 Moscow was told that Clayton 'has been given the task' of finding out more information about Throssell's posting 'and detailed information about his character'.148

According to departmental records, Throssell's posting to Moscow came about because the Australian legation there needed another officer to deal with 'political matters'.149 According to a former colleague, the officer who was at that time 'the senior man in charge of administration and postings', Peter Haydon, thought—in what he later said was 'an error of judgement'—that 'Throssell's a radical, so . . . let's post him to Moscow, let's see how he reacts to Russia on the ground. It will probably do him a great deal of good . . . Peter Haydon thought that exposure to the Russian system would cause him to drop the stars out of his eyes.'150 However, the Venona traffic suggests that Prichard had again intervened to secure Throssell's posting to Moscow—and, indeed, that Clayton had argued against this.151

Throssell stayed with his mother in Sydney for a couple of weeks before leaving for Moscow on 10 October 1945. During this brief but hectic period he called in at Evatt's office at Martin Place, where he talked with Dalziel and also met Bernie;152 he met Nosov at his mother's flat and received 'some advice as to the climate and what to wear';153 and, on 29 September 1945, he married Ellman Hague ('Bea') Gallacher.154 'Bea' was a 'steno at the Attorney-General's Department, in the next wing of West Block', and they had met about a year before.155 Their marriage was a simple affair, performed by 'an obliging nonconformist parson in his suburban sitting room',156 but obtaining her passport and visa, and organising her travel arrangements, was not easy. She was not eligible for travel aboard RAAF and Allied transport aircraft, and was not able to get a ship to Europe until 22 January 1946.157

Throssell had arrived in Moscow on 11 November 1945. The Australian legation in 1945–46 had only four or five official staff, a small remnant of the wartime Australian presence in Moscow. Throssell found 'little time for constructive research work', but was mainly occupied with 'the general administration of the Chancery' and supervision of 'the day to day affairs of the Legation', including 'the cyphering and decyphering of telegrams'.158 (The ASIO regional director, NSW, noted in February 1952 that 'the fact that he was responsible for codes and ciphers in the Australian Embassy, Moscow, is alarming'.[159]) He also became friendly with a Russian woman, Lydia Mertsova, who, it was (later) believed, worked for the NKVD.[160] Bea arrived in Moscow in March 1946, but after only four months she contracted polyneuritis and died. Throssell left Moscow on 25 October 1946 and arrived in Sydney on 3 December.[161]

He stayed with his mother at Greenmount until January 1947, then returned to the department in Canberra, where he stayed for the next two years.[162] By 1947, the post-hostilities planning section had been disbanded. Evatt had pronounced 'unswerving support for the United Nations' as the basic principle of his foreign policy, and Throssell went to work in the new United Nations division. Dr John Burton, a family friend, who had taken over as secretary, 'brought a driving intellectual vigour to the place', and Throssell 'whaled into the work'. He was 'convinced that the United Nations could bring peace and security to the world', and was enthusiastic about the leading role played by Evatt in the UN's formative years. In 1947, he told Evatt that 'I think Australia should declare itself permanently neutral. If the old world is determined to drag us into war again, we should keep out of it. We have no part in their disputes. Let them fight their own wars.'[163]

From early 1947 to February 1949, Throssell lived in the flat previously occupied by Doris Beeby. His mother came to live with him in April 1947, but returned to Western Australia in October, when he married Dorothy Jordan. During this six-month period, Throssell and Prichard talked often about international affairs, Australian politics and foreign policy, and Throssell's work. Sometimes he continued the latter at home, drafting speeches and broadcast scripts. Also at this time, he began to write a book with Jim Hill, with whom he had 'worked side-by-side in the department for a year or so', on the principles and practice of international cooperation and peaceful settlement of disputes; some eight chapters of the book were drafted before the department refused them permission to publish it, on the grounds that 'we had used too much official material', including drafts of ministerial speeches and departmental reports.[164]

Some time between Throssell's departure for Moscow in October 1945 and May 1948, when decrypted cables from Moscow to Canberra inquired about his present whereabouts and his 'opportunities', he was given the cover-name FERRO.[165] However, the Venona decrypts provide no further information about when, or in connection with what expressed or anticipated services, this occurred. Indeed, in June 1948, during the reorganisation of the KLOD group, Moscow Centre had several questions about Throssell's serviceability. First, it wanted to know whether it was 'advisable to bring FERRO into our work in view of the fact that his mother is well known . . . as an influential ACADEMICIAN'.[166] Second, it questioned some of the proposed liaison arrangements involving FERRO.[167] But in any case, as the opportunities available to Throssell were already being exploited by Hill, Moscow Centre must also have regarded him as redundant.

Milner, Hill, Jordan and Throssell represented a substantial network in External Affairs, holding positions where they had access to valuable information. Between 1945 and 1948, they—or at least Milner and Hill—provided a stream of material to Moscow. As some of them gained promotion in their respective areas they would have been of even more value to Moscow. However, by the beginning of 1948 Venona material had become available to security authorities in several countries. Their usefulness to Moscow was to be curtailed and eventually neutralised.

15

'our enquiries have met with no success'

BRITAIN'S SPYCATCHERS COME TO AUSTRALIA

ON 7 FEBRUARY 1948 THE director-general of MI5, Sir Percy Sillitoe, and the director of MI5's protective security division, Roger Hollis, stepped off the plane from Britain at Sydney airport.[1] Their mission was of the utmost importance. With them they carried the information, revealed by the Venona operation, that there was a Soviet spy ring in Australia. The network was evidently quite extensive. The Canberra–Moscow cables which had been decrypted by Arlington Hall at the end of 1947 had mostly been sent in 1945–46, but they included more than a dozen cryptonyms and names of members of the network. Specifically, Sillitoe and Hollis had information that two members of the department of External Affairs in Canberra, named MILNER and KhILL, had passed information about British documents to KLOD, who had in turn passed it to the NKGB resident in Canberra. The documents included the 'top secret' *Security in the Western Mediterranean and the Eastern Atlantic*, which had been prepared by the post-hostilities planning staff for the War Cabinet in London in May 1945,[2] and which had been provided to the Defence post-hostilities planning committee in Melbourne; and copies of telegrams from Whitehall to the department of External Affairs which also concerned British postwar strategic planning.

Sillitoe's mission had arisen as a result of efforts by the US administration in the latter part of 1947 to arrange Anglo-American talks on strategic cooperation in the Far East and Southeast Asia. On 16 December 1947 the British Foreign secretary, Ernest Bevin, suggested to the US secretary of State, George Marshall, that

Sir Percy Sillitoe, director-general of MI5, 1946–53, flew to Australia in February 1948 to warn Prime Minister Chifley that a Soviet espionage network was operating in Australia.

Australia and Canada be permitted to join the top-secret talks. Marshall readily agreed. However, within days British Foreign Office officials advised Bevin and Prime Minister Clement Attlee that the Americans had doubts about Australian security and that it was unlikely that they would agree to Dominion participation. It is probable that Attlee and Bevin discussed this matter on 8 January 1948; in any case they decided to postpone holding talks with the Americans.[3] Meanwhile, Sillitoe was to be sent to Australia to discuss the leakages of information personally with the prime minister and a handful of senior officials.[4] His mission was to determine whether Australia had the capacity to handle the investigation. If not, he needed to persuade the Australians to set up a new counter-espionage organisation along the lines of MI5. At the same time he could not afford to compromise the Venona operation. He already knew that the Soviets had penetrated both the department of External Affairs and the Commonwealth Investigation Service, so he could not reveal his sources to members of those agencies.

The investigation of the leaks in Australia, which later became known as 'the case', involved a very asymmetrical relationship between the intelligence and security authorities in Britain and Australia, which lacked any effective counter-espionage organisation anyway. The evidence for the leaks was produced in the US and Britain, but identification of the cryptonyms could only be done in Australia. No Australians were told about the Venona operation and the cryptanalytic source of the information about the leaks until February 1949, but they were expected to find other evidence that could be used in operations or in legal proceedings against the members of the espionage network when the cryptonyms were identified.

The Australian Venona operation involved the best officers the British intelligence and security community could offer. Management of the case, which was the responsibility of MI5, was exercised at the highest level. In 1948–50 it was one of MI5's highest-priority counter-espionage operations, and this was a period when it was being stretched investigating the large networks that the Venona material showed were operating in Britain itself. In 1948–49, several of the most senior MI5 officials visited Australia in connection with the case. After Sillitoe and Hollis, the principal officers involved included Dick Goldsmith White, Arthur Martin, Robert V. Hemblys-Scales, Courtenay Young and Derek Hamblen.

THE BRITISH SPYCATCHERS

Sillitoe served as the director-general of MI5 throughout the whole period of 'the case'. Two other officers, Goldsmith White and Hollis, later became successive directors-general of MI5, and White also served as chief of MI6. The other MI5 officers involved (Martin, Young and Hemblys-Scales) were among the best in the counter-espionage profession. These were the men who broke the Soviet intelligence offensive that had begun internationally during the war and continued through the early postwar period. They were officers who, through the period of 'the case', brought to successful prosecution numerous Soviet agents in Britain, including Dr Allan Nunn May and Dr Klaus Fuchs; who had determined that Donald Maclean was HOMER shortly before his defection; and who later identified H. A. R. ('Kim') Philby and Anthony Blunt as Soviet agents. Together with their colleagues in GCHQ, they were important figures in establishing the postwar Anglo-Saxon intelligence community (involving the United States, the United Kingdom, Canada, Australia and New Zealand, and generally known as UKUSA). To command attention in this league, the insights into Soviet intelligence operations provided by the Australian Venona material would have had to be of global significance.

Sillitoe had been appointed director-general of MI5 on 30 April 1946. His previous experience had been limited to regular police work. He had begun his career with some fifteen years in the British South Africa Police (1908–22). After returning to England at the end of 1922, he served as chief constable of Chesterfield in Derbyshire (1923–25); chief constable of the East Riding of Yorkshire (1925–26); chief constable of Sheffield in South Yorkshire

(1926–31); chief constable of Glasgow (1931–43), whose police force was second in strength to that of the metropolitan force of London, and where he was responsible for successful operations against both the Communist Party and the Irish Republican Army (IRA), both of which had been very active in Glasgow in the late 1930s; and then chief constable of Kent (1943–46), the front-line county in the war against Germany.[5]

When he became director-general of MI5, he said, 'I felt myself very much the new boy.'[6] His appointment was not welcomed by many of the 'professionals' in MI5, particularly those in B (counter-espionage) division, some of whom soon resigned, while others conducted 'a campaign of noncooperation and hostility'.[7] Chief among the latter group were Dick White and Roger Hollis.[8]

White had joined MI5 in 1936. He soon became the assistant director of B division and, in 1946, was promoted to director.[9] From the outset, he developed close working relations with colleagues in MI6 and the Government Code and Cypher School (GCCS), evincing a degree of collegiality that was quite rare in the British intelligence community in the prewar period. In 1939, he had conceived the 'Double-Cross' (XX) program, whereby German spies captured in Britain were 'turned around' rather than executed, and used to send false information to Germany.[10] By 1940, he 'had already established a reputation as the highest flier among the younger professionals within MI 5'.[11] As director of B division from 1946 to 1953, he oversaw the investigation of Klaus Fuchs (cover-named REST) in 1949–50, of Donald Maclean in the months before he defected with Guy Burgess in May 1951, of Philby later in 1951, and of Anthony Blunt in 1951–52.[12] Together with Roger Hollis, director of C (protective security) division from 1947 to 1953, he also oversaw the espionage case in Australia. On 1 September 1953, he succeeded Sillitoe as director-general of MI5, and in 1956 he was appointed chief of MI6,[13] which he headed until 1968, when he became the first incumbent of the new post of intelligence coordinator in the Cabinet Office.[14]

Hollis joined MI5 in 1938, and after a brief period in the Soviet counter-espionage section of B division he transferred to that part of F division responsible for monitoring the activities of the Communist Party of Great Britain (CPGB). He served as director of F division from 1940 to 1947, when he was promoted to director of C (protective security) division. By this time, he was generally reckoned to be the leading authority on Soviet counter-espionage in MI5. (Later, in September 1953, he was appointed deputy director-general of MI5, and he served as director-general from 1956 to 1965.)[15]

The three officers from MI5's B division who worked most directly on 'the case' were Arthur Martin, Robert V. Hemblys-Scales

Sir Roger Hollis, director-general of MI5, 1956–65. In 1948 he was director of MI5's Protective Security Division and visited Australia several times. In late 1948 and early 1949 he played a leading role in setting up the Australian Security Intelligence Organisation. (Press Association News)

and Courtenay Young. Hemblys-Scales spent eight months in Australia in 1948–49, and Courtenay Young lived there for two years in 1949–51.

Martin had first become involved with British intelligence during the war, when he served as an NCO with 1 Special Wireless Group, which had been established in 1940 to provide Sigint directly to the War Office and the relevant field commanders, as well as to provide German Enigma traffic to the cryptanalysts at Bletchley Park.[16] He later served with No. 53 Special Wireless Section in North Africa.[17] Although he was invited to join GCHQ after the war, he instead joined MI5, where he initially served as the officer in B division responsible for liaison with GCHQ. In this capacity, he was a central figure in the Venona operation, both assisting the cryptanalysts at GCHQ in the interpretation of the Venona decrypts and suggesting to GCHQ the time periods and pieces of traffic that could prove most fruitful for MI5 investigations.[18] The Venona material was stored in a 'special secure office' on the fifth floor of MI5 headquarters at Leconfield House, access to which was limited to Martin and his 'research officer', Evelyn McBarnet.[19] In the Australian Venona operation, Martin acted as the critical link in the process of matching information about Soviet agents (such as their access to particular areas of classified material) revealed in the partially decrypted Soviet cables with information provided from the MI5 representatives in Australia on possible suspects. Martin was able to inform GCHQ of dates on which it was likely that cable traffic from the Soviet embassy in Canberra to Moscow might contain espionage material and of the sorts of material most likely to be associated with particular cryptonyms (e.g., BUR and material on British postwar planning)—which, in turn, sometimes helped the cryptanalysts at GCHQ to make further breaks into the KGB cable traffic.

Martin was soon to earn a reputation as MI5's most 'celebrated molehunter'.[20] In September 1949, largely because of his contribution to the analysis of the Venona/Bride material, he was put in charge of the case against Fuchs.[21] In April–May 1951, Martin was instrumental in identifying HOMER as Donald Maclean when he advised the cryptanalysts at GCHQ to focus on particular sections of the KGB traffic from Washington to Moscow.[22] In June 1951, he accompanied Sillitoe to Washington to try to placate the US authorities over the defection of Maclean and Burgess to Moscow.[23] Through the second half of 1951, he led the investigation of Philby (cover-named STANLEY in the Bride material); he prepared the brief for and assisted with Philby's interrogation in November 1951.[24] In 1952, he was posted to Singapore, and then to Kuala Lumpur, where he served as director of Intelligence and commissioner of the Special Branch, as well as the local representative of MI5's E3 section, during the Malayan Emergency.[25] In January 1960, he was appointed director of DI (Soviet counter-espionage) branch in MI5.[26] In 1965, at the suggestion of White (then chief of MI6), he left MI5 and joined the counter-intelligence division of MI6.[27]

Robert Hemblys-Scales was a counter-espionage officer in the B2 section of B division. In 1945–46, he had been involved in the case against Dr Allan Nunn May, an atomic scientist (cover-named ALEK by the GRU) who confessed in February 1946 to having passed atomic secrets to the GRU from February to August 1945, including samples of enriched uranium and 'a written report on atomic research [in the US and Canada] as known to me'.[28] Nunn May was arrested on 4 March 1946, pleaded guilty at his trial on 1 May, and was sentenced to ten years' imprisonment.[29] Hemblys-Scales's first commission under Sillitoe was to compile an appreciation of Soviet espionage intentions, based on material provided by Igor Gouzenko (who had been debriefed by Hollis in September 1945 and again in early 1946) and information gleaned during the case against Nunn May.[30] In 1947 he headed a major MI5 study of captured material about the Gestapo's and Abwehr's investigations into the GRU's wartime 'illegal' network in Europe.[31] Hemblys-Scales retired from MI5 in 'the late 60s'.[32]

Courtenay Young was also a counter-espionage specialist, who had served in B16 (Far East) section of MI5's B division during the war;[33] then briefly as head of E3 (Far East) section of E (overseas operations) division[34] before returning to B division in 1946. He visited Australia at the end of October 1946 for several days for discussions with Australian security officials. He spent most of his time in Canberra at the headquarters of the Commonwealth Investigation Service. He also met with Evatt in his capacity as attorney-general.[35] In 1947, Young was put in charge of the interrogation of Alexander Allan Foote, who had joined the 'Z organization' of MI6 in 1936, been recruited by the GRU (and cover-named JIM) in 1938, served as the deputy controller of the GRU's Lucy ring in Switzerland during the war, worked with the GRU Centre in Moscow from 1945 to 1947, and 'defected' back to the British in West Berlin in August 1947.[36] Through 1948, Young worked with Foote on the latter's 'autobiography', which was designed by MI5 as an exposé of Soviet espionage practices and published under MI5 auspices in 1949.[37] In February 1949, Young was appointed the first MI5 security liaison officer (SLO) to the newly established ASIO. He returned to London in March 1951. After Maclean and Burgess's defection, Young was to play a central role in the British efforts to ascertain the extent of Soviet penetration of the British intelligence establishment. He was involved in the 1951 interrogation of Philby, and conducted a series of interviews with Blunt from 1952 through to 1964, having been convinced of Blunt's treason during the 'damage assessment' after the defection of Burgess and Maclean.[38] Young served as head of the Soviet counter-intelligence section of MI5 from 1956 to 1960.[39]

MI5 INFORMS AUSTRALIA

It is important to understand the global strategic situation when Sillitoe arrived in Australia in 1948. By then the Cold War had begun to intensify into a sharply defined confrontation. There were civil wars between communists and their opponents in a number of countries, such as Greece and China, and to many politicians and their advisers it seemed that war involving the US and the Soviet Union could break out at any time. Initially Australia's reaction was ambivalent, with Evatt trying to improve relations with the Soviet Union. On 25 February 1948 a new, predominantly communist government took power in Czechoslovakia, and on 10 March it was announced that the non-communist president, Jan Masaryk, had committed suicide; in truth he was murdered. The Chifley government refused to follow the British response of banning communists from its public service.[40] A senior British Foreign Office official reported that Chifley had said he preferred to 'deal with the communists in the open', and that 'no fascists or communists' were 'engaged in any job where there are security considerations'. Foreign

Secretary Bevin noted: 'I must await report'; presumably referring to the results of Sillitoe's mission.[41]

On 12 February 1948, Sillitoe and Hollis had their first meeting with Chifley. Four days later they met with the Defence secretary, Shedden. Sillitoe informed Shedden that he had come to Australia 'on the direction of the Prime Minister of the United Kingdom, to acquaint the Prime Minister of Australia with information, which had come to the knowledge of the United Kingdom Authorities', that copies of British postwar planning documents, and notably the paper on *Security in the Western Mediterranean and the Eastern Atlantic*, 'had come into the possession of the USSR'.[42] Evatt and John Dedman, the Defence minister, were informed in general terms of Sillitoe's mission, and on 20 February, the day he left Canberra to return to Singapore, Sillitoe again called on the prime minister.[43] While in Australia he also met Brigadier Chilton, the controller of joint intelligence in the department of Defence; Spry, the DMI; Longfield Lloyd, the director of the CIS; and Professor Kenneth Bailey, the secretary of the Attorney-General's department.

The Australian officials would have quickly realised the significance of Sillitoe's mission, for, as related in Chapter 8, throughout 1947 the Americans had progressively reduced the amount of information that they were passing to Australia. Shedden was both the senior official concerned with hosting and supporting Sillitoe's visit and, as the secretary of the Defence department, the official personally responsible for the 'control and distribution' of the documents the UK had provided to Australia. On 16 February, the day of his first meeting with Sillitoe and Hollis, Shedden conducted a preliminary investigation into the 'control and distribution' of British postwar planning documents, and submitted a 'progress report' to the minister for Defence.[44] That same day he called in Chilton, advised him that British material 'had somehow become known to Soviet Russia',[45] and directed him 'to investigate the matter'.[46] Chilton was given no details of what Sillitoe had told Shedden about MI5's knowledge of the leaks.[47]

On 27 February Chilton provided a comprehensive report to Shedden on 'the system of control, circulation, and custody of Secret documents received from the United Kingdom from the aspect of security',[48] and on 1 March he submitted a further report specifically on the paper on *Security in the Western Mediterranean*, referred to as PHP(45)6(0).[49] Chilton found that the circulation of secret documents within the department of Defence was rigorously controlled. Three copies (Nos. 109, 110 and 111) of PHP(45)6(0) had been received from London on 11 September 1945. Apart from the three service members and the secretary of Defence's post-hostilities planning committee, who evidently had not circulated the document any further, the only person who had had access to it was Ian Milner, who served as the External Affairs representative on that committee during the relevant period.⁵⁰ Milner had specifically requested a copy of the document on 6 November 1945.⁵¹ According to the register in the department of Defence, Milner had possession of one copy of the document (No. 110) from 15 November 1945 to 19 February 1946 and another (No. 109) from 6 March 1946 to 28 March 1946.⁵² When Chilton wrote this report he did not know Milner, nor anything about him, nor whether he might be a suspect.⁵³ Shedden provided Dedman with Chilton's report ('for the information of the Prime Minister') on 2 March 1948.⁵⁴

Chilton's reports also showed that Defence had received fourteen British post-hostilities papers, and that Milner had had access to seven of them:

> PHP(44) 22 (0), International Control of Germany—M. Massigli's proposal, dated 3 January 1945.
> PHP(45)4(0), Occupation of Berlin and Vienna, dated 17 February 1945.
> PHP(45)8(0), French Zone of Occupation in Germany, dated 10 February 1945.
> PHP(45)5, International Air Corps, dated 25 March 1945.
> PHP(45)6, World Organisation—Military Staff Committee, dated 25 March 1945.
> PHP(45)6(0), Security in the Western Mediterranean and the Eastern Atlantic, dated 19 May 1945.
> PHP(45)15(0), Security of India and the Indian Ocean, dated 19 May 1945.⁵⁵

Although the focus of Chilton's investigation was on the second last of these documents, a number of others would also have been of great value to the Soviet Union, especially during the period when it was negotiating with the Allies over postwar arrangements in Europe. The importance of the documents was emphasised by recent developments in the Cold War.

The Soviets would have found much of interest in the paper on security in the Western Mediterranean and the Eastern Atlantic, which they had received in March–April 1946. They would have learned that the British post-hostilities planning staff had produced a series of papers dealing with the strategic situation that might 'be expected to exist in the period 1955–60'. The paper referred to another paper, that covering the security of Western Europe and the North Atlantic, which had concluded 'that the only major threats to our interests would arise from a hostile USSR and/or a rearmed Germany'. The Western Mediterranean and Eastern Atlantic paper reiterated the views of the Western Europe and North Atlantic paper that US help would be vital. It was important that Spain remain friendly or neutral and that friendship be renewed with Italy so it did not look to the USSR for support.[56]

It was not long before the MI5 representatives advised the Australians that the Soviets had also received the paper covering the security of India and the Indian Ocean, and this too would have been of great interest. The paper stated that 'the USSR was the only major power which would be capable of threatening our interests in India and the Indian Ocean by 1955'. It added that the British position in India was expected 'to be vulnerable to Soviet strategic bombing' from bases in Russian Turkestan and that a Soviet advance through Persia and Afghanistan might prove irresistible.[57] Together these papers provided a window into top-level British official thinking about the security of Britain and the Commonwealth, and Britain's perceptions of the Soviet Union as a threat, at a time when the international situation was still in transition between the end of the Second World War and the outbreak of the Cold War. Chilton did not spell out the importance of these papers, but it would have been obvious to anyone with any understanding of defence planning.

Shedden had other material incriminating Milner, but he did not divulge it to Chilton. Earlier in February, Spry had provided him with two interesting pieces of information. The first was that 'the contents of a [post-hostilities planning committee] Planning Paper had been referred to at a Communist Party meeting in Sydney in December 1945'.[58] The second related to information that Spry had received from his predecessor, Combes, when he had taken over as DMI in April 1946. Between October 1945 and March 1946 Combes's brother-in-law, Major John Mathews, had been seconded from the Allied geographic section in GHQ SWPA to work in the post-hostilities section of External Affairs. He had noticed that Ian Milner, a senior officer in the section, had taken a top secret document out of the department over a weekend when he was visiting Melbourne. When Milner had been asked to produce the document he had taken 36 hours to do so. Spry had made a mental note of the incident, but no further action had been taken at that time.[59] Shedden directed Spry personally to relate this information on Milner to Sillitoe.

By early March Sillitoe and Hollis were back in Australia, no doubt to receive the outcome of Shedden's and Chilton's investigations. When Sillitoe returned to Britain on 20 March, Hollis remained in Australia. He had the more detailed knowledge of the Venona material and the limited information about the cryptonyms it contained. Remaining with him was Hemblys-Scales, whom Chilton has described as 'Sillitoe's bag-handler',[60] but who actually had a very good knowledge of Soviet espionage activities and operational techniques. On 7 April 1948 Hollis met with Chifley, Evatt, Dedman and Shedden to discuss 'the result of the investigation' and the need for the establishment in Australia of a security service along MI5 lines.[61] At a further meeting with Shedden on 10 April, the day he left Australia, Hollis reiterated his arguments for the establishment of an MI5-type organisation. Since the military distrusted the CIS, he believed that it could 'not be patched' up. On 15 April, after returning to London, Hollis reported that 'no practical planning had begun' in Australia.[62]

This may well have been the first proper report received in London, for although Sillitoe had left Australia a month earlier, he had been 'stranded by illness in Singapore'. In the absence of Sillitoe's advice, Bevin had decided to send another envoy, M. E. Denning, an assistant under-secretary of state at the Foreign Office, to Australia to discuss the possibility of arranging talks with the Americans on Far East security and 'to stress the importance of complete secrecy'.[63] Denning arrived in Canberra in the first week of May and met with Chifley, Evatt and Burton, the External Affairs secretary. When he raised the issue of Australian domestic security, Chifley detailed the security procedures that were in place and that he believed were adequate. Denning reported to London that he was not satisfied that official secret material passed to External Affairs was secure. He continued: 'Chifley went on to make disparaging remarks about sleuths who have to have something to show to earn their keep, and he seemed to have some doubts whether there was really any foundation to our story' that top-secret documents had been passed from External Affairs to the Soviets. Denning thought that Chifley took the matter a 'little light-heartedly'. Since Evatt and Burton were responsible for implementing policy, Denning doubted whether the Australians could keep the proposed talks secret.[64]

Meanwhile, investigations had continued in Australia. At the meeting with Hollis on 7 April Evatt had suggested, and Chifley had agreed, that Shedden should inform Burton about these matters insofar as the department of External Affairs was involved.[65] Shedden had little respect for or trust in Burton. He wrote to him that afternoon and informed him that Sillitoe had visited Australia in February to 'acquaint' the prime minister with information concerning the leakage of British documents (including *Security in the Western Mediterranean*) to Moscow, and that an investigation within the department of Defence had shown that Milner was the only person outside Defence who had had a copy of the document. Shedden told Burton nothing about any other evidence against Milner.[66]

On 9 April, Burton replied to Shedden that he had 'been making certain inquiries', but that 'before continuing them' he would be glad if Shedden could 'inform me in a little more detail of the circumstances referred to by the official of the United Kingdom Government', and that 'without knowing these things . . . I find it difficult to make any satisfactory enquiry'.67 Shedden did not bother to respond. The next week, Burton asked Colin Moodie, the Defence liaison officer in External Affairs, 'to ascertain with the utmost discretion anything I could about what happened to the document in the Department . . . and . . . to report to him verbally as soon as I could'.68 Moodie reported back to Burton a few days later that 'a careful search' of the files showed that Milner had had the document but it 'revealed nothing else . . . throwing any light on what happened to the document during its retention in the Department'.69

Burton's response to Shedden, on 22 April 1948, was pitiable. He acknowledged that 'No officer other than Mr. Milner would have seen the document under discussion', but noted that those officers in the department who knew Milner well 'all maintain that there is no reason to believe the papers held by him would not be in safe-custody'. He asked that no suggestion should be made in any report 'that Mr Milner was an officer to whom secret information could not safely be entrusted', and, more importantly, that any report should contain 'a firm assurance regarding the safe-custody of any secret information to the Department'.70 Having no inkling of Operation Venona and the decrypts, Burton felt obliged to speculate about other means by which 'an agent of another country' might have obtained the document in question.71 He also asked that Shedden arrange for him 'to see any draft report which might be returned by any channel to the United Kingdom authorities';72 but Shedden ignored his request.

Chifley wrote to Attlee on 7 June, giving him a full report on the status of the investigation undertaken since Sillitoe's visit in February and his meeting with Hollis on 7 April. He described in detail the investigations that Chilton and Moodie had made into the control and distribution of PHP(45)6(0), and cited at length the information about Milner which Burton had sent to Shedden on 22 April. The investigation, however, was still inconclusive. Chifley told Attlee that:

> In the absence of full particulars to enable me to study the specific information that came into the possession of the United Kingdom Government and to assess the credibility of the information [sic], we were placed at some disadvantage in dealing with the matter . . .
> Though every effort has been made to discover any possible source of leakage, our enquiries have met with no success.73

He noted in his last paragraph that consideration was being given to 'any additional measures that might be considered necessary for strengthening the check of all civilian and service personnel in the group of Departments dealing with Defence information of a secret nature'.[74]

When Shedden wrote to Burton on 9 June to tell him about Chifley's report to Attlee, he refused to show him a copy, saying only that the information Burton had provided about Milner had been included in the report.[75] Burton was livid; he protested to Shedden, as did Evatt to Chifley, about the 'impressions' of External Affairs 'embodied' in the report, and Chifley asked Shedden to put together an account of how the content of his report had been compiled.[76] As Burton has recalled, there ensued an argument between the departments of Defence and External Affairs which involved reciprocal accusations and which poisoned the working relations between them for another five years.[77]

Meanwhile, Australia's reputation for security continued to decline. By May 1948, the US authorities had decided to institute a complete embargo on the transfer of classified US information to Australia.[78] The decision was communicated to the Australian services in Washington 'suddenly, and without any reason given', at the end of June, and Canberra was informed of the US action on 3 July.[79] It was clear to Shedden, if not to Evatt, and perhaps not even to Chifley at this stage, that more action was necessary.

BRITAIN APPLIES PRESSURE

In early July 1948 Chifley visited London to discuss economic questions with the British government, but the British were more interested in strategic and security issues. The Soviet Union had imposed a total blockade of Berlin on 24 June and the British Foreign Office had already sought assistance from the dominions in the form of aircraft and men to help with the airlift to the beleaguered city. Attlee thought Chifley's visit so important that he cancelled a trip to Germany so he could be in London for the duration of Chifley's stay.[80] He had received a damning report on security arrangements in Australia from Sillitoe, who remained unimpressed with the Australian efforts to identify the leaker of PHP(45)6(0) and with Australian security arrangements more generally.[81] Sillitoe, moreover, had the benefit of additional Venona material, which GCHQ was now providing on a fairly regular basis. Attlee reportedly showed the Sillitoe report to Chifley (after first sanitising references to Venona material), and he and Sillitoe persuaded Chifley to accept an MI5 proposal to establish a new Australian security intelligence organisation to replace the CIS.[82]

Chifley also agreed that, in view of the doubts expressed by Attlee regarding the adequacy of security in Australia, two MI5 officers—Hollis and Hemblys-Scales—should be dispatched to check MI5's information about the leaks.[83] In an effort to align Chifley with British anti-Soviet policy, the British arranged for Chifley to visit Berlin for eight hours and to inspect the airlift.[84]

When Hollis and Hemblys-Scales left London on 28 July, the Venona operation had revealed much more information about the Soviet espionage activities in Australia. In addition to more material from the Canberra–Moscow cable traffic in 1945–46, a lot of traffic from 1947–48 was now available, some of it sent only a couple of months previously, which referred to SESTRA, BEN, TOURIST, PODRUGA, FERRO, MASTER and PROFESSOR.[85] In a letter written on 6 August 1948, Dedman advised Shedden that 'even the fact that they [Hollis and Hemblys-Scales] are out here is to be treated as "top secret".'[86] Dedman said that 'only five people know of it'.[87] These were Chifley, Dedman, Shedden, Longfield Lloyd, and Bailey, the solicitor-general, though Chilton, who by this time had moved to the position of second assistant secretary in the department of Defence, and Spry were also soon informed. Hollis met with Shedden and Chilton on 24 and 27 August and, according to the notes of the discussions, stated that 'there is no evidence of leakage from Defence sources' but that there were suspects in both External Affairs and the Attorney-General's department.[88] Shedden informed Dedman of his discussions with Hollis on 3 September, and emphasised to the minister 'that advantage should be taken of the presence of Mr Hollis to place our security organisation on a sound footing, which alone would now apparently satisfy the United Kingdom and United States in regard to the release of information to Australia'.[89]

Hollis then decided to meet with Burton. The secretary of the External Affairs department had previously served as acting secretary on several occasions (including 1 October to 15 November 1945 and 26 February to 27 March 1947), and in 1944–45 had been in the post-hostilities division, to which much of the Venona material pointed. Hollis needed to gain Burton's cooperation, but Burton was suspicious of security officers, dismissive of the importance of the material allegedly leaked, and very protective of the members of his department. Hollis, on the other hand, was less than candid. There was no question of informing Burton about the decrypts. He could only be given information consistent with a 'cover story', in his case that MI5's knowledge of the leaks came from a British mole in the KGB.[90]

The tenor of the discussions between Burton and Hollis, which also included Hemblys-Scales and Moodie—to whom Burton had 'given the job of keeping in touch with MI 5 on all matters connected or related to their enquiries'[91]—has been described by Burton as follows:

> Two representatives of British intelligence—MI 5—[Hollis and Hemblys-Scales] came to give the Australian authorities some information; in part, it was to check information which they had obtained. . .
>   These officers had certain information which gave them to believe the possible existence of a spy net-work. They had descriptions of people, code names and other details. . .
>   They had a list of nine to ten to twelve code names to which they had attached certain descriptions and they asked our help to try to help them identify the persons. . .
>   The information came through in somewhat curious way—in bits and pieces—details about a person, he may have been sick two years ago; he may have two children—little snippets such as that; and as they came through local attempts were made to identify the person on the basis of the information. . .
>   All those investigations were across the table between [Hemblys-]Scales and myself, or Moodie, later, and Scales.[92]

During this visit Hollis was able to confirm the identity of SESTRA. Decrypted cables sent from Canberra to Moscow on 25 April and 5 July 1945 suggested that SESTRA was 'FRANCISCA BURNY',[93] but MI5 wanted the Australians to provide the confirmation without being told the name. The decrypts had revealed that SESTRA/BURNY was a woman who worked 'at Evatt's', and that she had given information to KLOD from the end of 1944 to the beginning of 1946; there were (frequently incomplete) descriptions of some of this information, which Hollis described as 'confidential political information'; and there were certain personal details, including a reference to her marriage in 1945. Hollis and Hemblys-Scales discussed the matter with Burton, who told them 'there was no such person, because I thought I knew everyone who had been on the Minister's staff'.[94] However, Moodie investigated the staff records, and discovered that Frances Bernie, who had worked as a secretary in Evatt's office in Sydney from 1944 to 1946, but whom Burton had 'never met', fitted the details of SESTRA. Burton then 'informed MI 5 that we had been in error and in fact there was such a person who fitted that description'.[95] Only 'a few days' had lapsed between Burton's briefing by Hollis and Hemblys-Scales and the confirmation of Bernie as SESTRA. Hollis told Chifley 'directly', and Evatt was informed by Burton soon after.[96]

Hollis returned to London in mid September 1948, but Hemblys-Scales stayed in Australia 'to work full-time on the flow of important British and Australian data which was by then shown

Professor Sir Kenneth Bailey, solicitor-general and secretary of the Attorney-General's department, played an important role in the formation of ASIO in 1949. (NLA)

to be reaching the Soviet State Security Service'.⁹⁷ However, before Hollis departed, on 17 September the Defence committee recommended the formation of a separate security organisation on the ground that the CIS did not have the required 'counter-espionage capacity'.⁹⁸

On 20 September Chifley met with three of his Cabinet colleagues—Dedman, acting Attorney-General Nicholas McKenna (Evatt was in London), and Senator John Armstrong, the minister for Supply and Development—as well as Shedden, to discuss 'matters of leakages and internal security'. Chifley explained how he had arranged with Attlee for Hollis and Hemblys-Scales to be sent to Australia. He said that 'the position was that, except for the Milner incident which occurred in 1946, nothing can be discovered regarding any continuing leakages from Departments'. He proposed to write to Attlee to emphasise that 'any present doubts that existed [about leakages in Australia] had not been substantiated'. Armstrong, who had just returned from Britain and the US, interjected 'that he had not found Mr Forrestal, the [US] Secretary of Defense and other persons with whom he had discussed the matter [of the leakages], very forthcoming'. Chifley replied that he was willing to set up an Australian security organisation 'similar to MI 5', and that he was also willing to ask Attlee to post a British security intelligence officer to Australia to 'provide advice' to the new organisation.⁹⁹ This was a key meeting because for the first time Chifley had definitely committed the government to the formation of a new security service.

At the meeting Chifley added that the absence of Evatt and Bailey (who was also in London) might delay an early decision.

Evatt was attending a Commonwealth prime ministers' meeting (on Chifley's behalf). Solicitor-General Bailey and Longfield Lloyd were attending the first Commonwealth Security Conference, which had been called to 'counter the skilful and extensive infiltration measures which Russia is now carrying on, and the way in which these security authorities could assist each other in relation to the infiltration problem'. It was agreed that the security organisations would soon develop procedures for exchange of information.[100]

On 27 September Chifley wrote to Attlee about 'security in Australia and the stoppage of the flow of information from the USA.'[101] Chifley reported that, further to his letter of 7 June and his meeting with Attlee and Sillitoe in July, 'additional measures' had been instituted 'for strengthening the check of all civilian and service personnel in the group of Departments dealing with Defence information of a secret nature'; that Hollis had had discussions with Solicitor-General Bailey 'on the creation of a new Security Organisation along the lines of your MI5'; that he (Chifley) agreed 'with the strengthening of our Security Organisation along these lines'; and that he 'would also welcome the posting of an officer of your MI5 for liaison purposes and, in the early stages, his knowledge would be useful in assisting in the creation of this machinery'.[102] In his letter Chifley emphasised

> the serious repercussions of the stoppage of the flow of classified information on British Commonwealth and Australian Defence Policy. . . it is an invidious position for a Government to be placed in, if the flow of information is to be arbitrarily stopped, as has occurred at present . . .
> In regard to the leakage that is alleged to have arisen from Australia over two years ago, I would confidently assert that there has not been a country, at least of all the Great Powers, which has not had a similar experience of this nature. Even in the present instance, judging by press reports emanating from Washington, the Americans have not been able to safeguard the fact they have stopped the flow of information to Australia . . .
> I would therefore ask that either the embargo be lifted as soon as possible, or that I should be informed of the reasons why this cannot be done.[103]

Hemblys-Scales remained in Canberra until late February 1949 as the MI5 representative with the Security Section of the CIS, attempting to identify those persons, named or cover-named, on whom bits of information had been revealed in the Venona operation. His focus was on Milner and Hill/TOURIST, both known to be current or former members of the department of External Affairs. Although he continued to meet with Burton to discuss the matter, most of his dealings in the department were with Colin Moodie.

According to Moodie, Hemblys-Scales was then about 35 years old, 'skinnyish', about 5'9" or 5'10" tall, with a 'pimply, pasty face'.[104] Moodie and Hemblys-Scales met 'about once very fortnight', or twelve to fifteen times from mid September 1948 to mid February 1949. Hemblys-Scales would call in to Burton's or Moodie's offices unannounced, having walked some 800m from the Patents Building to West Block; some of the meetings were 'perfunctory' and others 'more purposeful'.[105]

Moodie's discussions with Hemblys-Scales primarily concerned Ian Milner. The MI5 officer also had information about TOURIST which pointed to Jim Hill, but Burton insisted that any questions concerning Hill were to be discussed only with him. As Burton later testified, 'the one matter which I reserved and handled myself was . . . Hill'.[106] Hill was still a member of his department, while Milner had left two years before and was no friend of Burton's anyway.

Hemblys-Scales was quickly able to persuade Moodie that Milner had leaked material to the Soviets. It took a little longer for Burton to be persuaded—partly, perhaps, because he had strenuously asserted Milner's loyalty only six months before. By October 1948, however, Burton conceded that he 'knew' Milner was 'a security risk',[107] and in his account of his later discussions with Hollis about Milner he suggests that he had no doubt about Milner's guilt—but that he thought Hollis had evinced little interest in the subject.[108]

HOLLIS AND THE ESTABLISHMENT OF ASIO

Roger Hollis returned to Australia again in late January 1949. His principal mission was to advise the government on the establishment of the new security organisation, including its charter, responsibilities, organisational structure, and senior appointments. He was accompanied this time by Courtenay Young, who was to replace Hemblys-Scales as the MI5 representative and to be the first MI5 Security Liaison Officer (SLO) with the new organisation. He also brought out all of the Venona material then available, including copies of decrypts, which was to be left with Young in Australia. Much of the new material concerned TOURIST.

Hollis' initial discussions about the new organisation and the appointment of the first director-general were with Solicitor-General Bailey. In December, Bailey had met with Justice Geoffrey Reed of the South Australian Supreme Court in Adelaide and had asked him for suggestions about the 'new security service'. Reed had had some limited experience with security matters, having been chairman of the South Australian committee dealing with objections

Justice Geoffrey Reed of South Australia was appointed first director-general of ASIO in March 1949. His principal task was to crack 'the case'. (Herald and Weekly Times, reproduced by permission)

to internment. In September–October 1943, he had conducted an inquiry into the lack of cooperation between the Commonwealth Security Service and Military Intelligence. His report appears to have been destroyed and its recommendations have not been revealed (apart from the demotion of Robert Wake, who had been the over-zealous head of the Security Service in Queensland).[109] Reed had also chaired a board of inquiry into breaches of the National Security Regulations in Hobart in 1944.[110] It was presumably through these inquiries that Reed's name had occurred to Bailey and Chifley.[111]

The foundations for the establishment of the Australian Security Intelligence Organisation (ASIO) were laid by the government in meetings among ministers and officials concerned with security matters in Canberra on 8 February 1949. The main meeting was attended by Chifley, Evatt, Dedman, McKenna (who had acted for Evatt as attorney-general at a previous meeting), Shedden, Chilton, Bailey, Hollis, Young and Scales. Hollis explained the functions, organisation and operation of MI5. The meeting agreed that an Australian security intelligence service should be set up along the same lines, that the next step should be appointment of a director, and that knowledge of the meeting was to be limited to those present. Hollis was not likely to have been very impressed by the security capacity of this group.

There was also a smaller, more secret meeting, involving Hollis, Young, Shedden, Chilton, and, at least for some part, Chifley, at which Hollis described the Venona operation and the extremely sensitive nature of the Venona material, and explained the role Young would play as special liaison officer with the Australian service. This was the first time Australian officials learned anything about Venona. Hollis had copies of the decrypts, which Chilton studied closely. When Chilton and Hollis had met in late August 1948, Hollis had told him 'some cock-and-bull story' about a defector's being the source of MI5's evidence, but to Chilton it had been 'obvious' that it came from decrypts. He was pleased to have his perspicacity confirmed.[112] It was agreed that knowledge of the Venona operation was to be restricted to those at this meeting, and that after Hollis left, Courtenay Young was to hold the Australian Venona material and that he was not to inform anyone in the new Security Service about the cryptanalytic source of this material.

By mid February Chifley, after further discussions with McKenna and Bailey, had decided that Reed himself should be 'requested by the Attorney General to form the new Security Service'.[113] In order to secure Reed's services, Chifley engaged in a 'tough horse-trade' with Sir Thomas Playford, the premier of South Australia. L. F. Crisp has recounted an incident in which one of Chifley's advisers found him chuckling to himself in his office in Parliament House and remarking: 'I have just traded three boilers with Tom Playford for two judges.'[114] Playford wanted three large steam boilers from a Commonwealth munitions establishment that had been run down after the war for a development project in South Australia; Reed was one of the judges involved in the trade.[115] On 24 February 1949, Chifley wrote to Playford to ask formally for Reed's services:

> An efficient system of internal security is an essential part of national defences. For this purpose a distinct security service was established during the recent war, but at the end of hostilities an attempt was made to provide for the necessary functions as merely an adjunct of the Commonwealth Investigation Service. Subsequent developments in the international situation, and consultation with other Governments of the British Commonwealth have convinced me that it is necessary to re-establish a distinct security service. I am convinced also that the new service should be organised under the leadership of a man of high standing and wide experience of affairs . . . .[116]

On 2 March, Chifley told Parliament that 'a great increase in Australian security tasks and responsibilities has made it necessary to re-establish a separate security service' and that Justice Reed had been appointed to 'establish and organise an Australian Security Service'.[117] Longfield Lloyd, the CIS director, had not been consulted about the formation of ASIO, and got the news from Bailey only four hours before hearing about it on the radio that evening.[118]

Hollis's principal task in March 1949 was to draft the charter for ASIO. This 'was based on that given to the UK Security Service [i.e., MI5]',[119] but there were some changes made to reflect the Australian situation, including the relationship between ASIO and MI5. (ASIO had been described by Shedden in December 1948 as 'the proposed MI5 Section'.)[120] Other details of the new organisation were worked out by Hemblys-Scales after discussions with Spry, the director of Military Intelligence, and two of his key officers, Colin Brown and Max Phillips; indeed as Brown recalled, they 'virtually did Hemblys-Scales's job for him'.[121]

Reed had visited Canberra briefly in February to discuss his appointment with Bailey, but had to return to Adelaide. He asked a close 'legal acquaintance' in Adelaide, Bernard G. Tuck, who had been a wartime member of the Security Service in Queensland, to go to Canberra in his stead and discuss the draft charter and proposed organisation with Hollis and Young. Robert Wake, the officer in charge of the CIS in Queensland and a personal friend of Tuck, was also invited to Canberra to join the discussion. Hollis, Young, Tuck and Wake prepared the draft charter and plan of organisation, which Reed approved when he returned to Canberra a few days later. McKenna, as acting attorney-general, suggested 'a small alteration', and Hollis and Reed then took the proposed charter to Chifley, who signed and issued it to Reed on 16 March 1949.[122]

Thirteen months had elapsed from the arrival of Sillitoe in Australia in February 1948 until the formation of ASIO in March 1949. Until then the Australian investigation had proceeded slowly. Although BUR, TOURIST and SESTRA had been identified, it was still not known whom KLOD, BEN, the 'influential ACADEMICIAN', FERRO and PODRUGA referred to, and Australia was still being denied important defence information by the Americans. However, the government had at last begun the formation of a counter-espionage organisation. It remained to be seen whether it could crack 'the case'.

16

'identification of the spymaster has been made'

ASIO AND 'THE CASE'

THE AUSTRALIAN SECURITY INTELLIGENCE ORGANISATION was established for two closely connected reasons: to persuade the British and the Americans that Australia was taking security seriously, and to crack 'the case'. As Reed, the first director-general of ASIO, wrote:

> CIS was for some years the body responsible for security measures. Two main tasks to which it was expected to attend were what is usually known as 'the case' and vetting. The decision to establish the new Security Service was arrived at largely because very little progress was being made with 'the case', and the position regarding security generally was not satisfactory.[1]

MI5's close involvement in planning the organisation was reflected in the proposed organisational structure which, like MI5's, was based around three activities—B1 (counter-subversion), B2 (counter-espionage), and C (protective security). In ASIO's case, B1 and B2 were to be based in Sydney, while C was to be split between C1, based in Canberra and responsible for C activities with respect to the public service, and C2, based in Melbourne and responsible for C activities with respect to the services and the department of Supply. Offices were to be established in Brisbane, Townsville, Darwin, Port Moresby, Adelaide, Perth and Hobart, responsible to directors in Canberra, Sydney and Melbourne. It looked neat on paper (see figure 16.1), but it proved unmanageable in practice.

Bernard Tuck and Robert Wake officially joined ASIO on 16 and 23 March respectively. Their first job was to implement the

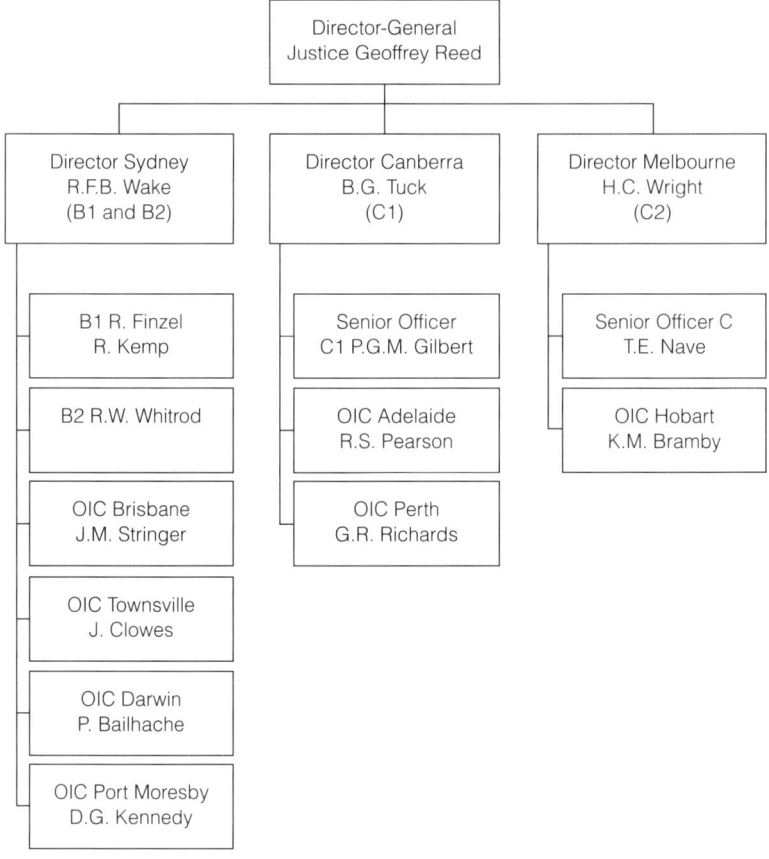

Figure 16.1 *Organisation of ASIO, 1949–50*

organisational plan which they had just helped draft—i.e., to find and furnish suitable accommodation and to decide on the senior appointments. ASIO's first office was in East Block in Canberra, just 400m from West Block. It had little furniture, no files or filing cabinets, and no safe. Wake obtained from the department of the Interior a safe with a two-drawer container (which had previously been used by the Italian consulate in Sydney). The new organisation's headquarters, however, were to be set up in Sydney. Canberra was too small to provide the organisation with sufficient cover. Melbourne was 'inaccessibly far' from Canberra. The main target was the CPA in Sydney. And most of the relevant files were maintained by the CIS there.[2] Wake was formally titled director Sydney, was responsible for all B1 (counter-subversion) and B2 (counter-espionage) activities, and was essentially the deputy director of ASIO in charge of operations. Tuck became director in Canberra, where he served in effect as the deputy director in charge of administration; he was also responsible for C1 activities.

Later in March, Hollis and Reed jointly prepared a report on 'The Australian Security Service'[3] which further spelled out the background of the 'unsatisfactory security situation' in Australia and the decision to establish ASIO, as well as the objectives, terms of reference, principles of activity and measures soon to be taken by the new organisation 'to strengthen security' in Australia. The Reed/Hollis report included several paragraphs on the status of 'the case' as at the end of March 1949, by which time the identities of 'two agents'—Ian Milner (BUR) and Frances Bernie (SESTRA) had been positively identified. According to the report:

> It is known that there is in existence in Australia a Soviet spy network which has, or had, means of obtaining information from Australian Government Departments. Two of the agents of the network have been identified. One worked in the Department of External Affairs and is known to have passed information to the Soviet intelligence machine which was available to him as a result of his work. The other worked in Dr Evatt's private office and, though not engaged on secret work, may have had access to official material. Neither of these two agents is now employed in any Australian Government Department.[4]

Early Progress

GCHQ was now progressing so well with the Venona operation that a large number of decrypts became available after Hollis and Courtenay Young had left London in January.[5] Dick White, director of B (counter-espionage) division, brought this new material to Australia at the end of March. It included a lot more information about the material supplied by KLOD and TOURIST, as well as further words and sentences about MASTER, FERRO (whose mother was 'an influential ACADEMICIAN'), and DZhON/PODRUGA.

By March 1949, MI5 had confirmed that TOURIST was Jim Hill. By the end of 1947 Arlington Hall had informed GCHQ that KhILL had provided copies of telegrams from Whitehall to the department of External Affairs in Canberra dealing with British postwar foreign policy. During 1948, information had been decrypted about TOURIST's membership of the Communist Party, his family relations and his continuing supply of important information.[6] When Hollis came back to Australia in January 1949, the Venona material he brought with him included 'a telegram number' which related to 'particular information' about British policy, and which 'was a matter of long discussion' between Hollis and Burton. After the movements of the numbered telegram were traced through the External Affairs files during the period before it was referred to in the Venona traffic, Hollis and Hemblys-Scales had concluded that TOURIST must be Hill. The Venona material White brought out left no doubt that they were right.

P. G. M. (Phil) Gilbert was appointed senior officer B1 in Canberra on 7 April 1949, and was immediately given responsibility for the investigation of Hill. Gilbert had worked as personal assistant to Bailey, the solicitor-general, in 1948–49, and had met Sillitoe, Hollis and Hemblys-Scales in February 1948; he had also been involved with arranging the telephone conversations between Bailey and Reed, and coordinating the transport for Reed, Tuck and Wake when they came to Canberra in February–March 1949.[7]

Before Hollis and White returned to London in late April, Hollis had another discussion with Burton about Hill. He told Burton that he was sure Hill was a source of leaks, and that he would have to be investigated. He also suggested that Hill be posted to London. It was thought that the fledgling ASIO might not yet be capable of matching the professional skills of the MVD or the well-developed tradecraft of the KLOD group, but that in London Hill and his contacts could be watched directly by MI5. Burton undertook to watch Hill 'carefully' and to keep in contact with Hollis concerning the question of posting Hill to London.[8]

In the second week of April 1949, Hollis and White prepared to leave Australia to report back to London on the Australian security developments. They briefed Chifley and Bailey in Canberra just before the prime minister himself left for London (on 15 April) to attend the dominion prime ministers' conference. Accompanied by Bernard Tuck, they spent Easter (around 15–18 April) in Adelaide, where they had further discussions with Reed. They then returned to Canberra with Reed for final discussions and farewells. One meeting in Canberra, which included Hollis, White, Courtenay Young and Reed, took place at the home of Gilbert (who had just transferred to ASIO).[9] By the time they left at the end of the month, Hollis and White must have been fairly satisfied with the recent progress on both the case and the establishment of ASIO.

In April 1949, ASIO acquired its first headquarters, a former Navy building at 12 Wylde Street in Potts Point, on Sydney Harbour. Called 'Agincourt' (but also nicknamed 'the Kremlin' and 'the Elephant House'), it was a three-storey building whose middle floor was at ground level and housed the offices of Reed, Courtenay Young, Wake and Ray Whitrod (who had transferred from the South Australian Police) and their secretaries. On the top floor were the B1 and B2 analysts; most of the files were stored on the bottom floor ('the salt mines'). A special Chubb safe was sent out from

'Agincourt'—also known as 'the Kremlin' or 'the Elephant House'—in Wylde Street, Potts Point, Sydney, was the first headquarters of ASIO. (E.O. Redford)

London for Courtenay Young; it was so large that it could only be got into in his office by knocking down part of the stonework around one of the outside windows. Within it Courtenay Young kept both the copies of the Venona decrypts and associated material, as well as his own codes for communication with MI5 and other agencies (such as the FBI in Washington, the Commissioner of Police in New Zealand, and the Royal Canadian Mounted Police). Courtenay Young acted as 'a self-contained unit' with his secretary, Pam Steibel, who had come out with him from MI5 and who was the only other person with access to his safe and personal ciphers. (Young's safe was presumably more secure than Reed's locally acquired one, whose combination he lost during a 'convivial lunch' about a week after it was installed, and which had to be broken open.)

On 20–25 April, while Agincourt was being cleaned and furnished, Reed, Wake, Tuck and Courtenay Young visited Melbourne. Reed and Courtenay Young met with Allan Fleming, the controller of joint intelligence, on 22 April, and Chilton, the second assistant secretary in the department of Defence, on 23 April to discuss the case. Arrangements were also made for the establishment of an office in Melbourne.[10]

By 1 July, ASIO had fifteen officers, but by June 1950 the number was to reach 141. The earliest appointments were those of the regional directors in Brisbane (J. M. Stringer, appointed on 26 May), Melbourne (Commander H. C. Wright, 24 June), and Perth (G. R. Richards, 20 June), and staff for the Sydney office to enable B1 and B2 operations to start there as soon as possible. The 'foundation members' of ASIO came mainly from the CIS

Ray Whitrod (left) joined ASIO from the South Australian Police in 1949. He recalled that the case 'was the reason for our existence'. He is shown here with the governor-general, Lord Casey, when he was commissioner of the Commonwealth Police in the 1960s. Later he was commissioner of the Queensland Police. (Australian Archives, CRS A1200/18, item L65482)

(e.g., Wake and Stringer), the services (e.g., Wright and Nave), and the state Police Special Branches and Criminal Investigation Branches (e.g., Ron Richards, Ray Whitrod and Ernest Redford). Most of the 'investigators' or field officers were from the CIS or had been police detectives. None of them had had any experience in counter-espionage.

Perhaps the most remarkable appointment was that of Wake as deputy director for operations, since the services had had severe doubts about both his capacity and integrity during the war. Probably Reed had formed a favourable impression of him when he was conducting the court of inquiry at the end of 1943. Also, Tuck, on whom Reed was relying, had worked with Wake in Brisbane during the war. Perhaps the fact that Wake had clashed with the Army made him an attractive prospect to people like Evatt who were suspicious of that service.

COURTENAY YOUNG AND 'THE CASE'

In its first fifteen months, ASIO's attentions and resources were devoted almost wholly to the case and to following leads provided by MI5. As Whitrod has recalled, the case 'was the reason for our existence; it occupied all our thoughts'.[11] Courtenay Young retained the Venona material, but its source was not disclosed to ASIO, the decrypts themselves were not shown to anyone in ASIO, and no detailed information was given to ASIO in written form. Courtenay Young would consult the Venona papers in his safe when ASIO officers sought clarifications. Young himself had to get MI5 approval of all steps taken to develop the case.[12]

Those who were directly involved in the case in Sydney, and whom Courtenay Young 'sub-briefed' (gave most of the detailed intelligence and told the source was authoritative, but not that it was decrypted KI cable traffic), would have a 'team conference' with him every two or three weeks.[13] The ostensible leader of the team was Wake, who has said that although he had 'not been advised' of the source of Courtenay Young's information, he 'presumed it was either material picked up by the FBI during the Fuchs case or came from a British Government cryptographic source'.[14] Tuck, although based in Canberra, attended 'occasionally'.[15] The other members of the team in Sydney were five 'investigators' (Whitrod, Richard (Dick) Gamble, Leo Parmeter Carter, William R. (Bill) Campbell, and Devereaux McDermott), who were responsible for the field activity and who were never given sufficient credit for their role in the case. After a while they began to suspect Wake's competence; indeed they doubted the existence of one of Wake's agents, known as 'Sydney Harbour'. Some of the intelligence officers gave Wake the nickname 'Fake'.[16]

Whitrod was recruited from the South Australian CIB by Tuck; he joined ASIO on 28 April 1949, and moved to Sydney as the senior officer B2 in June. Gamble was a CIS officer who had an encyclopaedic knowledge of the Communist Party in Sydney and who had succeeded in 'planting' an agent (a journalist, Mercia Masson) on the fringes of the party leadership in Sydney. McDermott had been in the NSW Police before joining the CIS. Carter was the son of a NSW Police superintendent, who became a police cadet in 1934 and had become a plain-clothes detective. Campbell was also a NSW Police detective.[17] There soon developed a division of labour among the 'footsloggers'. Whitrod, for example, concentrated on TEKhNIK, Gamble on KLOD, and McDermott on BEN.

As a basis for the team meetings, Courtenay Young had prepared a long columnar diagram which listed the cryptonyms together with whatever other information had been extracted about them from the Venona material (e.g., one informant was 'the husband of TOURIST's sister'; BEN had been in the 'Sydney security organs' in 1945), as well as any other supporting evidence that had been collected, and the possible identities of the subjects.[18] Milner, Bernie and Hill had already been identified. According to Whitrod, it took them 'a long time' (about three months) to work out that 'the influential ACADEMICIAN' was Prichard, as they were unfamiliar with the Soviet use of the term 'academician' and were looking for someone working in an Australian university.[19]

Gamble was the first 'to argue strongly' that KLOD (or POP, as Wake had named him for the purposes of the investigation) was Clayton. Gamble 'spent night-long hours' matching information Courtenay Young had supplied about KLOD's character and activities with material from CIS files, and by June 1949 he was convinced that 'Clayton's our man'.[20] A 'habitation check' to establish Clayton's whereabouts was ordered by Wake later that month. His address at 15a Awaba Street, Mosman, was located on 1 July,[21] but Clayton was not to be seen. Gamble spent much of the next fifteen months (until September 1950, when ASIO headquarters moved to Melbourne) trying to locate Clayton, but he could not find him. (Some of Gamble's colleagues thought Clayton had probably gone back to New Zealand.)[22] By the end of June, Reed and Courtenay Young had informed Chilton in Melbourne that 'a tentative identification of the principal spy master of the net-work has been made'.[23]

Meanwhile, Shedden had left Australia in April on a trip that would take him to Washington and London and whose purpose was, in part, to try to persuade the Americans and the British that security in Australia was now on a sound footing and that the embargo could be lifted. Throughout his trip he remained in regular contact with Chilton about both the case and the strengthening of security measures within the Defence group of departments. During three weeks in Washington, Shedden met President Truman, Secretary of State Dean Acheson, Secretary of Defense Louis A. Johnson, and Assistant Army Secretary Gordon Gray. On 11 April, he briefed Gray and representatives of the service intelligence agencies, the CIA, the Joint Chiefs of Staff and the State department, about the security situation. However, as he later informed the prime minister, the US authorities 'have not been able to agree to my request'.[24] Gray explained to Shedden on 28 April that 'the embargo had not been imposed arbitrarily, and it was not desired to continue it on a permanent basis', and hoped that 'the measures being taken in Australia will produce results'.[25] When Shedden told Defense Secretary Johnson later that day that he was personally extremely disappointed that the US would not restore the flow of classified information to Australia, Johnson replied that Shedden's visit had been 'premature', and said 'rather emphatically' that the embargo would remain.[26]

Gray suggested that the Australian authorities might provide the Pentagon with 'progress reports on the overall security situation', and Shedden said he 'would be glad to do so'.[27] In his telegram to Chifley on 29 April, Shedden requested that Chilton, 'who is

Sir Frederick Shedden meeting Major-General Robert Macon, deputy chief, Army Field Forces, during his visit to the USA in April 1949. Shedden tried to have the US embargo on sharing information with Australia lifted. He was told 'rather emphatically' that the embargo would remain. (Australian Archives, CRS A5954/1, item 1925/42)

conversant with the subject', prepare such a progress report and forward it to him in London.[28] On 9 May, while he was in New York, Shedden wrote to Chilton, stressing that 'it is very important that it should be quite convincing that we are vigorously pressing on with the job'.[29]

Chilton's initial report covered the period to 1 June. When he received it in London, Shedden made some minor updatings and 'modifications' and forwarded it to Gray, who received it in Washington on 8 July.[30] But events had been unfolding quickly: in early July Chilton forwarded a note to Shedden on the progress made during June, which Shedden sent to Gray on 20 July. It read in part:

> With regard to the Top Secret investigations being conducted by the Australian Security Service, some progress has been made.
> A tentative identification of the principal spy master of the net-work has been made, and his present activities are under active investigation. As a result of this tentative identification, new lines have been uncovered and the activities of certain other individuals who have been thrown up by ground investigation are being covered . . .
> Assuming that the identity of the principal spy master is correct, it is felt that the identification of other members of the

spy net-work connected with him will come to light in a comparatively short time.[31]

On 18 July, Shedden asked Chilton to prepare a further progress report,[32] and on 22 July Chilton wrote to Reed asking him to report on progress with the establishment of ASIO and the case as at that date.[33] Visiting Melbourne at the end of July, Reed briefed Chilton on ASIO but remarked that 'the Americans were more interested, at the moment, in the results of his special investigation than in the rapid build up of his staff, and he was therefore concentrating all possible effort on the investigation'.[34] In a letter to Shedden in London on 18 August, Reed said 'a good deal of progress' had been made with 'the case' over the previous two months, but 'it would be premature at this stage to give any details'.[35] However, Courtenay Young was not so reticent, and he kept Sillitoe informed about that progress.[36] It is clear that by the end of July 1949, nearly all the important members of the KLOD group had been identified.

By August 1949, there is no doubt that the British security intelligence authorities were fully satisfied with the security situation in Australia. On 4 April, Attlee had already written to Chifley, informing him that the UK chiefs of staff had provided the Australian chiefs with a paper on British defence policy and strategy and proposing that detailed discussions with respect to 'joint defence planning . . . *should start without necessarily waiting for the information you require from the United States'*.[37] Later in April, when Shedden was in Washington, he met with General Sir William Morgan, head of the British joint services mission in Washington, and reported to Chifley that Morgan believed the US embargo should be raised.[38] On 22 July, Shedden sent copies of several papers to Sillitoe, including his letters and progress reports sent to Gray on 30 June and 20 July, and asked for Sillitoe's opinion about the adequacy of the recent developments with respect to security in Australia. Replying on 22 August, Sillitoe expressed his 'delight' with progress with 'the new Security Service'[39] and disappointment that 'your Washington visit did not have the immediate result for which we hoped'. Noting that 'the Americans . . . apparently regard the clearing up of the situation of which we know as a prerequisite to the lifting of the embargo', he gave his personal assurance 'that I am giving all possible assistance in this matter'.[40]

SURVEILLANCE AND ALERTING OF THE RUSSIANS

In May 1949, under the direction of Courtenay Young, ASIO began to collect information on Nosov, the TASS representative who had been identified as TEKhNIK in the Venona material; and Makarov, who was reckoned to be EFIM, the KI resident in the Soviet embassy in Canberra. Nosov's mail was opened; his telephone records were obtained, with itemised long-distance calls (including eleven to the Soviet embassy in Canberra in April); and he was placed under occasional but very cautious surveillance.[41]

By coincidence, the surveillance of Makarov began in June, just as he was about to leave Australia, and it was clear that he was aware of the newly established ASIO's interest in his movements and contacts. After his ship, the SS *Stratheden,* left Sydney on 24 June it docked in Melbourne and Adelaide, and ASIO (in consultation with Courtenay Young) decided to monitor his movements in case he made any last-minute contacts. Whitrod and Ernest Redford (a Victoria Police officer who would join ASIO that August) attempted to follow him in Melbourne, but they could not match Makarov's expertise in counter-surveillance, and after they had traipsed up and down escalators and lifts in various large department stores, 'he quite clearly knew that we were tailing him'.[42] There is no doubt that by 28 June, the third day in Melbourne, he knew he was under surveillance.[43] This was probably the first inkling the KGB had that the new Australian security intelligence organisation was monitoring its activities.[44] ASIO attempted further surveillance of Makarov in Adelaide on 30 June, but 'he adopted all of the evasive tactics used by him in Melbourne'—including running to catch a moving bus and then jumping off two stops later, and alighting from the wrong side of a tram—and was again able to elude his 'shadowers'.[45]

In June 1949, with Chifley's approval, ASIO began a program of telephone interception. No warrants were required, but approval was to be 'sought and granted orally' for each telephone monitored. Fourteen approvals were given between 1 July 1949 and 17 July 1950, with 'people involved in the case' the primary targets.[46] Two of the first telephone numbers to be tapped were those of Nosov in Sydney (FA 2759) and the Soviet embassy.

ASIO also obtained permission to conduct 'audio surveillance' or 'bugging' operations. The first of these, in September 1949, involved installing a microphone in Nosov's flat in Darlinghurst. It was a 'crude technical operation', and was immediately discovered.[47] According to Whitrod, who was responsible for the operation, a married couple who worked for ASIO rented the apartment directly above Nosov's. Whitrod and his colleagues then bored a hole through Nosov's ceiling and put down a microphone, but when they looked down not only was the microphone visible but some of the plaster had fallen onto the floor. Whitrod hastily persuaded the caretaker of the building to let them into Nosov's flat to clean up the plaster, but Nosov 'would have known' that his premises had been violated.[48]

On 23 December, while the Nosovs were at the theatre, ASIO conducted a better-prepared entry into their flat. Notes and photographs were taken of the various entries in Nosov's 1949 desk calendar, and it was noted that 'Nosov keeps his bedroom padlocked (at least when he is out).'[49] Several further break-ins were conducted during the next six months.[50] From 5 December 1949 until their departure in August 1950, ASIO maintained daily logs on the Nosovs' movements, meetings, telephone calls and private conversations. Although the logs often amounted to several pages a day, the 'intelligence dividend' was disappointing. As an ASIO report on Nosov on 6 February 1950 noted:

> The equipment was gathered together from a variety of sources and installed in a hurry; conversations were frequently in Russian and no translator was available to cope with them; and . . . the Nosovs appear to indulge in routine security precautions to prevent the use of microphones, namely, the conducting of their confidential conversations against the background of a wireless.[51]

In January 1950, ASIO recruited Don Marshall, a White Russian émigré, to work full-time on translating the tapes of Nosov's conversations. Any leads concerning Nosov's contacts were given to Whitrod and his colleagues to pursue, but Nosov's activities with the KLOD group had stopped by this time.

THE INVESTIGATION OF HILL

The ASIO officer principally involved in the investigation of Hill was Phil Gilbert, the senior officer B1 and deputy to Bernard Tuck in Canberra. Besides reporting to Justice Reed and Tuck in Canberra, and indirectly through them to Courtenay Young in Sydney, Gilbert visited Sydney every few months for direct discussions with Young concerning the Hill aspect of the case.[52] Gilbert was never indoctrinated into Venona, and deduced from his sub-briefings that 'the source was American'. In 1965, when he accompanied Spry on a trip around the world, he put it to him that the British 'must have been breaking the Soviet codes', but Spry refused to confirm the proposition and Gilbert continued to believe in the US source.[53]

Gilbert knew Hill very well and quite liked him. The Hills' house in Froggatt Street, Turner, was only 200m from Gilbert's house in Ridley Street. Hill and Gilbert played cricket together ('Hill was a good slow bowler') and went to parties together. When Courtenay

Young first told Gilbert that Hill had been identified as an MVD agent, Gilbert was incredulous, saying 'it must be a case of mistaken identity'. It took Gilbert 'a couple of months' to accept the notion.54 Between April and November 1949, however, Gilbert maintained a very close surveillance on Hill. In April, he prepared a lengthy report on a party that Mrs Hill had given on the 2nd to celebrate Jim's 31st birthday, including the names of, and brief comments about, the two dozen guests. Later in April, he compiled a list of people (including both Ric Throssell and Dorothy Jordan) who had attended a party given by Hill in April 1947;55 to it he appended pen portraits of the dozen guests and accounts of the party games and 'some almost-baudy songs'.56 (Courtenay Young criticised Gilbert for this misspelling of 'bawdy'.)57 Gilbert had attended the party and participated fully in the party games, including 'Murder', in which he was the 'victim'.58 In mid September 1949, when Ian Milner visited Canberra, the ASIO surveillance operations against him and Hill came together when they met at a dinner party at the Canberra Tourist Lodge on the 15th.59

When Cecil Sharpley 'defected' from the party early in 1949, ASIO thought he might be a useful source of information about Hill. Sharpley had recruited Jim's brother, Ted, into the party, and had known Jim when he had lived in Melbourne and been a member of the Moonie Ponds branch in the late 1930s. In July Sharpley was interrogated by Whitrod and Redford at a 'safe house' in St Kilda Road, Melbourne, where he was being looked after by the Victorian Special Branch. Sharpley was unable to provide 'anything of use in the case' apart from the names and personal details of party members he knew.60 He described Hill as 'a "vicious" undercover member of the Party'61 and said he thought that Marjorie shared her husband's political beliefs.62 On 4 November, Sharpley told 'a Security Officer' that Hill was a member of the CPA (but 'never an open member') and that he 'is a man worth watching'.63

In about September 1949 MI5 had decided that Hill should be posted to London, and Burton was reminded of his discussion with Hollis in April about this. Burton wrote a private letter to Hollis in which he explained 'my conviction that Hill was a man who could be trusted' but said he 'would act in accordance with [Hollis's] wishes and would transfer Hill to London'.64 Burton received an immediate reply from Hollis, together with 'an acknowledgement' from Courtenay Young, ordering Hill's posting.65

On 22 November, in preparation for this move, Gilbert put together a report for Courtenay Young on Hill in which 'many previously known facts [were] re-hashed to give a clearer picture of Hill, his character and associates'.66 He noted that:

> Hill and his wife are to outward appearances a care-free happy-go-lucky couple. They frequently entertain and have many drinking parties. Mrs Hill is not a heavy drinker but her husband consumes considerable quantities.
>
> They both exhibit many likeable qualities. Hill is a good cricketer; he mixes well with other men although he is slow to make friends. When Throssell was in Canberra [in 1947–49] the two were always together.[67]

Hill and his wife and two children left Australia for the UK aboard the SS *Stratheden* on 6 January 1950; they arrived on 12 February, and Hill commenced duty the next day.[68] Burton told Hollis that Hill's superior officer at Australia House, Peter Heydon, had not been told that Hill might be a security risk or the real reason for his posting to London, and suggested that Hollis 'use his discretion as to what he should tell Heydon'.[69]

Hill's movements and contacts were closely monitored by MI5 over the next three months, but although he quickly established friendly social relations with members of the British Communist Party and the large Australian communist community in London, he made no contact with the Soviet embassy and engaged in no clandestine or illegal activity. By the end of April, MI5 decided that since the Venona operation had extracted everything possible about Hill/TOURIST from the 1945–48 cable traffic, and since the surveillance operation was proving unfruitful, it might as well submit him to direct interrogation. In preparation it asked ASIO to put together a report on Hill's background, character, social interests, and friends. Gilbert compiled a report from material collected by ASIO over the previous year, and took it to Courtenay Young, who then sent it to London.[70] ASIO was apprised of the decision and, as Spry later noted, Hill's interrogation 'had the approval of the relevant Australian authorities'.[71] On 2 June, Tuck informed Prime Minister Robert Menzies, whose Liberal–Country Party government had been elected the previous December, of MI5's intention to interview Hill. Menzies insisted that 'you must make it clear to him that it is to be done subject to his concurrence'.[72] On 5 June, Tuck called on Evatt, now deputy leader of the opposition, in his Sydney office and told him Hill was to be interviewed in London.[73] To coincide with the Hill interview, ASIO officers from all over Australia assembled in Sydney in the hope that if Hill identified any members of a spy ring there would be an immediate search for them.[74]

On Tuesday 6 June, Hill was unexpectedly ushered into a room by his superior at Australia House and introduced to William James (Jim) Skardon, the famed MI5 interrogator who had extracted a confession from Klaus Fuchs only six months before. Skardon wore a Homburg hat and carried a rolled umbrella. To put Hill at ease yet convey the impression that the Security authorities knew all about him, he began by mentioning Hill's cricket scores when he was at high school in Melbourne. But Hill did not crack. The most he would admit was that he might have been 'indiscreet' at a party attended by some left-wingers in Canberra. He insisted that he had never knowingly given information or taken documents home.[75]

In reality, Hill was 'unnerved' by the interview and by MI5's evident knowledge of both his personal life and his espionage activities. That evening he met with several British and Australian comrades at the home of Dr Eric Burhop to discuss the interview.[76] Aside from Hill and Burhop, the guests included Rupert Lockwood, Noel Counihan, R. Palme Dutt and 'another representative' of the British party who (according to Lockwood's recollection) was not introduced.[77]

Burhop was a physicist who had been born in Hobart, Tasmania, on 31 January 1911; had been a lecturer and research officer in Physics at Melbourne University from 1936 to 1942; worked at the CSIR's Radio Physics Laboratory in Sydney from 1942 to 1944; worked at the University of California at Berkeley as part of the British team involved in the Manhattan Project in 1944–45; and had taken up a lectureship in Applied Mathematics at London University in 1945. In 1941–42, he was closely associated with Ian Milner and was, like him, a secret party member.[78] They were both very active in the Australia–Soviet Friendship League in Melbourne in 1941–42,[79] and Burhop was president of the Civilian Air Raid Defence Association, of which Margot Milner was secretary.[80] After Burhop moved to Sydney in January 1942, Margot reported to the association that 'Dr Burhop had supplied the initiative of the organisation so much during the last year', and Ian moved a formal vote of thanks to him.[81] In August 1945, Clayton had informed the NKGB that Burhop had joined the party in 1937, and that he had worked 'on an assignment of the Party' within the Australian scientific community; Clayton had 'been given the task' of collecting further information on Burhop for the NKGB.[82]

Lockwood was in London on his way back to Australia after a meeting of the World Peace Council in Stockholm in March 1950, at which he had represented the CPA. Lockwood, who was 'staying with British Party people', had met Hill earlier that evening and had suggested the meeting at Burhop's house.[83] Lockwood had joined the party in September 1939, and got to know Clayton in Sydney in 1940–42, when the party was illegal. By 1942, he was the party journalist 'most prominently concerned with the Soviet Union', in which capacity he worked under Clayton's direction.[84] Lockwood had met Milner on the latter's first day in Australia.[85]

Noel Counihan was born in Victoria on 14 October 1913 and was in the 1950s Australia's leading political cartoonist and 'socialist realist' painter. He had joined the CPA during the Depression, and remained an active member for the rest of his life. He had known Lockwood since the early 1930s, when the latter was a cadet reporter on the Melbourne *Herald*.[86] In April–May 1949, Lockwood and Counihan had gone to Paris together as Australian representatives at the World Peace Congress.[87] Counihan had met Milner in Wellington in January 1940, and they had become very close friends;[88] like Milner, he had been a secret member of the Melbourne University branch of the CPA in 1940–44.[89] Counihan was deeply loyal to Milner. (He wrote to him in February 1986 informing him of his plans to visit him in Prague in mid year, but he died before he could make the trip.)[90]

Rajani Palme Dutt was an austere Anglo-Indian who was a graduate of Balliol College at Oxford, a founder member of the Communist Party of Great Britain, a member of the central (later the executive) committee of the party for more than 40 years, and the party's leading theoretician. He and Harry Pollitt, who was to serve as the general secretary of the party for nearly two decades, had been responsible for bringing the British party under firm Comintern direction in 1922. Palme Dutt had split with Pollitt in September–October 1939, after the German–Soviet non-aggression pact, Britain's declaration of war on Germany, and the Soviet intervention in Poland, when Pollitt had called for a frank discussion within the central committee. Palme Dutt had declared that the war was an 'imperialist war' (and not a people's anti-fascist war), and that 'every member' of the CPGB must become 'a fighting member of the Communist International', even if this meant assisting Britain's defeat by Germany.[91] By 1933–34, Palme Dutt and Pollitt had established clandestine courier services between London and the USSR for both the Comintern and the OGPU, and some means of fairly expeditious communications with the OGPU—presumably involving either a clandestine radio link or the OGPU residency in the Soviet embassy in London.[92]

At the meeting on 6 June 1950 the chief topics of discussion were the extent of MI5's knowledge of the membership and activities of the KLOD group, and what to do about the threat of arrest faced by Clayton and Milner. Skardon must have been incredibly incompetent to have alerted Hill to the intensity of the security interest in Clayton and Milner, though the gathering at Burhop's needed little prompting about who should be warned.

Lockwood borrowed money from the CPGB for the air fare from London to Sydney, and flew back to warn Clayton on 19 July. He believes, however, that Clayton was already aware of Hill's interrogation when Lockwood told him.[93] Lockwood also reported the episode to two other CPA leaders, Lance Sharkey and Jack Henry; they were already aware of ASIO's interest in Clayton, and concluded that British intelligence was trying to frame Hill and would attempt the same with Clayton.[94]

Hill was interviewed by Skardon on at least two other occasions between 6 and 13 June, including once at his flat and once (evidently on 10 June) when Skardon took him to a football match. However, he still refused to admit anything.[95] He made an unsuccessful attempt to contact Burhop on 20 June.[96] MI5 completed a report on Hill on 15 June, which included an assessment of his discussions with Skardon as well as the conclusion that there was nothing further to be gained by having Hill in London, and the report was cabled to the British High Commissioner in Canberra on 16 June.[97] On 4 July the Australian High Commission in London was asked to 'please arrange for J. F. Hill to return to Australia by earliest boat, together with family', and for him to take immediate leave 'pending departure of boat'.[98] Hill left London on 3 August and arrived back in Melbourne on 4 September.

Skardon's fame as an MI5 interrogator greatly exceeded his effectiveness. He had joined MI5 from the Special Branch in late 1940, and although he was affable and patient, and sometimes able to win the confidence of his subjects, he lacked an incisive intellect and mostly failed to obtain confessions when it came to espionage cases. He had come to public attention as the chief MI5 interrogator during the trial of Fuchs in February 1950; his skill was subsequently greatly exaggerated by Kim Philby and his followers, who have described Skardon as 'a brilliant master at his work'.[99] Skardon was really quite inept. He was also greatly disadvantaged by the fact that he was never informed about Venona. In 1947, he had interviewed Ursula Kuzchinski (SONIA), after Alexander Foote had identified her to Courtenay Young, and concluded she was innocent; she disappeared two days later, and lived for the rest of her life in East Germany.[100] Even in the case of Fuchs, Skardon had been persuaded that he was innocent, and was 'on the verge of giving up' when Dick White and Arthur Martin told him they 'knew' Fuchs was guilty and that he must continue his interrogation.[101] Later, in May 1951, he interviewed Melinda Maclean and accepted her lies about Donald Maclean's defection to Moscow.[102] In 1952, he interrogated John Cairncross, the fifth member of the Cambridge ring, but failed to obtain a confession.[103] At the end of 1952, he had more than half a dozen interviews with Kim Philby,[104] and through the 1950s, together with Martin and Courtenay Young, he interviewed Anthony Blunt on some eleven occasions, but he was never able to shake these members of the Cambridge Five either.[105]

Skardon's ineptitude with Hill in June 1950 heralded the end of 'the case'. As Gilbert has observed: 'The interrogation in London was a mess. Skardon tipped everything that MI5 had in its hand and left nothing.'[106]

17

'a clincher for Clayton as a spy'

THE END OF 'THE CASE'

THERE WAS NO SINGLE END point to the case. It was too multi-faceted, involving a complex combination of cryptanalysis and counter-espionage; and it was subject to decisions and events in Washington, London and Moscow that were at least as important as the developments in Australia itself. The new codebooks and cryptographic techniques introduced by Moscow Centre at the end of 1948, the decryption of most of the Canberra–Moscow cable traffic for 1943–48 by March 1949, and Philby's disclosures to Moscow about the Venona operation from September 1949 to June 1951, all helped to close the book on Venona. On the counter-espionage side, all of those involved in the KLOD group in 1943–48 had been identified by August 1949. By April 1951, when Valentin Sadovnikov (SAID) returned to Moscow, there was no member of the Residency in Canberra left who had worked with Makarov or had any personal knowledge of the members or activities of the KLOD group.

On 6 January 1950 the US began to restore the flow of classified information to Australia, beginning with 'selected information classified up to and including "Confidential"'; and on 29 August 1950 a security agreement was concluded between the US and Australian departments of Defence, providing for a more complete flow.[1] While the resolution of the case was important in restoring access to US information, equally so was the election of the Menzies Liberal–Country Party government in December 1949. The US mistrusted the Labor Party in general and Evatt in particular. Relations between

Colonel Charles Spry on his appointment as director-general of Security in July 1950. He reformed ASIO and served as director-general until 1969. (The Age, reproduced by permission)

the US and Australian Defence departments would grow stronger over the coming years.

CHARLES SPRY AND ASIO

When Reed had accepted the post of ASIO director-general in 1949, he had insisted that it be for only one year. However, after the election of the Menzies government he decided to continue until a successor was found. This was Colonel Charles Spry, the DMI, who formally began duty as the second director-general of ASIO on 17 July 1950. Spry already knew a lot about the case. Although he had not been formally indoctrinated into the Venona operation, he knew that it involved British Sigint/cryptanalysis. As DMI, Spry had a channel through which highly classified information could be sent from UK and US security and intelligence authorities marked for his 'eyes only'. Spry later recalled that one particular letter from the US had so many 'references' cut out of it that had it been played on a pianola it would have produced a 'cacophony of sound'.[2] Spry had worked with Poulden since the latter's appointment as head of the Defence Signals Branch in April 1947, and in 1948–49 they had liaised on several aspects of the case. At Spry's request, Poulden had searched the DSB 'archives' in Melbourne for any intercepted Soviet radio traffic that referred to Soviet espionage interests in Australia and that might mention any of the cryptonyms. Spry became the first ASIO officer and the fourth Australian to be told about the Venona operation when he was 'indoctrinated' by Courtenay Young soon after his appointment in July 1950.

By mid 1950, the case had lost momentum. Little new Venona decrypts and translations had become available since the material Dick White had brought out in March 1949, all of the important members of the KLOD group had been identified and there had been little progress with any of the evidently less important cryptonyms. The field activity was not producing any new evidence. The interrogation of Hill by MI5 in London had revealed the investigation to both the KLOD group and Moscow Centre. In any case, Moscow would have known of ASIO's interest in its activities since Makarov had reported the surveillance effort against him in Melbourne and Adelaide the previous June, and since Nosov had reported the intrusion into his flat the previous September. ASIO's surveillance capabilities and technical facilities were still very limited but were almost entirely occupied with activities concerning the case. The staff had reached 140 by 1 July 1950, but it was of very uneven quality.

Spry decided to make some major changes. A 'proper headquarters' was to be established and located in Melbourne, ASIO's structure was to be reorganised, and many of the personnel were to be changed. The headquarters officially moved to Melbourne on 29 September 1950. It was located in ASIO's branch office in the Theosophical Society Building in Collins Street until a new building was found at 8 Queens Road in November. Courtenay Young then moved to Melbourne, together with Pam Steibel, the Chubb safe, and the Venona material.

There were seventeen resignations and 63 recruitments between July 1950 and July 1951. The most important resignation, in September 1950, was that of Bob Wake. The military had a long-standing antipathy towards him, but there were also doubts about his competence and reliability. Furthermore, he was seen as being too close to Evatt. There were several important new appointments. Michael Thwaites was appointed director B2 (counter-espionage) on 10 October 1950. He was first acquainted with the case during a visit to Sydney with Spry to meet Courtenay Young, who had still not moved to Melbourne. Over the next several months Whitrod, now assistant director B2, briefed him on the operational details of the Sydney part of the investigation in 1949–50.[3] Also in October 1950, Spry transferred G. R. (Ron) Richards from Perth to Sydney to replace Wake as officer in charge in Sydney, and to take responsibility for the case there.

In March 1951, Courtenay Young returned to London and was succeeded by Derek Hamblen as the MI5 special liaison officer at ASIO headquarters. Hamblen stayed in Australia until just after the defection of the Petrovs in April 1954. In 1951, he represented MI5 and ASIO in Sillitoe's efforts to persuade the New Zealand government to establish a counterpart organisation in that country.[4] Hamblen inherited Young's secretary, safe and Venona material, and the case remained one of his principal responsibilities. In late 1951 or early 1952, Spry and Hamblen decided that the case might be reinvigorated if Thwaites were 'indoctrinated' into Venona and allowed to assist Hamblen directly with respect to its counter-espionage implications. He soon became very familiar with the Venona material in Hamblen's safe.[5] In November 1952 Hamblen indoctrinated Ron Richards into the Venona operation, and arranged for him to go to London to 'study the case material'.[6]

Hamblen also developed very close working relations with Ralph Thompson, who had succeeded Poulden as the first Australian director of the Defence Signals Branch in Melbourne in April 1950. The search of DSB archives for relevant Soviet traffic from the late 1940s was expanded, and the 'old ladies' recruited to sort and 'strip' the recorded traffic. However, Thompson was not indoctrinated into Venona, and only became aware of it, and then unofficially, when a senior traffic analyst directing the activity within the DSB apprised him of its likely purpose. According to Thompson, any relevant material found by the 'old ladies' was given to Spry rather than Hamblen.[7]

Before Hamblen returned to London in 1954, he thoroughly sorted all the Venona material in his possession. Copies of the translations which contained material of significance to the case were left with his successor, George H. Leggett; the larger portion, which included fragmentary and irrelevant decrypts, as well as earlier and less complete translations, he took back to London.

Spry ensured that Menzies was fully informed about any developments in the case, but also that Menzies understood 'the prime necessity to safeguard' the secret of Venona and 'the great obstacle' that this presented 'to the vigorous development of the "Case"'. Menzies was told about the British mission to Australia in 1948 which had revealed the existence of the espionage network and the nature of the documents supplied to Moscow, and about the roles of Makarov, Clayton, Nosov, Milner, Hill, Bernie, Hughes, and 'several other possibilities whose recruitment to the net has never been confirmed'.[8]

Frances Bernie Confesses

ASIO had known from its inception in 1949 that Bernie (by now Mrs Garrett) had passed on to Clayton 'information which she had

G.R. Richards, ASIO deputy director-general (operations) and Colonel Charles Spry, director-general of Security, leaving a hearing of the Royal Commission on Espionage in 1954. (The Age, reproduced by permission)

received in the course of her duties' in Evatt's office.[9] Her name and cover-name had been decrypted in 1947 and her identity confirmed by Hollis and Hemblys-Scales in August 1948, and from September 1948 to March 1949 she had come under surveillance by the CIS.[10] By August 1949 ASIO had begun a full investigation into her background and current activities, and from October 1949 throughout 1950, and again 'from 1952 onwards' she was placed under intensive survillance.[11]

However, it had been decided not to approach her since, without some other sufficient cause, she or Clayton or their Russian handlers might have been alerted to the ASIO operation against them. The opportunity to interview her arose in 1953 when she was nominated as a referee by an alien seeking naturalisation as a British subject. She was then interviewed on the ground that it was important to ascertain the loyalty of persons wishing to become naturalised.[12] The question of her integrity as a referee, given her Communist Party background, provided the lead-in to asking about her relationship with Clayton.

Bernie was interviewed by senior ASIO officers on at least nine occasions from June 1953 to December 1959, sometimes alone and sometimes with her husband. Nearly all of the interviews involved both Ron Richards, now regional director for NSW, and J. M. Gilmour, also from the Sydney office, and took place at the Garretts' home in Wahroonga. After her first interview, on 9 June 1953, Bernie was described by Richards as 'an attractive woman, intelligent and thoughtful', who remained composed throughout most of the interview but 'was very frightened' when her relationship with Clayton was pursued.[13] She readily admitted her membership of the Communist Party in 1941–44, but said that 'all that is behind me—I have tried to lock it away—it was a period of youthful idealism that has completely finished'.[14]

Bernie then went on to describe how, on only three or four occasions, she had taken material from Evatt's office and given it to Clayton at Marx House during her lunch hour.[15] She said the sorts of things she passed on were the fact that an ambassador, or other important person, had called at the office to see the attorney-general, and other 'odd bits of office chatter'.[16] She had also taken Clayton various 'scraps of paper, which I found around the office', but apart from an old copy of the by-laws from the (publicly available) National Security Regulations, she could not remember details.[17] She had presumed that Clayton needed the information 'to keep the Party up to date . . . about what was happening' in the government.[18] She had stopped seeing Clayton after she married and moved to Wahroonga in 1945, and neither Clayton nor any other party official had made any attempt to dissuade her when she stopped passing on information or decided to stop working in Evatt's office.[19] At the close of the interview, Bernie said she was 'seriously thinking of returning to Roman Catholicism', that she felt 'purged and relieved' for telling her story, and that she 'had now told us the whole truth'.[20] Richards, however, was sure that 'she has more to tell'.[21]

She had indeed much more to tell, but this interview was of singular importance. Bernie remains the only member of the KLOD group willing to admit their involvement with Clayton in espionage. Her confession on 9 June, notwithstanding its numerous shortcomings, was the first confirmation by ASIO of any part of the activities of the KLOD group as outlined in the Venona material. And unlike the latter, it could be used by ASIO directly in 'the case'.

ASIO had three more interviews with Bernie and her husband in June–July 1953. On 18 June, she provided further details about the information she had given to Clayton: typed summaries of documents she had seen in Evatt's office, typed accounts of conversations she had overheard there (such as those when a group of US Congressmen visited in June 1945), copies of the 'political correspondence' between Evatt and Dalziel, and copies of correspondence between the Attorney-General's department and other Commonwealth departments. Clayton had retained all the material Bernie took to him.[22]

Bernie was a little more forthcoming on 7 July. She admitted not only that she typed up her own summaries of documents and accounts of conversations but also that 'she "sometimes" took an extra carbon copy of her work if she thought it would be of interest to Clayton'. This was generally 'political matter dictated to me by

Dalziel or Mr. Hewitt'. She was also able to recollect some particular pieces of material. In February 1945, she had helped organise a conference of the Western Pacific Section of the UN Relief and Rehabilitation Agency (UNRRA), held at Lapstone in NSW. She said she did a 'lot of work on the Lapstone meeting—it went to Clayton'—including 'an agenda and a lot of notes I had to do which dealt with the agenda'. She insisted that 'after the Lapstone Conference I did not take any information to Clayton'—even after it was pointed out to her that she had previously admitted reporting to Clayton about the US Congressional visit in June 1945. Richards remained 'of the opinion that Mrs. Garrett is holding on to at least one act she did for Clayton which frightens her'.[23]

On 17 November 1959, after attending a Billy Graham evangelical crusade and praying for God's guidance, Bernie contacted ASIO to make a fuller confession and 'clean' her 'troubled conscience'. This time, according to a report of the interview, she said:

> She had omitted to inform us that whilst employed in Dr. Evatt's office she had taken information received on a tele-type machine and had handed same to Walter Seddon Clayton. This information was in code, but Clayton had expressed interest in it, and asked her to bring any such material she could . . . She had done this on at least one occasion and probably twice. The particular information had been received from Canberra.[24]

As the ASIO interviewer noted, 'this is a clincher for Clayton as a spy and she as knowing it'.[25] On 2 December 1959 she said that she 'had made copies in pencil of a few, possibly only two, teletype messages', and that this had occurred 'towards the end' of her employment in Evatt's office (much later than she had previously admitted to passing material to Clayton).[26]

Bernie has frequently been portrayed as an inconsequential person, and Allan Dalziel has claimed that she had no access to confidential material and could only have provided Clayton with unimportant or already public information.[27] However, from her evidence it is clear that she passed a large volume of material to him. While some of it was innocuous, much of it would have been very valuable to Moscow Centre, including the information on such seemingly mundane matters as the organisation of Evatt's Sydney office, the sources and types of advice received by Evatt, the overseas visitors and international meetings with which his office was involved, and the postings of Australian diplomatic personnel. Some of the material, such as the copies of encrypted cables from Canberra to Sydney, would have been of inestimable value. Moreover, it remains highly likely that the types and items of material instanced by Bernie are far from complete. Although she stated on 9 June

1953 that she had reported to Clayton 'only three or four times',[28] and on 8 September 1954 that she reported to him 'in all not on more than six occasions',[29] it is clear from her various accounts of her meetings with Clayton and of his reactions to the material she gave him that she reported more often than this—very likely on at least a dozen occasions from December 1944 to early 1946—and that on some of these she gave Clayton material of greater importance than she was ever prepared to confess.

PETROV'S STATEMENT ON LEAKS

Vladimir and Evdokia Petrov defected in early April 1954. They had arrived in Australia on 5 February 1951, he to take up the overt post of third secretary and consul but covertly to serve as the 'temporary' KGB (MVD) resident, and she to take up the overt post of embassy accountant and secretary to the ambassador but covertly to be responsible for cipher work and technical assistance in the Residency.[30] Although the activities of the Petrovs, their defection and the subsequent Royal Commission on Espionage essentially postdate the events of this story, the Petrovs and the royal commission were able to provide important details of the KGB Residency in the embassy, the means of communication between the Residency and Moscow Centre, the objectives of the KGB in Australia, and the contacts and means used by the KGB to collect intelligence; they were also able to confirm substantial parts of this story.

In a statement to Ron Richards, now deputy director-general (operations) of ASIO, on the day of his defection, Vladimir Petrov said:

> Before I came here the N.K.V.D. agent [Resident] in the Embassy at Canberra was Mr. Simeon Makarov, and his contact man was Fedor Nosov, the Tass Representative in Australia. Nosov was a secret agent of the N.K.V.D.—he obtained his information from one man—this man operated a group of agents in Australia, who reported information to him. . .
> Between 1945 and 1948 there was a very serious situation in Australia in the Dept. of External Affairs. The Communist Party here had a group of External Affairs officers who were giving them official information. The members of the group were bringing out copies of official documents, which they gave to a Communist Party member. This party man gave the documents to Mr. Makarov at the Soviet Embassy. Documents described the Australian foreign policy and also contained a lot of information about American and English foreign policy. I do not know the name of the Party man who at that time reported to Makarov—but his code name was [KLOD].[31]

Ric Throssell has repeatedly denied passing information to the Soviet Union. The Venona decrypts show that cover named FERRO, *he was regarded by the KGB in 1948 as an important member of the* KLOD *group. (NLA)*

When Petrov defected he brought with him a package of material which Valentin Sadovnikov had left in his safe when he had hurriedly departed in April 1951, some in Sadovnikov's handwriting and some copies which Petrov had made in his own hand. This material had been in an envelope marked *N* for *Navodki*, indicating persons and matters of interest to the KI, and particularly persons it 'aims' to use.[32] It comprised an aide-memoire made by Sadovnikov of the cover-names of seven Australians mentioned in correspondence from Moscow Centre;[33] an aide-memoire headed 'Contacts K', made by Sadovnikov from information received from Moscow concerning eleven Australians whom it had recorded as connected directly or indirectly to Clayton;[34] a note of Clayton's 'accommodation address';[35] another listing the cover-names of seven Australians;[36] a copy made by Sadovnikov of a paragraph from a Moscow Centre letter of 14 June 1948 directing further reports to be made concerning six Australians mentioned in it;[37] and a copy of an enclosure to a letter from Moscow Centre on 10 November 1949 containing for Sadovnikov's information 'dossiers' on 22 Australians in whom Moscow was interested.[38]

THE CASE CONCERNING THROSSELL

In February 1949 Ric Throssell was posted to the Australian legation in Rio de Janeiro, Brazil. For some nine months, from May 1950 to January 1951, he served as chargé (and sole officer in the legation) and 'would have had access to everything', including the ciphers.[39]

The Throssells left Brazil in May 1952 and arrived back in Canberra in August. While he was in Brazil, in about August 1949, Throssell was identified as 'the son of the influential ACADEMICIAN' and, later, FERRO. However, the Venona material contained no classified information of which he was reportedly the source, and ASIO could find no other incriminating evidence against him.

On 30 March 1953, after he returned from Rio, two senior ASIO officers interviewed Throssell in Canberra. It was not a very productive event. While the ASIO officers were not impressed with his deportment, they concluded that 'Throssell is a loyal subject and is not a security risk in the Department in which he is employed'.[40] Throssell was given a top secret clearance.[41]

In 1954 the Petrovs provided ASIO with some information about Throssell's relationships with KLOD and the KI in the 1940s, but it was sketchy, second-hand and inconsistent. Among the material that Petrov brought with him when he defected was a handwritten copy of a letter from Moscow Centre to the Canberra Residency in 1953, which listed FERRO as an agent who had 'transmitted valuable information to the Communists, and then they to us'.[42] In early 1952, when Petrov replaced Ivan Pakhomov as acting KI resident in Australia, Pakhomov reportedly told him 'that he believed that Throssell was an agent of the Soviet Union'.[43] In about December 1952 Petrov received a cable from Moscow Centre which 'stated that "FERRO" Throssell was very important, that during the war years he gave very important information to "KLOD" . . . who handed the information on to our MVD representative in Canberra'.[44] The cable directed the Canberra Residency to work out a plan to contact Throssell; 'operations were planned' but aborted by Moscow Centre.[45] In response to directions from Moscow, on at least two occasions in 1953 Petrov tried to contact Throssell, but he proved unapproachable; Petrov thought 'he is afraid'.[46]

In early May 1954, on advice from ASIO, Throssell 'was removed from any direct access to secret information from that time'.[47] Then on 22 July he was interviewed for a second time by Ron Richards. With the allegations and material provided by the Petrovs, Richards was able to be somewhat more specific in his questioning, but Throssell was still no more forthcoming. He denied saying on 30 March 1953 that Jim Hill had told him about his interview by security officers in London.[48] He refused to admit that he knew Walter Clayton, saying:

> To the best of my recollection I have not met him—the only place I can think of where I could have met him would have been at my mother's flat, 'Gwydir Flats' . . . in Sydney, during my

cadetship at the Department when I was doing my course [in June–December 1943].⁴⁹

He admitted that he had 'met Nosov, the Tass agent, at my mother's flat'.⁵⁰ He also admitted having had 'quite a talk' with his mother about his posting possibilities before he went to Moscow, but refused to say precisely what and when he had told her.⁵¹ But he insisted that he had '[never] disclosed . . . any official classified information to anyone who was not entitled to have it'.⁵² In his report to Spry, Richards concluded:

> In my opinion Throssell was not being frank with me during the interview. He had two very bad periods; the first on the discussion about his knowledge of Clayton, and the second on the discussion about passing over Departmental information which may subsequently have got into the hands of the Russians. He did not impress me as being entirely truthful in these two particular periods of the interview.⁵³

Throssell appeared before the Royal Commission on Espionage on 2 February 1955, but he was not very helpful and on some matters he was quite stubborn. He also indulged in some untruths. For example, when he was asked whether he had ever met Nosov, he said he was 'not sure', and that although he thought he had met 'the Tass man who was in Australia before I went to Moscow', he believed this was Mikheev rather than Nosov.⁵⁴ But Throssell had said in his ASIO interview on 22 July 1954 that he 'met Nosov, the Tass agent, at my mother's flat—the last time was just before I left for Moscow—he gave me some advice as to the climate and what to wear'.⁵⁵ He could not have forgotten that in his mother's letters to him in Moscow in December 1945 and January 1946 she had told him that she was going to a party at which the Nosovs were also expected, 'so there will be toasts your way, you may be sure';⁵⁶ that she had shown his letters to her from Moscow to the Nosovs;⁵⁷ that Nosov had helped her obtain a sheepskin coat, which Bea would bring to Moscow for him; and that Nosov was her 'usual source of help'.⁵⁸

The royal commission found in 1955 that the evidence provided by the Petrovs was all 'remote hearsay assertions' and that 'in face of Throssell's denial, it would be wrong to hold that he had been a member of "Klod's Group" or that he had wittingly given any information'.⁵⁹ However, it reported that

> it is quite possible that in the circle in which Throssell lived at Canberra he may have let drop information which he himself did not regard as important and may not even have been conscious of giving, but which was regarded as important by a Communist group

which included 'Klod', and through him was passed to the Moscow Centre.⁶⁰

After his access to secret materials was withdrawn in May 1954, Throssell's career stagnated. He could not work in the more central policy areas of the department, nor be promoted to any more senior position, since this would necessitate his having access to secret material. He was passed over for promotion in 1955, and for several years thereafter, on the grounds that 'the necessity . . . to limit his access to information' meant that he could not be declared 'to be fully efficient in all respects'.⁶¹ In 1961 he was promoted to head of the training and welfare section of the economic and technical assistance branch (later reorganised as the international training section of the Australian Development Assistance Agency), where he stayed for thirteen years, and where he was primarily responsible for the administration of Australia's Colombo Plan scholarship program.⁶² In November 1972 Throssell had a third interview with an ASIO officer, who had put together a file of all the Venona material relating to him. From 1974 to 1980, he served as assistant secretary in charge of the department's cultural relations branch; and he was director of the Commonwealth Foundation in London from 1980 until his retirement in 1983, after 40 years in the Australian foreign service.⁶³

It is very difficult, if not impossible, to determine precisely what information the NKGB/KI ever obtained from Throssell and the extent to which Throssell was ever a 'witting' participant in the KLOD group. In 1944–45, when 'the son of the influential ACADEMICIAN' was evidently a minor source of information, he was probably being used unwittingly by his mother. But important questions remain concerning the information he gave her, his relationships with other members of the KLOD group, and the nature of his alleged espionage activities in the late 1940s. Throssell may not have had the slightest inkling, at least at the beginning, that information he was giving his mother was being passed to the central committee, let alone the Soviets. The Venona material is incomplete. Many of the allegations by the Petrovs remain unsubstantiated. Throssell himself has not been very helpful, sometimes dissembling, sometimes contradicting himself, and sometimes refusing to answer questions that would have illuminated important aspects of the activities of the KLOD group without in any way incriminating him. For example, he dissembled about his knowledge of Nosov before the royal commission; he refused to admit that he had ever met Clayton, whereas the Venona material suggests otherwise; he contradicted himself about whether or not Jim Hill had told him about his interview with security officers; and he was unwilling to clarify the matter of his discussions with his mother concerning his posting to Moscow in September–October 1945.

Some of the ASIO officers most familiar with the Venona material and the investigation believe that Throssell was at least partially witting by 1947, when he was evidently aware that information he was giving his mother was going to the communists, that in 1948 he provided information knowingly to Clayton, and that in 1949–50, during his first year in Rio, he also assisted the KGB. Mrs Petrov stated in 1954 that she had been told in 1952 that Throssell had been 'an active agent for the Soviet' in Brazil.[64] It is believed that Throssell ceased all contact with the KGB following the interrogation of Jim Hill by MI5 in London in June 1950.

BURTON AND HILL

When Hill returned to Canberra from London in September 1950, one of the first people he told about his interrogation by MI5 was John Burton, who had now taken up sheep farming on a property near Canberra. Burton has said that Hill was 'dismayed and realised that he had no future in the Department and . . . wanted to get it off his chest', but that Burton was unresponsive and asked him no questions. Burton did, however, tell Evatt about it. Burton had, of course, been involved in posting Hill to London at the suggestion of MI5, but he has testified that he never told Hill about this, either before Hill left or when he returned.[65]

Burton has said that he did not know Hill until after Hollis's visit in 1948 (or 1949), and that 'then I was very closely associated with him quite deliberately'.[66] This is simply incredible. When Hill joined the department in June 1945, his section was headed by Burton. It is true that Burton was abroad for much of 1945–47, but in October 1946, he had recommended that Hill be appointed a permanent public servant.[67] In April 1948, when Burton was secretary of the department, he personally authorised Hill's promotion to second secretary.[68] In fact, Burton and Hill had become close friends well before 1948–49. As Phil Gilbert reported to Reed on 22 November 1949, Hill 'has for several years been a fairly frequent visitor to Burton's property, out of Canberra', and 'Burton has looked after Hill's children on occasions when the Hills have been away from Canberra'.[69] In late 1948, Burton decided that he would stand for the newly created Canberra seat in the 1949 federal elections, and when in January 1949 he attempted unsuccessfully to obtain ALP endorsement for the seat, Hill served as his 'organising secretary'.[70] In October 1949, when Hill took sick leave for stress, Burton reportedly said to Mrs Hill (in a telephone conversation taped by ASIO), 'Don't worry about money; I'll look after that.'[71]

When Hill returned to work in External Affairs he was given a temporary position (and excluded from classified information) for a few months until 12 February 1951, when he transferred to the legal service bureau of the Attorney-General's department in Melbourne.[72] In June 1953, Hill left the public service and went into private practice as a barrister and solicitor in Melbourne.

THE DEFECTION OF IAN MILNER

In July 1950—just three weeks after Hill was interrogated by MI5 in London—the Milners went to Czechoslovakia. Stalinist communists had seized control of the country just two years earlier. According to Milner, while they were on 'normal annual leave' in Switzerland, Margot 'was taken ill with a severe attack of rheumatism from which she had suffered for many years', and they went on an impulse to Prague because of its facilities for the treatment of rheumatic illnesses.[73] In September he was granted leave without pay from the secretariat. He soon found a temporary job as special lecturer in the department of English at Charles University in Prague, and at the end of August 1951 he tendered his resignation from the UN.[74] He has also said, in 1989, that the main reason he went to Prague was to follow up a relationship with a Czech diplomat, Jarmila Fruhaufova, whom he had met when she served with the Czech mission to the UN in New York.[75]

Milner was not mentioned either by name or cryptonym in any of the documents provided by Petrov. However, both the Petrovs signed statements, and Vladimir Petrov testified to the royal commission, to the effect that in about October (or November) 1953, Moscow Centre had sent a cable to Petrov which identified BUR as Milner; said that he had given information to KLOD, who in turn had given it to the Residency; said that 'whilst in New York he gave information to the Soviet about [the] Australian Delegation to the UN'; and asked Petrov to try to ascertain through his contacts in the CPA whether 'any action would be taken by the authorities in the event of his returning to New Zealand'.[76] Mrs Petrov thought that Moscow 'intended to send him to New Zealand as an agent'.[77] Petrov made some discreet inquiries, and informed Moscow that Milner was 'forgotten' and 'not now the subject of discussion in the Department [of External Affairs]', but he 'did not receive any further instruction' before he defected in April 1954.[78] The royal commission found, on the basis of both the testimony of the Petrovs and 'other material which we have seen', that Milner had given information to the NKGB through KLOD.⁷⁹

On 1 March 1956, Milner lodged a 'personal statement' at the British embassy in Prague (for forwarding by diplomatic pouch to the Attorney-General's department in Canberra) concerning the allegations of the Petrovs and the findings of the royal commission. He denied that he had ever 'consciously reveal[ed] official confidential information entrusted to me to the representative or national of any foreign Power' or 'consciously divulged any such material relating to defence to any unauthorized person'.⁸⁰ He said that he did not know and to the best of his recollection he had never met Walter Clayton.⁸¹ Indeed, he 'did not have any relations with Communists in Sydney'⁸² (though he must have known that Rupert Lockwood was a member of the party). The most he would admit was that

> During the war years I was acquainted with some Communists individually in Melbourne. Such association . . . was based either on personal friendly relations or it arose from my participation in public activities, supported by persons of all shades of opinion, aimed at bettering relations with Soviet Russia in the interests of the common war effort.⁸³

As the Venona material showed, Milner lied about both knowing Clayton and providing information to him for the Soviets. He also lied about his membership of the Communist Party. He was one of those members who remained 'secret' after the party became legal in 1942; but many of his former comrades have become less reticent over the past decade, and more than half the members of the Melbourne University branch in 1940–42 have now attested to his secret membership. Too much of the detailed information about Milner's party activities in Melbourne in 1940–1944 has been confirmed to leave any credibility in the Milners' denials.

In 1996 newly released secret files of the Czech ministry of the Interior revealed that in 1950 the Soviet intelligence service had decided to 'relocate' Milner to Czechoslovakia after information was received from an informer in 'the American counter-espionage agency about a possible repression against Milner working for us as agent'. The files showed that his wife's illness was a 'pretext'. In 1949, while employed by the United Nations in New York, Milner had also begun working for the Czech secret service, and once he arrived in Czechoslovakia he was paid 25 000 Czech crowns a month, compared with the normal university salary of 7000 crowns. With the cover-name DVORAK and the pseudonym A. Jansky, agent No. 9006, Milner continued working for the Czech secret service, reporting on academic and diplomatic acquaintances. The last report made available from the Czech archives shows that he was still working for Czech intelligence in March 1968.⁸⁴

Ian and Margot Milner were divorced in 1958, when Margot found out about his now longstanding affair with Jarmila. Margot moved to London, where she became 'an advocate of Czech musical culture' as well as 'an organiser of splendid parties', and where she died on 11 August 1995.⁸⁵ Ian married Jamila in 1958, and then began what his biographer described as 'the impressive and fruitful partnership in which the Milners did so much to make Czech poetry available to the West'.⁸⁶ He died in Prague on 31 May 1991, a week before his 80th birthday.⁸⁷ To the end, he denied that he had ever given secret material to the Russians and protested that he had been framed by ASIO. The closest he came to 'a guarded confession of his guilt' was in an off-the-record interview with Richard Hall in Prague in 1985, when he 'listened stony-faced' as Hall told him what he had found out about the Venona material, then said: 'If what you say is true, then things look bad for Ian Milner.'⁸⁸

Clayton's activities post 1949

During 1950 and 1951 Clayton was noticed in Sydney 'on several occasions' when he visited his former home at 15a Awaba Street, Mosman. However, he did not attend the 16th national congress of the Communist Party in Sydney in August 1951, and he was not re-elected to the central committee. He ceased being a party functionary 'towards the end of 1951'.⁸⁹ The most likely explanation for his departure from the party is that he had lost his Soviet patronage. Soon after this, as the NSW Special Branch noted in August 1952, 'Clayton disappeared somewhat mysteriously from Party circles and . . . no information can be obtained as to his present whereabouts.'⁹⁰ Towards the end of 1951 Clayton began building a house at 12 Railway Street in Baulkham Hills, but a year later he let it out and went to work as a farm labourer 'in the bush'.⁹¹ He sold the house in December 1954.⁹² From 1951 to March 1955, he used several false addresses and at least one alias ('Mr Roberts').⁹³

On 13 July 1954, the Royal Commission on Espionage issued a subpoena for Clayton to appear before it, and when he failed to do so there ensued a 'nationwide manhunt'.⁹⁴ Radio stations broadcast descriptions of him. One newspaper story carried the headline: 'This Man is Wanted: Who Can Uncover Comrade Clayton?'⁹⁵ The wanted man was secretly ensconced at a remote farm over the Budawang Mountains from the small town of Milton on the south

Wally Clayton in more recent years. He always denied any involvement in Soviet espionage, and later worked as a fisherman around Nelson Bay, NSW. (N. Whitton)

coast of NSW.⁹⁶ In March 1955 Clayton unexpectedly reported to the royal commission, explaining that he had 'been away where I have not had access to the newspapers or radio continuously'. He had 'heard a statement over the national ABC news which I regarded as a shocking slander' and that he wished 'to declare my complete innocence' regarding allegations made about him at the royal commission.⁹⁷

Clayton was in the witness box for four days.⁹⁸ He denied that he had ever been involved in espionage. He said he had never received any official documents or 'secret information' in his life, from Frances Bernie or from anyone else. He said he had never met or known Jim Hill, Ian Milner or Ric Throssell. He said he had never met Mikheev, Makarov, Nosov or any other Russian or member of the Soviet embassy. He had 'no idea' how his name and contact address had been found in the MVD safe in the Residency in Canberra and could not explain the various references to him in the Petrov material. And he refused to discuss any party or control commission activities in which he had ever been involved, or his whereabouts in 1951–55, or his use of pseudonyms or false addresses. He was, throughout the four days, in the words of one of the royal commissioners, 'evasive and dissembling'.⁹⁹ The royal commission found that Clayton was indeed the KLOD referred to in NKGB/KI communications, and that he was 'the principal channel' through which information from the department of External Affairs had been supplied to the Soviet intelligence service.¹⁰⁰

In December 1955, six months after Clayton appeared before the royal commission, Spry distributed a four-page memorandum which reviewed Clayton's past activities, described his current state of affairs, and expressed ASIO's continued interest in him. Spry noted that 'there is no evidence, or indeed probability, of current espionage activity by him', but that 'there is no doubt that he could supply vital information about espionage in Australia in the post-war years if he were willing to do so', and hence that 'Clayton's present and future whereabouts and behaviour and his attitude towards the Communist Party, the Soviet Union and to the Australian Authorities are of great concern to A.S.I.O., having in mind his possible defection [to the Soviet Union] or unconscious exploitation [by ASIO].'[101]

In February 1956 Clayton bought back his property in Baulkham Hills, on 1 March he married Peace Joy Gowland, and in July they moved into the house.[102] Clayton's marriage was extensively discussed within ASIO, and on 26 March 1956 Ron Richards wrote a five-page paper which noted that 'he has never appealed as a marrying type' and posited 'two possible reasons why this marriage should take place at this particular time'.[103] The first was that, as Clayton had been 'intimately connected' with Gowland 'during the last twelve months and during the time his former activities were under scrutiny by the Royal Commission', he may have confided to her 'something of the extent of these activities'; as Clayton's wife, 'she would not be compelled to give evidence against her husband on these matters'.[104] The second possible reason concerned the interests and intentions of Moscow Centre. Richards noted that so long as Clayton remained in Australia, 'he represents a risk to the Soviet M.V.D.', that Ted Hill was currently visiting the Soviet Union, and that he 'may well come back with an instruction from the Soviet authorities concerned that it may be a wise thing to encourage Clayton to leave Australia'.[105] If Clayton did not want to leave, then his marriage would make this 'encouragement' harder; and 'in the event of a more direct "persuasion" being attempted, it means that he would leave behind him a wife, who could no doubt ask embarrassing questions as to his whereabouts, etc'.[106] Arrangements were made (code-named Operation Pigeon) to confront Clayton directly if any information was received suggesting that he was either preparing to leave Australia or that he might consider cooperating with the Australian authorities.[107]

Towards the end of February 1957, Clayton and his wife applied for a passport to travel to England. At ASIO Headquarters, which was informed of the application within a couple of days, this was confirmation of the earlier conjecture. As Spry later recounted, Clayton 'had played such a vital role in a successful espionage network in Australia' that it was 'reasonable to assume' the Soviet intelligence service would want him out of Australia; hence, 'it was our belief that his planned departure for overseas was organised by the R.I.S. [Russian Intelligence Service] in order to secure their position here'.[108] Spry also noted the possibility that if Clayton was unwilling to leave he might 'seek protection against the R.I.S.'.[109] On 1 March, Spry informed the regional directors that 'there is now confirmed information that Clayton is planning to leave Australia for overseas in the very near future', and directed them to maintain the 'closest watch' on shipping lists, air bookings and 'any other travel checks which might reveal the future movements' of Clayton and his wife 'as a top priority matter'.[110] Over the next four weeks he was subject to the closest possible technical and physical surveillance. His house was bugged and his telephone tapped. His movements around his house, or when he went out shopping or drinking at his favourite hotels, were continuously watched and reported to ASIO's Sydney office on an hourly basis. Much of the surveillance was deliberately conspicuous and intimidatory.[111] The party soon arranged for Lachie Carr, 'the toughest man on the waterfront', to move into his house and serve as his bodyguard.[112]

By the beginning of April, ASIO had conceded that Clayton's reaction to its pressure was entrenching his hostility rather than engendering any cooperation. On 3 April, his new passport was officially cancelled,[113] and Clayton surrendered it to the department of Immigration the next day. Surveillance continued, off and on, until the end of August 1957. Thereafter, ASIO's interest in Clayton was only sporadic. In May 1958 ASIO's Sydney office received information that Clayton had purchased a 25-foot 'launch', which it investigated immediately.[114] ASIO may have thought that some significant move was afoot, but Clayton was planning a new career as a fisherman in the area around Nelson Bay, some 175km northeast of Sydney. An ASIO review of his case a week later noted that, despite his 'exceedingly long and painful illnesses', he retained 'great stamina and fortitude', and had 'no weaknesses that could be exploited with advantage'.[115]

In 1960–61, Clayton worked part-time at the CPA bookstore at 2a Sloane Street, Newtown, in Sydney.[116] He also wrote occasional articles for *Tribune*,[117] but he was spending increasing periods of time fishing around Nelson Bay and building a small house in the bush there. ASIO still did not leave him alone. In September 1962, the regional director, NSW, noted that 'Clayton and his wife are spending periods away from home and this may present an opportunity for a Technical Operation against his home', and reported to Richards that planning for such an operation was proceeding.[118] ASIO Headquarters still thought that 'valuable intelligence could be obtained by extending our coverage', and a 'technical operation', including the establishment of a 'listening post', was approved by Spry on

1 October 1962.[119] In 1997 Clayton was still living quietly near Nelson Bay.

ALFRED THOMPSON HUGHES

Although the Venona operation had by 1948 identified Hughes as BEN, the wartime Security Service officer who had provided information to Clayton and thence the NKGB from 1943 until at least the end of 1945, there was tantalisingly little in the Venona material about the nature of this information or the subjects of particular meetings with Clayton. He was investigated by ASIO from October 1949 to September 1952, and again in March–May 1957, culminating in some half dozen interviews with Hughes by Ron Richards. These investigations produced no real breakthroughs; rather, they raised new questions about the extent of Hughes's illicit activities and exposed a myriad of contradictions which cannot be resolved.

There are, for example, irreconcilable testimony and unexplored questions concerning Hughes's relationship with Justice Stanley Cassin Taylor, who served (from May to December 1942) as the first head of the Security Service in NSW (formally titled deputy director of security, NSW). Taylor had had a long career in industrial jurisprudence in Sydney, and in December 1942 he was appointed president of the Industrial Commission of New South Wales. On 28 January 1955 Taylor testified that he purposely remained ignorant of the counter-espionage functions of the service, apart from having to authorise its expenditures;[120] and that he had little recollection of Hughes.[121]

On the other hand, the head of Hughes's section has stated that 'while Mr. Taylor was Deputy Director of Security, Hughes appeared to be his constant advisor and personal friend and seemed to be entirely in the Deputy Director's confidence, and I have no doubt was used in connection with Mr Taylor's political activities'.[122] In March 1957, the then ASIO regional director in Queensland, who had worked in the same office with Hughes in the Security Service from 1942 to 1945, recalled that Hughes 'was then a very intimate friend' of Taylor.[123] Other former colleagues in the Security Service have stated that Hughes was a 'close confidant' of Taylor.[124] 'Hughes was on very friendly terms with Stan Taylor', they spent much of their spare time together, Hughes taught Taylor to drive a motor vehicle, and 'Taylor subsequently arranged for Hughes to be transferred to the Vice Squad after his Security duties had terminated at the end of the War'.[125] In June 1951, when Hughes applied (unsuccessfully) to join ASIO, he listed Taylor as one of his referees.[126] At least two former colleagues in the Security Service recalled in 1957 that there had been leakages of information from the service, and that Hughes had been suspected at that time of passing information to Taylor (after the latter had left the service), who passed it on to Evatt.[127]

It is clear that Hughes and/or Taylor were involved in at least one important leak from the Security Service to the Communist Party. In a message to Valentin Sadovnikov, the KI resident in Canberra, on 10 November 1949, Moscow Centre advised that Taylor had been described 'favourably' by 'K' (i.e., Clayton), and that during the period that Taylor was 'head of the security service in Sydney . . . [he] handed to the Communist Party a document which made possible the exposure of an agent provocateur in one of the regions of the Communist Party'.[128] On 28 January 1955, Taylor was asked by the royal commission whether he might be able to explain the report from Moscow Centre. He said he had never handed any document to the party, although it was possible that in his dealings with trade union officials (who might also be party members) concerning industrial security matters he might have been indiscreet and quoted from Security Service reports.[129] His fellow judges did not press him on the issue.

In December 1991, David McKnight obtained an unsolicited account from 'one of Clayton's close associates', Bill Callen, of Clayton having been shown his 'security file' during the war and of using information in it to identify a security informant in the party, who was immediately denounced by Clayton and expelled from the party.[130] Taylor might have provided information to Clayton. It is also possible that Hughes was the source, but that Taylor may have been the subject of discussion between Hughes and Clayton, and that a garbled account of the episode and Taylor's presumed connection was subsequently compiled at Moscow Centre.

The record is also contradictory about Hughes's relationship with Evatt. On the one hand, Hughes has said that: 'I have never met him. I have never spoken to him.'[131] On the other hand, some former colleagues have stated that Hughes and Evatt were personal friends. They probably got to know each other around the courts in Sydney during the 1930s, when Hughes sometimes served as a prosecuting officer and Evatt was a High Court judge, although one former colleague has suggested that they may have become friends as early as the 1920s. The same colleague, who worked with Hughes in 1949–50, has related how Evatt once rang Hughes and asked him to intervene on behalf of one of his political supporters who had been arrested for pawning stolen goods, which Hughes did.[132]

One of the principal objectives of ASIO's investigation of Hughes in March–May 1957 was to clarify his relationship with Frances

Bernie in the mid 1940s, but, again, the evidence was contradictory and ultimately inconclusive. Hughes had noted Bernie as early as September 1943, when, as a member of the Eureka Youth League (EYL), she was elected assistant secretary of the International Youth Council.[133] In May 1944, Hughes wrote a report on the EYL, of which Frances Bernie was then a member of the NSW state council and assistant national secretary. On 26 July 1944 he produced a report on the People's Council on Culture, another 'front' organisation of which Bernie was also secretary.[134] Hughes was first interviewed by ASIO officers about these reports and his sources for them on 11 and 29 March 1957. He reportedly said that he knew Bernie 'when she was working at the Doc's [Evatt's] and when she was with the EYL', and that he thought 'she wasn't a bad little lass';[135] that Bernie was the principal source for his reports on the EYL and the People's Council on Culture in May and July 1944, and that he had obtained the information from her over the counter at 40 Market Street.[136] However, in an interview in May 1957 Bernie had no recollection of any interview by security officers, was unable to recognise a photograph of Hughes, and denied that she would have been a source for him: 'This is inside Party stuff . . . I wouldn't give it away even if I knew it.'[137] On 3 May 1957, Hughes retracted most of his story about Bernie. He said that she had not been a source for him (that 'was another little girl' who he would not name), that he only ever met Bernie once and that was at 40 Market Street, and that he could not have met her at Evatt's office because 'I was never in his office.'[138]

This last claim was undoubtedly false. For example, a former colleague of Hughes in the Security Service stated on 22 September 1952 that 'I have seen Hughes in Dr Evatt's office on a number of occasions usually in the outer office with Dalziel and the typists.' This informant added that 'there was no doubt . . . that Security Service documents had been removed by Hughes from Security Service and made available for copying to [Dudley] Fitzpatrick [a close friend of Dalziel and an associate of Feodor Nosov].'[139]

In March 1957, ASIO decided to confront Hughes about his relationship with Clayton and his espionage activities in 1943–45. Ron Richards, the deputy director-general (operations), was given the task, which he pursued in some half dozen interviews and telephone conversations with Hughes over the next couple of months. The report of the interview on 29 March stated:

> Hughes was nervous from the start of the interview. He is a frightened man. He declined to eat lunch, but ordered tea and toast. During the interview he managed to crumple up nearly all his toast in his fingers. He found difficulty in swallowing any

tea. He looks unwell and complained that he has broken out in boils . . .

Not once during the interview did he show the slightest hostility, even when it was put straight to him that, unless he offered an acceptable explanation of his meetings with Clayton, it would be open to me to believe that the meetings were organised for more sinister reasons, bearing in mind Hughes' employment at the time and Clayton's position with the Russian Intelligence Service.[140]

Hughes had had legitimate reason to meet Clayton during the war. It was his job to monitor the movements and activities of senior party functionaries in Sydney and, indeed, to cultivate them as potential sources of information. On 31 August 1945, after consulting all the relevant records on Clayton held by both the Security Service and the NSW Special Branch, Hughes put together a report on Clayton which was remarkable for its vacuity. He reported that:

Since . . . 1941 . . . very little concerning him is recorded either here or at Police Headquarters, Sydney. It is known, however, that he is a tutor at Marx House and that he conducts classes for 'cadres' there. It has been further ascertained from contacts that Clayton does office work and also special journalistic work for the Tribune, and is still extremely active in Party work.[141]

Hughes denied meeting or otherwise having any connections with Clayton. He said on 1 April 1957, for example, that 'I don't know the bloke . . . ; I don't remember even knowing Clayton . . .; I only know Clayton . . . as a figurehead that you people tell me about.'[142] However, the Venona material showed that Hughes and Clayton had met clandestinely throughout the period from 1943 to 1948. Richards told Hughes, in an interview on 29 March, that 'there is absolutely no room for doubt' that he had met Clayton. Richards referred specifically to meetings during the 'winter of 1945', but added that 'you were in fact known to each other for longer than that—perhaps much longer', though he could not of course disclose his source of information to Hughes.[143] Hughes could make no satisfactory response. He asked whether there was information that he and Clayton had been 'seen in cars together', but Richards avoided answering. Hughes claimed that he had learned little about Clayton during 1940–46, when he was responsible for security operations concerning the party. He said that his report on Clayton on 31 August 1945 was based on 'stuff from the records', but when it was pointed out that his report had mentioned information from 'contacts', he said: 'Oh well, I had some contacts of course, [but] I can't disclose them.' In sum, he said: 'I can't remember that I ever used him [i.e., Clayton] as a contact. I can't account for it at all. Of course we all make mistakes.'[144]

Hughes was able to bluff his way through the ASIO interviews in March–May 1957. He had by then been in the NSW Police Force for nearly 22 years, including nearly fourteen years as a detective, and would have been a fair match for any interrogator. But he also had a major advantage—he knew, better than anyone else, not only what had been in the Security Service and NSW Special Branch files about CPA activities in 1942–45 but also how the information in those files had been compiled. When it came to the question of meetings with Clayton, for example, Hughes was fully cognisant of Clayton's file and knew that no such meeting had ever been recorded—or, indeed, that no substantial information whatsoever had been recorded about Clayton from 1941 to 1945, when Hughes was responsible for monitoring him. As Richards concluded, 'he will not be induced or persuaded into admissions unless stronger emphasis can be placed on the alleged associations between he [sic] and Clayton in the form of some precise details to back up the allegations'[145]—which insofar as they derived from the Venona operation was not possible.

Hughes retired as a detective sergeant 1st class and officer in charge of No. 2 sub-district (the Newtown/Campsie area) in 1960.[146] He died of a stroke in 1978.

The investigation of Hughes was a painful affair for ASIO. It was in some respects the successor organisation to the wartime Security Service, and the notion that a security officer responsible for monitoring the espionage and subversive activities of the Communist Party was himself a secret member of the party and working for the KGB was not easy to entertain. Spry, until his death in May 1994, maintained a forlorn hope that Hughes's membership of the KLOD group would not be publicised.[147]

18

'every counter-intelligence man's dream'

THE IMPORTANCE OF 'THE CASE'

IN THE 1930S AND '40S the Soviet Union established an international espionage network which was both unheralded in nature and unprecedented in scale. Hundreds of agents were recruited, by both the NKGB and GRU, in dozens of countries. The principal centres of activity were Germany, Japan, Britain and the US, but extensive networks were also established elsewhere in Europe, in Canada, in South America, and in Australia. The Australian network had about ten members, including both dedicated agents and 'in the dark' informants. By 1951, however, as Colonel Anatoli Gorsky (VADIM) complained, in a letter to the Canberra Residency on 6 June 1952, 'intelligence work in Australia . . . was actually at a standstill'.[1] Sigint was critical to the exposure of this Soviet activity. It provided the first intimation, in 1944, of Soviet espionage in Australia; later, during the Venona operation, it also both revealed the international dimensions of the Soviet activity and described some particular aspects of this activity in extraordinary detail, including the information being passed to Moscow and the people involved.

Sigint is generally the most lucrative form of intelligence. It can provide unique insights into an adversary's policies, plans, capabilities and operations. As former FBI special agent Robert Lamphere has said, 'every counter-intelligence man's dream is to be able to read the enemy's communications'.[2] It is like having an agent at the heart of an adversary's intelligence structure, but safer and more dependable.

Ultra intelligence had contributed significantly to the Allied victories against the Axis, and had shortened the war by perhaps as much as two years. The Venona operation was just as momentous in counter-espionage terms. However, while the intelligence derived from Sigint is often unique, it must invariably be complemented by other means and sources. This is especially the case with respect to espionage activities where, no matter how revelatory Sigint might be, sophisticated counter-espionage capabilities are necessary for its exploitation.

The Sigint personnel who intercepted and decrypted the Japanese diplomatic signals traffic from Harbin to Tokyo, and the Japanese Army traffic from Tokyo to field commands, in late 1944, which 'definitely proved that there are leakages of information from Australia',[3] could have had no idea about where any subsequent investigation might lead. With regard to the Venona operation in 1948, when Lamphere began working with Meredith Gardner, Lamphere has said, 'I stood in the vestibule of the enemy's house, having entered by stealth,' but that 'I had no idea where the corridors in the KGB's edifice would take us, or what we would find when we reached the end of a search.'[4] Gardner himself has observed that having decrypted various Soviet messages, 'I could tell what these people were up to, but I couldn't tell who they were.'[5]

Many of the leads had long detours and dead ends; much of the decrypted material was fragmentary, and was more tantalising than revelatory; many of the names and cryptonyms remained unidentified and the activities associated with them unsubstantiated. The Sigint itself was never complete; it was limited by the availability of radio intercepts and accessible cables, and in the case of the Venona operation, by the extent to which the duplicated Soviet OTP pages were recovered, as well as by the abilities of the cryptanalysts to decrypt them. Exploitation of the intelligence was greatly encumbered by the inherent dilemma of Sigint activities: the overriding necessity to protect the secret of the cryptanalytic operation itself. The number of counter-espionage personnel who could be fully indoctrinated into the secret had to be strictly limited, the information obtained from the decrypts had to be 'compartmentalised' from other relevant information, and no actions could be taken that might compromise the operation. It was inevitable, then, that important aspects of Sigint-dependent activities were inconclusive.

The leakages of information from Australia about which General Blamey advised the War Cabinet in January 1945 were never satisfactorily resolved. Although Australian Military Intelligence determined that the *AMF Weekly Intelligence Review* of 4 November 1944 was leaked to Tokyo when the Japanese intercepted the cables from Major-General Wang, the sources of the other leaks were more difficult to detect. As revealed in Blamey's letter of 6 January 1945, these included the 'Special Spy Report' from Harbin on

24 November 1944, which provided details of 'General MacArthur's plans for certain operations in the Philippines', and another Harbin report on 2 December 1944, which gave information of a similar nature. In each case the source was given as the Soviet legation in Canberra, but the method of transmission could not be determined. Possibly the details of the news background sheet, distributed to newspaper editors by the department of Information in November 1944, which was also the subject of a Harbin intelligence report, was obtained by the TASS correspondent Nosov, but there was no proof.

The investigation of these incidents does not seem to have been pursued beyond the end of the war. First, the prime focus had been on preventing the information from reaching the Japanese, and once the war was over this imperative disappeared. Second, there was the matter of the extreme secrecy and strict compartmentalisation of Sigint. Except for specific information given to the director-general, the Security Service was not given access to Sigint; and once the war was over Sigint from Allied countries was curtailed. Thirdly, postwar demobilisation and reorganisation resulted in the loss of expertise and a severe reduction in counter-espionage capabilities. Finally, it is possible that the Soviets passed only a small quantity of information to Tokyo. Furthermore, since the interception of Japanese signals was the only effective means of detecting the espionage, this means disappeared with the end of the war.

The Venona operation also left many questions unanswered. It proved beyond doubt that the Soviet intelligence agencies had penetrated Western foreign policy, defence and intelligence establishments on a vast scale, and were obtaining intelligence of the utmost importance—such as the material on various aspects of highest-level British policy-making provided by Kim Philby and the other members of the Cambridge ring in the UK; the material on US nuclear weapons development supplied by the 'atomic spies' in the UK, Canada and the US; and the top secret material about British postwar strategic planning obtained from Australia.

The story of the relationship between Sigint and counter-espionage in terms of the exposure of Soviet espionage activities in Australia in the 1940s is extremely important, and not just because of the value of the intelligence to Moscow. It highlights the dilemmas involved in the exploitation of Sigint, and the difficulties imposed upon counter-espionage operations, including the strict limits on the extent to which some incriminating matters are able to be investigated. But it is also very important because of light it throws on many controversial issues of historical political importance in Australia.

The importance of the Australian leaks

Australia in the 1940s was not a major player on the world stage. Australia had contributed substantially to the Allied war effort, in North Africa and Europe as well as in Southeast Asia and the Pacific; and in 1944-48 had been prominent in the establishment of the UN organisation. Nonetheless, it was a small power, remote from the principal theatres of the Second World War and from the front lines of the subsequent Cold War.

But if Australia itself was fairly unimportant, there were some very important secrets in Australia. During the war the Australian government had been given access to many top-level decisions of the major Allies, Britain and the United States, and this access continued after the war. Although Australia had not been closely involved in the Manhattan Project, by the late 1940s plans were being made to test missiles in Australia. Britain began developing its own atomic bomb in 1947 and it was likely that it would be tested in Australia (as it was five years later). Despite access to valuable information, the Australian government had a poor appreciation of the need for security, and this was recognised by the Soviet intelligence services in 1942-43.

From 1947, when US cryptanalysts discovered the leakage of British documents from Canberra to Moscow, Australia was subject to extraordinary attention by the most secret US and British Sigint and counter-espionage operations. Of course, the fact that the Venona operation was an astounding cryptanalytic achievement, and had by the late 1940s engaged the best cryptanalysts at both Arlington Hall and GCHQ, does not mean that the information garnered from the decrypts was necessarily important. It was an enthralling exercise. However, the worldwide commitment of Sigint resources to the interception and decryption of NKGB and GRU traffic would not have been maintained, at least as a high priority, unless its revelations were important. The US defence and intelligence authorities certainly regarded the Australian leaks as being sufficiently serious to warrant cutting off the flow of classified information to Australia in 1947-49 and threatening to abrogate cooperative arrangements with the UK (with regard, for example, to missile and atomic weapons secrets) unless the latter's relationship with Australia could be shown to be unimpeachable. The investigation of the Australian leaks and the establishment of an effective Australian security intelligence organisation was one of MI5's most important projects in 1948-49.

The value of the information obtained from Australia from Moscow's point of view will never be known. Neither the full extent of the information obtained nor the use made of it in policy-making in Moscow can be determined. Some of the most telling appreciations, made in closed meetings and private discussions in the Kremlin and at Moscow Centre, were probably not recorded. Whether or not all the material ever obtained from Australia remains held in one place, or is at least indexed or summarised somewhere in Moscow, are open questions. In any case, the Russian Foreign Intelligence Service, successor to the Foreign Intelligence Directorate of the NKGB, is uninterested in releasing any archival material relating to its predecessors' Australian activities. And nothing has ever been disclosed about GRU operations in Australia during this period. It is likely that the Venona material released in 1995–96 will remain the most authoritative basis for any assessment of the nature and importance of the Soviet espionage activities in Australia in 1944–49.

Two good indicators of the relative importance of the NKGB's espionage operations in a particular country are the size of the local Residency and the volume of cable traffic between the Residency and Moscow Centre. The number of KGB personnel reflects both the number of contacts being cultivated and agents being run by the Residency, and the value of the information to Moscow. Despite the desperate manpower and economic situation in the Soviet Union, Moscow Centre was able to send extra staff or 'co-opt collaborators' from other embassy posts (e.g., press, commercial attachés, guards, clerks, etc.) if the local circumstances were sufficiently promising. In June 1949, when Makarov was replaced as Resident by Sadovnikov, the Canberra Residency had grown to seven officers and 'co-opted collaborators' (including Nosov in Sydney). There were also at least two and probably three GRU officers in the embassy. This was a substantial intelligence establishment—not as large as the KGB and GRU Residencies in New York, Washington or London, but larger than anywhere else in the Anglo-American part of the world.

The volume of cable traffic reflects both the amount of important information being collected (and deemed necessary to report by telegraph), and the degree of attention Moscow Centre was prepared to devote to a particular area of operations. Telegraphic services were supposed to be used to report only the most important and most urgent intelligence. Material that was 'a year old', or was of 'minor importance', together with the copies of actual documents and notes, was to be sent by the less frequent courier services.

The Residencies in New York and Washington were the most communicative. The New York Residency sent some 1300 cables to Moscow Centre in 1942, and more than 2000 in 1943. The Washington Residency began in late 1943, taking over some of the operations previously conducted by the New York Residency, and in 1946 Washington sent more than 7000 cables to Moscow Centre. In return, Moscow sent about 1000 cables to New York and some 2650 to Washington in 1945. By comparison, in 1946, some 600 cables were sent from the Canberra Residency to Moscow Centre and over 300 from Moscow to Canberra (or about a third the number that Moscow sent to New York). In the early 1950s, on the other hand, the number of cables from Moscow to Canberra was down to an average of ten to fifteen a month, or about 150 a year.[6]

Moscow Centre was explicit in both its disdain for useless material and its praise for important intelligence. Sometimes when the Residency proposed the cultivation or recruitment of a particular individual (such as Mark Younger), Moscow Centre would declare that the person 'is of no direct interest to us' and ordered that any relationship be suspended or curtailed.[7] Some agents were dropped when their information was no longer found interesting. For example, PALM, the French consul-general who had arrived in Sydney in October 1944, provided the NKGB with important political information in early 1945 (such as details of the UNRRA meeting at Lapstone on 15–20 February, which he reported to the NKGB on 26 February, and which were sent from Canberra to Moscow in a long cable on 1 March).[8] However, in September 1945, Moscow Centre informed the Canberra Residency that 'PALM's information does not present any interest for us', and that meetings with him were to be limited to 'once in 1–2 months';[9] and in March 1946 Moscow instructed Canberra to 'cease all liaison with him'.[10]

In addition to articulating the intelligence collection priorities in Australia (i.e., 'the Department of External Affairs, the political parties and the intelligence and counter-intelligence organisations'),[11] Moscow Centre would sometimes ask for specific documents to be obtained, and it could be congratulatory about particular achievements (as in September 1945, for example, when the Canberra Residency was instructed to 'express appreciation to KLOD in our name for successful work', after Clayton had obtained 'detailed material . . . of operational interest' about the Security Service from Alfred Hughes).[12] Sometimes, Moscow Centre was so eager for material about a particular matter that it would ask its residencies to send the whole texts of documents by cable, regardless of the expense and encryption effort involved—as was the case with the two top secret British War Cabinet postwar planning papers, *Security in the Western Mediterranean and the Eastern Atlantic* and *Security of India and the Indian Ocean*, which Ian Milner had given to Clayton in March 1946.[13]

There is no doubt about Moscow Centre's interest in these particular documents. These are the ones about which Milner had told his NKGB controllers at the end of 1945 or the beginning of 1946, and which, evidently at the specific request of Moscow Centre, Milner obtained from the department of Defence on 6 March 1946. Makarov informed Moscow that he had photographed the two documents on 19 March, and on 21 March Moscow asked that the texts be telegraphed as soon as possible—a major encryption task, involving the transmission of twenty cables and some 12 000 words from Canberra to Moscow from 22 March to 3 April.[14]

More generally, the important information Moscow obtained from Australia can be categorised into five sorts. To begin with, there was the information about Allied war planning, including 'General MacArthur's plans for certain operations in the Philippines' and information dealing with 'the utilisation of Australian Forces', which Moscow obtained in 1944–45. Access to the US plans for the final campaigns against Japan, from Papua New Guinea and Borneo up through the Philippines to the Japanese archipelago itself, would have greatly assisted Soviet geostrategic planning. Stalin had decided by the beginning of 1945 to move manpower and materiel to the Far East in order to occupy the northern Japanese islands and to ensure a stake in any peace settlement before the US forced Japan's surrender; at the same time, however, he was determined to push his forces in Europe as far westward as possible before Germany's capitulation. With the details of MacArthur's plans, Stalin was able to prepare for the Far East campaign, and for a role in the Japanese surrender negotiations, with superb timing.

Indeed, Stalin may even have used the material on MacArthur's plans obtained from Australia to manipulate this timing. This material was somehow getting to Tokyo (from Harbin) fairly quickly, and the most likely explanation is that it was being passed directly to the Japanese by the Soviet authorities as part of a deception campaign designed to prolong the fighting in the south-west Pacific— regardless of the US and Australian casualties.

The second category of important information concerned British postwar strategic planning and foreign policy, of which the War Cabinet documents obtained by Moscow in March–April 1946 were highlights. These top-secret documents had a limited distribution and included discussion on policy for the occupation and control of Germany, proposals for a military staff committee for the United Nations, and British security planning in the Western Mediterranean and the Eastern Atlantic as well as India and the Indian Ocean. These papers would have been of great value to the Soviet Union, especially during the period when it was negotiating with the Allies over postwar arrangements in Europe.

The great bulk of the British material which Moscow obtained in 1945–46, and probably through to 1948 or 1949, consisted of copies of hundreds of cables from the Foreign Office in London to the department of External Affairs in Canberra, which were given to the NKGB by Jim Hill. Some of these went back to 1944 (e.g., cables 'dealing with the situation in Roumania and the attitudes of the British and U.S. Governments', which the Canberra Residency sent to Moscow in October 1945),[15] but in most cases they were never more than a couple of weeks old (e.g., the Foreign Office cable on Argentina of 16 October 1945, which was sent to Moscow on 8 November).[16] Some of the Foreign Office cables and papers obtained from Hill were top secret, but most were confidential. They would have provided Moscow with a detailed picture of the making of British foreign policy regarding numerous other countries (as far afield as Greece, Poland, Iceland, Argentina and Indonesia) and international issues. They would have confirmed and complemented the Foreign Office material that Moscow Centre had obtained directly from Donald Maclean and Guy Burgess during much of this period.

Third, Moscow Centre obtained an enormous volume of information about Australian politics and policies, including foreign policy, and about the personalities involved. Much of this was unimportant, such as the political gossip Prichard related to Clayton in 1944–45, and the material Clayton obtained from Frances Bernie during her first few months as an agent in early 1945.[17] However, some of it was top secret, such as a report prepared for Evatt on south-eastern Europe, which was based on secret British information and was obtained from Hill in September 1945.[18] In early 1945 British forces were fighting Greek communists in Greece, and by 1946 the Greek civil war against the communists was under way. The information also included the telegrams exchanged between Prime Ministers Attlee and Chifley concerning Australian policy on the Indonesian independence struggle, which were sent to Moscow in November 1945.[19] There is no doubt that, in addition to Hill, Ian Milner also gave the NKGB material of this sort. As the KGB informed the Czech ministry of the Interior after Milner's defection to Prague in 1950: 'During his employment in the Ministry of Foreign Affairs in Australia between 1944 and 1947, Ian Milner transferred to us through third persons *valuable materials* on political questions.'[20]

The fourth category consists of 'operational information' about the Australian Security Service, which Moscow Centre obtained from Alfred Hughes. This included detailed information about the structure and capabilities of the Security Service, its interests and activities (e.g., its surveillance of communist as well as fascist organisations), and the files compiled about particular operations and people of interest.[21] This was the sort of material Moscow regarded as being 'of operational interest', and for which it asked that Clayton be congratulated.[22] Hughes was able to show Clayton his own file, as well as those of Mikheev and Nosov.[23] He was in a position to stymie particular investigations, to remove incriminating material about Clayton or his associates from their files, and to warn Clayton of any security interest in their activities. In operational terms, Hughes's importance cannot be disputed.

The fifth category consists of Australian cryptographic material of use to the NKGB's cryptanalysts. Bernie confessed in 1959 to having given Clayton in 1945 copies of encrypted telegrams sent from Canberra to Evatt's office in Sydney;[24] and the reason for the NKGB's interest in Dorothy Jordan was her access to 'the entire correspondence of the Australian Department of External Affairs', including 'enciphered telegrams'.[25] Extensive sequences of clear and encrypted texts, whether archival or contemporary, would have been extremely useful to the NKGB's cryptanalysts working on Australian ciphers as well as the British ciphers from which they were derived.

SIGINT AND COUNTER-ESPIONAGE

The Venona operation represents the archetype of the exploitation of Sigint for counter-espionage purposes by the UKUSA countries in the postwar period. It involved an extraordinary cryptanalytic exercise, but it was instrumental in shaping the arrangements, conditions and processes whereby the most secret and sensitive intelligence sources and methods could be used in counter-espionage operations. It was a difficult regime to establish, and it was often unsatisfactory, particularly from the counter-espionage point of view. The basic working rules were designed to protect the Sigint secrets, the Sigint itself was invariably partial and inconclusive, and information based on the Sigint could not be used as evidence.

The Sigint controllers in both Britain and the US were mindful of the necessity for extreme secrecy. Their determination that the cryptanalytic activities should not be compromised for counter-espionage purposes was informed by the gross indiscretions the British government had committed in the 1920s, when decrypted Soviet diplomatic telegrams had been quoted in the House of Commons and in an official letter to the Soviet chargé d'affaires in London; this had led to the adoption by the Kremlin in 1927 of a one-time pad (OTP) encipherment system for high-grade Soviet diplomatic and OGPU cable traffic, which had remained unbroken by British and US cryptanalysts for nearly two decades. Even prime ministers were to be told as little as possible, if anything, about Venona.

The strictest 'compartmentalisation' was imposed on Venona material within the US and British security and intelligence communities, with a 'need to know' principle defined by Sigint interests. Few counter-espionage personnel were ever fully indoctrinated into the Venona operation. In Washington in 1948–49, seven counter-intelligence officers were visiting Gardner and his colleagues more or less often for direct acquaintance with the Venona decrypts (Mickey Ladd, Wesley Reynolds and Robert Lamphere from the FBI, Peter Dwyer and Kim Philby from MI6, and Dick Thistlethwaite and Geoffrey Patterson from MI5). There was considerable compartmentalisation among these; for example, Lamphere was told nothing about the decrypts involving Australia, even though these had figured centrally in Gardner's breakthroughs in 1947. Within MI5 in the late 1940s, there were about a dozen indoctrinated officers (including Sillitoe, White, Hollis, Thistlethwaite, Patterson, Martin, Courtenay Young, Hemblys-Scales and Evelyn McBarnet). However, Jim Skardon, MI5's renowned interrogator, was not told about Venona. In Australia, no member of ASIO was indoctrinated until 1950, although three senior officers (Spry, Michael Thwaites and Richards) had been by the end of 1952. From the counter-espionage point of view, they were too few and it took too long for the confidences to be shared. As a recent official account of the Venona operation has noted, the effort to use the decrypts 'remained understaffed and highly compartmented, and exploitation opportunities were almost certainly lost in consequence'.[26]

Sigint can offer unique insights, but from the counter-intelligence point of view it can also be extremely frustrating. Sigint and cryptanalysis are imperfect arts. The product is invariably partial and can sometimes take years to put together. It is not possible for Sigint agencies to cover all radio wavelengths, circuits and cable traffic. By the time Gardner and his colleagues at Arlington Hall realised the vast extent of Soviet espionage, in 1947, it had been underway for several years, and the earlier radio telegrams and cables had not all been collected. About 50 per cent of the NKGB cables from New York to Moscow in 1944 and of the GRU Naval cables from Washington to Moscow in 1943 were decrypted, but in the cases of most other Moscow–Residency circuits the success rate was much lower. About 5 per cent of the cable traffic between Moscow and Canberra in 1943–48 was decrypted to any substantial degree. The fragments recovered in more than 1000 other cables served only to intrigue.

There was considerable room for interpretation, on the part of the cryptanalysts and translators as well as the counter-intelligence specialists. Tradecraft expressions such as 'in the dark' informants, and 'bring [cover-name] into our work', required special comprehension.

The investigation of the Venona leads required the invention of plausible cover stories, which were undoubtedly a hindrance. It was intimated to Burton, for example, when he was secretary of the department of External Affairs, that Britain had a 'mole' within the NKGB whose existence would be prejudiced if any information about British knowledge of the Australian leaks ever became public or otherwise known in Moscow, but he found this 'somewhat curious'.[27] Significant leads remained off limits in the absence of plausible pretexts. For example, ASIO was unable to interview Bernie, and hence to obtain her confession and confirmation of Clayton as the spymaster, until the opportunity incidentally arose in 1953. There can be no doubt that when the royal commissioners inquired into Soviet espionage in Australia in 1954–55, their ignorance of the Venona material greatly diminished their report (as in the inability to identify BEN and PODRUGA).[28]

The prosecution of espionage cases inspired by Sigint and cryptanalytic activities is thus fairly uncommon. William Weisband was never prosecuted for revealing the Venona operation to the Soviets in 1947 because it would have involved an unprecedented public discussion of 'sources and methods' and the possibility of the Soviets' learning more about the scale and scope of the operation, the cryptanalytic techniques involved, and the particular findings.[29] In September 1949, Robert Lamphere found information in a newly deciphered NKGB 1944 message that incriminated Klaus Fuchs in atomic espionage; however, as Lamphere has recounted:

> [The British were] unsure of how to go after him. The problem was that there was no evidence that could be used in court; we couldn't reveal that the clue to his espionage and identity had come from the [Venona] messages. Unless Fuchs could be forced to confess, there would be no case.[30]

MI5 found a suitable pretext to interview him, and Skardon was able to obtain his confession, but this was a rare case.

But if it was imperative that no hint of Sigint or cryptanalytic activity be given to the courts, it was also true that the Venona material would have had little legal standing anyway. Sillitoe has noted that 'intelligence information is one thing; legal evidence sufficient to justify prosecution is another', and has emphasised that in the case of Burgess and Maclean (and notwithstanding his full knowledge of the Venona material), 'the inescapable truth [is] that no shred of legal evidence has ever been made available against either of them which could have served as grounds for the issuing of a warrant for their arrest.'[31]

The Venona material is manifold hearsay. It is the communications between Moscow Centre and the NKGB/KI Residency in

Canberra, based on what KLOD had told TEKhNIK and what he had told the Residency, or what the Residency had presumed about KLOD's sources. Despite the endeavours of Moscow Centre to clarify in detail the particulars of each piece of information obtained, there were undoubtedly some mistakes (e.g., the report about Major Mathews joining the department of External Affairs in 1946).[32] Venona, as authoritative as it is, would not stand up in court.

QUALIFICATIONS, MITIGATIONS, MOTIVES

No-one in Australia was ever charged with espionage or any other offence relating to the activities of the KLOD group, and the issue is now academic. However, some ethical and motivational considerations cannot be avoided.

The motives of those who supplied information to KLOD and thence to the NKGB/KI cannot be characterised simply. They were mostly quite different, invariably complex, and in some cases not possible to discern fully. It is not easy to recreate the extent of personal tragedy or the despair generated by the Great Depression, or the fear produced by the rise of fascism and its commitment to the destruction of communism and, indeed, liberal democratic systems. Anthony Blunt sneered at his MI5 interrogator when trying to explain why he and his fellow members of the Cambridge ring felt compelled to work for the KGB: 'You don't understand the 1930s.'[33] Within the CPA, there was a significant difference between 'a Depression communist' and 'a war-time communist'. As a wartime member of the party has observed: 'Those who experienced the Depression as active party members saw a much uglier side of the Janus face of capitalism . . . and became more committed.'[34] Several members of the KLOD group (including Clayton himself) had been active communists during the Depression; their commitment to the Soviet cause was the strongest.

For Wally Clayton, 'Communist activity is never improper';[35] 'he had' he told his NKGB controllers in May 1945, 'always considered it his duty to help our country'.[36] Some of his informants, on the other hand, were either uninterested in knowing that their information was destined for Moscow or were quite unconscious of their exploitation. (Ric Throssell was evidently in the latter category in 1945.)[37]

There is justification for some in the fact the Soviet Union was a wartime ally, whose survival had been vital to the Allied cause. Soon after the German attack on the Soviet Union in June 1941, Churchill said that the 'Russian danger is our danger'.[38] The following year General MacArthur referred to the Soviet Army's efforts as the greatest military achievement in history.[39] At a rally organised by the Australian–Soviet Friendship League in Melbourne in November 1943 to celebrate Soviet national day, messages were read from Evatt and Blamey.[40] But this was not the green light to pass information to the Soviets. Indeed, it was not the prerogative of relatively junior Australian public servants to decide what should and should not be passed to a foreign government even if it was an ally. And of course they had no control over what use might have been made of the information, such as the Soviets' apparent willingness to pass selected material to the Japanese.

Exculpation for others has been sought in the philosophy and practice of 'open diplomacy', of which John Burton, the secretary of the department of External Affairs from 1947 to 1949, was a fervent advocate. Burton believed it was very important that the Soviet Union understand Australia's policies concerning the construction of a new postwar international order. He thought that 'almost nothing' was really secret anyway; and he encouraged his departmental officers to be as forthcoming as possible with Soviet representatives in Canberra.[41] To some extent at least, Jim Hill was simply practising what some of his superiors were preaching. On the other hand, however, some of the material which Hill gave the Soviets was in fact 'most secret', and some concerned the details of Australian regional security policies rather than postwar international order more generally.[42] It is unlikely that when Hill met clandestinely with Clayton, following strict NKGB tradecraft, to give him the most up-to-date British and Australian foreign policy material, there was much thought of open diplomacy in his mind.

IRONIES AND GAPS

The story is replete with irony. The Australian informants who comprised the KLOD group did not know anything about the purposes for which their information would be used, even if they were aware that their information was destined for Moscow. Some of the more subtle and indirect consequences were simply inconceivable at the time; they became manifest only in the 1950s, sometimes in surprisingly different contexts.

It was quite perverse that the material which the Australian informants gave the Soviets about US and Australian forces and plans in the south-west Pacific in 1944–45 were apparently obtained by the Japanese and used to assist their operations in the South West Pacific Area in 1945, in which hundreds of Australian lives were lost. To what extent awareness of this would have perturbed the Australian informants can only be surmised. Some would surely have been anguished. But to the committed Stalinist internationalist, prolongation of the war in the Pacific and the loss of Australian lives were immaterial considerations. As the leadership of the CPA had secretly agreed in 1942, 'as Communists, we want a Russian victory, not necessarily an Allied victory'.[43] By 1945, the categorical consideration was the enhancement of the Soviet Union's geostrategic position in the postwar international order, whatever Australia's expense.

Some of the ironies were quite specific. For example, the NKGB's Australian operations provided critical material for the rapid progress of the Venona operation at Arlington Hall in 1947, and hence for the exposure of the Soviet worldwide intelligence offensive. The only successful decrypts of some of the circular telegrams from Moscow Centre to various Residencies in 1942–44 were those sent from Moscow to Canberra, such as the cable from Moscow on 12 September 1943 which gave detailed instructions for handling intelligence sources within the Communist Party after the dissolution of the Comintern,[44] and which has been described by a Venona expert as 'one of the most interesting and historically important messages in the entire corpus of Venona translations'.[45] The transmission of the 12 000 words of the two British War Cabinet documents in twenty cables to Moscow in March–April 1946, at VIKTOR's direct instruction, later enabled Gardner and his colleagues to reconstruct a large proportion of the NKGB's code groups, without which much of the Venona material could never have been recovered. In intelligence terms, these two documents may have been among the most important of the ones obtained from Australia; but obtaining them was ultimately at the expense of the integrity of Moscow's international espionage operations, and the loss of much more information.

The Soviet intelligence operations in Australia in the mid 1940s were ultimately responsible for the establishment of the Australian Security Intelligence Organisation in 1949. After the Second World War Australian defence officials had tried to establish an all-embracing security organisation, but without success. The government was not interested, and without evidence of espionage in Australia the efforts to establish such an organisation would have been fruitless. Without the discovery of the Australian leakages by Arlington Hall in 1947 and the US embargo on classified information to Australia, and the direct involvement of MI5 in the case in 1948–49, there would probably have been no ASIO. ASIO was established to deal with the case, and the case dominated its formative years. For several decades, the basic structure of ASIO, its operational interests and its areas of suspicion, and its operational technique and character, remained heavily influenced by the case. The KLOD group can be accorded great responsibility for the sorts of things which ASIO did for some forty years.

The case indirectly contributed to the maintenance of conservative government in Australia for some two decades. Venona was a very privileged secret. There is no evidence that it was ever used improperly by any Australian politician or official. Indeed, given the frustrations which so often occurred in efforts to investigate known informants, to clarify important issues, or to justify unpopular policies, this is remarkable. Prime Minister Menzies, like Chifley before him, would have been told little about Venona other than that it was a cryptanalytic operation providing unique and important intelligence, and requiring absolute secrecy. However, Venona gave ASIO the confidence to declare that Soviet espionage was taking place in Australia. Menzies was a politician, willing to exploit security issues for political advantage, and his confident statements, based on ASIO assessments, were widely believed. In the case of the defection of the Petrovs in April 1954, he did not conspire with ASIO to engineer their defection, or to use the royal commission to embarrass Evatt and the Labor Party, or even allow the royal commission itself to use any Venona material. But the issue contributed to his success in the 1954 election. The communist threat went beyond espionage in Australia. After all, Soviet and other communist activities could be seen in action around the world, in Europe, Northern and Southeast Asia and elsewhere. But the revelation of espionage in Australia gave the communist threat more immediacy. Menzies used anti-communist scare tactics to good political effect later in the 1950s and '60s.

The Soviet espionage operations undoubtedly also contributed to the development of the Cold War. The defection of Igor Gouzenko in Ottawa in September 1945 alerted the West to the existence of vast Soviet espionage networks in Canada, the US and the UK; the Venona decrypts not only confirmed in 1947 that the Soviet effort was worldwide and had been under way for several years, but also revealed that it was critically damaging Western defence and security interests. The scale of the Soviet intelligence offensive alone left no doubt that the Cold War was a reality.

The British intelligence service had, of course, revived its anti-Soviet activities in early 1944. GCHQ had resumed work on Soviet diplomatic and intelligence codes and ciphers in June 1944, and Philby had reported this to the NKGB in August 1944. The US Army Security Agency had begun work on Soviet codes in February 1943, and this had been reported to Moscow in November 1944. To Moscow Centre, the active British and US interest in Soviet codes and ciphers, when the end of the wars in both Europe and the Pacific were still a year away, would have been evidence that the Cold War was already under way in 1944.

Moscow's suspicions about postwar British and US strategic intentions would have been much exacerbated by the two British War Cabinet documents prepared in May 1945 which it had been so desperate to obtain in early 1946. These showed that even before the end of the war the British regarded the Soviet Union as a potential enemy. They would have confirmed to Moscow that Britain and the US would not retreat across the seas but would maintain a global approach to strategy.

There are many gaps remaining in this story. This is in fact an inherent feature of the subject of Sigint and counter-espionage. Sigint is inevitably partial, and investigations remain incomplete because of the need to protect 'sources and methods'. The Russian foreign intelligence service will never release all the relevant information about Soviet intelligence operations in Australia or their importance. A major gap concerns the activities of Viktor Zaitsev, the GRU Resident in Australia from 1943 to 1947 and an officer of creditable achievement in Japan beforehand. None of the GRU cables between Moscow and Canberra were ever decrypted in the Venona operation, and the GRU archive remains closed.

There remain many important questions concerning the KLOD group and its activities, some of which will never be clarified—such as the process whereby Clayton was selected to be the NGKB's spymaster in Australia, or the extent to which some of his particular informants were either witting or 'in the dark'. Most of the members of the group have died. Only one of them, Bernie ever confessed to collecting and providing material for Clayton, and her confessions, a decade and a half after the event, are incomplete in important respects. All of them have dissembled, whether (as in the case of Clayton) about the existence and operation of the group as a whole, or about particular matters concerning their activities or relations with Clayton or other members of the group. An already complex and difficult exercise, to explain and describe the motives and activities of a group operating half a century ago, has been rendered impossible by these deaths and dissemblings.

There are also important gaps in the Australian archival record which will undoubtedly inspire conspiracy theories. Perhaps the most tantalising gap concerns the records surrounding Blamey's 1945 letter, which began this story. For instance, after Blamey discussed the matter with Shedden on 2 January, the latter replied that he would like a copy of Blamey's statement 'in order that I may be able to link the matter with the Defence files which I brought to your notice'.[46] At the Cabinet meeting on 17 January Blamey read extracts from his top-secret file, and the following day Brigadier

Rogers gave Brigadier Simpson 'the suspected name of the Sydney agent'.[47] The file on which Blamey based his letter was not released until July 1997, but it does not contain all the intercepts such as the one revealing the leak of the news background sheet. The Defence files referred to by Shedden have not been located. The Australian government is only now releasing information about the Second World War 'diplomatic' section and what signals it might have intercepted.

In April 1956, Sir Arthur Tange noted, in a secret memo about the Soviet penetration of the department of External Affairs in the 1940s: 'This is a story about the leakage of information which is highly classified; indeed, so classified that I do not believe the Department of External Affairs has ever been told the full story.'[48]

The full story can never be told. But the shrouds of secrecy have now been mostly removed.

Appendix 1

AMF Weekly Intelligence Review No. 118, 4 November 1944

SECRET

AUSTRALIAN MILITARY FORCES WEEKLY INTELLIGENCE
REVIEW NO. 118
Compiled from information received from 1200 hours
27 Oct 44 to 1200 hours 3 Nov 44

TABLE OF CONTENTS	Page
PART I	
Summary of Significant Events	1
PART II	
Section 1 - Summary of Operations by Areas	
(a) Land	2
(b) Sea	4
(c) Air	10
Section 2 - Strengths and Dispositions of Enemy Forces	
(a) Land	12
(b) Sea	–
(c) Air	13
Section 3 - Enemy Organisation	13
Section 4 - Enemy Equipment	15
Section 5 - Tactics	–
Section 6 - Extracts from Captured Documents	19
Section 7 - General	22
PART III	
Other Fronts	–
PART IV	
Topographical	–
PART V	
Security	28
APPENDICES	
A.	
B. Type 100 82mm Mortar Fusse - Instantaneous or Delay	
C. Japanese Conventional Signs	

PART I

SUMMARY OF SIGNIFICANT EVENTS

Except for small enemy pockets, organised resistance has ceased in the LEYTE VALLEY. Further South, an Allied force is advancing along the ABUYOG–BAYBAY road towards the West coast against little opposition.

Subsequent to the Allied landing on LEYTE, no surprise would have been occasioned by reports of a redistribution of the enemy strength on MINDANAO, in order to strengthen the Northern coast of this island. It is of interest that as yet no information in support of this has been received.

It is apparent from the extent of the enemy's air reaction, that for the defence of the PHILIPPINE ISLANDS he is prepared to utilise some of his reserve air strength held in the JAPAN–MANCHURIA area, staging them in through FORMOSA. During the week continuous attacks were launched against our beach-head, shipping and airstrips, on a scale not encountered heretofore in the SWPA. These attacks interfered with airfield construction and the maintenance of our invasion forces. A feature of the tactics employed against our naval vessels was the frequent use of suicide crash dives. Though some success was achieved against our light naval forces, these methods proved unsuccessful against our heavy units.

Both aerial reconnaissance and ground reports lend weight to the belief that considerable reinforcements reached LUZON during the month of September. It is estimated that at least one major formation, probably a division, arrived during that period. Until our land based aircraft can close the waters of the PHILIPPINES to the enemy, it seems certain he will endeavour to reinforce still further his main bastion of defence—LUZON.

It is now estimated that in the recent naval battle off the PHILIPPINES, a total of 63 Japanese vessels were involved. Of these 47 were either sunk or badly damaged.

* * *

PART II

SUMMARY OF OPERATIONS BY AREAS

(a) LAND - SOLOMONS:

BOUGAINVILLE

Encounters on a slightly heavier scale have been reported in the Upper LARUMA VALLEY, where in a patrol clash on 26 Oct, 15 Japanese were killed. On the same day artillery fire was brought down on another enemy party of 75 in the same locality.

NEW BRITAIN:

WIDE BAY AREA

Natives have disclosed that during the MILIM engagements, the Japanese, after killing a number of them, forced the remainder to give information and act as guides to locate an Allied patrol.

NEW GUINEA:

MADANG AREA

Patrols operating in the BAGASIN area (26 miles SW of MADANG) on 28 Oct reported that several hundred natives were being trained under Japanese supervision in an area some five miles North of BAGASIN.

Native scouts stated that although few rifles were in evidence, they saw at least 100 natives armed with grenades.

WEWAK AREA

A report dated 25 Oct states that natives killed 20 Japanese near HAMBIKI (approximately 50 miles West of WEWAK).

A PW, 2nd Lt, 237 Infantry Regiment, 41 Division, who surrendered near ULAU on 29 Sep 44 confirmed previously known information regarding the locations of 18 Army formations with the exception of 20 Division. He stated that HQ 18 Army was located at BOIKEN, 41 Division in the vicinity of BALUP, 51 Division in the vicinity of WEWAK, and he had heard that most of 20 Division were at MARUI, whence they had moved from BUT.

PW stated that there were no fortifications at BALUP, as previous fortifications had been destroyed by Allied bombing, manual labour owing to malnutrition, as supplies of rice became exhausted on 10 Jul 44.

DUTCH NEW GUINEA:

During the past week scattered contacts only have been reported throughout the DUTCH NEW GUINEA area, and minor casualties inflicted on the enemy.

On BIAK ISLAND native patrols operating on the West coast between 9 and 26 Oct are now credited with killing 111 Japanese. These are in addition to previous casualty figures.

PHILIPPINE ISLANDS:

LEYTE ISLAND

Rapid progress has been maintained in the occupation of the island and heavy casualties have been inflicted on the enemy.

In the Northern Sector on 24 Oct a sharp counter-attack by about 100 Japanese took place at PALO. This was repulsed, 70 enemy being killed.

On the following day, another counter-attack three miles WNW of PALO was effectively dealt with. In the Southern Sector, Allied troops advancing from BURAUEN captured BURI airfield and town, two miles to the North, against stiff opposition. Progress Northward towards DAGAMI was hindered by enemy minefields.

Other Allied forces advancing along the coast from DULAG encountered opposition about 12 miles South of DULAG, but the enemy withdrew into the hills under Allied pressure.

On 26 Oct, Allied troops operating along the West shore of SAN JUANICO STRAIT occupied UBAN and patrols pushed forward to BABATNGON (9 miles Westward). In the PALO area, PASTRANA, SANTA FE (5 miles West of PALO) and ALANGALANG (11 miles WNW of PALO) were occupied by our forces.

On 27 Oct, Allied amphibious patrols landed unopposed at BARUGO and CARIGARA on the Southern shore of CARIGARA BAY, patrols pushing inland to SAN MIGUEL (7 miles East of BARUGO). Fifty Japanese were encountered just North of SAN MIGUEL, of whom 41 were killed.

In the Southern Sector, heavy enemy resistance continued in the CATMON HILL area, which had been by-passed by our forces advancing inland to BURAUEN.

At BURAUEN our advance Northward towards DAGAMI was stubbornly resisted, but progress was made to within 1,000 yards of DAGAMI.

There were indications at this time of a general enemy withdrawal to the West coast or to the mountains SW of LEYTE VALLEY.

Meanwhile, Allied forces on SAMAR ISLAND, pushing rapidly Northward were reported 10 miles North of CATBALOGAN, advancing against only slight enemy opposition.

In the PALO area good progress was maintained, and on 28 Oct a junction was made on the BINAHAAN RIVER with troops moving North from DULAG, thus linking up the Northern and Southern sectors.

Other forces moving inland from PALO approaching CAVITE (12 miles NW of PALO) encountered heavy machine gun and mortar fire. Meanwhile, a second thrust on DAGAMI by troops from TANAUAN successfully overcame strong enemy positions East of DAGAMI and reached the outskirts of the town.

In the Southern sector, the coastal town of ABUYOG (14 miles South of DULAG) was occupied and the Allied troops turned inland along the ABUYOG–BAYBAY road.

On 29 Oct heavy enemy attacks forced the Allied detachment to withdraw from CARIGARA to BARUGO, where 500 to 600 Japanese troops were reported in the area. Allied forces driving from the East captured CAVITE and JARO (4 miles SW of CAVITE) and continued their advance towards CARIGARA against enemy opposition.

The reduction of enemy positions on CATMON HILL proceeded steadily, the enemy offering stubborn resistance from numerous caves. By 30 Oct our troops were in occupation of the main features, with the enemy confined to the NW slopes and isolated cave positions, still to be mopped up.

In the DAGAMI area, Japanese troops offering stiff resistance in the town area were surrounded and annihilated, the town falling to our forces on 30 Oct.

By this time main activities were centred on the Western side of the island in the CARIGARA and ORMOC BAY areas.

It was reported that some 1,500 Japanese had landed at ORMOC BAY between 25 and 29 Oct. On 31 Oct enemy troops in the CARIGARA area were estimated at 2,000.

358   BREAKING THE CODES

The Allied advance from JARO to CARIGARA was met by considerable enemy opposition but by 31 Oct our troops had reached a point six miles SE of CARIGARA.

In the Southern sector, patrols met little opposition. The NW slopes of CATMON HILL were found to be clear of the enemy, while further to the South, our patrols from ABUYOG had penetrated four miles inland.

Forward movement was maintained during 1 and 2 Nov. By 2 Nov Allied troops, supported by heavy artillery, reached CARIGARA. CATMON HILL was considered clear of the enemy, while patrols from ABUYOG had crossed the island of BAYBAY.

Enemy casualties to 31 Oct:-

Killed   9,345

Captured   93

(b) SEA - SOUTH CHINA SEA:

The amount of shipping sighted in these waters during the week has remained at the same high level as that reported for the past weeks. The following shipping reports comprise only the major sightings made in this area.

On 26 Oct, seven carriers with 72 aircraft, two battle-ships, seven destroyers, two gunboats and six transports were reported at AMOY.

On the same day, one carrier, one light cruiser, three destroyers and nine merchant vessels were sighted 80 miles East of TONKON POINT (NE HAINAN ISLAND) on a course East by South. Half an hour later, the same reconnaissance aircraft spotted two destroyers and four freighters 65 miles SE of TONKON POINT on a course NE by East. During the night 26/27 Oct, a convoy of seven unidentified vessels was sighted 150 miles SE of TONKON POINT on a Northeasterly course. This convoy may have been identical with the convoy of three escort vessels and three or more merchant vessels observed 120 miles South by West of HONGKONG on a course ENE.

During the week, a number of convoys were sighted heading towards the PHILIPPINES. On 26 Oct, a large convoy, the composition of which was not reported, was seen 105 miles NNW of APARRI (North coast LUZON) on a Southerly course. Two days later, ten medium vessels with numerous escorts departed from NAHA (OKINAWA ISLAND) on a Southwesterly course. On 31 Oct, a convoy of four 7,000/8,000 ton freighter-transports and four 1,500/2,500 ton stack-aft vessels, with three escorts, was sighted 140 miles South by West of HONGKONG on a Southerly course.

On 26 Oct, ten transports, two tankers and two unidentified vessels were reported at SAIGON. On the following day, four transports proceeded North from SAIGON whilst 17 vessels laden with troops arrived. On 28 Oct, one 9,000/12,000 ton transport escorted by a destroyer was observed 300 miles West of BRUNEI BAY (NW BORNEO) on a course NW by West.

PHILIPPINE ISLANDS:

The following is a summary of events in the defeat by Allied naval forces of the Japanese Navy's endeavour to neutralise the Allied invasion of the PHILIPPINES.

On 24 Oct, the enemy warships appeared in the Western VISAYAS, and in two groups made sorties Eastwards towards the Allied positions. One force, comprising the following vessels, confirmed by photographs,

5 battleships (2 YAMATO, 2 KONGO, 1 NAGATO class)
5 heavy cruisers (2 MAGAMI, 2 ATAGO, 1 NACHI class)
1 heavy cruiser unidentified
1 light cruiser AGANO class
1 light cruiser unidentified
<u>13</u> destroyers
<u>26</u> warships

proceeded through MINDORO STRAIT, North of TABLAS ISLAND, through the SIBUYAN SEA to SAN BERNARDINO STRAIT, arriving the night 24/25 Oct.

The second force, believed to comprise

2 battleships FUSO and YAMASHIRO classes
2 heavy cruisers
2 light cruisers
10 destroyers
16 warships

proceeded South from MINDORO STRAIT, and on the same night reached SURIGAO STRAIT via the MINDANAO SEA.

Battle off SAMAR ISLAND:

The first force was contacted South of MINDORO at 0745 hours on 24 Oct, and throughout the day was attacked by Allied carrier aircraft. At 1400 hours, when 30 miles East of TABLAS ISLAND, the enemy units reversed their course Westwards. It was reported that the force was heavily damaged by numerous torpedo and bomb hits. However, it again headed Eastwards in the SIBUYAN SEA, and at the strength reported above, passed through the SAN BERNARDINO STRAIT during the night 24/25 Oct.

At daybreak, an Allied escort carrier group East of SAMAR ISLAND sighted the enemy approaching from the NW and soon after was under fire from heavy enemy units at 15 mile range, closing to 7 mile range. All the Allied aircraft were launched, whilst the carriers engaged the enemy with gunfire. At the same time, Allied naval units arrived in the area from the SURIGAO STRAIT battle.

Under smoke screens the carriers took evasive action, and at 0740 hours on 25 Oct, Allied destroyers and escorts of the carrier group attacked with torpedoes, whilst the carriers exchanged gunfire with the enemy cruisers. Some Allied vessels were straddled, the enemy fire being accurate as to range, but faulty in direction. At approximately 0930 hours, the enemy suddenly broke off the action and turned away.

In this unique engagement, which the Allied naval commander described as unbelievable, the carrier group turned back the heavy enemy force with relatively light losses and reported the following damage inflicted on the enemy:

1 heavy cruiser MOGAMI exploded and sank
2 heavy cruisers probably sunk
2 heavy cruisers damaged by torpedo hits
1 battleship damaged

Aircraft of another Allied carrier group later attacked the enemy units retreating from the SAN BERNARDINO STRAIT, contacting them in the MINDORO STRAIT—SIBUYAN SEA area, and expending 56 tons of bombs, 45 torpedoes and 80 rockets. The following results were reported:

Sunk
1 heavy cruiser
1 cruiser or destroyer
1 destroyer
1 9,000 ton seaplane-tender

Probably sunk
1 heavy cruiser
1 light cruiser
1 battleship

Damaged
4 battleships
2 heavy cruisers (at least)
7 destroyers

Battle off SURIGAO STRAIT:

During the afternoon of 24 Oct, carrier aircraft attacked the force approaching from the SW, scoring two hits on two battleships, and rocket hits on a cruiser and a destroyer. Allied aircraft continued their harassing attacks until about midnight when PT boats picked up the force South of BOHOL ISLAND and scored two torpedo hits.

The enemy entered SURIGAO STRAIT at 0230 hours on 25 Oct in two columns, the second four miles astern, with heavy units in each. Allied units, from PT boats to battleships disposed in the Northern end of the Strait, opened the action at 0330 hours with torpedoes from the lighter units. Torpedo hits slowed the enemy units from 20 to 12 knots. Ten minutes later, a further torpedo attack was launched, with several hits scored, and at 0405 hours, the heavy units opened fire, noting many flames and explosions at the targets.

At 0445 hours, the enemy force turned and attempted to escape; four vessels were seen burning and later sank. Later assessment confirmed the sinking of two battleships, one heavy and one light cruiser, and six destroyers.

During daylight 25 Oct, carrier aircraft attacked the remaining six retreating enemy units, sinking one large unit East of PANAY, but the attack on the Allied carriers off SAMAR ISLAND prevented further pursuit. However on 26 Oct, the remaining one heavy and one light cruiser and four destroyers were subjected to heavy attacks by a large force of Liberators, and all of these vessels were reported as being either sunk or badly damaged and probably sunk. An interesting feature of this action was the sinking of a destroyer by a strafing attack.

Whilst some of the enemy units which escaped from the area were probably returned to rear bases for repair, numerous sightings made during the week have indicated that a number of naval vessels are scattered about in Northern and Central PHILIPPINE waters. Some light units will possibly be retained in the PHILIPPINES to be employed for fast troop transportation missions to VISAYAN bases, as long as such missions can be carried out without escessive losses.

Battle off LUZON:

The third naval force, consisting of

2 battleships, with flight decks aft
1 aircraft carrier
2 small combat carriers
1 small combat or escort carrier
1 heavy cruiser
4 light cruisers
5/6 destroyers
16/17 warships

was engaged by Allied units on the morning of 25 Oct in the waters NE of LUZON. Detailed reports of this engagement have not been received, although the following damage inflicted on the enemy has been reported:

Sunk
4 carriers (types not specified)
1 light cruiser
1 destroyer

Probably sunk
1 light cruiser

Damaged
2 battleships
1 heavy cruiser
2 light cruisers
2 destroyers

Damaged and undamaged units of this enemy force escaped to the North.

It is estimated that a total of 63 first line Japanese naval units were actually engaged in combat by Allied surface vessels and aircraft. Although detailed total results of the three naval actions have not been received as yet, it is estimated that all but 18 of the 63 units were either sunk or badly damaged.

It is believed that the enemy had some troop concentrations for immediate transport to the Allied beachhead had his naval forces been able to gain control of the seas in the LEYTE area.

Sightings of enemy vessels in LUZON waters have been maintained at a high level. On 24 Oct, 19 large and eight small vessels were observed entering MANILA BAY, whilst three days later the following shipping was sighted in the Bay:

4 freighter-transports (1 large, 3 medium)
3 freighters (2,000 tons each)
2 tankers (9,000 tons each)
1 hospital ship
3 destroyers
1 cruiser

On the same day, Allied aircraft reported three light cruisers and two destroyers heading towards the Bay. On 29 Oct carrier aircraft probably sank one heavy cruiser, and damaged a cruiser and a tanker in the MANILA BAY area.

On 25 Oct, four large merchant vessels accompanied by five escorts were sighted 25 miles West of VIGAN (West coast LUZON) on a course NE by East. On the following day, photographs taken of a Southbound convoy 20 miles SE of CAPE BOLINAO (LINGAYEN GULF) showed the convoy to consist of four heavily laden merchant vessels totalling 39,400 tons, one 400 foot probable aircraft tender, three 220 foot gunboats and a PT boat.

Various sightings, mainly of naval vessels, were made in the VERDE ISLAND PASSAGE area, the principal sightings being made on 31 Oct and 2 Nov. The first sighting consisted of five light cruisers, five destroyers and four transports on an Easterly course. The second sighting comprised one battleship, three heavy and three light cruisers, and two destroyers in the BATANGAS BAY area.

Numerous sightings of naval vessels were made during the week throughout the VISAYAN SEA area. The majority of these warships are considered to have been connected with the withdrawal of the enemy naval force reported elsewhere. Many sightings of small groups of naval vessels in the CEBU—LEYTE area indicate a possible "TOKIO EXPRESS" run to Western LEYTE. On 2 Nov, two large merchant vessels, two light cruisers, three destroyers and seven landing barges were observed in North ORMOC BAY.

On 27 Oct, Lightnings and Thunderbolts sweeping the VISAYAS for enemy warships, set on fire a probable destroyer, heavily camouflaged, anchored off CEBU town. On the same day, ten 300/1,000 ton stack-aft vessels were sighted in TANON STRAIT (between NEGROS and CEBU ISLANDS), and five vessels, two of which were of 7,000 tons, were sighted 15 miles SSW of CEBU, on a Northerly course. On 1 Nov, nine midget submarines were reported at CEBU.

During the night 23/24 Oct, PT boats operated along the West coast of LEYTE ISLAND, sinking seven barges, three of which were troop laden, one 100 foot barge laden with machinery, and one lugger. In addition, two 150/300 ton vessels were badly damaged. On the morning of 26 Oct, an Allied warship sighted a periscope near Allied carriers in the LEYTE area. Attacks brought much oil and debris to the surface during the day, and the submarine was believed destroyed.

STRENGTHS AND DISPOSITIONS OF ENEMY FORCES

(a) LAND—Revised estimates of enemy strengths in the SWPA as at 1 Nov 44 are as follows:-

NW SECTOR	ESTIMATED STRENGTHS		REMARKS
PHILIPPINES LUZON			1. Changes LUZON due to re-assessment.
NORTHERN CENTRAL	47,000		
BATANGAS	51,200		2. Decrease LEYTE area due to deduction of casualties, attrition and some evacuation.
	47,000		
BICOL PENINSULA	15,000		
			3. Major formations in the PHILIPPINES include -
MINDORO	1,000	161,200	
CENTRAL			HQ Southern Army
			14 Area Army
PALAWAN	4,000		HQ 35 Army
PANAY	7,200		16 Division
NEGROS	12,500		26 Division
BOHOL-CEBU	15,200		30 Division
LEYTE-SMARMASBATE	13,000		100 Division
			102 Division
		51,900	103 Division
			105 Division
MINDANAO			An unidentified
NORTHERN	11,500		Independent Mixed
SOUTHERN	41,900		Brigade is believed to be
ZAMBOANGASULU			present in the
ARCHIPELAGO (incl.			ZAMBOANGA
TAWI TAWI)	7,500	60,900	PENINSULA.
TOTAL PHILIPPINES	274,000		
TIMOR		26,000	Increase due to re-assessment.
NORTH COAST DUTCH NEW GUINEA			
VOGELKOP (including MANOKWARI and SORONG)		11,000	Decrease due to attrition.
NE SECTOR			
EAST OF AITAPE		27,000	Decrease due to attrition.
	TOTAL NW SECTOR	464,400	
	TOTAL NE SECTOR	97,000	
		561,400	

NOTE: Strength estimates will in future be issued every ten days.

APPENDIX 1   363

(c) AIR - ENEMY LAND BASED AIRCRAFT STRENGTH:

Estimate of Enemy Land Based air strength in the areas listed below on information to 1700K/3 Nov 44.

AREAS	F	2E/F	SE/B	2E/B	F/B	F/P	Obsn	Total 3 Nov	Comparative 27 Oct	Totals 18 Oct
NEW BRITAIN NEW IRELAND SOLOMONS						10	2	12	12	12
PHILIPPINES:										
MINDANAO	6		6	3	2	6	7	30	26	61
VISAYAS	56	8	14	30	2	14	9	131	95	107
LUZON	128	29	80	95	2	13	6	353	156	281
								514	277	449
AMBON	4		3		2	9	4	22	26	26
CELEBES:										
MANADO AREA	4		2			6		12	12	19
KENDARI-MAKASSAR	20	8		6	3	12	4	53	65	79
								65	77	98
TIMOR-SOEMBA-SOEMBAWA-FLORES	10					3	3	16	16	16
JAVA-BALI-LOMBOK	4			12		15	5	36	36	36
BORNEO	68	18	18	48		12		164	188	172
	300	63	123	11		100	40	831	632	809

[The next fifteen pages, through to the end of the document, have been deleted. They cover energy organisation and equipment, extracts from captured documents, Japanese 'suicide' tactics, Japanese atrocities, Malaya under the Japanese, Chinese army organisation, and headquarters security in operation areas.]

Appendix 2

Department of Information Background Service

Department of Information

Background Service—New Series No 259 (6/11/44)

Greece: M. Papandreou proposes to form a Greek National Army by calling up the 1915 class which is to become a National Guard to replace the old Gendarmerie. This National Guard will take over from the R. A. M. Police organisation, which will then be declared illegal. All Greek guerilla forces will be disbanded on December 1 and shortly afterwards formal age groups will be called up for the National Army.

The British Ambassador, giving his preliminary impression of the internal situation, considers that the Communist influence is limited in Athens and the Piraeus, and that there is little evidence of fanaticism. Within the Government the Communist section is loyal and co-operative, and this policy has been strengthened by the correct attitude of Russia. The Soviet Government has made it clear that it does not intend to play an independent part in Greek affairs. Outside Athens, however, E.L.A.S. appears to be beyond the control either of M. Papandreou or E.A.M. In Athens itself no political party is at present prepared to dispute the authority of M. Papandreou.

Japan: Following the U.S. landings in the Philippines a special meeting of Japanese elder statesmen was held. Some significance is thought to attach to the absence of Baron Hiranuma, who is known to be anti-German and whose attempted assassination in 1941 was believed to be the work of a pro-German clique. It is also reported that Prince Konoye, who is closely associated with Baron Hiranuma, has declined the presidency of the House of Peers.

Spain: General Franco is reported to have determined to adopt a cautious attitude in regard to the pursuit of the Spanish Maquis across the French frontier.

Germany: While there is no confirmation of the Swedish report that Nazi leaders have decided that Hitler shall withdraw to Obersalzburg and will not appear publicly in future, it is thought that November 9, the anniversary of the Munich Putsch of 1923, should provide a good test. So far Hitler has never failed to make a speech on this occasion.

The following is to be given verbally to editors only: -

Philippines: All plans for the use of Australian troops in the Philippines have been scrapped. It now depends on the present operations on Leyte whether Australian troops will be used. Reconnaissance planes have confirmed earlier reports on the landings of heavy reinforcements in the Luzon sector.

China Coast: Several enemy convoys have been seen in the Saigon area. Troop transports have been pouring in reinforcements into Saigon and adjacent areas.

New Britain: Latest estimate of Japanese strength in the Rabaul area is 45,000. There will be no large-scale Australian operations in New Britain before December.

Solomons: Japanese strength on Bougainville is estimated at 13,000. Australian troops will commence operations there some time in December.

New Guinea: The Aitape–Wewak area contains 28,000 Japanese, according to latest reports. The Australian 6th Division is in movement into Aitape now. No large-scale operations are contemplated, but active patrolling will commence in about five weeks. The natives there are fifty per cent friendly. Australian and New Guinea Administrative Unit men are making contact and converting numbers to the Allied cause.

[The final edition of this circular has not been located but a teleprinter message (on which the above copy is based) is in AWM 123, item 752.]

Appendix 3

Security in the Western Mediterranean and the Eastern Atlantic: Report of post-hostilities planning staff, 19 May 1945

THIS DOCUMENT IS THE PROPERTY OF HIS BRITANNIC MAJESTY'S GOVERNMENT

Printed for the War Cabinet, May 1945

The Circulation of this paper has been strictly limited. It is issued for the personal use of ....

TOP SECRET Copy No.
P.H.P. (45) 6 (O) (Final.)
19th May 1945

WAR CABINET.

Post-Hostilities Planning Staff.

SECURITY IN THE WESTERN MEDITERRANEAN AND THE EASTERN ATLANTIC.

REPORT BY THE POST-HOSTILITIES PLANNING STAFF.

Introduction.

    1. As instructed,* we have revised our regional study of British Post-War Strategic Requirements in the Western Mediterranean and North-Eastern Atlantic+ in the light of the Joint Planning Staff's paper on the miliary aspects of our future relations with Spain.#

    2. Since our earlier study was written, we have submitted a regional study on Western Europe and the North Atlantic.$ The present paper has been prepared against the background of the latter and is, in effect, a supplement to it.

---

*   C.O.S. (44) 401st Meeting (O) item 2.
\+   C.O.S. (44) 483 (O) P.H.P.
\#   J.P. (44) 288
$ P.H.P. (44) 27 (O)

Object.

3. The object of this paper is to determine the long-term policy required to safeguard British strategic interests in the Western Mediterranean and the Eastern Atlantic. It relates to the situation that may be expected to exist in the period 1955–60 and is one of a series of regional studies intended to lead to a world-wide survey of the measures to safeguard the interests of the British Commonwealth and Empire.

Definition of Area.

4. The area under consideration is bounded on the east by the Sicilian Narrows, on the west by the Azores, and includes North-West Africa as far south as Dakar. (See map attached.)

Strategic Interests.

5. Our broad strategic aims in this are:-
(a) **Control of the vital sea communications in the Eastern Atlantic in order to:**
  (i) Protect the routes between the United Kingdom and West Africa and the South Atlantic, which are vital]] to the British Commonwealth and its European Allies.
  (ii) Enable an economic blockade on enemy-held territory in Europe to be imposed.
(b) **Control of sea communications in the Straits of Gibraltar and the Western Mediterranean in order to:-**
  (i) Prevent the use of the Straits of Gibraltar by enemy shipping, or by enemy forces from the Mediterranean which might attack our Atlantic communications.
  (ii) Protect our own shipping route through the Mediterranean. Although less important* than the Atlantic route, its loss might well prejudice our position in the Middle East and would certainly increase the strain on our shipping resources (particularly tankers), and thus impose a limitation on our war effort generally.
(c) **Maintenance of air transport routes to the Middle East, India, Australasia, and to West and South Africa, which are essential both in peace and war for:-**
  (i) Reinforcement of all types of aircraft by air.
  (ii) Movement by air of troops and supplies.

6. An additional factor which must be taken into consideration is that Gibraltar is an important focal point in the Imperial Cable system, in particular in the main cable route to India and the Far East.

The Threats.

7. In our study on Western Europe and the North Atlantic[+] we concluded that the only major threats to our interests would arise from a hostile U.S.S.R. and/or a rearmed Germany.

8. An enemy in Central Europe might:-
(a) attempt to occupy France and the Iberian Peninsula in order to obtain additional bases from which to attack the United Kingdom and our Atlantic Communications.
(b) Attempt to cut our Mediterranean communications either at the Sicilian Narrows, or at the Straits of Gibraltar.
(c) Attempt to gain access to the North-West African Coast and thereby add

---
]]   C.O.S. (45) 30 (O)
*   C.O.S. (45) 30 (O)
+   P.H.P. (44) 27 (O)

a further threat to our Atlantic communications and our bases in West Africa.

Need for Allies.

9. *France.*—French interests in maintaining control of the Western Mediterranean and in the defence of North Africa are as great as our own. It has already been accepted# that close co-operation with a friendly France is essential. We therefore assume throughout this study that she will co-operate with us fully in the measures required to ensure the security of this area.

10. *The U.S.A.*—The Staff Study+ on Security in Western Europe and the North Atlantic led to the conclusion that it is vital to us that the help of the United States should be forthcoming with the minimum delay in the event of a major threat to our interests in Western Europe. In view of the strategic importance which the United States attaches to the West African coast in relation to the defence both of the American Continents and of their Atlantic communications, the interests of the United States in the area under consideration are growing. Consequently it should not be difficult to obtain their co-operation in a common policy for the defence of North-West Africa.

11. *Portugal.*—Bases in the Azores would certainly be required for the protection of our Atlantic sea routes if an enemy were again to overrun Western Europe. Our long-standing alliance with Portugal should therefore be maintained. If, however, Spain were occupied by an enemy, Portugal would be unable to put up an effective resistance and it is most unlikely that we should be able to assist her on land.

Attitude of Spain.

12. *Friendly or Neutral.*—So long as Spain is friendly or effectively neutral, there will be no threat from bases in the Iberian Peninsula to our vital Atlantic communications, and the air threat to Gibraltar and the Straits will be limited to long-range attack.

13. A high degree of security against air attacks on Gibraltar or on our shipping passing through the Straits would, however, depend on radar facilities and airfields in Spanish Morocco. Under a multilateral regional agreement for the defence of the Straits, it might, with Spanish goodwill, be possible to arrange for such facilities to be available to us in war, even in Spain were nominally neutral. We could not afford, however, to insist on obtaining these facilities at the risk of incurring the enmity of Spain.

14. With Spain friendly or neutral, the denial of the Straits to enemy shipping should present no difficulty.

15. *In hostile hands or hostile.*—Although in the future, as in the past, Spain would probably be reluctant to go to war against us, a European aggressor who had already overrun France, might compel Spain to join forces with her. Unless we or our Allies could furnish powerful support, involving a major campaign in the Iberian Peninsula, it is unlikely that Spain would be able to resist effectively.

16. With Spain and probably Portugal overrun, the threat to our vital Atlantic communications would be extremely serious, and the passage of the Straits by our own shipping would be very difficult.

17. In such circumstances, it would be essential for us to obtain control of Spanish Morocco. Then, we could at least hope:—
   (a)   to prevent the development of the maximum threat to our vital Atlantic communications which would arise if the enemy obtained bases on the Atlantic coast of Africa.

\#   C.O.S. (45) 485 (O) P.H.P. and C.O.S. (44) 388 (0)
\+   P.H.P. (44) 27 (O)

(b)   to make it very difficult for enemy shipping to use the Straits of Gibraltar.

18. If the Spaniards were in fact friendly, Spain having been overrun against their will, it would be much easier for us to obtain our requirements in Spanish Morocco, and we might obtain the co-operation of Spanish forces in the defence of North Africa. In addition, Spanish goodwill would facilitate our occupation of the Spanish Atlantic islands and Rio de Oro.

19. Thus a friendly Spain is essential to the satisfaction of our strategic requirements in the Eastern Atlantic and Western Mediterranean.

Attitude of Italy.

20. It is doubtful whether Italy will ever be able to defend herself from attack by a major Power[*]; and, owing to her geographical position, she might constitute a serious threat to our interests in the Mediterranean. We should therefore renew our friendship with Italy and it would be greatly to our advantage that she should look to Western Europe and not to the U.S.S.R. for support.

21. If, however, Italy were to enter the war against us or were overrun, it would be highly desirable that we or our Allies should occupy Sicily and Sardinia in order to deny them to the enemy. Failure to do so would lead to a serious threat to our control of the Sicilian Narrows, and North Africa and Malta would be in danger of invasion. Under these circumstances, if the Peace Settlement had allowed Italy to retain some measure of control over Tripolitania, we and France might be faced with an additional commitment to occupy this territory.

Gibraltar.

22. The vulnerability of Gibraltar has been greatly increased by the improved range and technique of air attack. The fortress and port suffer from the following serious limitations:-
   (a)   Adequate air defence, based on Gibraltar alone, is impossible.
   (b)   The existing airfield is quite inadequate to fulfil the many air requirements; it is capable of but little expansion.
   (c)   The harbour, airfield and commercial anchorage are entirely overlooked from Spain, and the anchorage is difficult to defend.

23. Gibraltar will, however, be of great strategic value with Spain friendly or neutral. Even with Spain in hostile hands or hostile, Gibraltar would have some value.

Detailed Considerations.

24. We consider at Annex, in greater detail, the threats which might develop and the measures required to meet them, taking into account the possibilities that Spain and/or Italy might be for us or against us in varying degree; and we discuss the effect of a World Organisation upon our strategic requirements.

CONCLUSIONS.

25. Our main conclusions are:-
(a)   A friendly or neutral Spain is essential to the security of our vital Atlantic communications.
    Since the free use of the Straits and the security of the Western Mediterranean are of lesser importance, we should not insist on obtaining facilities for their protection if such action would incur the hostility of Spain.
(b)   If Spain is in hostile hands or hostile, we must ensure that the Eastern Atlantic Islands and the mainland of Africa are denied to the enemy.
(c)   It is essential for the security of our Mediterranean communications

---

[*]   P.H.P. (54) 10 (O), Annex 1.

that no hostile Power should be established in Sicily and Sardinia. We should, therefore, renew our friendship with Italy.

(d) A strong and friendly France is of paramount importance. With Spain or Italy in hostile hands or hostile, our whole position in the area would depend on facilities which only France can give us.

(e) The cooperation of the United States in the defence of the Atlantic sea and air communications, and of North and West Africa, must be assured.

(f) Bases in the Azores would be essential to us in war. The maintenance of our present alliance with Portugal should achieve this object.

(g) A successful World Organisation might facilitate the establishment of regional arrangements for the security of the Straits area. Under such arrangements, we would hope to obtain the facilities which we require in Spanish Morocco, the Tangier Zone and the eastern Atlantic islands.

(h) Gibraltar should be retained as a strongly fortified naval and air base, since, as long as Spain is friendly or neutral, it is likely to continue to be of considerable value to us. If Spain were in hostile hands or hostile, Gibraltar would be useless as a base. But, so long as it could hold out as a fortress, it could at least prevent free use of the Straits by enemy vessels.

26. Our further conclusions are:-
(a) The adequate defence of the Straits of Gibraltar area from air attack demands:-
  (i) The extension of the air defence belt covering Western Europe through the Western Mediterranean to French North Africa.
  (ii) *In war*, the use of radar facilities in Spanish Morocco, the Tangier Zone and French Morocco.
  (iii) *In war*, the use of airfields in Spanish Morocco and, possibly, in the Tangier Zone, as well as those in French Morocco.
(b) The French should be encouraged to develop Atlantic port facilities in French Morocco and West Africa, and land routes from these ports to the Mediterranean coast.
(c) We should continue to develop the Takoradi air route across Central Africa, which is strategically secure.
(d) Malta should be retained as an operational naval and air base for the control of the Sicilian Narrows. With Italy and Sicily in hostile hands, it would be required as an advanced base for aircraft, light naval craft and submarines. Its defences and protected accommodation should be developed to enable it to withstand all forms of attack.
(e) Air staging posts in the Azores, French Morocco and Tripolitania will be required in war as alternatives to Gibraltar and Malta.

Recommendation.

27. This paper replaces C.O.S. (44) 483 (O) P.H.P. and we, therefore, recommend that a copy be made available to the Foreign Office so that a summary may be forwarded, on the same conditions as before,* to His Majesty's Ambassadors in Madrid and Paris and to His Majesty's Consul-General in Tangier.

(Signed)

C. C. A. ALLEN.
F. C. CURTIS.
P. WARBURTON.

1, Richmond Terrace, S.W.1,
19th May, 1945

---

* C.O.S. (44) 477 (O) and C.O.S. (44) 179th Meeting (O) item 4.

ANNEX.

THE THREAT TO BRITISH STRATEGIC INTERESTS, AND THE MEASURES TO MEET THEM.

1. We consider below the threats to British strategic interests in the Western Mediterranean and the Eastern Mediterranean and the measures to meet them, under the following headings:-

A.–France friendly; Spain and Italy friendly or neutral.[*]

B.–France overrun; Spain and Italy friendly or neutral.[*]

C.–Spain in hostile hands or hostile.

D.–Italy in hostile hands or hostile.

A.–France Friendly, Spain and Italy Friendly or Neutral.[*]

Threat.

2. In these circumstances the threat, on the outbreak of war, to the area under consideration would be limited to air attack from Central European bases and to submarine, and possibly surface raider, attack on our sea communications. The scale of the threat would be dependent on relative forces available and cannot be assessed.

Defence of Atlantic Shipping.

3. The protection of our North Atlantic communications has already been dealt with in a previous study.[+] We shall require:-
   (a) A system of naval and air bases in Northern Europe and the Eastern Atlantic Islands, including the Azores.
   (b) An air defence belt across Western Europe.

Defence of Straits of Gibraltar and Western Mediterranean Sea Routes.

4. The extension of the air defence belt, either through Corsica, Sardinia and Sicily to Tunisia, or through the Balearics to Algeria, would greatly increase the security of Gibraltar and our sea routes in the Western Mediterranean.

5. *Straits of Gibraltar.*-With Spain friendly or neutral, we shall require fighter airfields and radar facilities in the vicinity of Gibraltar for the defence both of the base and of our shipping in the Straits. Ideally these should be situated in Spain, the Tangier Zone and Spanish Morocco. It is, however, unlikely for political reasons that we shall be able to obtain such facilities on the Spanish mainland unless Spain were an active ally in war.

6. For the defence of Gibraltar itself, airfields in either Spanish Morocco *or* the Tangier Zone would suffice[#], provided radar facilities were available in *both* these territories.

For the defence of our shipping in the Straits, a considerable measure of protection could be provided by the use of airfields in French Morocco, and of carrier-borne aircraft, provided radar cover from Spanish Morocco were available.[$] In order to provide a high degree of security for our shipping against a heavy scale of attack, fighter airfields would be required in Spanish Morocco and, possibly in the Tangier Zone, while radar facilities should be available in both these territories.

---

[*] By 'neutral', we mean a country which is genuinely neutral and does not afford favours or facilities to either side.
[+] P.H.P. (44) 27 (O), Annex.
[#] C.O.S. (45) 30 (O).
[$] Future developments of radar technique may eventually make such use of Spanish territory unnecessary, but we cannot count on this at present.

7. We, therefore, reaffirm our view* that we should endeavour, in co-operation with the United States and France, to obtain agreement to the establishment of radar installations and the development and use of airfields in the Tangier Zone.

8. *Western Mediterranean Sea Routes.*-Facilities available to us for the defence of our sea communications in the Western Mediterranean should be adequate since, in addition to our bases at Malta and Gibraltar, French airfields and naval bases on the North African coast would be available.

The requirements of our maritime air forces would be beyond the capacity of Gibraltar; the overflow would best be located in French Morocco and Algeria.

Security of Air Routes.

9. It is probable that Gibraltar alone would be inadequate as a main air staging post. It will be necessary to obtain from the French the use of airfields in French Morocco (*e.g.*, Port Lyautey and Ras el Ma, which have been available to us in the present war).

10. Malta would probably be available as a main air staging post. Should the scale of enemy attack restrict its use for this purpose, it would be essential that an airfield in Tunisia or Tripolitania (*e.g.*, Castel Benito) should be available to us.

B.–France Overrun, Spain and Italy Friendly or Neutral.

Threat.

11. If France were in hostile hands, the threat to our strategic interests, both in the Atlantic and the Western Mediterranean, would be increased as it was in this war when the French Atlantic ports were in enemy hands.

French North Africa.

12. It would greatly strengthen our position if the French continued to resist from their overseas possessions, and particularly from those in North Africa.

The use of air and naval bases in Algeria and Tunisia would probably prove essential to us in order to provide a high degree of security for our shipping in the Western Mediterranean against the increased threat resulting from enemy occupation of Southern France and, possibly, of Corsica.

Role of Gibraltar.

13. Since the threat from enemy forces operating from the French Atlantic coast would involve the routeing of our Atlantic shipping and aircraft well to the westward, Gibraltar would be too far from the main north-south Atlantic shipping lane to act as a convenient base for naval forces engaged in its protection. It would, however, be required as a naval operational base for the control of the Straits and the Western Mediterranean.

Portugal and the Azores.

14. Naval and air bases in the Azores would need substantial development before they would suffice both for the protection of our Atlantic shipping and as a staging post on our air reinforcement routes. It might also be desirable to acquire use of air and naval facilities in Portugal.

C.–France Overrun, Spain in Hostile Hands or Hostile.

Threat.

15. If Spain were in hostile hands or hostile, our vital sea and air routes in the Atlantic would be seriously threatened. They would be further endangered if Portugal also were occupied by the enemy.

---

*   C.O.S. (45) 30 (O).

16. If Spain were invaded, the retention by the Allies of a bridgehead on the Spanish mainland would contribute very materially to the security of Gibraltar and of our shipping in the Straits. However, the prospects of finding the forces necessary to hold an area sufficiently large to be of any military value are small.* We have, therefore, assumed that no attempt would be made to adopt such a course.

17. With the Spanish mainland and probably Portugal in enemy hands, the strategic importance of North-West Africa would be at its greatest. It would be essential to secure Spanish Morocco and, if Spain were actively hostile, this would be likely to entail a major operation. In addition, it would be necessary to deny the Rio de Oro and the Spanish Atlantic islands to the enemy; the capture and occupation of these would involve a further commitment for our forces.

If the Spaniards were in fact friendly, Spain having been overrun against their will, it would be much easier to obtain our requirements in Spanish Morocco, and we might obtain the co-operation of Spanish forces in the defence of North Africa and the Atlantic Islands.

In the following paragraphs we assume that, with or without Spanish assistance, Spanish Morocco has been denied to the enemy and we are in control of that territory.

Defence of Atlantic Shipping

18. The defence of our vital Atlantic communications against attack from enemy forces based on the Iberian Peninsula would be a more difficult problem than that which arose in the present war with French Atlantic ports in enemy hands. The protection of the sea routes, which would have to run far to the westward, would certainly require the use of bases in the Azores, and it would be necessary to occupy the other Atlantic islands, and to deny the West African Coast to the enemy.

Security of Air Routes.

19. Since Gibraltar would no longer be available as an air staging post in this area, we should have to rely on airfields in Spanish and French Morocco. Should we fail to maintain air superiority, the scale of enemy attack might force us to use airfields further south than Port Lyautey.

20. With the enemy in Spain and Portugal, it would be necessary to route our aircraft further to the west, and airfields in the Azores would be essential to meet our additional requirement of an intermediate air staging post between the United Kingdom and French Morocco.

Defence of Gibraltar and of our shipping in the Straits area.

21. With Spain hostile, or in hostile hands, the scale of attack against Gibraltar, whether by land bombardment or from Spanish airfields, could undoubtedly be such as to make Gibraltar inoperable as a naval and air base.

It has been agreed+ that the use of the Straits by our shipping would be governed by the measure of air and artillery bombardment and of attack by light craft to which it could be subjected. Possession of airfields in the Tangier Zone and Spanish Morocco would probably be insufficient to enable us to maintain air control over Gibraltar and the Straits. With Spain in enemy hands, the use of the Straits by our shipping would therefore be very difficult.

---

*   During the present war it was estimated that, even if Spain were friendly, some ten divisions would be required to hold a perimeter on the general line Malaga, Seville, Huelva, and that the maintenance of such a force through the available ports would have been difficult. J.P. (43) 122.

+   C.O.S. (45) 30 (O).

Denial of the Straits to the enemy.

22. It would still be important to deny the Straits, and, as far as possible, the Western Mediterranean, to the enemy in order:-
   (a) To protect our Atlantic shipping routes from attack from within the Mediterranean.
   (b) To render the invasion of North-West Africa more difficult.

23. Provided we remained in occupation of the southern shore of the Straits, we should be in a position to impose the maximum restriction upon enemy shipping attempting to use them. In any case, air forces based on French Morocco and Algeria, and naval forces based on Casablanca and Oran, would be able to exercise a considerable measure of control over the approaches to the Straits.

24. So long as Gibraltar remained in our hands as a fortress, its guns could prevent free use of the Straits by enemy surface vessels.* It is, therefore, desirable that it should be capable of withstanding a long siege.

Defence of North-West Africa.

25. With Spain in hostile hands, an attempt by the enemy to cross the Straits and establish himself in Spanish Morocco might be expected. If such an attempt were successful, not only would Casablanca, Dakar and our West African Colonies be endangered, but the threat of our vital Atlantic communications would be greatly increased. Hence the defence of the coast of North-West Africa is essential to prevent such a crossing.

26. So long as we could prevent an enemy from establishing air supremacy over the Straits and their approaches, the invasion of North-West Africa would be very difficult, if not impossible.

In order to defend North-West Africa and to prevent an enemy from gaining air supremacy in the area of the Straits, it would be necessary to secure Spanish Morocco and to develop a considerable air effort from airfields in North-West Africa. Even with the assistance of Spanish forces in Spanish Morocco, a heavy commitment would be entailed in denying North-West Africa to an enemy.

27. Forces defending North-West Africa would have to be maintained chiefly through French Moroccan ports on the Atlantic. The resources of Casablanca are likely to be severely taxed if it were used both as a supply base for such forces and as an operational base for naval forces controlling the Straits. In these circumstances, it would be to our advantage if we could make use of La Luz (Canaries) as a naval base, in addition to Casablanca, particularly for the use of escorts on the shipping routes to French Morocco. Madeira, although geographically well placed for this purpose, has practically no naval facilities.

There would be a substantial naval and air commitment for the defence of the sea routes to these ports and of the air bases in North-West Africa.

Use of Overland Communications in Africa.

28. With Gibraltar inoperable as a base and the use of the Straits virtually denied to us, it would be necessary to have the use of land and air routes between the Atlantic and the Mediterranean to maintain forces in Algeria, Tunisia and French and Spanish Morocco for the defence of the North African coast.

29. We should encourage the French to develop their railways:-
   (a) Casablanca-Rabat-Oran-Algiers-Tunis-Bizerta.
   (b) Dakar-Koulikouro-Colomb Bechar-Oran.

The latter would be the less vulnerable to air attack, but at present most of the trans-Saharan portion is unbuilt. The mountain sections on both routes would limit

---

* C.O.S. (45) 30 (O).

traffic unless supplemented by motor transport. Fair roads follow the alignment of each railway in these sections.

30. These projects would involve great labour and cost, but the Allied position in North Africa would essentially depend upon our ability to supply our troops there without using the sea route through the Straits. The above proposals are thus of great strategic importance as a reinsurance against the invasion of Southern Spain. Expansion of the ports of Dakar and Casablanca would be necessary and these would be expensive long-term projects. The U.S.A. might, however, be willing to continue to assist in the development of both the ports and the communications from them, as they have done during the present war.

31. In order to supplement the long sea route round the Cape, it would be possible to develop the Takoradi air route across Central Africa, which is strategically secure. As a land route it is not susceptible of major improvement.*

D.–Italy in Hostile Hands or Hostile.

Threat.

32. It is doubtful whether Italy will ever be in a position to defend herself from attack by a major Power,+ and, owing to her geographical position, she would directly influence the security of our interests in the Mediterranean.

33. If Spain and/or Southern France, in addition to Italy, were in enemy occupation, the threat to our security in the Western Mediterranean would be increased. If, in such circumstances, France failed to continue resistance in North Africa, or Spain were actively hostile, the situation would be more grave than at any time in this war. We assume in the following paragraphs that the French are resisting in North Africa.

Sicily and Sardinia.

34. Although it would be in our interests that the enemy's advance should be held as far north as possible, it is problematical whether Allied forces could be provided to assist Italy on the mainland.+

It would be essential to deny Sardinia and Sicily to the enemy in order to:-
    (a)   Defend the sea route through the Sicilian Narrows adequately.
    (b)   Counter the threat of invasion of North Africa.
    (c)   Defend British and Allied bases in Malta and Tunisia against air and airborne attack.

Defence of Malta and of our Sea Routes.

35. If Sardinia and Sicily, in addition to Italy, were under enemy control, the defence of shipping in the Central Mediterranean would demand the use of strong air forces and naval escorts based on North Africa and Malta.

It would be essential that our forces should have the use of bases and airfields in French North Africa, owing to the difficulty of providing adequately for the defence of Malta against an increased scale of air attack and owing to the congestion of its airfields. Malta would, however, still be required as an advanced base for aircraft, submarines, and light naval forces, for which protected accommodation would be necessary. The defences of Malta should therefore be designed so as to be capable of withstanding all forms of attack.

Use of Overland Communications in Africa.

36. It would probably be necessary to make use of overland communications

---
*   J.P. (44) 288.
+   P.H.P. (45) 10 (O), Annex I.

in Africa, since the hazards of passing personnel shipping through the Sicilian Narrows might be unacceptable.

Security of Air Routes.

37. It would probably be impossible to continue to use Malta as an air staging post, and it would then become essential for us to have the use of airfields on the North African Coast, such as Castel Benito.*

Defence of North Africa.

38. The security of the Allied position in North Africa, with Italy in hostile hands or hostile, would depend on factors very similar to those affecting our security in North-West Africa if Spain were in hostile hands or hostile.

If Italy had regained possession of Tripolitania as a result of the Peace Settlement, it would probably be necessary for the French and ourselves to occupy that territory.

39. In addition to the indirect support afforded to the French by our control of the Central Mediterranean, which constitutes the first line of defence against the invasion of North Africa, it might be necessary for us to give direct assistance to French land and air forces in the defence of Algeria and Tunisia.

The supply of such forces would be very difficult if the Straits of Gibraltar were closed to our shipping, and we should be dependent on the use of the land routes from the Atlantic and on air transport.

Effect of a World Organisation.

40. Although a World Organisation could not restrain a Great Power bent on aggression, it would, if successfully maintained, cement our Treaty with the U.S.S.R., and ensure the continued suppression of Germany. Moreover, a successful World Organisation might facilitate the establishment of regional arrangements for the security of this area. Under such arrangements, we should hope to obtain the facilities which we require in Spanish Morocco and the eastern Atlantic islands.

41. It appears that there is no practicable way for Great Britain alone to secure, in advance of an emergency, the agreement of Spain to the granting of the required facilities in Spanish Morocco in time of war.+ On the other hand, the Foreign Office consider that it might be possible to obtain them under a regional security system covering the area of the Straits.

From a military point of view, there would be little objection to such a solution, provided our exclusive control of Gibraltar were not compromised. It would be very desirable that, in addition to Great Britain, Spain and France, the U.S.A. and Portugal should participate in any such system.+

---

*   P.H.P. (44) 10 (O), Annex.
\+   C.O.S. (45) 30 (O).

Notes

Preface

1 D. M. Horner, 'Special Intelligence in the South-West Pacific Area in World War II', *Australian Outlook*, December 1978, vol. 32, no. 3, p. 325.
2 Whitlam and Stubbs, *Nest of Traitors*, pp. 164, 167.
3 Ward, *Australia Since the Coming of Man*, p. 201.
4 Frank Cain, 'Limited Intelligence Gives Scholar a Bad Name', *Weekend Australian*, 6–7 July 1991, Review p. 4.
5 Frank Cain, 'Thin Evidence Brands the Spy Who Never Was', *Weekend Australian*, 20–21 July 1991, p. 24.
6 Frank Cain, 'The Right to Know: ASIO, Historians and the Australian Parliament', *Intelligence and National Security*, vol. 1, January 1993, p. 90.
7 Gregory Pemberton, 'A Suspect Spy', *Sydney Morning Herald*, 6 July 1991, p. 42.
8 McMullin, *The Light on the Hill*, p. 250.
9 See Klehr, Haynes, and Firsov, *The Secret World of American Communism*.
10 Maurice Isserman, 'Notes From Underground', *The Nation*, 12 June 1995, pp. 846–56.
11 ibid, p. 856.
12 See Manne, *The Petrov Affair*, especially ch. 12.
13 See Lamphere and Shachtman, *The FBI-KGB War*, especially ch. 6.
14 See Wright, *Spycatcher*, pp. 179–8, 195–7, 283–6, 370–5.
15 Christopher Andrew, 'The Growth of the Australian Intelligence Community and the Anglo-American Connection', *Intelligence and National Security*, vol. 4, no. 2, April 1989, especially pp. 223–8.
16 Desmond Ball, 'The Spies and the Spied Upon', *Sydney Morning Herald*, 4 June 1994, Spectrum p. 11A.
17 Norman Abjorensen, 'Origin of Petrov's Contacts Queried by Expert', *Canberra Times*, 6 October 1996, p. 3.
18 Norman Abjorensen, 'Experts Debate Historical Import of "Petrov Affair"', *Canberra Times*, 13 October 1996, p. 2.

Chapter 1 Sigint and counter-espionage

1. Blamey to Acting Minister for the Army, 6 January 1945, Australian War Memorial (AWM): Blamey Papers, 3 DRL 6643, item 2/59.
2. US National Security Council Intelligence Directive no. 6, 'Signals Intelligence', 17 February 1972, sanitised version published in *Declassified Documents Reference System* (DDRS), 1976–168A.
3. Winterbotham, *The Ultra Secret*.
4. For a bibliography see Davies, *The British Secret Service*.
5. See Andrew and Dilks, *The Missing Dimension*, p. 1.
6. See, for example, John Ferris, 'Before "Room 40": The British Empire & Signals Intelligence, 1898–1914', *The Journal of Strategic Studies*, vol. 12, no. 4, December 1989, pp. 431–57.
7. David Kahn, 'Codebreaking in World Wars I and II: The Major Successes and Failures, Their Causes and Their Effects', in Andrew and Dilks, *The Missing Dimension*, p. 140.
8. Cave Brown, 'C', p. 671.
9. Christopher Andrew and David Dilks, 'Introduction', in Andrew and Dilks, *The Missing Dimension*, pp. 1–2; F. H. Hinsley, 'Introduction: The Influence of Ultra on the Second World War', in Hinsley and Stripp, *Codebreakers*, pp.11–3; and Cave Brown, 'C', pp. 671–2.
10. Hinsley, 'Introduction', in Hinsley and Stripp, *Codebreakers*, pp. 3–5.
11. ibid, p. 6.
12. ibid, p. 7.
13. For example see Layton, *"And I Was There"*.
14. For the best account see Drea, *MacArthur's ULTRA*.
15. Blair, *Silent Victory*.
16. Lee, *Marching Orders*; Boyd, *Hitler's Japanese Confidant*.
17. Cave Brown, *Bodyguard of Lies*, ch. 2.
18. Freyberg, *Bernard Freyberg*, pp. 285–8.
19. Hinsley, *British Intelligence in the Second World War, Volume Two*, p. 424; Lewin, *Ultra Goes to War*; p. 173.
20. Holmes, *Double-Edged Secrets*, pp. 128, 214.
21. Hinsley, *British Intelligence in the Second World War, Volume One*.
22. Benson and Warner, *Venona*, p. xxiv; and Meredith Gardner, interview with I. Livingstone, 7 October 1996.
23. 'Cracking a Soviet Cipher', *Newsweek*, 19 May 1980, p. 4; and Martin, *Wilderness of Mirrors*, pp. 41–53.
24. Lamphere, *The FBI-KGB War*.
25. Cited in Cockerill, *Sir Percy Sillitoe*, p. 185.
26. Volkman, *Spies*.
27. ibid, pp. 117–8; and Deacon, *Spy!*, p. 40.
28. See Foote, *Handbook For Spies*, pp. 120–30; Read and Fisher, *Operation Lucy*, pp. 175–8, 187–9; and West, *The Illegals*, p. 92.
29. See Hohne, *Codeword Direktor*, pp. 3–5, 93–107.
30. Masterman, *The Double-Cross System*.

Chapter 2 The formation of Australia's Security Service

1. Knightley, *The Second Oldest Profession*, p. 27. See also Andrew, *Secret Service*, ch. 2.
2. Coulthard-Clark, *A Heritage of Spirit*, p. 43.
3. For a description see Coulthard-Clark, *The Citizen General Staff*.
4. Jacqueline Templeton, 'Australian Intelligence/Security Services, 1900–1950', *Seventh Report of the Royal Commission on Intelligence and Security*, p. 33, CRS A8908/1, vol. 1, p. 19.

5 ibid, p. 43.
6 Scott, *Australia During the War*, p. 144.
7 The only exception, with respect to operational planning, was the small expedition to capture German New Guinea in August–September 1914.
8 Cain, *The Origins of Political Surveillance in Australia*.
9 D. M. Horner, 'Australian Estimates of the Japanese Threat', in Towle, *Estimating Foreign Military Power*, p. 142.
10 R. D. Walton, 'Feeling for the Jugular: Japanese Espionage at Newcastle 1919–1926', *Australian Journal of Politics and History*, vol. 32, no. 1, 1986.
11 Templeton, 'Australian Intelligence/Services, 1900–1950', p. 127.
12 Jones to Secretary, Attorney-General's Department, 7 March 1942, CRS A432/15, item 55/4432.
13 DMO&I memo S688, 10 August 1934, AWM 49, item 73.
14 'Eastern Command, History of Intelligence Activities, Sep 39 to Sep 45', p. 10, DMI file 123.19.
15 Cain, *The Origins of Political Surveillance in Australia*, p. 225.
16 Winter, *The Intrigue Master*, ch. 4.
17 Templeton, 'Australian Intelligence/Security Services, 1900–1950', p. 169.
18 Report of Interdepartmental Committee National Intelligence, CRS A1981/1321/1, folder 1.
19 Scott to Hughes, 29 June 1939; Jones to Hughes, 8 August 1939; Attorney-General's Department minute dated 16 August 1939, Hughes Papers, NLA: MS 1538, series 43, sub-series 3, folder 1, 1939.
20 For his biography see Winter, *The Intrigue Master*.
21 Chief of the Air Staff to Chief of the General Staff, 26 July 1940, CRS A1196/6, item 36/501/105.
22 Winter, *The Intrigue Master*, p. 44.
23 'Conference to Consider the Activities of the Communist Party', 23 January 1940, Hughes Papers, NLA: MS 1538, series 43, sub-series 3, folder 1, 1939. See also 'Significant Events in the History of Internal Security Intelligence Organisations in Australia up to the Formation of ASIO on 16 March 1949'. Typescript, by R. A. Swan, in ASIO records—hereafter Swan typescript.
24 Secretary of the Department of the Navy to the Secretaries of the Departments of the Army and Air, 2 February 1940, CRS A1196/6, item 36/501/105.
25 Meeting of the Inter-Service Committee to Consider the Formation of a Defence Security Organisation—Victoria Barracks, 19th February to the 6th March 1940, CRS A1196/6, item 36/501/105; Minute by Defence Committee at Meeting Held on Tuesday 7th May 1940, CRS A1981/132/1, folder 1; War Cabinet Minute 306, 5 June 1940, and Directors of Service Intelligence to Chiefs of Staff, in CRS A1196/6, item 36/501/105.
26 Directors of Intelligence to Chiefs of Staff, 8 July 1940, and War Cabinet Agendum 148/1940, 25 June 1940, CRS A1196/6, item 36/501/105; War Cabinet Minutes 369 of 26 June 1940, and 424 of 16 July 1940, CRS A2673.
27 War Cabinet Agendum 115/1940, 27 December 1940, CRS A1981/132/1, folder 1. See also MP 729/6, item 15/403/29.
28 Lt-Col J. C. Mawhood to Solicitor-General, 18 October 1941, CRS A432/15, item 55/4432.
29 War Cabinet Minutes 822 of 18 February 1941 and 880 of 5 March 1941, CRS A1981/132/1, folder 1.
30 Mrs B. Cohen to D. M. Horner, 26 April 1993.
31 'Eastern Command History of Intelligence Activities, Sep 39 to Sep 35', p. 10, DMI file 123.
32 Mrs Cohen to Horner, 26 April 1993.
33 Knowles to Attorney-General, 9 March 1942, MP 729/6, item 15/403/76.
34 For an outline of the Mawhood affair see Shirley Lithgow, 'The Strange Case of Lieutenant Colonel Mawhood', a paper presented to the Australian War Memorial Conference, 14 February 1986.
35 Mawhood to Knowles, 18 October 1941, CRS A432/15, item 55/4432.
36 See documents in PRO: FO 371/27788, 2961, and CRS A816, item 19/304/276.
37 Coulthard-Clark, *Edge of Centre*, p. 52.

38 Colonel L. H. Lemaire to General Blamey, 29 June 1943, 3DRL6643, item 3/92.
39 Templeton, 'Australian Intelligence/Security Services', pp. 116–7.
40 Mrs E. Wake to D. M. Horner, 26 May 1993.
41 Long to Wake, 20 August 1941, Wake Papers.
42 Report on Visit to Singapore August–September 1941, by Lt-Col R. F. B. Wake, and other documents in Wake Papers.
43 Report on the Visit of Colonel G. E. Grimsdale, General Staff, F.E.C.B., Singapore to Australia, 10th October to 23rd October 1941, PRO: WO 208/2062.
44 Longfield Lloyd to E. L. Piesse, 27 December 1920, NLA: Piesse Papers, MS882, series S, pp. 142–3.
45 Hasluck, *The Government and the People, 1939–1941*, p. 610.
46 Quoted in Spender, *Politics and a Man*, p. 123.

CHAPTER 3   THE SECURITY SERVICE AND THE WAR WITH JAPAN

1 Hasluck, *The Government and the People, 1939–1941*, p. 594. See also Bevege, *Behind Barbed Wire*; and Kay Saunders and Helen Taylor, 'The Enemy Within? The Process of Internment of Enemy Aliens in Queensland 1939–45', *Australian Journal of Politics and History*, vol. 34, no. 1, April 1988.
2 Hasluck, *The Government and the People, 1942–1945*, p. 718.
3 Muirden, *The Puzzled Patriots*, pp. 96–7.
4 Hasluck, *The Government and the People, 1942–1945*, p. 742.
5 'Eastern Command, History of Intelligence Activities, Sep 39 to Sep 45', p. 35, DMI file 123.
6 Duncan to Evatt, 7 January 1942 and attached report, MP 729/6, item 15/403/76.
7 Templeton, 'Australian Intelligence/Security Services, 1900–1950', p. 196.
8 Secretary, Department of the Navy to Defence Committee, 9 February 1942, CRS A2680/1, item 11/1943.
9 Jones to Secretary, Attorney-General's Department, 7 March 1942, CRS A432/15, item 55/4432.
10 Knowles to Attorney-General, 9 March 1942 MP 729/6, item 15/403/76.
11 P. J. Sadler to D. M. Horner, 25 February 1993. Sadler was the military reporting officer at Tatura.
12 Roberts to CGS, 4 March 1942, MP 729/6, item 15/403/76.
13 Sturdee to Minister for the Army, 9 March 1942, MP 729/6, item 15/403/76.
14 Long to Kevin, 16 March 1942, MP 729/6, item 15/403/199.
15 Undated note in ibid.
16 Forde to Evatt, 5 March 1942, MP 729/6, item 15/403/199. Kevin's draft is in the same file.
17 Notes for Minister for 9 March conference, MP 729/6, item 15/403/199.
18 Secretary, Department of the Army, to Minister, 9 March 1942, and Evatt to Forde, 11 March 1942, MP 729/6, item 15/403/199.
19 MacKay to Forde, 22 March 1942, MP 729/6, item 15/403/199.
20 Forde to MacKay, 9 April 1942, CRS A1981/132/1, folder 1.
21 Forde to Secretary, Department of Defence, 24 September 1942, MP 729/6, item 15/403/199.
22 MacKay to Forde, 22 May 1942, CRS A432/15, item 55/4432.
23 Swan typescript.
24 'Minutes of a Meeting Held . . . September 15th, 1942 . . .', MP 729/6, item 15/403/199.
25 The organisation formally came into existence on 1 February 1943. Memo G1 SD (Org) to DSD, 4 April 1944, AWM 54, item 883/21/45.
26 Cain, *The Origins of Political Surveillance*, p. 291.

27 For a full discussion of the command relationships see Horner, *High Command*, ch. 9.
28 For a description of the setting up and role of the AIB see ibid., ch. 10.
29 For a description of AIB operations see Powell, *War By Stealth*.
30 See Thorpe, *East Wind, Rain*.
31 Willoughby, *A Brief History of the G2 Section*, p. 78.
32 War Diary Advanced LHQ GS (Intelligence), AWM 52, item 1/2/2.
33 Horner, *Crisis of Command*, p. 104.
34 Memo, Rogers to Senior Australian Intelligence Officers, October 1945, DMI file 18/5/0.
35 Col K. A. Wills to Blamey, 25 August 1943, 3DRL6643, item 2/54.
36 Templeton, 'Australian Intelligence/Security Services,' p. 204.
37 ibid, p. 209.
38 The following account is from Lemaire to Blamey, 29 June 1943 and 8 July 1943 and attached documents in 3DRL6643, item 3/92.
39 Winter, *The Intrigue Master*, p. 178.
40 Lemaire to Blamey, 8 July 1943, 3DRL6643, item 3/92.
41 Templeton, 'Australian Intelligence/Security Services', p. 210.
42 War Diary of Advanced LHQ GS Intelligence, AWM 52, item 1/2/2.
43 Lemaire to Blamey, 8 July 1943, 3DRL6643, item 3/92.
44 Brigadier Sir Charles Spry to D. M. Horner, 17 June 1993 and other interviews.
45 Gorman to Blamey, 17 December 1943, 3DRL6643, item 3/92.
46 Security in this area was supervised by Lieutenant-Colonel Austin Laughlin, who described his activities in *Boots and All*. For details of a major security exercise in northern Queensland in September 1943 see CRS A7359/84, item MS186/5.
47 Templeton, 'Australian Intelligence/Security Services', p. 209.
48 Simpson to Chairman, Public Service Board, 17 October 1945, A373/1, item 6663.
49 For example, T. E. Nave to D. M. Horner, 24 February 1993; Sir Frederick Chilton to D. M. Horner and D. J. Ball, 2 March 1993; Spry to Horner, 17 June 1993.
50 Cain, *The Origins of Political Surveillance*, p. 292.
51 Templeton, 'Australian Intelligence/Security Services', p. 206.
52 ibid, p. 208.
53 'Extracts from a Report on a Visit to Australia 6 Mar–28 Mar 1944' by Captain Hillgarth, RN, Chief of Intelligence Staff, Eastern Fleet, PRO: PREM 3, 159/10.
54 Mrs Cohen to Horner, 26 April 1993.
55 Chief of the General Staff to Defence Committee, 9 February 1942, CRS A2680/1, item 11/1943.
56 According to a report prepared for the Advisory War Council on 10 February 1942, '12 illicit stations were disclosed early in the war by means of the detection organisation, but in none of the cases was there any suggestion of subversive activities'. CRS A2680/1, item 11/1943.
57 Lt-Col P. J. M. Stratton, 'Report to the Chairman of the Canadian "Y" Committee on a Visit to Australia, New Zealand and India by Lt. Col. P. J. M. Stratton, R Sigs, Radio Security Service', 18 October 1943, National Archives of Canada: RG 24, vol. 8125, item NSS–1282–85 (vol 2).
58 Barker, *Signals*, p. 165.
59 Lt-Col P. J. M. Stratton, 'Report to the Chairman of the Canadian "Y" Committee on a Visit to Australia, New Zealand and India by Lt. Col. P. J. M. Stratton, R Sigs, Radio Security Service', 18 October 1943, National Archives of Canada, RG 24, vol. 8125, item NSS–1282–85 (vol 2); Ballard, *On ULTRA Active Service*, pp. 233–4; War Diary 67 Australian Wireless Section, AWM 52, item 7/39/27.
60 Notes of Talks between Capt Kendall, Lt-Col Sandford and DMI, 1 October 1943, CRS A6923/3, item SI/9.
61 Minute of Defence Committee, 13 December 1943, ibid.
62 Quoted in Simpson to Deputy Adjutant-General, 14 April 1944, CRS A1981/1321/1, folder 1.

382   BREAKING THE CODES

63 Unit Location Statement Card, AWM 132, box 4.
64 C. K. Hart (wartime 2ic of 1 ADU) to D. M. Horner, 21 April 1993.
65 ibid.
66 'German Intelligence Activity in the Far East', 22 February 1945, NARA: RG 457, SRMA–014.
67 Sandford to ADMI, 1 May 1945, CRS A6923/3, item SI/3.
68 Simpson to Rogers, 26 April 1944, CRS A6923/3, item SI/9.
69 Simpson to Rogers, 5 May 1944, ibid.
70 Sandford to Blamey, 19 January 1945, CRS A6923/3, item SI/3. Sandford was undertaking some purely British Sigint work and he maintained a separate house as an office for this work. For convenience and to save on guards he and other staff engaged in this work lived in the house. The Foreign Office paid the rent directly, not through Sandford.

CHAPTER 4   THE DEVELOPMENT OF SIGINT IN AUSTRALIA

1 Cable 714, C-in-C China Station to Admiralty, 14 June 1941, WO 193/920.
2 Comments of Lieutenant-Colonel Sandford at a meeting of the Canadian "Y" Committee, 24 June 1943, National Archives of Canada: RG 24: vol. 8125, file NSS 1282–85 (vol. 2).
3 Winter, *The Intrigue Master*, p. 51.
4 Secretary, Naval Board, to Officer-in-Charge, Coonawarra, 16 February 1940, MP1185/8, item 2037/3/25.
5 Australian Naval Board to C.O.I.S. (R) D.N.I. Admiralty, 15 February 1940, MP1185/8, item 2037/3/25. Notes by Commander Newman, c. October 1941, MP1185/8, item 1937/2/415.
6 An Admiralty history of radio interception in the Far East noted that at the end of August 1939 interception was taking place at the 'Melbourne R.A.N. Barracks'. R. T. Barrett, 'H. M. S. Anderson and Special Intelligence in the Far East', ADM 223/284. See also Ballard, *On ULTRA Active Service*, p. 146, which refers to the RAN's 'small organisation with limited resources for interception and D/F . . . at the Navy Office', in early 1942.
7 Commander Newman to CNS, 14 May 1940, MP1185/8, item 2037/3/25.
8 Long to CNS, 15 May 1940, MP1185/8, item 2037/3/25.
9 Memorandum for Discussion at Singapore, c. October 1940, MP1185/8, item 1937/2/415.
10 For a description of the FECB see A. Hillgarth and R. T. Barrett, 'British Intelligence in the Far East—The Far East Combined Bureau. Hong Kong', in 'Far East and Pacific I, History', ADM 223/297. Long to CNS, 28 November 1939, CRS A6923/3, item 37/401/425.
11 Colvin to CGS and CAS, 12 December 1939, CRS A816, item 43/302/18.
12 Goble to Colvin, 21 December 1939; Squires to Colvin, 16 December 1939, CRS A816, item 43/302/18.
13 Simpson to CGS, 1 April 1944, MP 729/8, item 37/431/181.
14 War Diary Signals Southern Command, AWM 52, item 7/12/3.
15 'Units in focus: 6 Signal Regiment', *Signalman*, no. 5, 1980, p. 19.
16 Ballard, *On ULTRA Active Service*, pp. 43–5. War Diary 4th Australian Special Wireless Section, AWM 52, item 7/39/41. Initially the unit was known as the 1st Australian Special Wireless Section.
17 Jenkins, *Battle Surface*, p. 42 states that although the Army section was established in early 1940, the university professors did not join it until January 1941; but other research indicates that they joined earlier.
18 Combes to DMO&I, 3 October 1939, MP 729/6, item 50/401/69; see also CRS A6828, item 4/1938.
19 Major GS(I) Eastern Command to AHQ, 18 October 1940, CRS A6923/3, item 37/40/425.
20 Notes of interview of Dr A. P. Treweek by D. C. S. Sissons, 11 October 1990.

Professor A. D. Trendall to D. J. Ball, 10 May 1990. See also David Jenkins, 'Our War of Words', *Sydney Morning Herald*, 19 September 1992, pp. 37–8, and Jenkins, *Battle Surface*, pp. 42–7.
21 A staff officer in Navy Office wrote on a copy of this cabled letter: 'We are not proud of this.' MP 1185/8, item 1937/2/415.
22 Minute of Defence Committee, 15 February 1940; Cable 88, Prime Minister of Australia to Secretary of State for Dominion Affairs, 11 April 1940; Cable 198, Secretary of State for Dominion Affairs to Prime Minister of Australia, 15 October 1940, MP 1185/8, item 1937/2/415.
23 Nave's own account can be found in his unpublished autobiography, a copy of which is held by D. M. Horner.
24 R. T. Barrett, 'H.M.S. Anderson and Special Intelligence in the Far East', ADM 223/284.
25 Hilvert, *Blue Pencil Warriors*, p. 39.
26 Memorandum for Discussion at Singapore, and Comments by Paymaster-Commander Nave, n.d. MP 1185/8, item 1937/2/415.
27 Conference in Naval Board Room, 4th January 1941, MP 1185/8, item 1945/2/6.
28 Notes prepared by Nave and forwarded to Mr Douglas Menzies, Secretary of the Defence Committee, 12 November 1941, MP 1185/8, item 1937/2/415.
29 Newman to CNS, 19 March 1941, MP 1185/8, item 1937/2/415.
30 Quoted in 'Far East and Pacific, III, Special', ADM 223/297.
31 Quoted in Jenkins, *Battle Surface*, p. 45.
32 Sturdee to Minister for the Army, 3 June 1941, CRS A6923/3, item 37/401/425.
33 Minute by Defence Committee at Meeting Held on 28 November 1941, CRS A816, item 43/302/18.
34 Nave unpublished autobiography.
35 Bleakley, *The Eavesdroppers*, p. 7.
36 ibid, pp. 10–11.
37 Treweek to Sissons, 11 October 1990.
38 Durnsford to Shedden, 28 November 1941, with attached messages, CRS A5954, item 558/12.
39 Treweek to Sissons, 11 October 1990.
40 Quoted in Jenkins, *Battle Surface*, p. 49. See also Nave unpublished autobiography.
41 Durnsford to Shedden, 4 December 1941, CRS A5954, item 558/12.
42 Rusbridger and Nave, *Betrayal at Pearl Harbor*, p. 25; Winter, *The Intrigue Master*, p. 122.
43 Clausen and Lee, *Pearl Harbor: Final Judgement*, pp. 447–70.
44 A. B. Jamieson to D. J. Ball. D. M. Horner and D. C. S. Sissons, 24 February 1988.
45 Notes on message, attached to Durnsford to Shedden, 28 November 1941, CRS A5954, item 558/12.
46 Ballard, *On ULTRA Active Service*, ch. 9.
47 Comprehensive reports on the unit's operations in Crete are in the War Diary of the Headquarters Australian Special Wireless Group, AWM 52, item 7/39/3, October 1942.
48 Ballard, *On ULTRA Active Service*, pp. 71–2.
49 ibid, ch. 11.
50 Hinsley, *British Intelligence in the Second World War, Vol. 1*, p. 199.
51 Memo by Officer Commanding No 2 W/T Company, 26 July 1941, War Diary HQ Australian Special Wireless Group, AWM 52, item 7/39/3, September 1942.
52 No 2 Wireless Company to 4th Australian Special Wireless Section, 28 October 1941, AWM 52, item 7/39/3; W. McCue to D. M. Horner, 24 October 1995.
53 Hinsley, *British Intelligence in the Second World War, Vol. 1*, p. 196.
54 ibid. See also Skillen, *Spies of the Airwaves*, pp. 50, 496.
55 Cable 62009, Chiefs of Staff to Wavell, 4 January 1942, WO 106/3298. See also cable F4, Dominions Secretary to Prime Minister, 7 August 1942, CRS A816, 19/304/330.
56 Nave autobiography.

57 Graydon A. Lewis, *Intercept Station "C"*, Naval Cryptographic Veterans Association, Denver, 1983. For the destruction of the Purple machine see Vince Chamberlin, 'Corregidor The Final Days' p. 44 in ibid.
58 Evacuation of USN COMINT Personnel from Corregidor in World War II, 1–5, US National Archives and Records Administration (NARA), Washington, D.C.: SRH–207.
59 Trendall to Ball, 10 May 1990; Jenkins, 'Our War of Words', p. 37.
60 J. R. Green, 'Scholar and archaeologist of world rank', *The Australian*, 20 November 1995, p. 13.
61 Blair, *Silent Victory*, pp. 218–9; Nave to Horner, 25 January 1979; R. L. Bond to D. J. Ball, 29 September 1994.
62 Jamieson to Ball, Horner and Sissons, 24 February 1988.
63 Bond to Ball, 29 September 1994.
64 Thompson and Harris, *The Signal Corps*, p. 340.
65 Radio 1224, MacArthur to the Adjutant-General, 1 April 1942, NARA: RG 165, OPD Exec 10, item 7D.
66 Roberts to DCGS, 3 March 1942, CRS A6923/3, item SI/2.
67 Ballard, *On ULTRA Active Service*, p. 141.
68 ibid, p. 145.
69 Minutes of Meeting of Y Officers, 30 March 1942, CRS A6923/3, item SI/2.
70 Roberts to DCGS, 5 April 1942, ibid.
71 Minutes of Conference, 6 April 1942, ibid.
72 Willoughby, *Operations of the Military Intelligence Section*, p. 67.
73 Sherr to Sutherland, 22 October 1942, CRS A 6923/3, item SI/2.
74 Ballard, *On ULTRA Active Service*, p. 161.
75 ibid, pp. 217–23. See also Bleakley, *The Eavesdroppers* for an account of the RAAF units.
76 Ballard, *On ULTRA Active Service*, pp. 223–28.
77 Drea, *MacArthur's ULTRA*, p. 20.
78 Ballard, *On ULTRA Active Service*, p. 169.
79 Radio C1384, MacArthur to Marshall, 31 December 1942, NARA: RG 165, OPD Exec 10, item 23a.
80 MIS Memorandum, 2 February 1943, NARA: RG 165, OPD Exec 11, item 1.
81 MacArthur to Blamey, 20 January 1943, MacArthur Memorial Military Archives (MMMA): RG 4, Box 1B. On 26 August 1942 Blamey had written to MacArthur suggesting such an organisation. ibid.
82 ADMI to Camp Commandant, Victoria Barracks, 26 November 1942, CRS A6923/3, item 37/401/425. For reference to the move of SIB from Navy to Army control see Major-General Sutherland to Commander Allied Naval Forces, 19 January 1943, MMMA: RG 4, Box 1B.
83 G. H. O. Crowther to D. M. Horner and D. J. Ball, 22 February 1993; R. L. Bond to D. M. Horner, 23 February 1993.
84 Jenkins, 'Our War of Words', p. 38.
85 Correspondence in CRS A6923/3, item 37/401/425.
86 Bond to Ball, 28 September 1994.
87 Northcott to Hodgson, 14 June 1943, CRS A6923/3, item 37/401/425.
88 Nave to Horner, 25 January 1979.
89 Drea, *MacArthur's ULTRA*, p. 36.
90 The message is in AA (Melbourne): CRS B5555, file 5. It is published in Bleakley, *The Eavesdroppers*, p. 43. Quoting other documents from Hawaii, Drea, *MacArthur's ULTRA*, p. 37, puts the date as 18 May.
91 Blair, *Silent Victory*, p. 606; GHQ Intsum 23/24 May 1942, National Records Center, Suitland: RG 405, G3 Journal.
92 Quoted in Jenkins, 'Our War of Words', p. 37.
93 Magic Summary, 18 April 1942, NARA: SRS575.
94 Drea, *MacArthur's ULTRA*, p. 41.
95 The role of air force Sigint is described in Bleakley, *The Eavesdroppers*.
96 Drea, *MacArthur's ULTRA*, p. 68.
97 ibid, p. 105.
98 Minutes of Joint Intelligence Sub-Committee, Conference on Coordination of

Intelligence in the Far East, 8–14 September 1944, Blamey Papers 3DRL6643, item 2/54.2. See also J. D. Roger, 'Say Not the Struggle', unpublished manuscript.
99 Ballard, *On ULTRA Active Service*, p. 243.
100 Rogers to Berryman, 12 July 1944, Berryman Papers.
101 War Diary Advanced LHQ GS (Intelligence), AWM 52, item 1/2/2.
102 'Memorandum for the Special Security Officer, 20 December 1945', NARA: RG 457, SRH–032. The instructions governing the handling and dissemination of ULTRA produced or received in the SWPA were set out in a memorandum signed by General Sutherland on 26 December 1944, NARA: RG 457, SRH–044.
103 S. F. Burley, 'The Silent Guardians of Ultra', unpublished manuscript.
104 Horner, *High Command*, p. 245.
105 See for example ibid, p. 230.

CHAPTER 5   THE FIRST SECURITY LEAKS

1 Berryman Diary, 2 October 1944, AWM: PR84/370, item 4.
2 At the time Wang was usually described as Chih Wang, the family name being placed last in the Western fashion.
3 Brig Rogers to Lt-Col Taplin, LHQ, 2 April 1943; Taplin to Rogers, 15 April 1943, AWM 54, item 425/6/69.
4 Maj-Gen Wang Chih to D. M. Horner, Lansing, Michigan, 22 May 1993. For more details of Wang's career see David Horner, 'The Chinese Liaison Officer in Australia 1942–1945', *Journal of the Australian War Memorial*, no. 25, October 1994.
5 Blamey to Northcott, 4 December 1942, 3DRL6643, item 2/8.3. Blamey's letter refers to Captain Wang, but Northcott's reply refers to the Chinese liaison officer, who was Colonel Wang. Either way the point is clear.
6 Cable Hsinking (Umezu) to Bangkok, 15 August 1941, NARA: RG 457, SRH–018.
7 Memo by Brig-Gen Willoughby, dated 18 August 1944, US National Records Center, Suitland, Maryland (hereafter USNRC): RG 338, GHQ G2, General Correspondence, Box T1212, file 312.1.
8 Memo, 3 June 1943, by Captain A. H. McCollum, the Intelligence Officer of the US 7th Fleet, MMMA: RG 4 Box 6, Correspondence Allied Naval Forces. Also, McCollum to Executive G2 GHQ, 27 December 1942, USNRC: RG 338, GHQ G2, General Correspondence, Box T1211, file 211.
9 Wang Chih to Col Merle-Smith, 2 January 1943, USNRC: RG 338, GHQ G2, General Correspondence, Box T1211, file 211.
10 Wake to Brig Simpson, Director-General of Security, 8 March 1943, Australian Archives (Qld): BP 242/1, item Q30575.
11 Wake to Simpson, 9 March 1943, BP 242/1, item Q30575.
12 Wake to Simpson, 2 April 1943, BP 242/1, item Q30575.
13 One wartime intelligence officer has doubted whether the Chinese had an office in the LHQ building. Wang's name does not appear in the GHQ telephone book for May 1944, but his assistant, Lt Nan Yu Lu, is listed as having both office and residence phone numbers at St Lucia. MMMA: RG3, Box 2.
14 Brig Rogers to Lt Col Taplin, LHQ, 2 April 1943; Taplin to Rogers, 15 April 1943, AWM 54, item 425/6/69.
15 Simpson to Deputy Directors in Sydney, Melbourne and Brisbane, 9 September 1944, BP 242/1, item Q30575.
16 ibid.
17 Deputy Director, Victoria, to Acting Director, Commonwealth Investigation Service, 6 October 1946, A367/1, item C71546.
18 Simpson to Deputy Director of Security, Brisbane, 12 November 1943, and

386   BREAKING THE CODES

       Appendix C to Security Summary No 63 dated 23 December 1943, BP 242/1, item Q30600.
19 Full correspondence on these plans is found in USNRC: RG 338, GHQ SWPA G–2, Correspondence, Box S–243. For a Dutch view, see Bob de Graaff, 'Hot Intelligence in the Tropics: Dutch Intelligence Operations in the Netherlands East Indies During the Second World War', *Journal of Contemporary History*, October 1987.
20 For correspondence see USNRC: RG 338, GHQ SWPA G–2, General Correspondence, Box T1211, file 211.
21 P. J. Sadler to D. M. Horner, 15 February 1993.
22 When D. M. Horner visited Wang on 22 May 1993, Wang showed him his notebook from his time in Australia. Batchelor was written in it as an important contact.
23 Sadler to Horner, 15 February 1993.
24 Note on DO file GS Int HQ NGF, immediately before an item dated 18 January 1944, held by P. J. Sadler.
25 Sadler to Horner, 15 February 1993.
26 Signal, Landops to Landforces, 18 July 1944, AWM 54, item 425/6/69.
27 Rogers to senior staff officers LHQ, 4 August 1941, AWM 54, item 425/6/69.
28 Wang to Willoughby, 23 August 1944, AWM 54, item 425/6/69.
29 Willoughby to Wang, 27 August 1944, AWM 54, item 425/6/69.
30 US authorities had intercepted a message from the Japanese Consul-General at Canton to Tokyo, dated 6 July 1944, which gave details of B29 operations in China (NARA: Magic Diplomatic Summary No 843, 16 July 1944, RG 457, SRS–1365). Japanese knowledge of B29 operations was also revealed by Allied intercepts of messages passed between German agents in Canton and Shanghai (NARA: 'German Intelligence Activity in the Far East', 22 February 1945, RG 457, SRMA–014).
31 Simpson to Deputy Directors in Sydney, Melbourne and Brisbane, 1 September 1944, BP 242/1, item Q30575.
32 Memo dated 30 November 1944, AWM, item 425/6/69.
33 Blamey to Wang, 26 July 1944; PA to C-in-C to ADMI, 26 July 1944; Wang to PA to C-in-C, 21 August 1944, 3DRL6643, item 2/8.3.
34 Willoughby to Rogers, 2 September 1944, AWM 54, item 425/6/69; Blamey to Wang, 7 September 1944; Wang to Blamey, 14 September 1944, 3DRL6643, item 2/8.3.
35 R. L. Bond to D. M. Horner, 24 February 1993.
36 Mellnik, *Philippine Diary*, p. 276.
37 Willoughby to DMI LHQ, 6 October 1944, 3DRL6643, item 2/8.3. A copy of this memo is in USNRC: RG 338, GHQ SWPA G–2, General Correspondence, Box T1211, file 211.
38 Willoughby to DC/S USAFFE, 19 October 1944, RG 338, GHQ SWPA G–2, General Correspondence, Box T1211, file 211.
39 Lt-Col C. A. McVittie to Col F. T. Armstrong, 19 October 1944, RG 338, GHQ SWPA G–2. General Correspondence, Box T1211, file 211.
40 Berryman Diary, 22 November 1944, PR84/370, item 4.
41 Blamey to Acting Minister for the Army, 6 January 1945, 3DRL6643, item 2/59.
42 MBJ 30028, 25 November 1944, CRS A6923/3, item SI/8.
43 *Australian Military Forces Weekly Intelligence Review* no. 118, War Diary of Advanced LHQ GS Intelligence, AWM 52, item 1/2/2.
44 The reviews are in the War Diary of Advanced LHQ GS Intelligence, AWM 52, item 1/2/2; see also AWM 123, item 901.
45 Advisory War Council Minute no. 1485, Canberra, 8 February 1945, CRS A5954/1, item 429/15; also CRS A2682, vol. III.
46 C-in-C Diary, 24 November 1944, 3DRL6643, item 3/144.
47 Blamey to L. Hooke, AWA, 24 November 1944, 3DRL6643, item 2/8.3. As early as 1941 AWA had passed Japanese consular telegrams to the Australian Army's code-breaking group at Sydney University; A. P. Treweek to D. C. S. Sissons, 11 October 1990 (notes from Sissons).
48 Further evidence that the letter was written by the Americans is found in the

fact that it was addressed to Amalgamated Wireless 'Association', not '(Australasia)' which was the correct title.
49 Berryman Diary, 23 November 1944, PR84/370, item 4.
50 Berryman Diary, 24 November 1944, PR84/370, item 4.
51 Berryman Diary, 26 November 1944, PR84/370, item 4.
52 Berryman Diary, 27 November 1944, PR84/370, item 4.
53 Signal, DMI to Berryman, 28 November 1944, PR84/370, item 14. Berryman Diary, 29 November 1944, PR84/370, item 4.
54 R. L. Holmes to Horner, 8 January 1993; DMI to Berryman, 20 December 1944, 3DRL6643, item 2/54.
55 Drea, *MacArthur's ULTRA*, pp. 159, 166–7.
56 ibid, pp. 170–2.
57 A teletype copy of the circular is in AWM 123, item 752.
58 Blamey to Ministers for Defence and the Army, 14 November 1944, 3DRL6643, item 2/139.1.
59 Forde to Calwell, 20 November 1944; Calwell to Forde, 24 November 1944, CRS A5954, item 325/12.
60 Blamey to Acting Minister for the Army, 6 January 1945, 3DRL6643, item 2/59; and Capt I (a) GS (Int) to DMI, 13 December 1944, CRS A6923/3, item SI/8.
61 Blamey to Acting Minister for Defence, 23 December 1944, CRS A5954, item 429/15; also AWM 23, item 444.
62 ibid. See also Postmaster-General to Acting Minister for Defence, 5 January 1945, CRS A5954, item 429/15; also AWM 23, item 444.
63 Sandford to Little, 14 December 1945, A6923/3, item SI/8.
64 MBJ 30601, 12 December 1944, ibid.
65 C-in-C Diary, 3DRL6643, item 3/144; E. J. L. Ride to D. M. Horner, 22 January 1993. For a discussion of L. T. Ride's role see Edwin Ride, *BAAG*.
66 See for example the *Australian Military Forces Weekly Intelligence Review* no. 89 of 14 April 1944 in War Diary Advanced LHQ GS (Intelligence), AWM 52, item 1/2/2.
67 Rogers to Chief of Staff, copies to C-in-C and Lt-Col Holmes, 20 December 1944, 3DRL6643, item 2/54.
68 *Australian Military Forces Weekly Intelligence Review* no. 138, for week ending 19 May 1945, War Diary of Advanced LHQ GS Intelligence, AWM 52, item 1/2/2.
69 MBJ 30028A, 25 November 1944, CRS A6923/3, item SI/8.
70 Winterbotham, *The Ultra Secret*, p. 172.
71 Sandford to Little, 19 December 1994, CRS A6923/3, item SI/8.
72 Memo, 'Censorship Activities of CGS branch', CGS to C-in-C, 11 March 1944, 3DRL6643, item 3/24.
73 Blamey to Acting Minister for Defence, 23 December 1944, A5954, item 429/15; also AWM 23, item 444.
74 Acting Minister for Defence to Blamey, Minister for External Affairs and Postmaster-General, 30 December 1944, CRS A5954, item 429/15; also AWM 23, item 444.
75 Memo by Shedden, 3 January 1945, CRS A5954, item 325/12.
76 Blamey to Acting Minister for the Army, 6 January 1945, 3DRL6643, item 2/59.
77 For an example of the code see teleprinter messages in AWM 123, item 752.
78 Sandford to Little, 25 December 1945, CRS A6923/3, item SI/8.
79 MBJ 31454, 30 December 1944, ibid.
80 Memo by Shedden, 3 January 1945, CRS A5954, item 325/12.
81 Shedden to Blamey, 3 January 1945, A5954, item 429/15 and 3DRL6643, item 2/59.
82 Blamey memoirs, from T. R. Blamey.

Chapter 6 General Blamey's letter

1 For example, see Horner, *High Command*, p. 245; Hall, *The Rhodes Scholar Spy*, pp. 103–4; and McKnight, *Australia's Spies and Their Secrets*, p. 12.

2 The first files in the series CRS A6923 DMI (Special Intelligence) were released on 25 July 1997.
3 C-in-C Diary, 3DRL6643, item 3/144.
4 See intercepts in CRS A6923/3, item SJ/8.
5 G. H. O. Crowther to D. M. Horner and D. J. Ball, 22 February 1993.
6 Ashley to Forde, 5 January 1945, CRS A5954, item 429/5, and AWM 123, item 444.
7 For details see 3DRL6643, item, 2/54.8.
8 Blamey to Acting Minister for the Army, 6 January 1945, 3DRL6643, item 2/59.
9 ibid.
10 War Cabinet Minute 4013, 9 January 1945, A2673, vol. xv; also A5954, item 429/15.
11 War Cabinet Minute 4008, 9 January 1945, A2673, vol. xv.
12 Shedden notebook, CRS A5954, item 733/2; Port notebook, CRS A924/1, item set 2, vol. 14.
13 ibid.
14 War Cabinet Minute 4008, 9 January 1945, A2673, vol. xv.
15 C-in-C Diary, 3DRL6643, item 3/144; Shedden to the Acting Prime Minister, 13 January 1945, Acting Prime Minister to Evatt and Fraser, 16 January 1945, A5954, item 429/15, and AWM 123, item 44.
16 C-in-C Diary, 3DRL6643, item 3/144.
17 Rogers to Blamey, 17 January 1945, CRS A6923/3, item SI/8.
18 Notes on ibid.
19 C-in-C Diary, 3DRL6643, item 3/144.
20 This record is likely to be more correct than Blamey's diary, which was kept by his personal assistant, Major D. H. Dwyer, who was not present at the meeting.
21 Minute, 'Leakages of Information', 17 January 1945, A5954, item 429/15.
22 Ananias, the husband of Sapphira, died for lying to God. *Acts* Ch 5 v. 3 reads: 'Then Peter said, "Ananias, how is it that Satan has so filled your heart that you have lied to the Holy Spirit".'
23 Rogers to Blamey, 18 January 1945, 3DRL6643, item 2/59.
24 ibid.
25 ibid.
26 ibid.
27 George Crowther, then an officer on the DMI staff in Melbourne, recalled that at the time he knew that an enemy agent had been identified in Sydney. Crowther left the Army at the end of 1945. Crowther to Horner and Ball, 22 February 1993.
28 Copies are in CRS A6923/3, item SI/8.
29 Blamey to Simpson, 25 January 1945, 3DRL6643, item 2/59; C-in-C Diary, 3DRL6643, item 3/144.
30 Burley to Winterbotham and Blamey, 1 February 1944, CRS A6923/3, item SI/8.
31 Sandford to Rogers and Little, 25 January 1945, CRS A6923/3, item SI/8.
32 Little to Simpson, 3 February 1945, ibid.
33 Note for file by Little, 2 February 1945, ibid.
34 Memo, 'Chinese Naval, Military and Air Attaches', 2 February 1945, 3DRL6643, item 2/8.3.
35 Wake to Simpson, 12 February 1945, BP 242/1, item Q30575.
36 Wang to Horner, 22 May 1993.
37 Maj-Gen C. Wang to Blamey, 4 May 1945, 3DRL6643, item 2/8.3.
38 Wake to Simpson, 31 July 1945, BP 242/1, item Q30575.
39 Willoughby to G–2 USAFFE, 13 April 1945, USNRC: RG 338, GHQ G–2, General Correspondence, box T1211, file 211.
40 Willoughby to C-in-C and C/S, 6 August 1945, RG 338, GHQ G–2, General Correspondence, box T1211, file 211.
41 Little to Capt C. K. Wang, 4 June 1945; Capt C. K. Wang to Blamey, 27 July 1945, 3DRL6643 item 2/8.3.

42 Shedden to Forde, 18 January, 1945, CRS A5954, item 429/15.
43 Memo,'Leakages of Information, by Shedden, 20 January 1945, CRS A5954, item 429/15.
44 Shedden to Forde, 24 January 1945, CRS A5954, item 429/15.
45 Curtin to Ashley, Evatt and Forde, 30 January 1945, CRS A5954, item 429/15.
46 Blamey to Shedden, 7 April 1945, Shedden to Blamey 12 April 1945, CRS A5954, item 429/15. See notes dated 26 March 1945 on Shedden to Forde, 18 January 1945, AWM 123, item 44.
47 Blamey to Forde, undated, April 1945, 3DRL6643, item 2/54.8.
48 War Cabinet Minute no. 4043, Canberra, 9 February 1945, and War Cabinet Agendum no. 24/1945, CRS A2670, item 24/1845.
49 Winterbotham to Burley, 2 February 1945, CRS A6923/3, item SI/8.
50 For example see Wright *Spycatcher*; Pincher, *Their Trade is Treachery*, and *Too Secret Too Long*; and West, *MI6*.
51 Little to Blamey, 7 February 1945, CRS A6923/3, item SI/8.
52 Sandford to Little, 3 February 1945, ibid.
53 Little to Blamey, 7 February 1945, ibid.
54 Sandford to Little, 5 February 1945, ibid.
55 Little to Blamey, 10 February 1945, ibid.
56 Signals reproduced in Sandford to Little, 20 February 1945, ibid.
57 Blamey to Simpson, 19 February 1945, ibid.
58 Blamey to Sandford, 'Radio Security', 8 March 1945; (copies to Brig Simpson, Director-General of Security; Maj-Gen C. H. Simpson, Signal Officer-in-Chief; and Brig Rogers, DMI); 3DRL6643, item 2/54.7; Blamey to Director-General of Security, 6 April 1945, 3DRL6643, item 2/59.
59 'Army reply to Defence Committee Agendum 161/1945, Intelligence Activities in Australia (Aust Army), Appendix C: Schedule of WT Stations Used For Intelligence Purposes', attachment to lettter, Lt-Gen Northcott to Shedden, 'Intelligence Activities in Australia', 27 July 1945, A816, item 25/310/410.
60 Advisory War Council Minute no. 1566, Canberra, 20 June 1945, and Agendum no. 26/1945, A2680, item 26/1945.
61 Notes of Discussion with C-in-C SWPA, 30 September 1944, CRS A5954, box 3.
62 War Cabinet Minute no. 3850, Canberra, 10 October 1944, CRS A2672, vol xv.
63 Advisory War Council Minute no. 1444, Canberra, 16 November 1944, CRS A2670, items 515/1944, 521/1944, 538/1944.
64 Shedden to Blamey, 3 January 1945, 3DRL6643, item 2/59.
65 Military History Section, Headquarters, Army Far East, 'Japanese Intelligence Planning Against the Far East', June 1955, p. 73; reprinted in Detwiler and Burdick, *War in Asia and the Pacific, 1937–1949*, vol. 10.
66 Summary no. 788, 22 May 1944, Tokyo to Moscow, 13 May 1944, NARA: RG 457, SRS 1310, Magic Diplomatic Summaries. The authors have examined the copies of the Magic diplomatic summaries, and the intercepts of both the diplomatic cable traffic and the military attaché traffic, held by the US National Archives. It is clear that the diplomatic summaries, and the reports detailed in footnotes 67 and 69, could not have been been prepared without access to vastly more intercepts than have been released to Archives. It is not clear whether these additional intercepts are still held by the National Security Agency or have been destroyed.
67 'Japanese Signal Intelligence Service, Third Edition, 1 November 1944', NARA: RG 457, SRH–266.
68 Diplomatic Summary no. 18, 17–19 June 1945, PRO: HW 10/1.
69 Bennett, Hobart, and Spitzer, *Intelligence and Cryptanalytic Activities of the Japanese During World War II*, pp. 95–6. This is a republished version of a document entitled 'The Japanese Intelligence System', prepared by the Military Intelligence Service, 4 September 1945, NARA: SRH 254.
70 Magic Diplomatic Summary no. 1032, 21 January 1945, NARA: RG 145, SRS 1554.
71 Bennett, Hobart and Spitzer, *Intelligence and Crytanalytic Activities of the Japanese*, pp. 24–5.

72 Blamey to Acting Minister for the Army, 6 January 1945, 3DRL6643, item 2/59.
73 'Japanese Signal Intelligence Service, Third Edition, 1 November 1944', p. 50, NARA: RG 457, SRH–266. 'A' intelligence was from 'decryptographed codes' and 'B' from items intercepted in plain text. ibid, p. 39.
74 Bennett, Hobart and Spitzer, *Intelligence and Crytanalytic Activities of the Japanese*, p. 14.
75 ibid, pp. 77–81.
76 ibid, pp. 95–6.
77 Glantz, *Soviet Military Deception in the Second World War*, pp. 544–5. For the Japanese intelligence failure see Edward J. Drea, 'Missing Intentions: Japanese Intelligence and the Soviet Invasion of Manchuria, 1945', *Military Affairs*, April 1984.
78 Sudoplatov and Sudoplatov, *Special Tasks*, p. 159.
79 David M. Glantz, 'The Battle That Never Happened', *MHQ: The Quarterly Journal of Military History*, Summer 1997, vol. 9, no. 10, p. 48.
80 Capt W. J. Holmes to Captain Smith-Hutton, 21 January 1944, NARA: RG 457, SRMD–009, File of Administrative Letters/Correspondence January 1942–September 1945.
81 'Japanese Signal Intelligence Service, Third Edition, 1 November 1944', NARA: RG 457, SRH–266.
82 Bennett, Hobart and Spitzer, *Intelligence and Crytanalytic Activities of the Japanese*, p. 13.
83 J. W. M. Chapman, 'Japanese Intelligence 1919–1945: A Suitable Case for Treatment', Andrew and Noakes, *Intelligence and International Relations 1900–1945*, p. 149.
84 Edward J. Drea, 'Reading Each Other's Mail: Japanese Communications Intelligence, 1920–1941, *The Journal of Military History*, April 1991, p. 201. Louis Allen 'Japanese Intelligence Systems', *Journal of Contemporary History*, October 1987 p. 556, wrote: 'Claims have been made that Japanese cryptographers broke 95 per cent of China's codes'.
85 Wang to Horner, 22 May 1993.
86 'Chinese Naval Attaché, London', ADM 223/298.
87 'B.J. Series of Diplomatic Messages', ADM 223/298.
88 JIC (45) 135(O), 16 April 1945, CAB 81/128.
89 JIC (45) 187(O), 8 June 1945, CAB 81/129.
90 Message dated 22 November 1944, NARA: RG 457, SRA 13938.
91 Message dated 26 November 1944, NARA: RG 457, SRA 14204.
92 MBJ 31258, 25 December 1944, CRS A6923, item SI/8. See also Most Immediate ULTRA signal, TAG 152, DO 17. To: Hutton, 27 April 1945, 3DRL6643, item 2/59. (This file is concerned with leaks of Ultra intelligence.)
93 ibid.
94 Diplomatic Summary no. 6, 24–27 April 1945, HW 10/1.
95 Most Immediate ULTRA signal, TAG 152, DO 17. To: Hutton, 27 April 1945, 3DRL6643, item 2/59.
96 Rogers to Blamey, 26 June 1945, 3DRL6643, item 2/54.31.
97 Diplomatic summary no. 7, 28 April–1 May 1945, PRO:HW 10/1.
98 Diplomatic summary no. 20, 24–26 June 1945, HW 10/1.
99 Intercepts dated 22 April 1945 in NARA: RG 457, SRN–317, nos 257604–5 and 257625.
100 ULTRA signal GEN 0108, dated 27 April 1945, 3DRL6643, item 2/59.
101 Stanley, *Tarakan*, pp. 66, 253.
102 Rogers to Blamey, 17 January 1945, CRS A6923/3, item SI/8.
103 'Intelligence Derived From ULTRA', 21 December 1944, NARA: RG 457, SRH–59.

Chapter 7 Moscow Centre and Soviet intelligence

1 Andrew and Gordievsky, *KGB*, p. xii; and Dziak, *Chekisty*, pp. 184–6.
2 Dziak, *Chekisty*, p. 33.
3 ibid, p. 56; and Conquest, *The Great Terror: A Reassessment*, p. 486.

4 Conquest, *The Great Terror: Stalin's Purge of the Thirties*, pp. 699–713; and Conquest, *The Great Terror: A Reassessment*, pp. 485–6.
5 Knight, *Beria*, pp. 105–6.
6 'In Brief: Know Thy Neighbor', *Bulletin of the Atomic Scientists*, November/December 1995, p. 7.
7 Deriabin and Gibney, *The Secret World*, p. 210.
8 Conquest, *The Great Terror: A Reassessment*, pp. 180, 279.
9 ibid, p. 432.
10 Andrew and Gordievsky, *KGB*, p. 49.
11 Dziak, *Chekisty*, pp. 41–2.
12 Andrew and Gordievsky, *KGB*, pp. 56–9. See also Klehr, Haynes and Firsov, *The Secret World of American Communism*, pp. 70, 205–58.
13 See Sudoplatov and Sudoplatov, *Special Tasks*, ch. 4.
14 Knight, *Beria*, p. 100.
15 Sudoplatov and Sudoplatov, *Special Tasks*, p. 83 and ch. 7.
16 Andrew and Gordievsky, *KGB*, p. 208. See also 'The Committee of Information ("K.I."), 1947–1951', 17 November 1954, p. 10, CRS A6283/XR 1, item 86.
17 Andrew and Gordievsky, *KGB*, p. 208.
18 ibid, p. 195.
19 Borovik, *The Philby Files*, p. 124.
20 ibid, pp. 124–8.
21 ibid, pp. 233–4.
22 Andrew and Gordievsky, *KGB*, pp. 208–9.
23 ibid, pp. 315, 549.
24 Dzhirkvelov, *Secret Servant*, p. 64.
25 'The Committee of Information ('K.I.'), 1947–1951', 17 November 1954, pp. 1, 2, 8, CRS A6283/XR 1, item 86; Dziak, *Chekisty*, pp.128, 185; and Andrew and Gordievsky, *KGB*, p. 314.
26 'The Committee of Information ('K.I.'), 1947–1951', 17 November 1954, pp. 1, 2, 8, CRS A6283/XR 1, item 86.
27 Andrew and Gordievsky, *KGB*, pp. 315, 549.
28 Dzhirkvelov, *Secret Servant*, pp. 65, 140–1.
29 'The Committee of Information ('K.I.'), 1947–1951', 17 November 1954, pp. 2, 3, 4, CRS A6283/XR 1, item 86.
30 ibid.
31 Andrew and Gordievsky, *KGB*, p. 316; Sudoplatov and Sudoplatov, *Special Tasks*, pp. 214–6, 252–3; and Knight, *Beria*, pp. 184, 260, 272.
32 Andrew and Gordievsky, *KGB*, pp. 315, 549; and Knight, *Beria*, pp. 215–6.
33 Sudoplatov and Sudoplatov, *Special Tasks*, pp. 141–2; 'Identifications of Soviet Staff Formerly Stationed in the United Kingdom', 18 October 1954, p. 9, CRS A6283/XR 1, item 56; and 'The Committee of Information ("K.I."), 1947–1951', 17 November 1954, p. 11, CRS A6268/XR 1, item 56.
34 Andrew and Gordievsky, *KGB*, pp. 263, 322.
35 'The Committee of Information ("K.I."), 1947–1951', 17 November 1954, p. 14; 'Report of the Background History of Vladimir Mikhailovich Petrov', 28 June 1954, p. 8, CRS A6283/XR 1, item 80; and 'Brief Outline of the Organisation of the Intelligence Service of the M.V.D.', CRS A6283/XR 1, item 143. See also Deriabin and Gibney, *The Secret World*, p. 212; and Dzhirkvelov, *Secret Servant*, pp. 98–105.
36 'Identifications of Soviet Staff Formerly Stationed in the United Kingdom', 18 October 1954, p. 1, CRS A6283/XR 1, item 56.
37 'R.I.S. Penetration of Foreign Security Services', 20 May 1955, CRS A6283/XR 1, item 9.
38 ibid.
39 'The Committee of Information ("K.I."), 1947–1951', 17 November 1954, p. 11.
40 Andrew and Gordievsky, *KGB*, pp. 238–248; Modin, *My Five Cambridge Friends*, pp. 85–93, 99–103, 109–113; and Sudoplatov and Sudoplatov, *Special Tasks*, pp. 142–3, 227.

41 Deriabin and Gibney, *The Secret World*, pp.117–8; and Sudoplatov and Sudoplatov, *Special Tasks*, p. 227.
42 'Further Material Relating to Identifications of Soviet Personnel Stationed in the United Kingdom', 21 December 1954, p. 6, CRS A6283/XR1, item 7.
43 Deriabin and Gibney, *The Secret World*, pp. 117–8.
44 'R.I.S. Penetration of Foreign Security Services', 20 May 1955, p. 1, CRS A6283/XR1, item 9; and 'The Committee of Information ("K.I."), 1947–1951', 17 November 1954, pp. 11, 12, CRS A6283/XR1, item 56.
45 'Identifications of Soviet Staff Formerly Stationed in the United Kingdom', 18 October 1954, p. 1.
46 Petrov, *Empire of Fear*, p. 211.
47 See, for example, Klehr, Haynes and Firsov, *The Secret World of American Communism*, pp. 70, 205–58.
48 'Soviet State Security Service Foreign Intelligence Operational Techniques ('Legal' Residency System)', 18 May 1955, p. 8, CRS A6283/XR 1, item 9.
49 Central Intelligence Agency (CIA), *Foreign Intelligence and Security Services: USSR*, April 1975, p. 8.
50 Central Intelligence Agency (CIA), *Soviet Intelligence: KGB and GRU*, February 1984, p. 16.
51 For contemporary accounts of GRU organisation and activities by GRU officers during the late 1930s and the 1940s, see Krivisty, *I Was Stalin's Agent*; Akhmedov, *In and Out of Stalin's GRU*; Gouzenko, *This Was My Choice*; and Foote, *Handbook for Spies*.
52 Suvorov, *Inside Soviet Military Intelligence*, p. 179.
53 ibid.
54 ibid; and Central Intelligence Agency, *Soviet Intelligence: KGB and GRU*, February 1984, p. 19.
55 Suvorov, *Inside Soviet Military Intelligence*, pp. 179–80.
56 Central Intelligence Agency (CIA), *Soviet Intelligence: KGB and GRU*, February 1984, p. 17. See also Hohne, *Codeword: Direktor*; Perrault, *The Red Orchestra*; and Read and Fisher, *Operation Lucy*.
57 *The Defection of Igor Gouzenko*, pp. 450, 455.
58 Cited in West, *The Illegals*, p. 189.

CHAPTER 8   THE ARRIVAL OF THE RUSSIANS

1 Barrow, *Canberra's Embassies*, pp. 59–60. See also Desmond Ball, 'The Use of the Soviet Embassy in Canberra for Signals Intelligence (Sigint) Collection', (Working Paper No. 134, Strategic and Defence Studies Centre, Australian National University, Canberra, 1987), pp. 4–6.
2 Thwaites, *Truth Will Out*, p. 64.
3 ibid, p. 63; Petrov, *Empire of Fear*, p. 243; and 'Internal Organisation and Functions of a Soviet Embassy', CRS A 6283/XR 1, item 9.
4 Memo, Hughes to Sgt Swasbrick, 4 May 1945, CRS A6119/83, item 1510, f. 84.
5 Letter dated 3 October 1942 in 'Katherine (sic) Susannah Prichard (Mrs H. Throssell)', CRS A6119/XR1, item 44, part 2, f. 91.
6 'Feodor Nosov', CRS A6119/79, item 1246, f. 89.
7 *Fifth Venona Release*, vol. 3, pp. 188–90.
8 Statutory Declaration by Allan Dalziel, Sydney, 22 March 1955, CRS A6119/79, item 854, f. 119.
9 'Stanley Clive Perry Turnbull', Minute from Royal Commission Section to Deputy Director-General (Operations), 22 November 1954, CRS A6119/79, item 851, f. 133.
10 Mikheev to Lionel Wigmore, 1 April 1943, CRS SP112/1/1, item M50.
11 Allan Dalziel, in Flinders University Library, Adelaide: Evatt Papers, File: Correspondence Misc. 1946–47, p. 2.

12 Statutory Declaration by Colin Simpson, 8 December 1954.
13 Testimony of R. Chiplin, 24 February 1955, *Royal Commission on Espionage: Official Transcript of Proceedings*, Commonwealth Government Printer, Canberra, 1955, p. 2402.
14 Statement by Ian Gray MacInnes, CRS A6119/79, item 851, f. 169.
15 Statement by Forbes Keith Miller, 22 November 1954, CRS A6119/79, item 851, f. 134.
16 'Petrov Twenty Years On—Rupert Lockwood's Personal View', transcript of ABC radio interview, 26 May 1974.
17 Statement by Allan Dalziel, Evatt Papers, p.1. This is evidently a longer and unedited draft of a statutory declaration by Dalziel declared in Sydney on 22 March 1955, CRSA6119/79, item 854, ff. 117–120.
18 Statutory Declaration by Allan John Dalziel, 22 March 1955, p. 2, CRS A6119/79, item 854, f. 119.
19 'Interview with Frederick John MacLean . . . on 10th November, 1954', Memo from Royal Commission Section to ASIO Deputy Director-General (Operations), 11 November 1954,CRS A6119/79, item 851, f. 98.
20 Statement by Allan Dalziel, Evatt Papers, p. 2.
21 'Arrival of Alien Passengers in Sydney', 24 May 1943, Australian Archives, Sydney, CRS C417, item G3028/42, Part 2.
22 Throssell, *My Father's Son*, p. 208.
23 'Makarov, Semen Ivanovich', Minute for Regional Director, Victoria, ASIO Office, Melbourne, 19 January 1956; and 'Interrogation of Mrs Petrov: Semen Ivanovich Makarov', PSO, B2, ASIO Office, Sydney, 5 July 1956, CRS A6119/83, item 1481, ff. 81, 99.
24 'Semen Ivanovich Makarov', CRS A6119/83, item 1481, f. 107.
25 ibid.
26 'Report on the Internal Organisation and Functions of a Soviet Embassy', 28 February 1955, CRS A6283/XR1, item 9.
27 *Report of the Royal Commission on Espionage*, p.85.
28 Security Service Report for the State of South Australia, Fortnight Ending 26 April 1943, Australian Archives (Sydney): C128, box 4.
29 Mrs Cohen to Horner and Ball, 7 April 1994.
30 *Report of the Royal Commission on Espionage*, pp. 23, 89, 93. See also 'Report on the Background History of Vladimir Mikhailovich Petrov', 28 June 1954, pp. 12–13, CRS A6283/XR1, item 80, ff. 133–134; and 'Report on the Background History of Evdokia Alexeyevna Petrov', 2 July 1954, p. 8, CRS A6283/XR1, item 14, f. 133.
31 *Report of the Royal Commission on Espionage*, pp. 89–93; and 'Report on the Background History of Vladimir Mikhailovich Petrov', 28 June 1954, p. 14.
32 *Report of the Royal Commission on Espionage*, pp. 89, 93; and 'Report on the Background History of Vladimir Mikhailovich Petrov', 28 June 1954, p. 14.
33 'List of Amendments to the Report, Dated 21 July, 1954 on Personnel and Structure of Soviet Intelligence Services in Australia 1943–1954', 3 December 1954, CRS A6283/XR1, item 7.
34 'Soviet State Security Service Foreign Intelligence Operational Techniques ("Legal" Residency System)', 18 May 1955, p. 18, CRS A6283/XR1, item 9.
35 'Interrogation of Mrs. Petrov: Semen Ivanovich Makarov', PSO, B2, ASIO Office, Sydney, 5 July 1956, CRS A6119/83, item 1481, f. 99.
36 Extract from ASIO report dated 21 July 1952, CRS A6119/83, item 1481, f. 16.
37 Statement by Vladimir Petrov, 3 April 1954, CRS A6119/79, item 1035, f. 49; and statement by Vladimir Petrov, 12 September 1954, in ibid., f. 111.
38 CRS A6119/79, item 1247, ff 17–19.
39 'Nosov, Feodor Andreevich, and Nosova, Galina Nikolaevna', Memo from Director, New South Wales, to HQ ASIO B2, 24 May 1951, CRSA6119/79, item 1246, ff. 69–70.
40 Statement by Allan Dalziel, Evatt Papers, p. 2.
41 ibid, p. 3.

42 See, for example, 'Alan Dalziel—Feodor Nosov', Memo to ASIO B2, 6 March 1950, CRS A6119/79, item 851, f. 82.
43 Statement by Allan Dalziel, in Evatt Papers, pp. 2, 4.
44 ibid, p. 3.
45 Memo, Regional Director, New South Wales, to ASIO Director-General, 22 June 1953, p. 7, CRS A6119/79, item 798, f. 49.
46 'Frances Ada Garrett nee Burnie', Memo from B2 to ASIO Acting Regional Director, Sydney, 17 November 1959, CRS A6119/79, item 799, ff 182–183; and 'Interview with Frances Ada Garrett on 2 December 1959', Memo, B2 to ASIO Regional Director, Sydney, 2 December 1959, CRS A6119/79, item 799, ff. 195–197.
47 *Report of the Royal Commission on Espionage*, p.159.
48 'Interview with Frederick John MacLean . . . on 10th November 1954', Memo, Royal Commission Section to the Deputy Director-General (Operations), 11 November 1954, CRS A6119/79, item 1247, ff. 93–9.
49 Statement of Constantine Johannes Tenukest, CRS A6283/XR1, item 56, f. 127.
50 'Richard Prichard Throssell', Memo from G. R. Richards to ASIO Director-General, 26 July 1954, p. 3, CRS A6119/57, f. 76.
51 K. S. Prichard to R. Throssell, 20 January 1946, Throssell Papers, National Library of Australia: MS 8071, box 26, folder 183, f. 8.
52 K. S. Prichard to R. Throssell, 13, 20 and 27 January 1946, in ibid, ff. 13; 10–11; 22.
53 Statement by Forbes Keith Miller, 22 November 1954, CRS A6119/79, item 1247, ff. 134–5; and *Report of the Royal Commission on Espionage*, p. 194.
54 'Forbes Keith Miller', Memo, RCS, Sydney, to Deputy Director-General (Operations), 22 November 1954, CRS A6119/79, item 1247, ff. 134–7.
55 Statement by Ian Gray MacInnes, CRS A6119/79, item 851, f. 169; and *Report of the Royal Commission on Espionage*, pp. 194–5.
56 Statutory Declaration by Colin Simpson, 8 December 1954, CRS A6119/79, item 851, ff. 171–3; and *Report of the Royal Commission on Espionage*, pp. 195–6.
57 ibid, pp. 119, 198–206, 229–30.
58 ibid, pp. 196–7; and 'Clement Byrne Christesen [and] Nina Michaelovna Christesen', Memo to Deputy Director-General (Operations), 25 November 1954, CRS A6119/79, item 1247, ff. 155–7.
59 Vladimir M. Petrov, cited in *Report of the Royal Commission on Espionage*, p. 119; see also pp. 107–8.
60 *Report of the Royal Commission on Espionage*, p. 108.
61 'Stanley Clive Perry Turnbull', Minute from Royal Commission Section, Sydney, to Deputy Director-General (Operations), 22 November 1954, CRS A6119/79, item 1247, ff. 131–3.
62 'Mark Younger', Memo, Royal Commission Section, to ASIO Deputy Director-General (Operations), 23 March 1953, CRS A6119/79, item 1246, f. 82.
63 *Report of the Royal Commission on Espionage*, pp. 268–71.
64 Statement of Constantine Johannes Tenukest, CRS A6283/XR 1, item 56, ff. 124–8.
65 Statement by Allan Dalziel, in Evatt Papers, File: Correspondence Misc. 1946–47, p. 4.
66 Memo for the Secretary, Department of External Affairs, 24 March 1950, CRS A1838/2, item 1500/1/3/12, Part 1, f. 99; and Memo for the Director, 'D' Branch, Attorney-General's Department, Canberra, 20 April 1950, in ibid, f. 124.
67 Statement by Mrs E. A. Petrov, 14 September 1954, CRS A6119/79, item 1247, ff. 115–7.
68 Interview with V. Petrov, 26 May 1954, CRS A6119/79, item 1247, ff. 44–6.
69 ibid; and *Report of the Royal Commission on Espionage*, p. 268.
70 ibid, p. 208.
71 Statement by Constantine Johannes Tenukest, CRS A6283/XR1, item 56, f. 125.
72 Attachment to Memo on 'Nosov, Feodor Andreevich, and Nosova, Galina Nikolaevna', from Director, New South Wales, to HQ ASIO B2, 24 May 1951,

CRS A6119/79, item 1246, ff. 69–70; and Attachment to letter from Jack M. Davis to R. Williams, Deputy Director, Commonwealth Investigation Service, Melbourne, 16 June 1954, CRS A1533/1, item 54/946 Misc.
73 Statement by V. Petrov, 12 September 1954, CRS A6119/79, item 1247, f. 111.
74 Statement by Mrs E. A. Petrov, 14 September 1954, CRS A6119/79, item 1247, ff. 115–7.
75 ibid.
76 Statement by V. Petrov, 12 September 1954, CRS A6119/79, item 1247, f. 111; Galina Nosov, 'A Letter From Old Friends', *Friendship* (Newsletter of the Australia–Soviet Friendship Society), (vol. 2, no. 2), February 1958, p. 6. See also Memo from Regional Director, New South Wales, to ASIO Headquarters, 13 May 1958, CRS A6119/79, item 897, ff. 119–20.
77 *Report of the Royal Commission on Espionage*, p. 93.
78 Memo, Director, Canberra, to Director, Sydney, 28 July 1949, CRS A6119/83, item 1481, f. 15.
79 ibid.; 'Personnel and Structure of Soviet Intelligence Services in Australia 1943–1954', 21 July 1954, CRS A6201/1, item 92; and A6283/XR 1, item 23, f. 175.
80 'Report on the Internal Organisation and Functions of a Soviet Embassy', 28 February 1955, p. 18, CRS CRS A6283/XR 1, item 9.
81 *Report of the Royal Commission on Espionage*, p. 96.
82 Extract from 'Interview with Petrov at Safe House Commencing Tuesday, 6 April, 1954', CRS A6283/XR 1, item 23, f. 134.
83 'Chart B: Organisational Structure of the K.I. in Sadovnikov's Day Prior to Arrival of Petrov: mid 1949–February 1951', CRS A6201, item 92.
84 Manne, *The Petrov Affair*, p. 8.
85 'Report on the Background History of Vladimir Mikhailovich Petrov', p. 14. See also testimony of V. M. Petrov, *Royal Commission on Espionage: Official Transcript of Proceedings*, p. 155.
86 Manne, *The Petrov Affair*, p. 203.
87 ibid, p. 8.
88 'Report on the Background History of Vladimir Mikhailovich Petrov', 28 June 1954, pp.14–15; and 'Report on the Background History of Evdokia Alexeyevna Petrova', 2 July 1954, pp. 8–9.
89 *Report of the Royal Commission on Espionage*, p. 90.
90 'Report on the Background History of Vladimir Mikhailovich Petrov', 28 June 1954, p. 15; and *Report of the Royal Commission on Espionage*, pp. 89–93.
91 'Report on the Background History of Vladimir Mikhailovich Petrov', 28 June 1954, p. 17.
92 *Report of the Royal Commission on Espionage*, pp. 35–7, 361–81.
93 Statement by Mrs E. A. Petrov, 14 September 1954, in A6119/79, item 1247, ff. 115–17. See also A6283/XR 1, item 14, f. 255.
94 'Report on the Background History of Vladimir Mikhailovich Petrov', 28 June 1954, p. 17.
95 *Report of the Royal Commission on Espionage*, p. 70; and 'Personnel and Structure of Soviet Intelligence Services in Australia 1943–1954', 21 July 1954, CRS A6201, item 92.
96 Willoughby, *Shanghai Conspiracy*, p. 102; Deakin and Storry, *The Case of Richard Sorge*, pp. 211, 213, 255–6, 347; and Prange, *Target Tokyo*, pp. 312–13, 364, 366, 395, 414.
97 Willoughby, *Shanghai Conspiracy*, pp. 24, 119.
98 Deacon, *Spy!*, pp. 15–6.
99 ibid, pp. 18–23; and Volkman, *Spies*, pp. 114–5.
100 Deacon *Spy!*, pp. 26–32; Volkman, *Spies*, pp. 115–7; and Willoughby, *Shanghai Conspiracy*, pp. 45–7.
101 ibid, p. 61; and Deacon, *Spy!*, p. 36.
102 Willoughby, *Shanghai Conspiracy*, pp. 24, 61–2, 105.
103 Lisa Beyer, 'Red Eyes on the Rising Sun', *Asiaweek*, 11 October 1985, p. 74.
104 Volkman, *Spies*, pp. 112, 113.
105 Prange, *Target Tokyo*, p. 395.

106 Mendelsohn (ed.), *Covert Warfare;* Willoughby, *Shanghai Conspiracy,* p. 100.
107 Willoughby, *Shanghai Conspiracy,* p. 101; and Prange, *Target Tokyo,* p. 312.
108 Deakin and Storry, *The Case of Richard Sorge,* p. 211.
109 Prange, *Target Tokyo,* p. 414; and Deakin and Storry, *The Case of Richard Sorge,* p. 211.
110 Volkman, *Spies,* pp. 117–8; and Deacon, *Spy!,* p. 40.
111 ibid, pp. 46–7.
112 Deakin and Storry, *The Case of Richard Sorge,* p. 350.
113 ibid, pp. 211, 347.
114 'Subject: ZAITSEV Viktor Sergevitch', Military Intelligence Section, General Staff, GHQ, Far East Command, Tokyo, 25 November 1949, NARA: RG 319, item X8997838. See also Prange, *Target Tokyo,* p. 312.
115 Record of interrogation of Mrs Anna Klausen, in Mendelsohn, *Covert Warfare.*
116 'Subject: ZAITSEV Viktor Sergevitch', Military Intelligence Section, General Staff, GHQ, Far East Command, Tokyo, 25 November 1949, NARA: RG 319, item X8997838.
117 ibid.
118 FBI letter dated 28 May 1951, cited in 'Subject: Viktor Sergevitch Zaitsev, wa. "Serge"', Memo from Office of the Assistant Chief of Staff, G–2, Commander-in-Chief, Far East Command, Tokyo, 22 June 1951, NARA: RG 319, item X8997838.
119 'Subject: The Richard Sorge Case (Viktor Sergevitch Zaitsev)', Memorandum from John Edgar Hoover, Director, Federal Bureau of Investigation (FBI) to the Director of Intelligence, General Staff, Department of the Army, The Pentagon, Washington, D.C., 28 October 1949, NARA: RG 319, item X8997838.
120 'Personnel and Structure of Soviet Intelligence Services in Australia 1943–1954', 21 July 1954, CRS A6201, item 92.
121 Colin Moodie, letter (and attached 'Note Regarding Victor Zaitsev and the USSR Legation') to Ball and Horner, 21 August 1993.
122 ibid.
123 'Subject: Celebration of the Anniversary of the Signing of the Anglo-Soviet Treaty, Held at Sydney Town Hall on 26/5/43', Security Service, Sydney, 27 May 1943, CRS A6119, item 53, ff. 10–11.
124 J. M. Gilmour, Royal Commission Section, ASIO, 'Laurence Frederic Fitzhardinge', 29 November 1954, CRS, A6283/XR 1, item 56, ff. 205–206; and statement of L. F. Fitzhardinge, 26 November 1954, ibid, ff. 202–205.
125 ibid; and Royal Commission Section to PSO B2, ASIO, 29 November 1954, A/6119/79, item 1247, ff. 160–4.
126 Moodie to Ball and Horner, 21 August 1993.
127 Hasluck, *Diplomatic Witness,* p. 49.
128 Moodie to Ball and Horner, 21 August 1993.
129 ibid.
130 ibid.
131 Statement by S. R. Phippard, 26 November 1954, CRS A6119/79, item 1247, ff. 165–167.
132 A1066/1 IC45/4/2/9.
133 'Soviet Delegation', Memo from W. H. Barnwell to Deputy Director, Security Service, 3 January 1947, CRS A6119/79, item 851, f. 19.
134 Moodie to Ball and Horner, 21 August 1993.
135 Interview with Colin Moodie, 17 August 1993.
136 Memo on 'Richard Prichard THROSSELL' from G. R. Richards to the Director-General, ASIO, 26 July 1954, CRS A6119, Item 57, f. 76.
137 'Soviet Delegation', Memo from W. H. Barnwell to Deputy Director, Security Service, 3 January 1947, CRS A6119/79, item 851, f. 19.
138 Summary of interview with Mrs Beryl Jane Philpott, 21 June 1950, CRS A6119/77, item 799, f. 123.
139 Allan John Dalziel, Statutory Declaration, 22 March 1955, CRS A6119/79, item 854, f. 118.
140 'Soviet Delegation', Memo from W. H. Barnwell to Deputy Director, Security

Service, 3 January 1947, CRS A6119/79, item 851, f. 19; and Dalziel statement to the Royal Commission on Espionage.
141 'Soviet Delegation', Memo from W. H. Barnwell to Deputy Director, Security Service, 3 January 1947, CRS A6119/79, item 851, f. 19.
142 ASIO file on Allan John Dalziel, CRS A6119/79, item 854, ff. 129, 134.
143 'Subject: Viktor Sergevitch Zaitsev, wa. "Serge"', Memo from the Office of the Assistant Chief of Staff, G–2, Department of the Army, to Assistant Chief of Staff, G–2, Commander-in-Chief, Far East Command, Tokyo, 22 June 1951, NARA: RG 319, item X8997838.
144 Letter, USSR Legation to the Department of External Affairs, Canberra, 12 September 1947, CRS A 1067/1 item C46/4/2/2.
145 'Viktor Sergectich Zaitsev', Report by Joshua D. Ensor, Federal Bureau of Investigation (FBI), New York Office, 26 May 1951, NARA: RG 319, item X8997838.
146 Deakin and Storry, *The Case of Richard Sorge*, p. 211.
147 Testimony of V. M. Petrov, 2 July 1954, *Royal Commission on Espionage: Official Transcript of Proceedings*, Commonwealth Government Printer, Canberra, 1955, p. 106.
148 'Subject: ZAITSEV Viktor Sergevitch', Military Intelligence Section, General Staff, GHQ, Far East Command, Tokyo, 25 November 1949, NARA: RG 319, item X8997838.
149 'Subject: The Richard Sorge Case (Viktor Sergevitch Zaitsev)', Memo from John Edgar Hoover, Director, FBI, to Director of Intelligence, General Staff, Department of the Army, 28 October 1949, NARA: RG 319, item X8997838.
150 'Subject: Viktor Sergevitch Zaitsev, wa. "Serge"', Memo from Office of the Assistant Chief of Staff, G–2, Department of the Army, to Assistant Chief of Staff, G–2, Commander-in-Chief, Far East Command, Tokyo, 22 June 1951, NARA: RG 319, item X8997838.
151 'Viktor Sergevitch Zaitsev', Report by Joshua D. Ensor, FBI, New York Office, 20 December 1951, NARA: RG 319, item X8997838.
152 ibid.
153 Spry to Horner, 17 June 1993. See Willoughby, *Shanghai Conspiracy*, p. 102.
154 '"Illegal" Operations of the Soviet Intelligence Services', 25 August 1954, p. 13, CRS A6283/XR1, item 143, f. 169.
155 Interview with Colin Moodie, 17 August 1993.
156 *Report of the Royal Commission on Espionage*, pp. 71–72.
157 Testimony of V. M. Petrov, 5 July 1954, *Royal Commission on Espionage: Official Transcript of Proceedings*, p. 130.
158 ibid; *Report of the Royal Commission on Espionage*, pp. 85–86; and CRS A 6283/XR 1, item 5, ff. 9–14.
159 'Internal Organisation and Functions of a Soviet Embassy', CRS A 6283/XR 1, item 9, f. 27.
160 During the period covered in this story, cables from Canberra to Moscow were transmitted by means of two carriers (radio-telegraph and telegraphic cable), both of which operated via the General Post Office in London. The radio telegraph, which involved direct transmission by short-wave 'beams' between stations near Melbourne and at Poldhu in Cornwall, was established by Amalgamated Wireless (Australasia) Limited (AWA) in 1927. Telegraph cables, operated by Cable and Wireless Limited, went either westward from Cottesloe (near Perth) to London via Cocos Island, Mauritius and South Africa, or eastward from La Perouse in Sydney via Hawaii, Vancouver and Newfoundland. (Connections from Darwin via Banjoewangi and Batavia in Java, Singapore, Penang and Rangoon were out of service from February 1942 until the end of the Second World War.) The Overseas Telecommunications Commission (OTC) was established in August 1946. It assumed control of the AWA radio telegraph services on 1 February 1947, and the Cable and Wireless cable system on 1 July 1947.
See Harcourt, *Taming the Tyrant*, ch. 8–11; Graves, *The Thin Red Lines*, pp. 68–82; Amalgamated Wireless (Australasia) Limited, *AWA and the War*; J. C. Harrison, 'An Outline of the Development of Telecommunication Services Between

Australia and Places Overseas—Part 1', *The Telecommunication Journal of Australia*, (vol. 5, no. 2), October 1944, pp. 65–76; J. C. Harrison, 'An Outline of the Development of Telecommunication Services Between Australia and Places Overseas—Part 2', *The Telecommunication Journal of Australia*, (vol. 5, no. 3), February 1945, pp. 160–169; Wood, *Empire Telegraph Communications*, pp. 44–46; and information provided by Kimberly O'Sullivan, Archives Coordinator, Australian and Overseas Telecommunications Corporation (AOTC), Sydney, 9 February 1993 and 12 February 1993.
161 *Report of the Royal Commission on Espionage*, p. 86.
162 'M.V. D. Cables', CRS A 6183/XR 1, item 79, f. 139.
163 ibid.
164 Lamphere and Shachtman, *The FBI-KGB War*, p. 87.
165 Wright, *Spycatcher*, p. 184; and Martin, *Wilderness of Mirrors*, p. 48.
166 'M.V. D. Cables', CRS A 6283/XR 1, item 79, f. 139.

CHAPTER 9 POSTWAR SECURITY AND INTELLIGENCE IN AUSTRALIA

1 Holloway, *Stalin and the Bomb*, p. 222.
2 Crisp, *Ben Chifley*, pp. 1–11, 213–29.
3 ibid, p. 276.
4 ibid.
5 ibid, pp. 197, 238.
6 ibid, p. 238.
7 Edwards, *Prime Ministers and Diplomats*, pp. 171–3.
8 Dalziel, *Evatt the Enigma*, pp. 8–9.
9 Edwards, *Prime Ministers and Diplomats*, p. 173.
10 Dalziel, *Evatt the Enigma*, p. 16.
11 Winter, *The Intrigue Master*, pp. 38, 88.
12 'Dr John Wear Burton', ASIO, August 1952, CRS A6119/XR1, item 128, ff. 104–7.
13 Burton, *The Alternative*, p. 89.
14 ibid, p. 90.
15 ibid, pp. 12, 13, 25, 71.
16 Dalziel, *Evatt the Enigma*, p. 20.
17 Throssell, *My Father's Son*, p. 215.
18 Evatt Papers: External Affairs, Reports and Intelligence Summaries 1942–47.
19 Winter, *The Intrigue Master*, p. 179.
20 Hasluck, *Diplomatic Witness*, p. 30.
21 Katharine Susannah Prichard, 'Deakin and Evatt', *The Realist*, no. 30, Spring 1968, republished in Prichard, *Straight Left*, pp. 101–12; and attachment to letter from K. S. Throssell to Mrs. Evatt, 21 June 1968, in Evatt Papers, Correspondence Misc. 1946–47.
22 'Exhibit J', CRS A6202, Exhibit J, pp. 33, 37.
23 'Dalziel, Allan John', CRS A6119/79, item 854, ff. 133–4.
24 Submission by Dr J. Burton to the *Royal Commission on Espionage*, 5 January 1955, CRS A6213, item RCE/2/9.
25 Cable 59, Deschamps to Burton, 20 March 1947, Hudson and Way, *Documents in Australian Foreign Policy 1937–49, Volume XII: 1947*, p. 422.
26 Watt, *Australian Diplomat*, p. 106.
27 Dr John Burton, interviewed by John Highfield, 'When Gnomes Reared Their Heads', *Nation Review*, 6–12 April 1973, p. 769.
28 John Burton, 'Secrecy Cloaks Policy Malaise', *Canberra Times*, 3 July 1995, p. 11.
29 Testimony of Dr J. Burton, 2 November 1954, in *Royal Commission on Espionage: Official Transcript of Proceedings*.
30 ibid.
31 ibid.
32 ibid.

33 Edwards, *Prime Ministers and Diplomats*, p. 176.
34 Hasluck, *Diplomatic Witness*, p. 58.
35 Committee of Review [of] Civil Staffing of Wartime Activities, *Review of the Department of External Affairs*, 31 October 1945, in CRS A6119/XR1, item 18, ff. 61–5.
36 Hasluck, *Diplomatic Witness*, pp. 130–1.
37 'Defence Post-Hostilities Planning Committee: P.H.P. Organization', (D.P.H.P. (45) 2 (Final)), 7 March 1945, CRS A5954, item 604/7.
38 'Report of a Meeting of Representatives of the Services and the Departments of Defence and External Affairs at Canberra, January 18 and 19, 1945', CRS A5954, item 604/7.
39 'Defence Post-Hostilities Planning Committee: P.H.P. Organization', (D.P.H.P. (45) 2 (Final)), 7 March 1945, in A5954, item 604/7; and 'Post-Hostilities Planning Papers', Memo to the Secretary, Defence Committee, 21 April 1945, CRS A5954, item 604/1.
40 War Cabinet Agendum No 24/1945, 8 January 1945, CRS A2670, item 24/1945.
41 Advisory War Council Minute No 1566, Canberra, 20 June 1945, CRS A2680, item 26/1945.
42 For Airy's visit to Australia see Simpson to Kirkman, 4 August 1944, Australian Archives (Adelaide): Series D1919, item SS1093.
43 Swan typescript.
44 Committee of Review—Civil Staffing of Wartime Activities, 'Report on Security Service, 13 September 1945', ibid.
45 Simpson, to Deputy Director of Security, 18 September 1945, AA1981/132, item, box 1.
46 Lt-Col C. A. K. Cohen to ADMI, 25 October 1945, AA1981/132, item, box 1.
47 Lt-Col C. A. K. Cohen to ADMI, 1 November 1945, AA1981/132, item, box 1.
48 See papers in CRS A367/4, item C62544, part 2.
49 Documents held by ASIO.
50 For a description see Arneill, *Black Jack*.
51 Spry to Horner, 17 June 1993; Sir Frederick Chilton to D. M. Horner and D. J. Ball, 2 March 1993.
52 F. R. Sinclair to Secretary, Prime Minister's Department, 28 September 1945, CRS A461/1, item D318/1/2.
53 Adjutant-General to NSW L of C Area, 16 October 1945, AWM 54, item 721/1/34.
54 Maj-Gen C. H. Finlay to D. M. Horner, 1 March 1993.
55 'Report on Joint Intelligence Organisation—Post War, 1 November 1945', reproduced in Swan typescript.
56 ibid.
57 ibid.
58 These proposals are set out in Council of Defence Agendum 2/1946, 5 April 1946, and other associated documents in CRS A5954, item 2364/2.
59 Spry to Horner, 17 June 1993. Spry recalled that Shedden told him that the best the Army could do at this stage was to designate an officer to study 'combined operations'.
60 Attachment to Chiefs of Staff Minute No 3/1946, CRS A2364/2, item Signal Intelligence.
61 Council of Defence Minute, 9 April 1946, quoted in Swan typescript.
62 *Commonwealth Parliamentary Debates*, 1945–46, 20 March 1946, p. 417.
63 Shedden to Travis, 4 July 1946, CRS A5954, item 2364/2.
64 Cabinet Agendum No 1213 of 19 July 1946, Swan typescript
65 Shedden to Travis, 4 July 1946, CRS A5954, item 2364/2.
66 Documents held by ASIO.
67 Shedden to Secretary, Defence Committee, 2 August 1946, CRS A5954, item 2364/2.
68 Christopher Andrew, 'The Growth of the Australian Intelligence Community and the Anglo-American Connection', *Intelligence and National Security*, vol. 4, no. 2, April 1989, pp. 225–6.

69 'Review of the Joint Intelligence Organization to 31st January, 1949—Report by Controller of Joint Intelligence to Joint Intelligence Committee', CRS A5954, item 2364/5. An organisation chart is in CRS A5954, item 2364/2.
70 Rogers to Blamey, 14 August 1944, 3DRL6643, item 2/56.8. The conference began on 6 September 1944. A little later the Australian Director of Allied Air Intelligence for the SWPA, Air Vice-Marshal J. E. Hewitt, visited England for similar reasons. The RAAF had sent a squadron leader to accompany Rogers, but he had proved to be too junior.
71 Rogers to Blamey 14 August 1944, 3DRL6643, item 2/56.8.
72 Christopher Andrew, 'The Making of the Anglo-American SIGINT Alliance', in Hayden B. Peake and Samuel Halpern (eds), *In the Name of Intelligence: Essays in Honour of Walter Pforzheimer*, Naval Intelligence Book Centre, Washington DC, 1994, p. 103.
73 Sandford to Berryman, 16 November 1945, Berryman Papers, DRL4.11, personal correspondence file.
74 S. Mason to D. J. Ball, 7 July 1995.
75 S. Mason to D. C. S. Sissons, 26 June 1994.
76 Professor Ian Smith to D. C. S. Sissons, 29 September 1996.
77 Sissons to Ball, 22 May 1996.
78 M. A. Williams to D. J. Ball, 9 July 1995
79 Ballard to DMI, 30 January 1947, CRS A6923/3, item SI/7. Some of the correspondence is in CRS A5954, item 2364/5. Correspondence was channelled through Admiral Sir Louis Hamilton, RN, the Chief of the Australian Naval Staff.
80 Details of the visit are in CRS A5954, item 2364/5. See also West, *GCHQ*, p. 153; and Welchman, *The Hut Six Story*, p. 95.
81 Joint Intelligence Committee, 'Joint Intelligence Organisation—Post War Australian Sigint Centre', Report No 25/46, attached to Defence Committee Minute 26 November 1946, CRS A2364/2, item Signba Intelligence.
82 Richelson and Ball, *The Ties That Bind*, pp. 142-3.
83 A. P. Fleming to D. M. Horner, 17 June 1993.
84 Spry to Horner, 17 June 1993.
85 'Obituaries: Lt-Cdr Teddy Poulden', *Daily Telegraph* (London), 20 November 1992.
86 Andrew, 'The Making of the Anglo–American SIGINT Alliance,' p.105.
87 Andrew, 'The Growth of the Australian Intelligence Community and the Anglo-American Connection', p. 223.
88 Notes for Secretary on Defence Committee Agendum No 2/1950, 11 January 1950, CRS A5954, item 2364/5.
89 Thompson to Ball, 27 September 1994.
90 Ballard, *On ULTRA Active Service*, pp. 43, 47, 57, 65, 114, 136, 143, 161, 178-9, 183-4, 188-91, 304.
91 Thompson to Ball, 27 September 1994.
92 A. P. Fleming to D. J. Ball and D. M. Horner, 17 November 1993.
93 West, *GCHQ*, p. 182.
94 Ballard, *On ULTRA Active Service*, pp. 299-300.
95 War Diary, 29 August 1945, Advanced Land Headquarters, GS Intelligence, AWM 52, item 1/2/2.
96 Bamford, *The Puzzle Palace*, p. 424.
97 JIC (S) Report No 2/1949, CRS A5954, item 2364/5.
98 Finlay to Horner, 1 March 1993.
99 Sadler to Horner, 15 February 1993.
100 See correspondence in CRS A5954, item 2364/2.
101 Spry personal file, Central Army Records Office.
102 Stretton, *Soldier in a Storm*, p. 69.
103 Spry to Horner, 17 June 1993.
104 ibid.
105 Stretton, *Soldier in a Storm*, p. 69.
106 Memo of Conversation, 20 April 1949, Naval Aide to the President Files, Harry S. Truman Papers, Truman Library.

107 Spry to Horner, 17 June 1993.
108 For an account of the withdrawal of Major David Morris see Bernice Morris, *Between the Lines*.
109 Spry to Horner, 17 June 1993.
110 'Annual Confidential Report for the Year Ending 30 June 1949', Spry file, Central Army Records Office.
111 Spry to Horner, 17 June 1993.
112 Chilton to Horner and Ball, 2 March 1993.
113 Documents held by ASIO.
114 Quoted in documents held by ASIO.
115 ibid.
116 Finlay to Horner, 1 March 1993.
117 Swan typescript.
118 Documents held by ASIO.
119 Cable 835, Makin to Chifley, 27 June 1947, Hudson and Way, *Documents in Australian Foreign Policy 1937–49, Volume XII: 1947*, p. 408–9.
120 Hillenkoetter to the President, 27 January 1948, Harry S Truman Library, Independence, Missouri: Naval Aide to the President Files, Truman Papers.
121 Documents held by ASIO.
122 Hollis to Shedden, 10 March 1947, CRS A5954/1, item 1847/1.
123 Frank Cain, 'An Aspect of Post-War Australian Relations with the United Kingdom and the United States: Missiles, Spies and Disharmony', *Australian Historical Studies*, vol. 23, no. 92, April 1989, p. 201.

CHAPTER 10   OPERATION VENONA

1 Benson, *Introductory History of Venona*, p. 8; and Lamphere and Shachtman, *The FBI-KGB War*, pp. 80–101.
2 Benson, *The 1942–43 New York-Moscow KGB Messages*.
3 Wright, *Spycatcher*, pp. 182, 283–5; and *Fifth Venona Release*, vol. 2, pp. 245–78.
4 ibid, pp. 186–7, 238.
5 'The KGB and the GRU in Europe, South America and Australia', *Venona Historical Monograph No. 5*, Center for Cryptologic History, National Security Agency, Fort George G. Meade, Maryland, October 1996), p. 5. See also Wright, *Spycatcher*, p. 184.
6 John Ferris, 'Before "Room 40": The British Empire and Signals Intelligence, 1898–1914', *The Journal of Strategic Studies*, vol. 12, no. 4, December 1989, p. 437; Desmond Ball, 'Signals Intelligence in India', *Intelligence and National Security*, vol. 10, no. 3, July 1995, p. 377; Andrew, *The Growth of Intelligence Collaboration*, p. 3; and Stripp, *Codebreaker in the Far East*, p. 50.
7 John Ferris, 'Before "Room 40"', p. 441.
8 Christopher Andrew, 'Codebreakers and Foreign Offices: The French, British and American Experience', in Andrew and Dilks, *The Missing Dimension*, p. 45; West, *GCHQ*, p. 76; and West, *MI 6*, pp. 25–6. Fetterlein returned to Bletchley Park soon after the outbreak of the Second World War, and later worked on breaking German one-time pad ciphers. See P. W. Filby, 'Floradora and a Unique Break Into One-Time Pad Ciphers', *Intelligence and National Security*, vol. 10, no. 3, July 1995, pp. 412, 421.
9 Skillen, *Spies of the Airwaves*, p. 50; West, *GCHQ*, p. 92; and Hinsley, *British Intelligence in the Second World War, Volume 1*, p. 199.
10 West, *GCHQ*, p. 76.
11 Ullman, *The Anglo-Soviet Accord*, ch. VII.
12 'The "Daily Herald": Lansbury's Orders From Moscow', *The Times* (London), 19 August 1920, p. 10.
13 Andrew and Gordievsky, *KGB*, p. 55.
14 ibid.
15 Andrew, *Secret Service*, p. 296; and Andrew and Gordievsky, *KGB*, p. 55.

16 Baldwin, House of Commons, *Parliamentary Debates*, vol. 206, 24 May 1927, pp. 1847–52.
17 House of Commons, *Parliamentary Debates*, vol. 206, 26 May 1927, pp. 2195–326.
18 Hinsley, *British Intelligence in the Second World War, Volume 1*, p. 52; and Andrew, *Secret Service*, p. 332.
19 Denniston, cited in Andrew, *Secret Service*, p. 332.
20 Barker, *The History of Codes and Ciphers*, p. 69.
21 Hinsley, *British Intelligence in the Second World War, Volume 1*, p. 53; and Andrew, *Secret Service*, p. 332.
22 A. G. Denniston, 'Account of Origin and Work of the Government Code and Cypher School (G.C. and C.S.)', (1944), p. 10, in Churchill Archives Centre, Churchill College, Cambridge: A.G. Denniston Collection, DENN 1/4. See also A. G. Denniston, 'The Government Code and Cypher School Between the Wars', *Intelligence and National Security*, vol. 1, no. 1, January 1986, pp. 57–58.
23 Desmond Ball, 'Signals Intelligence (Sigint) in Pakistan', *Strategic Analysis*, vol. XVIII, no. 2, May 1995, p. 195; and Skillen, *Spies of the Airwaves*, p. 496.
24 Hinsley, *British Intelligence in the Second World War, Volume 1*, p. 199. See also Calvocoressi, *Top Secret Ultra*, p. 110; Pincher, *Too Secret Too Long*, p. 69; Wright, *Spycatcher*, p. 182 and Smith, *The Ultra-Magic Deals*, p. 144.
25 Hinsley, *British Intelligence in the Second World War, Volume 1*, p. 199.
26 West, *Molehunt*, p. 41.
27 Memo by Officer Commanding No. 2 W/T Company, 26 July 1941, and No. 2 Wireless Company to 4th Australian Special Wireless Section, 28 October 1941, War Diary HQ Australian Special Wireless Group, AWM 52, item 7/39/3, September 1942.
28 Robert Cecil, 'Five of Six at War: Section V of MI 6', *Intelligence and National Security*, vol. 9, no. 2, April 1994, p. 352.
29 'Reception of Stations in Russia, 24.6.43', PRO: WO 201/2837.
30 Memo, R. H. Owen, MEW, Office of the Minister of State, Cairo, to PAIC (L), GHQ MEF, 16 August 1943, WO 201/2837.
31 Memo, PAIC, Liaison Section, GHQ, MEF, to Col. E. P. J. Ryan, DDMI, GHQ, PAIFORCE, November 1943, WO 201/2837.
32 West, *GCHQ*, p. 119.
33 Hinsley and Simkins, *British Intelligence in the Second World War, Volume 4*, pp. 43, 72; Howard, *British Intelligence in the Second World War, Volume 5*, p. 14; and West, *MI 5* p. 137.
34 West, *GCHQ*, p. 119.
35 Hinsley and Simkins, *British Intelligence in the Second World War, Volume 4*, p. 72; and West, *MI 6*, p. 157.
36 West, *GCHQ*, pp. 125–6.
37 ibid, p. 166, 120, 200, 214; and Pincher, *Too Secret Too Long*, p. 68.
38 West, *MI 6*, p. 213.
39 Hinsley and Simkins, *British Intelligence in the Second World War, Volume 4*, p. 183.
40 ibid, p. 181.
41 Pincher, *Too Secret Too Long*, pp. 68–72; and West, *Molehunt*, p. 41.
42 Cave Brown, 'C', p. 616.
43 Cited in ibid.
44 ibid; and Cecil, 'Five of Six at War', p. 352.
45 Costello, *Mask of Treachery*, p. 437.
46 Cecil, 'Five of Six at War', p. 352.
47 Pincher, *Too Secret Too Long*, p. 68.
48 Cave Brown, 'C', pp. 321–4, 621–2; Costello, *Mask of Treachery*, pp. 438–40; and Philby, *My Silent War*, pp. 101–16.
49 Pincher, *Too Secret Too Long*, p. 68.
50 See Farago, *The Broken Seal*, p. 253; Bamford, *The Puzzle Palace:*, p. 311; and Richelson and Ball, *The Ties That Bind*, p. 137.
51 Clark, *The Man Who Broke Purple*, p. 119.
52 ibid, pp. 119–21; and Bamford, *The Puzzle Palace*, p. 312.

53 Richelson and Ball, *The Ties That Bind*, p. 137; and Stevenson, *A Man Called Intrepid*, pp. 177, 273.
54 Cited in Smith, *The Ultra-Magic Deals*, pp. 138, 144.
55 ibid, pp. 144, 155, 197–8.
56 Smith, *The Ultra-Magic Deals*, ch. 6; Bamford, *The Puzzle Palace*, p. 314; and Richelson and Ball, *The Ties That Bind*, pp. 138–9, 141–51.
57 Smith, *The Ultra-Magic Deals*, pp. 208–9.
58 Cave Brown, 'C', pp. 629–31; and Smith, *The Ultra-Magic Deals*, ch. 8.
59 Benson and Warner, *Venona*, p. xl.
60 Cited in Cave Brown, 'C', pp. 686–7.
61 ibid, p. 687.
62 Clark, *The Man Who Broke Purple*, p. 162.
63 Gladys Taylor, 'The Role of the ATS Special Operator', in Skillen, *The Enigma Symposium 1994*; and Barbara B. Littlejohn, 'Eavesdropping on the Enemy', in ibid.
64 Skillen, *Spies of the Airwaves*, p. 369.
65 Desmond Ball, 'Over and Out: Signals Intelligence (Sigint) in Hong Kong', *Intelligence and National Security*, vol. 11, no. 3, July 1996, p. 477.
66 Stripp, *Codebreaker in the Far East*, p. 60; and Alan Stripp, 'Japanese Army Air Force Codes at Bletchley Park and Delhi', in Hinsley and Stripp, *Codebreakers*, p. 295.
67 West, *GCHQ*, p. 223.
68 Granatstein, *A Man of Influence:*, pp. 180–1; and Scott Anderson, 'The Evolution of the Canadian Intelligence Establishment, 1945–1950', *Intelligence and National Security*, vol. 9, no. 3, July 1994, p. 461.
69 West, *GCHQ*, pp. 216, 221; and West, *A Matter of Trust*, p. 28.
70 Ralph Thompson to D. J. Ball, 27 September 1994.
71 West, *GCHQ*, p. 224.
72 Bamford, *The Puzzle Palace*, p. 246.
73 ibid. See also Lamphere and Schachtman, *The FBI-KGB War*, p. 87.
74 Notes of interview of Dr A. P. Treweek by D. C. S. Sissons, 11 October 1990; Professor A. D. Trendall to D. J. Ball, 10 May 1990.
75 Rogers to Blamey, 18 January 1945, 3DRL6643, item 2/59.
76 Joint Intelligence Committee (JIC) Report No. 10, 1946, 'Report on London Conference', p. 4, attached to 'Minute by the Chiefs of Staff at Meeting Held on Thursday, 4th July 1946', CRS A2364/2, item: Signal Intelligence, f. 68; and Ball, 'Over and Out: Signals Intelligence (Sigint) in Hong Kong', p. 480.
77 Bamford, *The Puzzle Palace*, p. 391. See also Richelson and Ball, *The Ties That Bind*, pp. 141–4.
78 Bamford, *The Puzzle Palace*, p. 391.
79 For discussion of the KGB encryption system during this period, see Kahn, *Kahn On Codes*, pp. 146–64; Martin, *Wilderness of Mirrors*, pp. 41–4; and Lamphere and Shachtman, *The FBI–KGB War*, pp. 82–7.
80 Wright, *Spycatcher*, pp. 180–1.
81 Lamphere and Shachtman, *The FBI–KGB War*, p. 83; Wright, *Spycatcher*, p. 179; and Kahn, *Kahn on Codes*, p. 157.
82 Benson and Warner, *Venona: Soviet Espionage and the American Response*, p. xv.
83 Benson, *The 1942–43 New York–Moscow KGB Messages*, p. 2.
84 ibid, pp. 8–9.
85 ibid.
86 Wright, *Spycatcher*, p. 184; and Martin, *Wilderness of Mirrors*, p. 48.
87 'M.V.D. Cables', CRS A6283/XR I, item 79, f. 139.
88 Benson, *Introductory History of Venona*, p. 1.
89 *The Origin and Development of the Army Security Agency 1917–1947*; and Brownell, *The Origin and Development of the National Security Agency*.
90 ibid, pp. 1–2; and Benson, *The 1942–43 New York–Moscow KGB Messages*, p. 1.
91 Benson, *Introductory History of Venona*, p. 2.
92 ibid, pp. 2 3; and Benson and Warner, *Venona*, p. xv.
93 Benson and Warner, *Venona*, pp. xiv-xvi, xxix.
94 Benson, *Introductory History of Venona*, p. 199.

95 Lamphere and Shachtman, *The FBI–KGB War*, p. 84.
 96 Gardner, interview with I. Livingstone, 7 October 1996.
 97 ibid.
 98 Benson, *Introductory History of Venona*, p. 2.
 99 ibid, p. 2.
100 ibid, pp. 3–4.
101 ibid, p. 4.
102 Benson and Warner, *Venona*, p. xxi.
103 ibid.
104 Meredith Knox Gardner, 'Special Analysis Report No. 1: Covernames in Diplomatic Traffic', (ASA, Washington, D.C., 30 August 1947), in Benson and Warner, *Venona*, pp. 93–104.
105 ibid; and Benson, *Introductory History of Venona*, p. 4.
106 Gardner, 'Special Report No.1: Covernames in Diplomatic Traffic', 30 August 1947.
107 ibid.
108 See 'War Cabinet Documents Obtained by "KLOD" Through Friends in "the Nook": Documents Photographed and Returned (1946)', Canberra to Moscow No. 123, 19 March 1946 in *Fifth Venona Release*, vol. 3, pp. 200–1.
109 Gardner, interview by I. Livingstone, 7 October 1996.
110 Benson, *Introductory History of Venona*, pp. 4–6; and Benson and Warner, *Venona*, p. xxii.
111 Benson and Warner, *Venona*, p. xxiii.
112 Lamphere and Schachtman, *The FBI–KGB War*, pp. 68–9.
113 ibid, p. 80.
114 ibid, pp. 87–8.
115 ibid, p. 88; Martin, *Wilderness of Mirrors*, p. 43; and Wright, *Spycatcher*, p. 182.
116 Lamphere and Shachtman, *The FBI–KGB War*, p. 88; and 'Cracking a Soviet Cipher', *Newsweek*, 19 May 1980, p. 34.
117 Benson, *Introductory History of Venona*, p. 6; and Benson and Warner, *Venona*, pp. xxiii, xli.
118 Benson and Warner, *Venona*, pp. xxiv-xxv.
119 Pincher, *Too Secret Too Long*, pp. 140–2; Hyde, *The Atom Bomb Spies*, p. 19; Lamphere and Shachtman, *The FBI–KGB War*, pp. 138–9; and 'Cracking a Soviet Cipher', *Newsweek*, 19 May 1980, p. 4.
120 Lamphere and Shachtman, *The FBI–KGB War*, pp. 30, 183, 217; and Venona decrypts of the 1944–45 Moscow–New York and Moscow–Washington traffic.
121 Benson and Warner, *Venona*, p. xxv.
122 ibid, p. 8.
123 Benson, *The 1942–43 New York–Moscow KGB Messages*, p. 7.
124 Benson, *Introductory History of Venona*, p. 8.
125 Benson, *The 1942–43 New York–Moscow KGB Messages*, p. 8.
126 ibid.
127 ibid.
128 Benson, *Introductory History of Venona* p. 10.
129 Lamphere and Schachtman, *The FBI–KGB War*, p. 63.
130 Benson and Warner, *Venona*, p. xxiii.
131 Robert Louis Benson, *Introductory History of Venona*, p. 10.
132 Lamphere and Schachtman, *The FBI–KGB War*, p. 69; and *Of Moles and Molehunters*, p. 39.
133 ibid.
134 Borovik, *The Philby Files*, p. 235.
135 Richard J. Aldrich, 'Secret Intelligence for a Post-War World: Reshaping the British Intelligence Community, 1944–51', in Aldrich, *British Intelligence, Strategy and the Cold War*, pp. 27–8.
136 Benson and Warner, *Venona*, p. xiv; and PRO, 'Release of Records of the Government Communications Headquarters: Signals Intelligence Relating to the Venona Project', 1 October 1996.
137 West, *GCHQ*, pp. 92–4, 102–3, 129, 205; and Bamford, *The Puzzle Palace*, pp. 171–2.
138 Lewin, *The American Magic*, pp. 136–7.

139 Information from Renee Frank, NSA, 24 January 1997.
140 PRO, 'Release of Records of the Government Communications Headquarters: Signals Intelligence Relating to the Venona Project', 1 October 1996.
141 Information from Renee Frank, NSA, 24 January 1997.
142 PRO, 'Release of Records of the Government Communications Headquarters: Signals Intelligence Relating to the Venona Project', 1 October 1996.
143 Meredith Gardner, interview with I. Livingstone, 7 October 1996; and Wright, *Spycatcher*, p. 195.
144 Richard Aldrich and Michael Coleman, 'The Cold War, the JIC and British Signals Intelligence, 1948', *Intelligence and National Security*, vol. 4, no. 3, July 1989, pp. 535–49.
145 ibid, pp. 537, 547.
146 Lamphere and Shachtman, *The FBI-KGB War*, pp. 131–3.
147 ibid.
148 ibid; and Bower, *The Perfect English Spy*, p. 91.
149 Philby, *My Silent War*, p. 153; and Cave Brown, 'C', p. 697.
150 'The KGB and the GRU in Europe, South America and Australia', *Venona Historical Monograph No. 5*, Center for Cryptologic History, National Security Agency, Fort George G. Meade, Maryland, October 1996, p. 5. See also Wright, *Spycatcher*, p. 184.
151 Cited in Costello, *Mask of Treachery*, p. 516.
152 Borovik, *The Philby Files*, p. 235.
153 Benson, *Introductory History of Venona*, p. 10.
154 Romerstein and Levhenko, *The KGB Against the 'Main Enemy'*, pp. 111–12; and Andrew and Gordievsky, *KGB*, pp. 230–1.
155 Smith, *The Shadow Warriors*, pp. 354–5; and Lamphere and Schachtman, *The FBI–KGB War*, pp. 86–7.
156 Benson and Warner, *Venona*, pp. xxvii-xxviii; 'Espionage Directed Against the United States', Memorandum from Kenneth E. Geisen, Chief, Legislative and Public Affairs Division (DI-3), Defense Intelligence Agency (DIA) to the Senate Committee on Governmental Affairs, Permanent Subcommittee on Investigations, 3 December 1984; Wright, *Spycatcher*, p. 184; and Martin, *Wilderness of Mirrors*, p. 46.
157 Martin, *Wilderness of Mirrors*, p. 46.
158 Borovik, *The Philby Files*, p. 259.
159 ibid, pp. 261–2.
160 Modin, *My Five Cambridge Friends*, p. 184.
161 Benson, *Introductory History of Venona*, p. 10.
162 Lamphere, *The FBI–KGB War*, pp. 134–5, 240.
163 ibid, pp. 254–5.
164 ibid, pp. 192–200, 255, 309.
165 Cable No. 915, New York to Moscow, 28 June 1944, in NSA, *Third Venona Release*, March 1996, vol. 1, p. 240; and Lamphere, *The FBI–KGB War*, pp. 239–41.
166 Andrew and Gordievsky, *KGB*, p. 307.

CHAPTER 11   VENONA AND SOVIET ESPIONAGE IN AUSTRALIA

1 Meredith Knox Gardner, 'Special Analysis Report No. 1: Covernames in Diplomatic Traffic', (Army Security Agency, Washington, D.C., 30 August 1947), pp. 3–4, in Benson and Warner, *Venona*, pp. 96–7.
2 ibid, pp. 96–100.
3 National Security Agency, *Fifth Venona Release*, October 1996, vol. 3.
4 ibid, pp. 206–8.
5 ibid, pp. 204–5.
6 ibid, p. 191.
7 ibid, p. 51.
8 ibid, pp. 5–6.
9 ibid, pp. 9–10.

10 ibid, p. 21.
11 ibid, p. 3.
12 ibid, pp.13–14, 51.
13 ibid, p. 224.
14 ibid, p. 312.
15 ibid, pp. 40, 329.
16 ibid, p. 77.
17 ibid, pp. 164–5, 216–7, 232–3, 289.
18 ibid, pp. 279–281.
19 Testimony of E. A. Petrov, 20 July 1954, *Royal Commission on Espionage: Official Transcript of Proceedings*, p. 2801.
20 ibid, p. 2802; and 'Soviet State Security Service Foreign Intelligence Operational Techniques ('Legal' Residency System)', 18 May 1955, p. 8, in CRS A6283/XR1, item 9, f. 139. See also *Fifth Venona Release*, vol. 3, p. 37.
21 ibid, pp. 37, 95.
22 ibid, pp. 142–3.
23 ibid, p. 153.
24 ibid, pp. 248–9.
25 ibid, p.151.
26 ibid, pp. 35–6, 132–3.
27 ibid, pp. 99–100.
28 ibid, pp. 119–21.
29 ibid, p. 123.
30 ibid, pp. 160–1, 166–7.
31 ibid, pp. 218–9.
32 ibid, p. 145–6.
33 ibid, pp. 179–80.
34 ibid, pp. 200–1.
35 ibid, pp. 136–7.
36 ibid, p. 137.
37 ibid, pp. 311–2, 321–30.
38 ibid, pp. 325–6.

Chapter 12 The Communist Party and Clayton

1 *Seventh Report of the Royal Commission on Intelligence and Security*, 1977, vol. 1, p. 169, CRS A8908/1.
2 Davidson, *The Communist Party of Australia*, pp. 3, 24.
3 ibid, p. 82.
4 ibid, pp. 51–3; and Playford, 'Doctrinal and Strategic Problems of the Communist Party of Australia', p. 24.
5 Davidson, *The Communist Party of Australia*, pp. 53, 99.
6 'Australian Communist Party', April 1945, p. 4, in CRS A1533/2, item 62/1964 Z.
7 Cited in Klehr, Haynes and Firsov, *The Secret World of American Communism*, p. 71.
8 ibid.
9 'Brief on the Work of the CPUSA Secret Apparatus', 26 January 1939, cited in ibid, p. 87.
10 Davidson, *The Communist Party of Australia*, pp. 78–9.
11 ibid, p. 79.
12 ibid, p. 80.
13 Brown, *The Communist Movement and Australia*, p. 115.
14 Sharkey, *An Outline History of the Australian Communist Party*, p. 44.
15 Davidson, *The Communist Party of Australia*, p. 83; and Playford, 'Doctrinal and Strategic Problems of the Communist Party of Australia', p. 24.
16 Quoted in Sharpley, *The Great Delusion*, pp. 28–9.
17 Gibson, *My Years in the Communist Party*, p. 101. See also Beverley Symons,

'All-Out for the People's War: Communist Soldiers in the Australian Army in the Second World War', *Australian Historical Studies*, No. 105, October 1995.
18 Sendy, *Comrades Come Rally*, pp. 14–8.
19 Brown, *The Communist Movement and Australia*, p. 130.
20 See Lang, *Communism in Australia*, chs V-VII.
21 Testimony of W. S. Clayton, *Royal Commission on Espionage: Official Transcript of Proceedings*, p. 2541.
22 ibid.
23 ibid, pp. 2481, 2490.
24 Walter Seddon Clayton, 'Statement', 27 August 1957, p. 3, in Evatt Papers; and Evan Whitton, 'For a Top Spy, Agent KLOD is a Great Cook', *The National Times*, 10–15 September 1973, p. 40.
25 'Walter Seddon Clayton', ASIO note, October 1952, CRS A6119, item 55, f. 88; and 'Walter Seddon Clayton: Summary of File', p. 3, CRS A6119, item 57, f. 13.
26 Wilde, *Courage a Grace*, p. 131; and Souter, *A Peculiar People*, p. 287.
27 'Hilda Clayton or Hilda Lane', Memo to ASIO Director, Sydney, 2 August 1949, CRS A6126/25, item 567, f. 8; deposition by Hilda Clayton, Supreme Court, Melbourne, 30 October 1945, CRS A6126/25, item 567, f. 6; and 'Husband's Going Shock, Says Singer', *Daily Mirror*, 30 October 1945, p. 9.
28 Handwritten note, 26 July 1954, CRS A1533/1, item 1954/946 Misc., f. 65.
29 Testimony of W. S. Clayton, 15 March 1955, *Royal Commission on Espionage: Official Transcript of Proceedings*, p. 2442.
30 'Walter Seddon Clayton', Memo from ASIO Director General, Melbourne, to ASIO Regional Directors, 19 December 1955, p. 1, CRS A6119/79, item 953, f. 30.
31 'Australian Communist Party—Walter Clayton', Memo (and attachments) from Deputy Director of Security for N.S.W., Sydney, to Director General of Security, August 1945, CRS A6119/XR1, item 53, ff. 18–22.
32 Deposition by Hilda Mary Clayton, 30 October 1945, CRSA6126/25, item 567, f. 6.
33 Memo to ASIO B2 on Doug Gillies, 4 April 1957, CRS A6119/79, item 1036, f. 123.
34 'Walter Seddon Clayton', Memo from ASIO Director General to ASIO Regional Directors, 19 December 1955, CRS A6119/79, item 953, f. 30.
35 'Walter Seddon Clayton: Activities', CRS A6119/XR1, item 57, f. 9.
36 Note on 'Clayton, Walter Sidon', 20 April 1943, CRS A6119, item 57, f. 9.
37 'Australian Communist Party—Walter Clayton', Memo from Sergeant A. T. Hughes to Inspector Swasbrick, Security Service, Sydney, 31 August 1945, CRS A6119, item 53, f. 17.
38 'Walter Seddon Clayton', October 1952, CRS A6119, item 55, f. 88; 'Walter Seddon Clayton: Summary of File', attachment to Memo for ASIO Director-General, Melbourne, to Regional Director, NSW, 7 May 1954, CRS A6119, item 57, f. 14; a summary note on Walter Seddon Clayton, CRS A6119/79, item 1035, f. 86; and 'Walter S. Clayton', Note to ASIO Director, Sydney, 7 July 1949, CRS A6119, item 53, f. 47.
39 Testimony of W. S. Clayton, 16 March 1955, *Royal Commission on Espionage: Official Transcript of Proceedings*, pp. 2499–500.
40 *Report of the Royal Commission on Espionage*, Commonwealth Government Printer, Canberra, 1955, p. 404.
41 ibid, p.146.
42 'Preliminary Report on the Central Control Commission', p. 2, CRS A6112/10, item 808, f. 14, pp. 2 7. See also the interview with Edna Ryan in Stevens, *Taking the Revolution Home*, p. 132.
43 'Preliminary Report on the Central Control Commission', pp. 9–14.
44 'Walter Seddon Clayton', October 1952, CRS A6119, item 55, f. 88.
45 'Walter Seddon Clayton, alias Seddon-Clayton', Memo from ASIO Regional Director, NSW, to Director-General, 2 October 1951, CRS A6119, item 55, f. 40.
46 Rupert Lockwood, in 'Petrov Twenty Years On—Rupert Lockwood's Personal

View', ABC Radio, 26 May 1973, (Radio Drama and Features Department, Australian Broadcasting Commission), transcript, p. 20.
47 *Fifth Venona Release*, vol. 3, pp. 9–10.
48 ibid, p. 40.
49 ibid, pp. 77–78.
50 'Subject: Clayton, Walter Seddon', Memo from ASIO Director-General, Melbourne, for ASIO Regional Director, New South Wales, 7 May 1954, and attachments, CRS A6119, item 57, ff. 11–16.
51 Memo from ASIO Regional Director, NSW, for ASIO Director-General, Melbourne, 22 June 1953, CRS A6119/79, item 798, f. 51.
52 'Walter Seddon Clayton: Activities', CRS A6119, item 57, ff. 6–9.
53 See, for example, Stevens, *Taking the Revolution Home*, pp. 102–3, 180–3, 228–9; and Hewett, *Wild Card*, pp. 161–2.
54 'Subject: Celebration of the Anniversary of the Signing of the Anglo-Soviet Treaty, Held at Sydney Town Hall on 26/5/43', Security Service, Sydney, 27 May 1943, CRS A6119, item 54, ff. 10–1.
55 See, for example, Stevens, *Taking the Revolution Home*, pp. 182–3.
56 'Hilda Clayton or Hilda Lane', memo to ASIO Director, Sydney, 2 August 1949, CRS A6126/25, item 567, ff. 4–6; and 'Husband's Going Shock, Says Singer', *Daily Mirror*, 30 October 1945, p. 9.
57 'Walter Seddon Clayton: Summary of File', Attachment to Memo from ASIO Director-General, Melbourne, to Regional Director, NSW, 7 May 1954, CRS A6119, item 57, ff. 7, 14.
58 'Subject: Clayton, Walter Seddon', Memo from ASIO Director-General, Melbourne, for ASIO Regional Director, NSW, 7 May 1954, and attachments, CRS A6119, item 57, ff. 11–6.
59 Testimony of W. S. Clayton, 15 March 1955, *Royal Commission on Espionage: Official Transcript of Proceedings*, p. 2447; and 'Death of Miss Shirley Howard', *Tribune*, 12 February 1946, p. 1.
60 *Fifth Venona Release*, vol. 3, pp. 179–80.
61 'Subject: Clayton, Walter Seddon', Minute from ASIO B2 to Director, B1, 13 May 1952, CRS A6119/XR1, item 55, ff. 53, 52.
62 See, for example, Stevens, *Taking the Revolution Home*, pp. 102–3, 180–3, 228–9; and Hewett, *Wild Card*, pp. 161–2.
63 Stevens, *Taking the Revolution Home*, p. 228.
64 'Record of Conversation between Regional Director, NSW, and Mr Max Garrett, . . . 1st July 1955', CRS A6119/79, item 798, f. 3.
65 ASIO Regional Director, NSW, to ASIO Director-General, Melbourne, 22 June 1953, p. 7, CRS A6119/79, item 798, f. 49.
66 Sharpley, *The Great Delusion*, p. 90.
67 Cited in 'Walter Seddon Clayton: Activities', October 1952, p. 6, CRS A6119, item 56, f. 47.
68 McKnight, *Australia's Spies and Their Secrets*, p. 33.
69 'Central Control Commission: Walter Seddon Clayton', Memo from ASIO Director-General to ASIO Regional Directors, 11 September 1952, CRS A6119, item 55, f. 76.
70 'Walter Seddon Clayton: Activities', in A6119, item 57, f. 7.
71 Testimony of W. S. Clayton, 15 March 1955, *Royal Commission on Espionage: Official Transcript of Proceedings*, p. 2448.
72 Testimony of G. W. Legge, 26 October 1954, *Royal Commission on Espionage: Official Transcript of Proceedings*, pp. 1395, 1397.
73 ibid, pp. 1395–97.
74 'Royal Commission on Espionage: June Barnett, Frederick Godfrey Rose', Memo from J. M. Gilmour, Royal Commission Section, to Principal Section Officer, B2, ASIO, 25 October 1954, CRS A6119, item 57, f. 212; *Report of the Royal Commission on Espionage*, pp. 132–134; and 'Frederick George Godfrey Rose', Memo from ASIO Director-General, 8 March 1956, CRS A6119/79, item 1011, f. 133.
75 Testimony of W. S. Clayton, 15 March 1955, *Royal Commission on Espionage:*

Official Transcript of Proceedings, pp. 2446, 2451; and 'Walter Seddon Clayton', October 1952, CRS A6119, item 55, f. 87.
76 Testimony of W. S. Clayton, 15 March 1955, *Royal Commission on Espionage: Official Transcript of Proceedings*, p. 2451. See also Ferrier, *As Good As a Yarn With You*, p.109.
77 'Walter Seddon Clayton: Activities', October 1952, CRS A6119, item 56, ff. 46–7.
78 Ferrier, *As Good As a Yarn With You*, p.109; and Beasley, *A Gallop of Fire*, pp. 126–9.
79 Testimony of W. S. Clayton, 15 March 1955, p. 2471.
80 'Walter Seddon Clayton: Activities', October 1952, CRS A6119, item 56, f. 46.
81 See, for example, *Fifth Venona Release*, vol. 3, pp.136–7.
82 McKnight, *Australia's Spies and Their Secrets*, p. 51; 'Subject: James Frederick Hill', Memo for ASIO Regional Director, Victoria, 7 August 1952, CRS A6119, item 91, f. 147; and extract from a report on Sydney Sommerville, 5 July 1949, CRS A6119/79, item 1238, ff. 7–8.
83 See *Fifth Venona Release*, vol. 3, pp. 294–5.
84 See the ASIO file on Doris Isobel Beeby, CRS A6126/24, item 243, ff. 1–21.
85 Testimony of W. S. Clayton, *Royal Commission on Espionage: Official Transcript of Proceedings*, p. 2471.
86 'Elfrida Margaret Newbegin', Memo, Deputy Director General ASIO to Regional Director, ACT, 14 January 1955, CRS A6119/70, item 435, ff. 50–51; statement by Clarence William Dakin, 6 December 1954, CRS A6119/70, item 435, ff. 45–46; and testimony of E. M. Newbegin, 7 February 1955, *Royal Commission on Espionage: Official Transcript of Proceedings*, p. 2089.
87 See the accounts from ASIO files in CRS A6126/24, item 243, ff. 13, 21.
88 Statement by Clarence William Dakin, 6 December 1954, CRS A6119/70, item 435, ff. 45–6.
89 Testimony of F. G. G. Rose, 25 October 1954, in *Royal Commission on Espionage: Official Transcript of Proceedings*, p. 1371.
90 ibid, pp. 1371–6.
91 'Frederick George Godfrey Rose', Memo from ASIO Director-General, 8 March 1956, CRS A6119/79, item 1011, f. 134.
92 ibid, f. 132.
93 ibid, f. 133.
94 Testimony of F. G. G. Rose, 25 October 1954, *Royal Commission on Espionage: Official Transcript of Proceedings*, p. 1374.
95 *Fifth Venona Release*, vol. 3, p. 153.
96 ibid, pp. 200–1.
97 ibid.
98 ibid, pp. 248–9.
99 ibid, pp. 252–3.
100 ibid, pp. 309–12.
101 ibid, pp. 325–6.
102 Statement by Mrs E. A. Petrov, 14 September 1954, CRS A6119/79, item 1247, ff. 115–7.
103 Interview with Rupert Lockwood, 13 July 1995.

CHAPTER 13   THE DEVELOPMENT OF THE KLOD GROUP

1 *Fifth Venona Release*, Vol. 3, pp.139–140, 329–30.
2 C. Hartley Grattan, 'Readers and Writers Down Under', *The New York Times Book Review*, 22 June 1947, p. 20.
3 Throssell, *Wild Weeds and Windflowers*, pp. xii, 160, 232–4, 246.
4 Prichard, *Child of the Hurricane*, p. 200.
5 ibid, p. 217.
6 Throssell, *Wild Weeds and Windflowers*, p. 38.

7 ibid, p. 232.
8 ibid, p. 233.
9 K. S. Prichard, cited in Throssell, *Wild Weeds and Windflowers*, p. 233.
10 ibid, p. 234.
11 ibid.
12 Modjeska, *Exiles at Home*, p. 21.
13 ibid, p. 118.
14 ibid, pp. 137–8.
15 Cited in Throssell, *Wild Weeds and Windflowers*, p. 65.
16 'Katharine Susannah Prichard (Mrs. H. Throssell)', CRS A6119, item 44, part 2, f. 69.
17 Roland, *Caviar for Breakfast*, pp. ix, 64; and Roland, *An Improbable Life*, pp. 158–9.
18 ibid, pp. 162–4.
19 Roland, *Caviar for Breakfast*, pp. 119–31.
20 ibid, p. 69.
21 Throssell, *Wild Weeds and Windflowers*, p. 71.
22 ibid.
23 Beasley, *A Gallop of Fire*, p. 114.
24 ibid, p. 120.
25 Modjeska, *Exiles at Home*, pp. 123, 140.
26 ibid, p.140.
27 Dorothy Hewett, 'Excess of Love: The Irreconcilable Katharine Susannah Prichard', *Overland*, no. 43, Summer 1969–1970, p. 30.
28 Cited in Modjeska, *Exiles at Home*, p. 140.
29 Throssell, *Wild Weeds and Windflowers*, p. 250.
30 ibid, p. 244.
31 ibid, p. 245.
32 ibid, p. 241.
33 ibid, p. 236.
34 'Katharine Susannah Prichard (Mrs. H. Throssel)', CRS A6119, item 44, part 2, f. 87.
35 Throssell, *Wild Weeds and Windflowers*, p. 236.
36 Security Service Report, State of Western Australia, week ended 3 July 1942, AA Sydney: C128, box 4.
37 'Katharine Susannah Prichard (Mrs. H. Throssell)', CRS A6119, item 44, part 2, f. 91.
38 Throssell, *My Father's Son*, pp. 186–7.
39 Throssell, *Wild Weeds and Windflowers*, p. 254.
40 ibid, p. 94.
41 ibid, p. 95; and Throssell, *My Father's Son*, pp. 162–163, 186–7.
42 Katharine Susannah Prichard, 'Deakin and Evatt', *The Realist*, No. 30, Spring 1968, republished in Prichard, *Straight Left*, pp. 101–112; and attachment to letter, K. S. Throssell to Mrs. Evatt, 21 June 1968, in Evatt Papers, File: Correspondence Misc. 1946–47.
43 Testimony of R. P. Throssell, 2 February 1955, in *Royal Commission on Espionage: Official Transcript of Proceedings*, p. 2016; and 'Richard Prichard Throssell', Memo, G. R. Richards, Deputy Director-General (Operations), to ASIO Director-General, 26 July 1954, CRS A6119, item 57, f. 77.
44 Throssell, *Wild Weeds and Windflowers*, p. 236.
45 Throssell, *My Father's Son*, pp. 198–9.
46 ibid, p. 279.
47 ibid, p. 200.
48 ibid.
49 *Fifth Venona Release*, vol. 3, pp. 139–40.
50 ibid.
51 K. S Prichard to R. Throssell, September 1946, in Throssell Papers, NLA: MS 8071, folder 183, F. 262.
52 See the letters from K. S. Prichard to R. Throssell, 13, 20 and 27 January 1946, Throssell Papers, MS 8071, folder 183.

53 *Workers Star*, 24 April 1947, p. 4.
54 Testimony of R. P. Throssell, 2 February 1955, in *Royal Commission on Espionage: Official Transcript of Proceedings*, pp. 2016–2017; testimony of Eileen Dorothy Throssell (nee Jordan), 4 February 1955, in ibid, pp. 2073–2075; and statement by Clarence William Dakin, 6 December 1954, CRS A6119/70, item 435, f. 45.
55 Cited in Throssell, *Wild Weeds and Windflowers*, p. 241.
56 ibid, pp. 244–5.
57 ibid, p. 251; and Dorothy Hewett, 'Excess of Love: The Irreconcilable Katharine Susannah Prichard', *Overland*, no. 43, Summer 1969–1970, p. 28.
58 Throssell, *Wild Weeds and Windflowers*, p. 234.
59 Throssell, *My Father's Son*, pp. 6–7; and Beasley, *A Gallop of Fire*, pp. 122–3.
60 ibid, pp. 124, 126–7; and Ferrier, *As Good As a Yarn With You*, p. 29.
61 ibid, pp. 127–8; and Stevens, *Taking the Revolution Home*, pp. 101–3.
62 Ferrier, *Point of Departure:*, pp. 268–70; and Beasley, *A Gallop of Fire*, pp. 126–9.
63 Modjeska, *Exiles at Home*, p. 152.
64 See Beasley, *A Gallop of Fire*, pp. 128–9.
65 Devanny to Miles Franklin, 9 January 1954, in Ferrier, *As Good As a Yarn With You*, p. 371.
66 A. T. Hughes, 'Personal Particulars', 29 June 1951, CRS A6119/83, item 1510, ff. 29, 30.
67 Alfred T. Hughes, 'Application to Enlist in the Australian Imperial Force', 28 June 1918; Alfred Thompson Hughes, 'Australian Imperial Force: Attestation Paper on Persons Enlisted for Service Abroad', p. 4, CRS, B2455; and Alfred Thompson Hughes, NSW Police Force, Service Record no. 1810, provided by Services Branch, NSW Police Service, 13 December 1993.
68 'Operation . . .', Interview with Mrs Evelyn Margaret Janet Hughes on 29 March, 1957, by Mr W. R. Campbell', 1 April 1957, CRS A6119/79, item 955, f. 108.
69 Alfred Thompson Hughes, NSW Police Force, Service Record no. 1810, provided by Services Branch, NSW Police Service, 13 December 1993.
70 ibid.
71 Copy of Marriage Registration of Alfred Thompson Hughes and Evelyn Margaret Janet Cowell, 4 June 1925, Registrar of Births, Deaths and Marriages, Sydney, 21 December 1993.
72 'Operation . . .', Interview with Mrs Evelyn Margaret Janet Hughes on 29 March, 1957, by Mr W. R. Campbell', 1 April 1957, CRS A6119/79, item 955, f. 108.
73 Alfred Thompson Hughes, NSW Police Force, Service Record no. 1810, provided by Services Branch, NSW Police Service, 13 December 1993; and letter, Norman E. Mason to Helen Wilson, SDSC, 16 July 1994.
74 'Security Service in NSW, 1942–1946', 3 October 1952, CRS A6119/83, item 1510, ff. 12, 13; and letter, Mason to Wilson, 16 July 1994.
75 'Security Service in NSW, 1941–1946', 3 October 1952, CRS A6119/83, item 1510, ff. 12–13.
76 Letter dated 28 March 1957, CRS A6119/83, item 1510, f. 173.
77 'Security Service in NSW, 1941–1946', 3 October 1952, CRS A6119/83, item 1510, ff. 12–13.
78 Copy of Marriage Registration of Alfred Thompson Hughes and Margaret Ann Clancy, 5 February 1949, Registrar of Births, Deaths and Marriages, Sydney, 21 December 1993.
79 'Alfred T. Hughes', Memo from Principal Section Officer, B2, to Assistant Director of ASIO, NSW, 19 September 1952; Minute on Hughes, CRS A6119/83, item 1510, ff. 37, 31; letter, Mason to Wilson, 16 July 1994; and record of telephone conversation between Chief Inspector (Retd) Jo Green and Helen Wilson, February 1994.
80 Hughes to Deputy Director, Australian Security, CRS A6119/83, item 1510, f. 21.
81 Spry to Hughes, 8 June 1951, CRS A6119/83, item 1510, f. 22.
82 Spry to Hughes, 18 June 1951, CRS A6119/83, item 1510, f. 24.

83 Alfred Thompson Hughes, 'Personal Particulars', 29 June 1951, CRS A6119/83, item 1510, ff. 26–9.
84 Cited in 'Operation . . .', file note by ASIO Deputy Director-General, Sydney, 1 April 1957, CRS A6119/79, item 1144.
85 'Alfred Thompson Hughes', Memo, ASIO Regional Director, N.S.W., to ASIO Director-General, 17 August 1951, CRS A6119/83, item 1510, f. 33.
86 'Information Suggesting Alfred Thompson Hughes was a Member of the Communist Party of Australia and/or was Associated with Walter Seddon Clayton and the R.I.S.', CRS A6119/83, item 1510, f. 210; transcript of telephone conversation with Alf Hughes, 1 April 1957, CRS A6119/79, item 1144; and telephone message from ASIO, NSW, to Regional Director, Queensland, 27 March 1957, CRS A6119/83, item 1510, f. 162.
87 *Fifth Venona Release*, vol. 3, pp. 43–4.
88 ibid, pp. 77–8.
89 ibid, pp. 99–100.
90 ibid.
91 ibid.
92 ibid, pp. 101–2.
93 ibid, pp. 105–6.
94 ibid, pp. 119–22.
95 Hughes to Inspector Swasbrick, 31 August 1945, CRS A6119/1, item 53, f. 17.
96 'Reports by A.T. Hughes', CRS A6119/83, item 1510, ff. 114–5.
97 'Record of Conversation Between . . . Regional Director and Mr Max Garrett . . . on 1st July 1952', CRS A6119/79, item 798, f. 43.
98 Draft statement by Frances Ada Garrett, 8 September 1954, CRS A6119/79, item 799, ff. 55–56; and Letter from McMaster, Holland & Co., Solicitors, Sydney, to Mr Gilmore, Security Department, Crown Solicitor's Office, Sydney, 21 October 1954, CRS A6119/XR1, item 57, f. 210.
99 ibid.
100 Memorandum from ASIO Regional Director, NSW, to ASIO Director-General, 10 June 1954, p. 3, CRS A6119/79, item 798, f. 11; and 'Frances Ada Gluck, nee Scott known as Bernie: Personal Data', CRS A6119/78, item 797, f. 33.
101 ibid.
102 ibid; and 'International Youth Committee', report by Alfred T. Hughes and Alfred L. Walsh, Security Service, Sydney, 14 October 1943, CRS A6119/83, item 1510, f. 67.
103 'Frances Ada Gluck, nee Scott known as Bernie: Preliminary Report', 25 May 1950, p. 4, in A6119/79, item 796, f. 110.
104 Memorandum from ASIO Regional Director, NSW, to ASIO Director-General, 10 June 1953, p. 3, in A6119/79, item 798, f. 11.
105 Statement by Frances Bernie, 8 September 1954, pp. 2–3, CRS A6119/XR1, item 57, ff. 172–3.
106 ibid.
107 Memo, ASIO Regional Director, NSW, to ASIO Director-General, 10 June 1953; and 'Extract from Shorthand Note-book', 9 June 1953, CRS A6119/79, item 798, ff. 10, 13.
108 Memo, ASIO Regional Director, NSW, to ASIO Director-General, 22 June 1953, CRS A6119/79, item 798, f. 53; and statement by Frances Bernie, 8 September 1954, CRS A6119/XR1, item 57, f. 174.
109 *Sydney Morning Herald*, 1 November 1944, p. 15; and *Sydney Morning Herald*, 2 November 1944, p. 10.
110 Statement by Frances Bernie, 8 September 1954, CRS A6119/XR1, item 57, ff. 170–1.
111 'Bernie, Frances', CRS A6119/1, A53–1, Section 7.
112 Testimony of Frances Bernie, 22 October 1945, in *Royal Commission on Espionage: Official Transcript of Proceedings*, p. 1333.
113 Memo, ASIO Regional Director, NSW, to ASIO Director-General, 22 June 1953, CRS A6119/79, item 798, f. 54.
114 McKnight, *Australian Spies and Their Secrets*, p. 3.

115 Statement by Frances Bernie, 8 September 1954, CRS A6119/XR1, item 57, f. 174.
116 'Max Garrett', Memo, Director, B1, to Director-General, 9 May 1952, CRS A6119/79, item 797, f. 82; and 'Frances Ada Gluck, nee Scott known as Bernie', 7 August 1951, CRS A6119/79, item 797, f. 33.
117 'Record of Conversation between . . . Regional Director, New South Wales, and Mr Max Garrett, . . 1st July, 1953', pp. 15–16, CRS A6119/79, item 798, ff. 31–2.
118 *Fifth Venona Release*, vol. 3, pp. 70–1.
119 ibid.
120 File note on 'Bernie, Frances', CRS A6691/1, A53–1, Section 7.
121 Draft statement by Frances Ada Garrett, 8 September 1954, pp. 5–6, CRS A6119/79, item 799, ff. 51–2.
122 *Fifth Venona Release*, vol. 3, pp. 68–9.
123 ibid, pp. 70–1.
124 'Questions Which Could be Asked of Mrs Garrett', 25 August 1954, CRS A6119/79, item 799, f. 34.
125 Statement by Frances Bernie, 8 September 1954; letter re Bernie from McMaster, Holland & Co., Solicitors, Sydney, to Mr Gilmore, Security Department, Sydney, 21 October 1954, CRS A6119/XR1, item 57, ff. 163, 210.
126 Memo, ASIO Regional Director, NSW, to ASIO Director-General, 10 June 1953, p. 6, CRS A6119/79, item 798, f. 8.
127 'Five More Fellows of Academy', *Coresearch* [CSIRO Staff Journal], no. 3, June 1959, p. 4.
128 *Fifth Venona Release*, vol. 3, pp. 329–30.
129 'Name: Christiansen, Wilbur Norman', CRS A6119/79, item 864, ff. 76–8.
130 W.N.C., 'World Student Congress', *Proletariat* (vol. IV, no. 2), July–September 1935, pp. 7–8, in A6119/78 (or 79?), item 864, ff. 21–2.
131 Cited in 'Vetting: Wilbur Norman Christiansen', Memo, ASIO Director, Melbourne, to ASIO Director, Sydney, 18 July 1950, CRS A6119/79, item 864, ff. 27–28. See also Testimony of W. N. Christiansen, *Royal Commission on Espionage: Official Transcript of Proceedings*, 27 January 1955, p. 1970.
132 J. C. Harrison, 'An Outline of the Development of Telecommunication Services Between Australia and Places Overseas—Part 2', *The Telecommunication Journal of Australia*, vol. 5, no. 3, February 1945, pp. 161, 167.
133 *AWA and the War*.
134 Harcourt, *Taming the Tyrant*, p. 268; and *Royal Commission on Espionage: Official Transcript of Proceedings*, p. 1970.
135 *Royal Commission on Espionage: Official Transcript of Proceedings*, pp. 1969–72.
136 'Subject: Christiansen, Wilbur Norman', CRS A6119/79, item 864, f. 54.
137 'Wilbur Norman Christiansen', ASIO Report no. 13504, 29 August 1958, CRS A6119/79, item 864, f. 108.
138 'Walter Seddon Clayton: Activities', October 1952, CRS A6119/79, item 56, f. 47.
139 ibid, ff. 46–7.
140 Davidson, *The Communist Party of Australia*, p. 81.
141 Cook, *Red Barrister*, p. 60.
142 Taft, *Crossing the Party Line*, p. 65.
143 ibid, p. 64.
144 Davidson, *The Communist Party of Australia*, p. 95.
145 Testimony of W. N. Christiansen, *Royal Commission on Espionage: Official Transcript of Proceedings*, 27 January 1955, p. 1971; and 'Dr Wilbur (Norman) Christiansen', 31 January 1956, CRS A6119/79, item 864, f. 87.
146 Testimony of W. N. Christiansen, *Royal Commission on Espionage: Official Transcript of Proceedings*, 27 January 1955, p. 1971.
147 'Subject: Christiansen, Wilbur Norman. Case Summary', CRS A6119/79, item 864, f. 49.
148 *Fifth Venona Release*, vol. 3, pp. 64–5.
149 'Subject: Christiansen, Wilbur Norman. Case Summary', CRS A6119//9, item 864, f. 49.

150 'Australian Invention Photographs Sun by Radio', *Tribune*, 31 July 1957, p. 7; and 'Five More Fellows of Academy', *Coresearch*, no. 3, June 1959, p. 4.
151 'Appointments to Sydney Uni Staff', *Sydney Morning Herald*, 22 April 1960, p. 4.
152 Spry to Longfield Lloyd, 19 April 1948, CRS A6119/79, item 864, f. 1.
153 ibid.
154 R. Williams, Deputy Director, CIS, Sydney, to Director, CIS, Canberra, 4 June 1948, CRS A6119/79, item 864, f. 2.
155 'Vetting: Wilbur Norman Christiansen', Memo, Director ASIO, Melbourne, to Director ASIO, Sydney, 18 July 1950, CRS A6119/79, item 864, f. 28.
156 ibid.
157 See letter from W. N. Christiansen to the Secretary, CSIRO, 6 July 1950, CRS A6119/79, item 864, f. 26.
158 'Security Check in the Public Service', letter from W. E. Dunk, Chairman, Public Service Board, to the Prime Minister, 27 April 1949, Dedman Papers, NLA.
159 'Vetting: C.S.I.R.', Memo, G. A. Cooke, Secretary, CSIR, to the Deputy Director, CIS, Sydney, 1 April 1949; 'Vetting: CSIR Presonnel', Memo from R. Williams, Deputy Director, CIS, Sydney, to Director, CIS, Canberra, 26 April 1948, CRS A6119/79, item 864, ff. 9, 11.
160 See 'Vetting: Wilbur Norman Christiansen', Memo, ASIO Director, Melbourne, to ASIO Director, Sydney, 18 July 1950, in A6119/79, item 864, f. 28.
161 ibid.
162 ibid.
163 'Subject: Christiansen, Wilbur Norman. Case Summary', CRS A6119/79, item 864, f. 49.
164 ibid. See also, for example, letter, W. N. Christiansen to the secretary, CSIRO, 6 July 1950, CRS A6119/79, item 864, f. 26.
165 'Vetting: Wilbur Norman Christiansen', Memo, ASIO Director, Melbourne, to ASIO Director, Sydney, 18 July 1950, CRS A6119/79, item 864, f. 27.
166 'Wilbur Norman Christiansen', Memo, ASIO Director, Sydney, to ASIO Director, Melbourne, 9 August 1950, CRS A6119/79, item 864, f. 30.
167 *Fifth Venona Release*, vol. 3, pp. 322–3.
168 ibid, pp. 64–5.
169 ibid, pp. 329–30.

CHAPTER 14 SOVIET ESPIONAGE IN EXTERNAL AFFAIRS

1 *Fifth Venona Release*, vol. 3, pp. 151–2.
2 ibid, p. 153.
3 ibid, pp. 136–7, 142–3.
4 ibid, pp. 136–7.
5 ibid.
6 ibid, pp. 211–2.
7 ibid.
8 ibid, pp. 212–3.
9 ibid, pp. 179–80.
10 ibid.
11 Hall, *The Rhodes Scholar Spy*, pp. 1–29.
12 ibid, p. 10.
13 ibid.
14 ibid, p. 17.
15 ibid, p. 26.
16 ibid, pp. 19–9.
17 ibid, p. 30.
18 ibid.
19 Phillip Knightley, 'Australian Diplomat Spied for Russians: Author Reveals Intimate Confession', *Sun-Herald*, 9 June 1991, p. 15.

20 Hall, *The Rhodes Scholar Spy*, pp. 48–50.
21 ibid, pp. 44–6.
22 ibid, p. 53.
23 ibid, pp. 59–66.
24 'Ian Frank George Milner', Memo, ASIO Acting Deputy Director to Director, 27 September 1949, CRS A6119, item 17, f. 25. See also Smith, *Noel Counihan*, pp. 149–50.
25 O'Sullivan, *Intersecting Lines*, p. 164.
26 Hall, *The Rhodes Scholar Spy*, pp. 70–6.
27 O'Sullivan, *Intersecting Lines*, p. 164.
28 Hall, *The Rhodes Scholar Spy*, p. 75.
29 O'Sullivan, *Intersecting Lines* p. 167.
30 ibid, pp. 167–71.
31 Clark, *The Quest for Grace*, p. 152.
32 Cain, 'The Making of a Cold War Victim', *Overland*, no. 134, 1994, p. 61.
33 'Ian Frank George Milner', ASIO report c. July 1954, CRS A6119, item 18, f. 11.
34 Hall, *The Rhodes Scholar Spy*, p. 84.
35 ibid, p. 77.
36 'Ian Frank George Milner', Memo, Acting Deputy Director to Director, ASIO, 27 September 1949, CRSn A6119/XR1, item 17; and Hall, *The Rhodes Scholar Spy*, p. 79.
37 ibid.
38 ibid.
39 ibid; and Commonwealth Investigation Branch, File No. V/23919.Q, CRS A6119/XR1, item 17, f. 58.
40 ASIO file note on 'Ian Frank George Milner', CRS A6119/XR1, item 18, f. 35F.
41 ibid; and 'Meeting of Victorian Youth Parliament, held in . . . Melbourne, on 31/10/41', Internal Memo, Criminal Investigation Branch (CIB), Special Branch, Police Department, Melbourne, 3 November 1941, CRS A6119/XR1, item 17, f. 18.
42 'Ian Frank George Milner', Memo, Acting Deputy Director to Director, ASIO, 27 September 1949, CRS A6119/XR1, item 17, f. 25; O'Sullivan, *Intersecting Lines*, p. 22; and Hall, *The Rhodes Scholar Spy*, pp. 85–7.
43 O'Sullivan, *Intersecting Lines*, p. 170.
44 ibid, pp. 22, 170.
45 Cited in 'Ian Frank George Milner', Memo, Acting Deputy Director to Director, ASIO, 27 September 1949, CRS A6119/XR1, item 17, f. 24.
46 'Ian Frank George Milner', CRS A6119, item 18, f. 35E.
47 Hall, *The Rhodes Scholar Spy*, p. 94.
48 ibid, pp. 80, 82.
49 Smith, *Noel Counihan*, pp. 97, 150.
50 Cook, *Red Barrister*, pp. 60–61.
51 Hall, *The Rhodes Scholar Spy*, p. 82.
52 'Ian Milner', ASIO Minute, July 1954, CRS A6119, item 18, f. 11.
53 ibid.
54 ibid.
55 Hall, *The Rhodes Scholar Spy*, pp. 118–9.
56 'Ian Frank George Milner', CRSn A6119/1, PS 3/1, section 7; and Hall, *The Rhodes Scholar Spy*, pp. 97–8.
57 Letter, Hasluck to Milner, 24 November 1944, CRS Series 2364/2.
58 ibid.
59 Letter, Milner to Hasluck, 28 November 1944, CRS Series 2364/2.
60 Letter, Milner to Hasluck, 4 December 1944, CRS Series 2364/2; information given to Richard Hall by Professor Manning Clark, 11 April 1991; and letter, Malcolm Templeton, Ministry of Foreign Affairs and Trade, New Zealand, to D. J. Ball, 22 July 1993.
61 Letter, Milner to Hasluck, 4 December 1944, CRS Series 2364/2.
62 ibid.
63 Letter, Milner to Hasluck, 25 December 1944, CRS Series 2364/2.

64 Letter, Milner to Hasluck, 25 January 1945, CRS Series 2364/2.
65 O'Sullivan, *Intersecting Lines*, p. 184.
66 ibid.
67 'Ian George Frank Milner', CRS A6691/1, PS 3/1, section 7.
68 ibid.
69 ibid.
70 *Fifth Venona Release*, vol. 3, pp. 200–1.
71 Hall, *The Rhodes Scholar Spy*, p. 150.
72 ibid, pp. 164–5.
73 Cited in Peter Hruby, 'The Secret Life of Agent 9006', *The Courier-Mail*, 30 November 1996, pp. 30–1.
74 Hall, *The Rhodes Scholar Spy*, pp. 164–5.
75 Statement by Ian Frank George Milner', 1 March 1956, p. 6, attached to letter, Milner to Evatt, 29 May 1956, in Evatt Papers, file, 'Petrov Affair: Correspondence Relating to Case'.
76 'Ian Frank George Milner', CRS A6119/XR1, item 18, f. 30.
77 'James Frederick Hill', CRS A6119, volume 1, item 91, f. 147; and 'List of Persons Present at Dinner at Canberra Tourist Lodge on Night of Thursday, 15th September 1949', CRS A6119, volume 1, item 91, f. 26.
78 'Ian Frank George Milner', CRS A6119/XR1, item 18, f. 30.
79 ibid.
80 'James Frederick Hill', CRS A6119/XR1, vol. 1, item 91, f. 148.
81 'Interview Report [on] Political Association of James Frederick Hill, Edward Fowler Hill [and] Harold Leslie Booley', Memo, ASIO Field Officer, 28 August 1952, CRS A6119/XR1, item 91, vol. 1, f. 160.
82 Testimony of James Frederick Hill, *Royal Commission on Espionage: Official Transcript of Proceedings*, 4 February 1955, pp. 2059–60.
83 'Subject: Meeting of Victorian Youth Parliament, held in . . . Melbourne, on 31/10/41', report by Policewoman Jessie J. Clarey to Criminal Investigation Branch, Police Department, Melbourne, 3 November 1941, CRS A6691/1, item P53/1, section 7; 'Re James F. Hill', Memo, ASIO Director Sydney, 1 June 1950, CRS A6119/XR1, item 91, f. 55; and 'J. F. Hill, Secretary, Victoria Youth Parliament', Memo, ASIO Director, Canberra, to ASIO Director Sydney, 31 May 1950, CRS A6119/XR1, item 91, f. 31.
84 'James F. Hill', Memo, ASIO Director Sydney, 2 June 1950, CRS A6119/XR1, item 91, f. 38. See also 'Ban on Youth Council To Stay: Anti War', *The Herald* (Melbourne), 12 August 1940, p. 3.
85 ibid.
86 'Summary for Counsel: James Frederick Hill', in CRS A6119/XR1, item 91, f. 98; and 'James F. Hill', CRS A6119/XR1, item 91, f. 48.
87 Testimony of James Fredick Hill, *Royal Commission on Espionage: Official Transcript of Proceedings*, 4 February 1955, p. 2059; and 'James Frederick Hill B.A., L.L.B.', 5 June 1950, CRS A6119/XR1, item 209, f. 56.
88 'James Frederick Hill', Memo, ASIO Director, Sydney, 6 June 1950, CRS A6119/XR1, item 91, f. 42.
89 Letter, J. F. Hill to Secretary, Department of External Affairs, 10 February 1945, in J. F. Hill, Unserialised Personal File, External Affairs.
90 'James Frederick Hill', CRS A6119/XR1, item 91, f. 148.
91 Letter, John Hood, Acting Secretary, Department of External Affairs, to J. F. Hill, 30 April 1945 in J. F. Hill, Unserialised Personal File, External Affairs.
92 Teleprinter Message, the Acting Secretary, Department of External Affairs, to the Secretary, Department of the Army, 30 April 1945 in J. F. Hill, Unserialised Personal File, External Affairs.
93 Letter, Hood, Acting Secretary, Department of External Affairs, to the Acting Secretary, Public Service Board, 25 June 1945 in J. F. Hill, Unserialised Personal File, External Affairs.
94 'James Frederick Hill', CRS A6119/XR1, item 91, vol. 1, f. 147; testimony of James Frederick Hill, 4 February 1955, p. 2058; and McKnight, *Australia's Spies and Their Secrets*, p. 51.
95 'James Frederick Hill', CRS A6119/XR1, item 91, f. 149.

96 'Extract from Report On P.50/999', CRS, A367/1, item C65833A.
97 'Re J. F. Hill', Memo to the Director ASIO, Canberra, 22 November 1949, CRS A6119, item 91, f. 30.
98 ibid.
99 'Extract From Report On P.50/999'.
100 'James Frederick Hill', CRS A6119/XR1, item 91, f. 147, B.F.
101 ibid.
102 Testimony of J. F. Hill, *Royal Commission on Espionage: Official Transcript of Proceedings*, 4 February 1955, p. 2057.
103 *Fifth Venona Release*, vol. 3, pp. 136–8.
104 ibid, p. 143.
105 ibid, pp. 145–6, 150.
106 ibid, pp. 160–1.
107 ibid, pp. 322–3, 325–6.
108 ibid.
109 'James Frederick Hill', 27 October 1950, CRS A367/1, item C65833A, f. 9.
110 'Re J. F. Hill', 22 November 1949, CRS A6119/XR1, item 91, volume 1, f. 29.
111 ibid.
112 Extract from Report On P.50/999', CRS, A367/1, item C65833A.
113 Letter (and attachment) to C. T. Moodie, Department of External Affairs, Canberra, 13 December 1949, CRS A6119/XRO, item 59.
114 Memo, Secretary, Public Service Board, to Secretary, Department of External Affairs, 1 September 1950, in J. F. Hill, Unserialised Personal File, External Affairs; and 'James Frederick Hill', 27 October 1950, attached to letter, the Commissioner, Public Service Board, to Professor K. H. Bailey, Solicitor-General, 31 October 1950, CRS M1505/1, item 538.
115 *Fifth Venona Release*, vol. 3, pp. 136–8.
116 Testimony of E. D. Throssell, *Royal Commission on Espionage: Official Transcript of Proceedings*, 4 February 1955, pp. 2072–73.
117 ibid., p. 2074.
118 ibid.
119 *Fifth Venona Release*, vol. 3, pp. 136–8.
120 ibid, pp. 325–26, 329–30.
121 Throssell, *My Father's Son*, p. 302.
122 Statement by Clarence William Dakin, 6 December 1954, CRS A6119/70, item 435, f. 45; and testimony of E. D. Throssell, *Royal Commission on Espionage: Official Transcript of Proceedings*, 4 February 1955, pp. 2073–4.
123 'Clarence William Dakin', 5 November 1953, CRS A6126/24, item 244, ff. 27–28; statement by C. W. Dakin, 6 December 1954, CRS A6119/70, item 435, ff. 44–45; and testimony of C. W. Dakin, *Royal Commission on Espionage: Official Transcript of Proceedings*, 3–4 February 1955, pp. 2037–51, 2064–71.
124 Testimony of E. D. Throssell, *Royal Commission on Espionage: Official Transcript of Proceedings*, 4 February 1955, pp. 2073–8.
125 *Report of the Royal Commission on Espionage*, p. 152.
126 Throssell, *My Father's Son*, chs 14 and 15; and letter, Department of External Affairs to the Legation of the USSR, Canberra, 24 September 1945.
127 Throssell, *My Father's Son*, p. 165.
128 'Ric or Richard Prichard Throssell', 5 May 1952, CRS A6119/95, f. 96.
129 'Extract of Service: Throssell, Richard Prichard', 13 May 1952, CRS A6119/95, f. 88.
130 ibid; and Throssell, *My Father's Son*, chs 17 and 18.
131 ibid, pp. 189–90.
132 ibid, pp. 190–1.
133 ibid, pp. 6–7.
134 ibid, p. 7; and Beasley, *A Gallop of Fire*, pp. 122–3, 166.
135 Throssell, *My Father's Son*, p. 7.
136 'Katharine Susannah Prichard (Mrs. H. Throssell)', CRS A6119, item 44, part 2, f. 87.
137 Throssell, *My Father's Son*, p. 199.
138 ibid, p. 198.

139 Letter, K. S. Prichard to Ric Throssell, 15 March 1948, in Throssell papers, NLA, MS 8071, folder 185, f. 46.
140 Throssell, *My Father's Son*, p. 195; and ASIO file note on 'Mr. R. P. Throssell', CRS A6119/95, f. 12.
141 Throssell, *My Father's Son*, p. 198.
142 ibid, pp. 204–5.
143 ASIO file note on 'Mr. R. P. Throssell', CRS A6119/95, f. 12.
144 Throssell, *My Father's Son*, pp. 204–6, 212–5.
145 ibid, p. 215.
146 'Richard Prichard Throssell', letter, G R. Richards, Deputy Director-General (Operations) to ASIO Director-General, 26 July 1954, CRS A6119, item 97, f. 75.
147 *Fifth Venona Release*, vol. 3, pp. 139–40.
148 ibid.
149 Memo to Acting Secretary, Public Service Board, 21 September 1945.
150 Department of Foreign Affairs file 1963/3/34, cited in Throssell, *My Father's Son*, pp. 369–70.
151 *Fifth Venona Release*, vol. 3, pp. 139–40.
152 Memo, ASIO Regional Director, NSW, to ASIO Director-General, 21 July 1953, CRS A6119/79, item 797, f.
153 'Richard Prichard Throssell', Memo, G. R. Richards, Deputy Director-General (Operations), to ASIO Director-General, 26 July 1954, CRS A6119, item 97, f. 75.
154 Letter, R. P. Throssell to The Accountant, Department of External Affairs, 2 October 1945.
155 Throssell, *My Father's Son*, pp. 210–11.
156 ibid, p. 220.
157 ASIO file note on 'Mr. R. P. Throssell', CRS A6119/95, f. 17.
158 Letter, R. P. Throssell, Australian Legation to the USSR, Moscow, to W. E. Dunk, Secretary, Department of External Affairs, 20 August 1946.
159 'Richard Prichard Throssell', Memo, ASIO Regional Director, NSW, to ASIO Director-General, 7 February 1952, cited in Ric Throssell, *My Father's Son*, p. 225.
160 Testimony of R. P. Throssell, 2 February 1955, *Royal Commission on Espionage: Official Transcript of Proceedings*, pp. 2022–23; and Throssell, *My Father's Son*, pp. 239–40.
161 ASIO file note on 'Mr. R. P. Throssell', CRS A6119/95, f. 12; and Throssell, *My Father's Son*, pp. 236–40.
162 Letter, K. S. Prichard to Miles Franklin, 15 January 1947, in Ferrier, *As Good As A Yarn With You*, p. 161.
163 Throssell, *My Father's Son*, pp. 242–5.
164 ibid, pp. 245–6.
165 *Fifth Venona Release*, vol. 3, pp. 325–6, 329–30.
166 ibid, pp. 329–30.
167 ibid.

Chapter 15   Britain's spycatchers come to Australia

1 Documents held by ASIO.
2 Post-Hostilities Planning Staff, *Security in the Western Mediterranean and the Eastern Atlantic: Report by the Post-Hostilities Planning Staff*, (PHP (45) 6 (0) Final, 19 May 1945), CAB 81/46.
3 Waters, *The Empire Fractures*, pp. 107–9.
4 Pincher, *Too Secret Too Long*, p. 135.
5 Sillitoe, *Cloak Without Dagger*, chs I–XVI.
6 ibid, p. 158.
7 Pincher, *Too Secret Too Long*, p. 133.

8 ibid, pp. 133–4.
9 Bower, *The Perfect English Spy*; and West, *A Matter of Trust*, ch. 3.
10 Andrew, *Secret Service*, p. 440.
11 ibid, p. 460.
12 West, *A Matter of Trust*, pp. 32–43.
13 Pincher, *Too Secret Too Long*, pp. 235–6; and West, *A Matter of Trust*, p. 61.
14 Andrew, *Secret Service*, p. 498.
15 West, *A Matter of Trust*, pp. 13–15, 19; and Pincher, *Too Secret Too Long*, pp. 45, 132–3, 213, 309.
16 West, *GCHQ*, p. 225.
17 West, *A Matter of Trust*, p. 41.
18 West, *GCHQ*, p. 225; and Pincher, *Too Secret Too Long*, pp. 173, 179.
19 Wright, *Spycatcher*, p. 187.
20 West, *Games of Intelligence*, p. 129.
21 Pincher, *Too Secret Too Long*, p. 140.
22 ibid, pp. 179–80.
23 West, *A Matter of Trust*, p. 40; and Pincher, *Too Secret Too Long*, pp. 197–8.
24 Philby, *My Silent War*, pp. 190, 192.
25 West, *A Matter of Trust*, p. 54.
26 ibid, p. 76.
27 ibid, pp. 123–4; and Pincher, *Too Secret Too Long*, pp. 387–8.
28 Cited in Hyde, *The Atom Bomb Spies*, pp. 67–9.
29 ibid, pp. 70–3.
30 West, *A Matter of Trust*, p. 28.
31 West, *The Illegals*, pp. 66, 122.
32 John Stubbs and Evan Whitton, 'Petrov: New Light on a Tragic Farce', *The National Times Magazine*, 3 September 1973, p. 15.
33 West, *MI 5*, p. 27.
34 West, *A Matter of Trust*, p. 19.
35 See the correspondence from Roland S. Browne, Acting Director, CIB, Canberra to Lt-Col S. H. Jackson, CIB, Sydney, 18, 21 and 23 October 1946, AA Sydney: C439, item 7; and correspondence from Browne to Secretary, Attorney-General's Department, Canberra, 21 and 23 October 1946, in Evatt Papers, File: Correspondence Misc 1946–47.
36 See Read and Fisher, *Operation Lucy*, pp. 25, 30–34, 208–16.
37 Foote, *Handbook For Spies*; West, *A Matter of Trust*, pp. 9–30; and Read and Fisher, *Operation Lucy*, pp. 222–3.
38 West, *A Matter of Trust*, pp. 43, 121; Pincher, *Too Secret Too Long*, p. 355.
39 ibid, p. 241.
40 Waters, *The Empire Fractures*, p. 121.
41 ibid, p. 225.
42 Shedden to Burton, 7 April 1948, CRS, A53/1, section 6, f. 3.
43 Chifley to Shedden, 20 February 1948, CRS, A5954/10, item 848/1.
44 Letter from Shedden, 2 March 1948, CRS A5945/10, item 848/1.
45 Brigadier F. O. Chilton, Top Secret 'In Camera' testimony, 1 November 1954, *Royal Commission on Espionage: Official Transcript of Proceedings*.
46 ibid; and Shedden to Chilton, 16 February 1948, CRS A5954/10, item 848/1.
47 Interview with Brigadier Sir Frederick Chilton, 2 March 1993.
48 Report by Chilton to Shedden, 'Control of Documents Received from the United Kingdom Government', 27 February 1948, p. 1, CRS A5954/10, item 848/1.
49 ibid. See also Brigadier F. O. Chilton, Top Secret 'In Camera' testimony, 1 November 1954, in *Royal Commission on Espionage: Official Transcript of Proceedings*.
50 Report by Chilton to Shedden, 'Control of Documents Received from the United Kingdom Government', 1 March 1948, pp. 1–3, CRS AA A5954/10, item 848/1.
51 Milner to the Secretary, Defence Post-Hostilities Planning Committee, Department of Defence, 6 November 1945, CRS A53/1.

52 Report by Chilton to Shedden, 'Control of Documents Received from the United Kingdom Government', 1 March 1948, pp. 1–3.
53 Interview with Chilton, 2 March 1993.
54 Shedden to Minister for Defence, 2 March 1948, CRS A5954/10, item 848/1.
55 Report by Chilton to Shedden, 'Control of Documents Received from the United Kingdom Government', 27 February 1948, Appendix A, CRS A5954/10, item 848/1.
56 Post-Hostilities Planning Staff, *Security in the Western Mediterranean and the Eastern Atlantic: Report by the Post-Hostilities Planning Staff*, (PHP (45) 6 (0) Final, 19 May 1945), CAB 81/46.
57 Post-Hostilities Planning Staff, *Security of India and the Indian Ocean*, (PHP (45) 15 (0) Final, 19 May 1945), CAB 81/46.
58 Memo by Shedden, 'Discussion with Colonel Colin (sic) Cohen, Melbourne, 15th November 1945', 15 November 1949, CRS A5954/10, item 848/1.
59 ibid. Spry's recollections of this incident are mentioned in a hand-written memo dated 3 November 1954, in CRS A6119, item 18, f. 33. Later W. J. Mathews was interviewed and he confirmed the story; memo, [name expunged] Royal Commission Section to Deputy Director-General (Operations) [ASIO], 14 March 1955, CRS A6283/XR, item 72, ff. 423–4.
60 Interview with Chilton, 2 March 1993.
61 Swan typescript.
62 Documents held by ASIO.
63 Waters, *The Empire Fractures*, p. 126.
64 ibid, pp. 128–9.
65 Shedden to Burton, 7 April 1948, CRS A53/1, section 6, f. 3.
66 ibid.
67 Burton to Shedden, 9 April 1948, CRS A53/1, section 6, f. 8.
68 Moodie to J. K. Waller, Secretary of the Department of External Affairs, 17 December 1954, CRS A53/1, section 6, f. 30.
69 ibid.
70 Burton to Shedden, 22 April 1948, CRS A53/1, section 6, ff. 9–10.
71 ibid; see also the draft letter prepared by Dr Burton but not sent, CRS A53/1, section 6, ff 4–5.
72 Burton to Shedden, 22 April 1948, CRS A53/1, section 6, ff 9–10.
73 Shedden to Burton, 9 June 1948, CRS A53/1, section 6, ff 11–12.
74 Shedden to Chifley, 'Draft Letter to Prime Minister of the United Kingdom from Prime Minister', 27 September 1948, CRS A5954/10, item 848/1.
75 Shedden to Burton, 'Security of Secret Defence Information', 9 June 1948, CRS A53/1, section 6, f. 12.
76 Shedden to Chifley, 11 June 1948; and Shedden to the Minister for Defence, 11 June 1948, CRS A6954/10, item 848/1.
77 Testimony of Dr J. W. Burton, *Royal Commission on Espionage: Official Transcript of Proceedings*. See also Watt, *Australian Diplomat*, p. 190.
78 Brian Toohey, 'The Security Scandal That Led to ASIO', *The National Times*, 20–26 April 1980, p. 38; and Cain, 'An Aspect of Post-War Australian Relations with the United Kingdom and the United States', pp. 189–90.
79 Telegram No. 38, for Prime Minister, Australian High Commissioner's Office, London, and Department of External Affairs, Canberra, from Australian Embassy, Washington D.C., 3 July 1948, CRS A3300/7, item 750.
80 Waters, *The Empire Fractures*, p. 138.
81 *Hansard (House of Representatives)*, 30 September 1948, pp. 1037–49.
82 ibid; Andrew, 'The Growth of the Australian Intelligence Community and the Anglo-American Connection', p. 228; and Hall, *The Rhodes Scholar Spy*, p. 154.
83 Swan typescript.
84 Waters, *The Empire Fractures*, p. 140.
85 See, for example, *Fifth Venona Release*, vol. 3, pp. 325–6, 329–30.
86 Dedman to Shedden, 6 August 1948, CRS A5954/10, item 848/1.
87 ibid.
88 ibid.
89 Swan typescript.

NOTES   421

90 See Manne, *The Petrov Affair*, p. 179.
91 Dr J. W. Burton, Top Secret 'In Camera' testimony, 2 November 1954, *Royal Commission on Espionage: Official Transcript of Proceedings*.
92 ibid.
93 *Fifth Venona Release*, vol. 3, pp. 68–71.
94 Dr J. W. Burton, Top Secret 'In Camera' testimony, 2 November 1954, *Royal Commission on Espionage: Official Transcript of Proceedings*.
95 ibid.
96 ibid.
97 Swan typescript.
98 Documents from ASIO.
99 Swan typescript.
100 ibid.
101 Shedden to Chifley, 27 September 1948; and 'Draft Letter to Prime Minister of the United Kingdom from Prime Minister', CRS, A5954/10, item 848/1.
102 'Draft Letter to Prime Minister of the United Kingdom from Prime Minister', CRS, A5954/10, item 848/1.
103 ibid.
104 Interview with Colin Moodie, Adelaide, 17 August 1993.
105 ibid.
106 Testimony of J. W. Burton, 2 November 1954, in *Royal Commission on Espionage: Official Transcript of Proceedings*.
107 ibid.
108 ibid.
109 Laughlin, *Boots and All*, p. 105; and *Seventh Report of the Royal Commission on Intelligence and Security*, (1977), vol. 1, ch. 7, p. 210, CRS, A8908/1.
110 The details are in the Evatt Papers.
111 Hall, *The Secret State*, p. 37.
112 Interview with Chilton, 2 March 1993.
113 Swan typescript.
114 Cited in Crisp, *Ben Chifley*, p. 273.
115 ibid.
116 ibid, p. 360.
117 Public Statement Chifley, 2 March 1949, *Digest of Decisions and Announcements and Important Speeches by the Prime Minister, the Right Hon. J. B. Chifley*, no. 142, 24 January 1949 to 6 March 1949.
118 Longfield Lloyd to Secretary, Attorney-General's Department, 3 March 1949, CRS A367/4, item C23512, Part 2.
119 Royal Commission on Intelligence and Security, *Fourth Report*, vol. 1, p. 2.
120 Shedden to Dedman, 20 December 1948, NLA: Dedman Papers, 987/9, f. 34.
121 Stretton to Ball, 25 February 1993.
122 Swan typescript.

CHAPTER 16   ASIO AND 'THE CASE'

1 Quoted in Swan typescript.
2 Swan typescript.
3 Mr Justice Reed and Roger Hollis, 'The Australian Security Service', March 1949, cited in Sir Frederick Shedden, 'Brief for Visit Abroad', 1 April 1949, Dedman Papers, MS 987/9, f. 108; and Andrew, 'The Growth of the Australian Intelligence Community and the Anglo-American Connection', p. 228.
4 Mr Justice Reed and Roger Hollis, 'The Australian Security Service', March 1949, CRS, A5954/10, item 848/1. See also Morton, *Fire Across The Desert*, pp. 105, 113 (note 17); Shedden, 'Brief for Visit Abroad', 1 April 1949, Dedman Papers, MS 987/9, folio 108; and Andrew, 'The Growth of the Australian Intelligence Community and the Anglo-American Connection', pp. 228, 255 (note 70).

5 Pincher, *Too Secret Too Long*, p. 136.
6 See, for example, *Fifth Venona Release*, vol. 3, pp. 322–3, 325–6, 329–30.
7 Letter, P. G. M. Gilbert to D. J. Ball, 2 March 1993; and interview with Gilbert, 16 August 1993.
8 Testimony of J. W. Burton, *Royal Commission on Espionage: Official Transcript of Proceedings*.
9 Gilbert to Ball, 2 March 1993.
10 Wake diary, entries for 20–25 April 1949.
11 Interview with Ray Whitrod, 16 August 1993.
12 Swan typescript.
13 Interview with Whitrod, 16 August 1933.
14 Wake, 'Re the Net', (summary of discussion between Wake and Prime Minister Chifley in 'about August 1949'), in Evatt Papers: Correspondence Misc. 1946–47.
15 Interview with Whitrod, 16 August 1993.
16 ibid; and McKnight, *Australia's Spies and Their Secrets*, p. 26.
17 Interview with Whitrod, 16 August 1993; and McKnight, *Australia's Spies and Their Secrets*, p. 23.
18 Interview with Whitrod, 16 August 1993.
19 ibid.
20 ibid.
21 'Walter Seddon Clayton: Summary of File', attachment to letter from ASIO Director-General to Regional Director, New South Wales, 7 May 1954, CRS A6119/XR1, item 57.
22 ibid.
23 'Australian Security Service: Note on Progress from 1st to 29th June, 1949', attached to letter Shedden to the Hon. Gordon Gray, 20 July 1949, CRS A5954, item 1795/3, f. 54.
24 Shedden to Chifley, 10 May 1949, CRS A5954, item 1795/2.
25 ibid.
26 ibid.
27 ibid.
28 ibid.
29 Shedden to Chilton, 9 May 1949, CRS A5954, item 1795/1.
30 Shedden to Gray, 30 June 1949, and Shedden to Minister for Defence, 18 July 1949, CRS A5954, item 1795/3.
31 Note attached to letter, Shedden to Gray, 20 July 1949, CRS A5954, item 1795/3.
32 Shedden to Minister for Defence, 18 July 1949, CRS A5954, item 1795/3.
33 Chilton to Shedden, 9 August 1949, CRS A5954, item 1795/3.
34 ibid.
35 Reed to Shedden, 18 August 1949, CRS A5954, item 1795/3.
36 Sillitoe to Shedden, 22 August 1949, CRS A5954, item 1795/3.
37 Attlee to Chifley, 4 April 1949 (emphasis in original), Dedman Papers, MS 987/9/94–987/9/96.
38 Shedden to Chifley, 10 May 1949, CRS A5954, item 1795/2.
39 Sillitoe to Shedden, 22 August 1949, CRS A5954, item 1795/3.
40 ibid.
41 'Feodor Nosov', CRS A6119, item 1246, f. 29.
42 Interview with Whitrod, 16 August 1993.
43 Letter, D Branch, Attorney-General's Department, Melbourne, to ASIO Director General, Sydney, 28 June 1949, CRS A6119/83, item 1481.
44 Interview with Whitrod, 16 August 1993.
45 Memo, Adelaide Office to ASIO Director General, Sydney, 4 July 1949, CRS A6119/83, item 1481.
46 Swan typescript.
47 ibid.
48 Interview with Whitrod, 16 August 1993.
49 'Feodor Nosov: Preliminary Report, 18th May, 1950', CRS A6119, item 1248.
50 ibid.

51 'Operation . . .', 6 February 1950, CRS A6119, item 1246, f. 40.
52 Gilbert to Ball, 2 March 1993; and telephone conversation with Gilbert, 17 May 1996.
53 Gilbert to Ball, 2 March 1993; and interview with Gilbert, 16 August 1993.
54 Telephone interview with Gilbert, 8 March 1993; and interview with Gilbert, 16 August 1993.
55 'James F. Hill', April 1949, CRS A6119/XR1, item 91, volume 1, f. 3.
56 'J. F. Hill': List of Persons Who Attended a Party . . .', CRS A6119/XR1, item 91, volume 1, ff. 5–21.
57 Telephone interview with Gilbert, 8 March 1993.
58 Telephone interview with Gilbert, 17 May 1996.
59 'Re J. F. Hill', 22 November 1949, and 'List of Persons Present at Dinner at Canberra Tourist Lodge on Night of Thursday, 15th September, 1949', CRS A6119/XR1, item 91, volume 1, ff. 29, 26.
60 Interview with Whitrod, 16 August 1993; and telephone conversation with Ernest O. Redford, 10 March 1993.
61 'Dr John Wear Burton', ASIO, August 1952, p. 29, CRS A6119/XR1, item 128, f. 100.
62 ibid.
63 'Summary for Counsel: James Frederick Hill', CRS A6119/XR1, item 91, f. 98.
64 Testimony of Dr J. W. Burton, 2 November 1954, in *Royal Commission on Espionage: Official Transcript of Proceedings*.
65 ibid.
66 'Re J. F. Hill', 22 November 1949, CRS A6119/XR1, item 91, volume 1, ff. 29–30.
67 ibid.
68 Memo, Australia House, London, to the Secretary, Department of External Affairs, Canberra, 15 March 1950, in J. F. Hill, Unserialised Personal File, External Affairs.
69 Testimony of Dr J. W. Burton, 2 November 1954, in *Royal Commission on Espionage: Official Transcript of Proceedings*.
70 Gilbert to Ball, 2 March 1993; interview with Gilbert, 16 August 1993; and telephone interview with Gilbert, 17 May 1996.
71 Cited in Anthony McAdam, 'Spry Lays An Old Spook To Rest', *The Bulletin*, 27 November 1984, p. 52.
72 Swan typescript.
73 ibid.
74 ibid.
75 ibid.
76 Interview with Lockwood, 13 July 1995.
77 ibid.
78 'Further Particulars Re Burhop', 12 December 1954, CRS A6119/2, item 50, ff. 149–153.
79 'Subject: Eric Henry Stanley Burhop', April 1953, CRS A6119/2, item 50, f. 100.
80 ibid, f. 98.
81 ibid.
82 Cable no. 313, Canberra to Moscow, 29 August 1945, in *Fifth Venona Release*, vol. 3, pp. 115–6.
83 Interview with Rupert Lockwood, 13 July 1995.
84 'Petrov Twenty Years On: Rupert Lockwood's Personal View', transcript of ABC radio interview, 26 May 1974, p. 20; and interview with Lockwood, 13 July 1995.
85 O'Sullivan, *Intersecting Lines*, p. 167.
86 Smith, *Noel Counihan*, p. 229.
87 ibid, pp. 229–31.
88 ibid, pp. 149–50, 535–6; and O'Sullivan, *Intersecting Lines*, pp. 162–3.
89 Cook, *Red Barrister*, p. 60.
90 Smith, *Noel Counihan*, pp. 535–6.
91 Hinsley and Simkins, *British Intelligence in the Second World War. Volume 4*,

pp. 305–7; Costello, *Mask of Treachery*, p. 105; and Boyle, *The Climate of Treason*, pp. 31, 88.
92 Roland, *An Improbable Life*, pp. 162–4; and Roland, *Caviar for Breakfast*, pp. 125–30.
93 Interview with Lockwood, 13 July 1995.
94 McKnight, *Australia's Spies and Their Secrets*, p. 50.
95 Testimony of Dr J. W. Burton, 2 November 1954, *Royal Commission on Espionage: Official Transcript of Proceedings*; and interview with Lockwood, 13 July 1995.
96 'James Frederick Hill', attachment to memo from ASIO Director-General to Regional Director, Victoria, 7 August 1952, CRS A6119/XR1, item 91, f. 145.
97 Letter, Commonwealth Relations Office, London, to United Kingdom High Commissioner, Canberra, 16 June 1950, and attached Report, 15 June 1950, in file A/459, Department of Prime Minister and Cabinet, Canberra.
98 Cable, Secretary, Department of External Affairs, Canberra, to External Affairs Officer, High Commissioner's Office, London, 4 July 1950, CRS A6691, item A53/2.
99 Borovik, *The Philby Files*, pp. 267, 299–301. See also Philby, *My Silent War*, pp. 192–3; and Knightley, *Philby*, pp. 185–8.
100 Bower, *The Perfect English Spy*, p. 86.
101 ibid, pp. 95–6.
102 ibid, p. 115.
103 ibid, pp. 134–5.
104 Knightley, *Philby*, pp. 187–8.
105 Bower, *The Perfect English Spy*, p. 325.
106 Interview with Gilbert, 16 August 1993.

Chapter 17 The end of 'the case'

1 Aide-memoire from US Embassy, Canberra, 6 January 1950, and 'Draft letter from Minister for External Affairs to United States Ambassador', CRS A1209, item 68/9509.
2 Swan typescript.
3 Interviews with Michael Thwaites, 19 October 1992, 1 February 1993 and 4 October 1996; and interview with Whitrod, 16 August 1993.
4 See Parker, *The S.I.S.*, pp. 17, 20.
5 Interviews with Thwaites, 1 February 1993 and 4 October 1996.
6 Swan typescript.
7 Interview with Thompson, 27 September 1994.
8 Spry to Menzies, 29 July 1953, CRS A6122/39, item 1427.
9 'Notes for Counsel: re Bernie', 22 October 1954, CRS A6119/79, item 799, f. 106.
10 'Frances Ada Gluck, nee Scott known as Bernie: Preliminary Report', 25 May 1950, p. 8, CRS A6119/79, item 796, f. 106.
11 Handwritten notation on 'Notes for Mr Windeyer: re Bernie', 22 October 1954, CRS A6119/79, item 799, f. 104.
12 'Notes for Counsel: re Bernie', 22 October 1954, CRS A6119/79, item 799, f. 106.
13 Memo, ASIO Regional Director, NSW to ASIO Director-General, 10 June 1953, pp. 8–9, in A6119/79, item 798, ff. 5–6.
14 ibid, f. 12.
15 ibid, ff. 6, 8.
16 ibid.
17 ibid, f. 7.
18 'Extract from Shorthand Note-Book', 9 June 1953, CRS A6119/79, item 798, f. 2.
19 Memo, ASIO Regional Director, NSW, to ASIO Director-General, 10 June 1953, pp. 6–7, CRS A6119/79, item 798, ff. 7–8.
20 ibid, ff. 6, 7; and 'Extract from Shorthand Note-book', 9 June 1953, ibid, f. 1.

21 Memo, ASIO Regional Director, NSW, to ASIO Director-General, 10 June 1953, p. 5, ibid, f. 5.
22 Memo, ASIO Regional Director, NSW, to ASIO Director-General, 22 June 1953, ibid, ff. 49–52.
23 Memo, ASIO Regional Director, NSW, to ASIO Director-General, 21 July 1953, CRS A6119/79, item 797, ff. 62–6.
24 Memo, SSO B2 to Acting Regional Director, 17 November 1959, CRS A6119/79, item 799, f. 183.
25 ibid.
26 Memo, B2 to ASIO Regional Director, 2 December 1959, CRS A6119/79, item 799, f. 197.
27 Dalziel, *Evatt the Enigma*, pp. 110–15.
28 'Extract from Shorthand Note-book', 9 June 1953, CRS A6119/79, item 798, f. 2.
29 Statement by Frances Bernie, 8 September 1954, CRS A6119/XR1, item 57, f. 169.
30 *Report of the Royal Commission on Espionage*, pp. 21–3.
31 ibid, pp. 119–20.
32 ibid, p. 57.
33 ibid, pp. 58, 401.
34 ibid, pp. 58, 402.
35 ibid, pp. 58, 404.
36 ibid, pp. 58–9, 404.
37 ibid, pp. 59, 405–6.
38 ibid, pp. 59, 407–10.
39 Throssell, *My Father's Son*, p. 263.
40 'Richard Prichard Throssell', CRS A6119/95, f. 83. See also 'Short Summary of Interview with Richard Prichard Throssell at Canberra, 30th March, 1953', CRS A6119/97, ff. 82–83.
41 A. H. Tange, Secretary, Department of External Affairs, to Spry, 11 May 1956, CRS A6119/XR1, item 91, f. 176.
42 Cited in *Report of the Royal Commission on Espionage*, p. 414.
43 Excerpts from statement by V. M. Petrov, 21 May 1954, CRS A6119/57, f. 26.
44 ibid.
45 ibid.
46 ibid, f. 28.
47 Note by C. C. F. Spry, 18 August 1954, CRS A6119/XR1, item 97, f. 79.
48 Memo, Richards to ASIO Director-General, 26 July 1954, CRS A6119/XR1, item 57, ff. 75, 77.
49 ibid.
50 ibid, f. 76.
51 ibid, f. 75.
52 ibid, f. 76.
53 ibid, f. 71–72.
54 Testimony of R. P. Throssell, 2 February 1955, in *Royal Commission on Espionage: Official Transcript of Proceedings*, p. 2016.
55 Memo, Richards to ASIO Director-General, 26 July 1954, CRS A6119/XR1, item 57, f. 76.
56 Prichard to Throssell, 30 December 1945, in Throssell Papers, MS 8071, box 26, folder 182.
57 Prichard to Throssell, 20 January 1946, in ibid, folder 183.
58 Prichard to Throssell, 13, 20 and 27 January 1946, in ibid.
59 *Report of the Royal Commission on Espionage*, pp. 141–2.
60 ibid, p. 143.
61 Tange to Spry, 23 May 1955, cited in Throssell, *My Father's Son*, pp. 325–7.
62 ibid, pp. 353–5.
63 ibid, pp. 381–2, 388, 393.
64 'Richard Prichard Throssell', attachment to Memorandum from ASIO Royal Commission Section to ASIO Director General, 11 October 1954, in A6119/XR1, item 97, f. 85.

65 Testimony of Dr J. W. Burton, 2 November 1954, in *Royal Commission on Espionage: Official Transcript of Proceedings*.
66 ibid.
67 'James Frederick Hill', CRS A6119/XR1, item 91, volume 1, f. 147.
68 See the three forms signed by John W. Burton on 9 April 1948, in J. F. Hill, Unserialised Personal File, Department of External Affairs, Canberra.
69 'James F. Hill', in CRS A6119/XR1, item 91, f. 49; and 'James Frederick Hill', in CRS A6119/XR1, item 91, vol. 1, f. 147.
70 'James F. Hill', in CRS A6119/XR1, item 91, f. 49; and 'James Frederick Hill', in CRS A6119/XR1, item 91, vol. 1, f. 147; and 'Dr John Wear Burton', ASIO, August 1952, Appendix A, p.25, CRS A6119/XR1, item 128, f. 104.
71 'James F. Hill', in CRS A6119/XR1, item 91, f. 49; and 'James Frederick Hill', in CRS A6119/XR1, item 91, vol. 1, f. 147; and Hall, *The Rhodes Scholar Spy*, p. 161.
72 'Subject: Transfer of Mr. J. F. Hill as Legal Officer, Grade 2', Memorandum from F. X. Schneider, Secretary, Public Service Board, to the Secretary, Attorney-General's Department, 16 January 1951, in J. F. Hill, Unserialised Personal File, External Affairs; and 'Subject: Transfer of Mr. J. F. Hill as Legal Officer, Grade 2', Memo for the Secretary, Attorney-General's Department, Canberra, 15 February 1951.
73 O'Sullivan, *Intersecting Lines*, p. 194.
74 ibid, pp. 194–5.
75 ibid, pp. 31–2.
76 'Ian Frank George Milner', CRS A6119/XR1, item 18.
77 ibid.
78 ibid.
79 *Report of the Royal Commission on Espionage*, p. 46.
80 Statement by Ian Frank George Milner, 1 March 1956, pp. 4, 6, attached to letter from Milner to Evatt, 29 May 1956, in Evatt Papers, file on 'Petrov Affair: Correspondence Relating to Case'.
81 ibid, p. 3.
82 ibid.
83 ibid.
84 Peter Hruby, 'Secret Life of Agent 9006', *Courier Mail*, 30 November 1996, p. 30.
85 John Thompson, 'Circles of Music and Espionage', *Evening Post* (Wellington), 14 September 1995, p. 5.
86 O'Sullivan, *Intersecting Lines*, p. 2.
87 ibid, p. 7.
88 Cited in Phillip Knightley, 'Australian Diplomat Spied for Russians: Author Reveals Intimate Confession', *Sun Herald*, 9 June 1991, p. 5.
89 Testimony of W. S. Clayton, *Royal Commission on Espionage: Official Transcript of Proceedings*, 15 March 1955, p. 2469.
90 Memo, Inspector L. Jones, NSW Special Branch, to the Commissioner of Police, NSW, 21 August 1952, CRS A6119/XR1, item 56.
91 Testimony of W. S. Clayton, *Royal Commission on Espionage: Official Transcript of Proceedings*, 15 March 1955, pp. 2457–541.
92 ibid, pp. 2491–2.
93 ibid, pp. 2455, 2459.
94 McKnight, *Australia's Spies and Their Secrets*, pp. 83–4.
95 'This Man is Wanted: Who Can Uncover Comrade Clayton?', *The Herald* (Melbourne), 30 October 1954, p. 10.
96 McKnight, *Australia's Spies and Their Secrets*, pp. 84, 309.
97 Testimony of W. S. Clayton, *Royal Commission on Espionage: Official Transcript of Proceedings*, pp. 2441–2.
98 ibid, pp. 2441–3.
99 Justice Windeyer, in ibid, p. 2485.
100 *Report of the Royal Commission on Espionage*, pp. 50–151.
101 Memo, ASIO Director General to ASIO Regional Directors, 19 December 1955, CRS A6119/79, item 953, ff. 27–30.

102 Memo, ASIO Regional Director NSW to Headquarters, ASIO, 23 February 1957; Walter Seddon Clayton and Peace Joy Gowland, 'Application for Marriage: Information Paper', 1 March 1956; Memo from B2 to Director, ASIO, 17 October 1956, in A6119/79, item 953, ff. 38, 32, 187.
103 Memo, ASIO Deputy Director-General (Operations), 26 March 1956, CRS A6119/79, item 952, f. 2.
104 ibid.
105 ibid.
106 ibid.
107 ibid.
108 Memo, ASIO Director General, to Regional Director, NSW, 18 April 1957, CRS A6119, item 955, f. 192.
109 ibid.
110 'Walter Seddon Clayton', Memo, ASIO Director General to Regional Directors, 1 March 1957, CRS A6119/79, item 952, f. 78.
111 See the ASIO logs for March–April 1957, CRS A6119, item 955, ff. 26–131. See also statement by Walter Seddon Clayton, 27 August 1957, p. 3.
112 McKnight, *Australia's Spies and Their Secrets*, p. 5.
113 See A6119, item 955, ff. 123, 127.
114 Memo, ASIO Regional Director, NSW, to ASIO Headquarters, 18 April 1958, CRS A6119/79, item 952, ff. 128–9.
115 'Walter Seddon Clayton; Peace Joy Clayton, nee Gowland', CRS A6119/79, item 957, f. 204.
116 See the ASIO B2 notes on Clayton in CRS A6119/83, item 1597, ff. 27, 65.
117 See, for example, Wally Clayton, 'Hookers Horrible Home', *Tribune*, 11 October 1961, CRS A6119/83, item 1597, f. 130.
118 Note from ASIO Regional Director, NSW, to Deputy Director General (Operations), 13 September 1962, CRS A6119/79, item 952, f. 140.
119 Memo, ASIO Director General to Regional Director, NSW, 1 October 1962, CRS A6119/79, item 952, f. 141.
120 Evidence by Stanley Cassell Taylor (in camera), 28 January 1955, *Royal Commission on Espionage: Official Transcript of Proceedings*, pp.7494–6, in A6213/1, item RCE/2/21, ff. 13–15.
121 ibid, ff. 11–12.
122 'Security Service in N.S.W., 1942–1946', 3 October 1952, CRS A6119/83, item 1510, f. 12.
123 Memo, ASIO Regional Director, Qld, to Deputy Director-General (Operations), 27 March 1957, CRS A6119/83, item 1510, f. 164.
124 ASIO file note on Alfred Thompson Hughes, 28 March 1957, CRS A6119/83, item 1510, f. 173.
125 Memo on A.T. Hughes, 26 March 1957, CRS A6119/83, item 1510, f. 160.
126 'Personal Particulars' form completed by Alfred Thompson Hughes, 29 June 1951, p. 4; Memo from Field Officer, ASIO B2, to Principal Section Officer, B2, Sydney, 25 August 1954, CRS A6119/83, item 1510, ff. 26, 124.
127 Telephone Message concerning Det Sgt Alf Hughes, from ASIO Regional Director, Queensland, to ASIO NSW, 27 March 1957; Memo, ASIO Regional Director, Queensland, to Deputy Director-General (Operations), 27 March 1957; ASIO file note on Hughes, 28 March 1957, CRS A6119/83, item 1510, ff. 163, 164, 173.
128 Cited in *Report of the Royal Commission on Espionage*, p. 407.
129 Testimony of Justice Stanley Cassin Taylor, 28 January 1955, *Royal Commission on Espionage: Official Transcript of Proceedings*, pp. 2889–90.
130 McKnight, *Australia's Spies and Their Secrets*, pp. 82, 309.
131 Extracts from record of telephone conversation between G. R. Richards and A. T. Hughes, 3 May 1957, in Minute to Director B2, 24 November 1959, CRS A6119/79, item 799, f. 189.
132 Chief Inspector (retd.) Jo Green, NSW Police Force, to Helen Wilson, Strategic and Defence Studies Centre, Canberra, February 1994.
133 Memo, Hughes and Alfred L. Walsh, Security Service, Sydney, 14 October 1943, CRS A6119/83, item 1510, f. 61.

134 Extract from report of telephone conversation with A. T. Hughes, 3 May 1957, in memo for B2, 24 November 1959, CRS A6119/79, item 799, f. 189.
135 'Operation . . .', file note by ASIO Deputy Director-General, Sydney, 1 April 1957, CRS A6119/79, item 1144.
136 Telephone Message from B2, 24 April 1954, CRS A6119/79, item 798, f. 110; and Report on interview with Alfred Thomas [sic] Hughes on 29 March 1957 by Deputy Director-General (Operations), Sydney, 1 April 1957, CRS A6119/79, item 1144.
137 Memo, B2 to Director, 23 April 1957; Memo, B2 to ASIO Director, 1 May 1957; and extracts from interviews with Frances Ada Garrett, 24 November 1959, in A6119/79, item 799, ff. 109, 114, 187, 188.
138 Extracts from telephone conversation with A. T. Hughes, 3 May 1957, in report to Director B2, 24 November 1959, CRS A6119/79, item 799, f. 189.
139 'Information Suggesting Alfred Thompson Hughes was a Member of the Communist Party of Australia and/or was Associated with Walter Seddon Clayton and the R.I.S.', CRS A6119/83, item 1510, f. 210.
140 'Operation . . .', file note by ASIO Deputy Director-General, Sydney, 1 April 1957, CRS A6119/79, item 1144.
141 Sergeant A. T. Hughes to Inspector Swasbrick, Security Service, Sydney, 31 August 1945, in A6119/83, item 1510, f. 112.
142 Transcript of telephone interview with Alf Hughes, 1 April 1957, CRS A6119/79, item 1144.
143 'Operation . . .', Memo by Deputy Director-General (Operations), Sydney, 1 April 1957, CRS A6119/79, item 1144.
144 ibid.
145 Deputy Director-General (Operations), CRS A6119/83, item 1510, f. 156.
146 Alfred Thompson Hughes, NSW Police Force, Service Record no. 1810, provided by Services Branch, NSW Police Service, 13 December 1993.
147 Spry to Horner, 17 June 1993.

CHAPTER 18 THE IMPORTANCE OF 'THE CASE'

1 Moscow Centre to Canberra, 6 June 1952, reproduced in *Report of the Royal Commission on Espionage*, p. 331.
2 Lamphere, *The FBI–KGB War*, p. 81.
3 Blamey to Acting Minister for the Army, 6 January 1945, 3 DRL 6643, item 2/59.
4 Lamphere, *The FBI–KGB War*, p. 89.
5 Gardner, interview with I. Livingstone, 7 October 1996.
6 'M.V.D. Cables', in CRS A6283/XR1, item 79.
7 See, for example, *Fifth Venona Release*, vol. 3, pp. 103–4, 110.
8 ibid, pp. 41–2.
9 ibid, pp. 132–3.
10 ibid, pp. 184–5.
11 ibid, pp. 151–2.
12 ibid, pp. 123–4.
13 ibid, pp. 200–1.
14 ibid.
15 ibid, p. 150.
16 ibid, pp. 160–1.
17 See, for example, ibid, pp. 70–1, 139–40.
18 ibid, pp. 136–7.
19 ibid, pp. 166–7.
20 Peter Hruby, 'Secret Life of Agent 9006', *Courier Mail*, 30 November 1996, p. 30.
21 *Fifth Venona Release*, vol. 3, pp. 99–100, 119–21.
22 ibid, pp. 123–4.

23 ibid, pp. 99–100; and McKnight, *Australia's Spies and Their Secrets*, p. 50.
24 Memo, SSO B2 to Acting Regional Director, 17 November 1959, CRS A6119/79, item 799, f. 183.
25 *Fifth Venona Release*, vol. 3, pp. 136–7.
26 Benson and Warner, *Venona*, p. xxiii.
27 Testimony of Dr J. W. Burton, *Royal Commission on Espionage: Official Transcript of Proceedings*, 2 November 1954; and Manne, *The Petrov Affair*, p. 189.
28 *Report of the Royal Commission on Espionage*, p. 152.
29 Martin, *Wilderness of Mirrors*, p. 46; and Michael Dobbs, 'American Counterspy Ends The Silence', *International Herald Tribune*, 22 October 1996, p. 2.
30 Lamphere, *The FBI–KGB War*, p. 140.
31 Sillitoe, *Cloak Without Dagger*, pp. 161, 172.
32 *Fifth Venona Release*, vol. 3, pp. 179–80.
33 Volkman, *Espionage*, p. 220.
34 Smith, *Noel Counihan*, p. 542.
35 Testimony of W. S. Clayton, *Royal Commission on Espionage: Official Transcript of Proceedings*, p. 2541.
36 *Fifth Venona Release*, vol. 3, p. 77.
37 ibid, pp. 139–40.
38 Quoted in Brown, *The Communist Movement and Australia*, p. 114.
39 Quoted in Sendy, *Comrades Come Rally*, p. 11.
40 Cook, *Red Barrister*, p. 68.
41 Testimony of Dr J. W. Burton, *Royal Commission on Espionage: Official Transcript of Proceedings*, 2 November 1955.
42 See, for example, *Fifth Venona Release*, vol. 3, pp. 136–8, 166–7.
43 Sharpley, *The Great Delusion*, pp. 28–29.
44 *Fifth Venona Release*, vol. 3, pp. 9–10.
45 Benson, *The 1942–43 New York–Moscow KGB Messages*, p. 2.
46 Shedden to Blamey, 3 January 1945, CRS A5954, item 429/15.
47 Rogers to Blamey, 18 January 1945, 3DRL6643, item 2/59.
48 A. H. Tange, Secretary, Department of External Affairs, 23 April 1956, CRS A53/1, item 6, f. 47.

Bibliography

INTERVIEWS AND CORRESPONDENCE

Bond, R.L., to D.J. Ball, 28 and 29 September 1994
Bond, R.L., to D.M. Horner, 23 and 24 February 1993
Brookes, Alfred, to D.J. Ball, 9 July 1996
Chilton, Sir Frederick, to D.M. Horner and D.J. Ball, 2 March 1993
Cohen, Mrs B., to D.M. Horner, 26 April 1993
Crowther, G.H.O., to D.M. Horner and D.J. Ball, 22 February 1993
Finlay, Maj-Gen C.H., to D.M. Horner, 1 March 1993
Fleming, A.P., to D.J. Ball, 21 October 1992 and 22 February 1993
Fleming, A.P., to D.J. Ball and D.M. Horner, 16 and 17 November 1993
Fleming, A.P., to D.M. Horner, 17 June 1993
Gardner, Meredith, to Ian Livingstone, 7 October 1996
Gilbert P.G.M., to D.J. Ball, 2 and 8 March 1993, 16 August 1993 and 17 May 1996
Green, Chief Inspector Jo (retd), NSW Police Force, to H. Wilson, February 1994
Hart, C.K., to D.M. Horner, 21 April 1993
Jamieson, A.B., to D.J. Ball, D.M. Horner and D.C.S. Sissons, 24 February 1988
Lockwood, Rupert, to D.J. Ball, 13 July 1995
Mason, Norman E., to H. Wilson, 16 July 1994
Mason, S., to D.C.S. Sissons, 26 June 1994
Mason, S., to D.J. Ball, 7 July 1995
McCue, W.J., to D.M. Horner, 24 October 1995
Moodie, Colin, to D.J. Ball, 17 August 1993
Moodie, Colin, (and attached 'Note Regarding Victor Zaitsev and the USSR Legation') to D.J. Ball and D.M. Horner, 21 August 1993
Nave, T.E., to D.M. Horner, 25 January 1979 and 24 February 1993
O'Sullivan, Kimberly, Archives Coordinator, Australian and Overseas Telecommunications Corporation (AOTC), to H. Wilson, 9 and 12 February 1993
Redford, Ernest O., to D.J. Ball, 10 March 1993
Sadler, P.J., to D.M. Horner, 15 and 25 February 1993
Sissons, D.C.S., to D.J. Ball, 22 May 1996

Smith, Professor Ian, to D.C.S. Sissons, 29 September 1996
Spry, Brigadier Sir Charles, to D.J. Ball, 22 February 1993
Spry, Brigadier Sir Charles, to D.M. Horner, 17 June 1993
Stretton, A.B., to D.J. Ball, 23 and 25 February 1993
Swan, R.A., to D.M. Horner, 25 June 1993
Templeton, Malcolm, Ministry of Foreign Affairs and Trade, New Zealand, to D.J. Ball, 22 July 1993
Thompson, Ralph, to D.J. Ball, 27 September 1994
Thwaites, Michael, to D.J. Ball, 19 October 1992, 1 February 1993 and 4 October 1996
Trendall, Professor A.D., to D.J. Ball, 10 May 1990
Treweek, Dr A.P., to D.C.S. Sissons, 11 October 1990
Wake, Mrs E., to D.M. Horner, 26 May 1993
Wang, Maj-Gen Chih, to D.M. Horner, 22 May 1993
Whitrod, Ray, to D.J. Ball and D.M. Horner, 16 August 1993
Williams, M.A., to D.J. Ball, 9 July 1995

Unpublished records

Australian Archives (AA)

- Canberra

CA 5; Attorney General's Department, Central Office, (c1929–)
CRS A432 Correspondence files, annual single number series, 1929–
CA 12; Prime Minister's Department, Central Office (1911–1971)
CRS A459 Correspondence files Class 1 and Class 3 (Staff), 1921–1930
CRS A461 Correspondence files, 1939–1950
CRS A1209 Prime Minister, annual single number series (Classified)
CA 18; Department of External Affairs [II], Central Office (1921–1970), CA 1382; Department of Foreign Affairs, Central Office (1970–1987), and CA 5987; Department of Foreign Affairs and Trade, Central Office 1987–1989)
CRS A1066 Correspondence files, multiple number series with year prefix, 1943–1944
CRS A1067 Correspondence files, multiple number series with year and letter prefixes, 1946–1946
CRS 1838 Correspondence files, multiple number series, 1948–1989
CRS A3300 Australian Legation, United States of America (Washington), Correspondence files, annual alphabetical series
CRS A6691 Limited access files maintained by Assistant Secretary/Senior Assistant Secretary of Division III/Management Services, 1954–1974
CA 35; Department of Air, Central Office (1939–1956)
CRS A1196 Correspondence files, multiple number series (Class 501) [501–539] (Classified), 1935–1960
CA 37; Department of Defence Coordination, Central Office (1939–1942), and CA 46; Department of Defence [III], Central Office (1942–)
CRS A816 Correspondence Files, multiple number system (Classified) 1935–1957
CRS AA1981/132 Black Folder containing miscellaneous Security Service and Intelligence records of the Second World War, 1940–1945
CP 320; Sir Frederick Geoffrey SHEDDEN KCMG, OBE
CRS A5954 Papers of Sir Frederick Shedden
CA 495; Advisory War Council (1940–1945)
CRS A2680 Advisory War Council Agenda Files, 29 Oct 1940–30 Aug 1945
CRS A2682 Advisory War Council Minutes (carbon copies), 29 Oct 1940–30 Aug 1945
CA 650; Commonwealth Investigation Service, Central Office, (1953–1960), CA 736; Commissioner, Commonwealth Police Force [II] (1960–1975), CA 1892; Australian Police, Headquarters (1975–1975), CA 2083; Office of the Commissioner, Common-

wealth Police (Force) [III] (1975–1979), and CA 2999; Australian Federal Police Headquarters (1979–)
CRS A1533 Correspondence files, annual single number series, 1953–
CA 747; Investigation Branch, Central Office, Melbourne and Canberra (1919–1946), and CA 650; Commonwealth Investigation Service, Central Office (1946–1953)
CRS A367 Correspondence files, single number series with 'C' prefix, 1927–1953, 1916–1953
CRS A373 Correspondence files, single number series, 1941–1949
CRS A8908 *Reports of the Royal Commission on Intelligence and Security, numerical series, 1 January 1976–*
CA 1297; Australian Security Intelligence Organization
CRS A6119 Personal files, alpha-numeric series, 1949–
CRS A6122 Subject files, multiple number series, 1949–1949
CRS A6126 Microfilm copies of personal and subject files (CRS A6119 and CRS A6122), 1960–
CRS A6283 Correspondence files, multiple number series (Royal Commission Section), 1954–1955
CA 1468; War Cabinet Secretariat (1939–1946)
CRS A2670 Reference set of War Cabinet Agenda with Minutes, annual single number series, 28 Aug 1939–19 Jan 1946
CRS A2672 War Cabinet Agenda Registration Books, 28 Aug 1939–19 Jan 1946
CRS A2673 War Cabinet Minutes (carbon copies), chronological series, 27 Sep 1939–19 Jan 1946
CA 1882; Royal Commission on Espionage (1954–1956)
CRS 6201 Exhibits, single number series, 1954–1955
CRS 6202 Exhibits, single letter series, 1954–1954
CRS A6213 Correspondence files, alpha-numeric series with 'RCE' Royal Commission on Espionage prefix, 1954–1956
CA 1907; Royal Commission on Intelligence and Security (01 January 1976–21 April 1977)
CA 2001; Australian Imperial Force, Base Records Office
CRS B2455 Personnel dossiers for first Australian Imperial Forces ex-service members, lexicographical series, 1914–1920
CA 2671; Army Headquarters, Department of Defence [II] (1933–1939), and CA 36; Department of the Army, Central Office (1939–1940)
CRS A6828 Chief of the General Staff's (Australia) periodical letters to the Chief of the Imperial General Staff, 1933–1940
CRS A6923 Directorate of Military Intelligence (Special Intelligence)
CA 3196; Australian Archives, ACT Regional Office (1987–1994), and CA 7970; Australian Archives, National Office
CRS A7359 unidentified and uncontrolled Commonwealth records in the ACT regional office, 1987–

- Sydney

CA 946; Security Service, New South Wales (1942–1945)
SP C417 General correspondence files; annual single number series with G prefix, 1942–1945

- Melbourne

CA 6; Department of Defence [I], and CA 19; Department of Defence [II]
MP 729/6 Secret Correspondence Files, 1936–1945
MP 729/8 Classified Correspondence Files, 1936–1945
CA 38; Department of the Navy, Navy Office
MP 1185/8 Classified Correspondence, 1923–1950
CA 7137; Fleet Radio Unit, Melbourne, (from 1942) also known as 'FRUMEL'
CRS B5555 Translations of cipher messages, 1945–1946

- Brisbane

CA 753; Investigation Branch, Queensland (1924–1942 and 1945–1946), CA 947;

Security Service, Queensland (1942–1945), CA 913; Commonwealth Investigation Service, Queensland (1946–1960), and CA 952; Commonwealth Police Force [II], District Office, Queensland
BP 242/1 Correspondence files, single number series with Q (Queensland) prefix, 1924–1961

- Adelaide

CA 905; Investigation Branch, South Australia (1942–1946), and CA 914: Commonwealth Investigation Service, South Australia
D 1919 Investigation case files, single number series with 'SS' prefix, 1942–1946

Australian War Memorial (AWM)

AWM 23 Australian Records Section General Headquarters 3rd Echelon and British Expeditionary Force (France) files, c1916–c1919
AWM 49 Army Records
AWM 52 AIF and Militia unit war diaries (1939–1945)
AWM 54 Written records (1939–1945)
AWM 59 A Brief History of the G2 Section GHQ SWPA and Affiliated Units
AWM 123 "Special Collection II", Defence Committee records
AWM 132 Order of Battle cards and lists and location statement cards (1939–1945)
Berryman Diary PR 84/370
Berryman Papers DRL4.11
Blamey Papers 3DRL6643

National Library of Australia (NLA)

Dedman Papers MS 987
Hughes (William Morris) Papers MS 1538
Piesse Papers MS 882
Throssell Papers MS 8071

Department of Defence

Directorate of Military Intelligence (DMI) files
Personnel Records Section, Air Force Office
File of Brig Sir Frederick Spry, Central Army Records Office

Department of External Affairs

Personal file, J.F. Hill

Australian Security Intelligence Organisation (ASIO)

"Significant Events in the History of Internal Security Intelligence Organisations in Australia up to the Formation of ASIO on 16 March 1949", typescript by R.A. Swan

New South Wales Police Service

Hughes, Alfred Thompson, NSW Police Force Service Record

Flinders University

Evatt Papers

University of Western Sydney (Macarthur)

Wake Papers

Public Record Office, Kew, United Kingdom (PRO)

- Cabinet Office
CAB 81 War Cabinet, Chiefs of Staff Committee

- Foreign Office
FO 371 General Correspondence after 1906, Political

- Prime Minister's Office
PREM 3 Operational Papers

- War Office
WO 106 Directorate of Military Operations and Intelligence
WO 193 Directorate of Military Operations Collation Files
WO 201 War of 1939 to 1945, Military Headquarters Papers, Middle East Forces
WO 208 Directorate of Military Intelligence

- Admiralty
ADM 223 Naval Intelligence Papers 1939–1947

- Records created and inherited by Government Communications Headquarters
HW 10 Government Code and Cipher School, Japanese Section

Churchill Archives Centre, Churchill College, Cambridge

A. G. Denniston Collection, DENN 1/4

National Archives and Records Administration (NARA), Washington, D. C.

RG 145
RG 165 Records of the War Department and Special Staffs
RG 319 Records of the Office of the Chief of Military History
RG 457 Records of the National Security Agency
SRA 13938 Individual Translations: Japanese Military attache messages
SRA 14204 Individual Translations; Japanese Military attache messages
SRH 018 Collection of Japanese Diplomatic Messages, 12 July 1938–21 January 1942
SRH 032 Reports by U.S. Army ULTRA Representatives with Field Commands in the Southwest Pacific, Pacific Ocean, and China-Burma-India Theaters of Operation, 1944–1945
SRH 044 Regulations Governing the Dissemination and Security of Communications Intelligence, 1943–1945
SRH 059 Selected Examples of Commendations and Related Correspondence Highlighting the Achievements of U.S. Signal Intelligence during World War II
SRH 207 Evacuation of USN COMINT Personnel from Corregidor in WWII
SRH 254 The Japanese Intelligence System
SRH 266 Japanese Signal Intelligence Service
SRMA 014 Intelligence Documents; German Intelligence Activity in Far East, Japanese Estimate of US Ground OB, Japanese Estimate of Allied OB
SRMD 009 JICPOA/F22 File of Administrative Letters/Correspondence, January 1942–September 1945
SRN 317 Individual Translations; Japanese Naval Messages
SRS 575 'MAGIC' Summaries
SRS 1310 'MAGIC' Diplomatic Summaries
SRS 1365 'MAGIC' Diplomatic Summaries
SRS 1554 'MAGIC' Diplomatic Summaries

U.S. National Records Center (USNRC), Suitland, Maryland

RG 338 US Army Commands; SWPA
RG 405 GHQ SWPA, G3 Journal

Macarthur Memorial Military Archives (MMMA), Norfolk, Virginia

RG 3 Records of General Headquarters, South-West Pacific Area, 1942–1945
RG 4 Records of General Headquarters, United States Army Forces, Pacific, 1942–1947
RG 15 S.B. Akin, Macarthur's Signals Intelligence Service

Truman Library, Independence, Missouri

Harry S. Truman Papers

National Archives of Canada

RG 24

Papers held privately

Nave, T.E., unpublished autobiography
Sadler, P.J., papers
Burley, S.F., 'The Silent Guardians of Ultra', unpublished manuscript
Rogers, J.D., 'Say Not the Struggle', unpublished manuscript
Wake R.B.F., diary and papers

Published records

House of Commons, Parliamentary Debates, various years
Commonwealth Parliamentary Debates, various years
Review of the Joint Intelligence Organisation to 31 January, 1949, Report by Controller of Joint Intelligence to Joint Intelligence Committee
Report of the Royal Commission on Espionage, Commonwealth Government Printer, Canberra, 1955
Royal Commission on Espionage: Official Transcript of Proceedings, Commonwealth Government Printer, Canberra, 1955
Royal Commission on Intelligence and Security, Fourth Report, Australian Government Publishing Service, Canberra, 1977
Seventh Report of the Royal Commission on Intelligence and Security, 1977, Vol 1
Central Intelligence Agency (CIA), *Foreign Intelligence and Security Services: USSR*, April 1975
Central Intelligence Agency (CIA), *Soviet Intelligence: KGB and GRU*, February 1984
National Security Agency/Central Security Service, *Second VENONA Release*, Fort George G. Meade, Maryland, 12 October 1995
National Security Agency/Central Security Service, *Fifth VENONA Release*, Fort George G. Meade, Maryland, October 1996

Books

Akhmedov, Ismail, *In and Out of Stalin's GRU: A Tatar's Escape from Red Army Intelligence*, University Publications of America, Frederick, Maryland, 1984
Amalgamated Wireless (Australasia) Limited, *AWA and the War*, AWA, Sydney, 1945
Andrew, Christopher and David Dilks (eds.), *The Missing Dimension: Governments and*

Intelligence Communities in the Twentieth Century, University of Illinois Press, Urbana, Illinois, 1984
Andrew, Christopher and Oleg Gordievsky, *KGB: The Inside Story of its Foreign Operations from Lenin to Gorbachev*, Hodder & Stoughton, London, 1990
Andrew, Christopher, *Secret Service: The Making of the British Intelligence Community*, William Heinemann, London, 1985
Arneill, Stan, *Black Jack: The Life and Times of Brigadier Sir Frederick Galleghan*, Macmillan, Melbourne, 1983
Ballard, Geoffrey St Vincent, *On ULTRA Active Service*, Spectrum, Richmond, 1991
Bamford, James, *The Puzzle Palace: A Report on NSA, America's Most Secret Agency*, Houghton Mifflin, Boston, 1982
Barker, Theo, *Signals: A History of the Royal Australian Corps of Signals, 1788–1947*, Royal Australian Corps of Signals Committee, Canberra, 1987
Barker, Wayne G., *The History of Codes and Ciphers in the United States During the Period Between the World Wars, Part II: 1930–1939*, Aegean Park Press, Laguna Hills, California, 1989
Barrow, Graeme, *Canberra's Embassies*, Australian National University Press, Canberra, 1978
Beasley, Jack, *A Gallop of Fire, Katharine Susannah Prichard: On Guard for Humanity*, Wedgetail Press, Sydney, 1993
Bennett, J.W., W.A. Hobart and J.B. Spitzer, *Intelligence and Cryptanalytic Activities of the Japanese During World War II*, Aegean Park Press, Laguna Hills, California, 1986
Benson, Robert Louis, *Introductory History of Venona and Guide to the Translations*, Center for Cryptologic History, National Security Agency, Fort George G. Meade, Maryland, July 1995
——*The 1942–43 New York–Moscow KGB Messages*, Venona Historical Monograph No. 2, Center for Cryptologic History, National Security Agency, Fort George G. Meade, Maryland, November 1995
Benson, Robert Louis and Michael Warner (eds), *VENONA: Soviet Espionage and the American Response, 1939–1957*, United States National Security Agency and Central Intelligence Agency, Washington, D.C., 1996
Bentley, Elizabeth, *Out of Bondage: The Story of Elizabeth Bentley*, Devin-Adair, New York, 1951
Bertrand, Gustave, *Enigma: ou, La plus grande enigma de la guerre 1939–1945*, Plon, Paris, 1973
Bevege, Margaret, *Behind Barbed Wire: Internment in Australia during World War II*, University of Queensland Press, St Lucia, 1993
Bialoguski, Michael, *The Petrov Story*, Mandarin, Melbourne, 1989
Blair, Clay, Jr., *Silent Victory: The US Submarine War Against Japan*, Bantam, New York, 1975
Bleakley, Jack, *The Eavesdroppers*, Australian Government Publishing Service, Canberra, 1992
Borovik, Genrikh, *The Philby Files: The Secret Life of the Master Spy—KGB Archives Revealed*, Little, Brown, London, 1994
Bower, Tom, *The Perfect English Spy: Sir Dick White and the Secret War 1935–90*, William Heinemann, London, 1995
Boyd, Carl, *Hitler's Japanese Confidant: General Oshima Hiroshi and MAGIC*, University Press of Kansas, Lawrence, Kansas, 1993
Boyle, Andrew, *The Climate of Treason*, Coronet Books, Hodder & Stoughton, London, 1979
Brown, Anthony Cave, *Bodyguard of Lies*, W.H. Allen, London, 1975
——*'C': The Secret Life of Sir Stewart Menzies, Spymaster to Winston Churchill*, Macmillan, New York, 1987
Brown, W.J., *The Communist Movement and Australia: An Historical Outline—1890s to 1980s*, Australian Labor Movement History Publications, Sydney, 1986
Brownell, George A., *The Origin and Development of the National Security Agency, 13 June 1952*, Aegean Park Press, Laguna Hills, California, 1981
Burton, John, *The Alternative: A Dynamic Approach to Our Relations with Asia*, Morgans Publications, Sydney, 1954

Cain, Frank, *The Origins of Political Surveillance in Australia*, Angus & Robertson, Sydney, 1983
Calvocoressi, Peter, *Top Secret Ultra*, Ballantine, New York, 1980
Clark, Manning, *The Quest for Grace*, Penguin, Ringwood, Victoria, 1990
Clark, Ronald W., *The Man Who Broke Purple: The Life of the World's Greatest Cryptographer, Colonel William F. Friedman*, Weidenfeld & Nicolson, London, 1977
Clausen, Henry C., and Bruce Lee, *Pearl Harbor: Final Judgement*, Crown, New York, 1992
Cockerill, A.W., *Sir Percy Sillitoe*, W.H. Allen, London, 1975
Conquest, Robert, *The Great Terror: A Reassessment*, Oxford University Press, Oxford, 1990
—— *The Great Terror: Stalin's Purge of the Thirties*, Macmillan, London, rev. ed. 1973
Cook, Peter S., *Red Barrister: A Biography of Ted Laurie QC*, La Trobe University Press, Melbourne, 1994
Costello, John, *Mask of Treachery*, William Collins, London, 1988
Coulthard-Clark, C.D., *A Heritage of Spirit: A Biography of Major-General Sir William Throsby Bridges*, Melbourne University Press, Melbourne, 1979
—— *The Citizen General Staff: The Australian Intelligence Corps 1907–1914*, Military Historical Society, Canberra, 1976
—— *Edge of Centre: The Eventful Life of Group Captain Gerald Packer*, Royal Australian Air Force Museum, Point Cook, 1992
Crisp, L.F., *Ben Chifley: A Political Biography*, Angus & Robertson, London, 1977
Dalziel, Allan, *Evatt the Enigma*, Lansdowne Press, Melbourne, 1967
Davidson, Alastair, *The Communist Party of Australia: A Short History*, Hoover Institution Press, Stanford, California, 1969
Davies, Philip H.J., *The British Secret Services*, Transaction Publishers, New Brunswick, 1996
Deacon, Richard and Nigel West, *Spy!*, Grafton Books, London, 1988
Deakin, F.W. and G.R. Storry, *The Case of Richard Sorge*, Chatto & Windus, London, 1966
Deriabin, Peter and Frank Gibney, *The Secret World*, Ballantine, New York, 1982
Detwiler, Donald S. and Charles B. Burdick (eds.), *War in Asia and the Pacific, 1937–1949, Vol. 10, Japan and the Soviet Union (Part 1)*, Garland, New York, 1980
Drea, Edward J., *MacArthur's ULTRA: Codebreaking and the War against Japan, 1942–1945*, University Press of Kansas, Lawrence, Kansas, 1992
Dzhirkvelov, Ilya, *Secret Servant: My Life with the KGB and the Soviet Elite*, Harper & Row, New York, 1987
Dziak, John J., *Chekisty: A History of the KGB*, Lexington Books, Lexington, Mass., 1988
Edwards, P.G., *Prime Ministers and Diplomats: The Making of Australian Foreign Policy, 1901–1949*, Oxford University Press, Melbourne, 1983
Farago, Ladislas, *The Broken Seal*, Random House, New York, 1967
Ferrier, Carole (ed.), *As Good As A Yarn With You: Letters Between Miles Franklin, Katharine Susannah Prichard, Jean Devanny, Marjorie Barnard, Flora Eldershaw and Eleanor Dark*, Cambridge University Press, Cambridge, 1992
—— *Point of Departure: The Autobiography of Jean Devanny*, University of Queensland Press, St. Lucia, Queensland, 1986
Foley, Stephen and Marshall Wilson, *Anatomy of a Coup: The Sinister Intrigue Behind the Dismissal*, Canterbury Press, Scoresby, Victoria, 1990
Foote, Alexander, *Handbook For Spies*, Museum Press, London, 2nd ed., 1953
Freyberg, Paul, *Bernard Freyberg, VC, Soldier of Two Nations*, Hodder & Stoughton, London, 1991
Friedman, William F. (ed.), *Cryptography and Cryptanalysis Articles*, Aegean Park Press, Laguna Hills, California, 1976, Vols 1 and 2
Gibson, Ralph, *My Years in the Communist Party*, International Bookshop, Melbourne, 1966
Gillison, Douglas, *Royal Australian Air Force 1939–1942*, Australian War Memorial, Canberra, 1962

Glantz, David M., *Soviet Military Deception in the Second World War*, Frank Cass, London, 1989
Gouzenko, Igor, *This Was My Choice: Gouzenko's Story*, Eyre & Spottiswoode, London, 1948
Granatstein, J.L. and David Stafford, *Spy Wars: Espionage and Canada from Gouzenko to Glasnost*, McClelland and Stewart, Toronto, 1990
Granatstein, J.L., *A Man of Influence: Norman A. Robertson and Canadian Statecraft, 1929–68*, Deneau Publishers, Toronto, 1981
Graves, Charles, *The Thin Red Lines*, Standard Art Book, London, 1946
Haldane, Robert, *The People's Force: A History of the Victoria Police*, Melbourne University Press, Melbourne, 1986
Hall, Richard, *The Rhodes Scholar Spy*, Random House Australia, Sydney, 1991
——*The Secret State: Australia's Spy Industry*, Cassell, Sydney, 1978
Harcourt, Edgar, *Taming the Tyrant: The First One Hundred Years of Australia's International Communication Services*, Allen & Unwin, Sydney, 1987
Hasluck, Paul, *Diplomatic Witness: Australian Foreign Affairs, 1941–1947*, Melbourne University Press, Melbourne, 1980
——*The Government and the People, 1939–1941*, Australian War Memorial, Canberra, 1952'
——*The Government and the People, 1942–1945*, Australian War Memorial, Canberra, 1970
Hewett, Dorothy, *Wild Card: An Autobiography, 1923–1958*, McPhee Gribble, Ringwood, Victoria, 1990
Hilvert, John, *Blue Pencil Warriors: Censorship and Propaganda in World War II*, University of Queensland Press, St Lucia, 1984
Hinsley, F.H. and C.A.G. Simkins, *British Intelligence in the Second World War, Volume Four: Security and Counter-Intelligence*, Her Majesty's Stationery Office, London, 1990
Hinsley, F.H., with E.E. Thomas, C.F.G. Ransom and R.C. Knight, *British Intelligence in the Second World War: Its Influence on Strategy and Operations, Vols 1 and 2*, Her Majesty's Stationery Office, London, 1979, 1981
Hohne, Heinz, *Codeword Direktor: The Story of the Red Orchestra*, Ballantine, New York, 1982
Holloway, David, *Stalin and the Bomb: The Soviet Union and Atomic Energy 1939–1956*, Yale University Press, New Haven, Connecticut, 1994
Holmes, W.J., *Double-Edged Secrets: U.S. Naval Intelligence Operations in the Pacific During World War II*, Naval Institute Press, Annapolis, Maryland, 1979
Horner, D.M., *Crisis of Command: Australian Generalship and the Japanese Threat, 1941–1943*, Australian National University Press, Canberra, 1978
——*High Command, Australia and Allied Strategy, 1939–1945*, Allen & Unwin, Sydney, 1982
Howard, Michael, *British Intelligence in the Second World War, Volume Five: Strategic Deception*, Her Majesty's Stationery Office, London, 1990
Hudson, W.J., and Wendy Way (eds.), *Documents in Australian Foreign Policy 1937–49, Volume XII: 1947*, Australian Government Publishing Service, Canberra, 1995
Hyde, H. Montgomery, *The Atom Bomb Spies*, Ballantine, New York, 1981
James, Admiral Sir William, *Intelligence and Cryptanalytic Activities of the British Navy in World War I: The Code Breakers of Room 40*, Aegean Park Press, Laguna Hills, California, n.d.
Jenkins, David, *Battle Surface! Japan's Submarine War Against Australia 1942–44*, Random House, Sydney, 1992
Kahn, David, *Kahn On Codes: Secrets of the New Cryptography*, Macmillan, New York, 1983
Klehr, Harvey, John Earl Haynes and Fridrikh Igorevich Firsov, *The Secret World of American Communism*, Yale University Press, New Haven, Connecticut, 1995
Knight, Amy, *Beria: Stalin's First Lieutenant*, Princeton University Press, Princeton, New Jersey, 1993
Knightley, Phillip, *Philby: The Life and Views of the K.G.B. Masterspy*, Andre Deutsch, London, 1988

——*The Second Oldest Profession: Spies and Spying in the Twentieth Century*, W.W. Norton, New York, 1986
Krivisty, W.G., *I Was Stalin's Agent*, Hamish Hamilton, London, 1939
Lamphere, Robert J. and Tom Schachtman, *The FBI–KGB War: A Special Agent's Story*, Berkley Books, New York, 1987
Lang, John T., *Communism in Australia*, Express Newspapers, Sydney, 1944
Laughlin, Lt Col Austin, *Boots and All: The Inside Story of the Secret War*, Colorgravure, Melbourne, 1951
Layton, Edwin T. with Roger Pineau and John Costello, *"And I Was There": Pearl Harbour and Midway—Breaking the Secrets*, William Morrow, New York, 1985
Lee, Bruce, *Marching Orders: The Untold Story of World War II*, Crown Publishers, New York, 1995
Lewin, Ronald, *Ultra Goes to War: The Secret Story*, Hutchinson, London, 1978
Lewis, Graydon A., *Intercept Station "C"*, Naval Cryptographic Veterans Association, Denver, 1983
Manne, Robert, *The Petrov Affair: Politics and Espionage*, Pergamon Press, Sydney, 1987
Martin, David C., *Wilderness of Mirrors*, Ballantine, New York, 1980
Masterman, J.C., *The Double-Cross System in the War of 1939 to 1945*, Ballantine, New York, 1982
McCue, Bill, *Spook Stuff*, published by the author, Canberra, 1996
McKnight, David, *Australia's Spies and Their Secrets*, Allen & Unwin, Sydney, 1994
McMullin, Ross, *The Light on the Hill: The Australian Labor Party 1891–1991*, Oxford University Press, Melbourne, 1991
Mellnik, Steve, *Philippine Diary 1939–1945*, Van Nostrand Reinhold, New York, 1969
Mendelsohn, John (ed.), *Covert Warfare: Intelligence, Counterintelligence, and Military Deception During the World War II Era—Volume 7: The Case of Richard Sorge*, Garland, New York, 1989
Modin, Yuri, *My Five Cambridge Friends*, Headline, London, 1994
Modjeska, Drusilla, *Exiles at Home: Australian Women Writers, 1925–1945*, Angus & Robertson, Sydney, 1981
Morris, Bernice, *Between the Lines*, Sybylla Cooperative Press, Collingwood, Victoria, 1988
Morton, Peter, *Fire Across The Desert: Woomera and the Anglo-Australian Joint Project 1946–1980*, Australian Government Publishing Service, Canberra, 1989
Muirden, Bruce, *The Puzzled Patriots: The Story of the Australia First Movement*, Melbourne University Press, Melbourne, 1968
O'Sullivan, Vincent (ed.), *Intersecting Lines: The Memoirs of Ian Milner*, Victoria University Press, Wellington, 1993
Of Moles and Molehunters: A Review of Counterintelligence Literature, 1977–92, Center for the Study of Intelligence, Central Intelligence Agency, CSI 93–002, October 1993
Parker, Michael, *The S.I.S.: The New Zealand Security Intelligence Service*, The Dunmore Press, Palmerston North, 1979
Perrault, Gilles, *The Red Orchestra*, Schocken, New York, 1969
Petrov, Vladimir and Evdokia, *Empire of Fear*, Frederick A. Praeger, New York, 1956
Philby, Kim, *My Silent War*, Ballantine, New York, 1983
Pilger, John, *A Secret Country*, Jonathan Cape, London, 1989
Pincher, Chapman, *Their Trade is Treachery*, Sidgwick & Jackson, London, 1981
——*Too Secret Too Long*, St. Martin's Press, New York, 1984
Prange, Gordon W., with Donald M. Goldstein and Katherine V. Dillon, *Target Tokyo: The Story of the Sorge Spy Ring*, McGraw-Hill, New York, 1984
Prichard, Katharine Susannah, *Child of the Hurricane: An Autobiography*, Angus & Robertson, Sydney, 1963
——*Straight Left: Articles and Addresses on Politics, Literature and Women's Affairs Over Almost 60 Years, from 1910 to 1968*, Collected and Introduced by Ric Throssell, Wild and Woolley, Sydney, 1982
Read, Anthony and David Fisher, *Operation Lucy: Most Secret Spy Ring of the Second World War*, Hodder & Stoughton, London, 1980
Richelson, Jeffrey T. and Desmond Ball, *The Ties That Bind: Intelligence Cooperation*

Between the UKUSA Countries—the United Kingdom, the United States of America, Canada, Australia and New Zealand, Unwin Hyman, Boston, 2nd ed., 1990
Ride, Edwin, *BAAG: Hong Kong Resistance 1942–1945*, Oxford University Press, Hong Kong, 1981
Roland, Betty, *An Improbable Life*, Collins Australia, Sydney, 1989
——*Caviar for Breakfast*, Collins Australia, Sydney, 1989
Romerstein, Herbert and Stanislav Levhenko, *The KGB Against the 'Main Enemy'*, Lexington Books, Lexington, Mass., 1989
Rusbridger, James and Eric Nave, *Betrayal at Pearl Harbor: How Churchill Lured Roosevelt into War*, Michael O'Mara, London, 1991
Scott, Ernest, *Australia During the War*, Angus & Robertson, Sydney, 1936
Sendy, John, *Comrades Come Rally: Recollections of an Australian Communist*, Thomas Nelson, Melbourne, 1978
Sharkey, L.L., *An Outline of the Australian Communist Party*, Australian Communist Party, Sydney, December 1944
Sharpley, Cecil H., *The Great Delusion: The Autobiography of an Ex-Communist Leader*, William Heineman, London, 1952
Sheymov, Victor, *Tower of Secrets: A Real Life Spy Thriller*, Naval Institute Press, Annapolis, Maryland, 1993
Sillitoe, Sir Percy, *Cloak Without Dagger*, Cassell, London, 1955
Skillen, Hugh, *Spies of the Airwaves: A History of the Y Sections During the Second World War*, Hugh Skillen, Pinner, Middlesex, 1989
Smith, Bernard, *Noel Counihan: Artist and Revolutionary*, Oxford University Press, Oxford, 1993
Smith, Bradley F., *The Shadow Warriors: O.S.S. and the Origins of the C.I.A.*, Basic Books, New York, 1983
Smith, Bradley F., *The Ultra-Magic Deals: And the Most Secret Special Relationship, 1940–1946*, Presidio Press, Novato, California, 1993
Souter, Gavin, *A Peculiar People: The Australians in Paraguay*, Sydney University Press, Sydney, 1981
Spender, Percy, *Politics and a Man*, Collins, Sydney, 1972
Stanley, Peter, *Tarakan: An Australian Tragedy*, Allen & Unwin, Sydney, 1997
Stevens, Joyce, *Taking the Revolution Home: Work Among Women in the Communist Party of Australia, 1920–1945*, Sybylla Co-operative Press, Melbourne, 1987
Stevenson, William, *A Man Called Intrepid: The Secret War 1939–1945*, Sphere Books, London, 1977
Stretton, Alan, *Soldier in a Storm*, Collins, Sydney, 1978
Stripp, Alan, *Codebreaker in the Far East*, Frank Cass, London, 1989, and Oxford University Press, Oxford, 1995
Sudoplatov, Pavel and Anatoli Sudoplatov, with Jerrold L. and Leona P. Schecter, *Special Tasks: The Memoirs of an Unwanted Witness—A Soviet Spymaster*, Warner Books, Little, Brown, London, 1995
Suvorov, Viktor, *Inside Soviet Military Intelligence*, Macmillan, New York, 1984
Taft, Bernie, *Crossing the Party Line: Memoirs of Bernie Taft*, Scribe, Newham, Victoria, 1994
The Defection of Igor Gouzenko: The Report of the Royal Commission to Investigate the Facts Relating to and the Circumstances Surrounding the Communication, by Public Officials and other Persons in Positions of Trust of Secret and Confidential Information to Agents of a Foreign Power, Ottawa, 27 June 1946, Aegean Park Press, Laguna Hills, California, 1984, Vol. 1
The Origin and Development of the Army Security Agency 1917–1947, US Army Security Agency, Washington, D.C., March 1948, published by Aegean Park Press, Laguna Hills, California, 1978
Thompson, G.R. and D.R. Harris, *The Signal Corps: The Outcome*, Office of the Chief of Military History, Washington, D.C., 1966
Thorpe, E.R., *East Wind, Rain*, Gambit, Boston, 1969
Throssell, Ric, *A Reliable Source*, Minerva, Port Melbourne, 1991
——*In A Wilderness of Mirrors*, Left Book Club, Sydney, 1992
——*My Father's Son*, Mandarin Australia, Port Melbourne, Victoria, 1990

——Wild Weeds and Windflowers: The Life and Letters of Katharine Susannah Prichard, Collins/Angus & Robertson, Sydney, rev. ed., 1990
Thwaites, Michael, Truth Will Out: ASIO and the Petrovs, Collins, Sydney, 1980
Ullman, Richard H., The Anglo-Soviet Accord, Princeton University Press, Princeton, New Jersey, 1972
Volkman, Ernest, Espionage: The Greatest Spy Operations of the Twentieth Century, John Wiley, New York, 1995
——Spies: The Secret Agents Who Changed the Course of History, John Wiley, New York, 1994
Ward, Russel, Australia Since the Coming of Man, Lansdowne Press, Sydney, 1982
Waters, Christopher, The Empire Fractures: Anglo-Australian Conflict in the 1940s, Australian Scholarly Publishing, Melbourne, 1995
Watt, Alan, Australian Diplomat: Memoirs of Sir Alan Watt, Angus & Robertson, Sydney, 1972
Welchman, Gordon, The Hut Six Story: Breaking the Enigma Codes, McGraw-Hill, New York, 1982
——A Matter of Trust: MI 5 1945–72, Weidenfeld & Nicolson, London, 1982
——Games of Intelligence: The Classified Conflict of International Espionage, Weidenfeld & Nicolson, London, 1989
——GCHQ: The Secret Wireless War, 1900–86, Weidenfeld & Nicholson, London, 1986
——MI 5: British Security Service Operations, 1909–1945, Bodley Head, London, 1981
——MI 6: British Secret Intelligence Operations, 1909–45, Weidenfeld & Nicolson, London, 1983
——Molehunt: The Full Story of the Soviet Spy in MI 5, Coronet Books, Hodder & Stoughton, London, 1987
——The Illegals: The Double Lives of the Cold War's Most Secret Agents, Coronet Books, Hodder & Stoughton, London, 1993
Whitlam, Nicholas and John Stubbs, Nest of Traitors: The Petrov Affair, Jacaranda Press, Milton, Queensland, 1974
Wilde, W.H., Courage a Grace: A Biography of Dame Mary Gilmore, Melbourne University Press, Melbourne, 1988
Willoughby, C.A. (comp), A Brief History of the G2 Section, GHQ, SWPA and Affiliated Units, GHQ, Far East Command, Tokyo, 1948
——(comp), Operations of the Military Intelligence Section, GHQ/FEC/SCAP, GHQ, Far East Command, Tokyo, 1948
——Shanghai Conspiracy: The Sorge Spy Ring, E.P. Dutton & Company, New York, 1952
Winter, Barbara, The Intrigue Master: Commander Long and Naval Intelligence in Australia, 1913–1945, Boolarong Press, Brisbane, 1995
Winterbotham, F.W., The Ultra Secret, Dell, New York, 1974
Wood, K.L., Empire Telegraph Communications, Cable and Wireless Limited, London, December 1938
Wright, Peter, The Spycatcher's Encyclopedia of Espionage, William Heinemann, Melbourne, 1991
Wright, Peter, with Paul Greengrass, Spycatcher: The Candid Autobiography of a Senior Intelligence Officer, Viking Penguin, New York, 1987

JOURNAL ARTICLES, BOOK CHAPTERS, THESES, ETC

Aldrich, Richard J., 'Secret Intelligence for a Post-War World: Reshaping the British Intelligence Community, 1944–51', in Richard J. Aldrich (ed.), British Intelligence, Strategy and the Cold War, 1945–51, Routledge, London, 1992
Aldrich, Richard and Michael Coleman, 'The Cold War, the JIC and British Signals Intelligence, 1948', Intelligence and National Security, Vol. 4, No. 3, July 1989
Allen, Louis, 'Japanese Intelligence Systems', Journal of Contemporary History, October 1987

Anderson, Scott, 'The Evolution of the Canadian Intelligence Establishment, 1945–1950', *Intelligence and National Security*, Vol. 9, No. 3, July 1994
Andrew, Christopher, 'Codebreakers and Foreign Offices: The French, British and American Experience', in Christopher Andrew and David Dilks (eds.), *The Missing Dimension: Governments and Intelligence Communities in the Twentieth Century*, University of Illinois Press, Chicago, 1984
——*The Growth of Intelligence Collaboration in the English-Speaking World*, Working Papers No. 83, International Security Studies Program, The Wilson Center, Washington, D.C., 1987
——'The Growth of the Australian Intelligence Community and the Anglo-American Connection', *Intelligence and National Security*, Vol. 4, No. 2, April 1989
——'The Making of the Anglo-American SIGINT Alliance', in Hayden B. Peake and Samuel Halpern (eds), *In the Name of Intelligence: Essays in Honour of Walter Pforzheimer*, Naval Intelligence Book Centre, Washington DC, 1994, p. 103.
Andrew, Christopher and David Dilks, 'Introduction', in Christopher Andrew and David Dilks (eds.), *The Missing Dimension: Governments and Intelligence Communities in the Twentieth Century*, University of Illinois Press, Chicago, 1984
Ball, Desmond, 'The Use of the Soviet Embassy in Canberra for Signals Intelligence (SIGINT) Collection', Working Paper No. 134, Strategic and Defence Studies Centre, Australian National University, Canberra, 1987
——'Over and Out: Signals Intelligence (SIGINT) in Hong Kong', *Intelligence and National Security*, Vol. 11, No. 3, July 1996
——'Signals Intelligence (SIGINT) in Pakistan', *Strategic Analysis*, Vol. XVIII, No. 2, May 1995
——'Signals Intelligence in India', *Intelligence and National Security*, Vol. 10, No. 3, July 1995
Cain, Frank, 'An Aspect of Post-War Australian Relations with the United Kingdom and the United States: Missiles, Spies and Disharmony', *Australian Historical Studies*, Vol. 23, No. 92, April 1989
——'The Making of a Cold War Victim', *Overland*, No. 134, 1994
——'The Right to Know: ASIO, Historians and the Australian Parliament', *Intelligence and National Security*, Vol. 8, No. 1, January 1993
Cecil, Robert, 'Five of Six at War: Section V of MI 6', *Intelligence and National Security*, Vol. 9, No. 2, April 1994
Chamberlain, Vince, 'Corregidor: The Final Days', in Graydon A. Lewis, *Intercept Station "C"*, Naval Cryptographic Veterans Association, Denver, 1983
Chapman, J.W.M., 'Japanese Intelligence 1919–1945: A Suitable Case for Treatment', in Christopher Andrew and Jeremy Noakes (eds.), *Intelligence and International Relations 1900–1945*, Exeter University, Exeter, 1987
de Graaff, Bob, 'Hot Intelligence in the Tropics: Dutch Intelligence Operations in the Netherlands East Indies During the Second World War', *Journal of Contemporary History*, October 1987
Denniston, A.G., 'The Government Code and Cypher School Between the Wars', *Intelligence and National Security*, Vol. 1, No. 1, January 1986
Drea, Edward J., 'Missing Intentions: Japanese Intelligence and the Soviet Invasion of Manchuria, 1945', *Military Affairs*, April 1984
——'Reading Each Other's Mail: Japanese Communications Intelligence, 1920–1941', *The Journal of Military History*, April 1991
Ferris, John, 'Before "Room 40": The British Empire & Signals Intelligence, 1898–1914', *The Journal of Strategic Studies*, Vol. 12, No. 4, December 1989
Filby, P.W., 'Floradora and a Unique Break Into One-Time Pad Ciphers', *Intelligence and National Security*, Vol. 10, No. 3, July 1995
Glantz, David M. 'The Battle That Never Happened', *MHQ: The Quarterly Journal of Military History*, Summer 1977, vol. 9, No. 4
Harrison, J.C., 'An Outline of the Development of Telecommunication Services Between Australia and Places Overseas—Part 1', *The Telecommunication Journal of Australia*, vol. 5, No. 2, October 1944
Harrison, J.C., 'An Outline of the Development of Telecommunication Services Between Australia and Places Overseas—Part 2', *The Telecommunication Journal of Australia*, vol. 5, No. 3, February 1945

Hewett, Dorothy, 'Excess of Love: The Irreconcilable Katharine Susannah Prichard', *Overland*, No. 43, Summer 1969–1970
Hinsley, F.H., 'Introduction: The Influence of Ultra on the Second World War', in F.H. Hinsley and Alan Stripp (eds.), *Codebreakers: The Inside Story of Bletchley Park*, Oxford University Press, Oxford, 1993
Horner, D.M., 'Australian Estimates of the Japanese Threat', in Philip Towle (ed.), *Estimating Foreign Military Power*, Croom Helm, London, 1982
——'The Chinese Liaison Officer in Australia 1942–1945', *Journal of the Australian War Memorial*, No. 25, October 1994
Kahn, David, 'Codebreaking in World Wars I and II: The Major Successes and Failures, Their Causes and Their Effects', in Christopher Andrew and David Dilks (eds.), *The Missing Dimension: Governments and Intelligence Communities in the Twentieth Century*
Lithgow, Shirley, 'The Strange Case of Lieutenant Colonel Mawhood', a paper presented to the Australian War Memorial Conference, 14 February 1986
Littlejohn, Barbara B., 'Eavesdropping on the Enemy', in Hugh Skillen (ed.), *The Enigma Symposium 1994*, Hugh Skillen, Pinner, Middlesex, 1994
Lockwood, Rupert, in 'Petrov Twenty Years On—Rupert Lockwood's Personal View', ABC Radio, 26 May 1973, (Radio Drama and Features Department, Australian Broadcasting Commission), transcript
Military History Section, 'Japanese Intelligence Planning Against the Far East', Headquarters, Army Far East, June 1955
Nosov, Galina, 'A Letter From Old Friends', *Friendship* (Newsletter of the Australia–Soviet Friendship Society), Vol. 2, No. 2, February 1958
Playford, J.D., 'Doctrinal and Strategic Problems of the Communist Party of Australia, 1945–1962', PhD Dissertation, Australian National University, Canberra, October 1962
Prichard, Katharine Susannah, 'Deakin and Evatt', *The Realist*, No. 30, Spring 1968
Saunders, Kay and Helen Taylor, 'The Enemy Within? The Process of Internment of Enemy Aliens in Queensland 1939–45', *Australian Journal of Politics and History*, Vol. 34, No. 1, April 1988
Stripp, Alan, 'Japanese Army Air Force Codes at Bletchley Park and Delhi', in F.H. Hinsley and Alan Stripp (eds.), *Codebreakers: The Inside Story of Bletchley Park*, Oxford University Press, Oxford, 1993
Swan, R.A., 'Significant Events in the History of Internal Security Intelligence Organisations in Australia up to the Formation of ASIO on 16 March 1949'
Symons, Beverley, 'All-Out for the People's War: Communist Soldiers in the Australian Army in the Second World War', *Australian Historical Studies*, No. 105, October 1995
Taylor, Gladys, 'The Role of the ATS Special Operator', in Hugh Skillen (ed.), *The Enigma Symposium 1994*, Hugh Skillen, Pinner, Middlesex, 1994
Templeton, Jacqueline, 'Australian Intelligence/Security Services, 1900–1950', *Seventh Report of the Royal Commission on Intelligence and Security*, CRS A8908/1, Vol. 1
'Units in focus: 6 Signal Regiment', *Signalman*, no. 5, 1980
Walton, R.D., 'Feeling for the Jugular: Japanese Espionage at Newcastle 1919–1926', *Australian Journal of Politics and History*, Vol. 32, No. 1, 1986

NEWSPAPER ARTICLES

Abjorensen, Norman, 'Origin of Petrov's Contacts Queried by Expert', *Canberra Times*, 6 October 1996
——'Experts Debate Historical Import of "Petrov Affair"', *Canberra Times*, 13 October 1996
Andrew, Christopher, 'How Baldwin's Secret Service Lost the Soviet Code', *The Observer*, 13 August 1978
Ball, Desmond, 'The Spies and the Spied Upon', *Sydney Morning Herald*, 4 June 1994
'Ban on Youth Council to Stay: Anti War', *The Herald* (Melbourne), 12 August 1940

Beyer, Lisa, 'Red Eyes on the Rising Sun', *Asiaweek*, 11 October 1985
Burton, John, 'Secrecy Cloaks Policy Malaise', *Canberra Times*, 3 July 1995
Cain, Frank, 'Limited Intelligence Gives Scholar a Bad Name', *Weekend Australian*, 6–7 July 1991
——'Thin Evidence Brands the Spy Who Never Was', *Weekend Australian*, 20–21 July 1991
Clayton, Wally, 'Hookers Horrible Home', *Tribune*, 11 October 1961
'Cracking a Soviet Cipher', *Newsweek*, 19 May 1980
'Death of Miss Shirley Howard', *Tribune*, 12 February 1946
Dobbs, Michael, 'American Counterspy Ends The Silence', *International Herald Tribune*, 22 October 1996
Grattan, C. Hartley, 'Readers and Writers Down Under', *The New York Times Book Review*, 22 June 1947
Green, J.R., 'Scholar and Archaeologist of World Rank', *The Australian*, 20 November 1995
Highfield, John, 'When Gnomes Reared Their Heads', *Nation Review*, 6–12 April 1973
Hruby, Peter, 'Secret Life of Agent 9006', *Courier Mail*, 30 November 1996
'Husband's Going Shock, Says Singer', *Daily Mirror*, 30 October 1945
'In Brief: Know Thy Neighbor', *Bulletin of the Atomic Scientists*, November/December, 1995
Isserman, Maurice, 'Notes From Underground', *The Nation*, 12 June 1995
Jenkins, David, 'Our War of Words', *Sydney Morning Herald*, 19 September 1992
Knightley, Phillip, 'Australian Diplomat Spied for Russians: Author Reveals Intimate Confession', *Sun-Herald*, 9 June 1991
McAdam, Anthony, 'Spry Lays An Old Spook To Rest', *The Bulletin*, 27 November 1984
'Obituaries: Lt-Cdr Teddy Poulden', *Daily Telegraph* (London), 20 November 1992
Pemberton, Gregory, 'A Suspect Spy', *Sydney Morning Herald*, 6 July 1991
Stubbs, John and Evan Whitton, 'Petrov: New Light on a Tragic Farce', *The National Times Magazine*, 3 September 1973
'The "Daily Herald": Lansbury's Orders From Moscow', *The Times* (London), 19 August 1920
Thompson, John, 'Circles of Music and Espionage', *Evening Post* (Wellington), 14 September 1995
Toohey, Brian, 'The Security Scandal That Led to ASIO', *The National Times*, 20–26 April 1980
Whitton, Evan, 'For a Top Spy, Agent KLOD is a Great Cook', *The National Times*, 10–15 September 1973

Index

Page numbers in italics refer to illustrations.

1st Australian Discrimination Unit, 45–6, 158
Abakumov, Viktor, Semyonovich, 119
Abwehr (German Military Intelligence), 8, 182
ACADEMICIAN, *see* Prichard
Acheson, Dean, 302
Advanced Land Headquarters (LHQ), moves to Brisbane, 39; and Cohen, 44; in Hollandia, 69, 70; and SLU, 71; and Ultra leaks, 73, 81, 99
Advisory War Council, 36, 39; powers of, 26; and Shedden, 26; and suspension of *AMF Weekly Intelligence Review*, 83; and security leaks, 101, 105; report on CPA, 103, 156; and Evatt, 152
Agincourt, *see* ASIO
Air Force, *see* RAAF
Air Force Code Group, 105
Airy, Lt-Col E. A., 156
Akin, Maj-Gen Spencer, 38, 61, *62*, *62*, *64*, 83, 84, 97
Allen, Maj-Gen A. S., 171
Allied Geographical Section (AGS), 38
Allied Intelligence Bureau (AIB), 37, 39, 70, 78, 159
Allied Intelligence Organisation, xx
Allied Land Forces, 99
Allied Security Bureau, 42
Allied Translator and Interpreter Section (ATIS), 38, 76, 77
Amalgamated Wireless Australasia (AWA), 52, 83, 185, 247–50
America, *see* United States
American Counter-Intelligence Corps, *see* US Counter-Intelligence Corps
AMF Weekly Intelligence Review, 82–5,

87–8, 94, 97, 100, 104, 108, 110, 354
Anderson, Geoffrey (YEGER), 133–5
ANTENNA, *see* J. Rosenberg
Archer, Henry, 60, 65
Argus, 100
Arlington Hall, 190; *see also* US Army Security Agency
Armstrong, Senator John, 289
Army Intelligence, *see* Military Intelligence
Ashby, Lt-Col James, Jr, 70, 82, 84
Ashley, Senator William, 93–4
Ashurov, German Ivanovich, 121
Association of Scientific Workers of Australia, 193
ATHLETES, 210
Attlee, Clement, and Venona, 6; telegram to Chifley leaked, 213, 344; and Dominion participation in top-secret US–UK security talks, 275; and Bevin, 275; and Chifley, 285–7, 289, 290, 304; and Sillitoe, 286–7, 290; and ASIO, 286–7, 290; and Hollis, 289; and Hemblys-Scales, 289
Attorney-General, department of, 14, 17, 20, 157; and Gallacher, 271; leakages from, 287
Auchincloss, Col S. S., 84
Australia, and intelligence sharing with US and UK, 73–4, 79, 174–6, 274–6, 284–6, 290, 301–4, 340, 350; poor appreciation of need for security, 151–3, 340
Australia First Movement, 30
Australia–China Cooperation Association, 77

445

Australia–Soviet Friendship League (Society), and Ferguson, 133; and Ian Milner, 257–8; support for war effort, 349
Australian Army, establishes Intelligence Directorate, 23; Japanese reports on location of, 111
First Army, 69
1st Aust Corps, formation of, 18, 51; and operational intelligence, 18; and 4th Aust Special Wireless Section, 59, 63; and the Philippines, 69; and Wang, 80; and CPA, 220
3rd Division, 111; Signals Company, 51–2
5th Division, 104, 111
6th Division, 18, 111
7th Division, 111
9th Division, 111
11th Division, 111
4th Aust Special Wireless Section, 46, 52, 58–9, 61, 181; and Ralph Thompson, 167
5th Aust Special Wireless Section, 61, 65
51st Aust Special Wireless Section, 63
52nd Aust Special Wireless Section, 63, 66
54th Aust Special Wireless Section, 63
55th Aust Special Wireless Section, 63
56th Aust Special Wireless Section, 63
1st Aust Field Censorship Company, 88
1st Aust Mobile Signals Company, and Clayton, 223–4
Field Security Police, and Wake, 24; and Grimsdale, 25
Australian Army Intelligence, estimates of Japanese strength in the Philippines, 1, 104–5, 113–14
Australian Association of Scientific Workers, 249, 251
Australian Communist Party, *see* Communist Party of Australia
Australian Counter-Espionage Bureau, 13; *see also* Special Intelligence Bureau
Australian Imperial Force, second (2nd AIF), 18, 35, 42
Australian Intelligence Corps (AIC), 12, 15, 35
Australian Labor League of Youth (ALLY), *see* Eureka Youth League
Australian Military Forces (AMF), 74, 93, 99
Australian Naval Board, 76
Australian Radio Security Service (RSS), 45
Australian Secret Intelligence Service, 102
Australian Security and Intelligence Organisation (ASIO), 10, 43, *296*, *299*; First Directorate's files on, 120; and Makarov, 136, 231, 304–5, 315; and Zaitsev, 143; and Dalziel, 143, 152; and Nosov, 152, 231, 304–5, 305–6, 315; establishment opposed by Burton, 153; and Brown, 171, 294; and Max Phillips, 171, 294; and Clayton, 221, 222, 223, 231, 329–31; and Vladimir Petrov, 223, 320–1, 322; and KLOD group, 231, 350–1; and Alfred Hughes, 242, 244, 332–6; and Christiansen, 248, 250–1; and Elsie Hill, 248, 250, 251; and Jim Hill, 250, 251, 262; and CSIRO, 250–1; and Ian Milner, 262; and Jordan, 267; and Dakin, 267; and Young, 280, 291, 292–3, 294, 298–9, 300–4, 315; and MI5, 286–7, 291, 295, 340, 350; and Sillitoe, 286–7; and Chifley, 286–7, 289, 292, 294, 305; establishment of, 291–4, 350–1; and Chilton, 292; and Dedman, 292; and Evatt, 292; and Bailey, 292; and Hollis, 292, 293, 294, 298; and Hemblys-Scales, 292, 294; and McKenna, 292, 293, 294; and Reed, 293, 294, 295, 298–9, 314; and Venona, 293, 295, 297, 298–9, 300–4, 346–7; and Longfield Lloyd, 293; and Shedden, 292, 293, 294; and Tuck, 294, 295, 296, 297; and Wake, 294, 295, 296, 298, 300, 315; purpose and organisation of, 295, 300–1; location of, 296; and CPA, 296; and CIS, 296; and Gilbert, 298; and MVD, 298; and White, 298; and Whitrod, 298, 300–1; 'foundation members' of, 299–300; and KGB, 305; and telephone monitoring, 305; and Soviet embassy, 305; breaks into Nosov's apartment, 306, 315; recruits Don Marshall, 306; and Spry, 294, 314–16; relocated to Melbourne, 315; and Hamblen, 315–16; and Bernie, 317–19, 347; and Ric Throssell, 322, 324; and Gowland, 330; and Robert Menzies, 351
Australian Security Service, *see* Commonwealth Security Service
Australian Special Intelligence Personnel Sections, 65
Australian Special Wireless Group (ASWG), 45, *66*; formation of, 62, 63; moves to Mornington, 165; intercepts Soviet traffic, 165, 185; and Ralph Thompson, 167; *see also*

INDEX   447

4th Australian Special Wireless Section, 5th Australian Special Wireless Section and Central Bureau
Australian Women's Army Service (AWAS), 46, 63, 165

Bailey, Professor Sir Kenneth, *289*; and communists in Army, 172; and Sillitoe, 281; and Hollis, 287, 289, 291; and Hemblys-Scales, 287; and Chifley, 289, 293; and Reed, 291–2, 294; and establishment of ASIO, 292; and Longfield Lloyd, 293; and White, 298
Baldwin, Stanley, 179
Ball, W. MacMahon, 256
Ballard, Cpl Geoffrey, 58
Baracchi, Guido, 235, 236
Barnes, Eric, 65
Barnett, June, 227–8, 230
Barnwell, W. H., 143
Barr, Joel, 202
Batchelor, Maj George, 79
Bath, Lt-Col W. J., 169
Beasley, John, 26, 94, 105
Beeby, Doris Isobel, 229–30, 238, 267, 272
BEN, *see* Alfred Hughes
Bentley, Elizabeth (GOOD GIRL), 121, 196–7, 200
Beria, Lavrentiy (PETROV), 116–17, 119, 120, 203, 205
Bernie, Frances (SESTRA), *212*, 244–7, 316–20; and Nosov, 132, 211, 246; and Gardner, 205; and NKGB/KI, 209, 251, 345; and Clayton, 211, 214, 215, 225, 228, 233, 244–6, 288, 316–20, 329, 344, 345, 347, 352; becomes inactive, 215; and CPA, 244–7, 318; and Eureka Youth League, 244–5, 334; and Sherden, 245; and Evatt, 245–6, 252, 288, 317, 318, 319, 345; and Dalziel, 245–6, 318, 319; and Beryl Hallett, 245–6; and McKnight, 245; marries Gluck, 246; changes name to Garrett, 247; and Ric Throssell, 271; and Venona, 205, 287, 318, 347; and Hollis, 288, 317; identified as SESTRA, 288, 297, 301, 317; and Burton, 288; confesses, 316–20, 347, 352; and ASIO, 316–20, 347; and Hemblys-Scales, 317; and CIS, 317; and Gilmour, 317; and Richards, 317–19; and KLOD group, 318; and UNRRA, 319; and Alfred Hughes, 334
Berry, Wing Cdr Hugh, 167
Berryman, Lt-Gen Frank, *74*; head of Advanced LHQ, 39; and Ultra leaks, 73; and Wang, 77, 81, 82, 84; and Sandford, 165
Berzin, Gen Yan Karlovich, 122, 139
Bevin, Ernest, 274–5, 281–2, 284
Biggs, E.T., 60
Blair-Cunynghame, Hamish, 166
Blamey, Gen Sir Thomas, 37, *64*; letter to Fraser, 6 January 1945, xx, 88–9, 92–114, 104–5, 106–7, 338–9, 352; commands 6th Australian Division, 18; commands 1st Australian Corps, 18; commander-in-chief of AMF, 35; and MacArthur, 36–7; and Curtin, 37; and Wills, 39; and Wake, 42; and Brig Simpson, 44, 94–8, 100, 103; and diplomatic intelligence, 65; and FRUMEL, 67; and Roberts, 70; and security leaks, 71, 76, 78, 83, 85–91, 104–5, 106–7, 113, 338; and Wang, 80; and Akin, 84; and telephone monitoring, 88–9, 96, 100–1, 114; and Forde, 88–9, 93, 100, 101; and Shedden, 89–90, 95, 100–1, 104, 352–3; and Fraser, 90–1, 92; and Rogers, 92, 96–8, 112; memo from Rogers, 113; and Sandford, 92; and Burley, 98; and Capt Wang, 100; and Evatt, 100; and Soviet leaks, 114, 129, 338–9; and Central Bureau, 164
Bletchley House/Park, *see* Government Code and Cypher School, and Government Communication Headquarters
Blunt, Anthony, 120, 276, 277, 280, 311, 348
Bond, Lt Ronald, 60, 65
Booth, Wing Cdr H. Roy, 56, 62, *63*, *64*
Brasch, Charles, 254, 255
Bridges, Maj William, 12
Britain, and geopolitical significance of Venona, 1, 351–2; development of Sigint in, 2, 3, 10, 11; Soviet spies in, 13, 147; Sandford in, 45; Australia's reliance on for Sigint, 49; and intelligence sharing with Australia, 74, 274–6, 284–6, 340; supplies intelligence to Chinese, 79; and Russian diplomatic traffic, 102; involvement in formation of DSB, 166; defence cooperation with Australia, 176; Sigint cooperation with US, 183–6; establishes Sigint station in Hong Kong, 184
British Army Aid Group China, 87
British Chiefs of Staff Committee, 184
British Counter-Espionage Bureau, 13; *see also* MI5

British Intelligence in the Second World War, 6
British Long Range Weapons Organisation, 174
British No. 1 Special Wireless Group, 278
British No. 2 Wireless Company, 59, 181, 182
British No. 53 Special Wireless Section, 278
British No. 101 Special Wireless Section, 58
British Pacific Fleet, 90
British Radio Security Service (RSS), 45, 46, 47, 184
British Secret Intelligence Service, 37
British War Cabinet, leaked documents of, 193, 206, 213–14, 230, 260–9, 274, 281–4, 342–3, 350, 351; and the Cold War, 352
Brown, Maj Colin, 171, 294
Browne, Maj Roland S., 15, 157
BRUSA Agreement, 183, 197
Bulganin, Marshal, 119–20
Burchett, George, 77
Burchett, Wilfred, 78
Burgess, Guy (HICKS), 120; and Philby, 201; and Modin, 201; defects, 202; and Maclean, 279; and Sillitoe, 279, 347; leaks information from Foreign Office, 344
Burhop, Eric, 309
Burley, Sqn Ldr Sidney, 71, 86, 98
BURNY, *see* Bernie
Burton, Dr John, Jnr., *151*; and Evatt, 150–1, 288, 325; appointed departmental secretary of External Affairs, 150; and Australia's post-war foreign policy, 151, 349; and 'open diplomacy', 151, 349; and United States, 151; and communism, 151; and security, 151–2, 153, 287, 349; refuses to join JIC, 152; opposes establishment of ASIO, 153; and Jim Hill, 153, 264, 291, 297, 298, 307, 308, 325–6, 349; and Shedden, 153, 284–5, 286; replaces Hasluck as UN division head, 260; and Ian Milner, 260, 262, 284, 285, 291; and Denning, 284; and leaked British War Cabinet documents, 284, 285; and Moodie, 285, 288; and Venona, 285, 347; and Hollis, 287–8, 297, 298, 307, 308; and Hemblys-Scales, 288, 290–1; and Young, 307; and Gilbert, 325

Cable & Wireless, and GCHQ, 185
Cain, Frank, 14, 16, 176

Cairncross, John, 120, 311
Callen, Bill, 333
Calwell, Arthur, 85, 95
Campbell, Professor Arthur, 26–7
Campbell, William R. (Bill), 301
Canada, Sigint stations in, 184
Carr, Lachie, 331
Carter, Leo Parmeter, 301
Central Bureau, 38, 46–7, 64–5; establishment of, 61–2; funding of, 62; and FRUMEL, 62, 158; moves to Brisbane, 64; reorganised, 65; size of, 66; and breaking of Japanese codes, 66–7, 69; move to Hollandia, 69; and special security officers, 70–1; and Ultra intercepts, 78, 84, 103, 112; and Russian Diplomatic traffic, 102; and development of Australian Sigint organisation, 159; moves to Manila, 164; and Blamey, 164; disbanded, 165; and Ralph Thompson, 168
Central Intelligence Agency (CIA), 119, 194, 196, 197
Chandler, H. B., 226
Chapman, Col James A., 22, 23, 25, 31
Cheka, 116, 117; *see also* Soviet State Security Service
Chew, Samuel P., 196
Chiang Kai-shek, 75, 78
Chief of the Air Staff, 19
Chiefs of Staff Committee, 39, 161
Chifley, Joseph 'Ben', *27, 148*; and Venona, 6, 292, 351; and War Cabinet, 26, 94, 104, 148; access to top secret operational information, 105; becomes prime minister, 147; and Curtin, 148; and Dedman, 148, 289; and McKenna, 148, 289, 293; and Evatt, 149, 150, 286, 289–90; and Shedden, 149, 286, 289, 304; discusses JIC proposal with British, 162; and decisions about signals intelligence, 162; receives report from Makin, 174; leaked telegram to Attlee, 213, 344; and banning of communists, 280–1; and Sillitoe, 281, 286–7; and Hollis, 281, 284, 287, 288, 289, 294, 298; and Denning, 284; and Attlee, 285–7, 289, 304; and Chilton, 285; and Moodie, 285; and ASIO, 286–7, 289, 292, 294; and Hemblys-Scales, 287, 289; and Armstrong, 289; and MI5, 289; and Bailey, 289–90, 293; and Longfield Lloyd, 289–90; and Reed, 292, 293, 294; and Young, 292; and Playford,

293; and White, 298; approves ASIO telephone monitoring, 305
Childe, Vere Gordon, 26
Childers, Erskine, 11
Chilton, Brig Sir Frederick, 163–4, *163*; and Longfield Lloyd, 158; appointed as CJI, 163; and Poulden, 167; and communists in Army, 172; and CIS, 173; and Sillitoe, 281; and Shedden, 281–2, 302–3; and leaked British War Cabinet documents, 281–3; and Ian Milner, 282; and Hemblys-Scales, 283, 287; and Chifley, 285, 302–3; and Hollis, 287, 293; and establishment of ASIO, 292; and Venona, 292–3; and Young, 292–3, 299, 302; and Reed, 299, 302, 304
China, Wang sends information to, 77, 84, 110; Soviet embassy in, 105, 106
Chiplin, Rex (CHARLIE), 127, 133
Christesen, Clement (CRAB), 133
Christesen, Nina Michaelova (EVA), 132, 133
Christiansen, Wilbur (MASTER), *212*, 247–51; and reorganisation of KLOD group, 215, 247, 251; and Clayton, 233, 247, 251; and AWA, 247–50; and CPA, 248, 250; and ASIO, 248, 250–1; and Elsie Hill, 248, 250, 251; and Jim Hill, 248–9, 251; and Ted Hill, 248, 251; and Australian Association of Scientific Workers, 249, 251; and CSIRO, 249; and CIS, 249–50; and Spry, 249–50; and Longfield Lloyd, 250; and Whitrod, 251; and Venona, 251, 287, 297; and Makarov, 251; and NKGB Canberra Residency, 251; and Soviet State Security Service, 251
Christie, Lt-Col Laurence, 80–1
Chungking, and Soviet intelligence leaks, 76, 107; Wang's messages to, 77–80, 82, 94, 107, 109–10, 111, 113, 114
Churchill, Sir Winston, 3, 182, 195
Cimperman, John, 198
Clancy, Margaret, 242
Clark, Charles Manning, 256–7
Clark, Lt-Col William, 33–4
Clarke, Brig-Gen Carter W., *193*, *194*
Clarke, Marcus, 129
Clarke, Sqn Ldr, W. (Bill) J., *63*
Clayton, Walter Seddon (K/KLOD), 10, *212*, 220–31, *221*, 328–32, *329*; and Mikheev, 127, 221, 224, 237, 328; and Venona decrypts, 127, 193, 221, 238, 297, 347; and Makarov, 129, 209–13, 215, 221, 226, 230–1, 237, 251, 253, 267, 321, 328; and Nosov, 131, 135, 211, 221, 224, 225, 230–1, 246, 328; and Lane, 141, 221, 225–6; and KLOD group, 141, 210–12, 228–9, 231, 232, 238, 352; and Gardner, 193, 203; and British War Cabinet documents, 193, 213–14, 230, 253, 261, 274, 342–3; and Soviet State Security Service, 209, 211, 223, 224, 225, 228, 230, 243, 266, 270, 274, 328, 330–1, 342, 343–5; payment of, 210; role of, 211, 214–15; and Prichard, 211, 214, 224, 225, 228, 230, 233, 237, 270, 344; and Bernie, 211, 214, 225, 226, 228, 233, 244–6, 288, 316–20, 328, 344, 345, 347, 352; and Ian Milner, 211, 214, 225, 251, 253, 254, 260, 261, 264, 327, 328, 342–3; and Jim Hill, 211, 213, 214, 225, 251, 261, 264–5, 310, 328, 349; and Alfred Hughes, 211, 213, 214, 228, 230, 233, 240, 242–4, 332–6, 342, 344–5; and External Affairs, 211, 214, 230, 251, 252, 253, 261, 328; suspended by Soviet State Security Service, 212, 230–1, 232; and Jordan, 214, 266; and CPA, 220, 222, 225, 226–7, 328, 331; and ASIO, 221, 222, 223, 231, 316–17, 329–31, 347; moves to Sydney, 222; and *Tribune*, 222, 229; and NSW Police Special Branch, 223; and CPA Central Control Commission, 223, 225; and 1st Australian Mobile Signals Company, 223–4; and CSS, 224; and Lockwood, 224, 231, 309, 310–11; espionage activities of, 224–5, 227–8; and Howard, 226; description of, 226; and Garton, 226; and Sharpley, 226, 228; and George Legge, 227; and Barnett, 227–8; and Ted Hill, 228, 248, 330; and Oke, 228; and Key, 229; and Beeby, 229–30, 238; and Rose, 230; and Christiansen, 233, 247, 251; and Ric Throssell, 237, 238, 270, 271, 322, 324, 325, 328; and Devanny, 239–40; and Margot Milner, 260; and Gamble, 301, 302; identified as KLOD, 302, 328; and Burhop, 309; and Vladimir Petrov, 320; and Valentin Sadovnikov, 321, 333; and Special Branch, 328; and Royal Commission on Espionage, 328–30; and MVD, 321, 328, 330;

and Spry, 329–31; and Gowland, 330; and Carr, 331; passport cancelled, 331; and Taylor, 333; and Callen, 333; motives of, 348
Clementson, Lt-Col W. G., 169
Cohen, Barbara, 129
Cohen, Lt-Col Colyn, *21*; and Security Service, 21; criticised by Mawhood, 23; service liaison officer to CSS, 33; and Brig Simpson, 44; and Zaitsev, 144; and Longfield Lloyd, 157; and undercover agents, 171
Colquhoun, Wing Cdr D., 169
Colvin, Admiral Sir Ragnar, 50, 52, 53–4
Combes, Brig Bertrand, 10, 16, *159*; becomes director of Military Operations and Intelligence, 18, 160; chairs conference of security bodies on CPA, 19; and establishment of Security Service, 20; criticised by Mawhood, 22; recommended by Sturdee as director-general of Security Service, 31; and Kendall, 52; and Rogers, 96–7; and Military Intelligence, 160, 170; and establishment of JIC, 160; recommends formation of secret service, 161; and Shedden, 170; retires, 170; knowledge of Ultra leaks, 172; and Spry, 283
Combined Communications Board, 175
Combined Operational Intelligence Centre (COIC), 38, 159
Comintern (BIG HOUSE), and Cheka/NKVD, 117–18; recruitment of Soviet agents, 121; network of clandestine stations, 180; dissolved, 181, 208; and Sharkey, 218; and CPA, 218, 223; and Dutt, 310; and Pollitt, 310
Commonwealth Investigation Branch (CIB), establishment, 14; and political surveillance, 14; surveillance of CPA, 14, 17; and Military Intelligence, 15, 171; surveillance of right-wing secret armies, 15, 17; Lloyd as head of, 15; and department of Defence, 17; relations with Security Service, 23, 171; and Wake, 23; under Evatt, 26; and internment of aliens, 29–30; criticised by Duncan report, 31; First Directorate's files on, 120; and Pinner report, 156; renamed CIS, 157, 174; allegations by Rowell concerning, 174; and Ian Milner, 257
Commonwealth Investigation Service (CIS), formed from CIB, 157, 174;

and Longfield Lloyd, 158, 250; and investigation of Soviet embassy leaks, 172; and DSB, 173; and Chilton, 173; and JIC, 173; ineptness of, 173–4; and Evatt, 173; and Clayton, 226; and Christiansen, 249–50; and CSIRO, 250–1; and Jim Hill, 265; and Sillitoe, 275; and Young, 280; and Hollis, 284; military distrust of, 284; and Defence Committee, 289; and Hemblys-Scales, 290; and ASIO, 296; and Bernie, 317; *see also* Commonwealth Investigation Branch
Commonwealth Police, 13, 14
Commonwealth Security Conference, 290
Commonwealth Security Service (CSS), formation of, 17–21, 31, 33; inquiries into, 21–5; relations with CIB, 21, 23, 28, 171; and Navy, 22; and Grimsdale report, 25; and Evatt, 26, 97, 156, 157; competition with CIB and three armed services, 28; and war with Japan, 29–47; and internment of aliens, 29–30; and Duncan report, 31; director-generalship of, 30–1; Navy urges creation of, 31; and Kevin, 32–3, 161; and Forde, 32–3; MacKay appointed director-general, 33; headquarters of, 33; and MI5, 33; and Knowles, 34; Brig Simpson appointed director-general of, 35; role between 1942–45, 40–7; and MPI, 40; conflict with Army and Military Intelligence, 34–5, 40–2, 44–7, 71–2, 90, 94–7, 100, 101–2, 156; 1st Australian Discrimination Unit established, 45–6; conflict with Central Bureau, 46–7; and Capt Wang, 77; and Australia–China Cooperation Association, 77; and district censor, 86; and security leaks, 88, 96–7; and communist spies, 103–4; and Soviet espionage, 114, 115, 129; surveillance of Nosov, 134–5; investigates Mikheev, 135, 213, 243; and Alfred Hughes, 135, 203, 213, 241–4, 252, 332, 333, 334, 336, 344–5; and Pinner report, 156–7; and Longfield Lloyd, 157; disbanded, 157; and Clayton, 224, 243; and Prichard, 236; and Ian Milner, 257
Commonwealth Sigint Organisation (CSO), 185, 186
Communication Intelligence Group, 105
communications intelligence (comint), definition of, 2

Communist Party of Australia (CPA) (Codename: FRATERNAL), 218–20; and espionage, 10, 103–4, 121, 217; CIB surveillance of, 14, 16; Menzies convenes meeting to consider activities of, 19; declared illegal, 27, 219; and Australia–China Cooperation Association, 77; and NKGB residencies in Australia, 125, 208, 217; and Makarov, 129; Brig Simpson reports on activities of, 103, 155; and undercover agents, 171; and Army, 172–3, 220; and Comintern, 218–19; and Nazi–Soviet Pact, 219; support for war effort, 219–20, 348–50; and Clayton, 220, 222, 225, 226–7, 328, 331; and Prichard, 220, 234–40; and Beeby, 229; and Ric Throssell, 237, 269, 322–3; and Daniel and Sinyavsky, 238; and Alfred Hughes, 241, 242, 243, 336; and NSW Police Force, 242; and Bernie, 244–7, 318; and Gluck, 246; and Christiansen, 248, 250; and Ted Hill, 248–9; and Australian Association of Scientific Workers, 249; and Margaret Milner, 257, 258, 259; and Ian Milner, 258–9, 327; and Jim Hill, 262–3, 297, 307; and Jordan, 266; and ASIO, 296; and Gamble, 301; and Masson, 301; and Burhop, 309; and Lockwood, 309; and Counihan, 310; and Taylor, 333; loyalty to Australia, 350

   Central Committee, and Prichard, 220, 237, 238, 239; and Clayton, 220, 223, 328; and Ted Hill, 248–9; and Ian Milner, 259

   Central Control Commission, 223; and Clayton, 223, 225; and Ian Milner, 259

   members (FELLOWCOUNTRYMEN), and Canberra NKGB Residency, 208; in AMF, 220; and Fitin, 224; and Chifley, 281; and the Depression, 348; and WWII, 348

Communist Party of Great Britain (CPGB), 277, 308, 310
Controller of Joint Intelligence (CJI), 162–3
Cooper, Arthur, 60
Coplon, Judith (SIMA), 195
Coral Sea, 3–4, 67
Council for Civil Liberties, 257–8
Council for Scientific and Industrial Research (CSIR) (Commonwealth), 193, 229, 309

Counihan, Noel, 309, 310
counter-espionage, definition of, 6–7; and Sigint, 7–9, 48–9, 338, 339, 345–8; examples of, 8–9; and Richard Sorge, 8; and Lucy ring and Rote Kapelle, 8; and Sigint, 8–9, 48–9; and 'Double Cross', 8; early history in Britain, 11; pre-WWII in Australia, 11–21; limitations of, 338–9
Coventry, 5
Cowell, Evelyn, 240–1
Cowen, Zelman, 92
Cowgill, Felix, 182–3
Crete, 5, 46, 58
Crisp, L. F., 293
Crowther, Lt George, 92–3
cryptanalysis, 2, 6, 7; in Australia, 54–5; of Japanese diplomatic traffic, 52, 65; of Chinese ciphers, 109, 110, 112; of Soviet signal traffic, 179–80, 183, 186–8, 346; limitations of, 346
CSIRO, 249, 250–1
Currie, Lauchlin, 200
Curtin, John, 27; becomes prime minister, 25–6; and Shedden, 26, 149; Prime Minister's War Conference, 36; and MacArthur, 36–7, 104; and Blamey, 37; and Japanese diplomatic cipher, 57; ill, 71, 88, 90; appoints Chinese liaison officers, 74; chairs War Cabinet and Advisory War Council, 101; and postmaster-general's letter, 101; and MacArthur's Philippines operations, 104; succeeded by Chifley, 147–8; and defence policy, 149
Curzon, Lord, 179

Dakin, William, 229, 267
Dalziel, Allan (DENIS), and Mikheev, 127; and Nosov, 127, 131–2, 152; and Zaitsev, 143; and ASIO, 143; and Evatt, 127, 151, 246; photographed leaving TASS office building, 152; and Prichard, 238; and Bernie, 245–6, 318, 319; and External Affairs, 245; and Jim Hill, 264; and Ric Throssell, 271; and Alfred Hughes, 334; and Fitzpatrick, 334
Daniel, Yuri, 238
Darlinghurst, 127, 131
Darwin, 45, 56, 64, 71, 103
Davies, John, 65
Dedman, John, and War Cabinet, 26, 94, 104, 105; access to top secret information, 105; and Chifley, 148, 289; and decisions about signals

intelligence, 162; and Sillitoe, 281; and Shedden, 282, 287; and Hollis, 284, 287; and Hemblys-Scales, 287; and establishment of ASIO, 292
Defence, department of, and national intelligence, 17; and CIB, 17; and security leaks, 90; and Curtin, 149; and Shedden, 149; and postwar strategic planning, 153–5; relations with External Affairs, 153–5, 286; communists in, 172; concludes security agreement with US Defence department, 313–14
Defence Committee, 45–6, 92; and Colvin, 52; and establishment of Defence PHP Committee, 155; and JIC, 160, 161; endorses proposals for joint intelligence organisation, 161–2; recommends formation of separate security organisation, 289; and CIS, 289
Defence Post-Hostilities Planning (PHP) Committee, established, 155; External Affairs representation on, 155; relations with PHP Division of External Affairs, 155; and Shedden, 155; and leaked British War Cabinet documents, 274, 281, 342–3
Defence Scientific Advisory Body, 161
Defence Signals Branch, 10, 164–9; established as Signals Intelligence Centre, 162–3; involvement of Britain in formation of, 166; coverage and organisation of, 166; choice of first director of, 167; and Poulden, 167, 311; and Ralph Thompson, 167, 185, 316; and Rendle, 168–9; JIC oversight of, 169, 173; and CIS, 173; and Soviet espionage, 314, 316
Dekanozov, Vladimir Georgievich, 118
Denning, M. E., 284
Denniston, A. G. (Alistair), 180
Devanny, Jean, 239–40
Dill, F. M. Sir John, 183
Diplomatic and Press Intercept Section, 61, 62
Directorate of Military Intelligence, *see* Military Intelligence
Directorate of Naval Intelligence, *see* Naval Intelligence
Dixon, Sir Owen, 31
Dixon, Richard, 218, 219–20
Dollis Hill, 197
'Double Cross', 8, 277
Doud, Col H. S., *64*
Drakeford, Arthur, 26
Drea, Ed, 68
Duncan, Alexander, 22, 25, 28, 30–1
Durnsford, Cdre J. W., 56, 57

Dutch East Indies, *see* Netherlands East Indies
Dutt, Rajani Palme, 235, 309–10
Dwyer, Peter, 198, 199, 346
Dzhirkvelov, Ilya, 119
DZhON, *see* Jordan

East Asia Communication Investigation League, 105
Eastcote, *see* Government Communication Headquarters
Eastern Command, 52
Easton, Jack, 200
Eden, Anthony, 182
EFIM, *see* Makarov
Eldridge, Miss, 65
Ellis, Lt-Col Charles (Dick), 102
EM (Emigrés), 117, 120, 129
ENORMOUS/ERNOMAZ, 195
Ettelson, Phillip, 88, 96
Eureka Youth League (EYL) 243–5, 334
Evatt, Dr Herbert Vere, 10, *27, 150*; and War Cabinet, 26, 104, 105, 152, 270; appointed attorney-general, 26; and Military Intelligence, 26–7; and Longfield Lloyd, 26, 158, 173; supports appeal of Thomas and Ratcliff, 27; and bugging of Japanese consulate, 27; and letter from Forde, 32–3; letter to Forde, 34; and Wake inquiry, 42; and SIB, 66; and Ultra information leaks, 71, 92–3, 94, 95, 100–1; suspension of *AMF Weekly Intelligence Review*, 83; and Blamey, 90, 95, 100; and phone monitoring, 97, 101; and Security Service, 97, 152, 156, 173; and Fraser, 100; and Army personnel in Security Service, 102; access to top secret operational information, 105; and Mikheev, 127; and Zaitsev, 142, 143; and Chifley, 149, 150, 286, 289–90; and foreign policy-making, 149, 150, 280; and department of External Affairs, 149–53; and Burton, 150–1, 287, 325; and security, 151–2; and Dalziel, 127, 151, 246; and Ric Throssell, 151–2, 269, 270, 272; and McGuire, 152; and Hasluck, 152, 260; and Prichard, 152, 236, 239, 269; and Watt, 153; and Shedden, 153; opposes formation of defence security organisation, 162; and decisions about signals intelligence, 162; and communists in Army, 172–3; and Spry, 173; and Bernie, 245–6, 252, 317, 318, 319, 345; and Jim Hill, 253, 264, 325, 344; and Vishinsky, 264; and

INDEX   453

Young, 280; and Soviet Union, 280; and Sillitoe, 281; and Hollis, 284; and Denning, 284; and establishment of ASIO, 292; and Wake, 300, 315; US mistrust of, 313; and Taylor, 333; and Alfred Hughes, 333, 334; and leaked report on south-eastern Europe, 344; and Robert Menzies, 351
External Affairs, department of (NOOK), Defence officials distrust of, 66; and Blamey's request for telephone monitoring, 86, 89, 90, 93; and Ultra leaks, 98; and Zaitsev, 141, 143; and Evatt, 149–53, 272; expansion of, 149; and Burton, 150–3, 260, 270; and postwar strategic planning, 153–5; relations with Defence, 153–5, 286; and JIC, 161, 169; Soviet informants in, 205, 251, 252–74, 287; and Clayton, 211, 214, 230, 251, 252, 253; and Newbegin, 229; and Makarov, 230, 253; and Ric Throssell, 237, 239, 268–73, 321–5; and Dalziel, 245; and Soviet State Security Service, 251, 252, 343–5; and Venona, 252; codenamed 'the Australian NOOK', 253; and Ian Milner, 253, 259–61; and Jim Hill, 253, 263–6, 325–6; and UN secretariat, 253; and Jordan, 266, 345; and leaked Foreign Office telegrams, 274, 343–4; and Sillitoe, 275; and Denning, 284; and Tange, 353
Post-Hostilities (Planning) division, see United Nations division
Post-War Reconstruction Section, see United Nations division
United Nations division, establishment of, 154; and Paul Hasluck, 154, 259; name changes of, 154; and Ian Milner, 154, 259, 283; and Jim Hill, 154, 263–4; and Ric Throssell, 154, 270, 271, 272; document access of, 154–5; relations with Defence PHP Committee, 155; and Burton, 260; and Matthews, 283

Fabian, Lt-Cdr Rudolph, 60, 63, 64
Fadden, Sir Arthur, 25
Far East Air Force, 71
Far East Combined Bureau (FECB), 23, 50, 53–5, 59
Far Eastern Liaison Office (FELO), 37–8, 152, 161
Far Eastern Security Service, 25
FBI, and Lamphere, 6, 194–5; and Zaitsev, 144; and Soviet cables, 185; and Gen Clarke, 193; and Gardner, 194–5; and Venona, 194–7; and Harvey, 196; and Bentley, 196; liaison with MI5 and MI6, 198–9; and Philby, 201; and Ian Milner, 261
Fedotov, Lt-Gen Pyotr Vasilyevich (IVANOV), 119, 206
FELLOWCOUNTRYMEN, see Communist Party of Australia, members of
Feoktistov, 121
Ferguson, Jean (RAPHAEL), 132, 133, 209, 210
FERRO, see Ric Throssell
Fetterlein, E. C. (Felix), 178, 179
Finlay, Maj-Gen Charles (Basil), 70, 160, 169, 170–1, 175
First (Anglo-American) Directorate, 119–20
Fitin, Lt-Gen Pavel Mikhailovich (VIKTOR), as Soviet foreign intelligence service and INO head, 118; establishes espionage networks, 118–19; and Gardner, 192, 203, 250; and Moscow–Canberra cables, 192–3, 205, 206–8, 250; and operational matters, 208; and Makarov, 210, 213–14, 224; and British War Cabinet documents, 350
Fitzgerald, A. A., 156
Fitzhardinge, Hope, 142
Fitzhardinge, Laurence, 142
Fitzpatrick, Dudley, 334
Fleet Radio Unit Melbourne (FRUMEL), 38; and US Navy Intelligence, 60; and Central Bureau, 62, 159; decrypts Japanese message, 67, 112
Fleming, Lt-Col Allan, 164, 167–9, 299
Foote, Alexander Allan (JIM), 280, 311
Forde, Frank, 27, 96; member of War Cabinet, 26; attitude to security issues, 27–8; and formation of Security Service, 32–3; letter to Evatt, 32–3; letter from MacKay, 34; letter from Evatt, 35; and intelligence leaks, 71, 85, 90, 94, 95, 100–1; and Blamey, 85, 88–9, 93, 95, 100, 102; and Ashley, 93–4; and phone monitoring, 93–4, 96, 101; and Shedden, 101; and Army personnel in Security Service, 102; recommends establishment of JIC, 162; and decisions about signals intelligence, 162
Foreign Department (INO), 117
Foreign Intelligence Directorate (INU), 117, 118, 119, 122, 341
FORMER, 210, 215

Forrestal, 289
Franklin, Miles, 235
Fraser, Senator James, *93*; receives letter from Blamey, 1, 88; and Blamey, 90–1; and security leaks, 94, 95, 100
FRATERNAL, *see* Communist Party of Australia
Freyberg, Gen Lord, 58
Friedman, William F., 184
Fruhaufova, Jarmila, 326, 328
FRUMEL, *see* Fleet Radio Unit Melbourne
Fuchs, Klaus (REST), and GRU, 123; identified, 195, 347; in Britain, 199; prosecuted, 276; and White, 277; and Martin, 279; and Skardon, 311, 347; and Venona, 347; and Lamphere, 347

Gallacher, Ellman Hague ('Bea'), 133, 271–2
Galleghan, Brig Sir Frederick, 15, 158
Gamble, Richard, 301, 302
Gardner, Meredith Knox, *192*; and Operation Venona, 190–5, 338, 346; and Lamphere, 190, 194, 195; reads NKGB messages, 191–2, 350; and War Department General Staff, 192; and Fitin, 192, 193; report to ASA, 192; decrypts Moscow–Canberra KGB traffic, 192–3, 203, *204*, 350; and EFIM, 193, 203; and BEN, 193, 203; and KLOD, 193, 203–4; and JCIC, 193; and FBI, 195; and HOMER, 202; and VIKTOR, 203; and PETROV, 203
Garrett, Frances, *see* Bernie
Garton, Gloria, 226
General Headquarters Southwest Pacific Area (GHQ SWPA), 36; and intelligence, 38; move to Brisbane, 39, 67; and AIB, 70; and Ultra information, 71; and Wang, 78, 79, 82; and Ultra leaks, 84, 97
George, David Lloyd, and Soviet decrypts, 179
German Enigma, 3, 59
German High Command, 9
Germany, 3–4, 14, 19, 27
Gestapo (Secret State Police), 8
Gilbert, P. G. M., 298, 305, 306–8, 312, 325
Gilmour, J. M., 317
GLORY, 210, 215
Gluck, Max, 246
Goble, Air Vice-Marshal S. J., 50
Gold, Harry (GUS/GOOSE and ARNO/ARNAUD), 195, 202
Gorman, Brig Eugene, 42–3

Gorsky, Col Anatoli Borisovich (KAP, HENRY and VADIM), 120–1, 337
Gouzenko, Igor, defection of, 162, 205, 206, 211, 351; and Hemblys-Scales, 279
Government Code and Cypher School (GCCS), at Bletchley Park, 53; and SIB, 55; and Freyberg, 58; and Australian Special Wireless Section, 59; deciphers Japanese message, 87–8; and Chinese cyphers, 110; replaced by GCHQ, 162; and Fetterlein, 178; and Soviet decrypts, 179–82; and White, 277
Government Communication Headquarters (GCHQ), and Chilton, 164; and RSS, 182; Sigint cooperation with US, 183, 193, 197–9, 297; resumes cryptanalysis of Soviet traffic, 183, 351; and Soviet decrypts, 184, 197–9; establishes Sigint station in Singapore, 184; agreement with Cable & Wireless, 185; and Operation Venona, 193, 197–9, 340; moves to Eastcote, 197; learns of US Venona Operation, 197; British Venona Operation established at, 198; and Australian Venona material, 205, 297; and Martin, 278–9; *see also* Government Code and Cypher School
Gowland, Peace Joy, 330
Gowrie, Lord, *27*
Grabeel, Gene, 189, *191*
Graves, Hubert, 60
Gray, Gordon, 302–3, 304
Greenglass, David (SHMEL/BUMBLEBEE and KALIBR/CALIBRE), 195, 202
Greenglass, Ruth (OSA/WASP), 195, 202
Griffiths, Judge, P. L., 33
Grimsdale, Col G. E., 25
GRU, *see* Soviet Millitary Intelligence
Gubanov (SANTO), 129, 137
GUGB, *see* Soviet State Security Service

Hall, Richard, 328
Hallett, Beryl, 245–6
Hallett, Shirley May, *see* Howard
Hallock, Lt Richard, 189
Hamblen, Derek, 276, 315–16
Harbin, interception of Japanese diplomatic traffic from, 66, 86, 87, 89, 102, 105–8, 135; Soviets pass information to Japanese in, 135, 343
Hart, Warrant Officer Keith, 46
Harvey, William K., 196, 197
Hashida, Major Sei, 23
Hasluck, Paul, 30; and Zaitsev, 142, 143; and Evatt, 152, 260; heads

INDEX   455

Post-War Reconstruction Section, 154; and Post-Hostilities division, 259; and Ian Milner, 259–60; replaced by Burton, 260; in New York, 260; and Ric Throssell, 270
Haydon, Peter, 271
Hemblys-Scales, Robert V., 279; and Australian Venona Operation, 276, 277, 287, 288–9, 290–1, 346; and MI5, 279, 290; and May, 279; and Gouzenko, 279; and GRU, 279; and Hollis, 283, 288; and Chilton, 283; and Spry, 287, 294; and Burton, 288, 290–1; and Moodie, 288, 291; and Attlee, 289; and Chifley, 289; and CIS, 290; and Ian Milner, 290–1; and Jim Hill, 290–1, 298; and establishment of ASIO, 292, 294; and Brown, 294; and Max Phillips, 294; identifies TOURIST, 298; and Bernie, 317
Henry, Jack, 311
Hewett, Dorothy, 236
Hewitt, Air Vice Marshal Joseph, 38
Heydon, Peter, 308
Hill, E. F. (Ted), and Clayton, 228, 248, 330; and Christiansen, 248, 251; and CPA, 248–9; and Sharpley, 248, 307; and Taft, 249; forms CPA (Marxist/Leninist), 249; and Ian Milner, 262; and Jim Hill, 262, 265–6
Hill, Elsie, and Christiansen, 248, 250; and Ted Hill, 248, 250, 251, 262; and Jim Hill, 248, 251, 262; and ASIO, 250, 251
Hill, James (Jim) (KhILL and TOURIST), 10, 212, 262–6, 306–12; and Burton, 153, 264; and Post-Hostilities (Planning) division, 154, 263–4; in Australian Venona material, 205, 251, 253, 254, 265, 274, 291, 297; and Clayton, 211, 213, 214, 225, 251, 253, 261, 264–5, 274, 310, 329, 349; and British Foreign Office telegrams, 213, 253, 264–5, 274, 297, 343–4; and KLOD group, 215, 249, 262, 265; and Key, 229, 264; and Lockwood, 231, 309; and MI5, 231, 307–12; and Elsie Hill, 248, 251, 262; and Christiansen, 248–9, 251; and ASIO, 250, 251, 262, 306–8; and External Affairs, 251, 253, 262–6, 325–6; and Ian Milner, 251, 253, 261, 262, 263, 264, 307, 310; and Evatt, 253, 264, 325, 344; and Ted Hill, 262, 265–6; joins ALP, 262; and CPA, 262–3, 297, 307; and Sharpley, 263, 307;

and Marjorie Royle, 263, 307; and Hood, 264; and Ric Throssell, 264, 272–3, 307, 322, 324, 325; and Shann, 264; and Dalziel, 264; and UN division, 264; and Vishinsky, 264; and Soviet State Security Service, 262, 265, 344; in New York, 265; and CIS, 265; promotion cancelled, 266; and Hemblys-Scales, 290–1; and Burton, 291, 297, 298, 307, 308, 325–6, 349; identified as TOURIST/KhILL, 297, 298, 301; and Hollis, 297, 298, 307, 308; and Gilbert, 298, 306–8, 325; and Jordan, 307; and Heydon, 308; and CPGB, 308; and Spry, 308; and Robert Menzies, 308; and Tuck, 308; interviewed in London by Skardon, 308–10, 311, 325; and Burhop, 309, 311; and Counihan, 309; and Dutt, 309; and leaked report on south-eastern Europe, 344; motives of, 349
Hill, Maj William, 46
Hillenkoetter, Rear Admiral R. H., 175
Hillgarth, Capt Alan, RN, 43–4
Hinsley, Sir Francis, 165
HMAS Coonawarra, direction-finding and intercept station at, 49–50, 54, 166; and Japanese naval traffic, 53; and interception of Soviet signals, 185
HMAS Harman, 45, 51, 53, 54, 103, 166
Hodgson, Lt-Col Roy, 66, 98, 142, 239, 269
HOK, 46
Hollis, Maj-Gen Sir Leslie, 176
Hollis, Roger, 277, 278; in Australia, 274; and MI5, 274; and Sillitoe, 274; and Venona, 274; and Ian Milner, 274; and Jim Hill, 274, 297, 307, 308; and Clayton, 274; and Australian Venona Operation, 276, 283, 287, 291; and MI5, 274, 276; and White, 277, 298; and MI5 B Division, 277; and MI5 C Division, 277; and MI5 F Division, 277; CPGB, 277; and Chifley, 281, 284–7, 288, 289, 294, 298; and Shedden, 281, 284, 287; and Hemblys-Scales, 283, 287; and Evatt, 284; and Dedman, 284; and CIS, 284; and Chilton, 287, 293; and Burton, 287, 297, 307, 308; identifies SESTRA, 288, 317; and Attlee, 289; and Bailey, 287, 290, 291, 298; and Young, 291, 292, 294, 298; and establishment of ASIO, 292, 293, 294; and Venona,

292, 346; and Reed, 294, 297, 298; and Tuck, 294, 298; and Wake, 294; report on Australian Security Service, 297; identifies TOURIST, 298, 299; and Gilbert, 298; and Heydon, 308
Holmes, Capt Jasper, 108
Holmes, Lt-Col Reginald, 70, 84
HOMER, see Maclean, Donald
Honda, Ryuhei, 141
Hood, John, 98, 142, 264
Hope, Justice R. M., 6
Howard, Shirley May, 226
Howse, Philip, 197
Hughes, Constable Alfred (BEN), 6, 10, 212, 240–4, 241, 332–6; and Nosov, 135, 243, 345; and Gardner, 193, 203; and Clayton, 211, 213–15, 225, 228, 230, 233, 240, 242–4, 332–6, 342, 344–5; and Security Service files, 213, 243, 333, 334, 336, 344–5; and Mikheev, 213, 243, 345; becomes inactive, 215; and Makarov, 230, 243; and NKGB, 240, 242–4, 251, 336; and Cowell, 240–1; joins MPI, 241; and Security Service, 135, 203, 213, 241, 242, 244, 252, 333–6; and CPA, 242–3, 336; and Special Branch, 241, 244, 336; rejoins NSW Police Force, 242; marries Clancy, 242; and ASIO, 242, 244, 332–6; and Miles, 242; asked by Brig Simpson to report on Clayton, 243; and Eureka Youth League, 243, 334; and Venona, 287, 332; and McDermott, 301; identified as BEN, 332; and Richards, 332, 334–6; and Taylor, 332–3; and Evatt, 333, 334; and Bernie, 334; and Dalziel, 334; and Fitzpatrick, 334; and Spry, 336; and KLOD group, 336; and Royal Commission on Espionage, 347
Hughes, William Morris, and Longfield Lloyd, 13–14; and Jones, 17; opposes establishment of defence security organisation, 20; and Evatt, 26

Ilichev, Ivan Ivanovich, 122
Indooroopilly, 46
Industrial Workers of the World, 13
Information, department of, 18, 85–6, 89, 113, 135
Intelligence Corps, 40
Intelligence Section General Staff (ISGS), 12, 15
Introductory History of Venona, 196, 201
INU, see Foreign Intelligence Directorate

Jackson, Lt-Col Samuel, 157
Jamieson, A. B. (Jim), 55, 57, 60
Japan, 1, 3–4, 10, 28; and China's intelligence needs, 79; and espionage in Australia, 14–15, 17
Japanese Signal Intelligence Service, 106
Jennings, Lt J., 61
Johnson, Louis A., 302
Joint Counterintelligence Information Center (JCIC), 193–4
Joint Intelligence Bureau (Melbourne) (JIB [M]), tasks of, 161; and Flemming, 164; and JIBs in New Zealand, Canada and Britain, 164; oversight of by JIC, 169; and Finlay, 170; and Storey, 170
Joint Intelligence Centre (JIC), 108; and Burton, 152; and Moodie, 152; established, 159, 162–3; and Combes, 160; proposals for, 161–2; opposed by Evatt, 162; establishment recommended by Forde, 162; oversight of DSB and JIB, 169; partial exclusion of External Affairs from, 169; and CIS, 173; report on Sigint Intelligence Requirements, 198
Joint Intelligence Sub-Committee, 110
Joint Planning Committee, and JIC, 161
Jones, Maj Harold, 14, 15, 17, 20, 23
Jordan, Dorothy (DZhON/PODRUGA), 6, 212; in Australian Venona material, 205, 266, 287, 297; and Clayton, 214, 266; and reorganisation of KLOD group, 215; and Ric Throssell, 238, 266, 272; and Beeby, 238, 267; and NKGB, 266, 345; works in Post-War Reconstruction department, 266; and External Affairs, 266, 345; transfers to Territories department, 266; and CPA, 266; and ASIO, 267; and Dakin, 267; and Royal Commission on Espionage, 267, 347; and Jim Hill, 307
Journalists' Club, 127, 129, 224

Kahn, David, 2
kana code, 56, 59
Kendall, Maj Roy, 52
Kevin, J. Charles, 32; and formation of CSS, 31–2, 161; establishes Organisations Section of CSS, 43; reports on CSS, 43; and Hillgarth, 44; and JIC, 161
Key, Kenneth Hedley, 229, 264
KGB, 115–22; *see also* Soviet State Security Service

INDEX   457

KhILL, *see* Jim Hill
KI (Committee of Information), 119–20, 122; *see also* Soviet State Security Service
Kirkman, J. H., 33
Klausen, Anna, 140
Klausen, Max (FRITZ), 140
KLOD, *see* Clayton
KLOD group, *207*, 210–16, *212*, 232–51; and Makarov, 130, 231; and Nosov, 134, 135–6; suspension of, 136; and Clayton, 141, 228–9, 231, 232, 321, 352; and KI, 206; reorganisation of, 214–16, 231, 238, 247, 251; and Jim Hill, 215, 249, 262; and ASIO, 231; and Soviet State Security Service, 232; and Prichard, 237, 238; and Christiansen, 247, 251; and Ric Throssell, 268, 324; and Young, 304; and MI5, 310; and Canberra Residency, 313; and Bernie, 318; and Valentin Sadovnikov, 321; and Alfred Hughes, 336; motives of members, 348–9, 352; and Ultra leaks, 349–50; and establishment of ASIO, 351
Knowles, Sir George, 20, 22, 31, *34*, 34
Krueger, Gen Walter, 85
Krutikov, 130, 137
Kubatkin, Petr (EVGENEV), 206
Kukin, Gen Konstantin Mikhailovich, 120, 121
Kuzchinski, Ursula (SONIA), 311
Kuznetsov, Col-Gen Fedor Fedotovich, 122, 123
Kwantung Army, 105

Labor Party, 313, 351
Ladd, Mickey, 346
Lamphere, Robert J., *194*; and Venona, 6, 190, 194, 195, 338, 346, 347; and Gardner, 190, 194, 195; and Rowlett, 190; and FBI, 194, 195; and Harvey, 197; meets with Dwyer and Thistlewaite, 199; and Philby, 201; and HOMER, 202; on Sigint, 337; and Fuchs, 347
Land Headquarters (LHQ), and GHQ SWPA, 36; and FELO, 38; and Northcott, 39; and Cohen, 44; and Mander-Jones, 70; and Wang, 76, 78–9, 80, 84, 88, 98
Lane, Hilda Mary, 141, 221, 225–6
Lane, William, 221
Latham, Sir John, 12
Layton, V-Admiral Sir Geoffrey, 49
Lazzarini, Hubert, 94, 104
League of National Security, 15
Legge, George, 227

Legge, Jack, 227
Leggett, George H., 316
Leigh, Margaret (Margot), *see* Margaret Milner
Lewis, Lt-Col R. R., 81
LIBERAL, *see* J. Rosenberg
Lietwiler, Lt John M., 59
Little, Lt-Col Robert, *41*; and Military Intelligence, 40, 44, 65; and Sandford, 90, 98; and Crowther, 92; and Brig Simpson, 98–9, 102–3; and Capt Wang, 100; and Spry, 172
Lloyd, Lt-Col Eric Longfield, 9, 15, *20*; head of Military Intelligence, 14; and Security Service, 20, 33; and Mawhood, 23; and Evatt, 26, 158, 173; and 'winds execute' message, 57; reviews CIB, 156; CIB director, 157; becomes director-general of Security Service, 157–8; and CIS, 158, 250; and Colyn Cohen, 157; and Spry, 158, 250; and Christiansen, 250; and Sillitoe, 281; and Hollis, 287; and Hemblys-Scales, 287; and Chifley, 289; and formation of ASIO, 293; and Bailey, 293
Lloyd, Maj-Gen Herbert, 80
Lloyd, Lt Ian Longfield, 55
Lockwood, Rupert (VORON/WARREN), and Mikheev, 127, 224; and Pakhomov, 138; types report in Soviet embassy, 152; and Clayton, 224, 231, 309, 310–11; and Jim Hill, 231, 309; and Ian Milner, 256, 260, 309, 327; and Margot Milner, 260; and Burhop, 309; and CPA, 309; and Counihan, 310; and Sharkey, 311; and Henry, 311
Loehnis, Cdr Clive, 165, 166
London, and Ultra intelligence, 70, 88, 97, 103; Chinese military attaché in, 109, 110
Long, Cdr R. B. M. ('Cocky'), *18*; and Naval Intelligence, 18, 38; meets with Military and Air Force Intelligence, 19; and Mawhood, 23; and Royal Navy, 23; and Wake, 25, 40–1; visits FECB, 25; and Dixon, 31; and British Sigint, 49; and genesis of Sigint in Australia, 50; and Nave, 54–5
Los Alamos, 195, 201
Lucy ring, 8–9, 123, 280
Lyalina, Lyudmila, 130, 137
Lyons, Richard, 52, 55

MacArthur, Gen Douglas, role of Sigint in victories of, 3; in Australia, 36; member of PM's War

Conference, 36; and Blamey, 36–7; and Curtin, 37; and Wills, 39; and special intelligence organisation in Australia, 60–1, 62, 63; and FRUMEL, 65, 67; and Milne Bay, 68; and Central Bureau, 69–70; and Ultra intelligence, 70; and Ultra information leaks, 71, 78, 343; and Wang, 99–100; operations in the Philippines, 104, 343; and Borneo, 112
McBarnet, Evelyn, 278, 346
McDermott, Devereaux, 301
McEwen, John, 83
McFarlane, Cdr J. C., 33
McGuire, Cdr D. P. (Paul), 152
MacInnes, Ian, 127, 133
MacKay, William, 16, 31, 33, 34, 35, 40
McKenna, Senator Nicholas, 149, 289, 292–4
Mackenzie, Col Kenneth, 20
McKnight, David, 245, 333
Maclean, Donald (HOMER), 120; identified, 195, 201, 202, 276; in Britain, 199; defects, 202; and White, 277; and Martin, 279; and Sillitoe, 279, 347; and Skardon, 311; leaks information from Foreign Office, 344
McLean, Frederick (LOT), 127, 132
McNamara, Capt Robert, 46, 103
Macon, Maj-Gen Robert, 303
Makarov, Semyen Ivanovich (EFIM), NKGB resident in Australia, 127–30, 206, 209; and CPA, 129, 217; and Clayton, 129, 209, 210–13, 215, 221, 224, 226, 228, 230–1, 237, 246, 251, 253, 267, 320, 329; and Nosov, 129, 130, 230, 246, 320; and KLOD group, 130, 231; cables Moscow Centre, 135; and ASIO, 136, 231, 304–5; granted rail permit, 142–3; and Gardner, 193, 203; and Australian Venona material, 206; and GRU, 206; and Zaitsev, 206; criticised by NKGB, 209; and Fitin, 210, 213–14, 224; and VNUK, 210; and Soviet State Security Service, 211–13, 230, 341; and Alfred Hughes, 230, 243; and External Affairs, 230, 253; and British War Cabinet documents, 230, 343; and Christiansen, 251; and Jordan, 267; and Ric Throssell, 271; followed by Whitrod and Redford, 305, 315; and Vladimir Petrov, 320
Makin, Norman, 26, 175
Malcolm, J. A., 260

Malik, J., 119
Mander-Jones, Col Evan, 70, 97, 170
Manhattan Project, 200, 309
Marshall, Don, 306
Marshall, Gen George C., 65, 183, 274–5
Martin, Arthur, 278–9; and Australian Venona Operation, 276, 277, 278–9; and British No. 1 Special Wireless Group, 278; and MI5, 278–9; and GCHQ, 278–9; and Venona, 278–9, 346; and McBarnet, 278; and Fuchs, 279; and Maclean, 279; and Sillitoe, 279; and Burgess, 279; and Philby, 279; and White, 279; and MI6, 279; and Skardon, 311; and Blunt, 311
Masaryk, Jan, 280
Mason, Lt-Cdr Redfield, 60
Mason, Sgt Steve, 165
Masson, Mercia, 301
MASTER, see Christiansen
Mathews, Maj John, 283, 348
Mawhood, Lt-Col John, 21–23
MAX, and Philby, 199, 201
May, Allan Nunn (ALEK), 123, 276, 279
Mellnik, Col Stephen, 81
Menzies, Douglas, 92
Menzies, Sir Robert, and Venona, 6, 316, 351; and CPA in 1940, 19; letter to British government, 52; defeats Chifley, 147; and Tuck, 308; and Jim Hill, 308; and Spry, 316; and ASIO, 351; and Evatt, 351; and Petrovs, 351; and Labor Party, 351; uses Soviet espionage for political advantage, 351
Menzies, Sir Stewart, 3, 102, 182, 200
Merry, Lt-Cdr Alan, 60
Mertsova, Lydia, 272
MGB, 116, 119, 120, 261; see also Soviet State Security Service
MI5 (Military Intelligence, section 5), and 'Double Cross', 8; and Australia, 10, 13; early history, 11; praised by Scott, 17; and CSS, 33; and Airy, 156; establishes (British) RSS, 182; B Division, 182, 277, 278, 279; and Venona, 197; liaison with FBI, 198–9; investigates Fuchs and Maclean, 199; and Jim Hill, 231, 307–12; and Sillitoe, 274, 276, 277; and Hollis, 274, 276, 277; and Australian Venona Operation, 276, 340; and White, 276, 277; and UKUSA, 276; C Division, 277; F Division, 277; and Martin, 278–9; and Young, 279–80, 291, 301; and proposal to establish ASIO, 286–7, 290; and

INDEX 459

Moodie, 288; and Chifley, 289, 290; and Hemblys-Scales, 279, 290; and ASIO, 291, 340, 350; and KLOD group, 310; and Skardon, 311; and Hamblen, 315
MI6 (Britain's secret intelligence service), 3, 90; and security leaks in Australia, 102; and Philby, 118; Section V, 182; Section IX, 182, 183; and RSS, 182; liaison with FBI, 198-9; and White, 276, 277; and Martin, 279
Mikhailov, Valentin Matveevich, *see* Sadovnikov
Mikheev, Vladimir, first TASS correspondent in Sydney, 126-7; and Prichard, 126, 224, 236, 237; and NKGB/GRU, 126-7; and Clayton, 127, 221, 224, 237, 329; and Dalziel, 127; and Nosov, 127; and Lockwood, 127, 224; and Alfred Hughes, 213, 243, 345; and Ric Throssell, 323
Miles, J. B., 218, 239, 242
Military Board, 35
Military Intelligence (Australia), development of, 12; early tasks, 12; role during WWI, 13; in 1920s, 14, 15; in 1930s, 15-16; surveillance of CPA and Nazi sympathisers, 16, 17; criticised by Scott, 17; and establishment of defence security organisation, 19; Spender requests inquiry into, 22; criticised by Mawhood, 22; surveillance of Hashida, 23; and Wake, 23; report on by Grimsdale, 25; urges proscription of CPA, 27; and Evatt, 27; and internment of aliens, 29-30; Roberts becomes head of, 31; structure of, 38; and counter-intelligence, 38; dispute with CSS, 71-2, 94-7, 100-1, 101-2; and Combes, 160, 170; and JIC, 161; in postwar period, 169-70; and Rogers, 169-70; and Finlay, 171; and Spry, 171, 173, 314; and CIB, 171; and Shedden, 172; and Soviet embassy investigation, 172; and Soviet cables, 185; and Ian Milner, 257; and Wang, 338
Military Operations and Intelligence, 16, 18, 52, 160
Military Police Intelligence (MPI), formation of in NSW, 16; and MacKay, 16; and Cohen, 21; arrests members of Australia First Movement, 30; and CSS, 34, 40;

and Alfred Hughes, 241; disbanded, 241
Miller, Forbes, 127, 133
Miller, Paymaster-Lt Keith, 54, 60
Milner, Ian (BUR, DVORAK), 10, *212*, 254-62, *255*; appointed to Post-Hostilities division, 154, 259; goes to Czechoslovakia, 202, 326-8; in Australian Venona material, 205, 253, 254, 260, 261, 274, 327, 328; and Clayton, 211, 213-14, 225, 230, 251, 253, 254, 260, 261, 264, 274, 326, 329, 342-3; and British War Cabinet documents, 213-14, 230, 260, 261, 274, 282-3, 342-3; becomes inactive, 215; and External Affairs, 251, 253, 259; and Jim Hill, 251, 253, 261, 262, 263, 264, 307; and UN secretariat, 253; and Brasch, 254, 255; visits Moscow, 255; and OGPU, 255; joins CPGB, 255; in New Zealand, 256, 260; and Ball, 256; and Lockwood, 256, 260, 309, 327; in Melbourne, 256-60; and Manning Clark, 256-7; and Margaret Milner, 257, 258, 326-8; and Security Service, 257; and Military Intelligence, 257; and CIB, 257; and Council for Civil Liberties, 257-8; and Australia-Soviet Friendship League, 257-8; and CPA, 258-60, 327; and Hasluck, 259-60; and Malcolm, 260; access to secret documents, 260, 282; and Burton, 260, 262, 284, 285, 291; and UN Security Council Secretariat, 260-1, 327; resigns from External Affairs, 261; and Greek Boundary Commission, 261; and Palestine Commission, 261; and UN Temporary Commission on Korea, 261; and MGB, 261; and FBI, 261; and ASIO, 262, 307; and Ted Hill, 262; and Chilton, 282; and Shedden, 283; and Matthews, 283; and Post-Hostilities Section, 283; and Moodie, 285, 291; and Hemblys-Scales, 290-1; identified as BUR, 297, 301; and Burhop, 309; and Counihan, 310; and Fruhaufova, 326, 328; and Vladimir Petrov, 326; and Evdokia Petrov, 326; defects, 326; and Royal Commission on Espionage, 326-7; and NKGB, 327, 344; denies espionage charges, 327; as Czech agent, 327-8; and Richard Hall, 328
Milner, Margaret (Margot), and Ian Milner, 257, 326-8; and CPA, 257,

258, 259; and Clayton, 260; and Lockwood, 260; and Burhop, 309
MININDEL, 146
Mitchell, Capt, and Soviet State Security Service, 254
Modin, Yuri Ivanovich (PETER), and Burgess, 201
Molotov, Vyacheslav, head of KI, 119
MONAKH, 138
Montgomery, F. M. Viscount, 3
Moodie, Colin, and Zaitsev, 141, 142, 143, 144; and JIC, 152; and Jim Hill, 265; and Burton, 285, 288; and Ian Milner, 285, 291; and Chifley, 285; and Hollis, 288; and MI5, 288; and Hemblys-Scales, 288, 291
Morgan, Gen Sir William, 304
Morshead, Lt-Gen Sir Leslie, 80
Moscow, 53, 102, 105
Moscow Centre, NKVD/KGB headquarters, 117; *see also* Soviet State Security Service
Mosely, Lt-Col H. D., 33
MVD, 116, 120; *see also* Soviet State Security Service

Nan, Lt Yu Lu, 77, 99
National Security Agency (NSA), 164, 185, 196, 197, 340; *see also* US (Army's) Signal Intelligence Service
National Security Regulations, 30
Naval Intelligence (Australia), early tasks, 12–13; and Japanese espionage, 17; criticised by Scott, 17; Long as director, 18; war-time role, 18, 38; and establishment of defence security organisation, 19; severs relations with CSS, 23; and counter-intelligence, 38; and Capt Wang, 77; and JIC, 161
Naval Ultra (US), production of, 67; importance of, 69; leaking of, 1, 71–91, 94–8, 102, 103, 105–14, 338–9, 343, 349–50; estimates of Japanese strength, 112; and Soviet State Security Service, 343; and Stalin, 343; and KLOD group, 349–50
Nave, Capt Eric, 10, 53–4, *54*, 166; and Long, 53–5; and SIB, 55, 56, 66; takes message to Durnsford, 57; and 'winds execute' message, 57; and FECB, 59; and FRUMEL, 60; joins Central Bureau, 64; possible DSB director, 167; joins ASIO, 300
Netherlands East Indies, and Hashida, 23; and AIB, 37–8, 78; interception of radio messages from, 50; and Ultra leaks, 112
Newbegin, Elfrida Margaret, 229, 238

New Guard, 15, 16
New Guinea, and Japanese intelligence, 17; and Wake, 24; and AIB, 37; and 55th Special Wireless Section, 63; role of Ultra intelligence in, 67–9; and Wills, 79; and Ultra leaks, 85, 86, 104, 111, 112, 113
Newman, Cdr Jack, and genesis of Sigint in Australia, 49–50; and Nave, 53; and FECB, 54–5, 59; and FRUMEL, 60; possible DSB director, 167
Nimitz, Adm Chester, 78
NKGB/KI, *see* Soviet State Security Service
Residency in Australia, *see* Soviet State Security Service
NKVD, 116–18, 120, 121; *see also* Soviet State Security Service
Noguchi, 88
NOOK, *see* External Affairs, Department of
Northcott, Lt-Gen John, 39, 95, 99
Nosov, Feodor (TEKhNIK), *131*, 130–6, *212*, 217; and Mikheev, 127; and Dalziel, 127, 131–2, 152; and Makarov, 129, 131; and Clayton, 131, 206, 209, 211, 221, 224, 225, 230–1, 246, 329; and Sadovnikov, 131, 134; and Bernie, 132, 246; and MacLean, 132; and Prichard, 132–3, 210–11, 230, 237, 238, 271, 323; and Ric Throssell, 132–3, 271, 323, 324; and F. Miller, 133; and C. Simpson, 133; and McInnes, 133; and Chiplin, 133; and C. Christesen, 133; and N. Christesen, 133; and Ferguson, 133, 209; and Turnball, 133; and Younger, 133; and Anderson, 133, 134; and Tenukest, 134–5; and KLOD group, 134, 135–6, 306; and Ultra information leakage, 135, 339; and Alfred Hughes, 135, 243, 345; and Pakhomov, 135–6; and Soviet State Security Service, 135–6, 230, 341; returns to Moscow, 137; and ASIO, 152, 231, 301, 304–6, 315; in Australian Venona material, 205; and CPA, 217; and Whitrod, 301, 305–6; and ASIO telephone monitoring, 305; and ASIO bugging, 305; apartment broken into by ASIO, 305–6, 315; and Vladimir Petrov, 320; and Fitzpatrick, 334
Nosov, Galina, 130, 132–5
NSW Police Special Branch, 223
Nurse, Brig H. S., 174

Ogilvie, Maj Clive, 46

INDEX 461

OGPU, and OTP cipher system, 179–80, 345; and Dutt, 235, 310; and Roland, 235; and Ian Milner, 255; and Pollitt, 310; *see also* Soviet State Security Service
Oke, Richard (Ric), 228
Oldfield, Maurice, 200
Old Guard, 15, 16
Oldham, Capt G. C., 169
OLGA, *see* Ollier
Ollier, Rose-Marie (OLGA), 137
OMS, 117
Operation Bride, *see* Venona Operation
Operation Drug, *see* Venona Operation
Operation Overlord, 3, 8
Operation Venona, *see* Venona Operation
O'Sullivan, Fergan (ZEMLIAK), 138, 152
OTP ('on-time pad') ciphers, adoption of, 179, 345; and OGPU, 179–80; attempts to decrypt, 180, 188; duplication of, 188, 196, 199, 202, 215, 338; and KGB's encryption system, 186–8; and Cecil Phillips, 189; and Dollis Hill, 197; changes to, 202, 313
Ovakimyan, Maj-Gen Gajk (GENNADIJ), 206

Packer, Wing Cdr Gerald, 23, 38
PAK, 46
Pakhomov, Ivan, 134, 135–6, 137–8, 322
PALM, 205, 213, 342
Park Orchards, 45, 57, 61, 62
Patents Office, 20, 33
Patterson, Geoffrey, 199, 201, 346
Petsamo, 196
PETROV, *see* Beria
Petrov, Evdokia (TAMARA), 6; and Raina, 120; replaces Gubanov, 129; on Makarov, 130; on Nosov, 134, 136; arrives in Canberra, 137; and KI Residency, 137, 320; and Ric Throssell, 325; and Ian Milner, 326
Petrov, Vladimir (MIHAIL), 6; and Raina, 120; and Moscow Centre reorganisations, 121; warned by Pakhomov, 134; takes over KGB/MVD Residency, 134, 137, 320; arrives in Canberra, 137; briefed by Pakhomov, 138, 322; and Zaitsev, 145; and ASIO, 223, 320–1, 322; and Richards, 320–1; and Makarov, 320; and Clayton, 320, 321; and Nosov, 320; and Valentin Sadovnikov, 321; and Ric Throssell, 322, 324; and Ian Milner, 326
Philby, H. A. R. ('Kim') (SONNY,

SOHNCHEN, STANLEY), 118, 120; made head of Section IX (MI6), 183; and MAX, 199, 201; replaces Dwyer, 199; and UKUSA, 199; informs KGB about British Venona, 199–201, 313, 351; meets with Menzies, Oldfield, and Easton, 200; and Burgess, 201, 202; in Washington, 201; and FBI, 201; and Lamphere, 201; and Patterson, 201; and Maclean, 202; identified, 276; and White, 277; and Martin, 279; and Skardon, 311; and Venona, 346
Philippines, and Ultra leaks, 1, 81, 83, 85, 86, 87, 98, 104; and AIB, 37, 70; US Navy intelligence in, 59, 60; US Army's Sigint in, 61; RAAF wireless units in, 64; and Wang, 74, 79, 99–100
Phillips, Cecil, 189, 197
Phillips, Maj Max, 44, 171, 294
Philpott, Beryl, 143
Phippard, Stanley Raymond, 142
Piesse, Maj Edmund, 12, 14;
Pinner, J. T., 156–7
Playford, Sir Thomas, 293
PODRUGA, *see* Jordan
Pollitt, Harry, 235, 310
Porter, Maj R. E., *64*, 92
Post-Hostilities Planning division, *see* External Affairs
Postmaster-General's department (PMG), 53; and telephone monitoring, 86, 88, 90, 93, 101
Post-War Reconstruction, department of, 230, 266
Post-War Reconstruction Section, *see* External Affairs
Poulden, Lt-Cdr J. E. (Teddy), *168*; first DSB director, 167, 168–9, 311; and Venona, 167; and Travis, 167; and Spry, 167, 314; and Chilton, 167; and Soviet espionage, 314
Powell, Lt-Col Reginald, 22
Prentice, Lt-Col John, 171
Prichard, Katherine Susannah (ACADEMICIAN), 10, *212*, 233–40, *234*; and Mikheev, 126, 127, 224, 236, 237; and Nosov, 132–3, 135, 210–11, 230, 237, 238, 271, 323; and Evatt, 152, 236, 239, 269; and Australian Venona material, 126, 205, 270, 297; and Ferguson, 210; and Clayton, 211, 214, 224, 225, 228, 230, 233, 237, 238, 239, 240, 270, 271, 344; and Ric Throssell, 211, 233, 236, 237, 238, 239, 268–72, 323, 324, 325; becomes inactive, 215; and CPA, 220,

234–40; and Hugo Throssell, 233, 235; and Baracchi, 235, 236; and Roland, 235; and Pollitt, 235; and Franklin, 235; and Hewitt, 236; and Soviet Union, 236; and Security Service, 236; and Special Branch, 236; moves to Sydney, 237; and KLOD group, 237, 238; and KGB Canberra Residency, 237; and Dalziel, 238; and Newbegin, 238; moves back to Perth, 238; in Canberra, 238; and prosecution of Daniel and Sinyavsky, 238; and Soviet invasion of Czechoslovakia, 239; and Hodgson, 239, 269; and Devanny, 239–40; and NKGB, 251, 270; identified as ACADEMICIAN, 302
Prime Minister's War Conference, 36
PROFESSOR, 215, 216, 287
Proud, J. C. R., 161
Radio Security Service (RSS) (British), 180–2, 184

Raina, Col Ivan Λ. (YUREV), 120, 206
Ratcliff, Horace, 27
Red Army, 122
Reddrop, Wing Cdr J. W., 169
Redford, Ernest, 300, 305, 307
Reed, Justice, 292; and Wake inquiry, 42; in First Directorate's files, 120; and Bailey, 291–2, 294; and Wake, 292, 300; and Chifley, 292, 293, 294; and ASIO, 293, 294, 295, 298–9, 314; and Playford, 293; and Tuck, 294, 298; and Hollis, 294, 297, 298; report on Australian Security Service, 297; and White, 298; and Gilbert, 298, 306, 325; and Young, 298, 299; and Fleming, 299; and Chilton, 299, 302, 304; and Shedden, 304
Rendle, John, 168–9
Reynolds, Wesley, 346
Richards, G. R. (Ron), 299–300, *317*; and Spry, 315, 323; and ASIO, 315; and Hamblen, 316; and Bernie, 317–19; and Vladimir Petrov, 320–1; and Ric Throssell, 322–3; and Gowland, 330; and Alfred Hughes, 332, 334–6; and Venona, 316, 346
Ride, Col Lindsay, 87
Roberts, Col Caleb, 31, 37, 61, 70
Robertson, Miss, 65
Rogers, Brig John, 10, 18, 39, *64*, *93*; Director of Military Intelligence, 37; and Allied Security Bureau, 42; and Max Phillips, 44; and Brig Simpson, 46–7, 96–8, 103, 352–3; and Central Bureau move to Hollandia,

69; and Ultra information leaks, 78, 79, 95, 106; and Willoughby, 81; and Ride, 87; and Winterbotham, 88, 90; and Blamey, 95–8, 112; memo to Blamey on 17 January, 113; and Sandford, 98, 164; and Ellis, 102; and JIC, 159; and formation of DSB, 165; recruits Finlay, 169; discharged, 170; and Spry, 171
Roland, Betty, 235
Rommel, F. M. Erwin, 3
Room, Professor Thomas, 52, 55, 64
Roosevelt, 195
Rose, Frederick G. G., 216, 230
Rosenberg, Ethel, 202
Rosenberg, Julius (ANTENNA/LIBERAL), 192, 195, 202
Rote Kapelle, 8, 123
Rowell, Lt-Gen Sir Sydney, 171, 173–4
Rowlett, Frank, 190
Royal Air Force (RAF), 59
Royal Australian Air Force (RAAF), intelligence organisation, 19, 23, 62; and breaking Japanese codes, 55–6
1st Wireless Unit, 64
Intelligence, and establishment of defence security organisation, 19; attitude to Security Service, 23; under Packer and Hewitt, 38; and counter-intelligence, 38; and JIC, 161
Signals Unit, 220
Royal Australian Institute of Architects, 193
Royal Australian Navy, 53, 76–7, 159
Royal Commission on Espionage, and Venona, 6, 347; description of Soviet Embassy cipher section in Report of, 129, 146; and Dakin, 267; and Beeby, 267; and Jordan, 267, 347; and Ric Throssell, 323, 324; and Ian Milner, 326–7; and Clayton, 328–30; and Taylor, 333; and Alfred Hughes, 347
Royal Navy, 23, 49
Royle, Admiral Sir Guy, 57
Royle, Marjorie, 263, 307–8
Rushbrooke, Rear-Admiral E. G. N., 165
Russian Embassy, *see* Soviet Embassy
Russian Foreign Intelligence Service, 341, 352
Ryan, Lt-Col Jack, 52, 61, 63, *63*

Sadler, Lt-Col Phillip, 70, 78, 170
Sadovnikov, Elizaveta (ZHENA SAID or SAID'S WIFE), 136
Sadovnikov, Valentino (SAID), replaces Makarov, 129, 136–7; and Nosov,

131, 134; and Soviet State Security Service, 134, 341; recalled to Moscow, 137, 313; and Ollier, 137; and Pakhomov, 137; and Vladimir Petrov, 321; and Clayton, 321, 333; and KLOD group, 321; and Taylor, 333

Sandford, Lt-Col Alastair (Mic), 45, 46, 47, 58, *63*; and establishment of Central Bureau, 61, 62, 65; and Central Bureau move to Hollandia, 69; and Ultra leaks, 84, 86, 102; and Winterbotham, 88, 103; and Little, 90, 98, 102; and Naval Ultra, 97; and Rogers, 98, 164; and Japanese deciphering of Soviet cables, 102; and formation of DSB, 164; memo to Berryman, 165; heads Diplomatic Section, 166; joins Anglo-Iranian Oil Company, 166; possible DSB director, 167

Sarafand, 59, 179, 180

Sarant, Alfred, 202

Savchenko, Sergei Romanovich, 119–20

Shchekoldin, Col Aleksei (ShchEK), 206

Scott, Ernest, 13

Scott, Lt-Col W. J. R. (Jack), 16, 17, 21, 22;

Scullin, James, 15

Second Department (of First Directorate), 121

Secret Intelligence Australia, 37

Section 22, 38

Security Service, *see* Commonwealth Security Service

SESTRA, *see* Bernie

Shann, Keith, 264

Sharkey, L. L., 218, 219, 311

Sharpley, Cecil, 226, 248, 262, 307

Shearer, Miss R., 65

Shedden, Frederick, *154*, *303*; secretary of War Cabinet and Advisory War Council, 26; and Curtin, 26; secretary of Prime Minister's War Conference, 36; and 'winds execute' message, 57; and Blamey, 89–90, 95, 100–1, 104, 352–3; and Forde, 100–1; and Curtin, 104, 149; and defence policy, 149; and Chifley, 149, 286, 289, 302–3, 304; and Evatt, 153; and Burton, 153, 284–5, 286; and Defence PHP Committee, 155; and establishment of postwar intelligence organisations in Australia, 159, 166; and Travis, 166; and Military Intelligence, 172; and British Long Range Weapons Organisation, 174; and Rowell, 174; and Leslie Hollis, 176; and Hollis, 281, 284, 287; and Sillitoe, 281, 304; and leaked British War Cabinet documents, 281–2, 284; and Chilton, 281, 302, 303–4; and Dedman, 282, 287; and Ian Milner, 283; and Spry, 283; and Hemblys-Scales, 287; and establishment of ASIO, 292, 293, 294; and Venona, 292; and Young, 292–3; and American embargo on intelligence sharing, 302–4; and Truman, 302; and Acheson, 302; and Gray, 302–3, 304; and Johnson, 302; and Reed, 304; and Morgan, 304

Shepherd, Maj Tony, 92

Sherden, Ida, 245

Sherr, Lt-Col Joseph R., 60, 62

Shpigelglas, M., 118

Shtemyenko, Gen Sergei Mutveevich, 122

Sigint (signals intelligence), definition of, 2; before and during WWI, 2, 178; and collapse of Tsarist regime, 3; in 1920s and 1930s, 3, 179–80, 345; during WWII, 3–4, 180–97; and the Pacific War, 3–4; in the Cold War, 4; effectiveness of, 4; improvements to in WWII, 4–6; and German bombing of Coventry, 5; and German attack on Crete, 5; and sinking of *Indianapolis*, 5–6; publications on, 5; and counter-espionage, 7–9, 48–9, 338, 339, 345–8; and 'Double Cross', 9; genesis of in Australia, 49–52; radio-direction finding, 49–50; wireless telegraphy intelligence, 50; importance of in WWII, 66–72; and Spry, 173; and Venona decrypts, 177, 337, 338, 345–8; and Soviet espionage in Australia, 337, 339; and Lamphere, 337; limitations of, 338–9, 345, 346–8

Sigint Continuation Agreement, 184

signals intelligence, *see* Sigint

Signals Intelligence Centre, *see* Defence Signals Branch

Sillitoe, Sir Percy, *275*, 276–7; on counter-espionage, 7; and Sigint, 8; in First Directorate's files, 120; mission in Australia, 274–5; and Hollis, 274; and Venona, 274, 275, 346; and Ian Milner, 274; and Jim Hill, 274; and Clayton, 274; and Soviet penetration of External Affairs, 275; and Soviet penetration of CIS, 275; and Australian Venona Operation, 276; and MI5, 274, 276, 277; and MI5 B Division,

277; and Martin, 279; and
  Maclean, 279, 347; and Burgess,
  279, 347; and Chifley, 281, 286–7;
  and Shedden, 281, 304; and Spry,
  281, 283; and Bailey, 281; and
  Chilton, 281; and Longfield Lloyd,
  281; and Bevin, 284; and Attlee,
  286–7; and ASIO, 286–7; and
  Young, 304; and limitations of
  Venona material as legal evidence,
  347
SILVERMASTER group, 200
SIMA, see Coplon
Simpson, Colin, 127, 133
Simpson, Maj-Gen Colin, 45, 50–1,
  61–2, *62*
Simpson, Brig William, *36*;
  director-general of CSS, 35;
  problems with Army over personnel,
  40, 94, 155–6; and Wake, 40–3;
  and Kevin, 43; and Hillgarth, 44;
  and Cohen, 44; and Blamey, 44,
  94–8, 103; and Rogers, 46–7, 96–8,
  103, 352–3; and Sandford, 46–7,
  103; and Wang, 76, 79–80; and
  Capt Wang, 77; and security leaks,
  94–5, 97–8; and Evatt, 97, 100;
  and Burley, 98; and Little, 98–9,
  102–3; and Ultra information,
  98–9, 102–3; reports on CPA,
  103–4, 156; reviews Security
  Service, 156; resigns as
  director-general, 157; and Soviet
  cables, 185; asks Alfred Hughes to
  report on Clayton, 243
Sinclair, Frank, 35, 95, 96, 101, 264
Sinkov, Maj Abraham, 62
SK, 120, 129
Skardon, William James (Jim), 308–10,
  311, 312, 347
Slutsky. A. A., 118
Solomon Islands, 17, 24, 68, 85, 111
Sorge, Richard (SONTER, RAMSEY, FIX,
  and INSON), 8, 10, 138–41
Sorge espionage ring, 123, 139–41, 144
South Pacific Command, 67
Soviet Embassy (in Australia), *126*;
  and leaking of Ultra material, 95,
  98–9, 102, 103–4, 105, 106, 107,
  113–14, 172, 338–9; establishment
  of, 125, 128; description of cipher
  section, 129; and enciphered cables,
  145–6; Lockwood types report in,
  152; cables to Moscow broken into,
  192–4, 203–5, 278–9; Alfred
  Hughes obtains security files on,
  243; and ASIO telephone
  monitoring, 305
Soviet (Russian) Legation, *see* Soviet
  Embassy

Soviet Military Intelligence (GRU)
  (Codename: NEIGHBOURS), 115, 119,
  122–4; and Lucy ring and Rote
  Kapelle, 8, 123, 280; re-established,
  119–20; residency in Australia, 123,
  125, 138, 218, 341; organisation of,
  123; and Sorge, 123; intelligence
  collection activities of, 123–4;
  'illegal' espionage networks of, 123;
  and Mikheev, 126–7; and Zaitsev,
  138, 141, 144, 144–5, 352;
  enciphered communications with
  GRU Resident in Australia, 145–6,
  352; communciations with
  Washington Resident, 196, 346; and
  CPA, 218; and Hemblys-Scales,
  279; and Foote, 280; activities in
  Australia, 341
Soviet State Security Service, 115;
  name changes, 116; history and
  activities of, 115–24; at Moscow
  Centre, 117; and Philby, 118; impact
  of reorganisations on, 121; and
  Gorsky, 121; and Mikheev, 126; and
  Makarov, 128, 206, 209, 211–13,
  230, 231, 341; cipher room in
  Canberra, 129; and Nosov, 131,
  135–6, 206, 230, 341; and KLOD
  group, 135–6, 206, 232; and
  Pakhomov, 138; communications with
  Resident in Canberra, 145–6, 192–3,
  202, 341, 346; and Lockwood
  report, 152; intercepting of signals
  from, 182–3, 184; encryption system,
  186–8, *187–8*; communications with
  New York Residency broken by
  Venona, 191–6, 202, 341, 346;
  encrypted messages and Gardner,
  191, 350; informed about Venona,
  199–200, 313, 351; code books
  changed, 200, 202, 313; and
  Shchekoldin, 206; and Zaitsev, 206;
  operational matters, 206–10; and
  recruitment in Australia, 209, 229,
  342; and Clayton, 209, 211, 223,
  224, 225, 228, 230, 232, 266, 270,
  329, 330–1, 342, 343–5; and Bernie,
  209, 251, 345; and Ric Throssell,
  209, 268, 270, 271, 272, 322, 324,
  325; espionage priorities in Australia,
  212–13, 217, 253, 342; reorganises
  KLOD group, 214–16, 231, 251, 267,
  272; and CPA, 217–18; and Alfred
  Hughes, 240, 242–4, 251, 336; and
  Prichard, 251, 270; and Christiansen,
  251; and External Affairs, 251, 252,
  343–5; and UN secretariat, 253; and
  Jim Hill, 262, 265, 344; and Jordan,
  266, 345; and Mertsova, 271;
  communications with Washington

Resident, 279, 341, 346; and ASIO, 298; aware of ASIO surveillance, 305, 313; and Vladimir Petrov, 320; and Ian Milner, 327, 344; value of information obtained in Australia, 340–1, 343–4; and Sadovnikov, 341; and Younger, 342; and PALM, 342; and British War Cabinet Documents, 342–3, 350, 352; categories of information obtained from Australia, 343–5; and Naval Ultra leaks to Japan, 343, 349–50; and MacArthur's plans, 343; and Foreign Office cables, 343–4; and leaked report on south-eastern Europe, 344; information obtained on Security Service in Australia, 344; and establishment of ASIO, 350–1; *see also* Cheka, KGB, GUGB, NKVD, MGB, KI, MVD, OGPU
Canberra Residency, 125, 128–9, 137–8, 141, 203, 205–6, 208, 215, 218, 232, 237, 320, 341; and CPA, 208; cables to Moscow, 205–6, 208–9, 232, 241–2, 341–2, 346, 350; and duplicated OTP pages, 215; and Key, 229; and Alfred Hughes, 242; and Gluck, 246; and Christiansen, 251; and Association of Australian Scientific Workers, 251; and Jordan, 266; and KLOD group, 313; size and importance of, 341–2; and Soviet State Security Service, 342–3; and Foreign Office cables, 343–4
Soviet Union, and geopolitical significance of Venona, 1, 351–2; and early British Sigint, 3; and Cold War Sigint, 4, 10; Australian concerns at formation of, 14; and non-aggression pact with Germany, 19; German attack on, 27, 59, 115; as an ally, 105; espionage organisations of, 115–24; establishes diplomatic relations with Australia, 125; spies in Britain, 147; spies in US, 147; Prichard's attitude to, 236; and British War Cabinet documents, 352
SOVPOSOL, 146
Special Branch, 236, 241, 244, 328, 336
Special Intelligence Bureau (SIB), 13, 55–7, 60, 66; *see also* Commonwealth Investigation Branch
Special Liaison Unit No. 9 (SLU9) (British), 71, 95, 166
Spender, Sir Percy, 20, 22, *24*, 31, 103
SPIRITED, 210, 215

Spry, Brig Sir Charles, 10, *170*, *314*; in First Directorate's files, 120; and Zaitsev, 144; and Longfield Lloyd, 158, 250; recommends formation of secret service, 161; and choice of first DSB director, 167; and Poulden, 167, 314; and JIC, 169, 173; and Finlay, 170–1; and Rowell, 171, 173; and Rogers, 171; knowledge of Ultra leaks, 172; and removal of communists in Army, 172; and Evatt, 172–3; and Military Intelligence, 171, 173, 314; and signals intelligence, 173; and Rose, 230; and Christiansen, 249–50; and Sillitoe, 281, 283; and Shedden, 283; and Combes, 283; and Hemblys-Scales, 287, 294; and Hollis, 287; and ASIO, 294, 314–16; and Brown, 294; and Max Phillips, 293; and Gilbert, 306; and Jim Hill, 308; and Venona, 314–15, 316; reorganises ASIO, 315; and Richards, 315, 323; and Hamblen, 316; and Thwaites, 316; and Ralph Thompson, 316; and Robert Menzies, 316; and Clayton, 329–31; and Alfred Hughes, 336
Squires, Lt-Gen E. K., 50–1
Stalin, Josef, 116, 119, 122, 181, 343
Stanley, Peter, 112–13
Steibel, Pam, 299, 315
Stewart, Lt-Col Earl C., 34
Stewart, Maj George, 13
Storey, Cdr A. S. (Donk), 170
Stratton, Lt-Col F. J. M., 45
Stretton, Maj-Gen Alan, 171–2
Stringer, J. M., 299–300
Sturdee, Lt-Gen Sir Vernon, 22, 31, 80
Sudbury, Geoffrey, 198
Sudoplatov, Pavel, 118
Sutherland, Lt-Gen Richard, 38, 63, 84
Sydney University, 52, 54, 55, 60
Synyavsky, Andrei, 238

Taft, Bernie, 249
Tange, Sir Arthur, 353
Tannenberg, 2
TASS news agency, and Ultra leaks, 97, 103, 105; establishment of Sydney office, 126; and Mikheev, 126; and Nosov, 127; and F. Miller, 133; and Dalziel, 152; Alfred Hughes obtains security files on, 243
Taylor, Stanley Cassin, 33, 332–3
TEKhNIK, *see* Nosov
Templeton, Jacqueline, 17, 31, 42
Tenukest, Constantine (TIKHON), 134–5
Thistlewaite, Dick, 198, 199, 346
Thomas, Max, 27

Thompson, Maj John R., 71
Thompson, Ralph N., 167–9, 185, 316
Thorpe, Col Elliott R., 38
THROSSELL, 205
Throssell, Capt Hugo, 233, 235, 268
Throssell, Ric (ACADEMICIAN's son/FERRO), 212, 268–73, 269, 321, 321–5; on Soviet diplomats, 128; and Nosov, 132–3, 271, 323, 324; and Gallacher, 133, 271–2; and Zaitsev, 143; and Evatt, 151–2, 269, 270, 272; and Post-Hostilities division, 154, 270; in Australian Venona material, 205, 270, 272, 287, 297, 322, 324; and NKGB/KI, 209, 268, 270, 322, 324, 325; unwitting informant, 210, 225, 268, 323–4; and Prichard, 211, 225, 233, 236, 237–9, 268–72, 323, 324, 325; and KLOD group, 215, 268, 324; and CPA, 237, 269; and External Affairs, 237, 239, 268–73, 321–5; and Clayton, 237, 238, 270, 271, 322–3, 324, 325, 329; posted to Moscow, 237–8, 271–2; and Newbegin, 238; and Jordan, 238, 266; and Beeby, 238; and Jim Hill, 264, 272–3, 307, 322, 324, 325; in Army, 268; and Hasluck, 270; and Makarov, 271; and Haydon, 271; and Dalziel, 271; and Bernie, 273; and Mertsova, 271; and NKVD, 271; and UN division, 272; given cover-name FERRO, 272; and Soviet State Security Service, 272, 322; in Brazil, 321–2, 325; identified as FERRO, 322; and ASIO, 322, 324, 325; and Vladimir Petrov, 322, 324; and Pakhomov, 322; and Richards, 322–3; and Mikheev, 323; and Royal Commission on Espionage, 323, 324; and Evdokia Petrov, 325; motives of, 348
Thwaites, Michael, 315, 316, 346
Tiltman, Col John H., 197
Tizard, Sir Henry, 174
Tokyo, monitoring of broadcasts from, 53; interception of diplomatic traffic from, 66, 67–8; and Ultra leaks, 82, 86, 94, 114; and Wang, 100, 105, 106, 108, 111
TOURIST, see Jim Hill
Travis, Sir Edward, discusses JIC proposal with Chifley, 162; visits Australia, 165, 166, 184–5; and Shedden, 166; insists on a British director of DSB, 167; and Poulden, 167; and Australian access to US Sigint, 176
Trencode, 60

Trendall, Professor Dale, 52, 60, 65, 166
Treweek, Maj Athenasius, and Japanese decrypts, 52, 57, 67; and SIB, 55, 65; and FRUMEL, 60
Tribune, 222, 224, 229
Trotsky, Leon, 116, 117–18
Truman, President Harry S., 6, 195, 302
Tuck, Bernard G., and Reed, 294, 298; and Hollis, 294, 298; and Young, 294, 301; and Wake, 294, 300; and ASIO, 294, 295–7; and White, 298; and Gilbert, 306; and Jim Hill, 308; and Robert Menzies, 308; and Evatt, 308
Turnball, Clive, 127, 133
Type C Sections (Australian Special Wireless Group), 45
Type D Sections (Australian Special Wireless Group), 45, 46
Tyrell, Maj Beauchamp, 33, 41

UKUSA agreement, establishment of, 4, 165, 185–6; and Rendle, 169; distribution of responsibilities under, 186; and Philby, 199; and MI5, 276; and Venona, 345
Ultra, and allied successes in WWII, 3, 337–8; rules on handling of, 4; knowledge of, 5–6; and Freyberg, 58; *see also* Naval Ultra (US)
Umezu, Gen Yoshijiroo, 75
United Kingdom, *see* Britain
United Nations division, *see* External Affairs
United Nations secretariat (MECCA), 253
United Nations Relief and Rehabilitation Agency (UNRRA), 319, 342
United Nations Security Council Secretariat, and Ian Milner, 260–1
United States (USA), and geopolitical significance of Venona, 1, 351–2; and Sigint in inter-war period, 3; and postwar development of Sigint, 10; passing of Australian Sigint to, 66; and intelligence sharing during WWII, 74, 79; and Ultra leaks, 106; Soviet spies in, 147; denies intelligence to Australia, 174–6, 302–4, 340, 350; and Australian Labor government, 176; Sigint cooperation with Britain, 183–6
Uritskiy, Gen Semen Petrovich, 122
US 126th Signal Radio Company, 64
US Army
 2nd Signal Service Company, 60–1
 Intelligence, G-2, 193

Military Intelligence Service (MIS), 46; and Ultra leaks, 106–7, 108–9, 111, 114
Security Agency ([US] ASA), 189; at Arlington Hall, *190*, 190; Sigint cooperation with GCHQ, 183, 193, 197–9, 297, 340; Gardner reports to, 192; and Canberra–Moscow Soviet diplomatic traffic, 192–3, 203, *204*, 205, 215, 297; and Jim Hill, 297; begins work on Soviet codes, 351
Signal Intelligence Service ([USA] SIS), 64; and OTP ciphers, 180; and Comintern messages, 180; decrypts Soviet signals traffic, 180, 182; and Stewart Menzies, 182; and Philby, 183; and British RSS, 184; and Venona, 188–9; becomes Signal Security Agency, 188–9; becomes Army Security Agency (USASA), 189; becomes Armed Forces Security Agency (AFSA), 189; becomes National Security Agency (NSA), 189
Signal Security Agency, 185; *see also* US Signal Intelligence Service
US Counter-Intelligence Corps, 38–9, 40, 41–2
US Defense, department of, 313–14
US Forces Far East, 38
US Navy, 59, 64, 67, 112
USSR, *see* Soviet Union
US State-Army-Navy-Air Force Coordinating Committee (SANACC), 175
US War Department, 70, 81

Venona Operation, knowledge of, 5–6, 197, 275, 346–8; and Royal Commission on Espionage, 6, 347; first publicly reported, 6–7; and Chifley, 6, 292, 351; and Robert Menzies, 6, 316, 351; and Prichard, 126, 205, 270, 297; and Clayton, 127, 135, 221, 238, 260, 270, 274, 297, 347; and Bernie, 132, 278, 288, 297, 318, 347; and Nosov, 135; and Poulden, 167; and Sigint, 177, 337, 338, 345–8; and Soviet espionage in Australia, 177–8, 192–3, 198, 199, 203–16, 274–5, 276, 278–9, 287, 288, 295, 297, 341; in US, 188–97; and Hallock, 189; and Cecil Phillips, 189; and Gardner, 190–6, 338, 346; and Lamphere, 190, 194–5, 338, 346, 347; factors in success of, 196; and Chew, 196; and MI5, 197, 340; and NSA, 196, 197; and GCHQ, 197, 297, 340; and CIA, 194, 196, 197; in Britain, 197–9, 278–9; British briefed on, 198; Australian Venona material, 203–9, 215, 252, 274–5, 278–9, 287, 293, 297, 300–4, 313, 315–16, 322, 341, 347–8, 352–3; and Christiansen, 251, 287, 297; and Ian Milner, 254, 260, 261, 274, 297, 327, 328; and Jim Hill, 254, 274, 287, 291, 297; and Jordan, 266, 287, 297; and Ric Throssell, 205, 270, 272, 287, 297, 322, 324; and Sillitoe, 274, 275, 346, 347; and Hollis, 274, 283, 291, 292, 346; and Martin, 278–9, 346; and Burton, 285, 347; and Alfred Hughes, 287, 332; and PROFESSOR, 287; and Hemblys-Scales, 289–91, 346; and Shedden, 292; and Chilton, 292; and Young, 292, 293, 298–9, 300–4, 346; and ASIO, 293, 298–9, 346–7; and White, 297, 346; and Gilbert, 306; closes, 313; and Philby, 313, 346; and Spry, 314–15, 316, 346; and Hamblen, 315–16; and Thwaites, 316, 346; and Richards, 316, 346; and Leggett, 316; limitations of, 339, 346–8; importance of information garnered, 340–1; and UKUSA agreement, 345; compartmentalisation of, 346; and Ladd, 346; and Reynolds, 346; and Dwyer, 346; and Thistlewaite, 346; and Patterson, 346; and McBarnet, 346; and Skardon, 346; and Weisband, 347; and Fuchs, 347; legal status of evidence gathered, 347–8; importance of Australian material, 350; and Australian federal politics, 351; and Labor Party, 351; and the Cold War, 351–2; gaps in, 352–3
Victoria Barracks, radio direction-finding station at, 50; and SIB, 55, *56*, 66; and RAAF Sigint, 55–6, 62; and Diplomatic Section, 166
VIKTOR, *see* Fitin
Vishinsky, Andrey, 119, 264
Vlasov, Andrei, 125
VNUK (GRANDSON), 210, 215
Vreeland, Maj Albert L., 39
Vysselsky (VASSILI), 130, 137

Wake, Lt-Col Robert Frederick Bird (Bob), 9, *24*; and FECB, 23–5; career in security services, 23–5; and Far Eastern Security Service,

23–5; director of CSS, 33; complaints against, 40–3; head of Security in Queensland, 40–3, 157–8; and US Security, 42; and Brig Simpson, 41–3, 157; and Wang, 76; and Pinner, 157; and Reed, 292, 294, 300; and Young, 294, 301; and Tuck, 294, 300; and Hollis, 294; and ASIO, 294, 295, 296, 298, 300; and Evatt, 300, 315; leaves ASIO, 315
Wang, Maj-Gen Chih, 73, 74–5; Australian concern about, 75–6; and Wake, 76; and Berryman, 77, 84; and Brig Simpson, 76, 79–80; and Ultra intercepts, 78–82, 84, 94, 97, 108, 109–10, 111, 112, 113, 114, 338; and LHQ, 80; and Willoughby, 81–2; and Mellnik, 81; in Sydney, 99, 111–12; in Manila, 99–100, 114
Wang, Capt Chi-Kuang, 74, 77, 100, 110
War Cabinet, 36, 39; and establishment of defence security organisation, 19; approves establishment of CSS, 20, 33; orders inquiry into Security Service, 22; members of, 26; and Advisory War Council, 26; distribution of *AMF Weekly Intelligence Review* to, 87; and security leaks, 94–7, 100–1, 105; and Army personnel in Security Service, 101–2; and MacArthur's plans in the Philippines, 104; and Evatt, 26, 104, 105, 152, 270
War Department General Staff, 192
War Office, 193
Washington, transfer of Sigint from Australia to, 60, 70; and FRUMEL, 63; Sigint handled by, 79; and Ultra leaks, 88, 103, 108
Watt, Sir Alan, 153
Weisband, William (ZVENO), 200, 347
White, Dick Goldsmith, 276–7, 297, 298, 311, 346
Whitrod, Ray, 251, 298, 300–1, 305–7, 315
Whittington, Lt-Col S. F., 33, 41
Williams, Lt Mostyn, 166
Willoughby, Brig-Gen Charles, and intelligence in SWPA, 38; and Central Bureau, 63; and Ultra, 67; and Berryman, 73; and Wang, 79, 81–2, 100; and Japanese withdrawal from Philippines, 85; and Rogers, 97; and Sorge, 139, 144; and Zaitsev, 144
Wills, Brig Sir Kenneth, 39–40, 61, 70, 79
Winterbotham, Frederick, publication of *The Ultra Secret*, 2, 5; and security leaks in Australia, 88; and Rogers, 90, 102; and Burley, 98; and Sandford, 103
Workers' Weekly, see Tribune
Worlledge, Col J. P. G., 182
Wright, Cdr H. C., 299–300
Wylie, Capt F. J., 54
Wynes, Anstey, 142–3

Yagoda, Genrik, 116
Yamamoto, Adm Isoruku, 68
YEGER, see Anderson
Yendall, Sqn Ldr Bob, 71
Yezhov, Nikolay, 116, 117, 122
Young, Courtenay, 279–80; and Australian Venona Operation, 276, 277, 279–80, 293, 298–9, 300–4, 346; and MI5, 279–80, 291, 301; and CIS, 280; and Evatt, 280; and Foote, 280; and ASIO, 280, 291, 292–3, 298–9, 300–4, 315; and Philby, 280; and Blunt, 280, 311; and Hollis, 291, 298; and Wake, 294, 301; and Tuck, 294, 301; and Gilbert, 298, 306–8; and White, 298; and Reed, 298, 299; and Steibel, 299, 315; and Fleming, 299; and Chilton, 299, 302; and Whitrod, 301; and Sillitoe, 304; and KLOD group, 304; and Burton, 307; and Skardon, 311; and Thwaites, 315; returns to London, 315
YOUNGER, 205
Younger, Mark, 133, 342
Y Service stations, 184

Zaitsev, Col Viktor Sergevitch (SERGE), 10, 130, 138–45, 217; and GRU, 138, 141, 144, 144–5, 352; and Sorge, 138–41; and Klausen, 140; and External Affairs, 141, 143; and Lane, 141, 225; and Honda, 141; and Moodie, 141, 142, 143, 144; and Evatt, 142, 143; and Fitzhardinge, 142; and Hasluck, 142, 143; and Hodgson, 142; and Hood, 142–3; and Wynes, 142–3; and Phippard, 142; and Ric Throssell, 143; granted rail permit, 142–3; and Philpott, 143; and Dalziel, 143; and Barnwell, 143; and ASIO, 143; and Vladimir Petrov, 144, 145; and FBI, 144; and Spry, 144; and Willoughby, 144; and Cohen, 144; and EFIM, 206; and CPA, 217; gap in knowledge about, 352
Zhukov, Marshal Georgi, 108
Zorin, V., 119